Keep this book. You will need it and use it throughout your career.

About the American Hotel & Lodging Association (AH&LA)

Founded in 1910, AH&LA is the trade association representing the lodging industry in the United States. AH&LA is a federation of state lodging associations throughout the United States with 11,000 lodging properties worldwide as members. The association offers its members assistance with governmental affairs representation, communications, marketing, hospitality operations, training and education, technology issues, and more. For information, call 202-289-3100.

LODGING, the management magazine of AH&LA, is a "living textbook" for hospitality students that provides timely features, industry news, and vital lodging information.

About the American Hotel & Lodging Educational Institute (EI)

An affiliate of AH&LA, the Educational Institute is the world's largest source of quality training and educational materials for the lodging industry. EI develops textbooks and courses that are used in more than 1,200 colleges and universities worldwide, and also offers courses to individuals through its Distance Learning program. Hotels worldwide rely on EI for training resources that focus on every aspect of lodging operations. Industry-tested videos, CD-ROMs, seminars, and skills guides prepare employees at every skill level. EI also offers professional certification for the industry's top performers. For information about EI's products and services, call 800-349-0299 or 407-999-8100.

About the American Hotel & Lodging Educational Foundation (AH&LEF)

An affiliate of AH&LA, the American Hotel & Lodging Educational Foundation provides financial support that enhances the stability, prosperity, and growth of the lodging industry through educational and research programs. AH&LEF has awarded millions of dollars in scholarship funds for students pursuing higher education in hospitality management. AH&LEF has also funded research projects on topics important to the industry, including occupational safety and health, turnover and diversity, and best practices in the U.S. lodging industry. For information, go to www.ahlef.org.

MANAGING HOUSEKEEPING OPERATIONS

Educational Institute Books

MANAGING HOUSEKEEPING OPERATIONS

Revised Third Edition

Aleta A. Nitschke, CHA
William D. Frye, Ph.D., CHE

American
Hotel & Lodging
Educational Institute

Disclaimer

This publication is designed to provide accurate and authoritative information in regard to the subject matter covered. It is sold with the understanding that the publisher is not engaged in rendering legal, accounting, or other professional service. If legal advice or other expert assistance is required, the services of a competent professional person should be sought.

— *From the Declaration of Principles jointly adopted by the American Bar Association and a Committee of Publishers and Associations*

Nothing contained in this publication shall constitute a standard, an endorsement, or a recommendation of the Institute or AH&LA. The Institute and AH&LA disclaim any liability with respect to the use of any information, procedure, or product, or reliance thereon by any member of the hospitality industry.

©2008
By the AMERICAN HOTEL & LODGING
EDUCATIONAL INSTITUTE
2113 N. High Street
Lansing, Michigan 48906-4221

The American Hotel & Lodging
Educational Institute is a nonprofit
educational foundation.

Printed in the United States of America
1 2 3 4 5 6 7 8 9 10 13 12 11 10 09 08

ISBN 978-0-86612-336-5

Editors: Bridgette M. Redman
         James Purvis
         Jessica Miller

Cover Design: Kim Ricciardo

Contents

Preface

NOTHING SENDS A STRONGER MESSAGE than cleanliness in a hospitality operation. No level of service, friendliness, or glamour can equal the sensation a guest has upon entering a spotless, tidy, and conveniently arranged room.

To send this message of quality, housekeeping must be endowed with the same professionalism as other hospitality functions. *Managing Housekeeping Operations*, Revised Third Edition, gives managers the tools to systematically achieve the standards expected by today's guests in today's lodging and food service establishments.

While primarily written for the executive housekeeper, this text can be a resource for any professional who makes housekeeping decisions on a daily basis. The book is also designed to provide important technical information for persons seeking careers in this pivotal area. Every attempt has been made to thoroughly cover the day-to-day complexities of the housekeeping profession—from planning and organizing to budgeting, to supervising and performing the work itself.

To do so, the book begins by introducing the role of housekeeping in hospitality operations. It explains the role housekeeping plays in creating an environmentally sound property and focuses on the planning and organization of various housekeeping tasks. It then emphasizes the importance of quality housekeeping staff by examining human resource management in the housekeeping department. Additional chapters illustrate the various challenges and management responsibilities facing the executive housekeeper. These chapters focus on managing inventories, controlling expenses, and monitoring safety and security functions. For properties with on-premises laundries, a chapter is included which discusses how to effectively oversee the various laundry operations.

Finally, the last several chapters showcase the details of housekeeping tasks. These chapters consist of technical reference chapters which cover the how-to's of cleaning. Chapters focus on the basics of cleaning guestrooms, public areas, ceilings, walls, floors, carpets, bathrooms—as well as considerations in selecting and cleaning furniture, fixtures, linens, and other special features or conveniences. Step-by-step task breakdowns follow most of the technical/reference chapters. While designed as guidelines only, these breakdowns show the actual application of many of the concepts narrated in the text.

To promote understanding, review questions and key terms appear at the end of most chapters. Most chapters list websites to visit for additional, up-to-date information. Many chapters also include case studies that focus on the real problems and situations hospitality managers face.

Textbooks of this scope could not be written without the continual support of a great many people. Several industry and academic professionals have contributed time and expertise through their collaboration and written contributions. Each contributor's work is identified through the use of endnotes and acknowledgments.

First, the authors wish to acknowledge the original contributions of the late **Margaret M. Kappa, CHHE,** Wabasha, Minnesota and **Patricia B. Schappert, CHHE,** Nashville, Tennessee to the initial editions of this text. Their lifelong contributions and leadership in the realm of hotel housekeeping are still recognized to this day.

The authors would like to particularly extend thanks to these hard-working experts who shared significant expertise and content: **Jesse Denton,** McGriff, Seibels & Williams of Georgia, Inc., Atlanta, Georgia; **Gail Edwards, CHHE,** Millennium Hotel, St. Louis, Missouri; **Raymond C. Ellis, Jr.,** Loss Prevention Management Institute, Houston, Texas; **Mary Friedman,** Edina, Minnesota; **Prof. Michael Gentile,** Niagara University, New York; **Glenn Hasek,** Green Lodging News™, Cleveland, Ohio; **Dr. John Hogan,** Phoenix, Arizona; **Doug Scouten,** Cleanfix Cleaning Systems, Wyckoff, New Jersey; and **Phil Sprague,** PSA Energy Consultants, Mound, Minnesota.

This edition also features the input of **Michael P. Sciarini, Ph.D.,** associate professor at Michigan State University, *The* School for Hospitality Business. He contributed his insight and knowledge to various sections in the first half of the textbook.

We are also grateful to **Dr. Sheryl Fried Kline** from the College of Hospitality, Retail, & Sport Management at the University of South Carolina for her initial work reviewing and augmenting the safety and security chapter in earlier editions. Her expertise has been carried forward into many aspects of Chapter 7 of this text.

In each chapter there are also reprints from *The Rooms Chronicle®. The Rooms Chronicle®* is a bimonthly journal that was created in July 1993 to provide an informative, educational tool to help hotel managers be better at their jobs and thus improve the hotel's profit while giving consistent, higher quality service to guests and improving operational efficiency. During the past 16 years, *The Rooms Chronicle®* has evolved from modest beginnings to where it is a significant outreach initiative to the lodging industry by the College of Hospitality and Tourism Management at Niagara University. The articles incorporated into this text were written by managers and other experts in the industry about issues they have faced and problems they have solved. The articles are reprinted with permission from *The Rooms Chronicle®.*

We hope this text meets its intended purpose as a practical resource for the executive housekeeper—and as a vehicle for promoting the professionalism of this important segment of hospitality.

Aleta A. Nitschke, CHA
Founder, *The Rooms Chronicle®*

William D. Frye, Ph.D., CHE
Associate Professor
College of Hospitality and Tourism
Management
Niagara University
and Executive Editor, *The Rooms Chronicle®*

About the Authors

Aleta A. Nitschke, CHA

Aleta A. Nitschke, CHA is the founding publisher of *The Rooms Chronicle*®, The #1 Journal for Hotel Rooms Management®. Ms. Nitschke has had the opportunity to see many hotel operations during her 30-year career, beginning with a summer job of cleaning rooms at a tiny resort inn. Over the years she worked for six companies, in ten cities, and thirteen hotels. She then served as Radisson Hotels' Corporate Director of Rooms where she supervised the rooms operations of more than 200 hotels. In 1993, she founded *The Rooms Chronicle*®. Although many publications existed for other hotel segments, she felt there was a need for hands-on, how-to information specifically for managers of the front office, housekeeping, and related departments. Ms. Nitschke currently writes and maintains the website for the journal, www.roomschronicle.com.

William D. Frye, Ph.D., CHE

William D. Frye, Ph.D., CHE is an associate professor of hotel management in the College of Hospitality and Tourism Management at Niagara University and is the Executive Editor of *The Rooms Chronicle*®, The #1 Journal for Hotel Rooms Management®. He teaches classes in hotel and resort management, hospitality and tourism law, club management, and advanced hotel operations. Dr. Frye has been published in various hospitality journals and currently conducts research in the areas of hotel overbooking, employee satisfaction, risk management, security issues, as well as lodging strategies. He is the editor of the *Electronic Journal for Hospitality Legal, Safety, and Security Research*. A former resort general manager, he is the current chair of the Lodging Special Interest Group for the International Council on Hotel, Restaurant, and Institutional Education and possesses more than 22 years management experience.

Chapter 1 Outline

Types of Hotels
    Economy Hotels
    Mid-Market Hotels
    Luxury Hotels
Hotel Management
Hotel Divisions and Departments
    The Rooms Division
    The Engineering and Maintenance
        Division
    The Human Resources Division
    The Accounting Division
    The Security Division
    The Food & Beverage Division
    The Sales and Marketing Division
Housekeeping and the Front Office
Housekeeping and Maintenance
    Types of Maintenance
Teamwork

Competencies

1. Classify hotels according to the level of service provided. (pp. 3–8)

2. Explain the responsibilities of hotel management and the major divisions and departments of a hotel. (pp. 8–15)

3. Explain the relationship between housekeeping and the front office. (pp. 16–20)

4. Explain the relationship between the housekeeping and maintenance departments. (pp. 21–28)

The Role of Housekeeping in Hospitality Operations

Efficiently managed housekeeping departments ensure the cleanliness, maintenance, and aesthetic appeal of lodging properties. The housekeeping department not only prepares clean guestrooms on a timely basis for arriving guests, it also cleans and maintains everything in the hotel so that the property is as fresh and attractive as the day it opened for business.[1] These are no small tasks, especially in light of the following statistics.[2]

There are an estimated 47,135 lodging properties in the United States, with a total of 4.4 million guestrooms available for sale each day of the year. Assuming that, on the average, 63.3 percent of the rooms available are actually occupied by guests, hotel housekeeping departments are responsible for cleaning 2,778,517 guestrooms each day. If, on average, a room attendant cleans 15 rooms a day, then there are at least 185,235 room attendants employed each day in housekeeping departments across the United States. Add to this figure the management staff of housekeeping departments; the housekeeping employees assigned to clean public spaces, back-of-the-house areas, meeting rooms, and banquet rooms; and the other housekeeping employees working in the hotel's linen and laundry rooms—and it's easy to see why there are usually more employees working in the housekeeping department than in any other hotel department.

The tasks performed by a housekeeping department are critical to the smooth daily operation of any hotel. Media outlets love to report negative publicity associated with poor housekeeping practices.[3] This chapter begins by briefly describing the roles that housekeeping performs within different types of hotels. Next, the structure of hotel management is described, and housekeeping's place within the overall organization of hotel operations is identified. This chapter goes on to describe the basic functions of various hotel divisions and departments and briefly examines housekeeping's relationship to them. The chapter ends by stressing the kind of teamwork that is crucial to successful hotel operations. It provides detailed examples of the teamwork that must exist between housekeeping and front office personnel and between housekeeping, engineering, and maintenance personnel.

Types of Hotels

Classifying hotels is not easy. The lodging industry is so diverse that many hotels do not fit into any single, well-defined category. Smith Travel Research has compiled the most comprehensive database of hotel performance currently available.

Exhibit 1   Size Classifications of Hotels

By Size	Properties*	Rooms**
Under 75 rooms	26,896	1,146,501
75–149 rooms	14,547	1,541,819
150–299 rooms	4,118	823,966
300–500 rooms	1,073	399,076
Over 500 rooms	501	478,081

*Based on a total of 47,135 properties
**Based on a total of 4,389,443 guestrooms
Source: Smith Travel Research

Source: AH&LA Lodging Industry Profile, 2007.

It classifies hotels using such characteristics as the property type (all suite, gaming, etc.), the price tier (upper, middle, or lower as defined by the property's relative rates compared to its market competitors), location, the type of guests (or markets) attracted, the kind of ownership structure or chain affiliation, the size, and the service level. From the point of view of housekeeping, the size and service level of a property are its most important characteristics. However, size and service level are not dependent on each other. The size of a property often has little to do with the level of service it offers.

The size of a property gives only a general idea of the amount of work performed by the housekeeping staff. Size characteristics may include the numbers of guestrooms, meeting rooms, and banquet rooms within the property; the square footage of public areas; and the number of divisions or departments within the hotel requiring housekeeping services. Exhibit 1 focuses on the number of guestrooms and provides statistics on five hotel classes based on size.

A more precise measure of the work performed by a hotel's housekeeping staff is the property's level of service. Indicators of service level include the kinds of furnishings and fixtures in the different types of guestrooms; the decor of public areas; and special features of a property's other facilities. While the levels of service offered by hotels vary tremendously across the lodging industry, properties can, for the sake of simplicity, be classified in terms of three basic service-level categories: economy hotels, mid-market hotels, and luxury hotels.

Economy Hotels

Economy hotels are a growing segment of the lodging industry. These properties focus on meeting the most basic needs of guests by providing clean, comfortable, and inexpensive rooms. Economy hotels appeal primarily to budget-minded travelers who want rooms with all the amenities required for a comfortable stay, but without the extras they don't really need or want to pay for. The types of guests attracted to economy hotels include families with children, bus tour groups, business travelers, vacationers, retirees, and groups of conventioneers.

The size of the typical economy property has increased from the 40- to 50-room hotel of the 1960s. Some economy hotels now have as many as 600 guestrooms; however, managerial considerations keep most properties between 50 and 150 guestrooms. The staff of small economy hotels generally consists of a property manager, several room attendants, front desk agents, and sometimes a maintenance person.

Low design, construction, and operating expenses are part of the reason economy hotels can be profitable. They incorporate simple designs that can be built economically and maintained efficiently. Economy hotels are usually two or three floors of cinder-block construction with double-loaded corridors (corridors with guestrooms on both sides). These structures are cheaper to build than the single-loaded corridors found in large hotels, where guestrooms may overlook elaborate atriums.

In comparison to the early 1970s when the only amenity offered may have been a black-and-white TV, most economy properties now offer color TV (many with high-definition or flat-screen sets), high-speed Internet access, continental breakfast, swimming pools, limited food and beverage service, small meeting rooms, and other special features. However, many economy properties do not provide full food and beverage service, which means guests may need to eat at nearby restaurants. Also, economy properties do not usually offer room service, uniformed service, banquet rooms, health clubs, or any of the more elaborate services and facilities found at mid-market and luxury properties.

Mid-Market Hotels

Hotels offering **mid-market service** probably appeal to the largest segment of the traveling public. Mid-market service is modest but sufficient, and the staffing level is moderate but not huge. Guests likely to stay at a mid-market hotel are business travelers on expense accounts, tourists, or families taking advantage of special children's rates. Special rates may be offered for military personnel, educators, travel agents, senior citizens, and corporate groups. Meeting facilities of the mid-market-service hotel are usually adequate for conferences, training meetings, and small conventions.

The typical hotel offering mid-market service is medium sized (between 150 and 300 rooms). These hotels generally offer uniformed service, airport limousine service, and full food and beverage facilities. They also frequently offer high-speed Internet access, a business service center, and exercise facilities. The property may have a specialty restaurant, coffee shop, and lounge that all cater to local residents as well as to hotel guests. The management staff of a mid-market property usually consists of a general manager and several department managers. The executive housekeeper manages the housekeeping department, the staff of which generally outnumbers that of any other department in the hotel.

A fast-growing segment of the mid-market category is the suite hotel. Typical hotel accommodations feature one room, an adjacent bathroom, a king-size bed or two double beds, a desk/dresser modular unit, and one or two chairs. A suite unit, on the other hand, offers a small living room or parlor area with a grouping of appropriate furniture (often including a sofa bed) and a small bedroom with a

The lobby of a world-class hotel may be elaborately furnished and decorated. (Courtesy of Opryland Hotel, Nashville, Tennessee)

king-size bed. Suite hotels provide temporary living quarters for people who are relocating, serve as "homes away from home" for frequent travelers, or appeal to families interested in nonstandard hotel accommodations. Professionals such as accountants, lawyers, and executives find suite hotels particularly attractive since they can work or entertain in an area that is separate from the bedroom.

Some guest suites include a compact kitchenette complete with cooking utensils, refrigerator, microwave unit, and a wet bar. These additional features mean that room attendants will need more time to clean a suite of rooms than to clean a standard guestroom. Therefore, housekeeping labor expenses may be higher for suite hotels than for other properties in the mid-market-service category. Due to these and other costs, suite hotels generally offer less public space and fewer guest services than other hotels.

Luxury Hotels

Luxury hotels offer **world-class service** providing upscale restaurants and lounges, exquisite decor, concierge service, and opulent meeting and private dining facilities. Primary markets for hotels offering these services are top business executives, entertainment celebrities, high ranking political figures, and other wealthy people. In catering to these types of guests, the housekeeping staff is generally responsible for dispensing oversize bath towels, bars of scented soap, special shampoos and conditioners, shower caps, and other guestroom and bath amenities. Bath linens may be replaced twice daily, and a nightly **turndown service** may be provided. In addition, these guestrooms contain furnishings, decor, and art work that is more expensive than guestrooms in the mid-market-service category.

Some mid-market-service hotels dedicate certain floors (usually the top floors) of the property to world-class service. Entry to these floors may be restricted by the use of special elevator keys that allow access only by authorized guests. The rooms provided on the "executive floor" are normally very large and deluxe. Hotels will typically upgrade the furnishings and decor of these guestrooms and provide additional guest services and amenities. The room or suite may be stocked daily with freshly cut flowers and fresh fruit. Bath amenities are generally similar to those provided by luxury hotels.

Hotel Management

Management guides the operation of the hotel and regularly reports the property's overall operating results and other pertinent information to the owner. The management team achieves specific objectives and goals by planning, organizing, staffing, directing, controlling, and evaluating functional areas within the hotel. Top management executives coordinate the activities of the various division and department managers.

The use of the terms "division" and "department" is not standard throughout the lodging industry. Large properties may call their main functional areas divisions and smaller functional areas departments. Other properties may call their main areas departments and refer to smaller areas as subdepartments. Neither method is better than the other. For consistency, this chapter will refer to the main functional areas as divisions and to the areas within divisions as departments.

The highest-ranking executive of a property is usually called the general manager, managing director, or director of operations. The general manager of a hotel reports directly to the owner or to an assigned person in the owner's company. Within hotel chain organizations, the general manager of a property may report to a district, area, or regional executive who supervises the properties in a particular group.

While the general manager is responsible for supervising all the divisions of a hotel, he or she may assign specific divisions or departments to the resident manager to oversee. Typically, resident managers are assigned to supervise departments in the rooms division of large hotels. When the general manager is absent from the property, the resident manager becomes the acting general manager. A manager-on-duty is often appointed to take responsibility when the general manager and the resident manager are both absent from the property.

All organizations require a formal structure to carry out their mission and objectives. A common method of representing that structure is the **organization chart**. An organization chart diagrams the divisions of responsibility and lines of authority. Some organizations list each employee's name on the chart along with his or her position title. Since no two hotels are exactly alike, organizational structures must be tailored to fit the needs of each individual property. Exhibit 2 shows

Exhibit 2   Sample Organization Chart for a Midsize, Rooms-Only Hotel

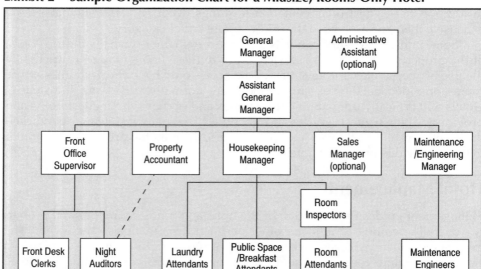

a sample organization chart for a midsize rooms-only hotel. Within this structure, all department managers report directly to the assistant manager.

Exhibit 3 shows a sample organization chart diagramming the management positions in a luxury hotel. Note that within this organizational structure, the executive housekeeper and the front office manager report directly to the rooms division manager. The rooms division manager ensures that the housekeeping and front office departments work as a team so that guestrooms are cleaned and made ready for arriving guests. The importance of effective communication between housekeeping and the front office is examined later in this chapter. The housekeeping department also works closely with the engineering and maintenance division. Since these functional areas do not usually report to the same manager, it is important that the executive housekeeper and the chief engineer establish a close working relationship. Communication between housekeeping and engineering and maintenance is also addressed later in this chapter.

Hotel Divisions and Departments

Departments within a hotel are classified according to a variety of methods. According to one method, each department is classified as either a revenue center or a support center. This method is especially useful for accounting purposes and in relation to the property's recordkeeping and information system. A **revenue center** sells goods or services to guests and thereby generates revenue for the hotel. The front office and food and beverage outlets are examples of typical hotel revenue centers. **Support centers** do not generate revenue directly but play a supporting role to the hotel's revenue centers. The housekeeping department

Exhibit 3   Sample Organization Chart for a Luxury Hotel

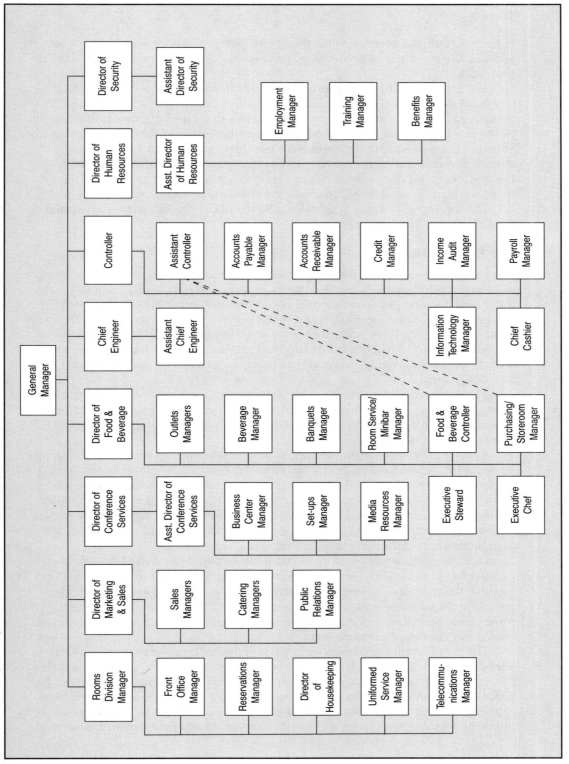

is a major support center within the rooms division. Other hotel support centers include the areas of accounting, engineering and maintenance, and human resources.

The terms **front of the house** and **back of the house** may also be used to classify hotel departments and the personnel within them. Front-of-the-house functional areas are those in which employees have a great deal of guest contact, such as the front office and food-and-beverage facilities. Back-of-the-house functional areas are those in which employees have less direct guest contact, such as accounting, engineering and maintenance, and human resources. Although members of the housekeeping department have some contact with hotel guests, the department is generally considered a back-of-the-house functional area.

The following sections briefly describe the major divisions and departments typically found in a large hotel.

The Rooms Division

The rooms division is composed of departments and functions that play essential roles in providing the services that guests expect during their stay. In most hotels, the rooms division generates more revenue than any other area in the hotel. The revenue center of the rooms division is the front office department. This department is usually the most important revenue center in a hotel. Other departments within the rooms division serve as support centers for the front office. These may include the housekeeping, reservations, telecommunications, and uniformed service departments.

The front office is the most visible department in a hotel and has the greatest amount of direct guest contact. The front desk itself is the focal point of activity within the front office department. Guests are registered, assigned rooms, and checked out at the front desk.

In some properties, the reservations and telecommunications functions may be separate departments within the rooms division. The reservations area is responsible for receiving and processing reservations for future accommodations. Reservations agents must maintain accurate records and closely track the availability of rooms to ensure that no date is overbooked. Many departments within the hotel—especially housekeeping—use reservations data and other rooms forecast information to properly schedule personnel.

Hotel switchboard operators in the telecommunications department, sometimes referred to as PBX (private branch exchange) operators, answer calls and connect them to the appropriate extensions. These operators relay telephone charges to the front office cashier for posting to the proper guest account and, in some properties, place wake-up calls, monitor automated systems, and coordinate emergency communication systems.

The hotel's uniformed service staff may include parking attendants, door attendants, transportation drivers, and bellpersons. Additionally, concierges who possess vast knowledge of the local area and extensive city-wide connections can handle guest requests from everything to theater tickets, dinner reservations, sourcing difficult to find items, or arranging personal services for hotel guests. As uniformed service staff meet and greet guests and help them upon their arrival and departure, these employees convey the first and last impression of the hotel guests recieve.

The Engineering and Maintenance Division

A hotel's engineering and maintenance division is responsible for maintaining the appearance of the interior and exterior of the property and keeping its equipment operational. This division is also typically responsible for swimming pool sanitation and the landscaping and upkeep of the property's grounds. Some hotels, however, staff a grounds division or an outdoor and recreation division to perform these and other tasks. Not all engineering and maintenance work can be handled by the hotel's staff. Often, problems or projects require outside contracting.

The housekeeping department works closely with the engineering and maintenance division to ensure that proper preventive maintenance procedures are carried out effectively. Since daily cleaning duties require that housekeeping personnel enter almost every guestroom every day, the housekeeping department is in a position to identify maintenance needs and initiate work orders for engineering.

The Human Resources Division

In recent years, hotels have increased investment in and dependence on human resources management. For larger hotels, the sizes and budgets of human resources divisions have grown steadily, along with their responsibility and influence. Recently, the scope of human resources management has changed in response to new legislation, the shrinking labor market, and the growing pressures of competition. Human resources functions may include employment (including external recruiting and internal reassignment), orientation and training, employee relations, compensation, benefits, labor relations, and safety.

Many properties are not large enough to justify the creation of a human resources division or department. In these properties, the general manager and department managers share many of the duties and responsibilities connected with the human resources function.

The Accounting Division

A hotel's accounting division is responsible for monitoring the financial activities of the property. Some hotels employ off-premises accounting services to complement the work of their internal accounting division. In this case, the hotel's staff collects and transmits data to a service bureau or to chain headquarters. A hotel that performs all of its accounting work in-house employs a larger accounting staff with a high level of responsibility.

The hotel's controller manages the accounting division. Accounting activities include paying invoices owed, distributing statements and collecting payments, processing payroll information, accumulating operating data, and compiling financial statements. In addition, the accounting staff may be responsible for making bank deposits, securing cash, and performing other control and processing functions required by the hotel's management.

In some properties, the purchasing manager and the storeroom manager may report to the hotel's controller. The executive housekeeper must often work closely with these managers, because the housekeeping department maintains inventories of cleaning supplies, equipment, linens, uniforms, and other items.

The controller and the general manager are responsible for finalizing the budgets prepared by division and department managers.

The Security Division

Security staff might include in-house personnel, contract security officers, or retired or off-duty police officers. Security responsibilities may include patrolling the property, monitoring surveillance equipment, and, in general, ensuring that guests, visitors, and employees are safe and secure at the hotel. The cooperation and assistance of local law-enforcement officials is critical to the security division's effectiveness.

A hotel's security program is most effective when employees who have primary responsibilities other than security also participate in security efforts. For example, housekeeping room attendants should follow the key control procedures of their properties. Also, when cleaning guestrooms, room attendants are usually responsible for locking and securing sliding glass doors, connecting doors, and windows. All employees should be wary of suspicious activities anywhere in the property and report such activities to an appropriate security authority. Since housekeeping personnel work in every area of the hotel, they are in a position to significantly contribute to the hotel's security efforts.

The Food & Beverage Division

A major revenue center in most hotels is the food & beverage division. There are almost as many varieties of food & beverage operations as there are hotels. Many hotels offer guests more than a single food and beverage outlet. Outlet types include quick service, table service, specialty restaurants, coffee shops, bars, lounges, and clubs. The food & beverage division typically supports other hotel functions such as room service, catering, and banquet planning.

The executive steward supervises most of the kitchen sanitation and cleaning duties. However, the housekeeping department may be responsible for cleaning specific areas of the hotel's dining rooms, banquet rooms, and some back-of-the-house food & beverage areas.

The Sales and Marketing Division

The sales and marketing staff in a hotel can vary from one part-time person to a dozen or more full-time employees. These personnel typically have four functions: sales, catering, advertising, and public relations. The marketing arm of the division researches the marketplace, competing products, and guest needs and expectations and then develops sales action plans by which to attract guests to the property. The primary goal of the division is to sell the products and services offered by the hotel.

Exhibit 4   Reasons Guests Give for Returning to a Hotel

Question: What are the most important factors in your decision to return to a hotel/motel?

Finding:

Reason for Returning	By Total Travelers	By Frequent Travelers
Cleanliness/Appearance	63%	63%
Good Service	42%	45%
Facilities	35%	41%
Convenience/Location	32%	38%
Price/Reasonable Rates	39%	35%
Quiet and Private	9%	8%

Source: "Bringing in the Business and Keeping It." Study done for Procter & Gamble by Market Facts.

Housekeeping's important contribution to the primary goal of the sales and marketing division often goes unrecognized. Successful sales departments maintain high percentages of repeat business. Exhibit 4 provides some data on the reasons guests return to a hotel. Note that the single most important reason a traveler returns to a hotel is the cleanliness and appearance of the property. The data also indicate that good service is second in importance. Housekeeping staff are among the most visible hotel representatives in this regard. Therefore, an important contribution of the housekeeping staff to hotel sales is the repeat business obtained by providing the level of cleanliness and service that meets or exceeds guest expectations.

Employees of sales and housekeeping share a mission: to create customers. Sometimes, the sales department, eager to reach annual goals, confirms bookings of groups that cause the housekeeping department difficulty. For example, a dog show that may result in a full house for several days. What salesperson could resist? But all those dogs have to go to the bathroom someplace. What hotel has lawn facilities to accommodate this? Are the dogs bathed before showing? And do they curl up with their owners for a snuggle on the couch or bed? Do they shed? Is there not a flea among all those animals?

What are the costs of this group? In addition to the cost of cleaning all the bedding, there are costs of shampooing the carpets and upholstery. Then add the costs of cleaning drainpipes for the next five years to remove pet hair. To make matters worse, suppose that sales has booked a full-house convention to arrive the day the dogs depart.

Other issues that cause problems for housekeeping are promises of early check-ins, late check-outs, and requests for guestrooms to be reset as meeting rooms.

Sometimes, the housekeeping department fails to provide a clean hotel for the sales staff to show. Or, it fails to follow through on something a group needs: extra towels, special amenities, or open connecting doors, for example. Caught between the demands of the guests and the performance of the housekeeping staff, salespeople often find themselves making excuses for housekeeping.

Employees respond to incentives provided by management. If a salesperson is rewarded exclusively for booking rooms without concern for the real costs of handling the groups, the hotel can expect problem groups. And if housekeeping managers are rewarded for cutting expenses without concern for the quality of cleaning, the condition of the hotel will suffer.

To cooperate with housekeeping, sales staff should do the following:

- Honor the people of the housekeeping department. Without them there would be no return business.

- Make the job of the housekeeping department easy. Before confirming a potentially difficult group, research the group's history with previous hotels. And if a previous hotel recommends NOT accepting the booking, refuse to confirm the group.

- Before confirming a group booking, meet with the department representative who will care for this group and solicit (not demand) his or her support.

- When housekeeping outlines how special accommodations for a group will cost more than the daily room rate, evaluate whether the group should be confirmed.

- Make it a habit to "pitch in" to support housekeeping while they are servicing a group. Help clean a room, help fold a towel, or help straighten the lobby. Rolling up sleeves and working beside people helps build bridges.

- If there is a problem in the way housekeeping is servicing a group, go directly to housekeeping to obtain the facts. Most problems can be resolved one on one if both departments make the effort.

- And say "thank you" to housekeeping—to the people who can make a salesperson a hero in the eyes of a meeting planner.

To cooperate with the sales department, housekeeping staff should do the following:

- Honor the people of the sales department. Without them, there would not be enough guests to make payroll.

- Make the job of the salesperson easy—keep a spotless hotel. Prepare show rooms every day, and make sure sales has a special set of keys on a ring at the desk.

- When sales says they need to research a group, call the housekeeping manager at the previous hotel and ask for his or her input. Share the comments with sales.

the Rooms CHRONICLE®

Ask Gail–Show Rooms for the Sales Department

Dear Gail:

Our sales department drives me crazy, always wanting a room fixed up for giving tours. Isn't there an easier way?

E.L., San Francisco, Calif.

Dear E.L.:

A great idea is to set up show rooms the first thing every morning. Ideally, have one of each room type available for sale. Have the lights on, music softly playing, fresh flowers or plants, and amenities. Make sure the front desk staff creates a ring of keys or key cards just for those rooms and mark it "Show Rooms." Put the rooms off-market so that they can't be used for check-ins. Sales associates can quickly stop by the front desk, sign out the keys, and be on their way. Your advance preparation can help sell the customer and make you a hero.

Source: *The Rooms Chronicle®*, Volume 3, Number 1, p. 9.
For subscription information, call 866-READ-TRC.

- When sales says they need special accommodations for a group, be positive about helping them meet and exceed the group's expectations.

- Make it a habit to "pitch in" to support sales. Arrange for meeting planners to tour the housekeeping department. Show the organization and cleanliness of the heart of the house with pride.

- Ask salespeople to inspect the hotel. Give them white gloves, invite them to touch surfaces in search of dirt, and ask for their feedback. Be open to their suggestions.

- Involve sales with housekeeping. Make them part of the family. And thank them for soliciting room nights that provide jobs for housekeeping employees.

Owners and general managers would be wise to review the incentive programs for these departments to ensure that the focus for both is creating customers.

Two things are certain in the hotel business: no matter how many guests a salesperson brings in the door, if housekeeping doesn't execute its function with excellence, the guests will not be back. And, no matter how clean the rooms, if the sales staff doesn't bring potential guests to the hotel, occupancy falls. There is nothing to be gained by these two staffs being at odds. No matter how different the departments may be, each must understand that it cannot exist without the positive support of the other.[4]

Exhibit 5   Sample Housekeeping Rooms Status Report

| Housekeeper's Report | | | | | | A.M. | |
| Date _____ , 20 _____ | | | | | | P.M. | |

ROOM NUMBER	STATUS	ROOM NUMBER	STATUS	ROOM NUMBER	STATUS	ROOM NUMBER	STATUS
101		126		151		176	
102		127		152		177	
103		128		153		178	
104		129		154		179	
105		130		155		180	
106		131		156		181	
107		132		157		182	
108		133		158		183	
120		145		170		195	
121		146		171		196	
122		147		172		197	
123		148		173		198	
124		149		174		199	
125		150		175		200	

Remarks:

_____

_____

_____

Legend:

✓	-	Occupied
000	-	Out-of-Order
―――	-	Vacant
B	-	Slept Out (Baggage Still in Room)
X	-	Occupied, No Baggage
C.O.	-	Slept In but Checked Out Early A.M.
E.A.	-	Early Arrival

_____
Housekeeper's Signature

Housekeeping and the Front Office

Within the rooms division, housekeeping's primary communications are with the front office department, specifically with the front desk area. At most properties, the front desk agent is not allowed to assign guestrooms until the rooms have been cleaned, inspected, and released by the housekeeping department. Typically, rooms are recycled for sale according to the following process.

Each night, a front desk agent produces an **occupancy report**. The occupancy report lists rooms occupied that night and indicates guests who are expected to check out the following day. The executive housekeeper picks up this list early the next morning and schedules the occupied rooms for cleaning. As guests check out of the hotel, the front desk notifies housekeeping about the change in room status. Housekeeping ensures that these rooms are given top priority so that clean rooms are available for arriving guests.

At the end of the shift, the housekeeping department prepares a **housekeeping status report** (see Exhibit 5) based on a physical check of each room in the

Exhibit 6   Room Status Definitions

Occupied: A guest is currently registered to the room.

Complimentary: The room is occupied, but the guest is assessed no charge for its use.

Stayover: The guest is not checking out today and will remain at least one more night.

On-change: The guest has departed, but the room has not yet been cleaned and readied for resale.

Do not disturb: The guest has requested not to be disturbed.

Sleep-out: A guest is registered to the room, but the bed has not been used.

Skipper: The guest has left the hotel without making arrangements to settle his/her account.

Sleeper: The guest has settled his/her account and left the hotel, but the front office staff has failed to properly update the room's status.

Vacant and ready: The room has been cleaned and inspected and is ready for an arriving guest.

Out-of-order: The room cannot be assigned to a guest. A room may be out-of-order for a variety of reasons, including the need for maintenance, refurbishing, and extensive cleaning.

Lock-out: The room has been locked so that the guest cannot re-enter until he/she is cleared by a hotel official.

DNCO (did not check out): The guest made arrangements to settle his or her account (and thus is not a skipper) but has left without informing the front office.

Due out: The room is expected to become vacant after the current day's check-out time.

Check-out: The guest has settled his or her account, returned the room keys, and left the hotel.

Late check-out: The guest has requested and is being allowed to check out later than the hotel's standard check-out time.

---

property. This report indicates the current housekeeping status of each room. It is compared to the front desk occupancy report, and any discrepancies are brought to the attention of the front office manager. A **room status discrepancy** is a situation in which the housekeeping department's description of a room's status differs from the room status information being used by the front desk to assign guestrooms. Room status discrepancies can seriously affect a property's ability to satisfy guests and maximize rooms revenue.

To ensure efficient rooming of guests, housekeeping and the front office must inform each other of changes in a room's status. Knowing whether a room is occupied, vacant, on-change, out-of-order, or in some other condition is important to rooms management. For example, if a guest checks out before the stated departure date, the front desk must notify the housekeeping department that the room is no longer a stayover but is now a check-out. Exhibit 6 defines typical room-status terms used in the lodging industry. While the guest is in the hotel, the housekeeping status of the guestroom changes several times. However, not every room status will occur for each guestroom during every stay.

Promptly notifying the front desk of the housekeeping status of rooms is a tremendous aid in getting early-arriving guests registered, especially during high-occupancy or sold-out periods. Keeping room status information up-to-date requires close coordination and cooperation between the front desk and the housekeeping department. The two most common systems for tracking current room status are mechanical room-rack systems and computerized status systems.

the Rooms
CHRONICLE®

Front Office Link to Housekeeping is Critical

Although the front office and housekeeping departments may be at opposite ends of the hotel, they share a mission: creating a return guest. These departments must work together seamlessly in order to fulfill their goals.

How can housekeeping and the front office work well together? The most successful hotels would answer that they have accomplished this by establishing excellent communication procedures. In fact, they work hard to have the departments integrated in a variety of ways. Here are some of their tips:

- Exchange managers between departments. This is most easily accomplished at the assistant manager or supervisor level but can be done with the executive housekeeper and the front office manager, given the right circumstances.

- Include time in the other department as part of each department's training program. Front desk employees could clean rooms, work in the laundry, or help prepare supplies. Room attendants could make up room packets, stuff confirmations in envelopes, or greet a bus tour. The objective is to get a sense of the activity and workflow of the other department.

- Keep communication efficient. Remember that every call to the other department takes employees away from their tasks and slows them in completing their assignments. Devise verbal and nonverbal ways to relay necessary information with a minimum of effort. For instance, in hotels with manual room-accounting systems, the front desk employees could set aside rack slips as guests check out. Housekeeping could stop by frequently to pick up the slips to update their staff.

- Think of the two departments as one team. Review combined progress toward joint goals of raising customer satisfaction, decreasing expenses, and increasing revenue. Treat the rooms division as one group, and pit the rooms group against food and beverage or marketing in friendly competitions.

- Avoid looking for someone to blame when problems arise. If a guest is checked into a dirty room, pointing fingers is less important than determining what part of the system didn't work and how can it be fixed.

- Create a good working relationship with the front office manager. A respect for one another's talents might result from working together on a project that is not related to either department.

- Schedule social time to bring the departments together. Potluck lunches, bowling tournaments, or charity drives are simple ways to have fun together.

Daily Communication

6 A.M.

> Front office to housekeeping:
> > Daily report of each room's status
> > Rooming lists and times for arriving groups
> > Special requests (adjoining rooms, rollaways), VIP rooms
> > Late check-outs
> > Early check-ins

(continued)

8 A.M.

> Front office to housekeeping:
> > Check-outs already departed
> > Update of special requests and VIPs
> > Assignment of show rooms for the day

10 A.M.

> Housekeeping to front office:
> > Results of vacant room check
> > Rooms that will not be cleaned today
> > Rooms on maintenance and the reasons

Throughout the Day

> Front office to housekeeping:
> > Late departures
> > Extended stays
> > Room changes
> > Check-outs which have departed
> Housekeeping to front office:
> > Continual reporting of vacant and ready rooms
> > Readiness of special requests
> > Status update of rooms found discrepant

Check-Out Time

> Housekeeping to front office:
> > Status of expected check-outs

During Check-In

> Front office to housekeeping:
> > Update on special requests
> > Rooms needed as soon as possible

End of the Day

> Housekeeping to front office:
> > Complete update of hotel status

Source: *The Rooms Chronicle*®, Volume 2, Number 5, p. 2.
For subscription information, call 866-READ-TRC.

The front desk may use a **room rack** to track the status of all rooms. A room rack slip containing the guest's name and other relevant information is normally completed during the registration process and placed in the room rack slot corresponding to the assigned room number. The presence of a room rack slip indicates that the room is occupied. When the guest checks out, the rack slip is removed and the room's status is changed to "on-change." An on-change status indicates that the room is in need of housekeeping services before it can be made available to arriving guests. As unoccupied rooms are cleaned and inspected, the housekeeping department notifies the front desk, which updates the room's status to "vacant and ready."

The cumbersome nature of tracking and comparing housekeeping and front desk room status information often leads to mistakes. For example, if a room rack slip is mistakenly left in the rack even though the guest has checked out, front desk agents may falsely assume that a vacant room is still occupied. This is an example of a room status discrepancy called a "sleeper"; the rack slip is "asleep" in the rack, and the potential revenue from the sale of the room is lost.

Problems may also arise from communication delays between the housekeeping department and the front desk. Spoken communication—over the telephone—relays information quickly, but without supporting documentation. A written report has the advantage of documenting the information but is time-consuming since it must be hand delivered.

In a computerized room-status system, housekeeping and the front desk often have instantaneous access to room status information. When a guest checks out, a front desk agent enters the departure into a computer terminal. Housekeeping is then alerted that the room needs cleaning through a remote terminal located in the housekeeping department. Next, housekeeping attendants clean the room and notify the housekeeping department when it is ready for inspection. Once the room is inspected, housekeeping enters this information into its departmental terminal. This informs the front office computer that the room is available for sale.

While room occupancy status within a computerized system is almost always current, reporting of each room's housekeeping status may lag behind. For example, the housekeeping supervisor may inspect several rooms at once but may not update the computer's room-status files until the end of a long inspection round. In a large operation, calling the housekeeping department after each room is inspected is generally inefficient, since answering the phone can be a frequent interruption. A delay may also occur when a list of clean, inspected rooms is furnished to the housekeeping office but not immediately entered into the computer system.

The problems in promptly reporting each room's housekeeping status to the front office can be eliminated when the computer system is directly connected to the guestroom telephone system. With such a network, supervisors can inspect rooms, determine their readiness for sale, and then enter a code on the room telephone to change the room's status in the hotel's computer system. No one needs to answer the phone since the computer automatically receives the relay, and there is little chance for error. Within seconds, the room's updated status can be displayed on the screen of a front-desk computer terminal. This procedure can significantly reduce not only the number of guests forced to wait for room assignment but also the length of their wait.

Teamwork between housekeeping and the front office is essential to daily hotel operations. The more familiar housekeeping and front office personnel are with each other's procedures, the smoother the relationship between the two departments is likely to be.

the Rooms
CHRONICLE®

Room Maintenance Is Not a Housekeeping Responsibility... Or Is It?

A good housekeeping manager is just as responsible for the hotel's maintenance as an engineering manager. In an ideal environment the housekeeping staff and managers should act as the eyes and ears of the engineering department. If damaged or broken items are not reported, they can't be fixed. Proper maintenance will make the perception of cleanliness easier to maintain and reduce guest complaints. Here are some key tactics to enable housekeepers to help their hotel's maintenance or engineering department.

Coordinate with the engineering department

A successful maintenance program requires teamwork and coordination with other departments including front desk and engineering. Housekeeping and other departments should be responsible for reporting maintenance issues to engineering. The engineering department must be familiar with the reporting procedure and be able to complete the work orders in a timely manner while being able to hold their staff accountable for unfinished work. The front desk must be aware of upcoming maintenance in specific rooms so that those rooms can be taken out of service. Other guestrooms that may be in close proximity may also be set aside to increase the efficiency of maintenance staff and eliminate any potential discomfort to guests (i.e., noise, paint fumes, unwanted debris and foot traffic) who would otherwise have been assigned to those nearby rooms. At slow times of the year an entire floor should be put out-of-order to conduct maintenance checks, perform deep cleaning, and reduce energy expense.

Order forms available to all employees

Make it easy for staff to report maintenance issues. Certainly, managers cannot be everywhere. Therefore, it is essential that they encourage their staff to find items that need maintenance and to report them in a timely manner. Timely reporting is best facilitated by ensuring that all employees have easy access to maintenance work order forms, that employees are trained in how to fill them out, and that the forms are delivered or deposited with engineering personnel for appropriate attention.

Punch lists for projects

Rooms division managers should have an accurate listing of all the rooms in the hotel earmarked for special projects. This can be accomplished best by entering key information onto a punch list spreadsheet. For example, the top of the spreadsheet should contain the title of the project, while underneath, separate columns are created that indicate the guestroom number, room type, start date of work, as well as columns to indicate that the work has been completed and inspected by management. The punch list will help track the progress of the project and track which rooms still need attention.

(continued)

(continued)

Evaluate housekeeping staff

A housekeeping department has tasks to complete throughout the majority of the hotel. In order for items to be repaired or attended to in a timely manner, they must be reported immediately to engineering. Again, since the engineering staff or the management of the housekeeping department cannot be everywhere at once, it is essential that all housekeeping employees participate in the work-order maintenance program by serving as engineering's "eyes and ears." Make it clear to housekeeping employees that if an item is broken or damaged they are expected to report that repairs are needed. To support this concept, housekeeping management must hold its employees accountable for fulfilling their role in the reporting process. This can be accomplished through room inspections, promotional contests, and daily reminders at the morning housekeeping briefing. Emphasize to the staff that maintenance is an important issue.

Demonstrate that items are reported

It is important for a housekeeping manager to record work orders that have been placed. An excellent way of doing this is to use a computerized spreadsheet. Recording maintenance requests will assist the engineering managers in holding their staff accountable for not completing work and show housekeeping staff that their maintenance reports are being taken seriously. The tracking process should be computerized and have the capability of being sorted by date, room number, type of request, and level of priority.

Another option is to create a maintenance tracking board. Use triplicate carbon-copy work order forms to report maintenance issues. Copies should stay with the reporting department, the engineering department, and the engineer to whom the repair is assigned. Once the work is completed the engineering copy should be returned to the reporting department. A good way to keep the work orders organized is a board with hooks or nails for the work orders. A sample layout is shown below.

Priority	1	2	3	Completed
Floor				
Back of House				
1				
2				
3				
4				
5				

Once a week a housekeeping manager should check several completed work orders with the engineering manager at random to make sure they have been completed.

Source: James Fields, *The Rooms Chronicle*®, Volume 12, Number 2, pp. 4–5.
For subscription information, call 866-READ-TRC.

Housekeeping and Maintenance

In most nonlodging commercial buildings, housekeeping and maintenance personnel generally report to the same department manager. This makes a great deal of sense because these functional areas have similar goals and methods and must have a close working relationship. In most midsize and large lodging operations, however, housekeeping personnel report to the rooms division manager, while engineering and maintenance constitute a separate division. Differing lines of accountability can become a barrier between these important support centers of a hotel.

It is unfortunate that support centers often seem to have an almost adversarial relationship. For example, housekeeping personnel sometimes resent having to clean up after various types of maintenance is completed, while engineering personnel may be upset if the misuse of chemicals and equipment by housekeeping personnel results in additional work for them. In order to ensure the smooth operation of both departments, housekeeping and engineering managers need to devote attention to improving the relationship between their departments.

Types of Maintenance

The housekeeping department often takes the first steps to maintenance functions for which engineering is ultimately responsible. There are three kinds of maintenance activities: routine maintenance, preventive maintenance, and scheduled maintenance.

Routine maintenance activities are those which relate to the general upkeep of the property, occur on a regular (daily or weekly) basis, and require relatively minimal training or skills. These are maintenance activities which occur outside of a formal work-order system and for which no specific maintenance records (time or materials) are kept. Examples include sweeping carpets, washing floors, cleaning readily accessible windows, cutting grass, cleaning guestrooms, shoveling snow, and replacing burned-out light bulbs. Many of these routine maintenance activities are carried out by the housekeeping department. Proper care of many surfaces and materials by housekeeping personnel is the first step in the overall maintenance program for the property's furniture and fixtures.

Preventive maintenance consists of three parts: inspection, minor corrections, and work-order initiation. For many areas within the hotel, inspections are performed by housekeeping personnel in the normal course of their duties. For example, room attendants and inspectors may regularly check guestrooms for leaking faucets, cracked caulking around bathroom fixtures, and other items that may call for action by engineering staff. Attending to leaking faucets and improper caulking around sinks and tubs can control maintenance costs by preventing greater problems, such as ceiling or wall damage in the bath below. Such maintenance protects the physical plant investment and contributes to guest satisfaction.

Communication between housekeeping and engineering should be efficient so that most minor repairs can be handled while the room attendant is cleaning the guestroom. In some properties, a full-time maintenance person may be

Exhibit 7   Sample Maintenance Work Order

DELTA FORMS - MILWAUKEE U.S.A.

(414) 461-0086

HYATT HOTELS ⊗   **MAINTENANCE REQUEST**

TIME _____   1345239

BY _____ DATE _____

LOCATION _____

PROBLEM _____
_____
_____
_____
_____
_____
_____

ASSIGNED TO _____
DATE COMPL. _____ TIME SPENT _____
COMPLETED BY _____
REMARKS _____
_____
_____
_____
_____
_____
_____

RPHK-04

HYATT HOTELS MAINTENANCE CHECK LIST
Check (☒) Indicates Unsatisfactory Condition
Explain Check In Remarks Section
BEDROOM - FOYER - CLOSET
☐ WALLS   ☐ WOODWORK   ☐ DOORS
☐ CEILING   ☐ TELEVISION ☐ LIGHTS
☐ FLOORS   ☐ A.C. UNIT   ☐ BLINDS
☐ WINDOWS   ☐ DRAPES
REMARKS : _____
_____
_____
_____

BATHROOM
☐ TRIM   ☐ SHOWER
☐ DRAINS   ☐ LIGHTS
☐ WALL PAPER   ☐ PAINT
☐ TILE OR GLASS ☐ DOOR
☐ ACCESSORIES   ☐ WINDOW
REMARKS : _____
_____
_____
_____

Courtesy of Hyatt Corporation, Chicago, Illinois

assigned to inspect guestrooms and to perform the necessary repairs, adjustments, or replacements.

Preventive maintenance, by its nature, sometimes identifies problems and needs beyond the scope of a minor correction. These problems are brought to the attention of engineering through the work-order system. The necessary work is then scheduled by the chief engineer. This type of work is often referred to as **scheduled maintenance**.

Scheduled maintenance activities are initiated at the property based on a formal work order or similar document. Work orders are a key element in the communication between housekeeping and engineering. A sample work order is shown in Exhibit 7. In many properties, work orders are numbered, three-part forms. Each part of the form is color coded for its recipient.

For example, when a member of the housekeeping department fills out a work order form, one copy is sent to the executive housekeeper and two copies to engineering. The chief engineer gets one of these copies and gives the other to the tradesperson assigned to the repair. The individual completing the task indicates the number of hours required to complete the work, any parts or supplies required, and other relevant information. When the job is completed, a copy of the

Exhibit 8   Sample Equipment History Record

		HISTORY OF REPAIRS				ACME VISIBLE CROZET VIRGINIA #60P01
DATE	W.O. NO.	DESCRIPTION OF REPAIRS		DOWN TIME	MAN HOURS	MATERIAL COST

TAG NO.	DESCRIPTION	WEEKLY CONTROL 1 2 3 4	MONTHLY INSPECTION CONTROL
			JAN FEB MAR APR MAY JUN JUL AUG SEP OCT NOV DEC

TYPIST PLEASE NOTE - START ALL TYPING AT SAME POINT ON SCALE THEN REMOVE THIS STUB   BE SURE YOU HAVE A WELL INKED RIBBON   CARE USED IN TYPING WILL IMPROVE REFERENCE DURING THE ENTIRE LIFE OF THE INDEX   TRY A FEW IN THE POCKETS TO SEE HOW THEY LOOK BEFORE TYPING THE ENTIRE LIST

RE-ORDER FORM NO. 60P01   ACME VISIBLE RECORDS   PRINTED IN U.S.A.
CROZET VIRGINIA

Courtesy of Acme Visible Records

tradesperson's completed work order is sent to the executive housekeeper. If this copy is not returned to the executive housekeeper within an appropriate amount of time, housekeeping issues another work order, which signals engineering to provide a status report on the requested repair.

Engineering generally keeps data cards and history records on all equipment operated by housekeeping personnel. Equipment data cards contain basic information about pieces of equipment. This information can include technical data, manufacturers' information, the item's cost, special instructions, warranty information, and references to other information as well (such as the storage location of manuals and drawings). Equipment history records (see Exhibit 8) are logs of the inspection and maintenance work performed on a given piece of equipment. History records may be separate cards or may be incorporated into the equipment data card. Their purpose is to provide documentation of all maintenance activity on a given piece of equipment. Many properties have computerized these record-keeping functions, making it easier for the executive housekeeper to retrieve pertinent information when requesting replacement or new equipment.

Teamwork

Teamwork is the key to successful hotel operations. Housekeeping must work closely not only with the front office and engineering but also with every other department

the Rooms
CHRONICLE®

Housekeeping and Engineering Work Together to Save Energy

The latest trend among both large and small hotels is to have one manager in charge of both engineering and housekeeping. Sometimes this manager's title is Director of Property Operations or Director of Services. It is no secret in the lodging industry that housekeeping and engineering sometimes have different opinions on how to save energy and implement a good preventive maintenance program. A good synergy between these departments can significantly improve efficiency of employees and the quality of the product by implementing guestroom repairs in a speedy manner.

Preventive maintenance program

Obviously, housekeepers generally go into all guestrooms in the hotel on an almost daily basis. Engineers are lucky to get into all of the guestrooms twice per year. This means that housekeepers observe maintenance items much quicker than do the maintenance engineers. With one department head, this encourages housekeepers to report potential guest complaints much more efficiently. Leaking faucets, burned out lights, mold in tubs, broken towel bars, etc., can go on for months if not reported to maintenance. This directly affects energy use and the guest experience.

A preventive maintenance (PM) program can range from an index card system to a computerized system, such as one provided by a company known as Espresso. PM systems can be extremely effective if implemented properly and have the cooperation of both the engineering and housekeeping departments. This is the area where the result of having one manager can be most effective. Rather than each department blaming each other for potential problems, the responsibility lays with the manager of the total operation.

The housekeeping and engineering departments literally control about 90 percent of the energy consumed in a hotel. The efficiency of energy and water use is directly related to how well these departments administrate the operation and maintenance of all components in the hotel.

The engineering department operates on the theory of preventive maintenance. This requires lists of items in the hotel that must be maintained at predetermined intervals. The housekeeping department identifies problems throughout the guestrooms that are more related to current maintenance problems in the guestroom. By blending current and predicted maintenance, a significant improvement will be noticed by the guest and all the components in the guestroom.

Both housekeeping and engineering must be involved in the preventive maintenance program, regardless of its type. Housekeepers should be capable of processing preventive maintenance work orders in a quick and easy manner. If a toilet is overflowing, a housekeeper should be capable of reporting it to maintenance very quickly and easily. In order to overcome bilingual problems, a simple numerical code checklist should be developed. For example, a leaking showerhead could be code number 6. In a more technical manner, computer software can enable a housekeeper to dial a specific extension from the guestroom phone and enter the code for repair. The computer will automatically generate a work order for engineers to respond to as quickly as possible.

The preventive maintenance program should also incorporate participation of the guest. Procedures should be developed whereby the guest can call one source, be it the operator or a predetermined extension, to report a problem that can be inserted into the preventive maintenance system immediately in order to ensure that the problem is corrected within a matter of less than 30 minutes. As one can see, there are significant overlapping responsibilities between housekeeping and engineering with regard to maintaining the quality of the hotel and conserving energy.

Energy conservation

Both engineering and housekeeping have firm control of the amount of energy the hotel consumes by implementing procedures. It is the responsibility of engineering to provide the proper temperature of water to the guestroom, while it is the responsibility of housekeeping to make sure the water is not leaking in the guestroom or being wasted in other ways. This partnership of services to the hotel further supports the theory of having one manager over both departments.

Depending on the type of hotel, the guestroom block typically consumes anywhere from 50 to 80 percent of the energy consumed in the total hotel. Both housekeeping and engineering have a direct responsibility for the energy consumed in these areas. The manager of the housekeeping department should develop firm procedures for housekeepers to set controls in guestrooms properly and follow other procedures.

For example, housekeepers should not set air conditioning on "max" while they are cleaning the room and housekeepers should set the thermostats properly after the room is cleaned. The housekeeping/engineering manager should be responsible for informing housekeepers on a daily or weekly basis how thermostats should be set in rooms. This is a frequent and severe problem with regard to wasting energy in hotels. Numerous on-site audits always discover guestrooms set to maximum cooling while they are unoccupied, or maximum heating during unoccupied periods.

One concept to eliminate this problem is a weatherboard. This involves the use of a placard in housekeeping where housekeepers pick up their carts or are issued keys and room assignments every morning. This placard will depict a sketch of how the thermostat should be set for that given day.

Obviously, housekeepers can implement many other simple procedures that will save a significant amount of energy and improve comfort in the guestroom. Blackout draperies should be closed to within 6 inches after the room is cleaned to provide some light, yet save energy due to heat lost through the windows. Housekeepers should not leave water running in sinks when they are cleaning the bathroom. And it is always a poor idea to leave the television on while the housekeepers are cleaning the rooms. This affects energy consumption and the efficiency of the housekeeper.

(continued)

(continued)

Synergy equals more control

From a global perspective, one can see that both housekeeping and engineering have the same Mission Statement related to their overall responsibilities. They are to maintain the property as efficiently as possible and control and reduce energy and water use wherever this can be accomplished without affecting guest comfort. The formal preventive maintenance system and specific procedures are the primary method of implementing this concept. Standardized procedures with regard to lighting, thermostats and other basic items are critical. The synergy between these two departments is almost instantaneously noticed by a guest upon entering the guestroom portion of the hotel. This concept will also provide the general manager with a more direct link with regard to monitoring the performance of these two departments.

Source: Phil Sprague, *The Rooms Chronicle®*, Volume 12, Number 6, pp. 12–13. For subscription information, call 866-READ-TRC.

in the hotel. Although the general manager is responsible for implementing the teamwork philosophy, each department and every employee can help.

Endnotes

1. As it is used in this chapter, "hotel" is a generic term for all types of lodging operations, including luxury hotels, motels, motor inns, and inns.

2. These statistics are published in the "2007 Lodging Industry Profile," a report prepared each year by the Communications Department of the American Hotel & Lodging Association.

3. "What's Hiding in Your Hotel Room?" Jan. 15, 2006, ABC News Report, abcnews. go.com.

4. This section was adapted from *The Rooms Chronicle®*, Volume 4, Number 5, p. 5.

Key Terms

back of the house—The functional areas of the hotel in which employees have little or no guest contact, such as engineering and maintenance.

economy hotel—A hotel property that focuses on the most basic needs of guests by providing clean, comfortable, and inexpensive rooms.

front of the house—The functional areas of the hotel in which employees have extensive guest contact, such as food & beverage facilities and the front office.

housekeeping status report—A report the housekeeping department prepares that indicates the current housekeeping status of each room, based on a physical check.

luxury hotel—A hotel property that offers world-class service, upscale restaurants and lounges, exquisite decor, concierge service, and opulent meeting facilities.

mid-market service—A modest but sufficient level of service that appeals to the largest segment of the traveling public. A mid-market property may offer uniformed service, airport limousine service, room service, a specialty restaurant, coffee shop, and lounge, and special rates for certain guests.

occupancy report—A report prepared each night by a front desk agent that lists rooms occupied that night and indicates guests who are expected to check out the following day.

organization chart—A schematic representation of the relationships between positions within an organization, showing where each position fits into the overall organization and illustrating the divisions of responsibility and lines of authority.

preventive maintenance—A systematic approach to maintenance in which situations are identified and corrected on a regular basis to control costs and keep larger problems from occurring.

revenue center—An operating division or department that sells goods or services to guests and thereby generates revenue for the hotel. The front office, food & beverage outlets, room service, and retail stores are typical revenue centers.

room rack—An array of metal file pockets designed to hold room rack slips arranged by room number. The room rack summarizes the current status of all rooms in the hotel.

room status discrepancy—A situation in which the housekeeping department's description of a room's status differs from the room status information at the front desk.

routine maintenance—Activities related to the general upkeep of the property that occur on a regular (daily or weekly) basis and require relatively minimal training or skills to perform.

scheduled maintenance—Activities related to the upkeep of the property that are initiated through a formal work-order or similar document.

support center—An operating division or department that does not generate direct revenue but plays a supporting role to the hotel's revenue centers. Support centers include the housekeeping, accounting, engineering and maintenance, and human resources functions.

turndown service—A special service provided by the housekeeping department in which a room attendant enters the guestroom in the early evening to restock supplies, tidy the room, and turn down the covers on the bed.

world-class service—A level of service that stresses the personal attention given to guests. Hotels offering world-class service provide upscale restaurants and lounges, exquisite decor, concierge service, opulent rooms, and abundant amenities.

Review Questions ————————————————————

1. Name the three basic service-level categories of hotels. What are typical characteristics of each?

2. What is the purpose of an organization chart?

3. What is the difference between a revenue center and a support center? What hotel departments typically fall under each category?

4. What is meant by the terms "front of the house" and "back of the house"? What functional areas are typically classified under each term?

5. What major divisions are typically found in a large hotel?

6. What important contribution does housekeeping make to a property's sales effort? How?

7. Why are two-way communications necessary between the front desk and housekeeping?

8. What are the systems used by the front desk and housekeeping to track current room status?

9. Compare the three kinds of maintenance activities.

10. What is the ideal relationship between housekeeping and maintenance? What is the actual situation in some properties?

 Internet Sites ————————————————————

For more information, visit the following Internet sites. Remember, that Internet addresses can change without notice. If the site is no longer there, you can use a search engine to look for additional sites.

Best Western International
www.bestwestern.com

Fairmont Hotels & Resorts
www.fairmont.com

Choice Hotels International
www.choicehotels.com

Doubletree Hotels – Hilton Hotels
doubletree1.hilton.com/en_US/dt/
index.do

Hyatt Hotels and Resorts
www.hyatt.com

Marriott Hotels, Resorts, and Suites
www.marriott.com

Radisson Hotels Worldwide
www.radisson.com

Sheraton Hotels & Resorts
www.starwoodhotels.com/sheraton/
index.html

Walt Disney World Resorts
disneyworld.disney.
go.com/wdw/index?bhcp=1

 **Case Study** ————————————————————————

VIP Gets Lost in the Service Shuffle, or How the ABC Hotel Dropped the Ball

Monday
10:00 A.M.

The eight o'clock Monday-morning sales meeting had been more tedious than most, Ms. Sarah Salesperson thought as she made her way back to her office. She poured herself a cup of coffee before sitting at her computer to compose a memo. The director of sales had hammered away at one of her pet themes that morning: "The secret to sales is, 'Don't drop the ball!'" I suppose she's right, Sarah mused as she began to type; dropping the ball is certainly easy enough to do at a 600-room hotel. In light of the morning meeting, she thought it might be wise to send a note about Mr. Bigbucks to Ray Smith, the front office manager. Mr. Bigbucks was a director at XYZ Corporation, an international firm that could mean $500,000 or more in room bookings in the next two years—if Mr. Bigbucks could be persuaded to place some of his group meetings and other business with the hotel. He was due to arrive at 1:30 P.M. today, and Sarah wanted everything to be perfect for him.

> Dear Ray:
>
> Just wanted to remind you that Mr. Bigbucks of the XYZ Corporation is arriving at 1:30 P.M. today for an overnight stay. *Please* make sure he gets the full VIP treatment. I've chatted with him on the phone a few times, and will meet with him in person next month about the possibility of booking some business with the hotel, but I won't be able to connect with him this visit—I'm flying to Dallas this morning.
>
> Don't worry—I remembered to fill out the VIP forms this time and everybody should have them by now!
>
> Sincerely,
> *Sarah*

10:30 A.M.

To make doubly sure Ray understood the importance of Mr. Bigbucks, Sarah walked down to the front office to deliver her memo in person, but Ray was not at his desk. Oh well, he'll probably be back in a minute, she thought. She left the memo on Ray's chair so he would notice it first thing.

11:10 A.M.

Ray finally escaped for a few minutes from a meeting the general manager called that morning, and went straight to his desk to check for messages. He read Sarah's memo and decided to drop it off at the front desk on his way back to the meeting.

11:20 A.M.

At the front desk, Evert was trying to stay calm and friendly despite the crowd milling in the lobby. He had only been a front desk agent for three weeks and still got nervous when tour buses pulled up outside the hotel. That morning two groups, the American Society of Poets and the Plate Glass Producers, were checking in; this afternoon the American Pharmaceutical Association would arrive for a four-day regional meeting. Evert didn't even notice Ray until Ray tapped him on the shoulder. "Make sure housekeeping knows about this," Ray said, and placed Sarah's memo beside Evert's computer keyboard. Evert half-turned and nodded while continuing to check in a guest.

11:45 A.M.

Evert took advantage of a lull to read what Ray had dropped off. He quickly picked up a walkie-talkie and called Gail, the executive housekeeper. "Hi Gail, it's Evert at the front desk. We've got a VIP, Mr. Bigbucks, arriving at 1:30 this afternoon. I'm changing room 816 from 'clean and ready' to 'out of order' until you can give it the VIP treatment, OK? Thanks."

11:50 A.M.

Why am I always at the other end of the hotel when I get a call like this? Gail thought as she hurried to the employee lunchroom. And why is it always when my staff is eating lunch or taking a break? She asked Mary and Teresa, two of her best room attendants, to interrupt their lunches and follow her to room 816. As the three of them were walking to the linen closet to get fresh bedspreads and blankets, she called Roger, the head of maintenance and engineering, and asked him to send someone to 816. Then she called George in the kitchen. "George, this is Gail. Are the amenities for 816 ready?" George said he was just finishing up and someone would drop them off soon.

1:20 P.M.

Gail stood in the doorway and cast a critical eye over room 816 one last time. The quiet and order she surveyed were in sharp contrast to the noise and bustle of the last hour and a half. A small army had descended on the suite and performed all the tasks needed to transform a guestroom from merely "excellent" to "perfect." As Mr. Thompson, the hotel general manager, had said to Gail on more than one occasion, "It's your job to put the "wow factor" in every VIP room. When they open that guestroom door for the first time, that's what I want them to think: 'Wow!'"

Gail reviewed her informal "wow" checklist in her mind. The clean bed linen, blankets, and bedspread were upgraded to freshly ironed sheets, new blankets, and a new bedspread. Mary edged the carpet with a whisk broom to get every speck of dust, the furniture was pulled out and the carpet vacuumed underneath, and the chair and chair cushions were vacuumed. Then the carpet was spot cleaned. All the drawers in the bedroom and bathroom were wiped out to make sure no dust or hair was hiding. As the drapes were taken down and replaced with freshly cleaned ones, Chris Jones arrived from maintenance and checked over all the room's mechanicals. While he was checking the bathroom, he noticed a small rust stain on the toilet seat. Teresa could not scrub it off, so Chris went off to find a new toilet seat to replace the old one. Nothing in the room made of wood escaped the polishing cloths. At around 1:00 P.M., Jessie arrived from the restaurant with the hotel's platinum amenities package: a miniature wicker chair about two feet high containing cheese, crackers, a bottle of wine, fruit, nuts, and bread sticks interlaced with packets of hard candy made by the hotel chef. Personalized matchbooks embossed with Mr. Bigbucks's initials, a vase of fresh-cut flowers, and a gilt-edged note signed by Mr. Thompson himself completed the amenities. The installation of the sparkling new toilet seat was completed just ten minutes before.

Gail gazed down at the undisturbed herringbone pattern in the carpeting, left by the vacuum Teresa ran as the last touch, and couldn't think of a thing she had missed. "Room 816's ready" she called in to the front desk, and went off to see if she could sneak in a few bites of lunch.

4:35 P.M.

Mr. Bigbucks arrived at the hotel looking a bit rumpled from the long plane trip and the taxi ride shared with four other people. The hotel lobby was crowded with pharmacists and late-arriving poets checking in at the conventions desk. He walked up to an unoccupied spot along the regular front desk area and waited until a front desk agent could break away from the group check-ins.

"Good afternoon, welcome to the ABC Hotel, my name is Joan. How can I help you?"

"Hi, my name is Bigbucks. I have a reservation for tonight."

"Let me check that for you." The computer keys ticked quickly. "Yes, you'll be staying for one night. Do you need help with your luggage?"

"No, I have just one small bag."

Joan finished the check-in process, smiling and remembering to make frequent eye contact, and gave Mr. Bigbucks the key packet to room 616.

4:40 P.M.

When Mr. Bigbucks opened the door to 616, he was mildly disappointed to find nothing waiting for him in the room. The room was spotless and fresh, but at most hotels he found flowers, chocolates, maybe a note to welcome him. Here…nothing. Maybe it's because I'm only staying one night, he thought, although he didn't know why that would make a difference. His flight had been delayed, so he arrived at the hotel much later than he'd planned and had just enough time to unpack and take a quick shower before heading out to dinner at the home of XYZ's president.

5:15 P.M.

Dr. Lucky, a dentist from Omaha, walked up to the front desk with a suitcase in each hand. He was in town for a three-day meeting at the city's convention center near the hotel. "I'd like a suite please," he said.

Dr. Lucky put his bags down while the front desk agent scanned the computer terminal. "We have a suite on the eighth floor available." A bell attendant started to place Dr. Lucky's bags on a luggage cart but Dr. Lucky stopped him. He liked to save money on his business trips whenever he could. He collected his room key, rode the elevator to the eighth floor, and followed the arrows to 816. He set his suitcases down and fumbled briefly with the electronic door lock before swinging the door open. He bent to pick up his bags. When he caught sight of the suite, he straightened up slowly, the bags forgotten. "Wow!" he sighed reverently.

5:35 P.M.

After hesitating a moment over stepping on the perfectly groomed carpeting, Dr. Lucky walked into the suite. He paused a moment to take it all in—the shining surfaces, the hint of fragrance from the flowers, the wicker basket (was that a tiny chair?)—before bringing in his suitcases, shutting the door, and opening up the wine. He usually didn't stay at hotels as nice as the ABC Hotel, but he decided to splurge a bit on this trip. I've got to do this more often, he thought, I had no idea ordinary guests were treated so well at these posh hotels. He was munching happily on the cheese and crackers and looking curiously at the candies—he'd never seen any quite like them before—when he noticed a note on the dresser:

Dear Mr. Bigbucks:

We hope you enjoy your stay with the ABC Hotel. If there is anything we can do to make your experience with us more pleasant, please let us know.
Jim Thompson, General Manager

Dr. Lucky stopped in mid-chew. Oh, no, he thought, I've already eaten half the stuff in the basket. Will I have to pay extra for this?

5:40 P.M.

Mr. Bigbucks got in the elevator and pushed the button for the hotel lobby. At the third floor, the elevator stopped and the hotel's director of sales got in. The director and Mr. Bigbucks rode in silence to the lobby, where they both got off and headed in opposite directions.

6:00 P.M.

Dr. Lucky changed into more casual clothes and decided to spend the evening finding the convention center and exploring the city around the hotel. It was an easy decision to wait until tomorrow morning to call the front desk and straighten out the mix-up.

Tuesday
8:00 A.M.

Dr. Lucky went down to the hotel restaurant for breakfast. Since he planned to go back to his room before leaving for the convention center, he decided he would call the front desk later to discuss the wine-and-flowers mix-up. At the restaurant, he ran into a dentist he knew. They ate breakfast together and shared a cab ride directly to the convention center. Dr. Lucky promised himself he would stop at the front desk and get things straightened out when he got back.

8:30 A.M.

Mr. Bigbucks picked up his bag and pulled the door to room 616 closed behind him. He hadn't slept well. He was hoping the all-day meeting at corporate headquarters would end early so he could change his seven o'clock flight back home to something earlier. At the front desk, the agent was exceptionally friendly and efficient. On the way out to his cab Mr. Bigbucks passed Ray Smith. Ray was in a hurry; he had another meeting with the general manager about improving guest service.

Discussion Questions

1. What did the ABC Hotel do wrong?

2. How could the hotel have recovered with Mr. Bigbucks had it discovered its mistake while he was still at the hotel? How can the hotel recover with Mr. Bigbucks now?

3. What procedures should the hotel put in place to avoid such a mix-up in the future?

The following industry experts helped generate and develop this case: Gail Edwards, CHHE, St. Louis, Missouri; Mary Friedman, Edina, Minnesota; and Aleta Nitschke, CHA, founder of *The Rooms Chronicle*®, Garfield, Minnesota.

Chapter 2 Outline

Sustainability and Green Philosophies
    Good Earthkeeping and Going Green
    Green Teams
    Certification Programs
Housekeeping's Role in a Green Property
    Communication
    Training
    Purchasing
Water Conservation
    Linen Reuse Programs
    Guestrooms
    Laundry
    Public Restrooms
Energy Efficiency
    Energy Management
    Lighting
Waste Management
    Reduce
    Recycle
    Reuse
Indoor Air Quality
    Indoor Air Quality Programs
    Fighting Mold
Cleaning Chemicals

Competencies

1. Explain why it is important for hospitality properties to adopt environmentally friendly policies, and list "green" strategies and organizations that can help hospitality properties be good stewards of the environment. (pp. 37–45)

2. Describe the role that housekeeping plays in a "green" property. (pp. 45–48)

3. List ways that hospitality properties can conserve water. (pp. 48–52)

4. Explain the steps hospitality properties can take to become more energy efficient. (pp. 52–57)

5. List the three main components of a waste management program. (pp. 57–60)

6. Describe the importance of indoor air quality and how it can be safeguarded. (pp. 60–63)

7. Explain how executive housekeepers can safely manage cleaning chemicals. (pp. 63–64)

2

Environmental and Energy Management

A majority of content in this chapter was contributed by Phil Sprague, President of PSA Energy Consultants, an energy consulting and hotel engineering audit company based in Mound, Minnesota.

ONE OF THE MOST DRAMATIC SHIFTS in the demands placed on executive housekeepers and other hospitality managers has been the increased need to know about energy management, sustainability, and environmentally responsible policies and procedures. Hospitality managers today must understand the role they play in ensuring their properties are wisely using resources, preventing waste, and contributing to an environment that is safe to reside in.

Why is there so much attention to "going green" in hotels lately? *Lodging Hospitality* says that environmentally friendly policies contribute to a **triple bottom line**: economic, environmental, and social.[1] Enacting environmentally sound policies increases the economic health of a property. The numbers are compelling and impossible to ignore. Properties that have instituted green policies have reaped millions of dollars in cost reductions. Economic benefits have included:

- Energy savings
- Waste reduction and lower disposal costs
- Eligibility for government incentives
- Reduced labor costs
- Reduced employee absenteeism
- Increased productivity

Environmental benefits include the conservation of limited resources. The actions that the hospitality industry takes to conserve water, save energy, reduce waste, and purify the air are making the world a healthier place to live. They reduce pollution and help preserve natural habitats. They ensure the long-term success of a property by helping to make tomorrow's world a sustainable environment.

The social benefits are also plentiful. Having environmentally sound management policies and initiatives—and publicizing those efforts—makes a property more attractive to its guests and to groups calling for environmental accountability. Green policies also can make the property more comfortable and healthy for guests. *Southern Hospitality* magazine cited the following ways hospitality properties can reap the benefits of environmentally friendly philosophies:

- Create a sense of pride in the community

- Increase the morale and health of employees

- Enhance a property's image

- Provide a competitive edge in the industry

- Establish a property as an environmental leader

- Create a deeper level of trust in guests, suppliers, and partners[2]

To explore the role that executive housekeepers and their departments play in a property's environmental policies, this chapter will examine sustainability initiatives and "green" philosophies, housekeeping's role in a green property, and specific policies that support water conservation, energy efficiency, waste reduction, clean air practices, and responsible cleaning chemical use.

Sustainability and Green Philosophies

The hospitality industry has been cited by the U.S. Environmental Protection Agency as a leader in environmentalism. Hospitality organizations have made an ever-growing commitment to the concept of **sustainability**—a way of doing business that says a company shouldn't take more than it gives back and should not sacrifice tomorrow for today's needs. Exhibit 1 tells the success stories of a few of the many hospitality properties that have made a commitment to sustainability.

A property's environmental policy must have commitment from not only the general manager, but from the owner(s) and central headquarters. The official sanction from top management will motivate employees and help them to realize that conservation is a part of their job responsibilities. They are also the ones who will conduct an environmental assessment, the first step to creating a property-wide environmental program. These assessments can establish baseline measurements and identify those areas in which the property can make the most improvement.

Good Earthkeeping and Going Green

The American Hotel & Lodging Association (AH&LA) has participated in several initiatives to help hoteliers demonstrate environmental leadership. The first initiative was launched in 2004—a partnership with the U.S. Environmental Protection Agency's (EPA) Energy Star. The program is called Good Earthkeeping, an educational program that provides resources and tools to help make hotels more profitable, competitive, and environmentally responsible through increased energy efficiency and ecological stewardship. The program helps hoteliers create a comprehensive strategic approach to energy management that assesses current energy performance, sets goals, tracks savings, and rewards improvements. It also makes available a series of Energy Star Webinars. Properties that participate in the Good Earthkeeping program become eligible for national recognition from the EPA.

A second initiative is Going Green, launched in July 2007 as part of a partnership with the International Tourism Partnership out of London, England. Going Green offers guidelines for hotels to set minimum standards to improve

Exhibit 1   Sustainability Success Stories

The Green Hotels Association and Energy Star, reported on several successful endeavors hospitality properties and organizations are making to help the environment:

- A lodge in Alberta, Canada, produces 50 to 90 percent of its electricity by solar and wind power, and 90 to 100 percent of its heat from solar energy and wood, resulting in a 90-percent reduction in fossil fuel use.

- Lodges in the Grand Canyon National Park compost more than 600 cubic yards of material each year; use non-toxic chemicals in transportation, cleaning, and food service; and encourage vendors to eliminate products that are harmful to the environment.

- The Columbus Hospitality Group reduced its energy bills and maintenance costs by $30,000 a year through a renovation that made its hotel more energy efficient. This included upgrading all lights; installing high-efficiency air conditioning units and pumps; installing occupancy sensors for lights and HVAC in offices and guestrooms; installing water-saving showerheads, toilets, and sinks; and installing energy-efficient TVs, VCRs, fax, and copy machines in rooms. Energy Star estimated that the property generated enough savings to increase its average daily revenue by $3.25.

- Marriott developed an auditing and inspection system for its properties to enhance their energy management systems and procedures. This resulted in a company-wide savings of $4.5 million annually.

- The Saunders Hotel Group began its environmental commitment in the 1980s when it pioneered ecotourism. It now involves staff members at all levels to conserve energy. The organization's most recent sustainability efforts included purchasing new energy efficient equipment for guestrooms and offices, and using energy management systems, motion sensors, fluorescent lighting, heat pumps, and ozone laundry systems in its properties.

- The Hyatt Regency Coconut Point Resort and Spa in Bonita Springs was the first Florida hotel to receive the state's two-palm certification in 2006. The property has reduced its water consumption by 28 percent, energy use by 1.8 percent, and waste disposal by 2.8 percent—after its initial one palm certification. The resort instituted a linen and towel reuse program and installed a laundry system that recycles water and steam and limits the water and detergent used. It donates leftover toiletries and used linens to charities.

Sources: Green Hotel Association, Energy Star, Florida Department of Environmental Protection.

sustainability and achieve goals for better environmental management. The Going Green program establishes six areas of focus for hospitality properties:

- *Policy and framework,* to develop a commitment from all employees
- *Staff training and awareness,* as a way to build a motivated staff
- *Environmental management,* aiming for the highest standards in terms of biodiversity protection, hygiene, safety, indoor air quality, and overall environmental management

the Rooms CHRONICLE®

States' Green Lodging Programs and Hotels' Eco-friendly Practices Plant the Seeds for Greener Bottom Lines

It has taken some time but the wait has been well worth it for hoteliers and current and future generations of guests. More and more states are following in the footsteps of California and are launching green lodging programs to preserve precious natural resources and recognize and reward hospitality businesses' eco-friendly practices.

In fact, the practice of eco-friendly practices has rippled from coast to coast to the point where states such as Florida, North Carolina, Pennsylvania, and Vermont also are getting green.

Pineapple Hospitality recently partnered with the Florida Department of Environmental Protection (DEP) to help the state's lodging industry create a healthier, safer indoor environment and reduce the generation of solid waste in hotels and motels. In the public-private partnership, Pineapple is providing hotels and motels with technical assistance on cost-saving green products and practices. Offering an arsenal of energy and water conservation, air quality improvement and waste reduction, recycling and reuse solutions, Pineapple is helping Florida DEP's nine certified Green Lodging facilities and 15 others currently enrolled and working toward the green designation to unearth a world of fresh ideas on how to help themselves while helping protect the environment.

Profits in the palm

Florida DEP'S Green Lodging Certification Program tiers its certified hotels into three levels:

One Palm Certification

To achieve this level of certification a hotel/motel must have completed the core activities representing a minimum set of best management practices in the areas of communication, water conservation, energy efficiency, waste reduction, and clean air. In addition, the property must obtain support from top management, form an active multi-disciplinary "green team," and operate in compliance with all applicable environmental laws and regulations.

Two Palm Certification

To achieve this level of certification a hotel/motel must have maintained the facility's one palm status for at least 12 consecutive months before applying for two palm certification. The hotel/motel had to have conducted an environmental baseline assessment, developed and enacted performance improvement goals, implemented at least one green project and evaluated its progress. If Two Palm certification status is not achieved within 24 months of obtaining the One Palm certification, the property may be moved to inactive status and will be removed from the Green Lodging Locator website: www.floridagreenlodging.com. A hotel in inactive status will no longer be able to consider itself a Florida Certified Green Lodge and will no longer be able to use the Florida Green Lodging Certification Program to promote the property.

(continued)

Three Palm Certification

To achieve this level of certification a hotel/motel must have maintained the facility's Two Palm certification and have demonstrated continual improvement for three consecutive years. To retain this certification level, the facility must continue to maintain or improve its high level of commitment to protecting the state's environment through the Florida Green Lodging program.

Who certifies these "Green Lodges"?

The Florida Department of Environmental Protection has trained Green Lodging Assessors (predominantly comprised of state and local government employees) throughout the state who visit the lodging facilities. The assessor verifies the facility's Green Lodging certification information via an onsite assessment. After a review by the DEP, the hotel or motel is certified if the lodge's information is complete, and correct, and the property meets all of the program requirements.

Green bandwagon

According to www.allstays.com, at least 35 states have documented lodging facilities that are "taking the right step forward for us and Earth one night at a time," including:

- Alaska
- Arizona
- Arkansas
- California
- Colorado
- Connecticut
- Florida
- Georgia
- Hawaii
- Indiana
- Iowa
- Kentucky
- Maine
- Maryland
- Massachusetts
- Michigan
- Montana
- New Hampshire
- New Jersey
- New Mexico
- New York
- North Carolina
- Ohio
- Oregon
- Pennsylvania
- South Carolina
- South Dakota
- Texas
- Utah
- Vermont
- Virginia
- Washington
- West Virginia
- Wisconsin
- Wyoming

As the Vermont Green Hotels Scorecard illustrates on the next page, Vermont's participating green hotels are using sound environmental management practices to reduce their impacts on the environment, improve their bottom lines, and satisfy customer demand for environmentally conscious lodging establishments.

Why get green?

The following are just a few reasons why hoteliers should consider adopting and implementing environmentally and ecologically friendly practices today:

- *Money Matters*—According to the U.S. Environmental Protection Agency (EPA), hotels and motels investing in energy-efficient lighting upgrades can expect to yield a profit of $6.27 on each dollar invested. Simple waste audits of lodging facilities can help one identify opportunities for reducing wastes, and recycling or reusing materials.

(continued)

(continued)

Green Hotels: 30 VBEP partners: 18			
Total participating properties: 48			

Environmental Policy & Mission	48	Towel/Linen Reuse Program	35
Energy Efficiency Upgrades	21	Composting	11
Using Recycled products	23	Using more enviro-friendly products	24
# of guest rooms for towel reuse	1758	Environmental Mgmt. Plan	30
Recycle & offer guests access & info	35	# of onsite assessments	11 in 0405

Saved Gallons of H_2O	Saved Gallons of Bleach	Saved Lbs. Detergent	Saved KWH	Saved Lbs. Recycled	Saved H_2O/gal. Propane
895,320	1,317	11,191.5	21,488	124,020	6,566

- *Win Customers*—According to the Travel Industry Association of America, within the United States alone 43 million people are self-proclaimed "eco-tourists" who are willing to pay 8.5 percent more to environmentally sensitive travel suppliers. A survey of U.S. travelers found 87 percent would be more likely to stay at "green" properties. By demonstrating that they care for the environment as well as their visitors' comfort, hoteliers can earn respect and customer loyalty and enhance their company's competitiveness.

- *Protect OUR Planet*—Lodging is the fourth most intensive user of energy in the United States' commercial sector. Improving energy efficiency in the hospitality industry will help reduce energy consumption, thereby reducing U.S. greenhouse emissions. Reductions in the use of hazardous cleaning materials, water consumption, and waste disposal will all contribute to protecting your state's land, air, and water resources.

- *Earn Recognition*—State DEPs and Pineapple can help green hotels and motels share their stories through positive public recognition. Green hotels and motels may be recognized through awards events, or in articles, news releases, newsletters, and other publications, both on the Internet and in print.

the Rooms
CHRONICLE®

(continued)

Creating eco-friendly guestrooms

Hopefully, after reading this article and careful consideration, ownership and management will seek to realize the full potential of cost-effective, eco-friendly practices. Many resource agencies, consultants, and private companies, including Pineapple, stand ready to assist. One advantage is that these individuals and organizations have typically developed close relationships with leading green product providers to save hoteliers money and time while maximizing any potential rebates from utilities and local governments.

Perhaps Pineapple's Eco Rooms demonstrate the extent of its involvement the best. Typically providing a complete payback in 12 months or less, these Eco Rooms include several of the following:

- Energy-efficient lighting solutions such as GE fluorescent lamp bulbs and The WattStopper occupancy sensor nightlight;

- Bathroom amenity dispensers using biodegradable, hypoallergenic soaps, body wash, lotion, shampoo, and conditioner;

- Recyclable/biodegradable plastic bottles filled with all-natural bathroom amenities and hand soap packaged in recycled paper;

- Programmable digital thermostats to control guestroom energy consumption without compromising guest satisfaction;

- Patented low-flow/high-pressure showerheads and sink aerators;

- Early-closer toilet flappers and tank diverter valves;

- The Nature's Mist deodorization system, which helps hotels guarantee non-smoking rooms no matter what a property's guests' preference mix is;

- In-room air filters;

- A towel and linens reuse program;

- Non-toxic, non-allergenic, all-natural cleaning products;

- Facial and bathroom tissues made from 100-percent recycled materials and at least 30-percent post-consumer waste paper;

- Recycling receptacles for guestrooms, lobbies, meeting rooms, restaurants, kitchens, and offices.

Conclusion

The bottom line is that money talks and people walk. Chances are that many of your hotel's competitors already are undertaking some or most of these eco-initiatives and making more money and a better name for themselves in the process. More importantly, they are helping to preserve the environment in the process. Where will you stand on this issue?

Source: Ray Burger, *The Rooms Chronicle®*, Volume 13, Number 6, pp. 4–6. For subscription information, please call 866-READ-TRC.

- *Purchasing,* to help properties work with suppliers for less wasteful practices
- *People and communities,* to encourage employees to look for environmental stewardship opportunities beyond the property
- *Destination protection,* to maintain a sense of place that supports the geographic character of a place—its environment, culture, heritage, aesthetics, and the well-being of its citizens[3]

Green Teams

Ensuring that a property follows environmentally sound policies means keeping track of a wealth of details that cross over many departments. Many hospitality properties have established committees or teams that work together to assess energy use, set goals, and monitor environmental activities.

The size of these "green teams" vary, but it is important that there is representation from top management and from those departments that have the greatest responsibility for resource management. These departments include:

- Housekeeping (and laundry).
- Engineering/ Maintenance.
- Kitchen.
- Front office.
- Purchasing.

In some properties, this team has a waste reduction subcommittee that establishes goals for reducing waste and training employees on the property's recycling program.

The green team is often responsible for establishing goals for the property and each department after an environmental assessment is conducted. It can also help increase staff awareness of goals by creating competitions, suggestion boxes, and reward programs.

Certification Programs

As the demand for greater environmental responsibility grows, regulatory and other bodies are beginning to place more demands on hospitality properties. For example, the Supreme Court recently strengthened the Clean Air Act, and Congress has increased demands that businesses behave responsibly. As a way of encouraging hospitality properties to enact environmentally sound policies, the EPA has announced that its $50 million earmarked for travel will go first to hotels and conference centers that self-certify on a 14-point environmental checklist.

Florida Green Lodging Certification Program. Some state environment departments are even offering certifications to properties that implement green strategies. One such state is Florida, which offers a Florida Green Lodging Certification Program through the Florida Department of Environmental Protection. Exhibit 2 lists the 10 steps in the department's certification program.

Exhibit 2   Florida Green Lodging Certification Program

1. Identify an environmental champion.
2. Obtain top management commitment and submit the admission application.
3. Create a Green Team.
4. Conduct an environmental assessment.
5. Establish goals and identify environmental improvement projects.
6. Submit your environmental baseline data to the FGLC Program Office.
7. Implement environmental improvement projects.
8. Evaluate and monitor the program.
9. Schedule on-site certifying visit.
10. Practice continual improvement.

Source: Florida Department of Environmental Protection

LEED Certification. The U.S. Green Building Council has established Leadership in Energy and Environmental Design (LEED) certification. The council promotes a comprehensive approach to sustainability that includes every element of a building's design and management. When new hotels are built, they can be awarded credits for such categories as sustainable sites, energy and atmosphere, water efficiency, indoor environmental quality, and materials and resources. This is a program that hotels have been slow to join until recent years.

Energy Star. The EPA rates energy efficiency in hotels. It scores hotels on how well they perform on a number of standards and provides those ratings to the public.

Green Leaf. Canada's Green Leaf and Audubon International have created the Audubon Green Leaf Eco-Rating Program that audits lodging facilities and awards them one to five Green Leaves, depending on whether they meet environmental best practices standards. The program began in 1998.

Housekeeping's Role in a Green Property

Given how much of the property housekeeping employees see and touch every day, they play a crucial role in identifying potential environmental opportunities throughout the hotel. The executive housekeeper in particular is responsible for a wide variety of environmental management duties, including:

- Communication.
- Training.
- Purchasing.

Communication

The housekeeping department's managers must determine how they are going to communicate the property's environmental initiatives to both staff and guests. To be most effective, multiple mediums can be used, such as newsletters, signs, websites, annual reports, placards in guestrooms, recorded messages on the television, and hint sheets that can be placed on guestroom carts. The executive housekeeper or another department representative can then be identified to communicate information to staff during pre-shift meetings, training sessions, and other staff meetings. It is also helpful to create a formal process for employees and guests to use for feedback on green practices. This could include an employee suggestion box or a guestroom survey form.

Bilingual Communication Issues. Housekeeping departments have always been among the most diverse departments in hotels and among the first to address multicultural issues. The hospitality industry as a whole employs a significant international population of employees.

The multiple languages spoken by employees can pose a unique challenge, since most of the training manuals, bulletin board material, and signs in the hotel are in a single language. The communication gap can result in situations where a significant amount of energy is wasted due to misunderstandings and ineffective communications. In a typical U.S. lodging property, the three key areas affected the most by this issue are housekeeping, laundry, and the kitchen.

Housekeeping employees visit every room of the hotel on a daily basis and have the responsibility for taking corrective action and reporting problems. There are specific procedures that room attendants follow to provide a quality product and conserve energy. They must be able to communicate these things no matter what language they speak.

The temperature setting on thermostats is the most common challenge for U.S. housekeeping departments with non-English-speaking workers. With most of the rest of the world on the Metric system, non-U.S. employees typically think in terms of Centigrade rather than Fahrenheit. This can cause difficulty in setting thermostats to the proper temperature. One solution has been to issue each room attendant a placard with a sketch showing a typical guestroom thermostat setting.

Room attendants are also responsible for turning off all lights and appliances, and closing the draperies after cleaning a guestroom. They should also report any potential plumbing problems that are noticed while cleaning the room.

Another housekeeping area where language can be an issue is in the on-premises laundry. Washing, drying, and ironing must be done properly to maintain the quality, comfort, and life of linens and to conserve energy, water, and chemicals. The executive housekeeper needs to find a way to communicate the preventive maintenance plan as well as develop checklists that can be used by employees regardless of the language they speak.

Training

Some estimates say that the annual cost of energy and water for a hotel can be reduced by as much as 10 percent by training employees to operate the hotel efficiently. Training can help a property reduce energy consumption without any capital investment.

Each hotel has its own personality and methods for conducting employee training. Executive housekeepers should design programs appropriate to the property's culture.

Housekeeping. Housekeeping staff members typically work throughout 80 percent of the hotel on a daily basis. Therefore, housekeeping training can be critical to the efficient operation of the guestroom block. Some "green" skills that training should cover include the following:

- Control of the heating, ventilation, and air conditioning, (HVAC) system of guestrooms is essential. Temperatures in vacant guestrooms should be set back according to season and geographical location parameters. Typically, HVAC settings should be 74 degrees Fahrenheit during the cooling season and 68 degrees Fahrenheit during the heating season. One important tool of housekeeping management is a weather-board to visually post for room attendants the HVAC settings for the day.

- Room attendants should turn off all exhaust fans and close all windows in vacant guestrooms. Entry of outside air during heating/cooling seasons causes a huge waste of energy.

- Room attendants should open the drapes to use free light while cleaning but close the blackout drapes to within six inches before leaving the room.

- Coffee pots, hair dryers, and irons should be unplugged before room attendants leave the guestroom. Disconnecting these items is a safety issue as well as an energy saver. Room attendants should also turn off all lights in every room and ceiling fans and whirlpool tubs (when present) when they exit.

- Room attendants should clean all light fixtures in guestrooms on a regular basis. They should especially ensure bathroom fluorescent fixtures with lenses are cleaned at least twice per year. This action will increase light output by approximately 25 percent.

- For hotels with through-the-wall heating/cooling units, room attendants should ensure all discharge air grills are clean and that drapes do not obstruct the flow of air from the unit.

Laundry. The laundry area (along with the kitchen) is one of the most intensive energy users in the hotel. The laundry and kitchen use about five times more energy per square foot than the rest of the property. The managers of these areas must be very conscious of training employees in the following basic energy-conservation strategies:

- Process full loads as recommended for both washers and dryers. If smaller loads are necessary, consider installing a residential-style washer and dryer.

- Lint screens and dryer exhausts must be cleaned on a frequent basis. Verifying that proper air flow is passing through the dryers will preserve the life of the burners.

- The flames on gas dryers should be checked regularly to ensure efficient burning. In conjunction, verify that the proper amount of combustion air is provided to the dryer to ensure a complete combustion of natural gas.

- Clean light fixtures and discharge air grills throughout the laundry on a regular basis. Lint buildup in the laundry area can reduce the efficiency of the equipment and present a fire hazard.

- Verify that the domestic hot water temperature for the wash wheel is set correctly and in accordance with detergent requirements.

Purchasing

Purchasing plays a major role in a property's environmental plan. **Eco-purchasing** involves evaluating purchasing practices and products on durability, reusability, recyclability, and content as well as the traditional price and quality standards. Packaging and delivery methods should also be evaluated.

Some experts suggest that **just-in-time buying** will reduce waste. Just-in-time buying is the practice of buying products just before they run out. Experts have said that employees will use more of a product if there is a large quantity of it on the shelf, while they will be more conservative with it if there is a small amount.

Things that an executive housekeeper can do to make the purchasing process more "green" include:

- Purchasing in bulk and concentrate.

- Requiring vendors to take back pallets and non-recyclable boxes and crates.

- Using local suppliers.

- Looking for simplicity in products and minimal packaging of items.

- Purchasing and maintaining more durable supplies that won't have to be replaced as often.

- Purchasing sheets with higher thread counts for longer wear.

Energy Star rates equipment based on its energy efficiency. The Energy Star website (www.energystar.gov) provides a calculator that can help housekeeping managers calculate how much energy savings a given piece of equipment can provide.

Water Conservation

Water conservation is one of the most cost-effective programs a hotel can implement. Not only does a property save water and reduce its water expense, but it also saves money in decreased electricity costs, sewage bills, and decreased chemical costs.

Hotels use a large volume of water, detergent, and cleansers every day. One AH&LA study found that, on average, each occupied room uses 209 gallons of water daily. Such high water use has made the issue of conservation increasingly important, especially in communities that have been hit heavily by drought.

In 2007, the South experienced heavy drought conditions that drained reservoirs to dangerously low levels. The Hyatt Regency Atlanta, a 1,260-room property that uses tens of millions of gallons of water each year, found itself searching for extra water conservation measures in addition to those it already had in place. It already outsourced its laundry to a facility outside of metro Atlanta (where the worse drought conditions were in effect), had a linen reuse policy, and guestrooms with low-flow fixtures. As the drought deepened, it began to irrigate its green plants with condensation from the cooling system and started putting fewer water pitchers in meeting rooms.

In 1992, the Environmental Protection Agency launched the Water Alliances for Voluntary Efficiency (WAVE). Endorsed by AH&LA, it's a country-wide program to promote efficient water use that initially focused on the lodging industry. WAVE encourages lodging properties to reduce water consumption by pointing out the economic and competitive benefits of doing so. Many of the WAVE partners—who include Westin, Hyatt, Sheraton, and LaQuinta—have reduced their water consumption by 30 percent annually.

Properties, especially resort properties with extensive landscaping demands, have also begun to use **effluent** or **reclaimed water**. Effluent water is water that is partially treated wastewater from community sewage or industry. It is usually cleansed of major pollutants, but still contains enough trace amounts of salt, minerals, and bacteria to render it undrinkable. This water can be used for irrigation, toilets, decorative fountains, and cooling towers.

Other common water conservation efforts include:

- Towel and linen reuse program in guestrooms.

- Low-flow faucets and showerheads in guestrooms.

- Low-flow toilets in guestrooms.

- Automatic faucets or toilets in public restrooms.

- Water-efficient clothes washing machines.

Linen Reuse Programs

Linen reuse programs are one of the most obvious and popular forms of water conservation. People at home rarely change their sheets and towels daily. Linen reuse programs remind guests of this and invite them to reuse their guestroom linens and towels rather than have them removed for washing. Since the early 1990s, hotels across the country have adopted various forms of reuse programs. They have been extremely popular with guests who appreciate that hotels are being environmentally conscious. Some hotels have reported 70 to 90 percent guest participation.

Exhibit 3   Linen Reuse Card

Help Us
Help the Environment

In our sincerest efforts to serve our guests, we also wish to pursue initiatives and policies that better serve the environment.

Upon check in, your room has been thoroughly cleaned and supplied with fresh linens. To contribute to the environment through the reduced usage of water, energy and potentially harmful detergents, please place this card on your pillow if:

**Fresh Linens
are Not Necessary Today**

Most estimates say that properties can save up to 13.5 gallons of fresh water and $6.50 a day per room with a linen reuse program. Such programs not only save water, but also electricity, gas, detergents, toweling, sheets, and labor.

Properties can create their own informational cards for guests or use one that is pre-designed by organizations such as AH&LA or the Green Hotels Association. These cards can be hung on a towel rack or placed on the bed. See Exhibit 3. They explain why the hotel has implemented a linen reuse program and how it works. Most hotels with linen reuse programs will not change sheets in occupied rooms unless a guest requests it or until three or four days have passed. Towels that are hanging on the rack will be left in the room while ones left on the floor will be changed. Sheets and towels are always changed upon check-out.

Guestrooms

The guestroom is one of the highest water-consuming areas of a hotel, primarily because of the bathrooms, which have a shower, toilet, and sink. The guestroom is also the place where the most inexpensive water conservation efforts can be made.

National standards now require that all showerheads in hotels consume no more than 1.75 gallons of water per minute. This can be tested by placing a bucket under the shower, running it for one minute, and then measuring the output. Unlike the old-style water conservation showerheads, the new ones provide a comfortable shower with an adequate supply of water. They typically pay for themselves in less than six months in saved water and the energy required to heat it.

Whoever is testing the showerheads should also look to see whether any water is also pouring out of the spigot into the tub when the shower diverter is turned on. If this is occurring, this is an indication that the diverter needs to be repaired immediately.

Older toilets consume as much as three to four gallons of water per flush. Water standards now require that toilets consume no more than 1.6 gallons per flush. This can be accomplished by installing new toilets or by installing a new flapper valve kit that will reduce the water consumed by an older toilet.

Flapper valves in guestroom toilets are the most notorious water wasters in hotels. A leaking flapper valve can cause numerous guest complaints because of the noise from constantly running water. All flapper valves in toilet tanks should be replaced at least every two to three years with a high-quality natural rubber flapper valve. The watertight seal of the flapper valve can be checked by placing food coloring in the tank and observing the bowl. If the coloring seeps through to the bowl, the flapper valve should be replaced immediately. Leaking flapper valves can cost about $150 per year per room in wasted water.

The flow rate at bathroom sinks should not exceed one gallon per minute. Flow rates can be reduced by installing an aerator that injects air into the water, causing an illusion of more water flowing. A simpler method is to turn down the hand valves under the sink to a minimal, but acceptable, level. This will conserve water and the energy to heat it.

Laundry

The largest consumers of water in an on-premises hotel laundry are the wash wheels (extractors). Here again, it is extremely important that employees wash only full loads. The wash wheels also have automatic fill valves that have a propensity to stick and waste a considerable amount of water. Laundry employees can listen for the continuous sound of water running and request that engineering repair any faulty valves immediately.

Water usage can also be drastically curtailed by decreasing the number of daily loads that are washed. This will require either the implementation of a voluntary linen reuse program in guestrooms or a change in standard operating procedures.

Laundry managers can work with appliance vendors to adjust washing machines to ensure the greatest overall energy efficiency. Increasing the spin cycle on the wash, for example, can decrease drying time by as much as one half.

Another way to save water is through major renovations. Many laundries are switching to an ozone-type washing system that uses less than half the amount of water of a traditional wash wheel.

Public Restrooms

Most public restroom toilets and urinals use a flush-valve type of flushing system. These toilets and urinals do not have water tanks, but flush by simply releasing water into the appliance to allow thorough flushing. It is now becoming standard

Exhibit 4   Energy Resource Demands

Market trends suggest that the demand for energy resources will rise dramatically over the next 25 years:

- Global demand for all energy sources is forecast to grow by 57 percent over the next 25 years.

- U.S. demand for all types of energy is expected to increase by 31 percent within 25 years.

- By 2030, 56 percent of the world's energy use will be in Asia.

- Electricity demand in the United States will grow by at least 40 percent by 2032.

- Currently, 50 percent of U.S. electrical generation relies on coal, a fossil fuel, while 85 percent of U.S. greenhouse gas emissions result from energy-consuming activities supported by fossil fuels.

Sources: Annual Energy Outlook (DOE/EIA-0383(2007)), International Energy Outlook 2007 (DOE/EIA-0484(2007)), Inventory of U.S. Greenhouse Gas Emissions and Sinks: 1990–2005 (April 2007) (EPA 430-R-07-002)

practice for many hotels to install ultrasonic motion sensors on these appliances that will automatically flush them with the proper amount of water each time they are used. While these devices do not necessarily save a lot of water, they do ensure that your facilities are flushed every time they are used and, therefore, help eliminate plugged lines.

Energy Efficiency

According to the American Hotel & Lodging Association, the hospitality industry spends $3.7 billion a year on energy. AH&LA estimates that reducing energy use by 10 percent across the hospitality industry would save the industry $285 million each year while increasing guest satisfaction. Exhibit 4 shows predicted demands for energy resources during the next 25 years.

Properties that are committed to energy efficiency not only decrease their consumption of natural resources, they also can save a great deal of money and improve their bottom line. Energy savings is a way of reducing costs without reducing guest service or satisfaction.

The Environmental Protection Agency estimates that every $1 in energy savings is the equivalent of increasing operating margins by $2 to $3. When Starwood Hotels & Resorts Worldwide implemented an energy management program, it was able to save $3.4 million in energy costs—the equivalent of renting 9,370 additional rooms.

When Hilton Hotels implemented an energy management plan, it saved nearly 43 million kilowatt-hours of electricity per year and prevented 65 million pounds of carbon dioxide emissions—the equivalent of removing 6,450 cars from the road for a year.

Energy Management

As mentioned earlier, Energy Star is an EPA program that helps to identify energy-efficient products. Hospitality managers can go online to consult the Energy Star rating of products before purchasing them. Energy Star also provides calculators that help determine the savings each item can provide to a property.

Computerized energy management systems have grown in popularity. These software programs help hotel managers collect and analyze data collected from major energy-consuming appliances. Such systems can help a property determine when a piece of equipment should be run, what its maintenance needs are, and whether it would be cost-effective to modify or replace it.

Common activities to ensure more efficient use of energy include:

- Using equipment rated as energy efficient by Energy Star.

- Using programmable thermostats.

- Using sensor lighting indoors and outdoors.

- Using energy-efficient lighting in both the front and the back of the house.

- Using a computerized energy management system.

- Installing renewable energy generating equipment (such as solar power).

- Purchasing green power through a local utility.

- Installing tinted or double-paned windows.

Exhibit 5 shows a list of ways housekeepers can affect the amount of energy a hotel consumes.

Sometimes energy efficiency is as simple as turning things off. When PSA Energy Consultants conducts full-service energy audits (see Exhibit 6 for the steps the company takes), it almost always identifies many energy-consuming items that can be turned off at key points during the day and night. The chief engineer or facilities services manager can identify air handling units, exhaust fans, lighting, air conditioners, and other items that can be turned off.

After these items are identified, the hotel can consider installing a seven-day or 24-hour time clock to control them automatically. If the hotel has a centralized energy control system, it may be cost-effective to add a time clock to the scheduling feature of this system. This is the single largest energy-saving idea that can be implemented in a hotel and can provide significant savings with very little capital expenditure.

Guestroom energy controls are becoming more reliable, easier to use, and less expensive. These energy controls typically turn off or set back heating and cooling levels during unoccupied periods. New wireless models are less expensive to install and provide additional technical features.

Public-space global controls for the entire property are also becoming less expensive, more effective, and easier to use. This is typically a capital expenditure; control systems vary considerably in size and may cost in the range of $50,000 to $150,000. The hotel will likely see a three- to five-year return on investment, depending on the application and the identified opportunities to save energy.

Exhibit 5   Housekeeping Activities that Promote Energy Efficiency

The following housekeeping procedures can save energy:	
1. Turn off or reset heating and cooling systems in unoccupied rooms.	Turning off heating and cooling systems in unoccupied rooms will help reduce costs without affecting the comfort of guests and staff.
2. Close draperies and shades when leaving guestrooms.	This will reduce heat loss in winter and heat gain in summer.
3. Turn off guestroom lights, televisions, and radios in unoccupied rooms.	Create reminder cards to remind guests to turn off lights, televisions, and radios when they leave the room.
4. Use natural lighting when cleaning guestrooms.	Remind housekeeping to close draperies when leaving guestrooms.
5. Clean lighting fixtures.	Bulbs will produce more light after cleaning.
6. Limit the amount of hot water used for cleaning.	Limiting the amount of hot water used for cleaning will save water heating costs.
7. Report any necessary equipment repairs.	Regular equipment maintenance will increase performance and decrease energy consumption.
8. Install Energy Star clothes washers.	Energy Star clothes washers use 50 percent less energy. They also use 40 to 50 percent less water, which means less water to heat and shorter drying times.
9. Capture and reuse waste heat from laundry operations.	Capturing and reusing emitted heat will decrease energy expenses.

Source: Florida Green Lodging Certification Program, Florida Energy Extension Service.

Lighting

Compact Fluorescent Lamps. Compact fluorescent lamps are the backbone of high-efficiency lighting. They are more energy efficient than incandescent bulbs, last about ten times longer, and do not emit lost energy through heat. Compact fluorescent lighting products continue to improve in terms of longer lamp life, better color, and a variety of sizes. The most common application for compact fluorescent lamps in hotels is in the guestroom. There are usually three to five table and floor lamps in a guestroom. A 20-watt spiral-type compact fluorescent lamp typically will provide higher light levels than 75-watt or 100-watt incandescent lamps.

To illustrate the energy expense savings, take a 300-room hotel with four 100-watt lamps per room and compare the energy cost for the old incandescent lamps to the new compact fluorescents. Assuming the lights operate about four hours per day, they will run a total of 1,460 hours per year. At $.08 per kilowatt-hour, the

Exhibit 6   Six Steps to Successful Energy Management

1. **Energy accounting.** Create a baseline and track the hotel's progress.
2. **Full-service energy audit.** Inventory every conceivable piece of energy-consuming equipment and then set priorities for projects that can help save energy.
3. **Implement.** Train employees, particularly in housekeeping and engineering, on procedures that will improve guest comfort and save energy.
4. **High-payback capital retrofit projects.** Implement capital projects such as lighting retrofits, lighting controls, energy efficient motors, time clocks, and adjustable speed drives.
5. **Capital projects specific to hotel.** These might include larger projects such as co-generation, free cooling, mechanical system upgrades, and computerized controls for all equipment in the hotel. Some of these may not be cost-effective, however.
6. **Ongoing security program.** Verify that savings have been made and then continue to upgrade the ideas in the full-service energy audit as technology improves.

Source: PSA Energy Consultants

annual cost of operating the old system is $14,016. But by converting all of the guest-room lamps in this 300-room hotel to 20-watt compact fluorescents, the hotel will save approximately $11,212 per year. Such a conversion program will also reduce labor costs associated with replacing burned-out lights by about 90 percent.

The cost to purchase the new energy-efficient compact fluorescents is estimated to be about $5 each, for a total conversion cost of $6,000. The project will, therefore, provide about a six-month return on investment. Many utilities will pay up to 50 percent of the cost of installing compact fluorescents. In that case, the project would have a three-month return on investment. This is a significant opportunity for hotels to reduce their electrical consumption and energy expense without affecting guest comfort.

Compact fluorescent lighting technology is also available in specialty lamps for decorative fixtures. These include flame, candle, and globe-type lamps that are available in wattages as low as 15 watts.

The majority of all public spaces in hotels, including ballrooms, corridors, lobbies, meeting rooms, and game rooms, are lighted with fixtures that are referred to as "recessed can down lights." These fixtures typically use a wide variety of incandescent lamps that range from 75 to 150 watts each. A large portion of these fixtures, especially those in meeting rooms, restaurants, and bars, are on dimmable switches known as rheostats. Dimmable compact fluorescent reflector lamps are evolving slowly, but product quality and reliability have been questionable thus far. Some of these lamps do not dim to required levels, and the purchase cost has been somewhat high. When they do become viable, dimmable compact fluorescent lamps will represent a major development and an opportunity to reduce energy use throughout a property's public space. Not only will these lamps save on direct energy costs (it will take less money to keep them burning), they will

C the Rooms
HRONICLE®

Straight Talk about Hotel Energy Myths

Fluorescent lights

Many people believe that turning fluorescent lights on and off consumes more energy than simply leaving them on continuously. This is absolutely not true. There is no greater energy savings than one hundred percent, which occurs whenever lights are turned off. Turning lights off and on frequently, however, will slightly shorten the life of the lamp.

Magnets and ozone

There are many vendors with some unusual products and concepts for saving energy. One vendor recommended putting magnets in the basin of a cooling tower as a form of water treatment, for example. He also recommended wrapping magnets around water supply pipes to swimming pools. The vendor touted the idea that the polarity of the magnets would perform some magic treatment to the water, therefore eliminating the cost of adding water treatment to the various water systems throughout the hotel such as pool water, laundry water, and chilled water for air conditioning.

Be very suspicious of vendors selling products to eliminate the need to treat water. Water treatment performed incorrectly can cost a substantial amount of money if equipment becomes corroded or if health problems result from improperly treated waters.

Over the years, there have been numerous ozone-related products introduced to the market whose worthiness could not be substantiated. Here again, water treatment was the most common application of ozone devices. Years ago, the Massachusetts Institute of Technology conducted extensive testing on many of these products and energy-enhancing concepts. They concluded that, in general, most ozone products did not work.

Today, ozone products have been developed to replace laundry detergent and to provide fresh air to guestrooms and public spaces. Some of these products are much improved over the older varieties. It is recommended, however, that whenever you are approached by a vendor offering any product that uses ozone to save money and purify air, you should thoroughly examine the product, research the purported technology, and obtain references from reliable people who are using it.

Light bulb buttons

Light bulb buttons are tiny disks that stick to the end of a light bulb before it is screwed into the socket. A light bulb button can reduce energy consumption in an incandescent light by 30 to 50 percent. Unfortunately, the light bulb button causes a corresponding reduction in light output.

Over-exaggerated savings

Vendors are known to either slightly or extremely exaggerate the savings of the products they were selling. This is why it is useful to consult an independent energy advisor when making capital expenditures on energy-saving devices.

The proper investment of time, research, and expertise early on can pay handsome dividends in the form of energy savings. Thorough testing and common

(continued)

sense should prevail when determining true energy savings. Keep in mind that the savings realized are not just based on the quality of the product or the source and type of energy consumed; they are also determined by the utility rates in each hotel's given area, which can vary substantially.

Source: *The Rooms Chronicle*®, Volume 14, Number 2, pp. 1–3.
For subscription information, please call 866-READ-TRC.

also provide indirect savings because they can significantly reduce the air conditioning load required in a hotel's public spaces.

Motion Sensors. One of the most abused energy wasters in hotels is lighting that is left on in unoccupied areas. To correct this, properties are installing light-switch motion sensors in areas such as room attendant closets, storerooms, and offices. These light-switch motion sensors typically cost less than $25, and can be installed by a maintenance engineer in minutes. Depending on the nature of the application, the typical return on investment by using these devices is less than six months. Ceiling motion sensors can also be used in areas such as meeting rooms, conference rooms, and public restrooms. These devices are more expensive and cost in the range of $200, but control a larger lighting load. Audits have revealed that lights are frequently left on in these areas when they are unoccupied.

Waste Management

The three R's of waste reduction—reduce, recycle, and reuse—are quickly becoming as well-known as their academic predecessors. Waste reduction programs that incorporate all three can help a property make a real difference in the world around it. According to the Florida Energy Extension Service, a large lodging property can generate as much as eight tons of waste per day—and up to 60 percent of this is recyclable. The most common source of waste is the kitchen.

To determine what and how to reduce, reuse, and recycle, many lodging managers begin by conducting a waste audit of each operational area. The executive housekeeper may be asked to conduct the audit in the housekeeping department and for guestrooms. This audit begins with a walk-through of every area to identify recyclable materials, the source of material, and the quantity of recyclable materials being collected or thrown away. The analysis should determine who collects waste, what type of waste is generated, when it is collected, where it is stored, and how the waste is collected at the source and diverted to recycling.

The waste reduction team can then create a plan from the audit and other information it collects. Each area of the property may be given its own waste reduction plan. There may be separate ones for the guestrooms, swimming pool and spa areas, public spaces, and the laundry.

Common waste reduction activities include the following:

- Recycling such materials as office paper, newspaper, aluminum cans, magazines, steel cans, and cardboard
- Purchasing products with recycled content, such as office paper, toilet tissues, paper towels, and paper napkins
- Purchasing in bulk
- Purchasing items that use reduced packaging or for which the supplier takes the packaging back and reuses it
- Using a trash compactor
- Composting yard trash and food waste

Reduce

Reducing waste is an area in which the housekeeping department can take an active role. As properties have looked for ways to reduce waste, the ideas have been as varied as the types of waste themselves.

One initiative that has been growing in popularity after initial resistance is the idea of shampoo and conditioner dispensers in bathrooms rather than the small bottles which create a great deal of waste and have to be thrown out after one use. Companies have developed tamper-proof models that protect the guests. Properties that use them have found that the cost savings means that they can purchase name-brand hair products that appeal to guests, thus making the program a popular one.

Bottled water, for all its popularity, also represents a source of potential waste because of the use of plastic bottles. Four Seasons Hotel in Jackson Hole, Wyoming, chose to start replacing the bottled water they put in guestrooms during turndown service with pitchers of local tap water.

Other amenities are also under examination. Many properties have removed underused amenities from guestrooms and offer them by request only. These include such things as shower caps, shoeshine cloths, sewing kits, and mouthwash. Some will also reuse items if the seal is not broken.

Tissues, toilet paper, and paper towels are also areas where many hotels have successfully reduced waste. In guestrooms, room attendants can be taught to not replace toilet paper until it is nearly gone. Instead, they can leave a second roll of toilet paper in the room for guests, ensuring that they will not run out. In public restrooms, some properties replace paper towels with electric hand dryers that are designed to minimize paper waste.

Environmental groups have encouraged properties to replace disposable glasses in guestrooms with reusable glasses. Properties that do this must ensure that they follow health and sanitation rules by removing these glasses from the room every day and washing and sanitizing them through the dishwasher. They should not be rinsed out or washed in the room.

Some properties that offer dry cleaning service have found ways to reduce the waste associated with this service. They return laundered clothes to guests in reusable garment bags or baskets, offering plastic wrap for dry cleaned clothing only upon request, and have eliminated the cardboard backing for laundered shirts.

Savings can also be found in the handling of chemicals. The executive housekeeper can set up mixing stations to reduce chemical spillage. The staff can be trained in how to mix liquid concentrates to ensure safety and save money. Along

Exhibit 7   Items for a Hotel Recycling Program

The following items are commonly included in a hotel recycling program:		
Aluminum cans	Fluorescent bulbs	Paint
Antifreeze	Food waste	Plastic bottles
Appliances	Freon	Plastic buckets
Batteries	Furniture	Radios
Building materials	Glass jars	Scrap metal
Cardboard	Landscape waste	Steel containers
Carpet	Magazines	Telephone books
Cell phones	Motor oil	Televisions
Cooking grease	Newspapers	Wood
Computers	Office supplies	

these same lines, housekeeping can use refillable pump spray bottles instead of aerosol cans.

Recycle

The second component in a waste management program is recycling and using recycled materials. (Exhibit 7 lists some of the items typically included in a hotel recycling program.) There are many ways a hospitality organization can participate in recycling. The Warwick Hotel in Seattle, Washington found that it saved a substantial amount of money by creating a recycling program. Thanks to recycling, it reduced the number of pickups for its five garbage containers from four times a week to two times a week, thus saving $730 a month in waste disposal bills.

Room attendants collect waste from guestrooms every day. Most commonly, this waste includes paper products, food-related wastes, and bathroom wastes. When first setting up a recycling program, the executive housekeeper (or some other housekeeping manager) will need to conduct a waste audit by selecting three random rooms and collecting garbage from them daily for seven days to determine the quantity and type of waste generated. This will let the manager know what type of volume of recyclables to plan for. Housekeeping management will have to decide where to store recyclables and how to train employees to collect and sort them.

Some properties now provide two trash cans in each guestroom—a recycling can or receptacle and a regular trash can. This helps save time for room attendants who won't have to sift through the waste. Room attendants can collect and sort recyclables as the room is cleaned. A housekeeping cart can be arranged to have separate bags on the side for trash and recycling.

In addition to recycling waste found in guestrooms, the housekeeping department can also recycle waste that it generates in its back-of-the-house areas. Cardboard boxes can be recycled, as can clothing hangers, plastic containers, and tissues.

The executive housekeeper can also evaluate the housekeeping products that the property is currently using and determine whether recycled products or products with recycled content can be purchased instead.

Exhibit 8   Take the Soap Home!

Bar soap is one amenity offered by all hotels. It's something that travel associations such as AAA and Mobil have as requirements for their ratings. Unused bars of soap are usually discarded by the housekeeper. Several reuse ideas have been attempted for used bars of soap, such as:

- Making it into liquid soap by chopping it or flaking it and soaking it in water
- Giving it to homeless shelters
- Using them in crafts projects to make carvings

However, these ideas save only a tiny percentage of the tons of bar soap discarded every day. Green Hotels Association suggests a simpler answer: Ask guests to take their partially used soap home. It recommends posting a sign in the bathroom that says "Save the Wrapper." The sign can explain the waste issue and encourage guests to save the wrapper they take off the new bar of soap so that they can take the soap home in the wrapper at the end of their stay and use the soap at home.

Newspaper Recycling Programs. Many properties—especially those serving a large number of business travelers—have begun newspaper recycling programs. Programs vary from property to property and range from simply recycling papers to reducing the number of newspapers provided. At some properties, guests are asked at check-in whether they would like to receive a complimentary newspaper. If they do not, then newspapers aren't delivered. Some properties also provide a door hanger in each guestroom that guests can put out if they do not want to receive a newspaper. Other properties put complimentary newspapers in a central location (such as on tables near elevators, in the breakfast lounge, at the front desk, etc.) rather than deliver them to every room. Properties doing this often find that they use fewer newspapers. Unread newspapers can sometimes be returned to the newspaper vendor. Newspapers can be donated to such places as animal shelters, pet stores, fish markets, mailing companies, moving companies, and paint shops. The hotel itself might be able to use old newspapers.

Reuse

Much of the waste generated by a hotel can be reused—by the property, by another organization, and even by guests (see Exhibit 8). Linens are a popular item for reuse. Stained tablecloths can be turned into napkins, room service tray place-mats, chef's aprons, or uniform ties. Retired sheets can be made into laundry bags. Retired terry can be made into hot pads or kitchen urn covers. Retired linens and towels as well as leftover bottles of shampoo, lotions, bar soap, and toilet paper can also be donated to schools, homeless shelters, humane societies, veterinarian offices, pet boarding houses, etc. Other items that can be donated include excess clothing hangers (or those left by guests in the room); these can be given to a local dry cleaner or thrift shop.

Indoor Air Quality

Lodging properties have been focusing on clean air concerns for decades. In 1995, AH&LA's Educational Institute published a manual on hotel air quality management—an action guide for engineers and managers. In it, R.A. Riedel wrote that the EPA says air inside buildings is sometimes as much as 100 times more polluted than the air outside. It's considered one of the most severe environmental risks to health in the United States.

Common clean air practices include:

- Using environmentally preferred cleaners.

- Using environmentally preferred High Efficiency Particulate Air (HEPA) filters.

- Cleaning all air handler units and coils at least annually.

- Venting exhaust fans to the outside.

- Running a dehumidifier.

- Making sure that rooms where smoking is permitted are well-ventilated or properly filtered.

A healthy indoor environment is one in which the surroundings contribute to productivity, comfort, and a sense of health and well-being. The indoor air is free of significant levels of odors, dust, and contaminants, and is circulated to prevent stuffiness without creating drafts. Temperature and humidity are appropriate to the season and the clothing and activities of the occupants.

Indoor air contaminants come from a number of sources. They can include contaminated outdoor air (pollen, dust, industrial pollutants, vehicle exhaust fumes), emissions from nearby sources (loading docks, dumpster odors, exhaust from the building, unsanitary debris near the outdoor air intake), soil gas (radon, underground fuel tank leakage, pesticides), moisture or standing water that promotes microbial growth (rooftops after rainfall, crawlspaces, air and moisture flow through the wall system, condensation within a wall, water-damaged furnishings, standing water from clogged or poorly designed drains), HVAC system, personal activities (smoking, cooking, body odors, cosmetic odors), housekeeping activities (cleaning materials and procedures, deodorizers and fragrances, airborne dust or dirt circulated by sweeping or vacuuming), chemicals and off-gassing from furnishings (carpets, wall coverings, ceiling tiles, interior paints and coatings), and redecorating/remodeling/repair activities (emissions from new furnishings, dust and fibers from demolition).

Indoor Air Quality Programs

Because there are plenty of potential indoor air contaminates to deal with, properties need to establish programs to manage their indoor air. Engineers and other property managers are often charged with creating an indoor air quality preventive maintenance program. Doing so will benefit guests and save unnecessary costs in the long run. **Indoor air quality** can be defined as:

- The introduction and distribution of adequate ventilation air.

- The control of airborne contaminants.

- The maintenance of acceptable temperature and relative humidity.

One challenge that hoteliers face is that some efforts to reduce energy costs contribute to poor indoor air quality. Hotel managers must make sure that adjusting one area doesn't cost the property in the other area.

Poor housekeeping practices that fail to remove dust and other dirt can cause indoor air quality complaints. On the other hand, some cleaning materials can produce odors and emit a variety of chemicals. Housekeeping staff may be the first to recognize and respond to potential air quality control problems as they work throughout the property. Housekeeping department managers should consider the following topics:

- *The importance of clean air.* Managers should understand both the financial factors and the human factors.

- *Cleaning schedules.* Managers should consider how cleaning activities are scheduled, particularly for public areas. Housekeeping managers may want to schedule the use of some cleaning agents during low occupancy periods, because they introduce strong odors or contaminants into the atmosphere.

- *Purchasing.* Housekeeping managers should become familiar with the chemicals in cleaning and other maintenance products and their potential toxicity, and make sure they select the safest available products. Much of the information needed for this type of research is provided by product labels and the products' material safety data sheets.

- *Materials handling and storage.* Managers should make certain that cleaning materials are used and stored properly by staff members.

- *Trash disposal.* Managers should make sure that staff members follow proper trash disposal procedures. If there is a restaurant at the property, perishable refuse should be disposed of daily. Managers should ensure that trash containers are covered, pest control is effective, and the trash collection area is cleaned at least daily.

All personnel should be trained on the importance of clean air practices. Housekeeping employees in particular should be familiar with and able to recognize crucial air quality factors such as gas leaks and improper exhaust emissions. When housekeeping employees are able to identify and properly report problems, the problems can be addressed as small concerns before they turn into larger, expensive problems.

Fighting Mold

Mold and mildew have become increasingly alarming problems for hotels, especially newer ones built in high-humidity climates. Several hotels that were either brand new or which added on major wings ended up closing their doors after only a few years because they became so infested with mold that the buildings were unlivable. It took years and millions of dollars in renovations before they could reopen.

Mold and mildew can lead to serious indoor air quality problems. Hotels, in particular their engineering departments, must take aggressive action to prevent mold growth. According to the Environmental Protection Agency, the following actions can help control moisture, which can help prevent mold:

- Fix leaks as soon as possible.

- Watch for condensation and wet spots and respond to them rapidly.

- Prevent moisture buildup in contained areas.

- Keep heating, ventilation, and air conditioning drip pans clean.

- Vent moisture-generating appliances.

- Maintain low indoor humidity.

- Perform regular inspections and maintain documentation logs.

Properties are also increasingly turning to low-moisture extractors when cleaning guestrooms as a way of preventing mold. Hotels do deep cleaning on guestroom carpets throughout the year. Typically, guestroom carpets took a long time to dry when the hotels used wet-extraction cleaning methods, because the rooms were in an enclosed space. The EPA advises that carpets need to dry within 48 hours to prevent mold and mildew; groups such as LEED say that carpets should dry in 24 hours or less. Low-moisture extractors reduce carpet-drying times to as little as 30 minutes while using fewer chemicals. Tankless low-moisture machines have the greatest efficiency, and carpets cleaned with them need the least amount of time to dry.

Cleaning Chemicals

A hotel's housekeeping and laundry personnel use more cleaning chemicals during the course of their daily tasks than any other staff members in a hospitality organization. This puts the responsibility for the care and proper use of these chemicals firmly on the shoulders of the executive housekeeper. The executive housekeeper must carefully manage chemicals from purchasing through use and disposal.

Executive housekeepers are increasingly choosing environmentally sound chemicals that are safer for employees and guests. Product labels provide information about how biodegradable the cleaning chemicals are, and suppliers should be able to provide cost information regarding environmentally responsible chemical choices.

Executive housekeepers should choose cleaning products with low levels of **volatile organic compounds**. They also want to look for cleaners that are non-toxic, biodegradable, and non-corrosive. Housekeeping employees must follow label instructions carefully. The executive housekeeper may want to conduct experiments by incrementally increasing or decreasing product use to calculate maximum efficiency in the use of the product. The rule of thumb is to use as little chemical as possible to get the job done.

The amount of hazardous chemicals stored at a property can be reduced by smart inventory practices. Just-in-time inventory can reduce the amount of time that cleaning chemicals and other potentially hazardous products have to be stored at the property.

Housekeeping employees need to clean up chemical spills, excesses, and run-offs quickly before the chemical soaks into carpets or other materials or gets trapped in the ventilation system. If the use of strong cleaning chemicals in a particular area will significantly affect that area's air quality, housekeeping should post warning notices for guests and others.

Finally, executive housekeepers need to make sure that when chemicals are disposed of that they go into the waste management system and not the storm sewer system.

Endnotes

1. Patricia Sheehan, "Seeing Green," *Lodging Hospitality*, July 1, 2007, pp. 22–24.

2. Shelli Johannes-Wells, "Moving Hospitality into 'Greener Pastures,'" *Southern Hospitality*, Summer 2007, Volume 30, Issue 2, pp. 14–16.

3. Kevin Maher, "Gone Green: The AH&LA's Environmental Partnership," *Lodging*, July 2007, p. 24.

Acknowledgments

Much of the information in this chapter was adopted from the following articles in *The Rooms Chronicle®*.

In particular, these issues provided a great deal of information:

- Volume 10, No. 3   Energy savings comes from employee training.

- Volume 11, No. 4   Water conversation can be invisible to the guest.

- Volume 11, No. 5   The top 10 energy-saving projects for a hotel.

- Volume 12, No. 2   2004 Lighting technology update.

- Volume 12, No. 3   Finding ways to minimize energy expense as gas costs keep rising.

- Volume 13, No. 4   It's time to reexamine energy saving capital projects.

- Volume 15, No. 4   Time to get serious about water conservation—Here are several steps to get started.

For information on subscribing to *The Rooms Chronicle®*, please call 866-READ-TRC.

Key Terms

eco-purchasing—Purchasing policies that evaluate products for durability, reusability, recyclability, content, packaging, and delivery methods.

effluent water—Partially treated wastewater from community sewage or industry.

just-in-time buying—The practice of buying products just before current inventory runs out.

reclaimed water—Partially treated wastewater from community sewage or industry.

sustainability—Reducing one's ecological footprint so that resources are not irresponsibly depleted.

triple bottom line—A three-pronged approach to sustainability that includes economic, social, and environmental management.

volatile organic compounds—Also known as VOCs, they emit gasses which can have short- and long-term adverse health effects. Examples include paint strippers, permanent markers, disinfectants, degreasers, and other cleaning supplies.

 ## Review Questions

1. What types of programs exist to help hospitality properties become better environmental stewards?

2. What role does the housekeeping department play in a property's environmental program?

3. How have linen reuse programs contributed to water conservation?

4. What is the most energy efficient form of lighting?

5. What are the three elements of a waste management program?

6. What are some important elements of indoor air quality programs?

7. What factors should an executive housekeeper consider when choosing cleaning chemicals?

 ## Internet Sites

For more information, visit the following Internet sites. Remember that Internet addresses can change without notice. If the site is no longer there, you can use a search engine to look for additional sites.

AH&LA's Good Earthkeeping
   Program
www.ei-ahla.org/content.asp?ID=146

Earth 911
www.earth911.com

EC3 Global
www.ec3global.com

Energy Star
www.energystar.gov

Florida Green Lodging
www.FloridaGreenLodging.org

Green Lodging News
www.greenlodgingnews.com

WasteWise
www.epa.gov/wastewise

Chapter 3 Outline

Identifying Housekeeping's Responsibilities
Planning the Work of the Housekeeping
    Department
       Area Inventory Lists
       Frequency Schedules
       Performance Standards
       Productivity Standards
       Inventory Levels
Organizing the Housekeeping Department
    The Department Organization Chart
    Task Lists and Job Descriptions
Other Management Functions of the
    Executive Housekeeper
       Coordinating and Staffing
       Directing and Controlling
       Evaluating
Supervisor Dilemma

Competencies

1. Identify typical cleaning responsibilities of the housekeeping department. (pp. 67–71)

2. Describe the tools the housekeeping department uses to plan its work. (pp. 71–83)

3. Explain the executive housekeeper's role in organizing the housekeeping department. (pp. 83–89)

4. Identify basic management functions of the executive housekeeper. (pp. 89–101)

3

Planning and Organizing the Housekeeping Department

Lɪᴋᴇ ᴀʟʟ ᴏᴛʜᴇʀ ᴍᴀɴᴀɢᴇʀs in a hotel, the executive housekeeper uses available resources to attain objectives set by top management executives. Resources include people, money, time, work methods, materials, energy, and equipment. These resources are in limited supply, and most executive housekeepers will readily admit that they rarely have all the resources they would like. Therefore, an important part of the executive housekeeper's job is planning how to use the limited resources available to attain the hotel's objectives.

The executive housekeeper uses objectives set by the general manager as a guide in planning more specific, measurable goals for the housekeeping department. For example, one of the executive housekeeper's first planning activities is to clarify the department's cleaning responsibilities and to map strategies for carrying out these responsibilities effectively. Strategies will identify the types of cleaning tasks and indicate how frequently the tasks must be performed.

This chapter begins by identifying some of the executive housekeeper's most important planning functions. The major cleaning responsibilities of the housekeeping department are identified, and suggestions for planning work within the department are presented. In addition, the chapter examines the organizational structure of several housekeeping departments and presents sample job descriptions for executive housekeeper positions. Job descriptions are also presented for typical housekeeping positions in a mid-market hotel. The chapter closes by showing how other important management functions of the executive housekeeper fit into the overall process of management.

Identifying Housekeeping's Responsibilities

Regardless of the size and structure of a housekeeping department, it is typically the responsibility of the hotel's general manager to identify which areas housekeeping will be responsible for cleaning. Most housekeeping departments are responsible for cleaning the following areas:

- Guestrooms
- Corridors
- Public areas, such as the lobby and public restrooms
- Pool and patio areas
- Management offices

- Storage areas
- Linen and sewing rooms
- Laundry room
- Back-of-the-house areas, such as employee locker rooms

Housekeeping departments of hotels offering mid-range and world-class service are generally responsible for additional areas, such as:

- Meeting rooms
- Dining rooms
- Banquet rooms
- Convention exhibit halls
- Hotel-operated shops
- Game rooms
- Exercise rooms

Housekeeping's cleaning responsibilities in the food & beverage areas vary from property to property. In most hotels, housekeeping has very limited responsibilities in relation to cleaning food preparation, production, and storage areas. The special cleaning and sanitation tasks required for maintaining these areas are usually carried out by kitchen staff under the supervision of the chief steward. In some properties, the dining room staff cleans service areas after breakfast and lunch periods; housekeeping's night cleaning crew does the in-depth cleaning after dinner service or early in the morning before the dining room opens for business. The executive housekeeper and the dining room managers must work closely together to ensure that quality standards are maintained in the guest service and server station areas.

The same cooperation is necessary between housekeeping and banquet or meeting services. The banquet or meeting services staff generally sets up banquet and meeting rooms and is responsible for some cleaning after the rooms are used. The final in-depth cleaning is left to the housekeeping department. This means that the final responsibility for the cleanliness and overall appearance of these areas falls squarely on the shoulders of the housekeeping staff.

The general manager typically designates which areas housekeeping will be responsible for cleaning. However, if areas of responsibility cross department lines, the managers of those departments must get together and settle among themselves any disputes about cleaning responsibilities. The agreement among the managers is then reported to the general manager for his or her approval. A good housekeeping manager can effectively solve problems with other managers, thereby relieving the general manager of day-to-day, operational problems.

It is a good idea for the executive housekeeper to obtain a floor plan of the hotel (either paper or digital) and "color in" those areas for which housekeeping is responsible. Different colors can be used to designate those areas for which other department managers are responsible. To ensure that all areas of the property have been covered—and to avoid future misunderstandings about responsibilities—copies of this color-coded floor plan should be distributed to the general

the Rooms
CHRONICLE®

Executive Housekeeper IS the Driving Force

Say it's Monday and the day is well under way. The roomkeepers are off doing their assignments, the laundry is humming, and the public space cleaners are started on their chores. The executive housekeeper decides the time is right for a walkdown. After all, it was a busy weekend, lots of guests in the house, and the executive housekeeper wants to review the property's condition.

This walkdown is one of the most important functions of the executive housekeeper. Undeniably, the executive housekeeper's number one job is to ensure a clean hotel, and inspections are the key to this goal. But exactly what is an executive housekeeper looking for during a walkdown? Clean hallways? Public space furniture arranged neatly? Litter-free grounds? Employees doing the right things in the right places? Yes. All of this and more. The executive housekeeper must look at the big picture.

For instance, when a public space cleaner patrols the hotel hallways, he concentrates on picking up litter and emptying ashurns. When an executive housekeeper walks the building, he or she is reviewing the physical state of the building.

It is big picture things like the condition of the upholstery on the lobby sofa or the scratches in the chair rail along the hallway that the executive housekeeper must notice. It is the role of the executive housekeeper to identify trends of decline in the state of the property and gather the resources necessary to make things right. Whether correcting the problem means coordination of efforts between other departments or preparation of a capital budget for money allocation, the executive housekeeper must be responsible for initiating activity.

Public areas

One maintenance item that can easily get out of control is nicks in doors and hallways. The best executive housekeepers trace the source of the nicks in order to eliminate the cause. Perhaps there's a sharp corner on one or more roomkeeper carts? A bellman's cart? Rollaway beds? Room service carts? The executive housekeeper surveys the hotel, decides the magnitude of the problem, and arranges with engineering to have the situation corrected. Redirecting painters, closing down sections of rooms, and communicating with various departments are actions that must be arranged in order to eliminate the shoddy-looking nicks.

The executive housekeeper worries about the general appearance of the building—what might be guests' first impressions? The condition of lobby furniture, the appearance of vending areas, the orderliness of roomkeeper carts—things that guests see before getting inside their rooms.

An executive housekeeper would notice that a vending machine is again out of a certain item(s) and would take responsibility for correcting the situation. An executive housekeeper would notice that the plant service has not been making regular visits as contracted. An executive housekeeper would notice that longer walk-off mats are needed at certain entrances.

Guestrooms

Within guestrooms, an executive housekeeper would be concerned not just with cleaning but with the general condition of the rooms. For instance:

(continued)

the Rooms
CHRONICLE®

(continued)

- Are mattresses, pillows, and bedspreads beginning to show wear and tear?

- Are the case goods holding up according to manufacturers' expectations?

- If air vents are collecting dust, an executive housekeeper asks "why?" Is the room attendant not performing cleaning tasks as assigned? Or is there a more serious problem within the air handling system?

- Are guestroom windows fogged? What is engineering's position on replacing them?

- Are balcony railings deteriorating? Do they need replacement, paint, or welding?

- What is the condition of draperies? What cleaning program should be employed? Vacuuming the drapes? Remove them to process through the dryer? Contract with an outside vendor to dry clean the drapes?

- What is the quality of bedmaking throughout the hotel? An executive housekeeper will tear apart a freshly made bed to inspect the condition of all components and the technique of the room attendant.

- Are the bathroom fixtures intact? No cracks or stains or leaks? Have room attendants been reporting problems? Has engineering been responding to the reports?

- Is the room overloaded with promotional materials? Pizza promotions, long distance dialing instructions, the latest frequent guest program—each flier takes up space in the guestroom and impacts the guest's impression of the room. It is an executive housekeeper's role to review the room, ensure that materials are current and necessary, and put a stop to clutter.

- Does the television work? The remote control? The telephone speed buttons? Are directions current and easy to follow?

Many of the items that an executive housekeeper must inspect require remedies that involve other hotel managers. Engineering, for example, must work hand in hand with housekeeping toward the general upkeep of the property. Accounting must be supportive in conducting inventories and preparing paperwork for building capital expenditure budgets. Purchasing must assist in gathering bids for replacement of inventory. And general managers must be involved in endorsing the improvements.

The condition of the property is the most valuable asset of the hotel. The executive housekeeper must be the driving force toward achieving perfection. In fact, the responsibility for getting things to happen must rest with the executive housekeeper.

In the real world the executive housekeeper often feels powerless to get other managers to help solve hotel problems. But the executive housekeeper is dependent upon others for cooperation. For instance, the front office must agree to close a section of rooms for deep cleaning. So, the executive housekeeper must continually work to gain commitment from all parties. It is the role of the executive housekeeper to not only see the big picture, but to enhance it at every opportunity.

Source: Mary Friedman, *The Rooms Chronicle*®, Volume 8, Number 3, pp. 4–5.
For subscription information, please call 866-READ-TRC.

manager and to all department managers. This way, everyone can see at a glance who is responsible for cleaning each area in the hotel. The color-coded floor plan also presents a clear and impressive picture of the housekeeping department's role in cleaning and maintaining the hotel.

Contemporary lodging properties are often attempting to "go green" in almost all aspects of their operations, including housekeeping. This may add another arc of responsibility for executive housekeepers. From encouraging guests to reuse linens to more comprehensive sustainability mandates, most hotels are or will likely move to adopt more environmentally friendly housekeeping standards.

Once housekeeping's areas of responsibility have been identified, planning focuses on analyzing the work required for cleaning and maintaining each area.

Planning the Work of the Housekeeping Department

Planning is probably the executive housekeeper's most important management function. Without competent planning, every day may present one crisis after another. Constant crises lower morale, decrease productivity, and increase expenses within the department. Also, without the direction and focus that planning provides, the executive housekeeper can easily become sidetracked by tasks which are unimportant or unrelated to accomplishing the hotel's objectives.

Since the housekeeping department is responsible for cleaning and maintaining so many different areas of the hotel, planning the work of the department can seem like an enormous task. Without a systematic, step-by-step approach to planning, the executive housekeeper can easily become overwhelmed and frustrated by the hundreds of important details. These details must be addressed in order to ensure that the work is not only done—but done correctly, efficiently, on time, and with the least cost to the department.

Exhibit 1 shows how the executive housekeeper can plan the work of the department. The exhibit lists the initial questions that focus the planning activities of the executive housekeeper and identifies the end result of each step in the planning process. The resulting documents form the plans that must be in place for the housekeeping department to run smoothly. The following sections examine each step in the planning process.

Area Inventory Lists

Planning the work of the housekeeping department begins with creating **area inventory lists** of all items within each area that will need housekeeping's attention. Preparing area inventory lists is the first planning activity because the lists ensure that the rest of the planning activities address every item for which housekeeping will be held accountable. Area inventory lists are bound to be long and extremely detailed. Since most properties offer several different types of guestrooms, separate inventory lists may be needed for each room type.

When preparing a guestroom area inventory list, it is a good idea to follow the sequence in which room attendants will clean items and in which supervisors will inspect items. This enables the executive housekeeper to use the inventory lists as the basis for developing cleaning procedures, training plans, and inspection

Exhibit 1   Basic Planning Activities

INITIAL PLANNING QUESTIONS	RESULTING DOCUMENTS
1. What items within this area must be cleaned or maintained?	Area Inventory Lists
2. How often must the items within this area be cleaned or maintained?	Frequency Schedules
3. What must be done in order to clean or maintain the major items within this area?	Performance Standards
4. How long should it take an employee to perform an assigned task according to the department's performance standards?	Productivity Standards
5. What amounts of equipment and supplies will be needed in order for the housekeeping staff to meet performance and productivity standards?	Inventory Levels

checklists. For example, items within a guestroom may appear on an area inventory list as they are found from right to left and from top to bottom around the room. Other systematic techniques may be used, but the point is that *some* system should be followed—and this system should be the same one used by room attendants and inspectors in the daily course of their duties.

Frequency Schedules

Frequency schedules indicate how often items on area inventory lists are to be cleaned or maintained. Items that must be cleaned on a daily or weekly basis become part of a routine cleaning cycle and are incorporated into standard work procedures. Other items (that must be cleaned or maintained biweekly, monthly, bimonthly, or according to some other cycle) are inspected on a daily or weekly basis, but they become part of a **deep cleaning** program and are scheduled as special cleaning projects. Exhibit 2 presents a sample frequency schedule for light fixtures found in a public area of a large convention hotel. Exhibit 3 presents a sample frequency list for special project duties carried out by housekeeping's night cleaning crew.

Tasks on an area's frequency schedule that are made part of housekeeping's deep cleaning program should be transferred to a calendar plan (whether computer- or paper-based) and scheduled as special cleaning projects. The calendar program guides the executive housekeeper in scheduling the appropriate staff to perform the necessary work. The executive housekeeper must take into account a number of factors when scheduling deep cleaning of guestrooms or other special projects. For example, whenever possible, days marked for guestroom deep cleaning should

Exhibit 2   Sample Frequency Schedule

PUBLIC AREA #2—LIGHT FIXTURES			
LOCATION	**TYPE**	**NO.**	**FREQ.**
Entrance #1	Sconce	2	1/W
Lobby	Chandelier	3	1/M
Entrance #2	Crown Sconce	2	1/M
Behind Fountain	Sconce	3	1/W
Catwalk	Pole Light	32	1/M
Lower Level	Pole Light	16	1/M
Fountain Area	Pole Light	5	1/M
Restaurant Courtyard	Pole Light	10	1/M
Restaurant Courtyard	Wall Light	5	1/M
Restaurant Patio	Half-Pole Light	16	1/W
Restaurant Entrance	White Globe Pole Light	6	1/W
Crystal Gazebo	White Globe Pole Light	8	1/W
2nd Stairs to Catwalk	White Globe Pole Light	2	1/W
Fountain	White Globe Pole Light	4	1/W
Lounge Patio	Wall Light	4	1/W
Restaurant Entrance	Chandelier	1	1/W

coincide with low occupancy periods. Also, the deep cleaning program must be flexible in relation to the activities of other departments. For example, if the engineering department schedules extensive repair work for several guestrooms, the executive housekeeper should make every effort to coordinate a deep cleaning of these rooms with engineering's timetable. Careful planning will produce good results for the hotel with the least possible inconvenience to guests or to other departments.

Performance Standards

The executive housekeeper can begin to develop **performance standards** by answering the question, "What must be done in order to clean or maintain the major items within this area?" Standards are required quality levels of performance. Performance standards state not only *what* must be done, they also describe in detail *how* the job must be done.

One of the primary objectives of planning the work of the housekeeping department is to ensure that all employees carry out their cleaning tasks in a consistent manner. A 2006 study indicated there may be large differences in the amount of cleaning products used by room attendants at the same hotel (or the same shift), reinforcing the importance of establishing, communicating, and measuring performance standards.[1] The keys to consistency are the performance standards which the executive housekeeper develops, communicates, and manages. Although these standards will vary from one housekeeping department to another, executive

Exhibit 3   Sample Frequency List for Night Cleaning Projects

| | Frequency | |
Special Projects	Per Week	Per Month
1. Wash down tile walls in restrooms	1	
2. Strip and wax the following:		
Restrooms (as necessary)		1
Basement hallway	1	
Lounge, lobby, and stairs		1
3. Shampoo the following:		
Registration area		1
Stairs		1
Restrooms		1
All dining rooms		2
All lounges		1
Coffee shop		1
Meeting rooms		1
Guest elevators		1
Employee cafeteria (as needed)		2
4. Spot shampoo the following:		
Front entrance		2
Side entrance		2
Front desk area		2
5. Wash windows in pool area		1
6. Dust louvers in pool area		1
7. Clean guest and service elevator tracks	1	
8. Polish kitchen equipment		1
9. Polish drinking fountains	1	
10. Clean outside of guest elevators	2	

housekeepers can ensure consistency of cleaning by demanding 100 percent conformity to the standards established by their departments. When performance standards are not properly developed, effectively communicated, and consistently managed, the productivity of the housekeeping department suffers because employees will not be performing their tasks in the most efficient and effective manner.

The most important aspect of developing standards is gaining consensus on how cleaning and other tasks are to be carried out. Consensus can be achieved by having individuals who actually perform the tasks contribute to the standards that are eventually adopted by the department.

Performance standards are communicated through ongoing training programs. Many properties have developed performance standards and have included them between the covers of impressive housekeeping procedure manuals. However, all too often, these manuals simply gather dust on shelves in the offices of executive housekeepers. Well-written standards are useless unless they

the Rooms
CHRONICLE®

To Give a 100-Percent Clean Appearance, Rotate Guestroom Tasks and Projects

Can a room cleaner clean 100 percent of every assigned room every day? Probably not! Shortage of supplies, time, or equipment may prohibit the room cleaner from doing perfect work in every room. But with a good daily job description and proper organization of tasks and projects, a room cleaner can consistently produce a high quality room.

The housekeeping manager should begin with a good room cleaner daily job description. Go to the guestroom and write all areas that need cleaning. Room cleaners should then test the items on the cleaning list with a time clock. With this information, a manager can decide what tasks will be included in the daily routine and which will be completed some other way.

The areas that don't need attention every day, such as changing bedspreads, washing walls, or shampooing carpets, become either special projects or deep cleaning items. Since guests do have expectations of a completely clean room when they arrive, room cleaners must be organized in a way that results in a room that appears as if it has been thoroughly cleaned that same day. To accomplish this, managers must have a frequency list for special cleaning tasks.

Many tasks fall into the category of deep cleaning. For instance, changing the sheer drapes is a deep cleaning task that may need to be done only biannually. An easy way to complete projects that fall into this category is to close down a block of rooms for deep cleaning. Thorough cleaning of a series of rooms is easily accomplished by having a cleaning team, supply inventory, and cleaning equipment ready. This is also a good time for engineering to review the rooms for preventive maintenance items.

There are various other ways to organize the completion of deep cleaning rooms. For instance, a deep cleaning team might be given a short schedule of check-out rooms. A hotel in downtown Minneapolis hires a group of workers with disabilities as their special clean team. They are assigned approximately six rooms per day to deep clean and are paid by the room.

Another deep cleaning method is to schedule every room cleaner with one room per day as a deep clean room. When the room cleaner accepts responsibility for deep cleaning one room per day, management may choose to institute a "perfect room" incentive to keep the quality high.

But there are other tasks that need to be done less often than every day but more often that deep cleaning: for instance, washing door frames, light switch plates, or bathroom air vents. One method of accomplishing these tasks is to highlight each as a special daily project that is announced at the morning meeting. Monday might be "wash the door frame" day so that each room cleaner will wash the door frame in every assigned room.

The difficulty of managing special cleaning tasks is tracking which rooms have been completed. For example, if on Monday the hotel is only 75 percent occupied, then 25 percent of the rooms did not get the door frames washed.

(continued)

C the Rooms HRONICLE®

(continued)

To overcome this dilemma, many housekeepers post a projects chart in the room cleaner closet on each floor. Room cleaners simply mark off which tasks have been accomplished in each room. With this system, relief room cleaners can easily see the status of the floor and participate in the project cleaning.

Although there are many variations on the rotation systems described above, all share the same goal—to present a thoroughly clean room to each arriving guest.

Source: Mary Friedman, *The Rooms Chronicle*®, Volume 5, Number 5, p. 4. For subscription information, please call 866-READ-TRC.

are applied. The only way to implement standards in the workplace is through effective training programs.

After communicating performance standards through ongoing training activities, the executive housekeeper must manage those standards. Managing standards means ensuring conformity to standards by inspection. Experienced housekeepers know the truth of the adage, "You can't expect what you don't inspect." Daily inspections and periodic performance evaluations should be followed up with specific on-the-job coaching and retraining. This ensures that all employees are consistently performing their tasks in the most efficient and effective manner. The executive housekeeper should review the department's performance standards at least once a year and make appropriate revisions as new work methods are implemented.

Productivity Standards

While performance standards establish the expected quality of the work to be done, **productivity standards** determine the acceptable quantity of work to be done by department employees. An executive housekeeper begins to establish productivity standards by answering the question, "How long should it take for a housekeeping employee to perform an assigned task according to the department's performance standard?" Productivity standards must be determined in order to properly staff the department within the limitations established by the hotel's operating budget.

Since performance standards vary in relation to the unique needs and requirements of each hotel, it is impossible to identify productivity standards that would apply across the board to every housekeeping department. Since the duties of room attendants vary widely among economy, mid-market, and luxury hotels, the productivity standards for room attendants will also vary.

When determining realistic productivity standards, an executive housekeeper does not have to carry around a measuring tape, stopwatch, and clipboard and conduct time and motion studies on all the tasks necessary to clean and maintain each item on an area's inventory list. The labor of the executive housekeeper and other management staff is also a precious department resource. However, housekeeping

Exhibit 4   Sample Productivity Standards Worksheet

Step 1

   **Determine how long it should take to clean
   one guestroom according to the department's
   performance standards.**

   Approximately 27 minutes*

Step 2

   Determine the total shift time in minutes.

   8 hours × 60 minutes = 480 minutes

Step 3

   Determine the time available for guestroom cleaning.

   Total Shift Time . . . . 480 minutes
   Less:
       Beginning-of-Shift Duties . . . . 20 minutes
       Morning Break . . . . 15 minutes
       Afternoon Break . . . . 15 minutes
       End-of-Shift Duties . . . . 20 minutes

   Time Available for Guestroom Cleaning . . . . . 410 minutes

Step 4

   **Determine the productivity standard by dividing the
   result of Step 3 by the result of Step 1.**

   $$\frac{410 \text{ minutes}}{27 \text{ minutes}} = 15.2 \text{ guestrooms per 8-hour shift}$$

   *Since performance standards vary from property to property,
   this figure is used for illustrative purposes only. It is not a
   suggested time figure for cleaning guestrooms.

managers must know how long it should take a housekeeping employee to perform the major tasks identified on the cleaning frequency schedules—such as guestroom cleaning. Once this information is known, productivity standards can be developed.

Let's assume that, at a mid-market hotel, the executive housekeeper determines that a room attendant can meet performance standards and clean a typical guestroom in approximately 27 minutes. Exhibit 4 presents a sample productivity standards worksheet and shows how a productivity standard can be calculated for room attendants working 8-hour shifts. Calculations within the exhibit assume that room attendants take a half-hour, unpaid lunch period. The exhibit shows that the productivity standard for room attendants should be to clean 15 guestrooms per 8-hour shift.

Quality and quantity can be like two sides of a coin. On one side, if the quality expectations (performance standards) are set too high, the quantity of work that can be done accordingly may be unacceptably low. This forces the executive housekeeper to add more and more staff to ensure that all the work gets done.

Experiment with Piece Rate Proves Positive for Northern Michigan Resort

With more and more employers competing for a shrinking work force, it has become difficult for housekeeping managers to find and retain top-notch staff, much less motivate them to do their work efficiently. But are external factors to blame? Or can something be done from within to attract and keep good staff?

Crystal Mountain Resort is a family-owned resort located in the smallest of Michigan's 83 counties. The four-season resort employs anywhere from 250 to 480 people (a large percentage of which are housekeepers) year-round. Even as the largest employer in the area, though, Crystal Mountain is not immune to the same problems encountered by housekeeping managers nationwide: retaining good help.

When Sharlene Thomas, director of facilities services at Crystal Mountain, took a look at their lodging forecast for the upcoming summer, she knew she had to make a few changes. She faced a record summer of overnight guests attributable to the resort's addition of a second golf course and booming conference business. Thomas knew that she needed to somehow motivate her staff to work efficiently and compensate them well enough to retain them, even when they were turning a record number of rooms. And she also knew that Crystal Mountain's current system, where her staff was paid an hourly rate, was not as powerful a tool as it should be to entice and retain quality staff; nor did it set her apart from other area employers who were competing for the same work force.

Having heard of the success that a nearby Michigan resort, The Homestead, had in its implementation of "piece rate" compensation for its staff, Thomas called the resort to inquire further. The Homestead's executive housekeeper came to meet with Thomas, as well as Crystal Mountain's executive housekeeper and personnel services director. All loved the idea of paying by the room.

The idea behind piece rate is that room attendants are paid for work based on the quantity of units cleaned. In Crystal Mountain's particular case, where they have many different types and sizes of lodging units, each unit is assigned a different value and time standard, and housekeepers' wages are determined not only by the number of units cleaned, but by the type as well.

Crystal Mountain started experimenting with piece work in March of 1998 with the Resort's spring cleaning. Prior to that, room attendants were paid an average of $6.95 an hour using the hourly pay rate. With the piece rate method of compensation, housekeepers have earned an average rate as high as $9.95 an hour.

"It was scary at first," admitted Thomas. "It was a big change for many people and at first we had to have several meetings and pow-wows to sort out the little details." Thomas noted that the housekeepers were concerned especially about the time they spent not actually cleaning units, i.e., stocking storerooms, making deliveries, and hauling linen. "We had to assure them that these rates included these little extras."

Crystal Mountain also took this time to make a few changes within the department to eliminate as many non-cleaning activities for the housekeepers as possible.

the Rooms CHRONICLE®

(continued)

In explaining the new system to her staff, Thomas stressed that piece rate would be much more beneficial to them. "Our housekeepers are able to make more money than they did with the hourly rate, providing they work hard and efficiently," she pointed out. "Piece rate also allows us to be more flexible in our scheduling. Several housekeepers have dropped to four days a week because they can now make the same amount of money in four days that they used to make in five. Yet we still schedule based on occupancy and demand.

"The piece rate system has allowed two room attendants to earn between $15 to $16 an hour, which allowed them to cut down to just four days a week of work," Thomas added.

And the benefits to Crystal Mountain? "Our people are more productive," said Thomas. "Productivity has increased 30 percent. There is no way that we could have turned over the volume we saw this summer without piece rate."

Quality is also a key element of piece work at Crystal Mountain, as credit is not given for work performed until quality standards have been met. Thomas or another supervisor checks every guest departure and any rework is performed by the person(s) who cleaned the unit.

New hires start at $6 an hour. After a week of training, they begin to be paid according to piece work standards. And should a room attendant work overtime, their overtime wage is calculated at time-and-a-half of their average hourly wage for that week.

Piece rate has not completely solved the problem of finding good room attendants. Crystal Mountain was still understaffed most of the summer, and during extremely busy times they contracted out for extra help. However, Thomas is convinced that piece rate has allowed her to retain her high-quality employees by keeping them happier. "In time, once the word spreads, I'm sure we'll entice more staff.

"Our housekeepers have a huge responsibility," Thomas says. "We demand high quality; however, it was hard to expect this when we were paying only $6 an hour." According to Thomas, roughly 99 percent of the room attendants love the new method of compensation. "We're still playing with it," she says. "It will take about a year to make it win-win."

(Authors' Note: The pay rates presented in this article were the prevailing wage scale when the article was published.)

Source: *The Rooms Chronicle®*, Volume 7, Number 1, p. 13.
For subscription information, call 866-READ-TRC.

However, sooner or later (and probably sooner than expected), the general manager will cut the high labor expense of the housekeeping department. This action would force the executive housekeeper to reduce the staff size and to realign quality and quantity by redefining performance standards in light of more realistic productivity standards.

On the other side, if performance standards are set too low, the quantity of work that can be done accordingly will be unexpectedly high. At first, the general manager may be delighted. However, as complaints from guests and staff increase and the property begins to reflect dingy neglect, the general manager may, once again, step in with a solution. This time, the general manager may choose to replace the executive housekeeper with a person who will establish higher performance standards and monitor department expenses more closely.

The challenge is to effectively balance performance standards and productivity standards. Quality and quantity each can serve to check and balance the other. For example, at some properties, eliminating redundant tasks from checkout and stayover rooms and training room attendants to concentrate on areas that guests really notice has helped reduce cleaning times in stayover rooms by eight to nine minutes while maintaining positive guest perceptions.[2] A concern for productivity need not necessarily lower performance standards—it can sharpen and refine current work methods and procedures. If room attendants are constantly returning to the housekeeping area for cleaning and guestroom supplies, there is something wrong with the way they set up and stock their carts. Wasted motion is wasted time, and wasted time depletes the most important and most expensive resource of the housekeeping department: labor. The executive housekeeper must be constantly on the alert for new and more efficient work methods.

Remember, an executive housekeeper will rarely have all the resources necessary to do everything he or she may want to accomplish. Therefore, labor must be carefully allocated to achieve acceptable performance standards and realistic productivity standards.

Inventory Levels

After planning what must be done and how the tasks are to be performed, the executive housekeeper must ensure that employees have the necessary equipment and supplies to get their jobs done. The executive housekeeper plans appropriate inventory levels by answering the following question: "What amounts of equipment and supplies will be needed for the housekeeping staff to meet the performance and productivity standards of the department?" The answer to this question ensures smooth daily housekeeping activities and forms the basis for planning an effective purchasing system. A purchasing system must consistently maintain the needed amounts of items in housekeeping inventories.

Essentially, the executive housekeeper is responsible for two types of inventories. One type stores items which are recycled during the course of hotel operations; the other type stores non-recyclable items. Non-recyclable items are consumed or used up during routine activities of the housekeeping department. Due to limited storage facilities and management's desire not to tie up cash in overstocked inventories, the executive housekeeper must establish reasonable inventory levels for both recyclable and non-recyclable items.

Recycled Inventories. Recycled inventories include linens, most equipment items, and some guest supplies. Recycled equipment includes room attendant carts, vacuum cleaners, carpet shampooers, floor buffers, and many other items. Recycled guest supplies include such items as irons, ironing boards, cribs, and refrigerators, which guests may need during the course of their stay. Housekeeping is responsible for storing and maintaining these items as well as issuing them as they are requested by guests.

the Rooms
CHRONICLE®

And the Standard Is Still 30 Minutes?

Recently the TRC staff visited with an executive housekeeper of a typical business hotel. Sitting in a guestroom, they glanced around at the amenities of the room. Amazing things have been incorporated into hotel rooms in the last decade. Consider the additional supply and labor costs of these items.

Comforters and duvets

Comforters and their covers, commonly known as duvets, are only part of the recent posh bed ingredients. Previously, hotel beds included only a mattress pad, two sheets, a blanket, and a bedspread. Consider the time necessary to change a posh bed versus a standard bed. Cah-ching.

Bed skirts

In recent years hotel owners have chosen the comforter/dust ruffle combination over the previously accepted bedspread. Sometimes called bed skirts, this move away from bedspreads adds difficulty and time to the bed-making process. Cah-ching.

Double pillows

Many hotels have increased guest comfort by providing twice the number of pillows. Double beds have four pillows, kings have six. This practice, well-appreciated by guests, doubles the time required to change the pillowcases while making the bed. Cah-ching.

Coffeemakers

Another guest convenience, coffeemakers, silently steals away precious room attendant minutes. Washing the pots, cleaning the baskets, wiping up the spills, restocking the accessories—adding a coffeemaker to the guestroom adds to the work load of the staff. Cah-ching.

China cups

Use of glass glasses was one upgrade requiring careful room attendant procedures. Adding china cups for the coffeemaker is another. Cups must be sanitized by washing in the kitchen's dishwashing machine and must be carefully carted to and from the guestrooms. Cah-ching.

Ironing boards and irons

Now that hotels have figured out how to hang ironing boards and irons in the guestroom closet; have identified cord-retracting, self-turn-off, self-cleaning irons; and have found a source for replacement ironing-board covers—now the guests are complaining that there is no place to plug in the iron. And managers are still working on ways of protecting the iron from theft. Cah-ching.

Mini kitchens

A set of four dishes, pots and pans, utensils, and refrigerators to clean, microwaves to wipe out, dishwashers to load and unload, more wastebaskets, more trash (read "yucky food trash"), more bug and rodent problems—and yes, guests are booking suite hotels and extended-stay facilities with more fervor every year. Cah-ching.

(continued)

(continued)

Pullout sofas

In previous times, guests who needed extra accommodations within their rooms requested a roll-away bed. Bingo, extra revenue for the hotel. Today, owners provide sofa beds in many rooms. Extra linen. Extra labor. No extra revenue. Cah-ching.

Bathrobes

When rates are high, amenities should be plentiful. And the addition of bathrobes is a wonderfully accepted guest treat. Managers just have to ensure the rate does actually withstand the cost of purchase, upkeep, handling, and replacement for the luxurious robes. Cah-ching.

Electronic equipment

Somewhere a few years ago when the fax machine was the hottest craze, many business hotels decided to place machines in guestrooms. Now, with technology advances, room attendants must not only dust the fax machines and provide supplies, they must also clean computer screens and keyboards/controls, organize electrical cords, and sanitize remote controls. Cah-ching.

Live plants

As hotel designers move the guestroom more to a residential look, live plants become a helpful corner filler. Sometimes rented and cared for by plant maintenance firms, most hotels have resorted to purchasing plants directly and assigning room attendant staff to care for them. Cah-ching.

Guest safes

Though guest safes do not require a lot of room attendant attention, staff training must still include the details of safe operation and staff must be vigilant about inspecting the safes in check-out rooms. Cah-ching.

Closet hangers

When hotels originally provided coat hangers for guest use, they were very basic, ball-top hangers. Now there are pant hangers, skirt hangers, and satin-padded hangers to straighten. And it's classy to use open-top hangers that are frequently taken home by guests. Cah-ching.

Summary

Isn't it interesting how the guestroom has evolved? Generally, items have been added to guestrooms to improve guest comfort. Or sometimes they were added to keep pace with the competition. In some cases, as with coffeemakers and irons, offering items free in the guestroom might actually have eliminated previously profitable services. Cah-ching.

How is the hotel compensated for the increased luxury of the guestroom? The remuneration for these amenities is received from increased room rates. Have room rates gone up over the last decade? Definitely, yes. But isn't it interesting that the accepted standard amount of time for cleaning a standard guestroom has remained at 30 minutes?

Source: *The Rooms Chronicle®*, Volume 10, Number 6, pp. 8–9.
For subscription information, call 866-READ-TRC.

The number of recycled items that must be on hand to ensure smooth operations is expressed as a **par number.** Par refers to the number of items that must be on hand to support daily, routine housekeeping operations. For example, one par of linens is the total number of items needed to outfit all the hotel guestrooms once; two par of linens is the total number of items needed to outfit all the hotel guestrooms twice; and so on.

Non-Recycled Inventories. Non-recycled inventories include cleaning supplies, guestroom supplies (such as bath soap), and guest amenities (which may range from toothbrushes and shampoos and conditioners to scented bath powders and colognes). Since non-recyclable items are used up in the course of operations, inventory levels are closely tied to the purchase ordering system used at the property. A purchase ordering system for non-recyclable inventory items establishes a par number that is based on two figures—a minimum quantity and a maximum quantity.

The **minimum quantity** is the fewest number of purchase units that should be in stock at any time. Purchase units are counted in terms of normal-size shipping containers, such as cases, drums, and so on. The inventory level should never fall below the minimum quantity. When the inventory level of a non-recyclable item reaches the minimum quantity, additional supplies must be ordered.

The actual number of additional supplies that must be ordered is determined by the **maximum quantity.** The maximum quantity is the greatest number of purchase units that should be in stock at any time. This maximum quantity must be consistent with available storage space and must not be so high that large amounts of the hotel's cash resources are tied up in an overstocked inventory. The shelf life of an item also affects the maximum quantity of purchase units that can be stored.

Organizing the Housekeeping Department

Organizing refers to the executive housekeeper's responsibility to structure the department's staff and to divide the work so that everyone gets a fair assignment and all the work can be finished on time.

Structuring the department's staff means establishing the lines of authority and the flow of communication within the department. Two important principles that should guide the organization of a department are:

- Each employee should have only one supervisor.

- Supervisors should have the authority and information necessary to guide the efforts of employees under their direction.

The executive housekeeper delegates authority to supervisors and must ensure that each employee recognizes the authority structure of the department. While the executive housekeeper may delegate authority, he or she cannot delegate responsibility. The executive housekeeper is ultimately responsible for the actions of department supervisors. Therefore, it is important that supervisors be well informed about hotel policies, procedures, and the limits of their authority.

Exhibit 5   Organization Chart for a Small Economy Hotel

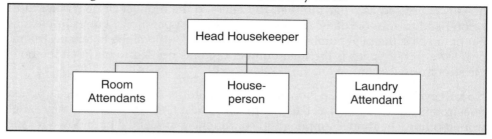

Exhibit 6   Organization Chart for a Large Mid-Market Hotel

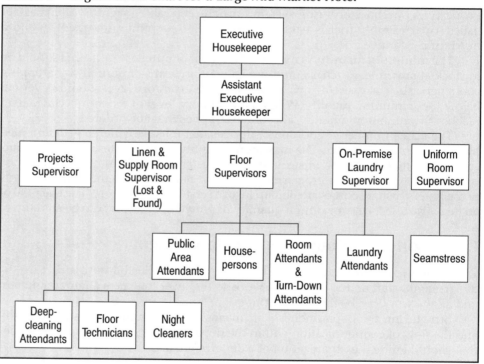

The Department Organization Chart

An **organization chart** provides a clear picture of the lines of authority and the channels of communication within the department. Exhibits 5 through 7 present sample organization charts for housekeeping departments of different sizes and service levels. At small economy properties, the title of the housekeeping department manager depends on the specific duties and responsibilities of the position. The position title is often "head housekeeper," or simply "housekeeper." When compared to the housekeeping departments of other types of hotels, the housekeeping staff of the economy property seems small. However, within the economy

Exhibit 7   Organization Chart for a Large Luxury Hotel

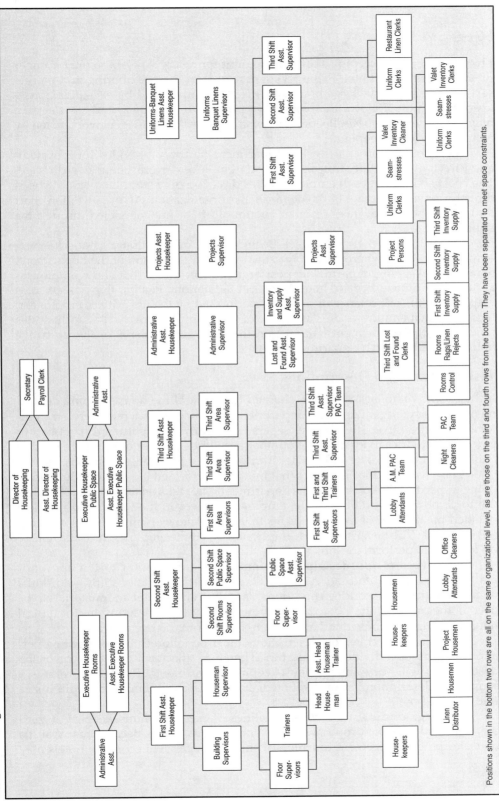

Positions shown in the bottom two rows are all on the same organizational level, as are those on the third and fourth rows from the bottom. They have been separated to meet space constraints.

Courtesy of Opryland Hotel, Nashville, Tennessee

property, the housekeeping staff may account for nearly half of the total number of employees at the hotel. Exhibit 6 suggests that properties offering mid-market service generally have large housekeeping staffs supervised by executive house-keepers. Exhibit 7 shows that very large properties offering world-class service may have a separate housekeeping division with several managers who are led by a director of housekeeping.

The organization chart of the department not only provides for a systematic direction of orders, but also protects employees from being overdirected. The chart shows that each employee takes direction only from the person who is directly above him or her in the department's organization. An organization chart also shows how grievances or other communications are channeled through the department.

A copy of the chart should be posted in an area so that all housekeeping employees can see where they fit into the overall organization of the department. Some housekeeping departments post organization charts that show employees at the top and the executive housekeeper at the bottom. Posting this type of chart emphasizes the importance of the work performed by the majority of employees; it conveys that employees are "at the top of the chart." Such a chart also illustrates how the entire department balances on the managerial talents of the executive housekeeper and other department managers.

Task Lists and Job Descriptions

If the executive housekeeper has planned the work of the housekeeping department properly, organizing the department staff becomes a relatively straight-forward matter. Executive housekeepers use information gathered from earlier planning activities to identify the number and types of positions that are needed and to develop task lists and job descriptions for each of these positions.

A task list identifies the tasks that must be performed by an individual occupying a specific position within the department. The tasks on the list should reflect the total job responsibilities of the employee. However, the list should not be a detailed breakdown of the procedures that the employee will follow in carrying out each task. The task list should simply state what the employee must be able to do in order to perform the job.

Some types of **job descriptions** simply add information to the appropriate task lists. This information may include reporting relationships, additional responsibilities, and working conditions, as well as equipment and materials to be used in the course of the job. Exhibit 8 presents sample job descriptions for typical housekeeping positions found at medium-size mid-market properties.

To be most effective, job descriptions must be tailored to the specific operational needs of individual properties. Therefore, the form and content of job descriptions will vary among housekeeping departments. Exhibit 9 presents a sample job description for the position of executive housekeeper at a medium-size mid-market hotel.

The range of duties and responsibilities of executive housekeepers at various sizes and types of properties varies enormously. This is because many of the housekeeping management functions at small, independent economy hotels may

Exhibit 8   Sample Job Descriptions for Typical Housekeeping Positions

ROOM ATTENDANT

Basic Function

Performs routine duties in the cleaning and servicing of guestrooms and baths under supervision of a floor supervisor.

Duties and Responsibilities

1. Enters and prepares the room for cleaning.
2. Makes the bed.
3. Dusts the room and furniture.
4. Replenishes guestroom and bath supplies.
5. Cleans the bathroom.
6. Cleans the closet.
7. Vacuums the carpet.
8. Checks and secures the room.

Relationships

Reports directly to the floor supervisor.

HOUSEPERSON

Basic Function

Performs any combination of the following tasks to maintain guestrooms, working areas, and the hotel premises in general in a clean and orderly manner.

Duties and Responsibilities

1. Cleans rugs, carpets, and upholstered furniture using a vacuum cleaner, broom, and shampoo machine.
2. Cleans rooms, hallways, and restrooms.
3. Washes walls and ceilings, moves and arranges furniture, and turns mattresses.
4. Sweeps, mops, scrubs, waxes, and polishes floors.
5. Dusts and polishes metalwork.
6. Collects soiled linen for laundering.
7. Receives linen supplies.
8. Stores linen supplies in floor linen closets.
9. Maintains housekeeping carts.
10. Removes trash collected by room attendants.

Relationships

Reports to the head houseperson.

LOBBY ATTENDANT

Basic Function

Keeps all lobbies and public facilities (such as lobby restrooms, telephone areas, the front desk, and offices) in a neat and clean condition.

Duties and Responsibilities

1. Cleans and maintains all lobbies and public restrooms.
2. Sweeps carpets.
3. Empties ashtrays and urns.
4. Polishes furniture and fixtures.
5. Vacuums and polishes elevators.
6. Keeps the front of the hotel free from trash.

Relationships

Reports to the floor supervisor.

LINEN AND UNIFORM ATTENDANT

Basic Function

Stores and issues uniforms, bed linen, and table linen; also takes inventory and maintains linen room supplies.

Duties and Responsibilities

1. Sorts items and counts and records number of items soiled.
2. Places linen and uniforms in containers for transport to laundry.
3. Examines laundered items to ensure cleanliness and serviceability.
4. Sends torn articles to the seamstress for repair.
5. Stores laundered linen and uniforms on shelves after verifying numbers and types of articles.
6. Issues linen and uniforms, which are both to be exchanged on a clean-for-soiled basis only.
7. Counts and records linen to fill requisitions.

Relationships

Reports to the linen room supervisor.

be carried out by the general manager. In the case of chain-affiliated properties, many housekeeping management functions are performed by staff at corporate headquarters. This leaves the task of implementing standardized procedures to the general managers and head housekeepers at individual properties.

Since job descriptions may become outdated as work assignments change, they should be reviewed at least once a year for possible revision. Properly written job descriptions can ease employee anxiety by specifying responsibilities,

Exhibit 9   Sample Job Description for the Executive Housekeeper at a Medium-Size Mid-Market Hotel

Executive Housekeeper

Job Description: The Executive Housekeeper is responsible for ensuring efficient operations of the Housekeeping Department, as well as supervising the entire House-keeping Department including rooms, front/back of house, public areas, and laundry.

JOB DUTIES

- Establish and maintain a key control system for the department.
- Monitor and direct all Housekeeping and Laundry personnel.
- Inspect rooms daily
- Review Housekeeping staff's worked hours for payroll compilation.
- Prepare employee schedule according to the business forecast, payroll budget guidelines and productivity requirements.
- Maintain required pars of all Housekeeping and Laundry supplies by ordering all needed supplies and amenities on a monthly/quarterly basis.
- Conduct monthly and quarterly Housekeeping inventories on a timely basis.
- Ensure guest privacy and security
- Motivate, coach, counsel and discipline all Housekeeping personnel.
- Maintain a professional working relationship and promote open lines of communication with other managers, employees and all other departments.
- Coordinates availability of rooms with Front Office Manager
- Monitors the responses on customer comment cards, identifies problem areas and formulates solutions.
- Conducts continual inspections to determine hotel's overall level of cleanliness; performs follow-up.
- Strives to reduce accidents within the department
- Schedules and supervises all rotational and special cleaning programs as required
- Monitors quality of rooms by conducting and documenting inspections of cleaned room
- Prepares maintenance work orders in regard to replacement or repair of furniture, fixtures, etc
- Insures completion by following through on orders, ensures compliance with accident/loss prevention programs, and health/sanitation standards.

Job Requirements:

- At least 1 year of progressive experience in a hotel or a related field.
- Supervisory experience required.
- Long hours sometimes required.
- Must be able to convey information and ideas clearly.
- Must maintain composure and objectivity under pressure.
- Must be effective in handling problems in the workplace, including anticipating, preventing, identifying and solving problems as necessary.
- Must be effective at listening to, understanding, clarifying and resolving the concerns and issues raised by coworkers and guests.
- Must be able to work with and understand financial information and data, and basic arithmetic functions.
- Adhere to all Hotel policies and practices.
- Report to work punctually and regularly.
- Work safely and successfully, including meeting productivity standards.
- Adhere to established grooming standards.
- Practice the Open Door Policy.
- Provide a picture perfect environment that encourages high standards and enthusiasm.
- Greet all Team Members and thank them for a job well done.

Management Position: Yes

Exhibit 10   Overview of the Management Process

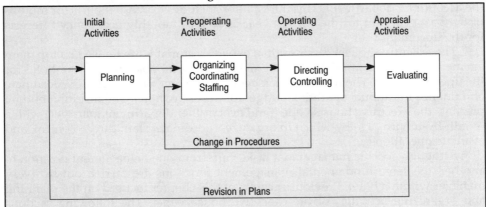

Source: Jack D. Ninemeier, *Planning and Control for Food and Beverage Operations*, 6th ed. (Lansing, Mich.: American Hotel & Lodging Educational Institute, 2004), p. 16.

requirements, and peculiarities of their jobs. Employees should be involved in writing and revising job descriptions for their positions.

Each employee of the housekeeping department should be given a copy of the job description for his or her position. A job description may also be given to all final job candidates before an employment offer is made. This is preferable to having someone accept the job and then decide the job is unsuitable because he or she was unaware of all of its requirements.

Other Management Functions of the Executive Housekeeper

Exhibit 10 presents an overview of the management process and shows how each management function contributes to the overall success of a hotel or, for that matter, any sort of business. Top executives must plan what the hotel is to accomplish by defining its objectives. The desire to attain these objectives leads to organizing, coordinating, and staffing activities. Once members of the hotel staff are selected, management can direct the course of their work and implement control systems to protect the hotel's assets and to ensure smooth, efficient operating activities. Finally, management must evaluate the extent to which the objectives of the organization have been attained. An analysis of actual operating results may lead to changes in organizing, coordinating, or staffing procedures. Also, as a result of evaluating all planning and operating activities, management may find that revisions to the organization's plans or objectives are needed.

An important planning activity of the executive housekeeper is drafting the housekeeping department's operating budget. The housekeeping operating budget estimates expenses of the department for the upcoming year. Expenses include labor, linens, laundry operation, cleaning compounds, some types of equipment, and other supplies. Initial expense estimates are based on information supplied by the accounting department. This information includes expense reports for months of the past year and for the current year as well as monthly occupancy forecasts for the upcoming year.

The executive housekeeper's initial expense estimates are revised by top management executives in relation to the overall financial objectives of the hotel for the upcoming year. The hotel's owner, general manager, and controller coordinate and finalize the annual operating budget for the entire hotel. The resulting budget presents the executive housekeeper (and every other department manager) with a month-by-month plan by which to organize, coordinate, staff, direct, control, and evaluate operations.

Although specific management tasks vary from one management position to another, the same fundamental management functions are carried out by every manager within a hotel. Previous sections of this chapter focused on the planning and organizing activities of the executive housekeeper. The following sections briefly examine the executive housekeeper's management responsibilities in the areas of coordinating, staffing, directing, controlling, and evaluating the operation of the housekeeping department.

Coordinating and Staffing

Coordinating is the management function of implementing the results of planning and organizing at the level of daily housekeeping activities. Each day, the executive housekeeper must coordinate schedules and work assignments and ensure that the proper equipment, cleaning supplies, linens, and other supplies are on hand for employees to carry out their assignments.

Staffing involves recruiting applicants, selecting those best qualified to fill open positions, and scheduling employees to work. Since labor is housekeeping's largest expense item, properly scheduling employees is one of the most important management responsibilities of the executive housekeeper.

Most housekeeping departments use some type of staffing guidelines. These guidelines are usually based on formulas that are used to calculate the number of employees required to meet operational needs at specific occupancy levels. The use of labor forecasting software has gained favor among lodging managers, with some evidence that it can help reduce the time that department managers spend scheduling employees.[3] However, the management function of staffing goes beyond simply applying a formula. Staffing must be adequate to meet the deep cleaning schedules for various areas of the hotel and to meet the needs of other special cleaning projects. Therefore, the executive housekeeper must be flexible and creative, establishing staffing patterns that permit the department to reach its goals within the limits of the budget plan.

Team Cleaning. Many years ago, team cleaning guestrooms was a hot new procedure in the hotel industry. But for many reasons, including lack of accountability of individual room attendants, enthusiasm for the procedure cooled, and it did not become standard practice. But now, it seems team cleaning guestrooms could be the solution to some of today's housekeeping challenges. With increasing concern for safety and security, assigning two people to clean a room could save many dollars in liabilities and lawsuits. Additionally, team cleaning might be a way to put some fun into a relatively mundane task.

Here's how it is being done. Teams of two people are usually assigned 30 to 35 rooms. Individuals rotate duties of bedroom and bathroom cleaning. Room attendants pick their own partners, and new employees become alternates until a new team is formed.

One hotel uses teams of three people and incorporates responsibility for the honor bar. The first person strips the soiled linens and restocks the in-room bar. Before going on to the next room, he or she helps the second person make the beds. The second person then finishes the bedroom while the third person cleans the bathroom. This technique is very fast-paced with approximately eight minutes being spent in each room.

Hotels that presently use team cleaning suggest that you let the idea come from the employees and that you give them ownership in the implementation process. Start with only one team and gradually, as systems are ironed out, add more teams. Keep a list of alternates in case team members are sick. Also, monitor the teams to ensure that partners work at the same speed. Advantages of team cleaning include the following:

- Fewer tools are needed; for example, one vacuum, one cart, and one caddy of cleaning supplies equip one team.

- Morale is higher. On days when someone doesn't feel 100 percent, having a teammate eases the stress.

- Attendance improves, as room attendants are less likely to let their partners down by calling in sick.

- Some special cleaning tasks are accomplished more easily with two people (for example, moving beds or pulling out credenzas).

- Very importantly, safety is improved with two people in the room.

- Getting new employees up to speed seems to be easier with teams because they have buddies to coach them along.

- Room attendants seem to like having more rooms in their "sections." A variety of room types breaks the monotony.

Careful planning is the key to success. Some of the considerations that executive housekeepers need to address include:

- Have linen and chemical inventories equally distributed so that teams are not fighting for supplies.

- If something stops a team, two or three people are stopped, as opposed to only one in traditional guestroom cleaning. Having supplies available is critical, as is giving teams an accurate list of room assignments.

- Some hotels save on labor costs due to team cleaners completing rooms faster than individuals. However, primary savings result from better attendance, less equipment, fewer accidents, and more employee interest in improving the process.

- Scheduling may require special effort to accommodate getting teams the same days off.

At a riverfront hotel, the executive housekeeper was able to give each team a separate locked cage with supplies, a cart, and a vacuum cleaner so that other employees would not disturb their things.

Another manager, at a northeastern inn, found that potential workers who were very nervous about their new jobs were comforted by working together. They were able to talk to each other and help each other become efficient. This manager has instituted team cleaning in other hotels. Incidentally, believing four eyes are better than two, he operates his hotels without supervisors, relying on the team members to check their own work. He credits team cleaning as contributing to longevity of service and high morale of housekeeping employees at his hotels.

One property has used team cleaning for more than 25 years and finds it contributes to low turnover of the housekeeping staff, better morale, and better speed. With two room attendants to a room, attendants are not working alone and feel safer. The room attendants also watch less TV in a room when there is someone to talk with. They vary the tasks—one dusts and vacuums while the other does the bathroom—and in the next room they switch. Four eyes are better than two for seeing items left behind or something not right in a room. An experienced worker may be paired with a new worker for training. Most of the room attendants change teams each day. The manager says the housekeeping staff is a happy group of workers, and many have been with the property for ten years or more.

Team cleaning works in hotels that are willing to make a change. Their key to success is involving the employees in the planning and giving room attendants the flexibility to get the work done.[4]

Directing and Controlling

Many people confuse the two very different management functions of directing and controlling. The easiest way to distinguish them is to remember that managers direct people and control things.

Directing is focusing employee activity on the goals established in the planning phase, using the strategies and organization established in the organizing, coordinating, and staffing phase. For an executive housekeeper, directing involves supervising, motivating, training, and disciplining employees. Motivating the housekeeping staff is a particularly important skill and is closely connected with the executive housekeeper's ability to lead the department. Motivation (or the lack of it) is contagious. Attitudes and work habits filter down to employees from their supervisors. The attitudes and work habits of supervisors are usually a reflection of the leadership provided by the executive housekeeper. A strong executive housekeeper personally expresses a genuine interest in everyone's performance and, thereby, creates an atmosphere in which motivation can thrive. On the other hand, an executive housekeeper who plays favorites with supervisors will find discontent everywhere as supervisors, in turn, play favorites with employees under their direction.

Controlling refers to the executive housekeeper's responsibility to devise and implement procedures that protect the hotel's assets. Assets are anything the hotel owns that has commercial or exchange value. An executive housekeeper helps safeguard the hotel's assets by implementing control procedures for keys, linens, supplies, equipment, and other items.

Evaluating

Evaluating is the management function of assessing the extent to which planned goals are, in fact, attained. Monthly budget reports prepared by the hotel's accounting staff are important evaluation tools for all managers in a hotel. These reports provide timely information for evaluating housekeeping operations, especially the department's monthly labor expense. The executive housekeeper uses these reports to compare actual departmental expenses to amounts estimated in the budget. Significant differences between actual amounts and budgeted amounts are called variances. Significant variances may require further analysis and action by the executive housekeeper.

In addition, the executive housekeeper needs information on a daily and weekly basis in order to closely evaluate the performance of the staff and the overall productivity of the department. Evaluation in these areas begins with performance and productivity standards developed by earlier plans. Daily inspection reports and quarterly performance evaluations are used to monitor how well the actual performance of employees compares with performance and productivity standards.

Supervisor Dilemma

The state of the economy has prompted a trend to eliminate middle managers. In the lodging industry, this trend has brought the position of housekeeping supervisor into question. General managers seem to be searching for more profit and, perhaps, a way to empower hourly employees. Is it possible to operate a clean and profitable hotel without housekeeping supervisors to inspect rooms?

Although the housekeeping supervisor position may have begun as a management extension of the executive housekeeper for larger properties, in the past twenty years, the job has centered on inspecting rooms. Is it, then, an essential role? Does the hotel get its money's worth from this position?

Key issues hotels must consider are:

- Did the hotel hire the right people to be supervisors?

- Do the hotel's systems support the responsibilities of the supervisor?

- Is the hotel's mission enhanced as a direct result of the position?

- How would the idea be introduced and then implemented?

the Rooms
CHRONICLE®

Team Cleaning Gets High Scores at Maine Hotel

To design a more efficient method of thoroughly cleaning guestrooms and to develop a new procedure for training new room attendants, all old standards and traditional taboos for the housekeeping department were set aside. For instance, the staff decided to:

- Focus on the room being cleaned to standards, not on the amount of time required

- Require room attendants to inspect their own rooms

- Eliminate section assignments based on seniority

- Assign two room attendants to work as a team

Implementation of these decisions was difficult. In fact, the new standards were perceived as radical. But the staff persevered. Two room attendants were chosen (not the best cleaners, but the best leaders) to try team cleaning. For one week they received double pay while they cleaned rooms together to smooth out the details of the procedures. They then were paired with other room attendants until all had been trained. Some employees were not able to adapt to team cleaning and found it better to resign.

With 117 rooms on two floors, six team setups were created, including three complete cart/vacuum sets on each floor. Sets were numbered one through six and contained most of the materials necessary to clean a room. Room attendants were instructed to stay within their stations, calling upon a runner to keep the cart supplied and remove soiled linen. Requests for more hangers or bedspreads or telephone books were to be called to the voice mail of the runner.

It has been three years since this system was put into place at the Ramada Conference Center in Lewiston, Missouri. The average room time, including lunch breaks and cart stocking time for room attendants and one floor runner, is approximately sixteen minutes.

Each morning the head housekeeper prepares room assignments using a base of twenty rooms or less per team. When room attendants arrive, they draw chits like in a lottery to determine their teammate and cart for the day (i.e., 1-A, 1-B, 2-A, etc.). The duties for cleaning a room are written step-by-step as "A" tasks and "B" tasks, with making the bed(s) as the only joint assignment. The task list includes follow-up inspections of their rooms, noting maintenance items, and moving an air-cleaning machine from room to room.

Not only has the quality and consistency of room cleaning improved, the staff has also been able to eliminate half of the necessary equipment, such as carts and vacuums. In addition, training of new room attendants has been cut to two days, throughout which they are totally productive. During the last Ramada quality inspection report, the housekeeping department lost only one point from a perfect score. Not only does management like the team system, but by now even the room attendants are believers.

Source: Gary Adams, *The Rooms Chronicle®*, Volume 7, Number 3, p. 4.
For subscription information, call 866-READ-TRC.

- Would the number of room inspections be reduced or would they be totally eliminated?
- Who would do room inspections if any are required?
- Who would conduct training?
- What changes would be made to job descriptions?
- How would quality standards be maintained or improved?
- What system would be used to ensure accurate room status updates?

The Rooms Chronicle® surveyed some of its readers on the topic of housekeeping supervisors. Some managers eliminated supervisors, only to be disappointed by a gradual decline in the condition of guestrooms. Others, after making the change, saw guest comments and employee morale improve.

One of the surveyed hotels reinstated inspections in 100 percent of the rooms after six months, another did so after one year. While some have been successful at keeping 50 to 75 percent of their room attendants working independently, others operate entirely without supervisors.

How Is the Program Initiated? Most hotels based their decisions to eliminate supervisors on a desire to save payroll, although many were motivated by the total quality management philosophy of empowerment. One hotel eliminated supervisors because it wanted to speed up reporting of clean rooms to the front desk.

The hotels that successfully eliminated housekeeping supervisors gave advance, careful thought to all ramifications and involved the employees in planning. Some approached room attendants with the question, How does it make you feel to have someone check everything you do? When some frustration was expressed, they began to explore alternative ways to operate, incorporating room attendants' ideas for working independently.

Are Any Rooms Inspected? One property surveyed operates without any room inspections. Management credits the work ethic of their room attendants for the attendants' ability to take full responsibility for the condition of their areas. Most hotels, however, inspect from one to five rooms per room attendant per week. As a rooms executive of a luxury hotel in the Midwest expresses it, "We conduct random verifications of our housekeepers' work. It should be like testing a pool for the level of chlorine—only a small sample is needed to know the condition of the entire pool."

Who Inspects If There Are No Supervisors? Most properties use housekeeping management to conduct random inspections, depending on the size of the hotel. Larger hotels retain one or more supervisors for this purpose. The general manager of a resort hotel in Florida involves the entire hotel staff. The general manager, sales department, bell staff, front desk agents (A.M. and P.M. shifts), guest service agent, housekeeping secretary—each inspects two rooms a day.

"I'm fortunate that in my present position we use supervisors," says an executive housekeeper of another resort, "but based on my experience at other hotels, there are many ways this concept can fail. If the room attendant base is not stable (for example, due to high turnover, or if many temporary employees are used), room quality can suffer." She added, "If unqualified room attendants are forced to work independently, an executive housekeeper may spend long hours trying to inspect all the rooms, and manager burnout or failure of the department in other areas may occur."

"The use of supervisors does not have to be an all-or-nothing decision," says a general manager of a midwestern resort. "We use supervisors only in the summer to work with our seasonal employees. During the rest of the year, our room attendants work independently. We've used this system for over a year and our comment card scores are still high, at 94 percent."

Are Job Descriptions Changed? The room attendant job description is usually changed to include final responsibility for cleanliness, readiness, and status updates for each room. The room attendant must check equipment in the room to ensure that a guest will not find something in disrepair. Some hotels add responsibility for the hallway area around the guestroom and specify who will do the running if a bedspread or some other supply item needs to be replaced. The houseperson or porter job description usually is changed to complement the new structure.

The executive housekeeper at a southern hotel instituted an "excellence team" on which room attendants earn a position through performance, attendance, and attitude. The job description includes all of the above, and team members sign a contract for performance.

How Do Pay Rates Change? Pay rates of room attendants are sometimes changed, with the majority of properties either setting rates according to quality of work or paying bonuses for exceeding quality standards. One hotel pays a $35 bonus biweekly if inspection scores are 90 percent or higher and if at least 1.9 rooms are cleaned per hour.

The general manager of one suites hotel has a program in which room attendants earn the right to work without supervisors by achieving high scores on quality, attendance, and uniform care and are then paid 25 cents more per hour. The "excellence team" members at the property mentioned earlier earn one dollar more per hour if they maintain the standards of their increased responsibility. At other hotels, in instances where the entire staff is structured to work independently, pay rates are not increased.

Who Does the Training? Since most hotels use supervisors to train new hires, who does the training if those jobs are eliminated? Housekeeping managers could be used, but in these days of high turnover, the training function is often a full-time job. One option is to designate one or more room attendants as on-the-job trainers. In other hotels, at least one supervisor is retained who concentrates on training and retraining. Because room attendants assume final responsibility for the condition of the room, an excellent training program is essential.

"If I hire the right people and conduct ongoing training, my staff will be able to meet our standards," says a rooms executive. "We rely on support and positive reinforcement to keep our housekeepers excited."

In all the surveyed hotels, if the quality of a room attendant's work declines, he or she goes through a retraining program in order to attain the improvements needed, and if standards are not met, routine disciplinary procedures are used.

What about Room Status? The morning check of vacant rooms is usually incorporated into the room attendant's job description by assigning him or her an area of responsibility rather than a list of dirty rooms. All rooms, hallways, vending areas, and elevator lobbies within this area are assigned. The room attendant will be the last person to see the rooms or area before the guest arrives or returns, so special care must be taken to ensure that the front desk always has the correct room status, whether occupied or vacant, clean or dirty.

Many property management systems are interfaced so a code can be entered on the guestroom phone to update the status. In other hotels, the room attendant must call either housekeeping or the front desk to change room status. When the front desk questions the status, someone is sent to double-check the room.

Without supervisors, expect to spend more time checking discrepancies. Room attendants might clean a room, thinking it is a stayover, but while they are in another room, the first room's guest could check out. If the hotel has not adequately planned for this aspect, payroll saved on supervisors could easily be lost by poor room inventory management.

Tips for Success. A well-thought-out plan will provide for the cleanliness, maintenance, and status reporting of every room. Since supervisors usually help prepare VIP rooms, do touch-ups on late check-outs, help with hurry-ups, assist with inventories, translate for room attendants who don't speak English, and clean rooms when there is a shortage of room attendants, all of these things must be accounted for in a successful plan.

Involve room attendants in the design of the program to help them have ownership. The plan must be a win-win situation, because employees are sensitive to management's efforts to save payroll at their expense. The program should be fine-tuned before implementation, because changes to pay rates or incentive plans after the fact serve as disincentives.

If the concept is planned to suit the property's needs and implemented carefully, the employees and the hotel will prosper.

How Can the Department Improve? IYADWYADYAGWYAG: "If you always do what you always did, you'll always get what you always got." If you have supervisors, but you are not satisfied with the results, step back to analyze what you've always done. If you have supervisors but are thinking of eliminating the positions, clarify the end results you want and think creatively about how to get where you want to be.

the Rooms CHRONICLE®

Hotel Wisdom: A Baker's Dozen Strategies for Directors of Housekeeping

1. **Learn to look at your hotel from an operational perspective as if you owned it.** The most successful housekeepers are those who take ownership of their property. Directors of housekeeping are critical to making the first impressions positive, whether it is in public space, the guestroom, or bathroom. Housekeeping has responsibility for corridors, pool and patio areas, management offices, storage and linen areas, the laundry, and many related areas. Strong and successful housekeepers plan the work of the department effectively, using inventory control, setting standards, and maintaining schedules.

2. **Honor the idea that the hotel guest is your guest, as if in your own home.** It is the sense of pride and hosting that makes a huge difference in whether someone has a *job* or a *career*. To do this:

   • Maintain your awareness over the entire property, even if it is outside of your particular direct area of responsibility. This includes parking areas, public areas, access points to the hotel, and the all-important curb appeal.

   • Work with the other property managers (as opposed to "hiding" in the office) because it takes the entire team to create a great experience for guests.

   • Effective directors of housekeeping show their pride by offering to assist senior management in other areas of discussion, even in sales, as appropriate. Remember, "everyone sells" should be a hotel's mantra for success; and housekeepers regularly come in contact with vendors and others who need hotel services.

3. **Know about the condition of the property from firsthand experience.** Personally and regularly inspect every type of accommodation in your hotel. Being aware of changes in the hotel can also help management to be better aware of potential problems. One executive housekeeper said she "always imagined that somewhere in the hotel there was a dirty washcloth hanging on the back of a bathroom door, on a wall hook or over a shower curtain rod." And she didn't want someone else to find it first.

4. **When recruiting people, pay attention to the "human" resource role. Balance "high touch" and "high tech."** Recruit and select people wisely. Encourage your general manager to pay competitively or better, and lead in incentives. As director of housekeeping, recognize your team regularly with "thank you's" and expressions of appreciation. Retain the champions by whatever it takes to keep them. Give them the training to succeed and then share in their successes with incentives and the chance to be part of a very cohesive and proud team. The greatest reward is recognition by others for a job well done.

the Rooms
CHRONICLE®

(continued)

5. **Maintain and increase training.** This element is crucial in housekeeping. The development of the staff to the point where guestroom attendants can be completely trusted to finish their jobs with "pizzazz" because they take pride/ownership in their rooms should be a goal for everyone. Allow guestroom attendants who pass and maintain cleaning inspections at the highest levels the privilege of self-inspection. A few other thoughts:

   - There is no excuse today for inadequately prepared or untrained housekeeping and laundry staff. There is enormous training support available at very low cost online from the major brands and a wealth of support from CDs, books, newsletters, and the Internet. When running high-occupancy, many mangers claim to be too busy to train. When occupancy is flat or declining, cutting ongoing training to save money will really cost more, as it will drive the best employees to consider leaving and the loyal customers to the competition because it appears you don't care. Remember, "the only thing worse than an untrained staff that leaves is an untrained staff that stays to service your customers."

   - Today's successful and confident director of housekeeping will also embrace technology in training. Use of computers, training DVDs, and even language-free videos should be the norm.

   - If appropriate to your market, recognize and address the language challenge that some housekeeping personnel face. This may include getting the hotel to pay for your learning of a new language to improve your effectiveness, offering an English as a Second Language course for employees, and/or investing in alternative language training materials.

6. **Clearly share with all staff members the expectations and goals provided by ownership and/or management.** Newcomers to the industry sometimes imagine huge profits when they compare their hourly wage with the room rates paid by guests. Those who have been in the industry for more than just a few years quickly realize that profits and losses go in cycles. The expenses of operating a successful hotel can be enormous. Therefore, it is important to share the realities of the cost of doing business with staff at all levels. All employees should understand the total costs of ownership, including payroll benefits, franchise or royalty fees, management company fees, the concepts of debt service, and more. Make those expectations understood, explain the value and rationale to all staff, and be certain these expectations can be measured fairly.

7. **Hold regular one-on-one sessions with all direct reports in housekeeping and laundry.** These sessions should not be formal reviews, but guideposts to reinforce positive actions or to correct a potentially dangerous course of action. When I first started doing these more than 20 years ago, the first time was awkward because people were gun-shy or afraid of hidden agendas. When it became apparent that these were honest dialogues, the sessions evolved into opportunities to address potential problems and to form plans for improved performance in a non-threatening manner.

(continued)

8. **Constantly assess time management.** The 80-20 rule of priorities and value remains true much of the time. Eighty percent of our problems often come from the same 20 percent of guestrooms or staff members. To fix the 20 percent is the problem. Research why things go smoothly with the remaining 80 percent, and then replicate that success. The question needs to be not, "Are we doing things right," but, "Are we doing the right things correctly?"

9. **Work with front office management to capitalize on forecasts for long-term efficiencies.** Operating budgets are usually approved by hotel ownership or its management company in a remote location. And typically, the housekeeping budget is tied to forecasted occupancy. Working with the front office allows an effective director of housekeeping to plan for deep-cleaning during slower periods and to replace capital items on a pre-planned schedule that does not interfere with periods of high activity.

10. **Master the art of inventory controls.** There are many inventories to attend to, including but not limited to:

    • Linens

    • F&B materials

    • Pillows and furniture

    • Uniforms

    • Cleaning equipment

    • Cleaning supplies

    • Guest amenity supplies

    • Guest loan items

Properly addressing the ordering, receipt, use, storage, and security of these (and other) items is a financial necessity.

11. **Study, embrace, and insist on proper safety and security.** Room and laundry attendants regularly deal with an array of chemicals. While most chemicals may initially be in the proper containers and concentrations, maintain care to continue to use them accurately and safely. Give training and provide follow-up checklists for linen rooms, on-premise laundry, housekeeping carts, and using equipment. Post and follow government regulations, such as OSHA and state/provincial guidelines. Specific security practices should be considered, reviewed, discussed, and constantly monitored. Housekeeping staff may be working in isolated areas and should be trained in the best ways to provide cleaning services safely.

12. **Embrace the brand standards and suppliers.** A majority of hotels in the U.S. today are part of a brand, and the trend is growing globally. The director of housekeeping should learn what the brand's requirements and expectations are as they pertain to housekeeping services and programs. Convey to your staff the brand's expectations and maintain its standards for all housekeeping services. After all, aside from the human capital aspect, the greatest asset any

Cthe Rooms
HRONICLE®

(continued)

branded hotel has is its brand name recognition by guests and their expectations that accompany it. With regards to suppliers, do you take the time to work with your general manager or purchasing manager to understand the brand's supply programs? If there is a better local price or distribution, have you made certain those products effectively do the job? For hotels that are affiliated with a brand, your local hotel association will likely know of qualified vendors, programs, or products to assist you in maintaining high standard levels.

13. **Know your budgets, costs, and results.** The housekeeping department usually employs the largest number of people in a hotel. The outstanding housekeeping managers are those who are often able to obtain higher compensation for their staff by effectively reducing turnover and managing their total budgets while exceeding guest expectations. Budgets need not be a mystery, and most caring general managers should be pleased to share information pertaining to operating budgets with applicable personnel because it helps everyone understand the bigger picture.

Source: John Hogan, Ph.D., CHA, MHS, CHE, *The Rooms Chronicle®*, Volume 14, Number 5, pp. 4–5. For subscription information, call 866-READ-TRC.

How can you improve hiring processes for both supervisors and room attendants so that their qualifications will strengthen the team? Single out the winning characteristics of your best employees and hire people who have the same traits.

How can you enhance room attendant training so that quality is not dependent on inspections? Manufacturing businesses usually cannot make a profit while performing quality inspections on 100 percent of their product. Systems are established to produce the product correctly the *first* time so that it is not necessary to spend hours and money checking, reworking, or scrapping product. Inspections are used only as random checks to ensure that systems are working properly. Should hotels operate any differently?

How can you revise the hotel's systems so that the entire team of supervisors and room attendants feels enthusiastic and responsible for promoting the hotel's mission of pleasing the guest? Find ways to allow the supervisor to be proactive as a teacher and communicator rather than negative as a police officer. Can a room attendant's pride be increased by having direct responsibility to the guest?

If there is room for improvement, it may be time to rethink the entire department and restructure job responsibilities appropriately. Short-term profit improvements gained by position eliminations may be insignificant compared to the results of creatively working toward the long-term goals of the hotel.[5]

Endnotes

1. Michael C. Sturman, "A New Method for Measuring Housekeeping Performance Consistency," *The Center for Hospitality Research Reports*, Cornell University, September 2006, pp. 6–13.

2. Rob Heyman, "Shaping up Hotel Housekeeping Programs, *Lodging Management*, October, 2006, www.lodgingmagazine.com.

3. Adam Kirby, "Spare the Spreadsheets," *Hotels Magazine*, May 2007. www.hotelsmag.com/article/CA6485309.html.

4. The section on team cleaning was adapted from Mary Friedman, *The Rooms Chronicle®*, Volume 2, Number 6, p. 4; and Marilyn Faulkner, *The Rooms Chronicle®*, Volume 2, Number 4, p. 13. For subscription information, call 866-READ-TRC.

5. The section on supervisors was adapted from *The Rooms Chronicle®*, Volume 2, Number 3, p. 5; and Mary Friedman, *The Rooms Chronicle®*, Volume 2, Number 5, pp. 4–5. For subscription information, call 866-READ-TRC.

 ## Key Terms

area inventory list—A list of all items within a particular area that need cleaning by or the attention of housekeeping personnel.

deep cleaning—Intensive or specialized cleaning undertaken in guestrooms or public areas. Often conducted according to a special schedule or on a special-project basis.

frequency schedule—A schedule that indicates how often each item on an area inventory list needs to be cleaned or maintained.

job description—A detailed list identifying all the key duties of a job as well as reporting relationships, additional responsibilities, working conditions, and any necessary equipment and materials.

maximum quantity—The greatest number of purchase units that should be in stock at any given time.

minimum quantity—The fewest number of purchase units that should be in stock at any given time.

non-recycled inventories—Those items in stock that are consumed or used up during the course of routine housekeeping operations. Non-recycled inventories include cleaning supplies, small equipment items, guest supplies, and amenities.

organization chart—A schematic representation of the relationships between positions within an organization, showing where each position fits into the overall organization and illustrating the divisions of responsibility and lines of authority.

par number—A multiple of the standard quantity of a particular inventory item that represents the quantity of the item that must be on hand to support daily, routine housekeeping operations.

performance standard—A required level of performance that establishes the quality of work that must be done.

productivity standard—An acceptable amount of work that must be done within a specific time frame according to an established performance standard.

recycled inventories—Those items in stock that have relatively limited useful lives but are used over and over in housekeeping operations. Recycled inventories include linens, uniforms, major machines and equipment, and guest loan items.

 Review Questions

1. What resources can the executive housekeeper use to attain the objectives set by top executives in a hospitality operation?

2. What areas are most housekeeping departments responsible for cleaning in a hotel?

3. What additional areas may housekeeping be responsible for cleaning, depending on the property's service level?

4. Why is it important for an executive housekeeper to take a systematic, step-by-step approach to planning?

5. What is the purpose of an area inventory list? What is an ideal way to sequence such a list?

6. What is a frequency schedule? How is it used in conjunction with a property's deep cleaning program?

7. What is the difference between a performance standard and a productivity standard?

8. What is the most important aspect of developing performance standards? How are standards best communicated once they are developed?

9. What two important principles should guide the organization of the housekeeping department?

10. What are the fundamental management functions that should be carried out by every hotel manager?

 Case Study

Under Pressure

Philip knocked tentatively on his general manager's office door. "You wanted to see me, Mrs. Smith?"

"Yes, Philip, please sit down." The general manager shifted some papers on her desk and handed Philip Stone, the executive housekeeper, a copy of the labor-cost budget. "Take a look at last month's report. Notice which direction the labor costs are going."

Philip quickly scanned the report he had previously studied in detail. "They're rising by about two percent, almost the same as the previous months of this quarter. In fact, they've been rising at about that monthly rate for the past year."

"Yes, Philip, I'm well aware of that. But that's why we hired you. You are supposed to turn these numbers around, and now—90 days after you started—there's no change in direction at all. I need you to do something about this immediately. I can't have this creeping overhead! Get back to me tomorrow with your action plan for how you're going to make sure labor costs are reduced next month."

Mrs. Smith then stood up and opened the door for Philip to leave.

Walking back to his office, Philip considered implementing a quick job-saving solution such as giving each room attendant an extra room to clean. As he mentally rehearsed breaking this news to the room attendant staff, Philip noticed his office was occupied.

"Betty! Jane! What can I do for you?" Philip asked, entering his office.

"Mr. Stone, we've been meaning to talk to you for a couple weeks," Jane said, "but we didn't want you to think we were a bunch of complainers, being as this job is new to you and all."

"Why, of course not, Jane. You two are some of the hardest-working room attendants in the department. You have the best productivity and set a wonderful example for all our other employees."

"Well, it's that productivity thing we want to talk to you about. We want to help make sure the rooms are done and done right, but you've been asking too much of us lately. We're burning out. And it's not just Betty and me. There are other employees who've been around a long time like us, and we can't keep up anymore. If you don't find a way to lighten the workload a little, you're going to kill us."

Betty chimed in, "I remember when we were expected to do only 17 rooms a shift. Now we're up to 22 rooms on a regular basis. I promise, Mr. Stone, we weren't slacking before. If we have to do more than 22 rooms, they're just not going to be clean, and I don't want a guest checking into any one of *my* rooms that isn't clean."

Philip felt a first-class headache coming on as he realized this would be a poor time to suggest room attendants take on extra rooms or spend less time per room. "Is there something specific that you think would help?"

"Yeah," said Jane. "Give us fewer rooms to clean so we don't all get ulcers!"

"Well, ladies, your break is over, you'd better get back to work. I appreciate your coming to talk to me. I'll let you know in a couple days what I decide to do," Philip said, looking at his watch in hopes of speeding the two women out.

The two room attendants exchanged disappointed glances. Betty shrugged and said, "OK, but you will get back to us, won't you? You're not just trying to get rid of us?"

"No. I'll get back to you by the day after tomorrow. Would that be OK?" Philip asked.

"If we don't have heart attacks first," Jane muttered as she and Betty left.

Philip sat at his desk with a sigh and pulled out his department's productivity standards. According to the information left him by the previous executive housekeeper, each room should take 26 minutes to clean. He decided to analyze how many rooms each room attendant was actually cleaning.

After a half-hour of analyzing productivity data, Philip identified the following problems:

- Forty percent of his room attendants were performing at the hotel's productivity standards or better

- Sixty percent of his room attendants were each cleaning fewer than 17 rooms a day and averaging longer than 26 minutes to clean a room

- The 60 percent performing below standards were all either new hires or still in training

- The housekeeping department has had 60 percent of its personnel in training or at new-hire status for the past ten months, due to high turnover

Philip then began to outline presentations for the general manager and for his own employees. First, he decided, he would explain the cause of rising labor costs to his general manager. "I'll have to tell her that turnover and poor training are causing lower productivity. We're not hiring the right people for the right positions, and then we're not bringing their productivity levels up to standards."

Philip determined he would tell Mrs. Smith she has to spend money to bring the labor-costs curve down. His suggestions included:

- Update job descriptions so new hires have more realistic expectations

- Provide more resources to the training department

- Organize training better so room attendants come up to speed within 30 days

- Terminate new hires if they do not meet productivity standards after 30 days

- Hold weekly recruitment meetings with human resources

He hoped that, although his suggestions wouldn't please Mrs. Smith, they would illustrate that the resources needed for the short term would be less costly than steadily increasing labor costs.

Philip struggled a little more over what to tell his room attendants. Ideally, he thought, he could encourage the more experienced 40 percent to pitch in and help bring the 60 percent up to speed. By doing just a little more now, they could reduce stress and tension in the long run. All he had to do, he thought, was convince them to give a little more a little bit longer. "At least I'm not giving them more rooms to clean," he decided.

As Philip set his presentation plans aside to go back to his daily work, he stopped and took one more look at them. "Hmmm," he thought. "Perhaps I should ask a few of my colleagues at other hotels how they would handle this."

Discussion Question

1. What feedback would executive housekeepers give Philip?

Case Study

Teams Can Triumph over Trials

Joanne Sommer has just been hired as the Ascot Hotel's executive housekeeper. The hotel's general manager, Jack Robbins, told Joanne he wants to maintain and improve the team cleaning system he had the previous executive housekeeper implement three months earlier for all housekeeping employees.

Mr. Robbins hadn't used team cleaning in the past and, as a "big picture" person who focuses on results, he shows little interest in the details of implementation. He was attracted to team cleaning by a management article that claimed team cleaning would cut costs, reduce turnover, improve attendance, and clean rooms faster. These are the results he wants.

Unfortunately, the initial implementation had not gone smoothly. The previous executive housekeeper switched the entire department over to teams at the same time, and immediately found herself with a scheduling nightmare. The goal of assembly-line efficiency was impossible to achieve because support systems were not effective. For example, when the laundry allowed torn or stained linens to be stocked on carts, team members often did not discover the problem until they put the sheets on a bed. Valuable time was lost as replacement linens were fetched, especially when the runners replenishing carts were also behind schedule, which seemed to happen frequently. Before, this situation would have put one employee behind schedule. Now, it puts two people behind schedule, costing the hotel more time and labor.

Teams find that they run out of supplies more quickly now and have to take extra trips to the housekeeping storage area to restock. Teams also lose time when they have to wait for a room to be vacated by a guest. While this was always an issue, now it holds up two people instead of one.

To make matters worse, some of the teams initially assigned are now experiencing personality conflicts. Several employees enjoyed working alone and resent being paired with other people. As a result of these and other problems, most housekeeping employees dislike the new system.

Joanne believes that the team cleaning concept could work at the Ascot Hotel if properly implemented. She recognizes that it was not properly implemented at the outset, and that mistakes have increased employee resistance and made successful implementation even more difficult.

Discussion Questions

1. What are some signs that, initially, the team cleaning system was implemented poorly?

2. What could Joanne do to gain employee buy-in and support? How might she be able to make working on teams attractive to housekeeping employees?

3. What issues must Joanne clarify with Mr. Robbins if team cleaning is to succeed at the Ascot Hotel? What kind of detail information would encourage Mr. Robbins to maintain a commitment to team cleaning?

The following industry experts helped generate and develop these cases: Gail Edwards, CHHE, St. Louis, Missouri; Mary Friedman, Edina, Minnesota; and Aleta Nitschke, CHA, founder of *The Rooms Chronicle®*, Garfield, Minnesota.

Chapter 4 Outline

Competencies

1. Explain why hotel housekeeping departments depend on effective diversity management. (pp. 109–114)

2. Describe several sources of potential employees including internal and external sources, creative recruiting tactics, and online sources. (pp. 114–126)

3. Explain how immigration reform affects the hospitality industry. (p. 126)

4. Describe the factors that should be taken into account when selecting employees. (pp. 126–127)

5. List the steps to skills training and what must be accomplished in each step. (pp. 127–146)

6. Describe the challenges involved in scheduling employees. (pp. 146–153)

7. Identify several methods of motivating employees. (pp. 153–161)

4

Housekeeping Human Resource Issues

Employees are the lifeblood of any hospitality operation; without them, an operation stands still. It stands to reason, then, that management must do all it can to recruit the right employees and offer employees the training they need to do their jobs well. Training is especially important in today's busy housekeeping departments, where skills must meet or exceed department standards in order to get the work done in a guest-pleasing manner.

Adults expect different things from training than teenagers and children do. Adults appreciate practical information, not theory. They want to know how to apply the training material and of what real-world value it is to them. Adults want to get involved. They learn by doing, not by being lectured to. Adults want their experiences to be appreciated. They bring with them a wealth of life and work experience. They appreciate it when this experience is respected and used in training. Finally, adults demand a meaningful, mature environment. They want to be treated as professionals and not talked down to.

Beyond training, housekeeping employees need to be scheduled efficiently to meet organizational goals; and if employees are motivated—if they really *want* to do their best—those goals will be more easily met. Efficient scheduling and employee motivation are more challenges for the executive housekeeper.

This chapter touches on all these human resource issues. It first covers diversity and turnover issues and addresses recruiting, selecting, training, and scheduling employees. The chapter then explores motivational techniques and methods.

Diversity

The success of lodging properties has always depended significantly upon the ability of managers to find and keep talented employees. Recent shifts in U.S. population demographics and forecast of continued changes in this regard combined with a progressively more complex and competitive marketplace has only increased the magnitude of the impact of employee performance in hotels. This need to find talent from among the entire range of potential employees (i.e. racial and ethnic background, language, age, religion, gender, sexual orientation, lifestyle, education and/or ability differences) is no longer an idealistic notion or merely "politically correct"—it has become a business imperative.

The potential benefits of positively managing employment diversity for hotels include access to first-hand information about a variety of current and potential guest target markets, increases in employee productivity and creation of a work force that mirrors the guests it serves. Examples of negative outcomes for hotels if management fails in efforts of inclusiveness and diversity are negative publicity, low employee morale and productivity, increased recruiting and training costs, loss of potential employees to the competition, and high turnover.

Lodging Industry Diversity Initiatives

The 1998 and 2004 American Hotel & Lodging Educational Foundation surveys on turnover and diversity in the lodging industry have documented the effect of diversity on lodging properties. These research reports serve to inform managers and industry decision-makers with solid data from which they may make well-informed choices about future resource allocations and serve as benchmarks by which future results may be assessed.

The American Hotel & Lodging Association (AH&LA) has also established the Multicultural and Diversity Advisory Council to promote diversity awareness, identify and encourage best management practices with regard to practices of inclusiveness and to support training and mentoring programs. Further, the AH&LA publishes Prism, a quarterly on-line newsletter of personal and in-depth articles featuring stories of actual individuals from diverse backgrounds who are building interesting and prosperous careers—contributing to their own success as well as the properties they work for and the lodging industry as a whole. Additional resources and information may be found at www.ahla.com/content.aspx?id=3312.

English-Only Requirements

Managing a diverse work force presents many opportunities and more than a few challenges for lodging managers. One of the recent issues that have challenged U.S. lodging managers has been policies on requiring English. This is especially relevant to the housekeeping department.

Establishing brand value in the hotel industry is critical. Active management of a hotel's basic elements, including its physical attributes and service delivery, has long been the key to unlocking this success. In theory, therefore, a hotel should be able to manage all aspects of guest interaction, including requiring that employees speak only English in the workplace. Such rules, however, may be in conflict with federal civil rights law and guidelines issued by the Equal Employment Opportunity Commission (EEOC).

This potential conflict is nowhere better reflected than in the March 20, 2006, settlement between the EEOC and the Melrose Hotel Co. of New York. In that case, the parties settled 13 employees' complaints of a hostile work environment, which included allegations that Hispanic employees were subjected to an "English-only" rule, for $800,000.

The EEOC receives hundreds of similar complaints. Accordingly, it is important for hotel owners, operators, and managers to consider how to best balance the interests in creating and delivering a unique brand experience with the rights and interests of an increasingly diverse work force.

The increasingly diverse work force in America makes the debate over "English-only" far from an academic exercise. For example, the number of persons of Hispanic or Latino ethnicity employed in the U.S. grew from 17.9 million and 18.6 million in 2004 and 2005, respectively, to more than 19.5 million as of May 2006. According to the American Hotel & Lodging Association Educational Foundation, 25.8 percent of the hourly recruits in the lodging industry in 2004 were Hispanic.

The federal Bureau of Labor Statistics provides an even further detailed breakdown of the percentages of persons of Hispanic of Latino ethnicity employed in 2005, including:

- 14 percent of all persons employed as hotel, motel, and resort desk clerks.

- 23.7 percent of all persons employed in the traveler accommodation industry.

- 30.6 percent of all building and grounds cleaning and maintenance occupations.

- 35.2 percent of all room attendants and housekeeping cleaners.

With an increasingly diverse work force comes an inevitably greater potential for a language barrier in the workplace. In fact, as of 2000, 10.3 million Americans spoke little or no English at home representing a 53 percent increase from the number reported in 1990. This language barrier has created a need in many hotels to implement programs addressing communication between management, associates, and guests. For example, Marriott International, Inc. announced on July 12, 2006, that it launched a 23-hotel pilot language program to teach workplace and life-skills English to its associates who speak English as a second language. The program's goals are to allow associates to enhance their English language skills to more comfortably and confidently interact with guests and management. The contrast between the Melrose Hotel case and the new Marriott program demonstrate that, for the hospitality industry in particular, decisions on whether to adopt policies regarding "English-only" and language skills in the workplace must be well thought out.

Title VII of the Civil Rights Act of 1964 prohibits discrimination in the workplace against any person based on, among other factors, one's national origin. The EEOC has issued guidelines identifying four general forms of national origin discrimination:

- Rules requiring employees to speak English at all times in the workplace

- An employer's refusal to hire an applicant based on the applicant's manner of speaking or accent

- Harassment that creates a hostile work environment in the form of ethnic slurs or physical conduct because of an employee's national origin

- Singling out applicants of a particular national origin and requiring only them to provide employment verification

Although the EEOC guidelines further state that any policy requiring "English-only" in the workplace is presumed to violate Title VII (thereby shifting the burden of proving the necessity of the policy to the employer), the guidelines allow for an exception. An employer may require employees to speak only English at certain times where the employer can show a business justification for the requirement.

There are several practices that hotel operators and owners should follow to ensure compliance with Title VII. The following practical tips will aid in developing a fair policy while allowing a hotel to better manage employee communications with guests.

First, do not have or enforce a blanket "English-only" policy. Such a broad policy will almost certainly violate Title VII. As with any other workplace policy, the adoption of this type of policy must be done for nondiscriminatory reasons. A policy that restricts the speaking of another language, for example, during lunch, in the employee break room, when making personal telephone calls, or before and after work if inside the building, will likely be seen as discrimination on the basis of national origin.

Second, any "English-only" policy should be limited to those situations which can be categorized as a business necessity. These situations may include:

- Communication with customers, co-workers, or supervisors who only speak English.

- Coordination of tasks in emergencies as better facilitated through a common language.

- Cooperative work assignments where an "English-only" rule is needed to promote efficiency.

- Enabling a supervisor who only speaks English to monitor the performance of an employee whose job duties require communication with coworkers or customers.

Therefore, in the context of hotel operations, if it is necessary for guest services personnel to use English when communicating with guests, a policy requiring English in those situations may be justified. Or, English may be required for communications with supervisors who speak only English. In establishing such a policy, however, a hotel should weigh and consider these business justifications against any possible discriminatory effects.

Third, any "English-only" policy should expressly contain exceptions for appropriate circumstances. This will ensure that the policy is flexible and adaptive to the business justifications of the hotel as they may change. This may include permitting or even encouraging employees to interact in their native tongue with international guests who prefer to communicate with staff fluent in their respective language.

Fourth, the work force must be put on notice of any "English-only" policy. It is important that the employees understand the reasons for such a policy, as well as the consequences that may occur if it is violated. According to its guidelines, the EEOC will consider any employer's application of an "English-only" policy, without effective notification, as discrimination on the basis of national origin.

Perhaps the best advice that can be offered, though, is if a policy is adopted, do not call it "English-only." It is a misleading title that raises unnecessary red flags. Some other title, such as "Guest Communications" or "Effective Employee Communication," more properly describes the desired goal of the policy. After all, effective communication within the hotel is what each hotel manager should be striving to achieve.[1]

Turnover

Each time a position is vacated, either voluntarily or involuntarily, a new employee must be hired and trained. This replacement cycle is known as turnover. As a result of current and impending labor shortages, employee turnover is now commanding the attention it deserves. Twenty or 30 years ago, hospitality managers seldom worried about where their employees would come from. At that time, turnover averaged about 60 percent annually for most hospitality companies, and triple-digit turnover was not uncommon. Even so, the supply of available workers always exceeded the demand.

Although turnover was too high even then, management always found reasons to justify it—seasonal work, young employees moving on to other careers, competition from new operations—all of which were valid then and are valid now. But the situation has changed today; turnover remains high, but the supply of available workers has diminished. As a result, the hospitality industry now finds itself critically short of employees. Even though this did not happen overnight, managers still wonder, "What happened?"

Two things happened. First, the baby boomers, many of whom were former hourly employees, grew up. They are now guests. Likewise, Generation X has also grown up and become guests rather than employees. Second, managers failed to address the "temporary employee issue" created by the view held by many hospitality employees that they were just passing through on their way to "real" jobs.

Today, the hospitality industry is still fighting high turnover rates. Much is already known about turnover. For instance, turnover is costly. One study projects that the cost of replacing an employee, whether manager, supervisor, or line-level, can be as high as 100 percent of the annual pay for that employee. Turnover has a significant negative impact on those employees who remain behind after friends and associates leave, and there is a significant positive relationship between high turnover and both low customer retention and investor disinterest. Research also shows a positive relationship between organizational stability and turnover, and that high turnover rates therefore create unwanted instability in organizations. Other research has shown there is a positive relationship between high turnover and organizational inefficiency. Unwanted turnover can contribute to an organization's inability to build an effective team of employees.

The Cost of Turnover

Turnover costs range from $3,000 to $10,000 per hourly employee, and can be even higher. Many companies equate the cost of losing one trained manager with the amount of that manager's annual salary; it typically takes about a year for a new manager to become fully productive.

Turnover costs can be classified as tangible or intangible. Tangible costs are incurred directly when replacing employees and range from uniforms to advertisements. Intangible, but in many cases significant, costs (such as lost productivity) do not relate directly to out-of-pocket expenses.

Separation costs are incurred directly with the loss of a current employee. These costs may include separation or severance pay and the costs associated with conducting exit interviews, maintaining files, removing names from the payroll, terminating benefits, and paying unemployment taxes.

Replacement costs are those associated with recruiting new employees: advertising, pre-employment screening, interviews, testing, staff meetings to discuss applicants, travel expenses for applicants, moving expenses for some applicants, medical exams, and other costs.

Training costs are those associated with orienting new employees, preparing and printing new employee information, creating or purchasing training materials, and conducting training. Lower productivity (on the part of those who are conducting the training as well as those who are being trained) is an intangible cost of training.

While recognizing problems associated with turnover, it is important to realize that not all employee turnover is bad and some level of turnover is inevitable. Even under the best of circumstances, employees may earn promotions or retire and if the hotel experiences an upsurge in business or expands, it will likely be necessary to add more staff. Therefore, whether turnover rates are high or low, housekeeping managers are generally well served by staying constantly prepared to recruit new employees.

Recruiting Employees

Employee **recruitment** is the process by which applicants are sought and screened concerning their suitability for positions in the operation. The process involves announcing job vacancies through proper sources, and interviewing and evaluating applicants to determine whom to consider for open positions.

In large properties, the human resources division assists the executive housekeeper in finding and hiring the most qualified individuals. However, many lodging properties do not have human resources divisions. Therefore, the executive housekeeper is often involved in such tasks as initial interviewing, contacting applicants' references, and related selection tasks. In all properties, the executive housekeeper should personally interview top candidates for open positions in the department. Depending on the property's organization, the executive house-keeper may either hire the applicant or make a recommendation to the manager at the next highest organizational level.

Finally, before recruiting from any external source, a property should conduct a job analysis and write job descriptions and specifications. Doing so can help ensure that the right people are identified, recruited, and hired.

The Pre-Recruitment Process

As Exhibit 1 shows, a great deal of recruiting actually takes place before any ads are placed in newspapers or notices are posted in employee lounges. The **pre-recruitment process** consists of a number of interrelated steps, beginning with defining job requirements and ending with evaluating recruiting methods.

- *Define job requirements.* To define the job and its requirements, a housekeeping manager needs to understand the primary responsibilities and tasks involved in the job, the background characteristics needed to perform the job, the personal characteristics required, the key features of the organization's culture, and the manager's managerial style.

- *Review job analysis, job descriptions, and job specification information.* Housekeeping managers should check that these tools are current, applicable, and complete. Changes and additions should be made when necessary.

- *Identify and review applicable laws and regulations.* Many issues associated with recruitment, selection, and promotion are subject to federal and state regulations. Housekeeping managers should review such regulations before recruitment begins.

- *Determine the message to convey to applicants.* The introduction of the business and the position are a critical part of recruitment. Many applicants are attracted to companies by recruitment advertising only to find that there is a considerable difference between the job in the ad and the job in the actual workplace. Businesses that carefully consider the message they want to send, and present the situation realistically, establish conditions that encourage long-term success.

- *Determine what should be learned from recruits about competitors and the community.* While identifying potential applicants is the primary purpose of recruiting, it is not the sole purpose. Recruiting also gives housekeeping managers a great opportunity to learn about the outside world. Applicants from other companies can provide valuable information about how the hotel's operation compares with the competition—as well as how the hotel's operation is perceived.

- *Decide whether to recruit internally, externally, or both.* Some companies have successfully established programs in which only entry-level employees are recruited from the outside. In these companies, all supervisory and management positions are filled by internal applicants. Such internal recruitment

Exhibit 1   The Pre-Recruitment Process

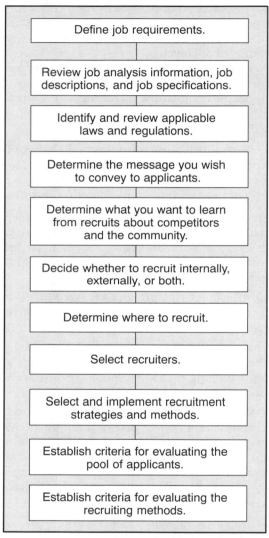

Define job requirements.

Review job analysis information, job descriptions, and job specifications.

Identify and review applicable laws and regulations.

Determine the message you wish to convey to applicants.

Determine what you want to learn from recruits about competitors and the community.

Decide whether to recruit internally, externally, or both.

Determine where to recruit.

Select recruiters.

Select and implement recruitment strategies and methods.

Establish criteria for evaluating the pool of applicants.

Establish criteria for evaluating the recruiting methods.

programs are designed to create career ladders that encourage personnel to remain with the company longer. Other companies have successfully established programs for the external recruitment of both managers and entry-level personnel. The advantages and disadvantages of internal and external recruitment are discussed later in this chapter.

- *Determine where to recruit.* Housekeeping managers should determine sources for both internal and external recruiting. For external recruiting, managers must determine the sites with the most potential for applicants—schools, competitors, apartment complexes, churches, and so on. Housekeeping managers must also identify productive sites for internal recruiting. Consider such efforts by a chain hotel that is searching for housekeeping supervisors. This property might find more success recruiting from the housekeeping departments of other hotels in their chain than from departments within their own property.

- *Select and implement recruiting strategies and methods.* Recruitment can take many forms. In some cases, word-of-mouth may work best; in others, it may be better to recruit through the mass media (radio, television, newspapers, and the Internet). Different approaches reach different markets. For that reason, the choice of approach is crucial to the recruiting process.

- *Establish criteria for evaluating the pool of applicants.* Too often, housekeeping managers simply toss out a recruiting net to see what they can catch. This approach can have two outcomes—both unproductive. First, while the right applicants may be caught in the net, others may be too. These others, however, may be unsuitable "catches" who waste management time on interviews. Second, this approach may not "catch" any applicants who really fit the criteria. In some cases, recruiters may think that they should select the most promising applicants from this pool—simply to justify the cost of recruitment. To avoid these pitfalls, establish clearly defined evaluation criteria at the outset of recruiting.

- *Establish criteria for evaluating the recruiting methods.* Costs, costs per hire, number of contacts made, acceptance-offer ratios, and salary-requested rates all vary depending on the type of method used. Before beginning a recruiting program, housekeeping managers should establish acceptable rates for each of these and other evaluation criteria.

As part of the pre-recruitment process, managers should also consider whether their personnel needs will be best met by internal or external sources of employees. The ultimate goal for a housekeeping manager is to balance internal promotions and external hires. To do so, managers need to understand the advantages and disadvantages of the sources that can be derived from **internal** and **external** **recruiting.**

Internal Recruiting

As mentioned earlier, some hotel companies generally recruit only entry-level employees from external sources; all supervisory and management positions are recruited internally—or, as some say, are "hired from within." Many hotel companies do the same. Companies reap several benefits through internal recruiting. Internal recruiting:

- Improves the morale of the promoted employee.
- Improves the morale of the staff who see opportunities for themselves.
- Provides managers with a better assessment of the abilities of internal recruits since their performance has been observed over time.

- Results in a succession of promotions for supervisory and management positions—meaning that one promotion is necessary to fill each job vacated by a promotion. These successions help reinforce the company's "internal career ladder."

- Is lower in cost than external recruiting.

- Reduces training costs since training for entry-level positions is generally less expensive than training for management positions.

  Internal recruiting also has its disadvantages. For instance, this method may:

- Promote inbreeding; after time, the flow of new ideas into the company diminishes.

- Cause morale problems among those employees who are passed over for promotion.

- Have political overtones; some employees attribute promotions to friendships and relations with managers and supervisors.

- Create a critical gap in one department when personnel are used to fill a gap in another.

External Recruiting

External recruiting—or hiring from outside sources—is usually easiest at the entry level since managers can readily evaluate the skills and abilities required for such jobs. External sources also include competitors. Experienced housekeeping managers are always looking for talented individuals employed at other companies.

Even though it costs more than internal recruiting, external recruiting has some distinct advantages. Among its major benefits, external recruiting:

- Brings "new blood" and new ideas into the company.

- Gives recruiters an opportunity to see how things are on the outside by talking with applicants from both direct and indirect competitors.

- Provides a fresh look at the organization, which sometimes reinforces the reasons current employees work in the hotel. Consider, for instance, the value of a recruit saying something like: "You keep your break room much cleaner than they do where I currently work," or "The light from the atrium certainly makes this a more pleasant place to work."

- Is sometimes cheaper than training.

- Avoids many of the political problems associated with internal recruiting.

- Serves as a form of advertising for the company. Newspaper ads, posters, bulletin board notices, presentations, and so on remind the public of the hotel's products and services.

Like internal recruiting, external recruiting has its dark side. Housekeeping managers should be aware that sometimes:

- It is more difficult to find a good "fit" with the company's culture and management philosophy through external recruiting.

- Morale problems can develop if current employees feel that they have no opportunity to advance in the organization.

- Job orientation for external recruits takes longer than it does for internal recruits who already know the goals of the company, how the payroll system works, and so on.

- External recruiting can lower productivity over the short run, since, in some cases, new employees cannot produce as quickly or as effectively as internal recruits.

- Political problems and personality conflicts can result when employees believe that they could do the job as well as the external recruit.

- External candidates may not prove to be as they first appear. Any external candidate is still an unknown risk. Managers will invariably know more about an internal applicant.

Recruitment Sources

Recruitment today is more difficult than in the past. Even though the aging of the Baby Boomers means that the industry can no longer rely on the traditional pool of 16- to 24-year-olds for the bulk of recruits, there are still many options left for creative managers to explore.

Internal Sources

Internal recruitment strategies often include career planning, skills inventories, and internal job-posting systems. Maintaining adequate skills inventories and replacement and succession charts makes internal recruiting easier; doing so gives managers a better idea of who has the skills for an open position and who might be interested in taking the job. These inventories and charts should be viewed as critical—especially in organizations that stress internal recruiting. So that current employees know about openings, many businesses:

- Post notices or actual **job postings** on bulletin boards or announce current job openings in newsletters or a company's Intranet site. Typically, postings or announcements include a job description and job specifications to inform employees of the responsibilities and skills required on the job. **Job bidding** results when employees sign a list indicating that they are interested in applying for posted positions.

- Use employees as referral sources. Some companies successfully use current employees as sources of information on external recruits. This method has the advantage of locating the friends and acquaintances of current employees who often have more realistic views about the advantages and disadvantages of the organization. In addition, employees tend to refer only those friends who they believe would really make good employees; they realize that referring poor applicants reflects on their own judgment. Although many companies report that they use **employee referral programs** to find new applicants, a study released in 1999 contends that they may not be doing this as much as they think or say they are—even though this can be one of the most cost-effective methods of recruitment today. For instance, this study found that too many managers do not know how to effectively recruit using referrals. Providing incentives and targeting employees for future promotions are effective ways to make referral recruiting better. Using referrals as the only source for recruiting can have unpleasant legal ramifications since this method may tend to discriminate against some protected groups. For instance, a hotel or restaurant located in a predominantly white neighborhood may naturally recruit or hire more white employees. If this company relied solely on employee referrals for recruitment, its policies might be construed as discriminatory.

Marriott successfully fills supervisory and managerial positions by emphasizing internal recruiting, effectively "growing its own" managers. Each hotel has a Management Candidacy Review Board composed of a department head and a member of the executive committee. The focus of this board is to review employees who may be near the level needed to train for management positions. If employees show managerial talent, the committee looks for opportunities for the employee to develop skills within the company. Marriott's Supervisor in Training and Manager in Training programs complement this activity by offering participants workbooks in which they record their learning experiences. The workbooks are later reviewed with mentors or coaches. These programs have proven so successful that each year approximately 30 to 40 percent of successful managerial applicants come from within Marriott's employee ranks.

External Sources

While local circumstances determine sources for external recruiting, sources that may be of value to housekeeping managers include the following:

- Employment agencies—state and private
- Schools—high school job fairs, managers as guest speakers in classes, notices with guidance counselors, personal contact with teachers and coaches, participation in work-study programs
- Colleges—job fairs, contact with placement counselors, guest speakers, contact with instructors and coaches, participation in work-study programs, contact with campus social and professional clubs, hospitality management programs, dormitory counselors
- Churches and synagogues
- Youth groups
- Apartment complexes—laundry room bulletin boards, "doorknob announcements"
- Apartment newsletters
- Local sports teams (sponsorship)

- Women's groups
- Child-care centers
- Professional and trade journals
- Craft centers
- Exercise centers
- Senior citizen groups
- Governmental division-on-aging unit
- Agencies for people with disabilities
- Student organizations—Family, Career and Community Leaders of America, Future Farmers of America, Distributive Education Clubs of America, and so on
- Sales, supply, and machinery representatives
- Community events
- Urban League and other agencies that provide skills training and job placement—Welfare-to-Work programs, Mexican-American Opportunity Foundation, and so on
- Government rehabilitation agencies
- Government veterans agencies
- Chamber of Commerce
- Social/health organizations such as YMCA or YWCA
- Social service organizations such as the American Red Cross or the Salvation Army
- Volunteer groups—League of Women Voters, homeless shelters, health agencies, and so on
- Welcome organizations—Welcome Wagon, Hello Club, Newcomers, and so on
- Military agencies—reserve and active units of the local National Guard
- Open job fairs
- Employees at other hospitality companies or service-oriented organizations met while dining out, shopping, or doing other day-to-day activities
- State American Hotel & Lodging Associations
- State restaurant associations
- Local and state assistance programs—for example, clothing and food drives for those in need
- Ads in local "pennysaver" and other low- and no-cost papers

Another source to consider is employees at same-chain properties who may be laid off during seasonal slowdowns. For instance, two Sonesta Hotels—one on

Sanibel Island, Florida, and another in Cambridge, Massachusetts—have worked out an arrangement to transfer employees during slow seasons.

Retired employees of the operation may be happy to help out and can provide an immediate source of expert knowledge during staff shortages or in other times of need. Likewise, former employees in good standing and current part-time employees might be available to fill in on a short-term basis.

Other methods used successfully by small businesses that could work for hospitality managers include:

- Telerecruiting.

- Talent scout cards.

- Point-of-sale messages.

- Direct mail campaigns.

- Database recruiting.

- Government funded programs.

- Information seminars.

- Referral incentives.

- Sign-on bonuses.

Regardless of the outlets targeted as sources for recruits, if a property wishes to advertise, it must first identify the potential legal ramifications and the types of people its advertising will attract. In many locations, a property must obtain permission before distributing job notices and bulletins to outside sources. To avoid unlawful discrimination, properties must also pay special attention to how their advertisements are worded.

Creative Recruiting Tactics

Several hospitality companies have developed creative ways of overcoming their labor shortages. For instance, Marriott has developed a program for recruiting and training homeless people. Also, its Pathways to Independence—a program in which Marriott offers basic skills and workplace assimilation training to welfare recipients—has proven to be a very effective recruiting tool. This program enables many potential employees to become more eligible for employment. Marriott has reported that employees who undergo this type of training have an 80 percent graduation rate, a 90 percent retention rate after 90 days, and a 55 percent retention rate after one year. Marriott uses the same type of approach in the technical hospitality skills high school that it champions and supports in the Washington, D.C., area.

Some state associations, such as the Florida Hotel & Lodging Association and the Texas Hotel & Lodging Association, have implemented successful high school work-study and internship programs for more than a decade. The educational arms of such national trade associations as the American Hotel & Lodging Educational

Institute and the National Restaurant Association Educational Foundation have developed high school curricula that prepare students for the adult working world before they graduate. The programs link what is learned in the classroom with on-the-job experiences. Skills learned at the workplace are then reinforced through practical classroom interaction.

Like many other companies, Marriott uses on-campus recruiting to locate many potential management candidates. Unlike some companies, however, Marriott likes to target universities with large international populations in order to attract students from other countries who may be employable back in their home country after graduation. Marriott is also developing regional recruitment centers in cities such as Washington, D.C., Phoenix, and Boston. These centers, located in downtown retail settings and on the ground floor where many potential employees pass by daily, offer one-stop shopping for potential job applicants.

The Employer Group, an alliance of three hospitality companies and 25 other major employers, has also developed a collaborative approach to recruitment.

In addition, some companies have found that keeping up with the times in recruitment can take on unusual aspects today. For instance, while it may sound like New Age propaganda, paying attention to employees' "mind, body, and spirit" can actually produce significant bottom-line results. This approach to employee management, which concentrates on transferring life skills, quality of life, and personal interest planning, has taken hold at traditional and nontraditional companies alike, where higher recruitment and retention rates are the payoff.

Online Recruiting

Recruiting through cyberspace is becoming more popular. Many companies recruit nationally through either online recruiting agencies or their own websites. Several studies have been conducted to determine which websites are most effective. The measures most commonly used to assess website quality include an examination of the site's readability and the organization's effectiveness in promoting itself to potential customers and to potential employees. If every potential visitor is viewed as a possible client or employee, as some websites do, it is imperative to include job announcement information on the website. This approach started with high-tech companies but has rapidly spread across the spectrum. As a result, potential applicants can learn about specific jobs, the company's potential for growth, orientation and compensation programs, and other factors that might influence them to apply with a specific company. Good websites include online applications or links to application sites.

One example of successful online recruiting is offered by Marriott International, with more than 131,000 employees. Marriott has found that using its website is a cost-effective method of encouraging both current and potential employees to look at recruitment options.

In addition to company-specific recruiting sites, the World Wide Web is replete with headhunter, job posting, and job referral sites. Monster.com, Aquent Partners, futurestep.com, employment911.com, careercentral.com, internweb.com, FutureCollegeGrads.com, jobsleuth.com, careermag.com, and many other sites offer complete job posting and résumé posting services.

the Rooms
CHRONICLE

Tips for Recruiting and Retaining Employees

Staffing continues to be the biggest challenge many housekeeping departments face. Yet even though unemployment numbers are very low across the United States, room cleaner applicants are still available. Managers who continuously evaluate and improve their recruiting and retention practices will be successful in maintaining adequate staffing levels.

Recruiting

- Without a doubt, employee referrals are the best method of recruitment. All employees have friends, neighbors and relatives who are potential candidates for hire. And because employees don't want to be embarrassed by recommending a poor performer they are likely to only offer referrals of people who will fit the hotel's standards. Management can encourage employee referrals by instituting a substantial reward for such action. Compensation for these referrals can be cheaper than any other means of recruitment and can have better results. It is not unusual for hotels to pay an employee $100 if their recommended new hire successfully completes 90 days of work. The best managers celebrate the success of the recruit by compensating the referring employee in front of all other employees at a staff meeting. This action will encourage others to give referrals.

- Current employees can also help with recruitment by posting hotel "help wanted" notices in their grocery stores, laundromats and churches.

- Managers should not underestimate the importance of a good benefits package for recruiting employees. Managers who are aware of what other hotels offer can structure a very competitive package. Even though health insurance and paid vacations are important, housekeeping employees may be more interested in the hourly rate, uniforms, scheduling flexibility and transportation.

- The best housekeeping managers are in contact with their colleagues at other hotels. In addition to sharing recruitment strategies, some job sharing may be arranged.

- Great managers also keep in contact with government agencies through phone calls, personal visits and faxing of hotel job openings.

- And finally, when staffing is a challenge, managers must always make time to see potential new hires. Always take time for interviews.

Retention

Once new staff members are hired, will they stay?

- First of all, it sounds incredibly simple, but many hotels miss this point completely—be very nice to the new hires. Everybody must be nice. The manager. The support staff. And the present employees. New hires should be given extra special attention. Greet them. Introduce them to others. Talk to them. Get them a uniform. Assign a trainer. Assign a buddy. Tell them about lunch and breaks. Give them a clean cart and supplies. Spend time with them. Give them positive feedback. Give them schedules. Ask them how it is going. Make sure the first paycheck is accurate and timely. And always show appreciation.

the Rooms CHRONICLE®

- Give employees a work schedule that is beneficial, profitable and desirable. If high occupancy on week-ends is the nature of the hotel, it's possible that the same employees are covering the work loads each week. This causes turnover. Instead managers should design schedules that permit alternating weekends off or some compromise of employees picking up one of the days supplemented with part-time student help for the balance. Or managers may drop rooms on Sunday if the hotel occupancy permits. If low occupancy threatens to disseminate the staff because they need more hours, the best managers work proactively to prevent turnover. They talk to their staff in advance of fluctuating occupancies. They may ask for volunteers to take time off. Or they arrange for everybody to give up a day. Or better yet, they have established a budget for cleaning projects to be accomplished as occupancies decline. Schedules should always be posted in advance so employees can plan ahead. And managers must be flexible. Regardless of how managers compromise with scheduling, they must establish and follow fair and consistent guidelines, remembering to discipline employees if schedules are abused.

- To increase retention rates, managers must make work fun. They can have birthday parties and special event celebrations. They can give out candy bars and cash to employees for doing things right. They insure the office area is bright, cheery and neat. They can plan competitive activities with carts, toilet paper or bedmaking contests. They can plan outings to take employees away from the hotel for bowling, picnics or socializing. They can encourage employees to bring in family pictures or vacation pictures to be posted. Also they can invite employees to bring in family food for a potluck luncheon.

- These ideas for recruitment and retention are tried and tested. When incorporated into a hotel's employee relations program, ideas such as these will increase morale, decrease turnover and bring more profit to the bottom line.

Source: Mary Friedman, *The Rooms Chronicle®*, Volume 9, Number 3, p. 4.
For subscription information, call 866-READ-TRC.

Employers wishing to learn more about other aspects of employee recruitment—for instance, outsourcing of staff—can easily find answers on the Internet as well. The Internet even provides information for those unfamiliar with certain aspects of recruiting. Finally, the Internet also provides ample opportunities to purchase or rent applicant tracking software, human resource information system software, and so on.

One of the advantages of Internet job posting is the potential for rapid response. Because information transfer on the Internet is virtually instantaneous, possible applicants can know about and apply (sometimes also by Internet) almost immediately. The American Hotel & Lodging Association has partnered with hcareers.com. Member hotels get a twenty percent discount on rates for job postings. It's a site that focuses on the hospitality industry and has a traffic of more than three million job seekers each month—all looking for hospitality-related jobs. In addition to these recruiting resources, many hospitality organizations offer direct contact with applicants through their own home pages.

Immigration Reform

Immigration reform became a hot political topic in the mid-2000s with many groups calling for tighter border control and less immigration. This has been an especially important issue for the hospitality industry. Personal service is the lifeblood of the lodging industry and particularly of the housekeeping department. Hiring workers to fill critical service positions is one of the hospitality industry's most urgent issues.

Modest growth in the lodging sector, which employed 1.4 million hotel property workers in 2004, is expected to result in the need for 300,000 additional workers by 2014 according to the U.S. Bureau of Labor Statistics. In recent years, hoteliers have sought to attract and retain employees through numerous initiatives. The industry is a leader in both welfare-to-work and school-to-work efforts, and the American Hotel & Lodging Association has partnered with prominent organizations such as America's Promise, the NAACP, and Esperanza USA to promote careers in lodging. Despite these efforts, the lodging industry faces widespread labor shortages.

Also of concern to the industry are workers who provide employers with false documentation. Every employee is required to provide proof that he or she is legally permitted to work in the United States. Federal law prohibits employers from verifying the validity of these documents if they appear genuine.

Selecting Employees

A successful recruiting process will result in candidates for open positions. The housekeeping manager's next challenge is to find the best fit. In the majority of hotel organizations, selection still falls to the housekeeping manager for whom the employee will eventually work.

Housekeeping managers should observe four principles when selecting employees:

- Explicitness. Be sure that everyone involved has a clear picture of the desired employee. Whether selecting two or ten people, the criteria should not change along the way. The more explicit the criteria, the more likely the hotel will find a suitable candidate.

- Objectivity. The entire hiring process must be quantifiable, from start to finish. Whenever possible, give the applicants numerical scores to let them know how they are faring in the process compared to the hotel's criteria for selection.

- Thoroughness. All selection processes must be thorough. All should include three phases: initial screening, interviewing and testing, and a meeting with the primary decision-maker.

- Consistency. A continuity of people, purpose, and procedures throughout the selection process will produce much better results.

The selection method a property uses will determine the length of the selection process. Housekeeping managers typically include at least some form of interview when selecting new employees. Details of conducting interviews are provided in the article beginning on page 128.

Skills Training

Ensuring that department employees receive proper training is one of the executive housekeeper's major responsibilities. This does not mean that the executive housekeeper must necessarily assume the duties and responsibilities of a trainer. The actual training functions may be delegated to supervisors or even to talented employees. However, the executive housekeeper should be responsible for ongoing training programs in the department.

Most managers and trainers understand that the goal of training is to help employees develop skills to do their jobs well. Many managers and trainers, however, are not sure of the best way to train. Often, they need a framework for training. The four-step training method provides that framework. The four steps in the method are "prepare," "present," "practice," and "follow up."

Whether training a group of new employees or experienced staff members, the **four-step training method** will work best.

Prepare to Train

Preparation is essential for successful training. Otherwise, the training may lack a logical sequence and key details may be omitted. A trainer may also feel more than normal anxiety regarding the training session. Before beginning training, review the job analysis that was performed prior to recruiting for the position. Based on this job analysis, develop the position's training needs.

Analyze the Job. The foundation for training employees and preventing performance problems is job analysis. **Job analysis** is determining what knowledge an employee must have, what tasks each employee needs to perform, and the standards at which he or she must perform them. Without complete knowledge of what each employee is expected to do, they can't be trained properly.

Job analysis involves three steps: identifying **job knowledge,** creating a **task list,** and developing a **job breakdown** for each task performed by each housekeeping position. The knowledge, lists, and breakdowns also form an efficient system for evaluating employee performance.

The job knowledge identifies what an employee needs to know to perform his or her job. To perform a job well, an employee needs to know about the lodging property, his or her department, and his or her position. For example, room attendants need to know knowledge for all employees, such as bloodborne pathogens and the Americans with Disabilities Act; knowledge for all housekeeping employees, such as telephone courtesy, OSHA regulations, and security; and knowledge for room attendants, such as unusual guest situations and deep-cleaning assignments.

The tasks on the task list should reflect the total job responsibility of the employee. Exhibit 2 presents a sample task list. Note that each line on the sample

C the Rooms
HRONICLE®

Here's a question for you...What questions should be asked during an interview?

Here's a question: Why are icebergs dangerous?

Answer: Because 90 percent of the iceberg is beneath the surface, sight unseen. You never know what you'll find underneath!

A second question for you: When are people most like icebergs?

Answer: When they are being interviewed for a job, for only 10 percent of the real person is seen with an application, resume, or interview. What you don't see is what you will really get!

So, how does a hotel manager find out what's beneath the surface when interviewing job applicants? How does one determine a candidate's true abilities, interests, personality and attitude?

In a recent study of screening factors of college students, criteria such as work experience, extra-curricular activities, and grade point average comprised about 50 percent of specific characteristics reviewed, thus indicating that recruiters often consider other factors just as important.

But what are these "other" factors? Often, "personality plus" candidates come to the top of the list with positive first impressions, with how they looked and how they talked coming in a close second.

Collecting information during an interview can be enhanced by following a few simple rules. The four basic rules are:

- Do your homework before the interview.

- Establish the appropriate setting.

- Establish a rapport.

- Know the job.

There are two primary types of interviews used today: structured and unstructured. Opinions vary on the value of unstructured interviews, yet it is probably the most common method used. Some believe that because it is less formal and more relaxed, it invites candidates to be open with their answers. However, sometimes, unstructured interviews are used for the wrong reasons or housekeeping managers are just poorly prepared.

Structured interviews are planned; questions are prepared in advance and are asked in the same way to each candidate. Structured questions will result in answers that are comparable between candidates. Taking the time at the beginning to ready for the interview will save time and money down the road because the housekeeping manager will be selecting the right person for the right job.

How does a housekeeping manager conducting job interviews choose the appropriate questions to find out the exact information they are seeking? There are five types of questions that should be asked: rapport building, behavioral, fitness, job competency, and closing.

Rapport-Building Questions. Especially at the beginning of an interview, managers will often attempt to put a candidate at ease through informal chit chat or small talk not related to the job. While putting a candidate at ease is ideal, it is also the easiest place to get into legal trouble by asking questions that may be inappropriate

the Rooms CHRONICLE®

(continued)

or have no bearing on the position the candidate has applied for. As a general rule, the focus should be on general comments and questions, and always avoid reference to the candidate's age, race, sex, religion, color, disability or national origin. Unless a bona-fide occupational qualification relating to gender, age, religion or national origin is associated with the position, stick to more general rapport building questions. Examples include:

- How has your day been?
- Can you tell me a little about yourself?
- Are you familiar with our property?
- What are three words that describe you?
- What do you know about our hotel?
- Tell me about a project that really excited you.
- What three adjectives would best describe you?
- What did you enjoy the most about your last job?

Behavioral Questions. These often begin with "Tell me about…" or "Describe a situation…" These are more focused questions that hold the candidate accountable for their past performance. Past performance is the most accurate predictor of future performance. Some sample questions:

- Tell me a time when you were creative in solving a problem.
- Describe your last supervisor's management style.
- Tell me about your worst customer service situation and how you handled it.
- If you could change two things in your last job, what would they be and how would you change them?
- In what ways do you expect your next job to differ from your present job?
- Describe a situation in which you were successful in getting people to work effectively together.
- How have you resolved problems you have encountered and what were the results?
- Tell me about a time when you were able to convince others that you had a better way of doing things.
- What is the most surprising objection you have ever received and how did you handle it?
- If you had a guest complaining about poor service, how would you handle it?
- Tell me about a situation with a guest that, in retrospect, you would have handled differently. What would you do differently now?
- What characteristics are the most important in a good manager?
- Tell me about a time when you handled a difficult situation with a coworker.

(continued)

the Rooms CHRONICLE®

(continued)

Fitness Questions. Personality, flexibility and commitment to quality work can all be determined by asking specific questions to determine an applicant's potential fit with the hotel's team and the company's work culture:

- How do you operate as a team player?
- How do you deal with people whose job backgrounds and value systems differ from yours?
- Do you prefer working with others or working alone?
- What two or three accomplishments have given you the most satisfaction and why?
- Describe your dream job.
- Why have you chosen this particular field?
- What can you bring to this job from your previous experience?
- What skill has been praised or rewarded in your past positions?
- What kinds of people do you prefer to work with?
- Why do you think you are a good match for this job?
- What would you peers say about you, both positive and negative?
- How comfortable are you with change?
- Define "cooperation."
- What makes you want to work hard?
- In your capacity as _____ at your last job, what was your job description?

Job Competency Questions. Job competency questions emphasize job and abilities. These are perhaps the easiest questions to ask. The interviewer has seen the candidate's cover letter and application or résumé , which claims he or she possesses the necessary skills for the position. Now it is time to ask a few questions to verify what they claim. Typically, these questions will ask "how" or "what"; they cannot be answered with a "yes" or "no" response. Listen to the answer to see how quickly the applicant answers, how complete/correct their answer is, and whether they actually answer the question that was being asked or if they went off on a tangent and answered something they were more familiar with. Some examples:

- What are the advantages of diversity in the workplace?
- What would you say to an interviewer who suggested that you do not have much organizational work experience?
- What are your team player qualities?
- What are the early morning priorities for a Guest Service Representative?
- Tell me how you clean a guestroom.
- How do you get along with your co-workers?
- How do you deal with guests who think they are right even when they're wrong?
- How do you show a guest that he or she is important?
- What qualities would you look for in hiring a person for this position?

the Rooms
CHRONICLE®

(continued)

- How would you go about writing a mission statement for your department?
- Can you tell me about a time you dealt with an ethical question on the job and how you handled it?
- What organizations in your life have earned your deepest sense of loyalty and why?
- If your manager gives you two projects to complete in a day but you have time to complete only one, how do you proceed?

Closing Questions. The number one closing question for all, at all times should be: "Do you have any questions for me?" Others may include:

- Is there anything else I should know about you?
- Is there any question I should have asked you but did not?
- What are the three most important contributions you have made to your current position?
- I've interviewed several capable candidates, including you. What is the one thing you would like me to remember about you when making my decision?

Source: Sue Garwood, *The Rooms Chronicle®*, Volume 15, Number 2, pp. 6–7. For subscription information, call 866-READ-TRC.

task list begins with a verb. This format stresses action and clearly indicates to an employee what he or she will be responsible for doing. Wherever possible, tasks should be listed in an order that reflects the logical sequence of daily responsibilities.

The job breakdown format can vary to suit the needs and requirements of individual properties. Exhibit 3 presents a sample job breakdown. The breakdown includes a list of equipment and supplies needed to perform the task; steps, how-to's, and tips explaining the methods of performing the task.

Employees should know the standards that will be used to measure their job performance. Therefore, it is important to break down job tasks and document the standards. In order to serve as a performance standard, each task must be observable and measurable. Exhibit 4 shows a sample Training Needs Evaluation for Current Employees that can be used as a performance evaluation. The executive housekeeper (or the supervising housekeeping manager) conducting a quarterly performance evaluation should be able to simply check the box matching the employee's performance.

Developing Job Breakdowns. If one person in housekeeping is assigned the responsibility of writing every job breakdown, the job may never get done, unless the department is very small with a limited number of tasks. Some of the best job breakdowns are written by those who actually perform the tasks. In properties with large housekeeping staffs, standards groups can be formed to handle the writing tasks. Group members should include department supervisors and several experienced room attendants and public area attendants. In smaller

Exhibit 2   Sample Task List

TASK LIST

Room Attendant

1.   Use your room assignment sheet.
2.   Get guest amenities for assigned rooms.
3.   Get cleaning supplies for assigned rooms.
4.   Keep your cart and work areas organized.
5.   Enter the guestroom.
6.   Prepare the guestroom for cleaning.
7.   Begin to clean the bathroom.
8.   Clean the tub and shower area.
9.   Clean the toilet.
10.   Clean the sink and vanity.
11.   Clean the bathroom floor.
12.   Finish cleaning the bathroom.
13.   Clean the guestroom closet.
14.   Make the bed.
15.   Dust the guestroom.
16.   Replenish supplies and amenities.
17.   Clean windows, tracks, and sills.
18.   Put finishing touches on the guestroom.
19.   Vacuum the guestroom and report room status.
20.   Exit the guestroom.
21.   Correct cleaning problems found during inspection.
22.   Complete end-of-shift duties.
23.   Rotate and flip mattresses.
24.   Set up or remove special guest service equipment.
25.   Clean multiroom guest suites.
26.   Provide evening turndown service.

properties, experienced employees might be assigned to write the job breakdowns alone. Exhibit 5 summarizes the process of developing job breakdowns.

Most hospitality organizations have a policy and procedures manual. Although this manual rarely contains the detail necessary to set up effective training and evaluation programs, portions of it may be helpful to members of a housekeeping standards group as they write job breakdowns for each department position. For example, if the procedure sections of the manual include job descriptions and job specifications, they may help a standards group in writing job lists and performance standards. The policy sections may be helpful sources of additional information that can be included in the job breakdowns.

The job breakdowns for tasks that involve the use of equipment may already be written in the operating manuals supplied by vendors. Standards groups should not have to write job breakdowns for operating floor buffers, wet vacuums, and other types of machinery, for example. Instead, the standards group may simply

Exhibit 3   Sample Job Breakdown

Clean the Toilet

Materials needed: Gloves, goggles, cleaning supplies, a damp sponge, a toilet bowl brush, dry cloths, a pen, and a room assignment sheet.

STEPS	HOW-TO'S
1. Put on protective gloves and goggles.	
2. Flush the toilet and make a note on your room assignment sheet if it does not flush and fill properly.	
3. Spray cleaning solution on the inside and outside of the toilet, the walls beside and behind the toilet, and under the vanity.	
4. Clean the area around the toilet.	❑ Wipe the walls around the toilet. ❑ Wipe the pipes leading to the toilet. ❑ Wipe the wall under the vanity and the drain pipe. ❑ Wipe the top, lid, seat, and outside of the toilet.
5. Clean the inside of the toilet.	❑ Use a toilet bowl brush to scrub the inside of the toilet bowl. Be sure to clean under the rim and the seat. ❑ Rinse the brush in the toilet when you are done and flush. This brush should only be used for cleaning the toilet.
6. Polish the toilet.	❑ Use a dry cloth to wipe the outside of the toilet. Polish the walls and pipes at the same time.

Source: Hospitality Skills Training Series, Room Attendant Guide, (Lansing, Mich.: American Hotel & Lodging Educational Institute).

Exhibit 4   Sample Needs Evaluation Form

Training Needs Evaluation for Current Employees

How well are your current employees performing? Use this form to observe and rate their work.

Part 1: Job Knowledge

Rate the employee's knowledge of each of the following topics:	Well Below Standard	Slightly Below Standard	At Standard	Above Standard
Knowledge for All Employees				
Quality Guest Service				
Bloodborne Pathogens				
Personal Appearance				
Emergency Situations				
Lost and Found				
Recycling Procedures				
Safe Work Habits				
Manager on Duty				
Your Property's Fact Sheet				
Employee Policies				
The Americans with Disabilities Act				
Knowledge for All Housekeeping Employees				
Working as a Team With Co-Workers and Other Departments				
Telephone Courtesy				
Security				
Housekeeping Keys				
OSHA Regulations				
Using Cleaning Supplies Correctly and Safely				
Maintenance Needs				
Special Cleaning Requirements				
Housekeeping Inventories				
Knowledge for Room Attendants				
What Is a Room Attendant?				
Superior Performance Standards				
Tip Sharing				
Unusual Guestroom Situations				
Deep-Cleaning Assignments				
Room Status Codes				

refer to (or even attach) appropriate pages from the operating manual supplied by the vendor for in-house training.

Developing job breakdowns involves breaking down each task on each housekeeping job list by writing the performance standards that state the specific

Exhibit 4 *(continued)*

Training Needs Evaluation for Current Employees *(continued)*

Part 2: Job Skills

Rate the employee's skills in performing each of the following tasks:	Well Below Standard	Slightly Below Standard	At Standard	Above Standard
Use Your Room Assignment Sheet				
Get Guest Amenities for Assigned Rooms				
Get Cleaning Supplies for Assigned Rooms				
Keep Your Cart and Work Areas Organized				
Enter the Guestroom				
Prepare the Guestroom for Cleaning				
Begin to Clean the Bathroom				
Clean the Tub and Shower Area				
Clean the Toilet				
Clean the Sink and Vanity				
Clean the Bathroom Floor				
Finish Cleaning the Bathroom				
Clean the Guestroom Closet				
Make the Bed				
Dust the Guestroom				
Replenish Supplies and Amenities				
Clean Windows, Tracks, and Sills				
Put Finishing Touches on the Guestroom				
Vacuum the Guestroom and Report Room Status				
Exit the Guestroom				
Correct Cleaning Problems Found During Inspection				
Complete End-of-Shift Duties				
Rotate and Flip Mattresses				
Set Up or Remove Special Guest Service Equipment				
Clean Multi-Room Guest Suites				
Provide Evening Turn-Down Service				

observable and measurable steps an employee must take to accomplish the task. The executive housekeeper should assist the standards group in writing performance standards for at least two or three positions within the housekeeping department. While assisting the group, the executive housekeeper should stress

Exhibit 5   Developing Job Breakdowns

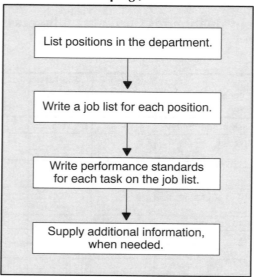

that each performance standard must be observable and measurable. The value of each performance standard can be tested by asking whether a supervisor or manager can evaluate an employee's performance by simply checking "Yes" or "No" in the quarterly performance review column.

After the standards group has written job breakdowns for two or three tasks, the writing of job breakdowns for the other housekeeping tasks should be assigned to individual members of the group. Within a specified time, they should submit their work to the executive housekeeper or the executive housekeeper's assistant, who then assembles the breakdowns, has them typed in a single format (perhaps similar to that shown in Exhibit 3), and provides copies to all of the group's members. A final meeting can then be held, with the standards group carefully analyzing the breakdowns for each position within the department. After the job breakdowns have been finalized, they should be used immediately to train the department's staff.

Analyze New Employee Training Needs. The task list is an excellent tool with which to plan any new employee training. Realistically, new employees cannot be expected to learn all of the tasks before the first day on the job. Before beginning training, study the task list. Then, rate each task according to whether it should be mastered (1) before working alone on the job; (2) within two weeks on the job; or (3) within two months on the job.

Select several of the tasks that were rated as "1" and plan to cover those in the first training session. After the employee understands and can perform these, teach the remaining tasks in subsequent training sessions until the employee has learned all of the tasks. Exhibit 6 shows a sample training schedule based on the task list found in Exhibit 2 and a list of "need to know" topics.

the Rooms
CHRONICLE®

Five Ways to Help Non-English-Speaking Housekeepers Be More Productive

Today, in hotels everywhere, communications in the housekeeping department can be challenging. Whether answering a hotel guest asking for extra towels, or a housekeeping supervisor wanting the carpet vacuumed, the response from an employee who does not understand English may be the same: a shoulder shrug, a smile, and no action.

Yet the same housekeeping employees who do not speak English may have many wonderful qualities—good cleaners, eager to work, excellent attendance, friendly smiles. Here are five things that can help a non-English-speaking employee become a valuable member of the team.

1. **Hire More Than One.**

   Just to make the environment less intimidating, try to hire more than one employee of the same nationality. It can be comforting to have someone to talk to, eat lunch with, or learn new tasks with.

2. **Make It Easy For Employees.**

   At a northern hotel, the housekeeping supervisors carry flash cards with simple requests printed in different languages. When a room attendant has neglected a routine task, the supervisor will point on the card to the proper request for the employee to dust, vacuum, change the bedspread, or whatever. A housekeeping coordinator says, "The cards work very well. As an employee gains tenure and knowledge of the language, the cards are needed less and less."

   The flash cards are easy to make. A local school, employment agency, library, or bilingual employee can translate a list of room attendant tasks. Some hotels use drawings to convey the meaning of the supervisor's request. Whatever method is chosen, the card should be laminated and included on each room attendant's cart.

3. **Make It Easy For Guests.**

   Non-English-speaking employees often have difficulty understanding guest requests. At a West Coast hotel, the staff has made communication easy. All room attendants carry on their cart a clipboard with basic guest requests written in English and other languages including those for soap, towels, and directions. When guests approach a room attendant, they can simply point to their request and the employee can immediately take action. This has made communications more personable, and "with the clipboard, there are not guest complaints," says the director of housekeeping. "We've eliminated the need for the guest to call the front desk."

4. **Offer Classes in English.**

   Many immigrants want to learn to speak English. Most local education and community centers offer classes designed to help a person of any nationality to learn to speak English as a second language (ESL).

(continued)

the Rooms CHRONICLE®

(continued)

With the help of a state literacy council and some ambitious employee volunteers, one hotel opted to offer ESL at the work site. Classes were offered three mornings a week prior to the workday beginning. At first employees learned greetings, then guestroom and/or restaurant terminology. Understanding simple requests and giving clear directions were also taught. By the end of the class, students were able to communicate about their families and backgrounds. The benefits of teaching ESL include making the employee feel important. This raises employee productivity and helps them become more involved in the team's efforts.

5. **Learn about the Employee.**

Americans who travel to foreign countries understand how comforting it can be to have someone say, "Good morning," in English. Those same feelings can be seen on the faces of non-English speaking employees when their supervisor learns a few words of their native language. Saying "Please," "Thank you," "Have a nice evening," and "Well done" in the employee's language can dramatically raise morale.

One executive housekeeper has 11 different countries represented on her staff. "It's important to learn the basics of their culture," she says. "We try to honor their holidays, acknowledge their customs, and empower them to share their culture with the rest of the staff. Taking the time and interest for them to tell us about their lives engenders loyalty and helps build a stronger team."

Many tremendous workers are available whose only barrier to work is not speaking English. Housekeepers who take the time to educate and train these people are not only increasing guest satisfaction but also enhancing their staff by the addition of new cultures.

Source: Mary Friedman, *The Rooms Chronicle®*, Volume 3, Number 4, p. 4.
For subscription information, call 866-READ-TRC.

Once it has been determined which tasks will be taught in each training session, turn to the job breakdowns. Think of the job breakdown for each task as a lesson plan for training or as a learning guide for self-directed study. Because the job breakdowns list all the steps employees must perform, they tell exactly what needs to be done during the training. Job breakdowns can direct the instruction and make sure that critical points or steps are not overlooked.

The knowledge an employee must know is usually written on a single page. Assign new employees nine or ten knowledge sections or job breakdowns at a time to study. Do *not* ask an employee to read all the knowledge sections and all the job breakdowns at once. This will overwhelm the employee and he or she won't remember enough information to perform the job well.

Analyze Current Employee Training Needs. Executive housekeepers sometimes feel that there's a problem with an employee's work or with several employees' work, but they're not exactly sure what it is; or they feel that something is not quite right with the staff, but don't know where to start making improvements. A training

the Rooms CHRONICLE®

A Ten-Day Training Checklist for New Room Attendants

For the housekeeping executive who has been planning to write a training program but just hasn't gotten around to it, here are a few basics. This list is designed for the training of a new room attendant without previous housekeeping experience.

Although the order of this checklist will change for each hotel, and special items may be added (such as balconies or kitchen dishes) these are the basic skills each new room attendant must acquire. Many housekeepers recommend that the employee learn only one task at a time so the job does not seem overwhelming. For instance, teach how to make a bed and let the employee concentrate on that until competency is achieved. When the pieces are in place, teach the routine of cleaning the entire room with a limited number of trips to the cart. Trainers are usually paid an incentive during the first two weeks, and he or she continues to tutor the new hire throughout the probation period.

The bottom line is that employees who are thoroughly trained on an ongoing basis will return the investment many times over.

Source: Gail Edwards, CHHE, *The Rooms Chronicle*®, Volume 3, Number 4, p. 5. For subscription information, call 866-READ-TRC.

Day One Orientation	Tour of all public space, employee space, and sample guestrooms Department goals and mission statement Introduction of department staff Expectations of performance Scheduling, time clock, breaks Safety procedures including chemical use Security procedures including keys Lost and found
Day Two, Three, Four, and Five Assigned to trainer for skills training	Use of protective equipment Stripping dirty linen Emptying wastecans and ashtrays Defrosting refrigerator Making a bed Making a sofa bed Making a rollaway Checking underneath bed Dusting furniture, drawers, pictures, sills Cleaning lamps, checking bulbs Checking TV remote and channel sticker Cleaning wastebaskets Cleaning window frames and windows Cleaning upholstered chairs Placement of furniture Cleaning and locking adjoining doors Cleaning the telephone Setting the time on digital clocks Proper paper supplies and placement Cleaning the bathtub, tile, chrome

(continued)

C the Rooms HRONICLE®

(continued)

Day Two, Three, Four, and Five
Assigned to trainer for skills training

Cleaning tile grout
Cleaning a toilet, seat, base
Cleaning bathroom walls, floors
Cleaning a vanity, sink, stopper
Cleaning a vanity mirror
Cleaning bathroom lights
Folding towels, tissues, and toilet paper
Placing clean glasses and ice bucket
Proper bathroom amenities and placement
When to replace toilet paper, soaps
Vacuuming carpets
Pulling beds and furniture
Placing hangers and laundry bags
Checking condition of iron and board
Cleaning coffee machine and restocking
Cleaning fingerprints on doors and walls
Cleaning air vents and corners for cobwebs
Proper placement of drapes
HVAC settings
Changing status of room
Special needs of stayover guests
Procedures for rooms with pets
Order of completing assignment
Do Not Disturb handling
What if phone rings while in room
Cleaning hall area near room
Emptying a vacuum
Handling keys
Fulfilling guest requests
Limiting access to guestrooms
Making maintenance reports
Making notes for missing linen or furniture
Lost and found
Package pass requests
Late, absent procedures
Inspection routine
Entrance/exit use
Care of cart and supplies
Lunch break procedures
Supply replenishment
Safety rules on guest floors
Communicating with other workers

Day Six-Ten
Full Routine

At the conclusion of Day Five, the trainer should review the checklist with the room attendant and the supervisor to assess progress and receive feedback from the employee. Beginning Day Six, the room attendant should be assigned a short set of rooms, perhaps eight. Then each day assign two more until the new hire has gained confidence and proficiency. Generally speaking, under the guidance of a trainer, a new hire should be able to clean 16 rooms a day by the end of the second week.

Exhibit 6   Sample Training Schedule

Suggested Training Schedule for New Employees

A training schedule is only effective it it fits the hotel's needs and the needs of the trainee(s). The following is a *suggested* training schedule. Read it carefully and adapt it as necessary to organize your training sessions. A trainer may want to give employees any Job Knowledge sections and Job Breakdowns to study at least one day before these materials are to be covered in a training session.

Day 1:

Department Orientation

Knowledge for All Employees:
- Quality Guest Service
- Bloodborne Pathogens
- Personal Appearance
- Emergency Situations
- Lost and Found
- Recycling Procedures
- Safe Work Habits
- Manager on Duty
- Your Property's Fact Sheet
- Employee Policies
- The Americans with Disabilities Act

The Task List for room attendants

Day 2:

Review Day 1 (Plan additional training time, if necessary)

Knowledge for All Housekeeping Employees:
- Working as a Team With Co-Workers and Other Departments
- Telephone Courtesy
- Security
- Housekeeping Keys
- OSHA Regulations
- Using Cleaning Supplies Correctly and Safely
- Maintenance Needs
- Special Cleaning Requirements
- Housekeeping Inventories

The Job Breakdowns for Tasks 1 - 5:
Task   1   Use Your Room Assignment Sheet
Task   2   Get Guest Amenities for Assigned Rooms
Task   3   Get Cleaning Supplies for Assigned Rooms
Task   4   Keep Your Cart and Work Areas Organized
Task   5   Enter the Guestroom

(continued)

---

needs assessment can help uncover the weaknesses of individual employees within a team or department.

To conduct a needs assessment of a single employee, observe present performance for two or three days and record it on a copy of a form similar to the one in

Exhibit 6 *(continued)*

Suggested Training Schedule for New Employees *(continued)*

Day 3:

Review Day 2 (Plan additional training time, if necessary)

Knowledge for Room Attendants:
- What Is a Room Attendant?
- Superior Performance Standards
- Tip Sharing
- Unusual Guestroom Situations
- Deep-Cleaning Assignments
- Room Status Codes

The Job Breakdowns for Tasks 6 - 12:
Task 6 Prepare the Guestroom for Cleaning
Task 7 Begin to Clean the Bathroom
Task 8 Clean the Tub and Shower Area
Task 9 Clean the Toilet
Task 10 Clean the Sink and Vanity
Task 11 Clean the Bathroom Floor
Task 12 Finish Cleaning the Bathroom

Day 4:

Review Day 3 (Plan additional training time, if necessary)

The Job Breakdowns for Tasks 13 - 21:
Task 13 Clean the Guestroom Closet
Task 14 Make the Bed
Task 15 Dust the Guestroom
Task 16 Replenish Supplies and Amenities
Task 17 Clean Windows, Tracks, and Sills
Task 18 Put Finishing Touches on the Guestroom
Task 19 Vacuum the Guestroom and Report Room Status
Task 20 Exit the Guestroom
Task 21 Correct Cleaning Problems Found During Inspection

Day 5:

Review Day 4 (Plan additional training time, if necessary)

The Job Breakdowns for Tasks 22 - 26:
Task 22 Complete End-of-Shift Duties
Task 23 Rotate and Flip Mattresses
Task 24 Set Up or Remove Special Guest Service Equipment
Task 25 Clean Multi-Room Guest Suites
Task 26 Provide Evening Turn-Down Service

Employee cleans one complete room while the trainer observes

Day 6:

Employee cleans a small number of rooms on his or her own

Add more rooms as the employee progresses

Exhibit 4. Areas in which the employee scores poorly are those areas that should be targeted for refresher training.

Develop Your Department Training Plan. It's a good idea to make a training plan four times a year, every three months or so. And it is best to complete each plan one month before the beginning of each quarter.

Follow these steps to prepare for training sessions:

- Carefully review all knowledge sections and job breakdowns that will be used in training.

- Make a copy of each knowledge section and job breakdown for each trainee.

- Establish a training schedule. This will depend on who is being trained and the training method that will be used. Remember to limit each training session's information to what employees can understand and remember.

- Select a training time and location. When possible, conduct training at the appropriate work stations during slow business hours.

- Notify the employee or employees of the dates and times of the training sessions.

- Practice the training presentation.

- Gather all the necessary supplies for demonstrating tasks.

Present

Well-developed job breakdowns provide all the information will be needed to conduct the "present" step of the four-step training method. Use the job breakdowns as a training guide. Follow the sequence of each step in each job breakdown. For each step, show and tell employees what to do, how to do it, and why the details are important.

Give employees a chance to prepare. Let new employees study the task list to get an overview of all the tasks they will learn to perform. If possible, give the list to them at least one day before the first training session. At least a day before each training session, let new and current employees review the job breakdowns that will be covered in that session. Then begin each training session by going over what the employees will do. Let them know how long activities will take and when their breaks will be.

When explaining each step of training, demonstrate them. Make sure employees can see exactly what is being demonstrated. Encourage employees to ask questions whenever they need more information.

Be sure to take enough time when presenting the training. Go slowly and carefully. Be patient if employees don't understand right away. Go over all the steps at least two times. When you show a step a second time, ask the employees questions to see if they understand. Repeat the steps as many times as necessary.

Avoid jargon. Jargon is language that is technical or specific to an industry, such as "railroad schedules" for public space cleaners. Use words that employees who are new to the hospitality industry or to the hotel property can understand. They can pick up the jargon later.

Ask Gail—Consistency through Training

Dear Gail:

How can I get consistency among room attendants? Everyone seems to have their own style.

B.C.

Dear B.C.:

The easiest way to have consistency throughout the department is to use one trainer to work with everyone. If you have conveyed to that trainer the exact way you want the rooms to be cleaned, then he or she can reinforce good habits with everyone else. You should have one-on-one training for everyone (not just new hires), because we all need a refresher course occasionally.

Next, you should have lots of visual reinforcements available: pictures of the correct linen placement, amenity setups, etc. It's easier to remember a picture than a list of words.

Another idea is to make a game of inspecting. You can preset a room with certain things wrong, and then ask each employee one at a time to fill out an inspection form of the room. Give prizes for those who find all the wrong things. And for those who don't find the errors, keep working with them. Repetition is the mother of habit.

Source: *The Rooms Chronicle®*, Volume 2, Number 4, p. 9.
For subscription information, call 866-READ-TRC.

Practice

When the trainer and trainees agree that they are familiar with the job and able to complete the steps acceptably, trainees should try to perform the tasks alone. Immediate practice results in good work habits. Have each trainee demonstrate each step of the task presented during the training session. This will indicate whether they really do understand. Resist the urge to do the tasks for the employees.

Coaching will help the employee gain the skill and confidence necessary to perform the job. Compliment the employee immediately after correct performance. Gently correct them when they perform incorrectly. Bad habits formed at this stage of the training may be very difficult to break later. Be sure that the trainee understands and can explain not only how to perform each step, but also the purpose of each step.

Follow Up

There are a number of things managers can do to make it easier for their employees to re-enter the workplace after training. Some of these options include:

• Provide opportunities to use and demonstrate new skills during and after training.

- Have employees discuss the training with their co-workers.

- Provide ongoing, open communication on progress and concerns.

Continue Coaching on the Job. While training helps employees learn new knowledge and develop new skills and attitudes, coaching focuses on the actual on-the-job application of what has been learned in the training sessions. As a coach, you challenge, encourage, correct, and positively reinforce the knowledge, skills, and attitudes learned during the training session.

Some on-the-job coaching tips:

- Observe employees while they work to ensure that they are performing tasks correctly.

- Make casual suggestions to correct minor problems.

- Tactfully correct employees when they make major mistakes. Typically, the best way to do this is in a quiet location.

- If an employee is using an unsafe procedure, correct the problem right away.

Give Constant Feedback. Feedback is when a manager tells employees how well they are performing. Two types of feedback are positive feedback, which recognizes a job well done; and redirective feedback, which recognizes incorrect performance and reviews how the employee can improve.

Some tips for giving both types of feedback:

- Let employees know what they are doing correctly and incorrectly.

- Tell employees when they perform well after training. This will help them remember what they learn. It will also encourage them to use those behaviors and that information on the job.

- If employees are not meeting performance standards, first compliment them for the tasks they are doing correctly. Then, show them how to correct their bad habits, and explain why it is important that they do so.

- Be specific. Describe behavior by stating exactly what the employee said and did.

- Choose the words used for feedback carefully; the feedback should sound helpful, not critical.

  Don't say, "You used quality guest service when you asked the guest who seemed lost if you could help, but you should have known the restaurant's hours of operation. Study your copy of the property's fact sheet."

  Do say, "You used quality guest service when you asked the guest who seemed lost if you could help, and you could give even better service by learning the restaurant's and other facilities' hours of operation. Let me get you another copy of the property's fact sheet."

- A manager should demonstrate that they understand what the employee is saying. Say something such as, "What I'm hearing you say is…"

- Make sure the employee understands the feedback. Say something such as, "I'm not sure I explained everything clearly. Let me hear what you think I said."

- Always be sincere and tactful with all comments. Employees appreciate an honest compliment about a specific behavior. And no one likes to be embarrassed or put down by criticism.

- Tell employees where to find help when you are not available.

Evaluate. Evaluate employees' progress. Use the task list as a checklist to confirm that all tasks have been mastered. Provide further training and practice for tasks that have not been mastered.

Get employees' feedback. Let employees evaluate the training they received. This can help a manager improve training efforts for them and other employees.

Keep training records for each person who receives training. Track each employee's training history and keep a copy of a training log in that employee's personnel file.

Scheduling

Since labor is the greatest single housekeeping expense, one of the most important managerial functions of the executive housekeeper is to ensure that the right number of employees is scheduled to work each day. When too many employees are scheduled to work, the department is overstaffed. Overstaffing results in excessive labor costs that decrease hotel profits. When too few employees are scheduled to work, the department becomes understaffed. While understaffing decreases labor costs, it may also decrease hotel profits because performance standards will not be met, resulting in dissatisfied guests and lost business.

The first step toward efficient **scheduling** is to determine which positions within the housekeeping department are fixed and which are variable in relation to changes in occupancy levels at the hotel.

Fixed staff positions are those that must be filled regardless of the volume of business. These positions are generally managerial and administrative in nature, such as executive housekeeper or assistant executive housekeeper. Employees occupying these positions are usually scheduled to work at least 40 hours a week, regardless of the occupancy level of the hotel.

The number of **variable staff positions** to be filled varies in relation to changes in hotel occupancy. These positions include:

- Supervisors.

- Room attendants (day and afternoon shifts).

- Housepersons (day and afternoon shifts).

- Floor supervisors.

- Lobby attendants.

The number of employees scheduled to work in these positions is determined primarily by the number of rooms occupied during the previous night. Generally, the higher the previous night's occupancy, the more employees must be scheduled to work the next day. The number of housepersons and lobby attendants needed for any given shift may also vary in relation to meeting room and banquet functions, convention business, and the volume of business at the hotel's restaurants.

In order to schedule the "right" number of employees occupying variable staff positions within the department, the executive housekeeper should develop a staffing guide.

The Staffing Guide

A **staffing guide** is a scheduling and control tool that enables the executive housekeeper to determine the total labor hours, the number of employees, and the estimated labor expense required to operate the housekeeping department when the hotel is at specific occupancy levels.

Developing a Staffing Guide for Room Attendants. The following sections present a step-by-step procedure for developing a staffing guide for day-shift room attendants at the fictional King James Hotel, a 250-room property providing mid-range services.

Step 1. The first step is to determine the total labor hours for positions that must be scheduled when the hotel is at specific occupancy levels. This can be calculated by using **productivity standards.** Let's assume that the productivity standard for day-shift room attendants at the King James Hotel is approximately 30 minutes (.5 hours) to clean one guestroom. Given this information, we can calculate the total number of labor hours required for day-shift room attendants at various hotel occupancy levels.

For example, if the hotel is at 90 percent occupancy, there will be 225 rooms to clean the next day (250 × rooms .9 = 225). It will take a total of 113 labor hours to clean them (225 rooms × 5 hours = 112.5 labor hours, rounded to 113). At 80 percent occupancy, there will be 200 rooms to clean (250 rooms × .8 = 200). It will take 100 labor hours to clean them (200 rooms × .5 hours = 100 labor hours).

Step 2. Determine the number of employees that must be scheduled to work when the hotel is at specific occupancy levels. The staffing guide expresses this number only in relation to full-time employees.

Since the productivity standard is .5 hours to clean one guestroom, a day-shift room attendant at the King James Hotel is expected to clean 16 guestrooms during an 8-hour shift. Given this information, the number of full-time, day-shift room attendants that must be scheduled at different occupancy levels can be determined by dividing the number of occupied rooms by 16.

For example, when the hotel is at 90 percent occupancy, there will be 225 rooms to clean the next day. Dividing 225 rooms by 16 indicates that 14 full-time, day-shift room attendants will be needed to clean those rooms (225 rooms ÷ 16 = 14.06, rounded to 14). When the hotel is at 80 percent occupancy, there will be 200 rooms to clean. It will take 13 room attendants to clean them (200 rooms ÷ 16 = 12.5 room attendants, rounded to 13).

The actual number of room attendants scheduled to work on any given day will vary depending on the number of full-time and part-time employees the executive housekeeper schedules to work. For example, when the hotel is at 90 percent occupancy, the executive housekeeper could schedule 14 full-time room attendants, or 10 full-time room attendants (each working 8 hours) and 8 part-time room attendants (each working 4 hours). Either scheduling technique would approximate the required total of 113 labor hours.

   Step 3. The third step in developing a staffing guide is to calculate the estimated labor expense required to operate the housekeeping department when the hotel is at specific occupancy levels. This can be done for day-shift room attendants at the King James Hotel simply by multiplying the total labor hours by the average hourly rate for room attendants. Assuming the average hourly rate to be $10.00, when the King James Hotel is at 90 percent occupancy, the next day's estimated labor expense for day-shift room attendants is $1,130 (113 total labor hours × $10.00/hour = $1,130) Regardless of the combination of full-time and part-time employees that is eventually scheduled to work, the total labor expense for day-shift room attendants should not exceed $1,130, when the hotel is at 90 percent occupancy.

Developing a Staffing Guide for Other Positions. Similar calculations must be made for other variable staff positions in the housekeeping department. Let's assume that the executive housekeeper at the King James Hotel has reviewed the productivity standards for other full-time positions and has determined that during one 8-hour shift:

- One floor supervisor is needed for every 80 occupied rooms, yielding a productivity standard of .1 (8 hours ÷ 80 occupied rooms = .1).

- One day-shift lobby attendant is needed to service public areas when 100 rooms are occupied, yielding a productivity standard of .08 (8 hours ÷ 100 occupied rooms = .08).

- One day-shift houseperson is needed for every 85 occupied rooms, yielding a productivity standard of .094 (8 hours ÷ 85 occupied rooms = .094).

- One afternoon-shift room attendant is needed for every 50 occupied rooms, yielding a productivity standard of .16 (8 hours ÷ 50 occupied rooms = .16).

- One afternoon-shift houseperson is needed for every 100 occupied rooms, yielding a productivity standard of .08 (8 hours ÷ 100 occupied rooms = .08).

   These productivity standards are multiplied by the number of occupied rooms to determine the total labor hours required for each position when the hotel is at specific occupancy levels. Dividing the total labor hours for each position by 8 determines the number of full-time employees that must be scheduled to clean the hotel the next day. Multiplying the required labor hours by an average hourly rate determines the estimated labor expense for each position. Exhibit 7 presents the complete staffing guide for variable staff positions at the King James Hotel.

Productivity Complications

In many hotels, the payroll in the housekeeping department equals one-fourth to one-third of the total payroll. Within the department, the payroll typically includes public space, supervisors, turndown staff, and room attendants, with the largest share belonging to room attendants.

Exhibit 7 Sample Variable Staffing Guide

King James Hotel										
Occupancy %	100%	95%	90%	85%	80%	75%	70%	65%	60%	55%	50%
Rooms Occupied	250	238	225	213	200	188	175	163	150	138	125
Room Attendants (A.M.)											
(Productivity STD = .5)											
Labor Hours	125	119	113	107	100	94	88	87	75	69	63
Employees	18	17	16	15	14	13	13	12	11	10	9
Expense	$1,250	$1,190	$1,130	$1,070	$1,000	$940	$880	$820	$750	$690	$630
Housepersons (A.M.)											
(Productivity STD = .08)											
Labor Hours	20	19	18	17	16	15	14	13	12	11	10
Employees	3	3	3	2	2	2	2	2	2	2	1
Expense	$200	$190	$180	$170	$160	$150	$140	$130	$120	$110	$100
Lobby Attendants											
(Productivity STD = .07)											
Labor Hours	18	17	16	15	14	13	12	11	11	10	9
Employees	3	2	2	2	2	2	2	2	2	1	1
Expense	$180	$170	$160	$150	$140	$130	$120	$110	$110	$100	$90
Inspectors											
(Productivity STD = .07)											
Labor Hours	23	21	20	19	18	17	16	15	14	12	11
Employees	3	3	3	3	3	2	2	2	2	2	2
Expense	$230	$210	$200	$190	$180	$170	$160	$150	$140	$120	$110
Room Attendants (P.M.)											
(Productivity STD = .09)											
Labor Hours	35	33	32	30	28	26	25	23	21	19	18
Employees	5	5	5	4	4	4	4	3	3	3	3
Expense	$350	$330	$320	$300	$280	$260	$250	$230	$210	$190	$180
Housepersons (P.M.)											
(Productivity STD = .07)											
Labor Hours	18	17	16	15	14	13	12	11	11	10	9
Employees	3	2	2	2	2	2	2	2	2	1	1
Expense	$180	$170	$160	$150	$140	$130	$120	$110	$110	$100	$90
Total Labor Hours	239	226	215	203	190	178	167	155	144	131	120
Total Expense	$2,390	$2,260	$2,150	$2,030	$1,900	$1,780	$1,670	$1,550	$1,440	$1,310	$1,200

When the budget is written for room attendants, management relies on certain productivity measures to project how many hours will be required and how many rooms can be cleaned per employee per shift. These numbers are based on the size of the guestroom, the presence of patios, kitchens, whirlpool tubs, or double bathrooms, or the standard of care expected.

When the budget is approved, the housekeeping manager must pay close attention to house counts and must schedule accordingly. Even managers who are excellent at scheduling must be prepared to cover extra rooms at any time due to absenteeism or increase of house count. However, extra room cleaners too frequently will cut into profits. These aren't the only complications.

Trainees/Turnover. A housekeeping manager cannot expect a new person to complete a full load on the first day or even during the first week of his or her employment. But there must be benchmarks to measure the trainee's productivity progress. Most hotels will expect one hundred percent productivity within two to four weeks.

Often the human resources department pays for the trainee's orientation to the hotel, but usually the cost of training the new employee must be borne by the housekeeping department. When the housekeeping department does carry the training payroll, remember that assigning any individual less than the number of budgeted rooms will affect the productivity of the entire department negatively.

A housekeeping manager must evaluate employee performance within the probationary period and address employees who are not producing at the required rate.

Send Backs. Room attendants who are routinely sent back to correct items they missed during their first cleaning of the room are a definite negative effect on productivity. As with trainees, room attendants who cannot meet the standards of the hotel should not be retained. The cost of checking behind them is too great.

Meetings. If the human resources department picks up the payroll for ongoing training and meetings, or if housekeeping has a separate budget line for such things, the housekeeping manager may feel more free to have morning, weekly, or monthly meetings. However, if a one-half hour meeting means one less room accomplished per room attendant, the housekeeper is challenged to cover this time somehow. The best housekeeping managers have very brief daily morning meetings but use different means to communicate other topics. For instance, printed memos handed out with paychecks, posters on bulletin boards, or one-on-one conversations while helping to make a bed.

Messy Rooms. When a room attendant finds a "trashed" room, more time is required for cleaning. A supervisor or public space person can assist the room attendant to help him or her stay on schedule. Also, the room attendant might cut corners in a normal room to still complete the daily assignment. Too many trashed rooms in one section will cost productivity.

Since weekend guests generally create messier rooms than weekday business guests, a smart manager can plan ahead to have the trashed room stripped of garbage and linen but held over to be cleaned the following day. (Weekends generally have late check-outs, so plan ahead with a flexible start-time schedule for cleaners.)

Suites. In the big picture of hotel occupancy, a suite is one room. But on the housekeeping assignment sheet, a suite could very well be the equivalent of two or three rooms in labor hours required for cleaning. This conflict will definitely affect productivity and should be addressed in future budgeting processes. Since generally more revenue is achieved for a suite, it is only fair to assign proportionately more labor for cleaning.

Late Check-Outs and Room Changes. Many large hotels will staff a second shift to care for late check-outs and room changes. These large hotels budget for a fixed number of hours per night for base staff and a variable additional amount of hours for busy nights. With the fixed hours, many leftover tasks of the day can be handled.

Smaller hotels without a second shift will keep track of late check-outs and room changes. They might always have one room attendant work a later shift than the rest.

Many small hotels depend on their housekeeping manager to pick up the late check-outs and room changes. This is acceptable only if the other tasks assigned to this manager can be accomplished within a reasonable work period.

Maintenance Rooms. Engineers, painters, and maintenance people constantly make repairs in guestrooms. Typically, they put the room out of order while they are working. The property management system is programmed to roll out-of-order rooms to dirty so that housekeeping is notified to check the room. The best hotels have excellent communication between engineering and housekeeping: the worker alerts housekeeping to exactly how much labor (if any) will be required to make the room ready.

Show Rooms. Generally, the sales department likes to set special guestrooms aside each day for use as show rooms for prospective group clients. Although these rooms may not be occupied, they still require a minimum of once-a-day touch up by housekeeping.

Review Daily Assignments. One other important, but perhaps hidden, source of productivity loss is rooms found dirty that do not show revenue. Most hotels perform a daily check of clean/vacant rooms. Sometimes, rooms that should be vacant are found to have been used. Although this may be the result of late check-outs or room changes, there are other causes that should be examined. For instance, perhaps a guest was registered, but the front office recorded a different room number. In this case, there will also be a room found clean that shows occupied on the housekeeping report. Another cause of rooms found dirty is unauthorized employee use. Perhaps an employee slipped into a vacant room for a nap or to watch television. Or worse, perhaps a bell attendant or a night auditor is selling rooms and pocketing the cash.

To ensure that these kinds of unauthorized uses are not occurring, the executive housekeeper should check each room attendant's and supervisor's work assignments at the end of the day. If "found dirty" rooms appear on the work sheets but do not appear on the occupancy report, investigate the cause.[2]

Developing Employee Work Schedules

Occupancy forecasts generated by the rooms division are used in conjunction with the staffing guide to determine the "right" number of employees to schedule each day for every position in the housekeeping department. Executive housekeepers have found the following tips helpful when developing employee work schedules:

- A schedule should cover a full workweek, which is typically defined as Sunday through Saturday.

- Schedules should be posted at least three days before the beginning of the next workweek.

- Days off, vacation time, and requested days off should all be indicated on the posted work schedule.

- The work schedule for the current week should be reviewed daily in relation to occupancy data. If necessary, changes to the schedule should be made.

- A copy of the posted work schedule can be used to monitor the daily attendance of employees. This copy should be retained as part of the department's permanent records.

Alternative Scheduling Techniques. Alternative scheduling, as its name implies, involves a staffing schedule that varies from the typical 9:00 A.M. to 5:00 P.M. workday. Variations include part-time and flexible hours, compressed work schedules, and job sharing.

Part-time employees. Part-time employees may include students, young mothers, or retirees who for various reasons are unable to work full-time hours. Employing part-time workers can give businesses extra scheduling flexibility. It can also reduce labor costs, because the benefits and overtime costs usually decrease.

Flexible work hours. Flexible work hours, or **flextime,** allow employees to vary the times at which they begin and end workshifts. Certain hours of each shift necessitate the presence of all employees. The rest of the shift can be flexible, allowing employees to determine for themselves when their shifts begin and end. Of course, the executive housekeeper must make sure that each hour of the housekeeping day is covered. The benefits of flextime include heightened staff morale, productivity, and job satisfaction. Moreover, the property will be more attractive to quality employees.

Compressed work schedules. Compressed work schedules offer housekeeping employees the opportunity to work the equivalent of a standard workweek in fewer than the usual five days. One popular arrangement compresses a 40-hour workweek into four 10-hour days. Compressed work schedules are usually inflexible, but many employees prefer inflexible hours for four days with an extra day off per week to flexible hours for five days. Primary benefits from the employer's viewpoint include enhanced recruiting appeal and employee morale, and reduced absenteeism.

Job sharing. In job sharing, the efforts of two or more part-time employees together fulfill the duties and responsibilities of one full-time job. The workers involved usually work at different times, but some overlap of work hours is desirable so that the workers can communicate. Job sharing may alleviate department turnover and absenteeism and increase employee morale. In addition, the department profits, because, even if one job-sharing partner leaves, the other usually stays and can train the incoming partner.

Motivation

Management in any organization is responsible for creating a work environment that fosters the professional growth and development of its employees. This includes providing training, guidance, instruction, discipline, evaluation, direction, and leadership. If management fails to perform these basic functions, employees may become passive, critical, and indifferent to organizational objectives. Such feelings manifest themselves in absenteeism, poor productivity, and high turnover.

A major challenge facing hospitality managers is motivating employees. Current changes in the labor market and the high cost of employee turnover demand that organizations seek ways to retain good employees. One way to accomplish this objective is to practice effective motivational techniques.

What Is Motivation?

Hundreds of definitions probably exist for the term **motivation.** For the purpose of this chapter, motivation can be described as the art of stimulating a person's interests in a particular job, project, or subject to the extent that the individual is challenged to be continually attentive, observant, concerned, and committed. Motivation is the end result of meeting and satisfying those human needs associated with feeling a sense of worth, value, and belonging to an organization or department.

Methods of Motivating Employees

Managers can select a number of ways to motivate employees. The end result should be that an employee's perception of his or her value and worth has increased from engaging in a particular activity. Employees who make a positive contribution to the success of an operation and receive recognition and praise for their efforts will more than likely be motivated, top performers. The following section suggests a number of motivational techniques.

Training. One surefire way to motivate employees is to get them involved in an effective training program. Training sends a strong message to employees. It tells them that management cares enough to provide the necessary instruction and direction to ensure their success with the organization. Training significantly reduces the frustration employees may feel when they do not have a clear-cut idea of what they are doing—or the proper tools and supplies to do the job well. Effective training educates employees about the job itself and about the use of any necessary tools and supplies. Managers should take the time to invest in employee training since it can result in employees who are more productive, efficient, and, essentially, easier to manage.

Cross-Training. Cross-training simply means teaching an employee job functions other than those he or she was specifically hired to do. Cross-training has many advantages—both for the employee and the manager. From the employee's perspective, it prevents feeling locked into a particular job and allows him or her to acquire additional work skills. From the manager's perspective, it increases flexibility in scheduling. Cross-trained employees become more valuable to an organization or department because they can perform many job functions instead of just a few. Cross-training can be a valuable motivational tool and can remove many of the obstacles associated with an employee's growth and advancement.

Recognition. Positive guest comments and repeat business reflect a staff that works together to satisfy guest needs. Managers should relay this type of information to the staff as recognition for a job well done. Graphs and charts are also effective motivators, since they provide staff with visual cues of achievements and progress. Written room inspection reports are also powerful motivators. Room attendants with high scores may be recognized through a room-attendant-of-the-month program or some type of financial reward.

Communication. Communication is a key to any motivational program. Keeping employees informed about goings-on in the department and property will reap positive results. Employees who are aware of events taking place feel a greater sense of belonging and value than those who are not.

Developing a department newsletter is an excellent way to keep lines of communication open. Some properties allow housekeeping employees to develop the newsletter and provide their own articles. Write-ups might be job related or personal, including such topics as:

- Promotions.
- Transfers.
- New hires.
- Resignations.
- Quality tips.
- Special recognition.
- Employee-of-the-month.
- Birthdays.
- Marriages.
- Engagements.
- Births.
- Potlucks.
- Upcoming parties.

A bulletin board provides a place to post schedules, memorandums, and other pertinent information in a clear, easy-to-understand manner. Bulletin boards

Retaining Staff through Recognition and Incentives

Many hotels are now facing a severe shortage of room attendants and are scrambling to retain the employees they have. The best way to reduce turnover is to keep employee satisfaction high. Here are some ideas.

Throughout the Day

Don't forget to provide the basic tools required for employees to get their jobs done. Regular inventories should be taken to ensure par levels of linens and chemicals are maintained. Employees also need training and visual aids to help them understand the work expected of them. Provide uniforms that look neat and fit well. Communicate with the staff at morning meetings; tell them about arrivals, departures, groups in-house, VIPs, and hotel goals. One-on-one, spend time listening to them about their families, their work needs, and their dreams.

Employees like schedules they can count on, including regular days off. If a hotel manager has to ask an employee to work overtime, it should be just that, a request. Part-time and weekend room attendants should be hired so that regular staff can have at least one weekend day off. When possible, carry dirty rooms to the next day to stabilize staffing.

Keep Work Exciting

Many hotels provide incentive points that can be cashed in for merchandise or hotel benefits. Some of the criteria used might include a month without an accident, high comment-card scores, perfect attendance, and proper appearance. Some hotels give room attendants incentive points based on room inspections or zero complaints about guestrooms. It's a good idea for a general manager to walk into a guestroom and reward the room attendant in cash for excellent work.

Other perks that require very little and yet mean so much to employees include birthday cards mailed to their homes, an employee newsletter with family pictures and notes, a cold soda on a hot day, a candy bar on a busy day, personalized note cards for them to leave messages for their guests, colorful bulletin boards, being called by name, a greeting of "Good morning" or "Good night," and a sincere "Thank you."

Most hotels have employee-of-the month programs. The housekeeping manager should nominate a department member every month. Even if he or she does not win, the recognition is important.

Lost and found can be a fun motivator for employees. If guests have not claimed items according to the hotel's guidelines, let the room attendants keep the items they have found. Some hotels permit room attendants to keep aluminum cans collected from guestrooms.

Have Fun after Work

Employee retention is dependent on recognition. It's that simple. Recognition for consistently excellent work can be fun and inexpensive. One hotel took room attendants bowling. With a department composed of Vietnamese, Cambodian, Laotian, Chinese, Hispanic, and American employees, most had never held a bowling ball or had never seen the game played. The afternoon was filled with laughter,

(continued)

Cthe Rooms
CHRONICLE®

(continued)

challenge, exchanges of "Bravo," and lots of support. The cost was minimal, and they continued talking about their games for months.

Source: Mary Friedman, *The Rooms Chronicle*®, Volume 3, Number 3, p. 4.
For subscription information, call 866-READ-TRC.

are most effective when they are in an area accessible to all employees and when employees are told to view the boards daily.

Incentive Programs. Employees in almost every organization need special appreciation for the work they perform. Sometimes a simple thank you demonstrates sincerity when an employee's performance meets or exceeds expectations. Other times, it's not enough. An **incentive program** is one of the most effective methods of rewarding and recognizing employees who excel in their jobs. Several basic guidelines should be considered when developing incentive programs. Managers should:

- Develop an incentive program that is appropriate for the department or organization.

- Outline the specific goals and objectives for the program.

- Define the conditions and requirements that employees must meet in order to receive the recognition and rewards.

- Brainstorm a variety of rewards and get the necessary approvals if financial expenditures are involved.

- Determine the date and time to begin the program. Make sure every employee participates and make it as much fun for them as possible.

Incentive programs offer special recognition and rewards to employees based on their ability to meet certain conditions. Among the rewards managers may consider offering are:

- Commendation letters.

- Certificates of appreciation.

- Cash bonuses.

- Pictures taken with the general manager and the department head that will be posted in public and back-of-the-house areas.

- Recognition dinners, potlucks, or picnics.

- Dinners for two in the hotel's restaurant.

- Gift certificates.

- Complimentary suites for a weekend in company-owned or -operated hotels in nearby cities or states.

the Rooms
CHRONICLE®

Keep 'em Going With Lots of Rewards

When a manager is running absolutely dry for new ideas for keeping employees energized, there's nothing better than an afternoon at a book store to roam the shelves. One great paperback book is called *"1001 Ways To Reward Employees"* by Bob Nelson (Workman Publishing Company: NY, 1994.) How can a manager reward an employee for a job well done? Here are some ways:

- Perform the least desirable work task for a day.

- Buy a huge ugly old bowling trophy from a garage sale and use it as a pass-around award—"You really bowled us over!"

- Tie balloons all over the cart of a room attendant with an excellent inspection.

- Post a flip-chart near the employee entrance and write thank you's and success stories for all to see.

- Offer sit-down massages for free in the employee cafeteria all day after a successful property inspection.

- Invite an hourly employee to represent the hotel at a Chamber of Commerce meeting.

- Rent a sports car for an employee to drive for a week.

- Hire a photographer to take employee family pictures in the ballroom one day.

- Create a party kit for employees to take home for children's birthdays: signs, candles, table linen, favors, balloons, and, of course, a cake.

- Name something after an employee for a week: The Edna Polaski Employee Cafeteria, the V.J. Patel Hotel Laundry.

- Buy a classified ad in the local paper to express thanks.

- Give cash bonuses.

Nelson writes that 95 percent of American workers consider a cash bonus a positive and meaningful incentive. Sixty-three percent also appreciate merchandise. But the best managers know that 100 percent of employees appreciate a thank you. The more creative it is, the more it is appreciated.

Source: *The Rooms Chronicle®*, Volume 8, Number 3, p. 5.
For subscription information, please call 866-READ-TRC.

- Special parking privileges for 30 days.

- Recognition plaques.

Incentive programs vary in structure and design and are an excellent way to award exceptional performance beyond the paycheck. Properties should develop and establish incentive programs that result in a "win-win" situation for the employee, the guest, and the company. The program should be challenging and create a spirit of competition among the staff.

Building Room Attendant Allegiance to Guests

Many years ago, the room attendant was viewed only as someone to clean a room. Now, the room attendant is one of the most important entities in the hotel.

Housekeeping managers must make certain that room attendants understand that it is not the owner, vice president, general manager, or executive housekeeper who pays his or her salary. It is the guest. If the guests aren't happy, they won't return. If guests don't return, the hotel isn't busy. If the hotel isn't busy, there are no hours for room attendants.

Clean Rooms

Clean rooms are the number one priority. If a guest checks in to what he or she considers a dirty room, nothing else about the stay will overcome that negative impression of the hotel. Make sure the room attendant understands the importance of taking pride in maintaining quality in his or her workplace. Other actions to encourage responsibility and help ensure clean rooms are:

- Give personalized cards to each room attendant, perhaps including a photo, with which to welcome each guest.
- Assign cleaning sections that do not change frequently.
- Allow personalization of the room, perhaps chair or lamp placement, or towel arrangement.

Communication

Room attendants must understand how to communicate with the guest. If there is a language barrier, the manager should have laminated translation cards for each employee. Universal symbols exist for many of the basic requests a guest might have, such as towels, shampoo, or blankets.

- Procedures must be set for handling guest requests for items such as rollaways or irons promptly.
- Proper etiquette and formal speech must be observed when interacting with guests: "Yes, ma'am," "Please," "May I help you," and "Thank you." Proper grooming is also essential.
- If a guest asks a room attendant to come back later, he or she should inquire about what time would be convenient. The response should be written on the assignment sheet and honored.

Follow-Up

Room attendants must be required to follow up on guest requests. For example, if a guest asks not to be disturbed until after 10 a.m., the room attendant must relay this request to supervisors and other appropriate employees. Or, if a guest requests to have his or her room cleaned by 8 a.m., the manager should allow the room attendant to adjust the work schedule to accommodate that request.

Cross-Training

Managers should create situations to allow the room attendant to see the guest from other perspectives. During slow times, a room attendant should spend one

C the Rooms HRONICLE®

(continued)

day at the front desk so that he or she understands the guest's expectations of the hotel as well as the front desk staff's need to have rooms clean when the guest arrives. Conversely, the front desk staff must spend time cleaning rooms to understand the room attendant's perspective of trying to turn rooms quickly.

Informative Meetings

Short daily meetings with room attendants are important. Telling them what groups are arriving or departing, how the hotel performed yesterday, or what VIPs are expected can help them be more involved in the total efforts to please the guests. Other things that can be done at the meeting include the following:

- Invite a salesperson to talk about their heads-in-beds philosophy.

- Invite the general manager to read the great comment letters the hotel has been receiving.

- Invite a regular guest to explain how wonderful it is to stay in a spic and span room.

Hotel companies that make it mandatory for each employee to attend a guest service training program ensure that their employees understand the importance of serving the guest with excellence. Housekeeping managers who go further-who weave relationships between their room attendants and the guests-build loyalty with employees and create lifetime guests.

Source: Wanda Kittles, *The Rooms Chronicle®*, Volume 4, Number 3, p. 4.
For subscription information, please call 866-READ-TRC.

There is an element of surprise associated with incentive programs. A pre-shift meeting or departmental staff meeting presents the best opportunity to announce the award recipients. Such announcements should be planned and presented in such a way that the recipients feel very good about themselves and the work they do.

A good incentive program:

- Recognizes and rewards exceptional performance.

- Motivates employees to be more productive.

- Demonstrates the organization's commitment to guest satisfaction by providing a work environment that encourages employees to take care of the guest.

- Says thanks for a job well done.

Performance Appraisals. Employees need to know where they stand at all times so they can feel secure in their job and know that the boss is pleased with their performance. Consider what happens in the following scenario:

> Sam applied for the position of night cleaner in a large downtown convention hotel. During his interview with Mr. Doe, the executive housekeeper, he demonstrated enthusiasm about the job and promised that the

hotel would be more than pleased with his services. Mr. Doe hired Sam to work specifically on tile floors during the night shift.

Sam worked very hard to please his boss. But even though the floors were beautiful and shined, there was a small problem: in the three months' time since he'd been hired, Sam hadn't heard one comment from his immediate supervisor. One day he decided to disguise his voice and call the hotel. When connected to housekeeping, he asked to speak with Mr. Doe.

"Mr. Doe," he said when the executive housekeeper answered, "My name is Jim. I noticed several months ago that you ran an ad in the newspaper for a night shift cleaner."

"Yes, we did," Mr. Doe replied.

When "Jim" asked if the position had been filled, the executive housekeeper said that it had.

"Tell me," Sam asked, "how is the employee doing?"

"The young man is doing a wonderful job," Mr. Doe said enthusiastically. "He's improved the appearance of the hotel 110 percent. He has excellent floor-care skills and everyone likes him. He's productive and gets the job done effectively every night he works."

"That's wonderful," Sam said.

"Why do you ask?" inquired Mr. Doe.

Pausing, Sam continued with a friendly laugh, "Because this is Sam—the guy you hired. I just wanted to see how I was doing!"

Interaction between an employee and a manager can affect an employee's perception of the job and an employee's self-image. A performance appraisal is one of the best tools a manager can use to increase employee motivation and morale. The reason this particular technique is so effective is that it:

- Provides the employee with formal written feedback on his or her job performance.

- Identifies strengths and weaknesses in performance and provides plans for improvement.

- Gives the manager and the employee the opportunity to develop specific goals and due dates to accomplish the desired results.

- Recognizes and rewards outstanding performance through possible promotions, wage increases, and additional responsibilities.

- Reveals—in some cases—whether that employee is actually suitable for the position.

An effective performance appraisal focuses on an employee's job performance and the steps the employee can take to improve job skills and performance. Appraisals should be fair, objective, and informative. While it is important to point out weaknesses, it is not necessary to dwell on them. The experience should be positive for the employee. When the process is completed, the employee should clearly understand the areas in which he or she is doing very well and those in which he or she needs to improve.

There are numerous methods and techniques for evaluating employee performance. Every organization must tailor its own appraisal program to meet particular needs and goals.

Endnotes

1. Adapted from David E. Morrison and Michael L. Sullivan, *The Rooms Chronicle®*, Volume 14, Number 4, pp. 1, 3. For subscription information, please call 866-READ-TRC.

2. Adapted from Mary Friedman, *The Rooms Chronicle®*, Volume 6, Number 4, pp. 4–5. For subscription information, please call 866-READ-TRC.

Key Terms

alternative scheduling—Scheduling staff to work hours different than the typical 9:00 A.M. to 5:00 P.M. workday. Variations include part-time and flexible hours, compressed work schedules, and job sharing.

coaching—An extension of training that focuses on accomplishments, job duties, and factual observations by providing positive or redirective feedback to an employee.

cross-training—Teaching employees to fulfill the requirements of more than one position.

employee referral program—A department or property program that influences employees to encourage friends or acquaintances to apply for a position. Such programs usually reward employees who refer successful candidates to the property.

external recruiting—A process in which managers seek outside applicants to fill open positions, perhaps through community activities, internship programs, networking, temporary agencies, or employment agencies.

fixed staff positions—Positions that must be filled regardless of the volume of business.

flextime—Flexible work hours that allow employees to vary the times at which they begin and end workshifts.

four-step training method—A training model used to implement an on-the-job training program. The four steps are prepare, present, practice, and follow up.

incentive program—A program offering special recognition and rewards to employees based on their ability to meet certain conditions. These programs vary in structure and design and are a way to award exceptional performance beyond the paycheck.

internal recruiting—A process in which managers recruit job candidates from within a department or property. Methods available include cross-training, succession planning, posting job openings, and keeping a callback list.

job analysis—Determining what knowledge each position needs, what tasks each position needs to perform, and the standards at which the employee must perform the tasks.

job bidding—The result of employees signing a list indicating that they are interested in applying for posted positions.

job breakdowns—A form that details how the technical duties of a job should be performed.

job knowledge—Information that an employee must understand in order to perform his or her tasks.

job posting—A formal announcement of a job opening.

motivation—Stimulating a person's interest in a particular job, project, or subject so that the individual is challenged to be continually attentive, observant, concerned, and committed.

performance appraisal—The process by which an employee is periodically evaluated by his or her manager to assess job performance and to discuss steps the employee can take to improve job skills and performance.

pre-recruitment process—Recruiting that takes place before advertisements or notices are posted. The process consists of a number of interrelated steps, beginning with defining job requirements and ending with evaluating recruiting methods.

productivity standard—An acceptable amount of work that must be done within a specific time frame according to an established performance standard.

recruitment—The process by which applicants are sought and screened concerning their suitability for positions.

scheduling—A process in which the appropriate number of employees are assigned to fulfill necessary duties and positions each workday.

staffing guide—A system used to establish the number of labor hours needed.

task list—A list identifying all the key duties of a job in the order of their importance.

variable staff positions—Positions that are filled in relation to changes in hotel occupancy.

Review Questions

1. What sources of labor will executive housekeepers be likely to draw upon to staff housekeeping departments?

2. What methods of recruiting would most benefit your department or projects?

3. What is the last step of the four-step training method, and why is it important?

4. What is the difference between fixed-staff and variable-staff positions?

5. What purpose does a staffing guide serve?

6. What are some alternative scheduling techniques?

7. Why do both properties and employees welcome cross-training? What are the benefits of cross-training to both properties and employees?

8. How could an incentive program be used as a motivational technique for housekeeping employees?

9. Performance appraisals are conducted for what reason(s)?

Case Study

Hiring Headaches in Housekeeping

Tim MacFarlane has been general manager for six weeks at the Executive Inn, a 200-room downtown property. While he's still learning about the property and its personnel, one department stands out in need of immediate attention: housekeeping. Rooms are not getting cleaned on time, shifts are running short-staffed, and the department is paying a lot of overtime to employees who stay late to try to catch up. This morning Mr. MacFarlane has called Helen Redman, the executive housekeeper, to his office for a meeting.

Helen has been the executive housekeeper at the hotel for 17 years. She has been plagued constantly by staffing shortages during those years. Not enough people want to work as room attendants, it seems. When she meets with Mr. Mac-Farlane, she tries to explain to him that constantly losing people and having to hire and train new employees is a fact of life in the housekeeping department. "It's hard to find people willing to work full time. Jesse will back me up on that."

"Let's have him join us," Mr. MacFarlane says, and has his secretary page Jesse.

Jesse Rodriguez, the hotel's human resources director, has been at the hotel almost as long as Helen. He tells Mr. MacFarlane that Helen is right, housekeeping is a hard department to staff. "You should see my advertising budget; I run an ad in the newspaper every week! No one applies. Every hotel in town is looking for room attendants."

"I may be new, but I know we've got to have good people to be the best we can be," Mr. MacFarlane replies. "I challenge you both to be creative. In a city of almost a million people, there have to be enough good people out there to staff our housekeeping department. I'm willing to do what I can to help. What kind of support do you need from me?"

Discussion Questions

1. How can Helen and Jesse be creative about recruiting top-notch people for the housekeeping department?

2. What kind of support should Helen and Jesse ask the general manager to provide?

The following industry experts helped generate and develop this case: Gail Edwards, CHHE, St. Louis, Missouri; Mary Friedman, Edina, Minnesota; and Aleta Nitschke, CHA, founder of *The Rooms Chronicle*®, Garfield, Minnesota.

Chapter 5 Outline

Par Levels
Linens
    Types of Linen
    Establishing Par Levels for Linens
    Six Steps to Perfect Linens
    Determining When to Change Linens
    Inventory Control of Linens
    Taking a Physical Inventory of Linens
Uniforms
    Establishing Par Levels for Uniforms
    Inventory Control of Uniforms
    Uniform Challenges
Guest Loan Items
    Types of Guest Loan Items
    Establishing Par Levels for Guest Loan
       Items
    Inventory Control of Guest Loan Items
Machines and Equipment
    Types of Machines and Equipment
    Establishing Par Levels for Machines
       and Equipment
    Inventory Control of Machines and
       Equipment
Cleaning Supplies
    Types of Cleaning Supplies
    Establishing Inventory Levels for
       Cleaning Supplies
    Inventory Control of Cleaning Supplies
Guest Supplies
    Types of Guest Supplies
    Establishing Inventory Levels for
       Guest Supplies
    Inventory Control of Guest Supplies
    Printed Materials and Stationery

Competencies

1. Define par, par levels, and par number. (p. 165)

2. Identify the challenges to inventory control for linens in a housekeeping operation. (pp. 165–184)

3. Describe how to establish par levels and inventory control for uniforms. (pp. 184–192)

4. Describe how to establish par levels and inventory control for guest loan items. (pp. 192–194)

5. Describe how to establish par levels and inventory control for machines and equipment. (pp. 194–196)

6. Describe how to establish par levels and inventory control for cleaning supplies. (pp. 196–199)

7. Describe how to establish par levels and inventory control for guest supplies. (pp. 199–207)

5

Managing Inventories

THE EXECUTIVE HOUSEKEEPER is responsible for two major types of **inventories**. **Recycled inventories** are those items that have relatively limited useful lives but that are used over and over again in housekeeping operations. Recycled inventories include linen, uniforms, guest loan items, and some machines and equipment. **Non-recycled inventories** are those items that are consumed or used up during the course of routine housekeeping operations. Non-recycled inventories include cleaning supplies, small equipment items, and guest supplies and amenities.

This chapter describes the types of inventories maintained by the housekeeping department and explains how par stock levels are established for each type of inventory item. This chapter also discusses important inventory control measures.

Par Levels

One of the first and most important tasks in effectively managing inventories is determining the par level for each inventory item. **Par** refers to the standard number of inventoried items that must be on hand to support daily, routine housekeeping operations.

Par levels are determined differently for recycled and non-recycled inventories. The number of recycled inventory items needed for housekeeping functions is related to the operation of other hotel functions. For example, the par level of linen depends upon the hotel's laundry cycle. The number of non-recycled inventory items a property needs is related to the usage rates of different items during daily operations. For example, par levels of particular cleaning supplies depend upon how fast they are depleted through routine cleaning tasks.

Inventory levels for recycled items are measured in terms of a **par number**— or a multiple of what is required to support day-to-day functions. Inventory levels for non-recycled items are measured in terms of a range between minimum and maximum requirements. When quantities of a non-recycled inventory item reach the minimum level established for that item, supplies must be reordered in the amounts needed to bring the inventory back to the maximum level established for the item.

Linens

Linen is the most important recycled inventory item under the executive housekeeper's responsibility. Next to personnel, linen costs are the highest expense in

the Rooms CHRONICLE®

Inventory Systems Can Control Costs

It's Friday afternoon—a quick check on supplies for the weekend, then—uh-oh, a scramble with vendors to locate that one necessary missing item. Sound familiar? Reduce this stress by taking inventories on a regular (weekly, monthly, quarterly) basis and maintaining par levels of stock.

The hardest part of taking inventory may be to get organized, but once a system is in place, it becomes easy to manage. One mark of an excellent executive housekeeper is the ability to maintain minimum supplies, yet never run short. Since supplies on a shelf represent dollars, a general manager appreciates department managers who keep their inventories as low as possible.

- Set up centralized storage areas for cleaning supplies, guestroom supplies, laundry supplies, etc. Secure these storage areas, giving access only to designated housekeeping personnel.

- Organize the items in a logical order, perhaps alphabetically, by vendor, or by size. Leave room for all items.

- List the items on the inventory in the order of storage. Include the vendor, the quantity per case, the price per item, etc., to make ordering a quick process. Note the sample inventory format below.

- Review specials which suppliers may offer. They often want you to buy excess cases in order to receive a price break. Study it carefully to ensure that it will not mean too many dollars "sitting on the shelf."

- When striving for minimum inventories, it is important to allow proper lead times. How much time passes from the moment the purchase order leaves the hotel until the product is received?

- Study shipping costs and other supplier add-ons. Some companies will ship at no charge when you order a specified unit number. Other companies will charge a few pennies more for the same item, but waive the shipping charge. Try to arrange for local distributors to give free delivery with a minimum purchase.

Remember to weigh all the factors: special pricing, lead time, shipping and freight cost, storage space, and consumption.

Sample Inventory Format

1. Count every item and record the number under "Beginning Inventory."

2. Select a responsible employee to record all items purchased and received. Before new items can be placed in storage, they must be recorded on the inventory as "Items Received This Period."

3. At the end of the month (or whatever time frame is used), again take inventory. Count every item in the storage room and record totals under "Total Items in Stock." Multiply each by its "Price per Item" and record under "Total Dollars in Stock."

(continued)

Sample Inventory Format

1- Item	2- Vendor/ Phone #	3- Items Per Case	4- Price Per Item Price Per Case	5- Beginning Inventory	6- Items Rec'd This Period	7- Total Items In Stock	8- Total $ In Stock	9- # Of Items Used	10- $ Value Of Items Used	11- Items Used Per Occ Rm	12- Forecast Item Needed

(continued)

4. From the sum of "Beginning Inventory" and "Items Received this Period," subtract "Total Items in Stock." This will be the number of items consumed during the month (Number of Items Used). Multiply each by its "Price per Item" and record results under "Dollar Value of Items Used."

5. Divide "Number of Items Used" by the number of rooms occupied during this inventory period to get "Items Used per Occupied Room." This figure can now be multiplied by the number of rooms expected for the next period to yield the "Forecast Item Need," and orders can be placed.

Source: Mary Friedman, *The Rooms Chronicle®*, Volume 1, Number 2, p. 4.
For subscription information, call 866-READ-TRC.

the housekeeping department. Careful policies and procedures are needed to control the hotel's inventory of linen supplies. The executive housekeeper is responsible for developing and maintaining control procedures for the storage, issuing, use, and replacement of linen inventories.

Types of Linen

The executive housekeeper is generally responsible for three main types of linen: bed, bath, and table. Bed linens include sheets (of various sizes and colors), matching pillowcases, mattress pads or covers, and duvets. Bath linens include bath towels, hand towels, specialty towels, washcloths, and fabric bath mats. The housekeeping department may also be responsible for storing and issuing table linens for the hotel's food & beverage outlets. Table linens include tablecloths and napkins. Banquet linens are a special type of table linen. Due to the variety of sizes, shapes, and colors, banquet linens may need to be kept separate from other restaurant linens in the inventory control system. The basic principles and procedures for managing linen inventories also apply to blankets and bedspreads.

Establishing Par Levels for Linens

The first task in effectively managing linens is to determine the appropriate inventory level for *all* types of linen used in the hotel. It is important that the inventory level for linens is sufficient to ensure smooth operations in the housekeeping department.

Shortages occur when the inventory level for linens is set too low. Shortages disrupt the work of the housekeeping department, irritate guests who have to wait for cleaned rooms, reduce the number of readied rooms, and shorten the useful life of linens as a result of intensified laundering. Although housekeeping operations run smoothly when inventory levels are set too high, management will object to the inefficient use of linen and to the excessive amount of cash resources tied up in an overstock of supplies.

The par number established for linen inventories is the standard stock level needed to accommodate typical housekeeping operations. One par of linens equals the total number of each type of linen that is needed to outfit all guestrooms one time. This is a number that has recently been revised upward in those hotels that have adopted triple sheeting and extra pillows for each bed. One par of linen is also referred to as a **house setup**.

Clearly, one par of linen is not enough for an efficient operation. Linen supplies should be several times above what is needed to outfit all guestrooms just once. Two par of linens is the total number of each type of linen needed to outfit all guestrooms two times; three par is the total number needed to outfit all guestrooms three times; and so on. The executive housekeeper must determine how many par of linens are needed to support efficient operations in the housekeeping department. When establishing a par number for linens, the executive housekeeper needs to consider three things: the laundry cycle, replacement linens, and emergency situations.

The hotel's laundry cycle is the most important factor in determining linen pars. Most hotels change and launder much of their linens daily (the old "wash everything, every day" rule has been relaxed in many hotels—usually with guest approval—because of environmental concerns). At any given time, large amounts of linen are in movement between guestrooms and the laundry. When setting an appropriate linen inventory level, the executive housekeeper must think through the laundry cycle in terms of the hotel's busiest days—when the hotel is at 100 percent occupancy for several days in a row. If housekeeping manages an efficient on-premises laundry operation, the laundry cycle indicates that housekeeping should maintain three par of linens: one par—linens laundered, stored, and ready for use today; a second par—yesterday's linens, which are being laundered today; and a third par—linens to be stripped from the rooms today and laundered tomorrow. Executive housekeepers also need to figure in guest requests for extra linens, and linens for rollaway beds, sofa beds, and cribs.

The laundry cycle in properties that use an outside commercial laundry service will be somewhat longer than the cycle in properties with their own in-house laundry operation. The frequency of collection and delivery services from the commercial laundry will affect the quantities of linen the property needs to stock. The more frequent the service, the less stock is needed to cover the times when the hotel's linen is being transported to and from the laundry service. A typical turnaround time for a commercial laundry is 48 hours. In this situation, the executive housekeeper may need to add another par of linen to cover linens that are in transit between the hotel and the outside linen service. In addition, some commercial laundries will not collect and deliver on weekends. This means that extra stock will be required to cover those days.

The second factor to consider when establishing linen par levels is the replacement of worn, damaged, lost, or stolen linen. Since linen losses vary from property to property, executive housekeepers will need to determine a reasonable par level for linen replacement based on the property's history. The need for replacement stock can be determined by studying monthly, quarterly, or annual inventory reports in which losses and replacement needs are documented. A general rule of thumb is to store one full par of new linens as replacement stock on an annual basis.

Finally, the executive housekeeper must be prepared for any emergency situation. A power failure or equipment damage may shut down a hotel's laundry

Exhibit 1   Sample Par Calculation

This is a sample calculation of how to establish a par stock level for king-size sheets for a hotel that uses an in-house laundry operation and supplies three sheets for each of the property's 300 king-size beds.

300 king-size beds × 3 sheets per bed = 900 per par number

One par in guestrooms	1	×	900	= 900
One par in floor linen closets	1	×	900	= 900
One par soiled in the laundry	1	×	900	= 900
One par replacement stock	1	×	900	= 900
One par for emergencies	1	×	900	= 900
Total number				4,500

4,500 sheets ÷ 900 sheets/par = 5 par

operation and interrupt the continuous movement of linens through the laundry cycle. The executive housekeeper may decide to hold one full par of linens in reserve so that housekeeping operations can continue to run smoothly during an emergency.

Therefore, the hotel's laundry cycle, linen replacement needs, and reserve stock for emergencies suggest that a minimum of five par of linen should be maintained on an annual basis. Properties using an outside commercial laundry service will need to add a sixth par to cover linens in transit.

Exhibit 1 illustrates a sample par calculation for the number of king-size sheets required for a hotel with 300 king-size beds. In this example, 4,500 king-size sheets should be in the hotel linen inventory at all times. Similar calculations need to be performed for every type of linen used in the hotel.

Six Steps to Perfect Linens

What exactly does "perfect linens" mean? The bedcover, blankets, sheets, pillowcases, and mattress pad must be absolutely spotless and free of rips or tears. There must be no indication from the bed linens that other guests have used them.

Housekeeping management must ensure that there is no breakdown along the linen processing cycle that permits stained or torn linen to be used in guestrooms.

First Step—Notice and Treat Stains. The first line of defense against stained linen is the room attendant. As the bed is stripped and linens are gathered from the bathroom, room attendants visually inspect used linens. Properly trained employees will:

- Notice stains. They keep a close eye on linens while removing them from the bed and from the bathroom.

- Separate stained linen. They place stained linen in a designated bag on their cart.

Housekeeping managers also need to review their room attendant incentive programs to ensure that their rewards for speed don't create a lack of attention to stained linen. The incentive program ought to include rewards for identifying and treating stains as well.

This first line treatment has two additional benefits: stains that are treated early have a better chance for complete removal; and the stain removal spray has time to work while the linen is being transported from the room attendant's cart to the laundry.

Second Step—Laundry Awareness. The laundry is the second line of defense against stained linens. Laundry employees handle the linen several times while processing-sorting, loading the washer, moving linen from washer to dryer, removing from dryer, and folding. Each handling provides an opportunity to spot stains or tears.

Third Step—Repair or Remove. Linen is considered unacceptable for guest use when it is stained, torn, or threadbare. Standards help laundry personnel identify unacceptable linens.

Many hotels instruct employees to place torn or threadbare linens in a special hamper for supervisors to review later. Some properties create rag stock from torn linen while others reclaim torn linen by having the seamstress perform minor repairs. While repair of a torn hem could result in an acceptable pillowcase, stitching a rip in the center of a bed sheet would not be acceptable.

Housekeeping staff must specially handle stained linen. Professional laundry chemical vendors provide stain removal kits with training materials. Most laundries contain a stain-removal area for pre-treating and soaking. Typically, one member of the laundry staff is specially trained as a stain-removal expert. This person processes the stained items set aside by the rest of the staff, first by pre-treating and then using special wash cycles.

Most laundry chemical companies routinely set hotel wash formulas to clean 97 to 98 percent of the daily soil. Why not 100 percent? In theory, increasing the amount of time and chemical necessary to clean 100 percent would not be economical for the hotel. The additional chemicals required would expose the linen to unnecessary abuse and premature aging.

Therefore, approximately two to four percent of every wash load will need re-processing. (This is not true for large, highly automated laundries that compensate for the lack of human contact with the linen by increasing the power of the wash chemical program.)

A special re-wash formula, including stronger chemicals and longer cycles, is used by hotel laundries for reprocessing. Such a "second wash" will generally remove the soil not purged by the first wash. A stain-removal expert may evaluate items that remain stained after a second wash.

Fourth Step—Investigate Reoccurrences. When the laundry staff identifies rips or stains occurring frequently or in the same places, further investigation should occur. Often, in cooperation with the engineering department, a source of the problem can be found.

For instance, perhaps a rough edge in the laundry chute is causing linen tears. Perhaps a washing machine's chemical injector is clogged, causing incomplete chemical action. Perhaps an ironer is dripping grease or wax, causing linen stains. Or perhaps staff somewhere in the hotel is abusing the linen. When the laundry staff finds the source of a problem, they can make changes to eliminate the damage to linens.

Fifth Step—Management Support. Hotel management must whole-heartedly support the concept of perfect linens. When soiled and torn linens are removed from inventory, additional purchases will be necessary. Adequate pars of linen are an essential element to a successful stain removal program. If room attendants have to choose between placing a stained sheet on a bed or waiting until late in the afternoon to get another sheet, generally they will use the stained sheet. Or if the laundry staff has only two-par of bath towels, they will be reluctant to remove stained towels from service.

If the hotel has not had an ongoing program to identify unacceptable linens, a sizable percentage of linen may be targeted for removal, resulting in a large expense to replace linens. However, when the program is in place, early identification of stains will increase the reclaim percentage, and early detection of the sources of problems will reduce the amount of linen damaged.

Sixth Step—Ongoing Inspections. How can a manager know that perfect linens are being provided for guests?

- Guests may tell management through comment cards.

- Contracted quality assurance inspectors may write up reviews of their visits. Or, managers may find out for themselves through guestroom and laundry inspections—a part of any successful hotel operation.

- Room inspections should frequently include tearing down the guest bed to inspect the linens.

- Laundry inspections should include a review of prepared linens before they are released for use.

When stained or torn linens are found, all the related processes should be examined. If employee carelessness is to blame, disciplinary action should be taken.

It takes commitment from everyone—owners, managers, and employees—to ensure that guests receive perfect linens.[1]

Determining When to Change Linens

Should a hotel change bed sheets in occupied rooms every day? Or is it acceptable to change sheets every second or third day? Riding the coat-tails of the environmental movement in the United States, some hotel managers are asking housekeeping executives to implement a policy to change sheets on alternate days. With increasing hotel rates and increased guest expectations on one side of the debate, and increased environmental awareness and responsibility and increased profitability on the other, can hotels create a win-win situation for everyone?

In a recent survey, half of all respondents stated they already had a policy of changing bed sheets on the second or third day of a guest's stay. Since all types of hotels were represented in the group of respondents, the decision does not seem to be based upon price levels.

Hotel management must decide what policy to adopt. Some hotels will change sheets in every occupied room every day. Others will place a card on the bed or the doorknob and let the guest decide, the guest can indicate on the card if he or she wants the sheets changed. Still other hotels will mandate sheet changing only every second or third day of a stay and will not inform the guest or request guest input.

There are only a few pros and cons to weigh in this policy decision. First and foremost, what does the guest want? Since serving the guest in a way that will create return business and positive word-of-mouth publicity is a hotel staff's first mission, it is important to measure guest feedback on this question. Although hotels that currently change sheets on alternate days report that they do have some guest complaints, the majority of their guests support the effort to limit the use of water and chemicals to help protect the environment. Hotels must obtain feedback from *their own* guests.[2]

Beyond just seeking feedback, research[3] has shown that the message on the cards left for guests may influence their choice to reuse their linens or not. The most effective message tested (resulting in about a 45 percent participation rate by guests) stated, "We're doing our part for the environment. Can we count on you? Because we are committed to preserving the environment, we have made a financial contribution to a non-profit environmental protection organization on behalf of the hotel and its guests. If you would like to help us recover the expense while conserving natural resources, please reuse your towels during your stay."

Second, what procedures can be implemented to ensure that the room-cleaning process remains acceptable and invisible to guests while retaining quality controls?

Third, will the cost savings in labor, chemicals, or energy cover any extra costs in guest complaints, labor to redo early departures, or other efforts to maintain the system? Some hotels have realized as much as a 1.8-room improvement in productivity per day, but many report no change.

Some operational issues include:

1. Housekeeping employees who have been trained to change bed-sheets daily or face disciplinary action or termination must be retrained. Although most room attendants are happy to avoid changing every bed, communicating *which* beds should be changed and which should not can be difficult. Hotels with employees who speak little or no English face an even greater communication challenge.

2. A system must be devised to record which beds have been changed and which have only been made up. The system must include a

code that identifies the status of *each* bed in two-bed rooms. This system must provide for guests who were supposed to stay over, but departed early. The room attendant (if he or she is still on the property) should return to the room to make the bed again, but with fresh linen. If the room attendant has departed for the day, someone else must remake the bed before the room can be noted as clean and vacant.

3. If bed linen is changed only on alternate days, establish a system to note on the room attendant's daily assignment sheet which beds to change that day. This can be accomplished when the person preparing the morning report reviews the arrival date of each stayover and highlights or marks the rooms in which to change sheets.

4. Since some hotels give the guest a card to indicate whether he or she wants the linen changed, the room attendant must mark the assignment sheet as to whether the sheets were changed. If a guest returns to the room after business hours and complains that the bed was not changed, the staff member on call will have to quickly remake the bed and later check the day's records to investigate the complaint.

5. Room attendants must learn *how* to decide whether to change sheets on days when it is not required but when the sheets are not acceptably clean. For instance, would makeup on a sheet mean changing the linen? What if there were an ink pen mark on the pillowcase?

6. Because most hotels want the guest to feel like the bed has been changed, they tuck the bedspread over the pillows. A different approach might be to leave the bed with a turndown look that is welcoming to guests but also signals staff that the sheets have not been changed.

7. If the staff chooses to let the guest decide whether to have the sheets changed, the language of the information card or door hanger should be carefully selected. There are groups that will provide collateral materials, such as the American Hotel & Lodging Association. One card offered in AH&LA's materials is designed for towels and asks guests to put the towel back on the rack if they are willing to use it again. The second card is for bed sheets. Usually, the cards are laminated for longer life and contain translations in English, French, German, Japanese, and Spanish.

The percentage of sheets left unchanged may vary among hotels, depending on the average length of stay and type of guest. If, for instance, the hotel's average length of stay is 2.8 days, and the policy is to change sheets every three days, in effect, the policy is to change sheets in checkouts only.

General managers want to know how this change in policy affects the bottom line. While room-cleaning productivity may remain relatively unchanged, some hotels project that linen life may be prolonged by 15 percent and outside laundry costs may be reduced by 9 percent. In fact, real savings come from the laundry. In a national survey conducted by Ecolab, the average cost of cleaning hotel guestroom linens is $0.232 per pound. These cost factors were compiled with laundries operating at maximum efficiency. Considering that a king sheet weighs about 1.8 pounds; a double sheet 1.2 pounds; and a pillowcase .3 pounds; there is a minimum potential savings of 3 pounds, or almost a dollar per room.

The most important factor is for the staff to be honest with themselves and the guests. Is saving the environment the issue? Or is it saving the bottom line? Guests may not appreciate a reduction in service if they do not see consistent environmental actions in other areas (such as compact fluorescent light bulbs, recycling bins, or motion sensors to control HVAC). Will guests stop staying at a hotel just because their sheets are not changed? Can we expect guests to ask during reservation calls, "Do you change your bed sheets every day?" Will we see advertisements with the tag line "We change sheets daily"? Probably not. In fact, if a hotel provides proper training, thorough operational procedures, and related environmental efforts, it can save many gallons of water, tons of detergent, and vast amounts of energy—and still please guests. *If* guests are supportive of the efforts, it is a win-win situation.[4]

Inventory Control of Linens

To effectively manage linen inventories, the executive housekeeper needs to develop standard policies that govern how and where linens will be stored, when and to whom linens will be issued, and how to monitor and control the movement of linens through the laundry cycle.

The executive housekeeper must cooperate with the laundry supervisor to maintain an accurate daily count of all linens sent to and received from the laundry. Effective communication with the laundry supervisor can help the executive housekeeper spot shortages or excessive amounts of linen.

Storage. Much of a hotel's linen supply is in constant movement between guestrooms and laundry facilities. Laundered linens should rest in storage for at least 24 hours before being used. This helps increase the useful life of linens and provides an opportunity for wrinkles to smooth out in permanent press fabrics. Linen is stored in the department's main linen room, in distribution rooms near the laundry, and also in floor linen closets for easy access by room attendants.

Linen storage rooms need to be relatively humidity-free and have adequate ventilation. Shelves should be smooth and free of any obstructions that could damage fabric, and should be organized by linen type. Sufficient room is required to prevent linens from being crushed or crowded. Linen storage rooms should be kept locked, and all standard key control procedures should be followed. Special security measures should be taken with new linens that are stored in the main linen room but have not yet been introduced into service.

Issuing. An effective method for controlling linen is to maintain floor pars for all floor linen closets. A **floor par** equals the quantity of each type of linen that is required to outfit all rooms serviced from a particular floor linen closet. Linen pars should

Exhibit 2   Sample Linen Control Form

Guestroom Linen to Laundry		
Date _____		
Item	**Color**	**Number**
Pillowcases	Ivory	
King Sheets	Blue	
Queen Sheets	Blue	
Twin Sheets	Ivory	
Bath Mats		
Bath Towels		
Hand Towels		
Washcloths		
Room Attendant _____		

be established and posted in each floor linen closet. Issuing procedures ensure that each floor linen closet is stocked with its par amount at the start of each day.

The occupancy report generated by the front desk can be used to determine linen distribution requirements for each floor linen closet. With information from this report, the executive housekeeper can create a linen distribution list that indicates how much linen is needed to bring each floor linen closet back up to par for the next day. This list functions as a requisition form for replenishing floor pars. The list is delivered to the laundry supervisor, who sets aside the required amount of clean linens and stores excess clean linens in the laundry distribution room.

Some hotels require room attendants to record the number of soiled linens, by type, that are removed from guestrooms and delivered to the laundry. Exhibit 2 is a sample worksheet that can be used for this purpose. The total number of linens removed from guestrooms should be consistent with the occupancy report.

At the end of the day shift, a member of the housekeeping evening crew restocks the floor linen closets with the linen set aside by the laundry supervisor.

This brings each floor linen closet back up to full par in preparation for the next day's work. Supervisors can spot-check floor linen closets to ensure that standard procedures have been followed. In this way, linens are issued daily only in the amounts needed to bring each floor linen closet up to its par level.

Special procedures are also required for linen that needs replacement. Any clean linen item that is judged unsuitable due to holes, tears, stains, or excessive wear should not be used in guestrooms. Nor should such damaged linens be placed in soiled linen hampers. Instead, room attendants should place damaged linens in a special discard container and hand-deliver them to the main linen room or housekeeping office. A special linen replacement request form should then be filled out detailing the type of linen involved, the nature of the damage, the linen closet in which it was stored, and the name of the room attendant who noted the damage. The laundry supervisor will increase the floor distribution count the next day to accommodate the need for replacement.

Clean but damaged linen should be held separately and delivered to the laundry supervisor (or other appropriate personnel) who determines whether it is unusable or whether it can be repaired. Careful records must be kept of all linen items that are condemned and discarded. Exhibit 3 shows a sample linen discard record that can serve as an important inventory control tool. The linen discard record should be kept in the laundry area and used by employees who sort damaged linens. The form provides columns for recording the specific types and numbers of discarded linen items. At the end of the accounting period, the form is dated and transferred to the executive housekeeper. The executive housekeeper reviews the record and transfers the totals to the master inventory control chart for linens when a physical inventory is taken. Automated/computerized systems may speed this process and provide easy access to historical data for forecasting, but the manual card system is the basis for success in this process.

Inventory control procedures for table linens should be designed in much the same way as for room linens. A par stock level of all table linens used in each food and beverage outlet should be established. Soiled linens should be counted nightly, and a list of items sent to the laundry should be prepared. Both the laundry supervisor and the executive housekeeper can use the list as a control and as an issue order for the next day. Each food and beverage outlet should be brought back up to its par level of table linens on a daily basis. Linen needs for special events can be noted on the nightly count sheet and included on the next day's delivery of table linen.

Taking a Physical Inventory of Linens

A physical inventory of all linen items in use and in storage is the most important part of managing linen inventories. A complete count should be conducted as often as once a month. At the very least, physical inventories should be taken quarterly. Typically, the physical inventory is taken at the end of each accounting month to provide the executive housekeeper with important cost-control information needed to monitor the department's budget.

As a result of regular physical inventories, the executive housekeeper has accurate figures on the number of all items in use, as well as those considered

Exhibit 3   Sample Linen Discard Record

LINEN DISCARD RECORD

HOUSEKEEPER'S INITIALS: _____

GENERAL MANAGER'S INITIALS: _____

PERIOD ENDING: _____

DATE	Bath Towels	Hand Towels	Wash-Cloths	Bath Mats	Shower Curtains	Double Sheets	King Sheets	Double Pillow-Case	King Pillow-Case	Double Pillow	King Pillow	Double Blanket	King Blanket	Double Mattress Pad	King Mattress Pad	Double Bed-Spread	King Bed-Spread	Crib Sheet		
Total Dis-carded																				

(continued)

Exhibit 3 Sample Linen Discard Record (Back of Page) *(continued)*

DISCARD METHODS			
ITEM	HOW DISCARDED	ITEM	HOW DISCARDED

COMMENTS: ____

____

____

____

____

____

BY: ______________________________
(EXECUTIVE HOUSEKEEPER)

Courtesy of Holiday Inn Worldwide

the Rooms CHRONICLE®

Housekeeping Logistics and Guest Service

They faced a challenge. Slow elevators were prompting guests complaints and costing the property repeat business. A team of employees at the beach hotel worked together to find a solution.

With representatives from the front desk, housekeeping, reservations, security, the switchboard, maintenance, and bell service, the team discovered that their own procedures were causing the elevator congestion. Porters were delivering linen when guests were trying to use the elevators. By rearranging work schedules to deliver supplies before 7 A.M., the elevators were made available for guests during prime morning hours.

But the team wasn't finished. Now they needed storage on each floor. Although closets were available, they were stuffed with miscellaneous hotel collectibles, such as accounting records and old sales brochures. The team got everyone involved in cleaning out the closets and volunteered their own time to reorganize the space and build shelves. They made it more fun by painting the areas according to each room attendant's personal preferences.

The general manager said, "When you add it up, it meant $84,000 to the hotel in increased guest satisfaction and improved staff productivity. The employee team deserves all the credit."

Source: *The Rooms Chronicle®*, Volume 2, Number 1, p. 5.
For subscription information, call 866-READ-TRC.

discarded, lost, or in need of replacement. This control is vital for maintaining a careful budget and for ensuring that the housekeeping department has adequate supplies to meet the hotel's linen needs. The need to replenish the hotel's linen supply is determined on the basis of each physical inventory.

Typically, the physical inventory is conducted by the executive housekeeper and the laundry supervisor working together. In large hotels, other housekeeping staff may be recruited to help count linen supplies. In most cases, the inventory is taken by staff members working in teams. One person calls out the count for each type of linen, while the other records the quantity on an inventory count sheet. It is not unusual for the hotel's controller or a representative of the accounting department to be involved in spot-checking counts and verifying the accuracy of the final inventory report. When the inventory is complete, a final report is sent to the hotel's controller or general manager for final verification and entry.

All linens in *all* locations must be included in the count. The executive housekeeper should plan to take the inventory at a time when the movement of linen between guestrooms and the laundry can be halted. This typically means that the inventory is taken at the end of a day shift after the laundry has finished its work, after all guestrooms have been made up with clean linens, and after all floor linen closets have been brought back to their par levels. All soiled linen chutes should be sealed or locked to avoid any further movement of linen.

The next step is to determine all the locations in the hotel where linens may be found. The executive housekeeper needs to take all possible locations into consideration, including:

- Main linen room.

- Guestrooms.

- Floor linen closets.

- Room attendant carts.

- Soiled-linen bins or chutes.

- Soiled linen in laundry.

- Laundry storage shelves.

- Mobile linen trucks or carts.

- Made-up rollaway beds, cots, sofa beds, cribs, etc.

The executive housekeeper should prepare a linen count sheet which can be used to record the counts for every type of linen in each location. Space should be allocated at the top of each count sheet for the date, location, and names of the staff members performing the count. Down the left side of each count sheet should be a list of every type of linen item to be counted. In making up the inventory list for the count sheets, the executive housekeeper should be sure to differentiate among all types, sizes, colors, and other linen features. In addition, the counting process will be quicker and easier if the inventory listing is organized in the same way as linen items on storage shelves. Exhibit 4 shows a sample count sheet for recording linen quantities in a floor linen room and on corresponding room attendant carts.

Using the count sheets, two-person teams can conduct the physical inventory at each linen location. One person should count and call out the number corresponding to a particular kind of linen, while the other person records the quantities in the appropriate place on the standard count sheet. A third person might spot-check counts to ensure accuracy.

After the counting process is completed and all standard count sheets have been filled out, the executive housekeeper should collect the sheets and transfer the totals to a master inventory control chart. Once the totals are collected, the results of the inventory can be compared to the previous inventory count to determine actual usage and the need for replacement purchases.

Exhibit 5 shows a sample master inventory control chart for linens. Across the top of this master control chart in the first part of the form is a line for listing all inventory items in the hotel's linen supply. This listing should correspond to the listing of linen items used on the standard count sheets.

The second line on the chart identifies the date that a physical inventory was last taken. The executive housekeeper should transfer linen counts from previous inventory records onto this line.

The third line on the chart is used to record the numbers of new linen items received since the last physical inventory. These figures should include both

Exhibit 4   Sample Linen Count Sheet

Inventory Count Sheet Guestroom Linens				
Name	**Date**		**Floor**	
Item	**Closet**	**Cart 1**	**Cart 2**	**Cart 3**
Pillowcases				
King-Size Sheets				
Queen-Size Sheets				
Twin Sheets				
Bath Mats				
Bath Towels				
Hand Towels				
Washcloths				

unopened linen shipments received and new linen items that have already been put into use.

The fourth line totals the on-hand quantities from the previous physical inventory (line 2) and the quantity of newly received linen items (line 3).

Next, line five is used to record the number of linen items known to have been discarded since the last physical inventory. These totals can be obtained by examining the linen discard record (see Exhibit 3).

By subtracting the numbers of discarded linens (line 5) from the subtotals (line 4), the executive housekeeper knows the totals for each linen type that can be expected to be on hand. These expected totals are recorded on line 6.

The second part of the form provides spaces for recording the totals counted for every linen type at each of the linen locations. These totals are obtained by tallying and transferring the totals listed for each linen type on the standard count sheets. The quantities of each linen type counted at every location are totaled on line 15 of the form. These figures represent the actual on-hand quantities for every type of linen in the hotel's inventory.

The third part of the form helps the executive housekeeper analyze the results of the physical inventory. By subtracting the counted totals for each linen item

Exhibit 5 Sample Master Inventory Control Chart

HOUSEKEEPING LINEN INVENTORY

| LOCATION NAME: _____ | | PREPARED BY: _____ |
| LOCATION NUMBER: _____ | GENERAL MANAGER'S INITIALS: _____ | INVENTORY DATE: _____ |

PART I											
1. ITEM											
2. LAST INVENTORY DATE ( )											
3. NEW RECORD											
4. SUBTOTAL 2 + 3											
5. RECORDED DISCARDS											
6. TOTAL 4 − 5											
PART II											
7. STORAGE ROOM											
8. STORAGE ROOM											
9. STORAGE ROOM											
10. LINEN ROOM											
11. LAUNDRY											
12. ON CARTS											
13. IN ROOMS											
14. ON ROLLAWAYS, CRIBS, ETC.											
TOTAL ON HAND 15. ADD 7 THROUGH 14											
PART III											
16. LOSSES 6 − 15											
17. PAR STOCK _____ TURNS											
18. AMOUNT NEEDED 17 − 15											
19. ON ORDER											
20. NEED TO ORDER 18 − 19											

Courtesy of Holiday Inn Worldwide

(line 15) from the corresponding expected quantities (line 6), the executive house-keeper can determine an accurate number lost for each linen item. This figure is recorded on line 16. Linen loss is the variance between the totals from the previous inventory (plus new purchases received) and the results of the current inventory. While the physical inventory reveals the losses for linen items, it does not show *why* these losses occur. If the variance between expected and actual quantities is high, further investigation is needed.

After each physical inventory, the executive housekeeper should make sure that the par levels are brought back to the levels originally established for each linen item. The par numbers for each linen type are recorded on line 17. These figures represent the standard numbers of each linen type that should always be maintained in inventory. By subtracting the actual quantities of each linen type on hand (line 15) from the corresponding par levels (line 17), the executive house-keeper can determine the quantities of each linen type that are needed to bring inventories back up to par. These amounts are recorded on line 18. By subtracting quantities of linen items that are on order but not yet received (line 19), the execu-tive housekeeper knows precisely how many of each linen type still needs to be ordered to replenish the par stock. This figure is recorded on line 20. As a result of the physical inventory, the executive housekeeper can determine which linens and what amounts of each type are needed to replace lost stock and maintain established par levels.

The completed master inventory control chart should be submitted along with the linen discard record (Exhibit 3) to the hotel's general manager. The general manager will then verify and initial the report before transferring it to the account-ing department. The hotel's accounting department will provide the executive housekeeper with valuable cost information related to usage, loss, and expense per occupied room. This information is useful in determining and monitoring the housekeeping department's budget.

Physical inventories of table linen used by the food & beverage department should be handled in much the same way as room linens. The same general rules and procedures should be followed—and the same general forms used. Inventory lists should be prepared for each food and beverage outlet—including banquet facilities—that itemize all types, sizes, and colors of table linens the hotel uses. The inventory should be taken when the movement of table linens to and from the laundry can be halted and each food and beverage outlet is fully stocked to its established par levels. By following the same procedures used for room linens, the total inventory of table linens can be calculated, and the executive housekeeper can determine the need for replacement stock.

Uniforms

Many hotel departments have uniformed staff members. Sometimes, each depart-ment is responsible for maintaining its own inventory of uniform types and sizes. More typically, the housekeeping department stores, issues, and controls uniforms used throughout the property. This can be a very complex responsibility—especially in a large hotel with many uniforms of varying types, quantities, and sizes.

Establishing Par Levels for Uniforms

Determining the number of types and sizes of uniforms to have on hand can be very difficult. Among the factors that can make the task a true challenge are varying department needs, uneven distribution of size requirements, unavoidable turnover, and unpredictable damage from accidents.

The executive housekeeper can ensure that a sufficient supply of all types of uniforms is placed into service based on information supplied by the department heads. To establish par levels for all types of uniforms, the executive housekeeper needs to know how many uniformed personnel work in each department, what specific uniforms they require, and how often uniforms need cleaning. Sizing problems can be handled by having uniforms tailored when they are first issued to new employees.

Another factor to consider in establishing par levels is the turnaround time required by the laundry for processing uniforms. The par level for uniforms depends, in large part, on how frequently uniforms need laundering. If, for example, uniforms are laundered only once a week, each employee would have to be issued five uniforms weekly. In this unlikely situation, each employee would exchange five soiled uniforms for five cleaned uniforms at the beginning of each week. Counting the uniform worn on the day of the exchange, this would require maintaining a par of eleven uniforms for each employee.

A more likely scenario would involve laundering uniforms on a daily basis and exchanging a clean uniform for a soiled one each day. In this situation, a minimum of three par of uniforms would be required. One par is worn by employees, another is turned in to be cleaned, and a third is issued in exchange. Daily washing would be more practical and less costly than laundering uniforms on a weekly basis. Every employee would have a spare clean uniform (in addition to the one being worn) in case it was needed during the day. Uniform rooms could be staffed for daily uniform exchanges at the beginning of each shift.

The executive housekeeper may decide that five par is more reasonable. This would keep an adequate supply on hand for new employees and for replacing uniforms for existing personnel. Five par would also ensure that an adequate supply of spare uniforms was available during the day in case of accidents or unexpected damage.

The executive housekeeper may also want to consider the needs of uniformed personnel across various departments. Since front-of-the-house employees are continuously in the public eye, their need to be neat and clean all day is particularly important. The executive housekeeper may want to maintain higher uniform pars for front office employees, since they may need to change uniforms more frequently. Similarly, chefs, stewards, and other kitchen personnel may need two daily changes of uniforms, since cleanliness is important for hotel staff dealing directly with food.

In many hotels, the employees themselves are responsible for the maintenance of the uniforms. However, since the law may require that employees be compensated for uniform cleaning, a hotel may be able to reduce costs by processing uniforms through the property's own laundry service.[5]

C the Rooms
HRONICLE®

Whether for Costumes or Uniforms, Pick a System

It's a typical day in Central Florida: warm, sunny, thousands of people moving around. At Walt Disney World in Orlando there are also thousands of cast members completing or beginning their shifts. *Costumed* cast members. Disney has about 40,000 cast members per week, more than 7,000 costume items, all coming and going. A dirty costume is turned in, a clean one retrieved. Cinderella, Mickey Mouse, the park maintenance crew—everyone is totally costumed.

The enormous Disney costume operation is controlled with barcodes or radio chips and scanners. But, what about the Acme Hotel with 150 employees? What choices should the Acme's managers make for operating a uniform system? Should they set up a manual system, an automated system, or have no system at all?

Manual System

In a manual system, all the tracking and reporting is done by pen and paper. For instance, an employee might come to the uniform room area with a dirty uniform, sign a log-in sheet, identify his or her employee number to the uniform room attendant, and receive a clean uniform.

Here's an example of how a manual system works:

- Each employee is fitted for three to five complete uniforms, which are numbered to match the employee.

- Each employee receives a numerical sticker for the back of the employee ID card.

- By showing the employee ID card with the number sticker, the employee is issued one clean uniform.

- When that uniform is dirty, the employee returns it to the uniform room, records the uniform number on the dirty uniform tracking sheet, and receives a clean uniform in exchange.

- If the employee does not need a clean uniform at that moment, the employee is given a ticket to surrender at a later date to receive a clean uniform.

- If an employee needs a clean uniform but does not have either a dirty uniform to turn in or a ticket, the clerk will research prior paperwork to ascertain whether the employee legitimately should have a clean uniform issued or whether a uniform has been lost from the system.

There are challenges to a manual system that include lack of employee cooperation and human error and inefficiency. These often add up to significant costs in time and money.

Automated System

Technology can almost entirely automate the hotel uniform room processes. Typically, a barcode or radio chip is installed in each uniform piece so that it can be easily scanned as it moves through the dirty-to-clean-to-issuance-to-retrieval cycle.

The computer is linked to human resources, purchasing, accounting, and other departments so that instant, real-time information is available. For instance, if an

(continued)

employee is terminated, human resources can update the system and accounting can check whether all uniforms have been returned before issuing a final paycheck. The computer system can monitor par levels and notify management when an order should be placed. Purchasing can check the inventory levels of all uniform types before issuing replacement orders. Housekeeping can e-mail a list for the contract cleaner to justify the return of all pieces sent for laundering. Automation simplifies the uniform-handling systems.

No System at All

Some major hotel corporations have adopted the "no system at all" system, meaning that the hotels do not maintain a daily process of issuing and retrieving uniforms. When new employees are hired, they are issued their complete set of uniforms, usually two to five sets. Throughout their employment, staff must maintain and be accountable for their own uniforms. When employees retire, resign, or are fired, they are responsible for returning all uniforms. Sometimes known as home care, this non-system has eliminated huge, expensive, bureaucratic nightmares within hotel uniform departments.

The home-care system can work when set up appropriately with human resources and accounting for the proper compensation issues of requiring employees to clean their own uniforms. Employees must be counseled to maintain the uniforms neatly, and measures should be established for daily appearance. Unless a uniform needs to be repaired or replaced, the hotel staff does not deal with the garment between the time of the employee's hiring and termination.

"In a ten-month survey, home-care garments were in better condition than hotel-care uniforms," says Paula Reno, consultant to the uniform industry. "This may be related to the strong chemicals and washing action of commercial laundries versus the more gentle care of home machines." This lengthened uniform life extends the hotel's bottom line.

Health issues are another important aspect of the home-care system. The hotel is liable for skin rashes or other chemical reactions that may result from commercial cleaning. Such liability is not present when employees are responsible for their own cleaning processes.

Another Variation

Some prominent casino companies instruct their employees to purchase their uniforms on a buy-out system with the casino. For instance, a table-game dealer will purchase the black pants and white shirts that are required and take care of the daily maintenance. At termination, the employee keeps the uniforms. In this scenario, the hotel does offer to repair rips and tears, but the employee maintains responsibility for the uniform.

When considering which system to use for uniform programs, hotels should project the up-front costs of establishing the system as well as on-going maintenance costs. With the goal of presenting employees whose appearances support the ambiance of the hotel, managers must choose carefully.

Source: Gail Edwards, CHHE, *The Rooms Chronicle*®, Volume 7, Number 6, pp. 4–5. For subscription information, call 866-READ-TRC.

Exhibit 6   Sample Uniform Inventory Control Card

> **Uniform Inventory Card**
>
> Name _____   Date _____
>
> Position _____   Dept. _____
>
> Uniform _____   No. _____
>
> I understand that the uniform(s) issued me are my sole responsibility and that if I should change positions or leave the company, I will return the complete uniform(s). I authorize the company to deduct from my paycheck the cost of any missing items or the cost of repairing uniforms damaged from other than normal wear. I further understand that these uniforms will *NOT* be taken off hotel property at any time.
>
> Employee
> Signature _____
>
> Housekeeping
> Signature _____   Date _____

Inventory Control of Uniforms

All uniforms should be issued and controlled through the uniform room. Adequate storage space should be provided for stocking the different sizes and quantities of uniforms. In addition, the room should be well-organized. Uniforms should be categorized by department so as to save time and hassle when employees exchange uniforms at the start and end of each shift. The executive housekeeper needs to establish specific operating procedures for uniform control. A system should be in place for receiving uniforms for cleaning and for providing both the uniform room and laundry with a record of items received. The uniform room attendant should submit to the laundry a daily record of uniforms to be cleaned that day.

For control purposes, most hotels establish a policy whereby a clean uniform is issued only when exchanged for a soiled one. In some hotels, uniforms will be issued to an employee only with a special request form signed by a department manager.

Employees should receive a receipt when they turn in a uniform. If an exchange system is used, the employee receipt may simply be a clean uniform. When uniforms are first issued, all employees should acknowledge in writing the number and type of uniforms received. A card similar to Exhibit 6 can be used for this purpose and kept on file for each uniformed employee. Such uniform-control cards can be kept by the uniform room itself or by the employee's assigned department. Some properties also keep uniform records in the employee's personnel file. A master record of all uniforms issued to employees should be kept by the housekeeping department.

At the time of issue, the employee assumes full responsibility for the custody, care, and control of the uniform. When an employee leaves the hotel's employ, he or she is expected to turn in all uniforms in his or her custody. The uniform room attendant should submit a statement to the accounting department that states whether the employee has properly returned all issued uniforms or the employee's final paycheck should be adjusted to compensate for uniforms that have not been returned.

The executive housekeeper is responsible for seeing that all uniforms are kept in a state of good repair. Uniformed employees themselves are most aware of the repairs that their uniforms need. A simple repair request form could be used to notify the uniform room attendant. The employee should complete the form when exchanging a soiled uniform for a clean one, and the uniform room attendant should hang the repair tag where the clean uniform is usually hung. Information on the repair tag may include employee name, number, department, uniform item, repair request, date received, and the date the uniform is needed. When the soiled uniform is returned from the laundry, the repair tag alerts the uniform room attendant to send the uniform for repairs. If the damaged uniform is beyond repair, the executive housekeeper should condemn the uniform and put a replacement uniform into service. As in the case of discarded linens, records for discarded uniforms should be kept by the executive housekeeper.

All uniforms should be inventoried at least on a quarterly basis. The same general principles that pertain to taking physical inventories of linen supplies apply to counting uniforms. The uniform room should be closed to prevent movement of uniforms. Records should be consulted that account for uniforms issued to employees' custody and for uniforms that have been taken out of service due to damage. All locations, including employee locker areas, need to be considered when counting uniforms. Uniform inventories are generally taken with the help of all hotel departments.

The executive housekeeper can collect accurate counts of each type and size of hotel uniform by using a uniform inventory control form such as the one shown in Exhibit 7. By comparing current on-hand quantities with those from previous inventories, the executive housekeeper can determine the number and kinds of uniforms that have been lost or discarded. In this way, quarterly uniform inventories can be used to establish an annual usage rate. The number and kinds of replacement uniforms needed can be determined by comparing on-hand quantities to the par level for each type of uniform.

Uniform Challenges

Although necessary for the pristine presentation of hotel staff, uniforms are the bane of most housekeeping operations. Hotels and casinos throughout the industry too often allow the organization and care of uniforms to be an afterthought, resulting in a tremendous loss to their bottom line.

Here are just a few of the problems encountered with uniform systems:

- Employees need a clean uniform when there are none available.

Exhibit 7 Sample Uniform Inventory Control Form

QTY.	SIZE	DESCRIPTION	UNIT COST	QTY.	SIZE	DESCRIPTION	UNIT COST
		UNIFORMED SERVICES				FRONT DESK	
		Bell Staff Jacket				F.O. Male Suit	
		Bell Staff Pant				F.O. Male Vest	
		Bell Staff Tie				F.O. Male Tie	
		Parking Att. Jacket				F.O. Female Suit	
		Parking Att. Pant				F.O. Female Scarf	
		Parking Att. Jac-Shirt					
		Parking Att. Tie					

- Employees don't return uniforms.
- Department managers terminate employees without retrieving uniforms.
- It is difficult to inventory what employees supposedly have been given.
- Management is unwilling to buy a three-par for every position.
- Cleaning bills are outrageous.
- Cleaners damage uniforms.
- Vendors are back-ordered in required sizes.
- Vendor billing is inaccurate.
- Frustrated department managers take back responsibility for uniform disbursement.
- A seamstress is unavailable for repairing damaged uniforms.
- The storeroom is full of discontinued (but still included in inventory) uniforms.

There are ways to reclaim a uniform system that is in shambles:

- *Prepare an employee roster.* Compare a current employee roster to whatever listings or employee cards were previously used in the uniform system. Move terminated employee names to a separate file and add new hires to the system. Ideally, this is done in the property management system.

- *Take inventory.* Count items in the uniform room, at the laundry, and in the employees' possession. Record totals by department, color, description, style number, and size in the hotel's inventory database program. Include uniforms that have been damaged or discontinued due to change of style (used and/or never worn), but mark these separately on the inventory.

- *Verify sizes.* Ensure that the sizes recorded for each employee are accurate. Measure to verify when necessary.

- *Assign numbering system to items.* If a new numbering system is needed, keep it simple and track each uniform separately through the life of the uniform. Assign each department a letter A to Z. For example, housekeeping might be assigned "H." Then assign each item a number. For instance, if there are 100 room attendant shirts and 100 pants, the shirts might be numbered H01 to H100 and the pants numbered H101 to H200. If more shirts are ordered in the future to exceed the 100 in inventory, they can be assigned a number above the highest assigned item number. If a damaged shirt is removed from inventory, a new shirt can be assigned the number of the damaged shirt.

- *Place order.* Review the inventory against current needs for uniforms and compile an order for new items. To extend the life of the uniforms and to ensure the employees always look fit regardless of turnaround shift assignments or accidental spills/tears, order a 3-par of uniforms.

- *Have fittings.* When the uniforms arrive at the property, schedule each employee for an individual fitting.

- *Issue uniforms.* Keep the records for issuing simple. Spreadsheet and database programs work very well. Each employee should have an entry listing the items they have been issued. For example:
  Shaw, Bill: banquets, employee number 43867
  - black pants, size 36, style #566030-90, issued 8/1/08—B213, B214, B215
  - white shirt, size L, style #102115-38, issued 8/1/08—B424, B425, B371

Each uniform item should also have an entry that includes the details of the item. It is in this entry that repairs to the item are listed as well as future employee assignees, and the date it is removed from inventory due to wear and tear.

All items should be included on a master inventory form with the total items on hand for each type of uniform. Columns can include department, color, item description, style number, vendor, size, price, number in circulation, number in storage, total quantity, par required, number discontinued due to damage, and number discontinued due to change of style.

- *Eliminate unusable uniforms.* When uniform items have been damaged or the item is no longer the recommended uniform for the position, the item is called discontinued. Housekeeping managers work with the accounting department to remove these items from inventory on a timely basis. There are many possibilities for old uniforms:

  - Call a rag company. They often pay for discarded uniforms and linens to be processed into rags for resale.
  - Donate the items to charity.
  - Allow employees to purchase items that might be usable for personal wear.[6]

Guest Loan Items

As a service to guests, hotels provide a variety of equipment that travelers commonly need. This equipment is loaned to guests upon request and at no charge. The housekeeping department is typically responsible for maintaining the inventory of guest loan items, responding to loan requests, and tracking the items to make sure they are returned.

Types of Guest Loan Items

The types of items that a hotel makes available for guests to borrow vary from hotel to hotel. Such items typically include refrigerators, sewing kits, air purifiers, white noise machines, cribs, bed boards, computer and phone charge cords, and voltage adapters. Other items kept on hand for guests may include vases, curling irons, a variety of pillows and blankets, specialty communication and alarm devices for guests with disabilities, rollaway cots, and tables and chairs.

Establishing Par Levels for Guest Loan Items

The types of guest loan items maintained at the hotel generally depend upon the hotel's level of service and the typical needs of its clientele. The quantities maintained in inventory depend on the size of the hotel and the anticipated volume of guest requests. The frequency of guest requests for specific items varies according to the type of hotel, the hotel's occupancy level, the arrival/departure pattern of the day, and the types of guests staying in the hotel at any given time (business, leisure, extended-stay, etc.). The executive housekeeper needs to work with the hotel's general manager and marketing department to identify the kinds and quantities of guest loan items that need to be maintained. The executive housekeeper is responsible for maintaining an adequate supply to meet guest requests.

Exhibit 8   Sample Log for Guest Loan Items

Date	Room No.	Loan Item Requested	Call Received		Delivered		Picked Up	
			Time	Who	Time	Who	Time	Who

Inventory Control of Guest Loan Items

The executive housekeeper should develop procedures for maintaining accurate inventory records of guest loan items, responding to guest requests, tracking items on loan, and ensuring that borrowed items are returned.

The executive housekeeper needs to maintain a complete and accurate list of all guest loan items stored in the housekeeping department. For each item, the inventory record should reflect the item's name, manufacturer, supplier or vendor, date of purchase, purchase cost, warranty information, and storage location. The record should also note the par number for each item. This master inventory record of guest loan items should be kept up-to-date as worn or broken items are taken out of service and new items are put into use.

Specific policies and procedures for issuing guest loan items—and for tracking items in use—must be developed. Procedures will be shaped by the nature of the property's usual clientele and the history of loss or theft of loan items. Whatever method is used to track on-loan items, a balance must be reached between the need to control hotel losses and the need to provide good guest service.

The executive housekeeper can monitor requests for loan items by maintaining a log such as the one shown in Exhibit 8. This log records the type of item loaned; the guest's room number; and the times of the item's request, delivery, and return. The guest's expected check-out date can also be noted to help track items such as special pillows and bed boards that are generally loaned for the duration of a guest's stay. By using this kind of log, the executive housekeeper can determine what items guests request most, the times particular items are requested, and how long different items remain on loan. This log also helps the executive housekeeper track the locations of items in use and ensure that all items are returned.

Some hotels require that guests sign a receipt for loan items. In this situation, housekeeping employees who deliver loan items to guestrooms should record the type of item, guest name and room number, and the date and time of delivery on the receipt. The employee should also obtain the guest's signature. In addition, some hotels require that guests pay a deposit. The amount of the deposit will vary according to the type of item. In this situation, housekeeping employees who deliver loan items to guestrooms should explain that the amount of the deposit will be charged to the guest's folio in the event the loaned item is not returned. Some hotels require that prepaying guests with no charge privileges pay a cash deposit for loaned items. In this situation, the guest should be required to come to the front desk to pay the deposit. Under no circumstances should housekeeping personnel or bell staff receive or handle cash deposits.

Receipts for deposits should be taken to the front desk for placement in the guest folio, but the amount should not be posted at this time. When guest items are returned, it is important that the receipt be removed from the guest's folio and immediately destroyed. If this is not done, guests may be charged for a loaned item even though it was returned.

Several other procedures should be considered standard for controlling guest loan items. Whenever possible, any guest requesting items should receive a follow-up call to confirm that he or she received the items and to see if any further assistance is needed. When items are delivered to guestrooms, the guest should be asked to call housekeeping later that same day to arrange for pickup. If housekeeping does not hear from the guest for several hours, the guest should be called to check on the status of the loan item. In most cases, items should not be loaned out overnight.

Each guest loan item should be checked regularly to see that it is in proper working condition and safe for guest use. Each item should also be tested on the day it is loaned to ensure that the guest will be able to use it for its intended purpose. Worn, damaged, or broken items should be replaced on an as-needed basis.

Machines and Equipment

The executive housekeeper is responsible for seeing that members of the housekeeping department have the proper tools to carry out their assigned tasks. These tools include major pieces of machinery and equipment to clean guestrooms and public areas. All machines and equipment must be maintained in proper working order so employees may use them safely and effectively. The executive housekeeper needs to develop systems and procedures for controlling the hotel's inventory of machines and equipment.

Types of Machines and Equipment

A variety of machines and equipment is used by the housekeeping staff on a daily basis. Room attendant carts are among the more basic—and more visible—pieces of equipment that employees will use. Employees may also use a number of types of vacuum cleaners for specific cleaning tasks. These include room vacuums, backpack vacuums, corridor vacuums, space vacuums, electric brooms, and wet vacuums. Carpet shampoo equipment, pile lifters, and rotary floor scrubbers are also essential to proper floor care. In addition, laundry equipment, sewing machines, and a variety of trash-handling equipment may be maintained and controlled through the housekeeping department.

Establishing Par Levels for Machines and Equipment

The number and types of equipment that need to be maintained in-house will depend on the hotel's size and cleaning needs. The executive housekeeper may decide to rent—rather than purchase—equipment that is highly specialized or infrequently needed. Equipment needs are also affected by the number of guestrooms and their locations, the kinds of floor and wall coverings, and the size of the laundry operation.

With the help and advice of the hotel's general manager, the executive housekeeper can determine the machines and equipment—and the number of each kind—that must be maintained in inventory. The executive housekeeper should also keep a complete list of all machines and equipment stored in the housekeeping department.

Inventory Control of Machines and Equipment

Controlling the department's stock of major machines and equipment involves maintaining accurate inventory records, establishing issuing procedures, and ensuring that storage areas are secure.

An effective way to control inventories is to use an inventory card system. An inventory card should be prepared for each piece of major machinery or equipment used in housekeeping. The card should specify the item name, model and serial numbers, manufacturer, supplier from whom it was purchased, date of purchase, purchase cost, expected life span (usually measured in terms of work hours), warranty information, and local service contact information. These records help determine when a piece of equipment needs replacement. The card should list all the accessories that can be used with the machine and that are owned by the hotel. Any spare parts (hoses, belts, etc.) that are kept in inventory should also be listed. The proper storage or work areas where the equipment, accessories, and spare parts are kept should be indicated on the card.

Repair logs should be kept and filed along with the corresponding inventory cards. Repair logs should record the date the item was sent for repair, a description of the problem, who performed the repairs, what repairs were made, which parts were replaced, the cost of the repairs, and the amount of time that the equipment was out of service. These records help pinpoint problems that should be addressed with the service representative. The executive housekeeper can also use these records to estimate repair costs and downtime during the useful life of the machine or equipment.

After issuing procedures have been established, equipment logs should be maintained to record all equipment that is issued and returned on a daily basis.

The date, items issued, person to whom the equipment is issued, location in the hotel where the equipment will be used, and the time the items are returned should be noted on the log. Ideally, all equipment should be issued from a central location with one staff member assigned responsibility for issuing the equipment. Each employee should sign for receipt of the equipment and sign again when the equipment is returned.

Security is a major concern in determining storeroom requirements for major machines and equipment. When not in use, all equipment should be stored and locked. In-house equipment should never be permitted to leave the hotel. When machines or equipment are loaned to other departments, the executive housekeeper should keep careful records and follow up to ensure the equipment is returned.

Physical inventories of all major machines and equipment should be taken on a quarterly basis. To do so, a time should be established when all equipment and machinery will be stored and locked. Inventory cards should be consulted and the proper location of all pieces verified. All accessories and spare parts should be counted and recorded on the appropriate inventory card. Finally, all machines and equipment should be tested to ensure they are in good working order.

Cleaning Supplies

Cleaning supplies and small cleaning equipment are part of the non-recycled inventory in the housekeeping department. These items are depleted in the course of routine housekeeping operations. Controlling inventories of all cleaning supplies and ensuring their effective use is an important responsibility of the executive housekeeper. The executive housekeeper must work with all members of the housekeeping department to ensure the correct use of cleaning materials and adherence to cost-control procedures.

Types of Cleaning Supplies

A variety of cleaning supplies and small equipment is needed to carry out the tasks of the housekeeping department. Basic cleaning supplies include all-purpose cleaners, disinfectants, germicides, bowl cleaners, window cleaners, metal polishes, furniture polishes, and scrubbing pads.

Small equipment needed on a daily basis includes applicators, brooms, dust mops, wet mops, mop wringers, cleaning buckets, spray bottles, rubber gloves, protective eye covering, and cleaning cloths and rags.

Establishing Inventory Levels for Cleaning Supplies

Since cleaning supplies and small equipment are part of non-recycled inventories, par levels are closely tied to the rates at which these items are depleted in the day-to-day housekeeping operations. A par number for a cleaning supply item is actually a range between two figures: a minimum inventory quantity and a maximum inventory quantity.

The **minimum quantity** refers to the fewest number of purchase units that should be in stock at any given time. Purchase units for cleaning supplies are counted in terms of the normal shipping containers used for the items such as cases, cartons, or drums. The on-hand quantity for a cleaning supply item should never fall below the minimum quantity established for that item.

Minimum quantities are established by considering the usage factor associated with each item. The usage factor refers to the quantity of a given non-recycled inventory item that is used up over a certain period. The rate at which cleaning supplies are consumed by housekeeping operations is the chief factor for determining inventory levels for these non-recycled items.

The minimum quantity for any given cleaning supply item is determined by adding the lead-time quantity to the safety stock level for that particular item. The **lead-time quantity** refers to the number of purchase units that are used up between the time that a supply order is placed and the time that the order is actually received. Past purchasing records will show how long it takes to receive certain supplies. Executive housekeepers should keep in mind not only how long it takes suppliers to deliver orders, but also how long it takes the hotel to process purchase requests and place orders. The **safety stock** level for a given cleaning supply item refers to the number of purchase units that must always be on hand for the housekeeping department to operate smoothly in the event of emergencies, spoilage, unexpected delays in delivery, or other situations. By adding the number of purchase units needed for a safety stock to the number of purchase units used during the lead-time, the executive housekeeper can determine the minimum number of purchase units that always needs to be stocked.

The **maximum quantity** established for each cleaning supply item refers to the greatest number of purchase units that should be in stock at any given time. An executive housekeeper should consider several important factors when determining maximum inventory quantities for cleaning supplies. First, he or she must consider the amount of available storage space in the housekeeping department and the willingness of suppliers to store items at their own warehouse facilities for regular shipments to the hotel. Second, the shelf lives of certain items need to be taken into account. The quality or effectiveness of some products deteriorates if they are stored too long before being used. Third, maximum quantities should not be set so high that large amounts of the hotel's cash resources are unnecessarily tied up in an overstocked inventory.

Inventory Control of Cleaning Supplies

Controlling the inventory of cleaning supplies involves establishing strict issuing procedures to regulate the flow of products from the main storeroom to the floor cleaning closets. It also involves maintaining accurate counts of the products on hand in the main storeroom.

The executive housekeeper can establish a system of par levels for floor cleaning closets from which room attendants supply their carts. (Properties without floor closets generally issue a day's worth of cleaning supplies to a room attendant at the beginning of the shift.) Based on usage rates for the various cleaning supplies under different occupancy levels, the executive housekeeper can determine par levels for every floor station so that each station has enough cleaning supplies to last a week. Cleaning supplies can be issued from the main storeroom to replenish par levels established for each floor station. By tracking the amounts of cleaning supplies issued from the main storeroom to the floor stations, the executive housekeeper can monitor usage rates and spot instances of under- or overuse. Floor cleaning closets can be inspected on a regular basis to ensure that par levels are maintained. Shortages of cleaning supplies in floor cleaning closets can result in inspection deficiencies, inconvenience to guests, and lost labor hours as room attendants search for supplies they need to do their job. Once par levels have been established, the executive housekeeper should regularly review and adjust them to accommodate changes in operation or occupancy.

The executive housekeeper needs to ensure that all storage facilities are secure and that all staff members strictly adhere to standard issuing procedures. The minimum and maximum quantities established for each cleaning supply item should be posted where each item is kept on the storeroom shelves. This enables the executive housekeeper to quickly determine whether an adequate amount of cleaning supplies is on hand.

A **perpetual inventory** of all cleaning supplies is often used in conjunction with the par stock system. The perpetual inventory provides a record of all materials requisitioned for supply closets. Together, these two systems enable the executive housekeeper to keep tight control over supplies used by housekeeping personnel in their cleaning assignments. As new purchases are received by the main storeroom and as quantities are issued to floor cleaning stations, the amounts of cleaning supplies are adjusted on the perpetual record. When the perpetual record shows that on-hand quantities for particular cleaning supplies have reached the reorder point, requisitions for sufficient quantities can be placed to bring the quantities back up to the maximum levels.

Regular physical inventories should be made of each property storeroom. A monthly physical inventory of all cleaning supplies will enable the executive housekeeper to determine order quantities. More frequent physical inventories need to be made for those items that are depleted more quickly. An inventory record, such as the one shown in Exhibit 9, can be used as a worksheet for taking the physical counts of all cleaning supplies. By identifying the minimum and maximum inventory levels for each item and tallying the on-hand totals from different storeroom locations, the executive housekeeper can easily determine how much to order of each item to bring supplies back up to the established maximum quantities. Physical inventories are quicker and easier if the items listed on the inventory record are in the same order as they are arranged on storeroom shelves.

By recording both purchases and issues of cleaning supplies, the executive housekeeper can monitor the actual usage rates for each product kept in inventory. Exhibit 10 shows a form the executive housekeeper can use to determine the expected inventory for each cleaning supply and equipment item. The results of the previous physical inventory are listed in the beginning inventory column for the next month. Monthly purchases are added to these initial quantities, while the amounts of supplies issued are deducted. The total—or ending inventory column—estimates the quantity of each item that should be in stock at the end of the month. The results of the physical count can be compared to the expected ending

Exhibit 9   Sample Inventory Record

			INVENTORY						
ITEM DESCRIPTION	STD. UNIT	MIN./ MAX	STORE ROOM	1	2	3	TOTAL INV.	UNIT COST	TOTAL COST

HOTEL: _____
LOC. NO. _____
DEPT.: _____

※ **Holiday Inn**
INVENTORY RECORD
DATE _____

CALLED BY _____
RECORDED BY _____
APPROVED BY _____
PAGE _____ OF _____

Courtesy of Holiday Inn Worldwide

inventory. The variance between the actual quantities on hand and the amounts expected to be on hand represent the loss of cleaning supplies and equipment during the month. If this variance is unacceptably high, the executive housekeeper should investigate whether proper storage, issuing, and recordkeeping controls are being followed.

Guest Supplies

Hotels provide a variety of guestroom supplies and amenities for the guest's needs and convenience. The executive housekeeper is typically responsible for storing, distributing, controlling, and maintaining adequate inventory levels of guest supply items and amenities.

Types of Guest Supplies

To a large measure, the types and quantities of guest supplies that a hotel routinely provides depend on the hotel's size, clientele, and service level. Guest supplies and amenities for which the housekeeping department is responsible typically include bath soaps, facial soaps, toilet tissue, facial tissue, and hangers. Other supplies may include glasses, plastic trays, water pitchers, ice buckets, matches,

Exhibit 10   Sample Form for Calculating Expected Inventories

Month _____

**HOUSEKEEPING DEPARTMENT
SUPPLIES AND EQUIPMENT
INVENTORY CALCULATION SHEET**

Item	Beginning Inventory	+ Purchases	− Issues	= Ending Inventory
CLEANING SUPPLIES				
All-purpose cleaner				
Dusting solution				
Glass cleaner				
Wastebasket liners				
Carpet shampoo				
Stain remover				
Cleaning cloths				
Sponges				
Work gloves				
Eye covering				
EQUIPMENT				
Mops				
Brooms				
Dustpans				
Vacuums				
Buckets				
Bowl mops				
Carpet shampooers				
Window brushes				

Exhibit 11   Comparison of Par Stock and Actual Usage for Guest Supplies

	Guest Supplies Par Stock for One Month				
Item	Potential Usage per Occupied Room	×	Forecasted Number of Occupied Rooms	=	Par Stock Required
Shampoo	1.0	×	450	=	450
Bathfoam	1.0	×	450	=	450
Small soap	1.0	×	450	=	450

	Actual Usage for One Month							
Item	Potential Usage per Room	×	Occupied Rooms	=	Potential Consumed	−	Actual Consumed	= Variance
Shampoo	1.0	×	450	=	450	−	370	= <80>
Bathfoam	1.0	×	450	=	450	−	513	= 63
Small soap	1.0	×	450	=	450	−	752	= 302

ashtrays, and wastebaskets. Some hotels may provide all guestrooms with lotions, shampoos, conditioners, bathfoam, shower caps, shower mats, sewing kits, shoe-shine cloths, disposable slippers, and other items. Laundry bags, plastic utility bags, sanitary bags, emery boards, and candy mints may also be included on the list. Pens, stationery, and a variety of printed items, such as "do not disturb" signs, fire instructions, guest comment forms, and hotel or area marketing material may also be regularly distributed.

Establishing Inventory Levels for Guest Supplies

Each hotel will have its own room setup requirements for guest supplies. One par of guest supplies would be the quantity of each guest supply item needed to outfit all occupied rooms in the hotel one time. By knowing the forecasted number of occupied rooms, the executive housekeeper can determine the quantity of each guest supply item that will be needed to outfit guestrooms in the month ahead. However, since guest supplies are part of the hotel's non-recycled inventory, usage rates are the most important factor for pinpointing inventory levels. Exhibit 11 shows a sample monthly par stock requirement for three guest supply items based on the number of occupied rooms forecasted for that month. Exhibit 11 also shows the actual usage of these guest supply items during the month. Notice that actual usage can far exceed the quantities expected to be used on the basis of par stocks required for room setups. If inventory levels for these guest supply items were based solely on the quantities needed to stock occupied rooms with the par amounts, severe shortages would result.

Like cleaning supplies, minimum and maximum inventory levels are used to establish and control the hotel's stock of guest supplies and amenities. Both occupancy levels and usage rates need to be considered in establishing minimum and maximum quantities for the hotel's inventory of guest supply items. As an

the Rooms CHRONICLE®

Bathrobes as an Amenity

Subscribers to *The Rooms Chronicle*® shared their experiences with placing bathrobes in guestrooms as an amenity:

- Most hotels that offer bathrobes as an amenity place one robe in each room and will deliver a second robe upon request. Hotels that have an average guest count of two or more per room place two robes.

- Robes are replaced upon checkout or more often if a guest requests.

- Most hotels keep a two or two-and-one-half par of robes to enable turnover on busy check-out days.

- The type of robe used ranges from extra thick terry cloth (difficult to stuff into a suitcase) to waffle weave 100-percent cotton. Some luxury hotels embroider their logo on the chest pocket.

- Wash cycles must be handled with care—some bathrobes require cold water washes to prevent shrinking and color loss.

- The processing time necessary for turn around of robes sometimes slows with the care of the robe's belt, which may need pressing.

- Robes are generally presented by hanging them in the closet, belts neatly tied. But some luxury hotels present them at turndown, folded neatly on the edge of the bed.

- Losses reported ranged from 2 percent per year to 10 percent every quarter to one par per year, including wear and tear as well as theft.

- Printed cards are often placed on the hanger or in the bathrobes's pocket to inform guests how they might purchase a robe if they are interested. For example: "This robe is provided for your pleasure during your stay. If you'd like to purchase one of these special XYZ luxury robes, please dial extension 493 or stop by our gift shop." And then there are the cards that say, "If this robe is found missing from your room upon checkout, $89 will be added to your account balance."

- Hotels should be careful about threatening to post a charge for a missing robe. One hotel reported nine out of ten credit cards that were charged for missing robes later disputed the charge. Where's the balance between offering an amenity and creating a guest dissatisfaction issue?

As room rates rise and guest expectations increase, providing bathrobes is certainly an amenity to consider for a luxury experience.

Source: *The Rooms Chronicle*®, Volume 7, Number 2, p. 7.
For subscription information, please call 866-READ-TRC.

example, consider how minimum and maximum inventory quantities are calculated for bath soap.

Since minimum and maximum quantities are calculated in terms of purchase units, the first step is to determine how many bars of soap usually compose a standard package. Suppose that one case of bath soap contains 1,000 bars.

The second step is to calculate how many bars of soap will be used on an average day during the hotel's peak season. This, of course, depends on the number of occupied rooms and on the amount of the item that will be used in each room each day. Suppose that the average number of occupied rooms during the hotel's peak season is 200 and that one bar of soap is used in each occupied room each day. This means that the hotel's guests will use up 200 bars of soap each day.

The third step is to determine how many days it will take for the hotel's guests to use a standard purchase unit of soap. Since there are 1,000 bars of soap in each case, and 200 bars of soap will be used up every day, it will take five days to use up one case of soap (1,000 ÷ 200 = 5). This means that one purchase unit of bath soap will be used up every five days.

The fourth step is to determine the minimum number of purchase units of soap that should always be in stock at any given time. The minimum quantity for any guest supply item is determined by adding the lead-time quantity to the safety stock level established for that particular item. Suppose that the executive housekeeper determines that an appropriate safety stock level for soap is one case—or a five-day supply. The executive housekeeper knows that soap has a relatively short shelf life and determines that a five-day supply is sufficient to cover any emergency, spoilage, or delivery delay. To determine the quantity of soap needed to cover the period between placing and receiving an order, the executive housekeeper has to consider how long it takes the hotel to process and approve a purchase request and how long the supplier needs to process and deliver the order. Suppose the executive housekeeper determines that it takes five days to process and get delivery on an order of soap. Since the amount of soap used in five days is one case, the executive housekeeper sets the minimum quantity at two cases (1 case safety stock + 1 case lead-time = 2 cases). Thus, the reorder point for soap is two cases.

The fifth step is to determine the maximum quantity of soap—or the greatest number of cases that should be in stock at any given time. In addition to concerns about storage space and conserving the hotel's cash outlay for inventoried products, the chief factor affecting the maximum inventory quantity for soap is the frequency of orders. A maximum inventory quantity can be calculated by dividing the number of days between orders by the number of days it takes to use one purchase unit, and then adding the minimum quantity. Suppose the executive housekeeper orders soap once a month. The amount of time from one order point to the next is 30 days. Since the number of days it takes to use one case of soap is five, the amount of soap that will be used in 30 days is six cases (30 ÷ 5 = 6). Adding the previously established minimum quantity of two cases, the maximum inventory quantity for soap can, in this case, be established as eight cases (6 + 2 = 8).

When the number of cases of soap in inventory reaches the minimum level, the executive housekeeper should place an order for enough soap to bring the inventory level back up to the maximum quantity. When the supply of soap reaches two cases, the executive housekeeper should place an order for six cases in order to bring the inventory level back up to the maximum of eight cases (8 − 2 = 6).

Minimum and maximum inventory quantities can be determined in a similar way for all guest supplies and amenities. The key factors affecting the calculations are occupancy levels, usage rates, storage space, cash available for supplies, and the frequency with which supplies are to be reordered.

C the Rooms HRONICLE®

Purchasing Facts and Tips—Shampoo and Lotion

- Personalized, bottled amenities often create a lasting impression with hotel guests. Not only are they reminded of your property when they use these amenities throughout their stay, but amenity bottles are frequently refilled at home for future trips. Thus, guests are repeatedly reminded of the hotel.

- Hotels with extended-stay guests will find it cost-effective to order bottled amenities for guests to use over a period of days. Properties with shorter guest stays will find it cost-effective to provide single-use packets of amenities.

- When ordering shampoo and conditioner, one money-saving possibility is to order a "shampoo-plus-conditioner" product. The conditioner is included in the shampoo, and conditioning shampoo is only slightly more expensive than regular shampoo.

- When ordering bottled amenities, be careful to avoid items that may give a guest an allergic reaction.

- When deciding whether to order generic or name-brand shampoo or lotion, ask for samples for testing by hotel staff and selected regular guests. Selections can vary greatly in water content, texture, sudsing quality, smell, and pouring ease.

- Most distributors offer to either silk-screen a property's logo and message on the bottled amenity or imprint the logo and message on a label.

- There is a price reduction for large orders of bottled amenities. Ordering extra-large quantities could reduce the per unit price by five percent or more.

- When receiving amenity shipments, always weigh a few sample bottles to ensure the accuracy of the order.

Source: *The Rooms Chronicle®*, Volume 4, Number 5, p. 16. For subscription information, please call 866-READ-TRC.

Inventory levels and usage rates for guest supply items should be carefully monitored and adjusted as necessary. A number of considerations may lead the executive housekeeper to adjust the minimum and maximum inventory levels for guest supplies and amenities. Seasonal changes in occupancy levels need to be considered, because fewer supplies will be needed when occupancy decreases. Since occupancy levels may vary considerably from month to month, executive housekeepers may use occupancy forecasts to calculate par levels of guest supplies and amenities on a monthly basis.

The standard packaging for some items also affects the determination of minimum and maximum inventory levels. For example, shower caps may be sold in quantities as high as 1,000 caps per case. This item may be so inexpensive that the executive housekeeper may decide that an overstock is much less serious than the effects of any shortages.

Some guest supply items—such as drinking glasses—are actually recycled inventory items. Par levels for this kind of guest supply should be determined

Exhibit 12   Sample Par for Room Attendant's Cart

12 Small Soap	12 Matches	6 Large Soap	12 Pencils
12 Shampoo	3 Sewing Kits	12 Bathfoam	6 Postcards
6 Shower Caps	3 Security Cards	12 Laundry Bags	12 Envelopes
6 Plain Notepads		12 Letterheads	3 Magazines
3 Room Service Menus		3 Fire Instructions	12 Guest Comment Cards

in a manner similar to that for room linens and other recycled inventory items. Considering the cleaning cycle alone, at least three pars of glasses may be needed to stock all guestrooms: one par of glasses will be clean, wrapped, and ready for distribution; a second par will be in guestrooms, soiled, and ready for collection; and a third par of glasses will be in the process of being cleaned and prepared for distribution on the following day. Considering theft, breakage, and potential guest requests for additional glasses, the executive housekeeper may decide that four or five pars of glasses are required.

Inventory Control of Guest Supplies

Since most guest supply items are among a hotel's non-recycled inventories, inventories are controlled in much the same way as cleaning supplies. Par levels are established, physical inventories are taken, and records are maintained. The principles of control and procedures for gathering accurate information about usage rates and inventory levels are substantially the same.

In addition to establishing par levels for the main storeroom and floor service closets, most hotels also establish par levels for room attendant carts. Exhibit 12 shows a sample par of guest supplies for a room attendant cart servicing 12 to 14 guestrooms. Inventory control procedures for issuing guest supplies and amenities to room attendants will depend on whether supplies are issued daily from the main storeroom in par levels established for room attendant carts, or whether supplies are issued on a weekly or other basis to replenish par levels established for floor service areas. In either case, the control procedure is the same: occupancy levels and usage rates determine the par levels needed, and supplies are issued only in quantities sufficient to replenish par stocks. Control forms, such as the one shown in Exhibit 13, can be used to monitor the quantities of guest supplies issued from the main storeroom.

Printed Materials and Stationery

Printed materials and stationery are distributed to guestrooms along with other guest supplies and amenities. Although the hotel's marketing department is usually directly involved in designing and producing these items, housekeeping is responsible for their distribution and for their inventory levels.

Writing paper, envelopes, notepads, postcards, telephone message forms, and fax cover sheets are examples of printed materials that a hotel may supply for the guest's use and convenience. "Do Not Disturb" signs, instructions for fire and

Exhibit 13   Sample Control Form for Issuing Guest Supplies

Guestroom Supplies Requisition

Item	Par Stock	Reorder Point	Requisition (same as par)	Cost of Item Requisition
Bar soap	1 case	$^1/_2$ case		
Tissue	1 case	$^1/_2$ case		
Toilet paper	1 case	$^1/_2$ case		
Shower caps	100	50		
Matches	6 boxes	3 boxes		
Pens	1 box	$^1/_2$ box		
Memo pads	2 pkgs	1 pkg		
Pencils	1 box	$^1/_2$ box		
Do Not Disturb signs	30	15		
Glasses	1 case	$^1/_2$ case		
Room folders	30	15		
Wastebaskets	6	2		

other emergencies, room service menus, maps, brochures on area restaurants or attractions, TV listings, and forms for guest comments or evaluation of hotel services may also be provided.

The frequency with which printed materials and stationery need to be changed or replaced will affect the minimum and maximum inventory levels for these items. Some printed items are relatively permanent features of the guestroom. These items do not need to be changed or redesigned very frequently and rarely need to be replaced except in the case of damage or wear. Instruction sheets for emergencies and for equipment such as the telephone, TV, and heating and air conditioning system fall into this category. Inventory levels for these printed materials will likely depend upon printing costs.

Some printed materials, such as TV listings or special event calendars, may need to be replaced on a daily basis. Other materials, such as room service menus, may need to be changed less frequently. Excess inventories of such printed items will be sheer waste as they become outdated.

Other printed items with relatively limited life spans are marketing brochures and flyers related to hotel services. The marketing department generally has established schedules for the redesign and replacement of such promotional materials. The executive housekeeper has to work closely with marketing personnel to determine adequate inventory levels for such items.

Par stock levels for stationery items such as notepads, letterheads, envelopes, and postcards are established in the usual manner for non-recycled inventory items. Occupancy levels, usage rates, safety levels, lead-time quantities, and purchasing schedules should be considered when determining minimum and maximum inventory levels.

Endnotes

1. Source: Mary Friedman, *The Rooms Chronicle*®, Volume 10, Number 5, pp. 4–5. For subscription information, call 866-READ-TRC.

2. Source: Mary Friedman, *The Rooms Chronicle*®, Volume 4, Number 4, pp. 4–5. For subscription information, call 866-READ-TRC.

3. Noah J. Goldstein, Vladas Griskevicius, and Robert B. Cialdini, "Invoking Social Norms: A Social Psychology Perspective on Improving Hotels' Linen-Reuse Programs," *Cornell Hotel and Restaurant Administration Quarterly*, Volume 48, Issue 2, May, 2007, pp. 145–150.

4. Friedman, Volume 4, Number 4, pp. 4–5.

5. According to the Fair Labor Standards Act, if cleaning costs would reduce an employee's weekly earnings to under minimum wage, the employer must clean the uniforms or pay the employee to do so.

6. Source: Gail Edwards, CHHE, *The Rooms Chronicle*®, Volume 7, Number 5, pp. 8–9. For subscription information, call 866-READ-TRC.

Key Terms

floor par—The quantity of each type of linen that is required to outfit all rooms serviced from a particular floor linen closet.

house setup—The total number of each type of linen that is needed to outfit all guestrooms one time. This is also referred to as one par of linen.

inventories—Stocks of merchandise, operating supplies, and other items held for future use in a hospitality operation.

issuing—The process of distributing inventory items from the storeroom to authorized individuals by the use of formal requisitions.

lead-time quantity—The number of purchase units consumed between the time that a supply order is placed and the time that the order is actually received.

maximum quantity—The greatest number of purchase units that should be in stock at any given time.

minimum quantity—The fewest number of purchase units that should be in stock at any given time.

non-recycled inventories—Those items in stock that are depleted or used up during the course of routine housekeeping operations. Non-recycled inventories include cleaning supplies, guest supplies, and guest amenities.

par—The standard quantity of a particular inventory item that must be on hand to support daily, routine housekeeping operations.

par number—A multiple of the standard quantity of a particular inventory item that must be on hand to support daily, routine housekeeping operations.

perpetual inventory system—An inventory system in which receipts and issues are recorded as they occur; this system provides readily available information on inventory levels and cost of sales.

recycled inventories—Those items in stock that have relatively limited useful lives but are used over and over in housekeeping operations. Recycled inventories include linens, uniforms, major machines and equipment, and guest loan items.

safety stock—The number of purchase units that must always be on hand for smooth operation in the event of emergencies, spoilage, unexpected delays in delivery, or other situations.

 Review Questions ―――――――――――――――――――――――――

1. What are some of the typical items in recycled and non-recycled inventories?

2. What is the basic premise for establishing par levels for recycled inventories? for non-recycled inventories?

3. What three factors should be considered when setting par levels for linen?

4. What are some of the typical ways the executive housekeeper and the laundry supervisor work together to control linen inventories?

5. What are the main benefits of conducting physical inventories? How often should physical inventories be taken?

6. What factors make it difficult to establish par levels for uniforms?

7. What type of information should be listed on an inventory card for a piece of major machinery or equipment?

8. What is meant by minimum quantity? Maximum quantity?

9. How do the concepts of minimum quantity and maximum quantity work together to control non-recycled inventories?

Chapter 6 Outline

Competencies

1. Identify the executive housekeeper's responsibilities in relation to the budget planning process. (pp. 211–213)

2. Explain how the executive housekeeper uses the operating budget as a control tool. (pp. 213–214)

3. Describe hotel income statements and rooms division income statements, and identify the line items on a rooms division income statement that are affected by expenses incurred by the housekeeping department. (pp. 214–220)

4. Explain how the executive housekeeper estimates department expenses during the budget planning process. (pp. 220–228)

5. Identify four actions that an executive housekeeper can take to control expenses. (p. 228)

6. Describe purchasing responsibilities of the executive housekeeper, identify factors to consider when determining the size of an annual linen purchase, and discuss capital budgets. (pp. 229–237)

7. Identify issues that an executive housekeeper should address when considering the use of outside contractors to perform cleaning services. (pp. 237–240)

6

Controlling Expenses

SINCE HOUSEKEEPING IS NOT A REVENUE-GENERATING DEPARTMENT, the executive house-keeper's primary responsibility for achieving the property's financial goals is to control the department's expenses. In addition to salaries and wages, inventoried items are a key area for the executive housekeeper's exercise of cost control measures.

This chapter describes the budgetary process and explains how budgets are determined for the operational expenses that fall within the executive housekeeper's responsibility. The chapter also examines the executive housekeeper's responsibility for controlling the costs associated with housekeeping operations. The role of the executive housekeeper in formulating capital budgets will also be discussed.

The Budget Process

The operating budget outlines the financial goals of a hotel. The purpose of the operating budget is to relate operational costs to the year's expected revenues. The yearly operating budget is broken down into budgets for each month of the fiscal year. In addition, each department prepares its own monthly budget. These budgets cover individual areas of responsibility and serve as a guide for how the department will achieve its expected contribution to the property's financial goals.

Essentially, a budget is a plan. It projects both the revenues the hotel anticipates during the period covered by the budget and the expenses required to generate the anticipated revenues. The executive housekeeper's responsibility in the budgetary process is twofold. First, the executive housekeeper is involved in the planning process that leads to the formulation of the budget. This entails informing the rooms division manager and general manager what expenses the housekeeping department will incur in light of forecasted room sales. Second, since the budget represents an operational plan for the year, the executive housekeeper ensures that the department's actual expenses are in line with budgeted costs and with the actual occupancy levels.

As a plan, a budget is not "set in stone." It may need to be adjusted in light of unforeseen or changing circumstances. If anticipated room sales do not materialize, then expenses allocated to different departments will need to be adjusted accordingly. If occupancy levels exceed expectations, then increased expenses need to be planned for and incorporated into a revised budget. If unexpected expenditures are required, their effect on the overall plan needs to be assessed. New ways may need to be determined for the property to meet its financial goals and objectives.

As a plan, a budget is also a guide. It provides managers with the standards by which they can measure the success of operations. By comparing actual expenses with allocated amounts, the executive housekeeper can track the efficiency of housekeeping operations and monitor the department's ability to keep its expenses within the prescribed limits.

Types of Budgets

Two types of budgets are used in managing a hotel's financial resources: capital and operating budgets. The difference between the two essentially lies in the types of expenditures involved.

Usually, a **capital budget** plans for the expenditure of company assets for items costing $1,500 or more. Typically, these items are not used up in the normal course of operations; instead, they have a life span that exceeds a single year. Furniture, fixtures, and equipment are typical examples of **capital expenditures**. Capital expenditures in equipment for the housekeeping department may include room attendant carts, vacuum cleaners, carpet shampooers, pile lifters, rotary floor scrubbers, laundry equipment, sewing machines, and trash-handling equipment. In addition, major initial purchases of recycled inventory items—such as linen, towels, blankets, and uniforms—are capital budget items since they have a relatively long useful life and are not used up in the course of normal operations.

An **operating budget** forecasts revenues and expenses associated with the routine operations of the hotel during a certain period. **Operating expenditures** are those costs the hotel incurs in order to generate revenue in the normal course of doing business. In the housekeeping department, the most expensive operational cost is salaries and wages. The costs of non-recycled inventory items, such as cleaning and guest supplies, are also considered operational costs.

Planning the Operating Budget

The budgeting process begins far in advance of the start of the period for which the budget is planned. The process of planning an annual operating budget generally takes several months. It involves gathering information, formulating initial plans, reconsidering goals and objectives, and making final adjustments. The budget-planning process requires a closely coordinated effort of all management personnel.

Operating budgets are typically prepared for each fiscal year; the annual operating budget summarizes the anticipated year-end results. Monthly operating budgets are also prepared for the property's fiscal year. This enables managers to clearly outline seasonal variations in expected revenues and corresponding expenses. It also provides managers and department heads with valuable tools to monitor actual results.

In budget planning, the first step is always to forecast room sales. The reason for this is twofold. First, room sales generate the revenue for operating various departments. Second, and more important, most of the expenses that each department can expect—and the ones that departments are most able to control—are most directly related to room occupancy levels. This is especially true of the housekeeping department where salaries and wages and the usage rates for both recycled and non-recycled inventory items are direct functions of the number of occupied rooms. The concept of "cost per occupied room" is the major tool the executive housekeeper uses to determine the levels of expense in the various categories. Once the executive housekeeper knows predicted occupancy levels, expected expenses for salaries and wages, cleaning supplies, guest supplies, laundry, and other areas can be determined on the basis of formulas that express costs in terms of cost per occupied room.

Occupancy forecasts are generally developed by the front office manager, who works closely with the property's general manager. The forecast is based not only on past levels of occupancy (and their distribution among the budget periods), but also on information supplied by the marketing department concerning the anticipated effect on room sales of special events, advertising, and promotions. Some hotels generate forecasts for room sales that predict the level of occupancy for each day of the coming year.

Once occupancy levels are predicted, the departments whose costs fluctuate with occupancy levels can forecast expected costs and submit prepared budgets to the general manager and controller for review. Upper management analyzes and adjusts the departmental budget plans so they reflect the property's goals and objectives. Often, budgets are returned to department heads with comments and recommended adjustments. Such feedback primarily reflects the concern of upper management to maximize profits and control expenses while maintaining appropriate levels of service.

By specifying expense levels in relation to room sales, the budget actually expresses the level of service the hotel will be able to provide. In this regard, it is important for department heads to report how service levels will be affected by budget adjustments. This is especially important for the executive housekeeper. If upper management tones down the operating budget submitted by the executive housekeeper, the executive housekeeper should clearly indicate what services will be eliminated or downgraded in order to achieve the specified reductions.

The cycle of feedback and discussion continues as department heads revise their budgetary plans and provide additional input in response to recommended adjustments. It is through this back-and-forth process that agreement is ultimately reached. The final budget represents the forecasts, goals, and constraints that everyone adopts. Each department is then committed to operating under the limits expressed in the budget and achieving its contribution to the overall plan. Once approved, the operating budgets set a standard by which departmental performance can—and will—be evaluated.

Using the Operating Budget as a Control Tool

An operating budget is a valuable control tool with which to monitor the course of operations during a specified period. Each month, the hotel's accounting department produces statements reporting actual costs in each of the expense categories. The form of these statements is nearly identical to that of the operating budget; actual costs are listed alongside budgeted costs. Such reports enable the executive housekeeper to monitor how well the housekeeping department is doing in relation to the budgeted goals and constraints.

Controlling expenses in the housekeeping department means comparing actual costs with budgeted amounts and assessing the variances. When comparing actual and budgeted expenses, the executive housekeeper should first determine whether the forecasted occupancy levels were actually achieved. If the number of occupied rooms is lower than anticipated, a corresponding decrease in the department's actual expenses should be expected. Similarly, if occupancy levels are higher than forecasted, the executive housekeeper can expect a corresponding increase in housekeeping expenses. In either case, the adjustment in expenses should be proportional to the variation in occupancy levels. The executive housekeeper's ability to control housekeeping expenses will be evaluated in terms of his or her ability to maintain the cost per occupied room expected for each category.

Small deviations between actual and budgeted expenses can be expected and are not a cause for alarm. Serious deviations from the budgeted plan require investigation and explanation. If the actual costs far exceed the budgeted amounts while the predicted occupancy level remains the same, the executive housekeeper needs to find the source of the deviation. In addition to discovering why the department is "behind budget," the executive housekeeper needs to formulate a plan to correct the deviation and get the department back "on budget." For example, a re-examination of staff scheduling procedures or closer supervision of standard practices and procedures may be necessary. Other steps might include evaluating the efficiency and cost of products being used in the housekeeping department, and exploring the alternatives.

Even if the executive housekeeper finds that the department is far "ahead of budget," it is not necessarily a cause for celebration. It may indicate a deterioration of the service levels that were built into the original budget plan. *Any* serious deviation from the plan is a cause for concern and requires explanation. Identifying and investigating such deviations on a timely basis is one of the most valuable functions an executive housekeeper can perform in terms of the operating budget.

Operating Budgets and Income Statements

An operating budget is identical in form to an **income statement**. An income statement—or statement of income—expresses the actual results of operations during an accounting period, identifying revenues earned and itemizing expenses incurred during that period. The difference between an income statement and an operating budget is that the first expresses the actual results of operations for a period that has ended, while the second expresses the expected results of operations for a current or coming period. The one is a report of what actually occurred, while the other is a forecast or plan for what is to come. The operating budget is a plan for the period in the sense that it predicts or anticipates what the income statement will actually show at the end of that period. The success of the hotel's plan as expressed in the budget is determined by how closely its forecasted numbers match the numbers on the end-of-the-period income statement.

In the budget-planning process, upper management collects information from the various department heads to prepare a budget for the entire property. This budget takes the form of an income statement for the coming period. Income statements that predict the results of current or future operations, as opposed to reporting actual results, are often referred to as **pro forma income statements**.

The Hotel Income Statement

The statement of income provides important financial information about the results of hotel operations for a given period. The period may be one month or longer, but cannot exceed one business year. Since a statement of income reveals

Exhibit 1   Summary Income Statement—Vacation Inn

Vacation Inn
Summary Income Statement
For the year ended December 31, 20XX

	Schedule	Net Revenue	Cost of Sales	Payroll and Related Expenses	Other Expense	Income (Loss)
Operated Departments						
Rooms	1	$1,041,200	$ 0	$ 185,334	$ 79,080	$ 776,786
Food	2	420,100	160,048	160,500	44,013	55,539
Beverage	3	206,065	48,400	58,032	22,500	77,133
Telephone	4	52,028	46,505	14,317	6,816	(15,610)
Total Operated Departments		1,719,393	254,953	418,183	152,409	893,848
Undistributed Operating Expenses						
Administrative and General	5			104,244	48,209	152,453
Sales and Marketing	6			33,231	33,585	66,816
Property Operation and Maintenance	7			31,652	49,312	80,964
Utilities	8			0	88,752	88,752
Total Undistributed Operating Expenses				169,127	219,858	388,985
Gross Operating Profit		$1,719,393	$254,953	$ 587,310	$372,267	504,863
Rent, Property Taxes, and Insurance	9					200,861
Depreciation and Amortization	10					115,860
Net Operating Income						188,142
Interest Expense	11					52,148
Income Before Income Taxes						135,994
Income Tax	12					48,707
Net Income						$ 87,287

Source: Raymond S. Schmidgall, *Hospitality Industry Managerial Accounting,* 6th ed. (Lansing, Mich.: American Hotel & Lodging Educational Institute, 2006), p. 100.

the bottom line—the net income for a given period—it is one of the most important financial statements used by top management to evaluate the success of operations. Although the executive housekeeper may never directly use the hotel's statement of income, this statement relies in part on detailed information supplied by the housekeeping department.

The sample statement of income shown in Exhibit 1 is often called a summary statement because it presents a composite picture of all the financial operations of the hotel. Rooms division information appears on the first line, under the category of operated departments. The amount of income generated by the rooms division is determined by subtracting payroll and related expenses and other expenses from the amount of net revenue produced by the rooms division over the period covered by the income statement. Payroll and related expenses charged to the rooms division include the wages, salaries, and benefits paid to housekeeping *and* front office staff, reservation agents, and uniformed service staff. Since the rooms division is not a merchandising facility, there is no cost of sales to subtract from the net revenue amount.

The revenue generated by the rooms division is often the largest single amount produced by revenue centers within a hotel. Using the figures shown in Exhibit 1, the amount of income earned by the rooms division during the year was $776,786, or 86.9 percent of the total income of $893,848. Since the rooms division is generally the hotel's major source of income, and since housekeeping is a major source of expense incurred by the rooms division, the executive housekeeper plays an important role in the hotel's overall financial performance.

The Rooms Division Income Statement

The hotel's statement of income shows only summary information. More detailed information is presented by the separate departmental income statements prepared by each revenue center. These departmental income statements are called **schedules** and are referenced on the hotel's statement of income.

Exhibit 1 references the rooms division as Schedule 1. This rooms division income statement appears in Exhibit 2. The figures shown in Exhibit 2 for rooms division Net Revenue, Payroll and Related Expenses, Other Expenses, and Departmental Income are the same amounts that appear on Exhibit 1 for the rooms division under the category of operated departments.

The format and specific line items used by the rooms division for its departmental income statement will vary with the needs and requirements of individual properties. The following sections briefly describe typical line items found on a rooms division income statement.

The first heading on the rooms division income statement records revenue from room sales during the period. The second heading, Allowances, identifies rebates, refunds, and overcharges of revenue. These are generally not known at the time that room sales are recorded. Instead, allowances are adjusted at a later date and may not appear as a budgeted line item on a pro forma income statement.

Net Revenue is arrived at by subtracting Allowances from Total Revenue. It is the Net Revenue figure that is transferred to the hotel's income statement as sales derived from the hotel's lodging operation.

The executive housekeeper is directly concerned with many of the line items listed in the expense sections of the rooms division's income statement. The largest single expense category listed is Salaries and Wages. The personnel costs associated with the housekeeping department are incorporated into this total, which also includes payroll costs for all rooms division employees. Regular pay, overtime pay, vacation pay, severance pay, incentive pay, holiday pay, and employee bonuses are included in this expense category.

The expense item referred to as Employee Benefits is generally calculated by the personnel or accounting departments. It includes payroll-related insurance expense, pension, and other related personnel costs. The share of Employee Benefit expense that belongs to the housekeeping department is included in this line item.

Many of the expense items listed under the heading Other Expenses fall under the direct responsibility of the executive housekeeper. These include the following:

* Contract Services
* Laundry and Dry Cleaning
* Linen
* Operating Supplies
* Uniforms

Exhibit 2   Sample Rooms Department Schedule

Vacation Inn	**Schedule 1**
Rooms	
For the year ended December 31, 20XX	
Revenue	
Transient—Regular	$ 543,900
Transient—Group	450,000
Permanent	48,000
Other	2,000
Allowances	(2,700)
Net Revenue	1,041,200
Expenses	
Salaries and Wages	159,304
Payroll Taxes	10,420
Employee Benefits	15,610
Total Payroll and Related Expenses	185,334
Other Expenses	
Cable/Satellite Television	4,900
Cleaning Supplies	3,200
Commissions	5,124
Contract Services	3,100
Guest Supplies	5,126
Laundry and Dry Cleaning	12,706
Linen	9,494
Miscellaneous	3,000
Operating Supplies	12,742
Reservations	9,288
Telecommunications	4,685
Training	4,315
Uniforms	1,400
Total Other Expenses	79,080
Total Expenses	264,414
Departmental Income	$ 776,786

Source: Raymond S. Schmidgall, *Hospitality Industry Managerial Accounting,* 6th ed. (Lansing, Mich.: American Hotel & Lodging Educational Institute, 2006), p. 99.

Contract Services includes the cost of contracting outside companies to clean lobbies and public areas, wash windows, and exterminate and disinfect areas of the rooms division. The pros and cons involved in the executive housekeeper's decision to employ contract cleaning services will be discussed at the end of this chapter.

The Laundry and Dry Cleaning expense item refers to the cost of both outside and in-house laundry and dry-cleaning services. It includes the cost of dry cleaning curtains and draperies as well as washing or cleaning awnings, carpets, and rugs in areas of the rooms division. All the expenses incurred by the property's in-house laundry facility (except salaries, wages, and benefits) are reflected in this expense item. The costs of supplies used to keep the house laundry in a clean and sanitary condition are included—plus the costs of all supplies used in the laundry operation itself. In addition, printing and stationery costs associated with laundry lists, printed forms, service manuals, and office supplies used by in-house laundry personnel are included. Finally, the cost of purchasing or renting uniforms for in-house laundry employees, along with the costs of uniform cleaning or repair, are incorporated in the total expense recorded in this category. Many hotels use a separate schedule to itemize all the costs within this expense category.

The Linen expense item includes the replacement costs or rental fees for sheets, pillowcases, towels, facecloths, bath mats, blankets, and other items included in the linen inventory.

The Operating Supplies expense item includes the cost of guest supplies, cleaning supplies, and printing and stationery items. All guest and cleaning supplies fall within the executive housekeeper's area of responsibility, and their inventories are maintained in the housekeeping department.

The Uniforms expense item includes the cost of purchasing or renting uniforms for all employees of the rooms division as well as other related costs.

Some of the expense categories listed under the heading Other Expenses fall outside the executive housekeeper's areas of responsibility. The Commissions expense refers to remunerations paid to outside sources, such as travel agents and online distribution channels such as Orbitz®, Expedia®, Travelocity® and Priceline. com® who market and secure rooms business for the hotel. Reservations includes the cost of a reservations service and a central reservation system involving telephone, fax, and Internet expenses. Fairly common Other Expenses line items not shown in the sample statement include Cable/Satellite Television, Telecommunications, Training, and Guest Transportation.

In the budget-planning process, the rooms manager will solicit information from the executive housekeeper concerning the expense categories that fall under the housekeeping department's areas of responsibility. In particular, the rooms manager will be interested in assessing expected expenses as a percentage of the revenue forecasted for room sales. Every controllable cost can be expressed as a percentage of revenue. For each expense category, the rooms manager will have a standard percentage that is considered to be an appropriate level of expense in relation to generated revenues. The rooms manager will expect that all projected expenses fall within an acceptable range of standard cost percentages for each category. The rooms manager may also build improvements on past cost percentages into selected expense categories, assuming that greater efficiencies will be achieved through better training, closer supervision, and tighter controls. The rooms manager's goal is to maximize the department's income by minimizing its expenses while still preserving or enhancing the service levels. Crucial to achieving this goal are the executive housekeeper's calculations of anticipated expenses and comments on how budget adjustments may affect the quality of service.

The operating budgets under which the executive housekeeper operates take the form of monthly income statements for the rooms division. Projected revenues and expenses for each month of the budgeted period will represent the rooms division's operational plan. The executive housekeeper will be held accountable for controlling the expense areas that fall within the housekeeping department's areas of responsibility. As the budgeted period progresses, monthly

Exhibit 3   Sample Monthly Rooms Division Budget Report

Vacation Inn
Budget Report Rooms Division
For January 20XX

			Variances	
	Actual	Budget	$	%
Revenue				
Room Sales	$156,240	$145,080	$11,160	7.69%
Allowances	437	300	(137)	(45.67)
Net Revenue	155,803	144,780	11,023	7.61
Expenses				
Salaries and Wages	20,826	18,821	(2,005)	(10.65)
Employee Benefits	4,015	5,791	1,776	30.67
Total Payroll and Related Expenses	24,841	24,612	(229)	(0.93)
Other Expenses				
Commissions	437	752	315	41.89
Contract Services	921	873	(48)	(5.50)
Guest Supplies	1,750	1,200	(550)	(45.83)
Laundry and Dry Cleaning	1,218	975	(243)	(24.92)
Linen	1,906	1,875	(31)	(1.65)
Operating Supplies	1,937	1,348	(589)	(43.69)
Reservations	1,734	2,012	278	13.82
Uniforms	374	292	(82)	(28.08)
Other	515	672	157	23.36
Total Other Expenses	10,792	9,999	(793)	(7.93)
Total Expenses	35,633	34,611	(1,022)	(2.95)
Departmental Income (Loss)	$120,170	$110,169	$10,001	9.08%

income statements will be produced that show the actual amounts alongside the amounts originally budgeted.

Exhibit 3 shows a monthly budget report for rooms that indicates both budgeted forecasts and actual results. The last two columns in Exhibit 3 show dollar and percentage variances. The dollar variances indicate the differences between actual results and budgeted amounts. Dollar variances are considered either favorable or unfavorable based on the following situations:

	Favorable Variance	Unfavorable Variance
Revenue	Actual exceeds budget	Budget exceeds actual
Expense	Budget exceeds actual	Actual exceeds budget

For example, the actual amount of salaries and wages for rooms division personnel in the month of January was $20,826, while the budgeted amount for salaries and wages was $18,821, resulting in a variance of $2,005. The variance is bracketed to indicate an unfavorable variance. However, if the revenue variance is favorable, an unfavorable variance in expenses (such as in payroll) is not necessarily negative. Rather, it may merely indicate the greater expense of serving more guests than were anticipated when the budget was created.

Percentage variances are determined by dividing the dollar variance by the budgeted amount. For example, the 7.61 percent variance for net revenue shown in Exhibit 3 is the result of dividing the dollar variance figure of $11,023 by the budgeted net revenue amount of $144,780—and then multiplying by 100.

Virtually all actual results of rooms division operations will differ from budgeted amounts for revenue and expense items on a budget report. This is only to be expected because any budgeting process, no matter how sophisticated, is not perfect. Executive housekeepers should not analyze every variance. Only significant variances require management analysis and action. The general manager and controller should provide the executive housekeeper with criteria for determining which variances are significant.

Budgeting Expenses

The budgeting process begins with a forecast of room sales. Since expense levels in all the expense categories on the departmental income statement vary with occupancy, everything in the operating budget depends upon how accurately occupancy levels are forecasted.

Early in the budget-planning process, the rooms manager will give the executive housekeeper the yearly forecast of occupancy levels, broken down into monthly budget periods. This information may be delivered on a form such as the one in Exhibit 4. Using historical data, along with input from the hotel's marketing department, the rooms manager will predict the occupancy percentage for each budgeted period. The second column of the form translates the anticipated occupancy percentage into the actual number of rooms expected to be occupied. By multiplying the number of expected occupied rooms by the average rate per room, the rooms manager can forecast the amount of revenue anticipated from room sales. For the rooms manager, this projection of revenue is the most important part of the operating budget. The appropriateness of all expenses expected will be measured in terms of the percentage of revenue represented by each expense category.

For the executive housekeeper, the most important information in the rooms manager's forecast is not so much the total expected sales dollars, but the projected number of occupied rooms for each budget period. This is because nearly all the expense levels for which the executive housekeeper is responsible are directly dependent upon the number of occupied rooms the housekeeping department will have to service.

The executive housekeeper can predict a certain level of expense for each expense category when he or she knows: (1) the cost per occupied room for each category of expense and (2) the number of occupied rooms forecasted for each budget period. At this point, the budgeting process simply involves relating costs per occupied room to the forecasted occupancy levels.

Exhibit 4   Summary of Forecasted Rooms Sales

Budget Period	Occupancy Percentage	Number of Occupied Rooms	Average Price per Room	Total Rooms Sales
1.				
2.				
3.				
4.				
5.				
6.				
7.				
8.				
9.				
10.				
11.				
12.				

Months of the Year

Salaries and Wages

Salaries and Wages expense for the housekeeping department is related to such positions as executive housekeeper, assistant housekeeping managers, supervisors, linen room attendants, room attendants, housepersons, lobby attendants, and others employed in the housekeeping operation.

By using a staffing guide, the executive housekeeper can determine how many labor hours in each job classification are needed to ensure smooth operations at varying levels of occupancy. When planning the Salaries and Wages expense for the operating budget, the executive housekeeper can use the staffing guide in conjunction with the occupancy forecasts to determine staffing needs for each budget period. After determining the number of labor hours needed for each job category, the executive housekeeper can multiply the number of hours by the position's average per-hour wage to calculate the expected cost for that job category. By summing the calculations for all positions, a total wage cost can be determined for each budget period. Costs associated with salaried positions in the housekeeping department can be averaged into each monthly budget period. In forecasting salary and wage costs, the executive housekeeper will need to account for any scheduled salary and wage increases as well as any cost-of-living adjustments planned by the property.

the Rooms
CHRONICLE®

Tips for Keeping Housekeeping Productivity in Line With Budgeted Expectations

Late check-outs, trashed rooms, trainees, temporary workers. There is no end to the drain on room attendant productivity. Considering all the issues that affect housekeeping's efficiency, is it still possible for a good manager to maintain budgeted productivity? Absolutely. Here are some of the tricks:

"No show" rooms. The front office staff will check-in guaranteed reservations before the date rolls on the property management system. But, before the audit shift ends in the morning, they will check the rooms out. These rooms are included in the total number of rooms occupied, but they do not require cleaning. These are bonuses for housekeeping, and in larger hotels can often account for a full person's load.

Supervisors, public space, and other housekeeping staff. In case of emergency, there are a number of people who can clean rooms yet who are not included in budgeted productivity. Using supervisors, public space, or laundry workers can help a housekeeping manager in critical times, but because those people have other responsibilities, if this trick is over-used, the other areas will suffer.

"No service" rooms or Do Not Disturbs. When a room attendant encounters a guest who does not desire service, the room is a bonus for productivity. Room attendants should be given incentives to request another room assignment, to go home early, or to help in another area of the hotel where their wages can be transferred.

Selling rooms. In some hotels, selling rooms to room attendants is a very common practice. In other words, room attendants are paid a predetermined flat amount per room to pick up extra rooms beyond their assignment. Since employees are eager to earn the additional money, if the rooms are cleaned within their eight-hour day, this system will improve productivity. However, keep in mind that the extra wage will negatively affect housekeeping (when the total room revenue is flat) if the department is measured by percent of sales.

Assign extra rooms daily. One of the easiest ways to maintain budgeted productivity is to assign an extra room. For instance, if the budget is for 15 rooms per eight hour shift, establish 16 as the standard assignment. The one extra room will cover the time used by trainees, meetings, suites, and so on.

In the same way, when productivity is in line, find times to assign one less room. Room attendants will appreciate the occasional lighter load.

Another option is to assign one extra room mid-week and one less on weekends. This works well in hotels that have messy weekend guests and neat weekday business travelers.

Communicate with other departments. Housekeeping managers are obligated to maintain excellent communication with all other departments. Too often it is the impact of other departments that causes a drop in room attendant productivity. Establish solid working relationships with other managers. For instance, the sales department may require that all the poolside guestrooms be converted to exhibit space. The housekeeping manager should reply that this can be accomplished—if sales will pick up the cost of the labor.

Or, perhaps the housekeeper discovers a large number of discrepant rooms each day. (Discrepant rooms are those that are marked clean, but are found to be dirty or vice versa.) Meet with the front office manager to explain the actual cost of the errors made by his or her staff. To help the front office manager resolve the problems, offer to give immediate feedback on room status conflicts. And suggest that someone on the front office staff payroll be sent to check every discrepant room and update the status appropriately.

Or, perhaps it is unclear how accounting is charging various payroll items. Meet with the controller to analyze every line of the previous month's budget and to check the coding on each employee. Often a room attendant is assigned to clean offices or public bathrooms and is not re-coded for such work. Make sure to have a crystal-clear understanding of how accounting assigns the costs of housekeeping.

Or, it could be that if engineers were given access to rags and cleaning spray bottles, they might give a quick wipe-up of their mess when making repairs in guestrooms. Often, (especially when housekeeping makes an extra effort to keep the engineers' office or shop clean) maintenance workers will clean behind themselves totally without bothering housekeeping.

Analyze Daily Routines

In analyzing room attendant productivity, perhaps the review of their daily routines is most important. For example, one hotel found that the slowness of their service elevators accounted for one hour of lost productivity for each room attendant each day. (Fifteen minutes to get to their stations in the morning, fifteen to go to lunch, fifteen to return, and fifteen at the end of the day.) Another hotel found that room attendants were making at least two trips per day to the laundry for linen that should have been delivered to their cart by linen runners. Another found that room attendants were sharing vacuum cleaners and constantly running between sections. Another found that they were paying for lunch breaks.

After these operational issues are discovered, solutions can be instituted. For instance, the elevator problem was resolved by staggering the start/break times of room attendants, by keeping the carts on the guestroom floors and by adding a person in the evening to restock the carts and closets.

In one hotel, it was the daily soap operas that were costing productivity. Room attendants were sneaking a half-hour break in an empty room to watch their favorite television show. They rushed to complete their rooms in the morning (but did not mark on their sheets that the rooms had been cleaned) and then relaxed in the afternoon. This problem was remedied in part by temporarily adding muscle to the inspection process with management checking almost immediately behind each room attendant. A notation was made on each room attendant's assignment sheet of the time each room was inspected. The natural "pace" of each room attendant soon became clear and productivity measures were revised accordingly. (Of course, there were disciplinary measures also taken.)

It is the responsibility of the executive housekeeper to know exactly how each employee's time is allocated. Only with this knowledge can the manager truly control productivity.

Source: Mary Friedman, *The Rooms Chronicle*®, Volume 6, Number 5, pp. 4–5.
For subscription information, please call 866-READ-TRC.

Employee Benefits

Calculations related to employee benefits depend on the number of labor hours expected to be scheduled, the types of job classifications involved, and the property's policies regarding employee benefits. The kinds of benefits in this expense category may include charges for the cost of holiday or vacation pay, employee meals, payroll taxes, medical expenses or insurance, social insurance such as pensions, and staff parties or social events. With the help of human resources or accounting staff, the executive housekeeper can determine what levels of expense to budget for employee benefits.

Outside Services

If the hotel employs any outside contractors for major cleaning projects or for laundry and dry-cleaning services, then the costs of these services are averaged throughout the budget periods. The executive housekeeper can consult current contracts or past invoices to determine the expense levels to budget.

In-House Laundry

The executive housekeeper needs to work closely with the laundry supervisor to budget laundry expenses. The forecasts of occupancy levels provided by the rooms division, along with the property's staffing guide, will be the basis for determining all expenses related to salaries, wages, and benefits for laundry personnel.

The cost of operating the hotel's on-premises laundry is directly related to the volume of soiled items to be processed. This, in turn, is a direct function of the hotel's occupancy levels. Therefore, the cost of laundering room linens and uniforms can be budgeted on the basis of historical information that shows the cost per occupied room of laundry operations. Multiplying the cost per occupied room for laundry operations by the number of occupied rooms forecast for each budget period will provide a figure for the expected laundry expense during the budget period.

Linens

Although linen supplies in the housekeeping department are a recycled inventory item, their life spans are ultimately limited. New linens must be purchased throughout the year as older linens are removed from service due to loss, damage, or wear. Replacement cost for new linens is an expense that needs to be worked into the budget-planning process.

Monthly physical inventories of linens show the executive housekeeper how long the existing stock of linens lasts and how much of each type of linen needs to be reordered to maintain appropriate par levels. The results of physical inventories of linens are submitted to the hotel's general manager, who routinely transfers the information to the hotel's accounting department. In turn, the accounting department regularly processes the information and provides valuable statistical information related to usage rates, losses, and expenses per occupied room. The executive housekeeper can use the cost per occupied room for replacement linen to forecast linen expense for the periods covered by the operating budget. Multiplying

the Rooms
CHRONICLE®

Payroll Dollars: Where Do They Go?

Two frequent causes of wasted payroll dollars in housekeeping are employee time spent traveling and time spent searching for supplies. These can be remedied by better department organization.

Travel time is defined as the amount of time an employee spends on his or her way somewhere, as opposed to time spent accomplishing a task. For instance, a room attendant may have to rotate between room assignments on various floors or in various buildings. Perhaps slow elevators mean long waits to get to work areas. Or it may be a long walk from the work area to the break room or cafeteria. Other causes of excessive travel time are a late check-out, which requires going back to an area already completed, and a supervisor sending a room attendant back to a room that was improperly made up.

Travel time is also a factor with public space cleaners, for whom the order of task assignments may mean excessive travel time.

Employees must have proper tools to effectively complete their tasks. When time is spent in search of supplies, payroll dollars are being wasted. For instance:

- Does a room attendant have to rummage through a pile of pillowcases to find one without stains?

- Does he or she have to seek out a vacuum cleaner that works?

- Does it take a half hour for the employee to load the cart with amenities and supplies?

- Does the room attendant stand in the laundry area, waiting for towels to dry?

- Is the room attendant returning to housekeeping for toilet paper, matchbooks, soap, etc.?

In the case of public space cleaners, time is often wasted when they have to change equipment between tasks. For instance, does the cleaner leave the department with a vacuum, return 10 minutes later for a broom and dustpan, return again for the buffer, and so on?

- Explain to the front desk how randomly assigning guests to rooms throughout the property during low occupancy periods can mean that payroll dollars are needlessly spent on travel time. Devise a system to restrict available rooms to certain predetermined areas as much as possible, while still making different types of rooms available for guests.

- In times of low occupancy, do not assign stray rooms in a particular section for cleaning. After a day or two, there may be enough dirty rooms in that area to warrant sending a room attendant.

- Instruct all room attendants to stay in their sections and use the telephone to call in their supply needs. Items not needed urgently can be picked up at break time. Urgently needed items should be delivered to the room attendants by a designated "on call" person (a laundry worker, public cleaner, or someone on a beeper for easy contact.)

(continued)

the Rooms
CHRONICLE®

- Stagger the start times and breaks of room attendants. This can help if slow elevators delay room attendants getting to work areas. Staggering starts also allows for coverage of early cleaning requests or late checkouts.

- Ensure that the room attendant training programs are minimizing the need to send cleaners back into a room that has been improperly done.

- Install quality control programs in the laundry to eliminate the possibility of stained linen being sent to the floors.

- Begin a preventive maintenance program on vacuum cleaners to keep them operational. Buy new equipment on a regular basis to replace worn-out vacuums.

- Maintain adequate linen pars. It is often the case that the labor dollars spent due to shortages of linen exceed the dollars necessary to purchase an additional par. Present a proposal to the management team to demonstrate this.

- Assign one evening houseperson to restock the room attendant carts with linens, toilet paper, tissues, and glasses.

- Prepare supply or amenity baskets in your central storage area to be issued each morning to room attendants. They carry these to their carts and are immediately ready to begin cleaning rooms. Replenish the baskets at lunchtime, if necessary.

- Organize public space carts so they carry the most frequently used items.

- Organize public space equipment in storage locations that make the most efficient use of the cleaners' time.

- Organize public space assignments in a way that makes sense not only by location, but also by task.

- Be on the lookout for things that steal your employees' time, and find solutions to correct those situations.

Source: Gail Edwards, CHHE, *The Rooms Chronicle®*, Volume 1, Number 3, p. 5.
For subscription information, please call 866-READ-TRC.

the cost per occupied room for linen replacement by the number of occupied rooms forecasted for the budget period will yield the linen expense to be built into the operating budget.

Operating Supplies

The operating supplies expense category for the housekeeping department includes non-recycled inventory items, such as guest supplies and amenities, cleaning supplies, and small equipment. As with the other housekeeping expense categories, the executive housekeeper can budget for the costs of these items on the basis of cost per occupied room.

Guest supplies include pens, stationery, matches, soap, shampoo, toilet and facial tissue, garment bags, and other amenities the hotel provides in each room for the convenience and use of its guests. The cost per occupied room for guest supplies is the same as the cost of one room par for these items. Budget amounts for guest supplies are determined by multiplying their cost per occupied room by the number of occupied rooms in the budget's forecast.

Cleaning supplies include not only chemical cleaners, polishes, and detergents, but also small equipment needed on a daily basis such as applicators, brooms, brushes, mops, buckets, spray bottles, and a variety of cleaning cloths. By following inventory control procedures, the executive housekeeper has an effective system for tracking the usage rates for the various cleaning supply items at different levels of occupancy. By dividing the cost of the number of purchase units used each month by the number of occupied rooms that month, a cost per occupied room can be established for each item in the cleaning supply inventory. Summing the results for all inventoried items yields a cost per occupied room for cleaning supplies. Multiplying this figure by the number of occupied rooms forecasted for the budget period provides the cleaning supply expense for the operating budget.

Uniforms

Provisions must be made in the operating budget for the cost of new and replacement uniforms. In addition, the cost of washing or dry-cleaning uniforms, as well as costs associated with repairing damaged uniforms, may need to be reflected in the operating budget.

Like linens, uniforms are a recycled inventory item. But unlike linens—whose usage rates and replacement needs are very predictable—the need for new uniforms during the budget period depends on factors such as personnel turnover and new hirings. To help organize information for the operating budget and for future purchasing, the executive housekeeper should maintain an itemized list of all types of uniforms maintained in the department's inventory. The cost information should be itemized for each part (for example, shirt, blouse, pants, skirt) of each type of uniform. The number of people working in each uniformed position may be obtained from human resources. Since men and women in the same position may require different uniforms—sometimes at different costs—the executive housekeeper also needs to consider the number of men and women occupying each uniformed position.

There are some rules of thumb that the executive housekeeper can use when budgeting for uniform purchases. While these rules of thumb may be helpful, executive housekeepers should keep in mind that uniform par levels vary from property to property.

The executive housekeeper should start by budgeting for one complete uniform for each person. Next, for uniforms that are dry-cleaned, the executive housekeeper should budget for one additional uniform per person. For uniforms that are washed, the executive housekeeper should budget for two additional uniforms per person, since laundering greatly reduces a uniform's useful life span. As a final rule of thumb, the executive housekeeper should budget three additional sets of uniforms for cooks. Taking into consideration an annual plan for replacing uniforms, the executive housekeeper should divide the cost of new uniforms into those months during the budget period in which they will be purchased.

In determining the cost of repairing uniforms, the executive housekeeper needs to consider not only the materials needed for repairs, but also the cost of the time spent by the supervisor or seamstress to repair the uniforms. Records of past repairs and productivity standards for repair can provide information relevant to the executive housekeeper's estimate for budgeting the cost of repairs.

Controlling Expenses

Controlling housekeeping expenses means ensuring that actual expenses are consistent with the expected expenses forecast by the operating budget. There are basically four methods the executive housekeeper can use to control housekeeping expenses: accurate recordkeeping, effective scheduling, careful training and supervision, and efficient purchasing.

Maintaining accurate records is the first step in controlling expenses and identifying problems in relation to managing inventories. Accurate recordkeeping enables the executive housekeeper to monitor usage rates, inventory costs, and variances in relation to standard cleaning procedures.

Effective scheduling permits the executive housekeeper to control salaries and wages and the costs related to employee benefits. It is important to schedule all housekeeping employees according to the guidelines in the property's staffing guide. Since the staffing guide bases its guidelines on the level of room occupancy, it ensures that personnel costs stay in line with occupancy rates. At the same time, the need for adequate staffing to maintain the desired level of service leaves the executive housekeeper little room to "cut corners" by scheduling fewer employees than the staffing guide recommends. The executive housekeeper can ensure that the approved guidelines expressed in the property's staffing guide are consistently followed in all employee scheduling decisions. Adjusting weekly work schedules in light of anticipated occupancy levels is an ongoing responsibility of the executive housekeeper.

Training and supervision should not be overlooked as a cost control measure. The recommendations in the property's staffing guide are based on the assumption that certain performance and productivity standards are consistently achieved. Effective training programs that quickly bring new hires "up to speed" can significantly reduce the time during which productivity is lower than the standards set for more experienced personnel. Close and diligent supervision, as well as refresher training, can ensure that performance and productivity standards are met—and may even bring about improvements. Finally, effective training and supervision are an important part of controlling the cost of inventoried items. For example, training employees in the proper use of cleaning supplies can improve usage rates and, over time, lower the cost of cleaning supplies per occupied room.

Efficient purchasing practices afford the executive housekeeper the greatest opportunity to control department expenses. The executive housekeeper bears an important responsibility to make sure that the hotel's money is well spent and the maximum value is received from products purchased for use.

Purchasing Systems

Efficient purchasing practices can make a significant contribution to the executive housekeeper's role in controlling housekeeping expenses. In fact, the most controllable expenses under the executive housekeeper's responsibility involve the various items whose inventories are maintained by the housekeeping department. Inventory control procedures enable the executive housekeeper to know when to buy and how much to buy for each inventoried item. Deciding what to buy, whom to buy it from, and exactly how to purchase it requires careful consideration on the part of the executive housekeeper.

Although the actual purchasing may be done by the hotel's purchasing department, quantities and specifications are submitted to the purchasing department by department heads. When ordering items for the housekeeping department, the executive housekeeper will need to fill out and sign a purchase order such as that shown in Exhibit 5. This order form then has to be approved by the controller and general manager. For all items purchased for the housekeeping department, the recommendation of the content, quantities, and source of a purchase is made by the executive housekeeper. Although various properties have various procedures for processing and approving purchases, the evaluation of what's needed, when it's needed, how much is needed, and from whom it is needed fall under the responsibility of department heads. The executive housekeeper needs to know how to obtain the best value when purchasing the items needed by the housekeeping department.

Linen Replacement

Next to salaries and wages, linens are the highest expense item in the housekeeping budget. The initial purchase of linens for the hotel will greatly influence the costs of replacing linens that become lost or are taken out of service due to damage or excessive wear. The fabric type, size, and color will influence both initial purchases and replacement costs. Colored items are usually more expensive and have shorter life spans than white ones since the colors fade through repeated washings.

The physical inventory records show the executive housekeeper how long the existing stock of linens will last and how much of each type of linen needs to be reordered to maintain par levels. Typically, linen purchases are made annually with deliveries scheduled to be drop-shipped on a quarterly basis. This arrangement enables the executive housekeeper to conserve available storage space by using a supplier's warehouse facilities while periodically receiving replacement stock.

Planning linen purchases on a yearly basis can also result in considerable savings. Linen brokers provide a convenient and quick way to purchase linens, but they are expensive. Ordering larger quantities in bulk can often win lower per-unit prices. Planned annual linen purchases also enable large hospitality chains to order linen supplies directly from linen mills. Although these orders require considerable lead time to prepare, a property saves on the premiums charged by linen brokers to process orders and arrange deliveries. Unforeseen emergency needs could then be filled through a linen broker.

Exhibit 5 Sample Purchase Order

Purchase Order					

Purchase Order
Number: _____

Order Date: _____

Payment Terms: _____

To: _____
(supplier)

From/
Ship to: _____
(name of operation)

_____
(address)

_____
(address)

Delivery Date: _____

Please Ship:

Quantity Ordered	Description	✓	Units Shipped	Unit Cost	Total Cost

Total Cost _____

Important: This purchase order expressly limits acceptance to the terms and conditions stated above, noted on the reverse side hereof, and any additional terms and conditions affixed hereto or otherwise referenced. Any additional terms and conditions proposed by seller are objected to and rejected.

_____
Authorized Signature

The quantity of linen to purchase is determined by assessing the hotel's quarterly requirements to maintain linen at the proper par level. Physical inventories of linens can be used to calculate an annual consumption rate that shows how much linen is "used up" either by normal wear and tear, damage, loss, or theft. With this information, the executive housekeeper can use the following formula to determine the size of annual linen purchases:

$$\text{Annual Order} = \text{Par Stock Level} - \text{Linen on Hand}$$

the Rooms
CHRONICLE®

Tips to Remember, Mistakes to Avoid When Purchasing

Whether it is for a 60-room limited-service property or a 1,500-room, full ser-vice resort, all managers inevitably face the challenge of procuring goods. As an agent dedicated to protecting the financial interests of the owner or operator, it is essential to produce the greatest output or service and to reduce costs to achieve a healthy bottom line. A strong purchasing program can effectively save money for the hotel and accomplish this goal.

Size Does Matter

The size of the hotel, either as a stand-alone property or collectively as part of a larger ownership or management portfolio, is the starting point for effective pur-chasing decisions. Remember that many pricing structures are based on volume.

Be realistic when negotiating prices for anything from bedding to linens and carpets to curtains. A 2,000-room resort will have a much higher usage rate and will be able to command much lower prices than the 300-room hotel just down the street. Realistically estimating one's buying leverage will save the buyer and the seller time and negotiation troubles as well as lost goodwill or good faith.

If intent on saving money on linens for example, the prudent manager should consider purchasing twice the supply now to obtain a lower price today, as opposed to purchasing two orders six months apart and paying a higher price. This could save a large amount of money, but there are drawbacks. A larger sum of capital is required to buy linens, and if it is tied up in linen inventory on the shelf, the hotel may not be able to commit the money to other needs or projects. The ultimate decision depends on what management values most: the savings derived from one large order or realizing the benefits of other investments that can be made with the funds.

Credibility Counts

During the bidding process, be truthful about the hotel's estimated usage. If the property is expecting to replace 100 mattresses in the next year do not tell sup-pliers that the estimated usage will be 125 or 150 mattresses. The deceiving hotel manager may find himself enjoying a large savings today but the long-term con-sequences will eventually bring a greater negative impact than the short-term eco-nomic benefit. The manager's credibility will likely become questionable and his hotel's purchasing reputation could be tarnished with that supplier.

Keep in mind that there are only a relatively small handful of hotel suppli-ers and institutional vendors in each market. And contrary to the assumed laws of competition, suppliers *do* talk to each other and share feedback regarding questionable accounts. Yes, the first year will be good while the hotel revels in its purchasing prowess. However, the vendor who feels that he or she was taken advantage of by an unscrupulous client will quietly increase that hotel's prices for supplies in the future, thus decreasing their bank account.

Rebates and Purchasing Promotions

If a purchasing manager is able to negotiate a custom price for a product, such as in-room coffee makers, he should not assume that the hotel will also be able to

(continued)

the Rooms
CHRONICLE®

(continued)

collect manufacturer's rebates and thus make the final acquisition price even lower. Many times, by buying certain products at the right time, a hotel can collect points towards future purchases. These points may not be available on already low negotiated prices. When faced with this situation, the manager must determine what is most important to the hotel: a lower price now or a greater discount later. The price will only go so low; it may go low in different promotions, but there is a bottom price.

Communicate Clearly

Effective communication is a key to success in every aspect of business and can be especially helpful in purchasing. Consider purchasing custom printed letterhead as well as purchase specification forms and bid request fax sheets. Make sure the hotel's purchasing policies, payment terms, and receiving hours are clearly outlined on the forms used during the bid process. This is important for several reasons.

First, exact purchase specifications and purchase quantity are necessary to enable competing suppliers to fairly and accurately bid on the exact same product. Also, this information will assist each vendor in determining whether they can fulfill the order according to the terms dictated. Without this information, problems invariably arise as one vendor may be bidding to supply the hotel with high-grade paper while another may be submitting a bid to supply lower-grade paper.

More significant than the probable price spread, the hotel may actually receive a different product than which it intended to acquire. This will require additional time, labor, and expense by both the hotel and the vendor to handle the refused goods, process the credit for refused merchandise, and to fulfill the original order as intended. More than likely, the vendor may actually lose money on the transaction to keep the hotel satisfied by providing the higher quality goods. A pattern of refusals by the hotel or misfulfillment by the vendor will inevitably lead to harsh feelings by both parties.

It's About Business

Finally, remember why the hotel is in business. The basic purpose of any business, including the hotel, is to make money by earning a profit through transactions. Now, remember why the hotel's suppliers are in business: to make money and earn a profit. Both parties need each other to survive; and both need strong communication and understanding from each other to grow their company.

The hotel and its vendors are not competitors; so work together, be honest, and communicate effectively, and both sides will be stronger in the end.

Source: Louis A. Quagliana, *The Rooms Chronicle®*, Volume 12, Number 2, p. 14. For subscription information, please call 866-READ-TRC.

The executive housekeeper is expected to carefully select suppliers and linen products to ensure that the hotel receives good value for money spent. The most important considerations are the suitability of the products for their intended uses and whether the products are economical. Regarding linen, the expected useful life of the linen is often more important than purchase price in determining whether alternative products are economical or not. The cost of laundering linens over their useful life is usually much greater and more important than their initial price.

The life span of linen is measured in terms of how many times it can be laundered before becoming too worn to be suitable for guestroom use. Linen that is purchased at bargain prices but that wears out after only moderate laundering will damage guests' perceptions of quality, increase annual linen usage rates, and increase costs in the long run. Durability, laundry considerations, and purchase price are the main criteria to use in selecting linen. A cost per use can be calculated in order to evaluate alternative linen purchases using the following formula:

$$\text{Cost per use} = \frac{\text{Purchase Cost} + \text{Life span Laundering Costs}}{\text{Number of Life span Launderings}}$$

The laundering costs over the life span of a linen product can be determined by multiplying the item's weight by the hotel's laundering cost per pound—and then multiplying again by the number of launderings the item can withstand before showing excessive wear.

When orders of new linens are received, shipments should be checked against purchase orders and inspected to ensure that the linens meet all quality and quantity specifications. Newly received linen orders should be immediately moved to the main linen room for storage. In the main linen room, new linens that have not yet been put into service should be stored separately from linens that are already in use.

Inventories for all new linen received and issued at the hotel should be kept on a perpetual basis. This means that a running count should be kept for on-hand quantities of every type of new linen stored in the main linen room. The inventory record should show the linen type, specific item, price, storage location, and dates of ordering and receiving. As linen items are put into service to replace worn, damaged, lost, or stolen linen, the quantity recorded on the perpetual inventory record should be adjusted accordingly.

The executive housekeeper is responsible for placing new linen in use on an as-needed basis to maintain the par level for each linen item. Issuing new linen to be used in daily operations typically occurs each month on the basis of shortages revealed by a physical inventory. New linen may also be issued between physical inventories to replace discarded linens. Some hotels inject a predetermined quantity of new linen into circulation at preestablished intervals based on past usage rates. New linens should be placed into service on a "first-in, first-out" basis. New linen not in service should be under the control of the executive housekeeper or laundry supervisor in the main linen room or another secure place.

Uniform Replacement

Uniforms need to be replaced when they become damaged or worn. The executive housekeeper needs to establish a procedure for issuing new or replacement uniforms. A notation could be made on the employee's uniform card that a damaged uniform was received and discarded, and that a new uniform was issued. The date and the employee's signature should be recorded on the inventory card.

The executive housekeeper is generally responsible for receiving, storing, and controlling all new uniforms held in the hotel's custody but not placed into service. The executive housekeeper is also responsible for placing new uniforms into service to ensure that all uniform requirements are met, clean uniform replacements are available, and the laundry is not unduly burdened with clean uniform processing.

As with linens, the main criteria for purchasing replacement uniforms are durability, life span, and the quality of materials. The purchase price of uniforms is a secondary consideration. Comfort, practicality, and ease of maintenance are also important considerations. New uniforms should be purchased to maintain the par levels established for uniforms. Comparing the on-hand quantities with the established par levels will show the executive housekeeper how many replacement uniforms should be ordered.

Purchasing Operating Supplies

Some hotel chains have centralized, national purchasing systems for major housekeeping items in order to achieve quantity discounts. Other hotels may join together in purchasing groups to achieve savings on bulk purchases of commonly used items. But, for the most part, operating supplies are purchased by the individual property and with the direct involvement of the executive housekeeper.

Inventory tracking forms can be used to create an exhaustive list of operating supplies that the executive housekeeper will need to purchase on a regular basis. Inventory control procedures will show how often and in what quantities supply items will need to be purchased to maintain par levels. Usage rates and cost-per-occupied-room figures can be determined from the inventory records. This information can form the basis for an effective purchasing system. By following careful purchasing procedures, the executive housekeeper can help the hotel control costs while ensuring that adequate supply levels are maintained.

Before buying any product, the executive housekeeper should obtain samples in order to test the product and determine whether it meets specifications. Suitability for the intended task, quality, ease of handling, and storage requirements are just as important as the price in determining whether a product is economical.

Value—not price—should be the leading consideration in making purchase decisions. An inexpensive cleaning agent that has to be used in much larger quantities than a more expensive one may actually cost more in the long run. The crucial concern is to obtain the best value for the money.

Selecting the right vendors can often make the executive housekeeper's purchasing systems more efficient. The executive housekeeper needs to competitively shop suppliers and vendors for the products to be purchased on a regular basis. When asking for price quotations, the executive housekeeper needs to be as precise as possible regarding such specifications as weight, quality, packaging, size, concentration, quantities, and delivery times.

In evaluating alternative suppliers, the executive housekeeper needs to be concerned with how well the supplier will service the hotel's account. It is important that the vendors selected appreciate the operations of a hotel's housekeeping department, fully understand the products they sell, and be able to provide demonstrations and even training in how to use the products. It is not unusual for the executive housekeeper to select one vendor for all guest supply items, another for cleaning products, and still another for all paper products. By limiting the number of suppliers with whom the housekeeping department has to deal, the executive housekeeper can streamline the purchasing process, reduce paperwork, and use time more efficiently. In addition, concentrating business with a limited number of suppliers often achieves greater purchasing—and thereby bargaining—power, resulting in improved quantity discounts and better service.

Another consideration in selecting vendors is whether they will be able to stock the products the hotel purchases at their own warehouse facilities and drop-ship the products to the hotel on an as-needed basis. This enables the executive housekeeper to achieve savings by purchasing products in bulk whenever possible and, at the same time, solve the problem of limited storage space.

In the process of reordering operating supplies, the executive housekeeper needs to periodically reevaluate the suitability of existing products for their intended purposes. Meeting with housekeeping staff who use the product can help determine any problems that may lead to a reconsideration of quality or functionality. The functionality of the product should be tested, and the executive housekeeper should determine whether the existing specifications for the product should remain the same. Alternative products should be investigated and compared to existing products in terms of performance, durability, price, and value.

Worksheets can be used to monitor usage rates and costs for the various types of operating supplies kept in inventory. Exhibit 6 illustrates one such worksheet for tracking the use of various chemical cleaners. For each product, the Monthly Chemical Use Report identifies the vendor, the product name, and its intended use. Each month, physical inventories provide the executive housekeeper with information concerning how many purchase units of each chemical cleaner have been used. Multiplying the number of units used by the cost per unit yields the total cost of the product used during the month. Dividing the total cost by the number of occupied rooms yields a cost per occupied room figure for each product. By reducing the size of each purchase unit (e.g., gallons, cans, pints, quarts) to a common-sized unit (e.g., ounces) and multiplying the number of purchase units used by the common-sized amounts, the total amount used for each product can be determined in terms that render the different-sized products comparable. After using a common measure to calculate the actual amounts used, the executive housekeeper can divide by the number of occupied rooms to determine the usage of each product per occupied room. In this way, the Monthly Chemical Use Report enables the executive housekeeper to compare the relative efficiency of using various products for similar tasks. By comparing the costs per occupied room and the usage per occupied room achieved by alternative products, the executive housekeeper can evaluate which products yield greater cost savings and make purchasing decisions accordingly.

Capital Budgets

Purchases of most inventoried items in the housekeeping department occur monthly. These costs appear in the operating budget as expenses against the revenue

Exhibit 6   Monthly Chemical Use Report

For April, 20XX Number of Occupied Rooms 25,410									
VENDOR	**PRODUCT**	**INTENDED USE**	**UNITS USED**	**COST PER UNIT**	**TOTAL COST**	**COST PER OCC. ROOM**	**AMOUNT PER UNIT**	**TOTAL UNITS**	**USAGE PER OCC. ROOM**
Johnson	G.P. Forward	All-purpose cleaner	108 gal.	$15.48	$1,671.84	$.066	128 oz.	13,824	.544
Johnson	Spartan	Degreaser	39 gal.	17.02	663.78	.026	128 oz.	4,992	.196
Johnson	Brady	Floor stripper	48 gal.	25.28	1,213.44	.048	128 oz.	6,144	.242
Armstrong	S-490	Special area stripper	5 gal.	25.88	129.40	.005	23 oz.	115	.005
Johnson	Complete	Composition floor wax	142 gal.	26.32	3,737.44	.147	128 oz.	18,176	.715
Johnson	Fortify	Porous floor seal	67 gal.	34.20	2,291.40	.090	128 oz.	8,576	.338
Johnson	Snap Back	Spray buff	.5 gal.	40.00	20.00	.001	128 oz.	64	.003
Johnson	Conq-R-Dust	Dust mop treatment	10 can	4.58	45.80	.002	128 oz.	1,280	.050
Dillon Chem	Waterless Cleaner	Wood floor stripper	35 gal.	12.80	448.00	.018	128 oz.	4,480	.176
Ecolab	Revitalize	Carpet shampoo	17 gal.	26.01	442.17	.017	128 oz.	2,176	.086
Amrep	Misty	Steam cleaner	6 gal.	11.61	69.66	.003	128 oz.	768	.030
Johnson	Carpet Odor Eliminator	Powdered deodorant	3 can	3.65	10.95	.001	24 oz.	120	.005
Core	Unbelievable	Carpet spotter	70 pints	6.72	470.40	.019	16 oz.	1,120	.044
SSS	Gum Remover	Tar & gum remover	61 can	4.86	296.46	.012	12 oz.	732	.029
Dumond C	Lift Away	Graffiti remover	3 can	14.95	44.85	.002	15 oz.	45	.002
Zep	Once Over	Wall & vinyl cleaner	27 can	5.95	160.65	.006	22.5 oz.	608	.024
Ecover	Ecological	Bathroom bowl cleaner	3 quart	4.69	14.07	.001	32 oz.	96	.004
P-G	Safeguard Dispenser	Dispenser soap	12 gal.	15.31	183.72	.007	128 oz.	1,536	.060
Johnson	Lemon Shine Up	Furniture polish	35 can	11.04	386.40	.015	15 oz.	525	.021
3M	Stainless Steel Polish	Metal cleaner	52 can	11.04	574.08	.023	21.5 oz.	1,118	.044
3M	Tarni-Shield	Brass cleaner	43 bottle	9.42	405.06	.016	10 oz.	430	.017
	Vinegar	Neutralizer	26 gal.	1.59	41.34	.002	128 oz.	3,328	.131

generated over the same period. Major purchases of machines and equipment in the housekeeping department are not included on operating budgets. Instead, purchases for items with relatively high costs and long life spans are planned as part of capital budgets because they involve additional capital investments by the hotel.

Capital budgets are prepared annually. The executive housekeeper will be asked to specify the need for funds to purchase machines and equipment for the housekeeping department. It is crucial that the executive housekeeper be prepared to justify any requests for capital expenditures. Although such requests may be part of an overall modernization or renovation program, they more typically involve a need to replace existing machines or equipment.

Typically, the need to replace major machines and equipment is discovered when a particular item cannot be repaired. However, the executive housekeeper can effectively predict the useful life of each machine in the housekeeping department based on how often it is used and its estimated number of working hours, provided by the machine's manufacturer and supplier. Executive housekeepers should be aware, however, that machines and equipment that receive high usage will not live up to the guarantees and estimates of useful life provided by suppliers.

When purchasing housekeeping equipment, executive housekeepers need to focus on long-range considerations. Major purchases of machines and equipment represent a capital expense for the hotel, and planning is required. Whenever possible, it is important to choose a supplier who can service the machines in a quick and efficient manner. If such a supplier cannot be found, the executive housekeeper will need to order an adequate number of replacement parts so that the hotel itself will be able to service the machines.

The executive housekeeper is expected to be able to recommend the proper type, quality, and quantity of equipment needed to keep guestrooms and public areas clean and attractive. The housekeeping department needs equipment that will last through continuous use with a minimum of maintenance. Cost effectiveness is the most important consideration. As always, purchase price needs to be considered along with the quality and durability of the product.

Contract vs. In-House Cleaning

A number of outside contractors offer a variety of cleaning services to hotels. Outside contractors are available for nearly any cleaning task that needs to be done, including outside laundry and dry-cleaning services, floor cleaning and care, outside window cleaning, overhead cleaning, masonry cleaning, and descaling and scouring of restroom fixture traps. Given these services, a hotel could even use outside contractors for its entire housekeeping operation.

An important decision that arises in an increasing number of contexts is whether to contract outside services for cleaning tasks or undertake them as in-house operations. The issue is often approached in terms of how to best control costs while ensuring that necessary tasks are accomplished and quality standards are maintained. In many situations, the issue is one that involves both capital budget and operating budget considerations.

While wages and materials are monthly expenses that can be budgeted, the equipment needed to start an in-house cleaning program is a capital expense that occurs all at once. Often, after the initial start-up cost for machines and equipment, the monthly expense that the hotel will incur with an in-house cleaning program is less than the monthly expense it would incur with an outside contractor. In addition, many executive housekeepers believe that an in-house staff will perform higher-quality work than an outside contractor because of the opportunity for increased control.

The executive housekeeper may be asked to demonstrate how long it would take to recover the initial start-up costs for machines and equipment through the monthly savings achieved by an in-house cleaning program. By dividing the savings achieved each month into the total amount of capital expenditure for the needed equipment, the executive housekeeper can calculate how many months it would take to pay back the initial investment. In determining monthly expenses that an in-house operation would incur, the executive housekeeper needs to consider the costs of salaries and wages, employee benefits, materials and supplies, training, and supervision. The decision as to whether the initial investment is possible and worth the monthly savings is one that belongs to the hotel's upper management and ultimately to the owners.

In some situations, the initial start-up costs are deemed too high for the monthly savings achieved. In other cases, the nature of the cleaning task may be so specialized or infrequent that initiating an in-house cleaning program is not reasonable or cost-efficient. In still other situations, the monthly expense for outside contractors is lower than the monthly expenses an in-house operation would incur in performing the same tasks. There are always pros and cons to consider when assessing the need for contracted cleaning services.

For whatever reason, the executive housekeeper will sometimes be charged with the task of arranging for outside contractors to perform some cleaning service. The initial problem is choosing the appropriate contractor. The executive housekeeper should request cost estimates from at least three different contractors. For area cleaning tasks, contractors base quotations on the exact size of the area to be cleaned; the executive housekeeper cannot collect comparable cost quotations until exact measurements are obtained. For laundering tasks, quotations are based on dry weight or on a per-piece basis. Quotations also specify the frequency of the service desired as well as collection and delivery times. For any kind of contract cleaning, the executive housekeeper should obtain cost quotations on the basis of carefully defined needs, precise descriptions of work, and clear indications of the frequency of service. The same specifications should be submitted to each contractor to ensure that cost estimates are fully comparable.

Both previous and current clients of each contractor should be checked for reports on the quality and efficiency of the services. The reputation and ability of the contractor's local organization, as opposed to the credentials of the home office, should be assessed. Visiting the contractor's place of business may provide insights into the kind of operation the contractor runs.

After selecting an appropriate contractor, it is important to establish the precise nature and frequency of the services desired in the written contract. The terminology describing the task, frequency, and expected performance needs to be as clear and precise as possible. All contracts should incorporate a cancellation clause. Certain contracts should also have penalty clauses to ensure compliance with all specifications.

After contracting an outside cleaning service, it is essential to monitor the quality of the contractor's work. Routine inspections and regular meetings with the contractor will enable the executive housekeeper to identify and discuss any problems or concerns in a timely manner. Assigned tasks and completion dates should be discussed clearly and documented in writing. It is also important to monitor invoices received from outside contractors; invoices should be checked for accuracy before being submitted to the accounting department for payment.

While the use of outside contractors for cleaning services appears to be increasing in the hospitality industry, the executive housekeeper should periodically assess whether replacing outside services with in-house operations can be justified as a cost control measure. After the initial capital investment in machines

Can Contract Cleaning Save the Day? Or Should the Hotel Save Its Money?

Whether the hotel is large or small, sometimes there are cleaning jobs that require outside help. It may be that the staff does not have the equipment, supplies, time, or personnel to perform the job.

That's when contract cleaners are called. Love them or hate them, contract cleaners play an important role in the hotel industry. Some of the more common jobs contracted are window washing, carpet shampooing, kitchen cleaning, third-shift public space cleaning, and renovation cleanup. Here are some things to consider before signing an agreement.

Advantages of Using Contract Cleaners

- They provide generally skilled laborers, well trained in their areas of expertise.
- They provide all supplies and equipment.
- They provide uniformed workers and have responsibility for all wages and benefits.
- Their workers stay on the job until it is done.
- They are accountable for the results.

Disadvantages of Using Contract Cleaners

- Workers are not representatives of the hotel and may not have skills for guest interaction.
- Workers may not show up within the time frame designated.
- Contract cleaners may not meet the hotel's standards for quality.

Tips for Making It Work

1. Obtain at least three bids for the job. Make sure a representative of each company visits the property to review the project before bidding. Ask the companies to list the equipment and supplies that will be used.
2. Work only with companies that are well established and recommended. A minimum of five years in the business should be required.
3. Check references thoroughly, and visit other job sites.
4. Inquire about the training provided to each company's workers.
5. Write time expectations for the job into the contract.
6. Write the hotel's quality expectations into the contract.
7. Verify insurance coverage for workers, guests, hotel employees, and assets.

(continued)

the Rooms
CHRONICLE®

(continued)

8. Greet the cleaners when they arrive, and review the job parameters.

9. Visit the job site shortly after work has begun to ensure that the hotel's expectations are being met.

10. Give the project a walk-down at completion to review the contractor's work.

11. Never pay in advance.

Source: Mary Friedman, *The Rooms Chronicle*®, Volume 3, Number 5, p. 4. For subscription information, please call 866-READ-TRC.

and equipment is recovered through monthly savings in operating expenses, the reduced costs and increased control that often accompanies in-house operations can be of significant value to the property.

Key Terms

capital budget—A detailed plan for the acquisition of equipment, land, buildings, and other fixed assets.

capital expenditures—Items costing $1,500 or more that are not used up in the normal course of operations, and that have a life span that exceeds a single year.

income statement—A report on the profitability of operations, including revenues earned and expenses incurred in generating the revenues for the period covered by the statement.

operating budget—A detailed plan for generating revenue and incurring expenses for each department within the hospitality operation.

operating expenditures—Costs incurred in order to generate revenue in the normal course of doing business.

pro forma income statement—A report that predicts the results of current or future operations, including revenues earned and expenses incurred in generating the revenues for the period covered by the statement.

schedule—A report which gives supporting detail to a property's financial statements.

Review Questions

1. What are the basic responsibilities of the executive housekeeper in the budget process?

2. What is the difference between a capital budget and an operating budget?

3. Why is forecasting occupancy levels such a critical part of the budget-planning process?

4. How can the operating budget be used as a tool to control expenses?

5. What is the relationship of an operating budget to an income statement?

6. What are some of the typical expenses (or line items) an executive housekeeper might encounter when preparing the department's budget?

7. What two factors can help the executive housekeeper predict a certain level of expense for each expense category?

8. What are the four basic methods an executive housekeeper can use to control expenses?

9. What basic responsibilities does the executive housekeeper have in terms of purchasing operating supplies?

10. What types of situations should be assessed when deciding whether to use outside contractors for cleaning services?

 ## Case Study

Dangerous Discrepancies

Herbert McMurtry, the general manager of the Hotel Commodore, convened a 10:00 A.M. meeting with the hotel's front office manager, executive housekeeper, and chief engineer. Mr. McMurtry was frustrated because that morning's report revealed six vacant rooms charged to guests who had already left a day or two earlier, an error that has become too common.

As his imposing figure entered the small meeting room, Mr. McMurtry opened the meeting: "I want to thank you all for meeting with me this morning because I have a number of things to cover and I don't want to hold you up from your jobs... Oh," he paused, furrowing his brow, "Where's Todd?"

Just as Mr. McMurtry finished his question, Todd, the front desk manager, burst into the room, "I'm so sorry to be late, Mr. McMurtry," Todd said. "I had another darn discrepant room to deal with."

"That's just why I wanted to speak with all of you." Mr. McMurtry continued. "I'm getting pretty upset because the property has been losing revenue due to chargebacks. To make matters worse, last week I had to deal with a very angry Ms. Spencer, of the Spencer Spinet Company, who flew here all the way from New York just to check into a dirty room. She is a regular, high-paying customer of our hotel and now she'll probably take her business elsewhere. And this wasn't the first time I had to face this sort of complaint. I'd like to find out what's going on here. I have a feeling your departments aren't communicating. If this keeps up, it's going to affect our bottom line *and* your bonuses."

Todd quickly spoke up, "Well, most of the time we get a chargeback because a guest neglects to notify the front desk upon checking out, sometimes days before the expected check-out time. We bill guests as originally booked but, if they claim that they checked out earlier, we have to reimburse them, their room is never rented, and we lose out. I think we should physically check all the rooms for occupancy each afternoon."

Isabel, the executive housekeeper, immediately responded, "I don't know, Todd, you have to consider the increased labor costs and the demands on my staff. Room checks are just Band-Aids to cover up bigger problems. There must be a better way to handle it. Let's think of ways to encourage guests to let us know when they've checked out. Perhaps the housekeeping staff can help."

"I don't know about chargebacks," Tomas, the hotel's chief engineer said, "but I think if everyone just followed our established procedures for out-of-order rooms, we wouldn't have problems with guests checking into unready rooms."

"Oh, c'mon Tom," Todd chimed in. "I'm under pressure to fill rooms. Frankly, maintenance can be too slow for me. If I have a potential sell-out, my staff checks the out-of-order rooms. If one looks good, I sell it."

Mr. McMurtry cast Todd an irritated glance. "While we can't afford to have rooms sitting vacant, giving someone an out-of-order room is just plain bad for business, Todd," he stressed. "There's no guarantee that your staff will know what's wrong with the room from a brief visual check. We need a more experienced eye than yours."

Tomas agreed, "Remember when the Paper Clip Manufacturers Association was in town for a convention and we checked someone into a room with a plumbing leak? The room was out-of-order when he checked in but, because we were at full capacity, we used the room anyway. We had to move him to another hotel because he wound up with two inches of standing water in the bathroom!"

"There's also the problem with discrepant rooms you faced before coming to this meeting, Todd," Isabel added, "My staff cleans rooms by noon and then an hour later the rooms are listed as dirty. How does that happen?"

"If guests check into rooms and then aren't satisfied," replied Todd, trying not to get defensive, "I move them to other rooms. The computer is programmed to default their original rooms as dirty."

"But I know that some of those guests never even *see* the room," Isabel replied. "They just change their minds right at the front desk. It would be better for all of us if the front desk would automatically redesignate those rooms as clean and vacant."

"I see your point," Todd said, trying to be patient, "but my staff is really busy too and it interferes with our other work if we are constantly switching back and forth on our computer screens. The worst thing I can do is keep guests waiting while I fiddle with the computer."

Mr. McMurtry quickly responded to Todd's last point, "Yes, but there's also no sense in hurrying guests to unprepared rooms or making them wait for rooms that are ready."

The conversation was heating up and Mr. McMurtry could see that they might be sitting there for the rest of the day if he didn't cut it short. "We've talked about a lot here. Now I want you all to agree on at least three solutions to these problems and come back to me with an action plan by the end of the day." With that he excused his managers and waited for the good news to roll his way.

Discussion Questions

1. What solutions would you suggest for reducing chargebacks within the hotel?

2. How can the different divisions within the Hotel Commodore cooperate to resolve conflicts over room status?

3. What are some ways in which the front office could eliminate room discrepancies?

Case Study

Lean Profits in a Land of Plenty

The 600-room Knightsrest Hotel, a property catering largely to business travelers, is in a good location near an airport and a busy government facility. Though the hotel seldom reaches full occupancy, it does good business. Still, the owners have been disappointed by the profit margins. The general manager, Nancy Wood, has determined that one element contributing to the hotel's unacceptable financial performance is that housekeeping expenses are way out of line. When she mentioned this to Sue Miller, the executive housekeeper, they agreed to hire Bonnie Hansen, a housekeeping consultant, to come in and look at the Knightsrest's housekeeping operations.

Bonnie begins her consultation by asking Sue how supplies are ordered. Sue explains that the hotel has a standing order placed every two weeks to replace supplies "assumed" to have been used.

As Bonnie walks around the property, she notes a number of things. All room attendants have access to the main storeroom, which is left open, and are expected to stock their own carts. Throughout the hotel, most housekeeper caddies are stocked with the same brand name cleaning supplies (purchased, as Sue explains to Bonnie, at great savings from a discount house), although the amount of supplies on each cart varies widely. Bonnie hears some room attendants explain that they occasionally stock their carts with extra supplies because the main storeroom too frequently runs out of certain items. Some carts have brand name items Bonnie did not see in the main storeroom. Bonnie also notes that the linen closets on each floor are filled with housekeeping supplies; in fact, housekeeping supplies seem to be stored in just about every nook and cranny available, including telephone equipment rooms. Some supplies are crammed so tightly into spaces that they are damaged. This is particularly true of guest stationery items imprinted with the hotel's logo.

As Bonnie looks through the guestrooms, she notes that the same high-quality amenities are used in all rooms. In stayover rooms, new soap and shampoo are left every day. She sees a room attendant using furniture polish on Formica™ surfaces. The room attendant tells her that this is her own personal touch. "They want us to use just water," explains the room attendant, "but this smells nice." This room attendant also explains to Bonnie that the cleaning chemical provided by the hotel for use on bathtubs refuses to suds up, so she and many other room attendants add the hotel guestroom shampoo to improve the chemical's effectiveness.

Throughout the day, Bonnie observes housekeeping staff using only large 3.0 mil garbage bags, many only half-filled when discarded. Walking through the kitchens, she notes employees wearing shower caps with hotel logos over their hair. She watches as the public space cleaner, Tom Harper, runs back and forth for supplies. First, Tom notices a bit of mud on the floor, so he leaves to get a mop and bucket. After cleaning up the mud, he notices some smudged windows, so he returns the mop and bucket and eventually returns with window cleaning supplies. Finally, he leaves once more and returns a few minutes later with a vacuum cleaner. The vacuum's suction is weak; apparently the bag is full.

On her rounds, Bonnie sees several employees reading *USA Today* during their breaks. Sue explains to her that the hotel orders one copy per room. Bonnie also notes that virtually all employees—including managers—use the hotel's logo notepads, ordered as guestroom amenities.

On her way to the general manager's office to talk with Ms. Wood and Sue, Bonnie sees that each of the executive offices has its own coffee maker and everyone seems to use the single-serving coffee supplies that are charged to housekeeping for guestroom use. Bonnie sees guestroom hand lotion bottles sitting on many desks as well as tissue boxes, pens, and desk organizers like those she saw stocked in the main housekeeping storeroom.

Discussion Questions

1. What problems and weaknesses is Bonnie likely to identify in her discussion with Ms. Wood and Sue?

2. What suggestions might she make to address these problems and weaknesses?

The following industry experts helped generate and develop these cases: Gail Edwards, CHHE, St. Louis, Missouri; Mary Friedman, Edina, Minnesota; and Aleta Nitschke, CHA, founder of *The Rooms Chronicle*®, Garfield, Minnesota.

Chapter 7 Outline

Safety
    Insurance and Liability Concerns
    Employee Morale and Management
      Concerns
    Potentially Hazardous Conditions
    Job Safety Analysis
    Safety Training
Common Housekeeping Chemicals
    Water
    Bathroom Cleaners
    All-Purpose Cleaners
    Safety Equipment for Using Chemicals
OSHA Regulations
    Work Areas
    Means of Egress
    Sanitation
    Signs and Tags
    First Aid
    Bloodborne Pathogens
    OSHA Inspection
OSHA's Hazard Communication Standard
    Listing Hazardous Chemicals
    Obtaining MSDSs from Chemical
      Suppliers
    Labeling All Chemical Containers
    Developing a Written Hazard
      Communication Program
Security
    Security Committees
    Suspicious Activities
    Meth Labs
    Theft
    Bomb Threats
    Fires
    Key Control
    Lost and Found
    Guestroom Cleaning

Competencies

1. Identify safety procedures that relate to tasks commonly performed by the housekeeping staff. (pp. 247–264)

2. Identify common cleaning chemicals used by housekeeping operations and what safety equipment should be worn when using those chemicals. (pp. 264–266)

3. Explain how OSHA regulations apply to hotel operations. (pp. 266–269)

4. Describe how housekeeping departments comply with OSHA's Hazard Communication Standard. (pp. 269–276)

5. Identify housekeeping's security responsibilities in relation to theft, key control, lost and found procedures, and emergencies. (pp. 276–292)

7

Safety and Security

R<small>ITA IS CLEANING</small> a badly stained toilet bowl with an ammonia-based cleaner. She scrubs vigorously at the stains, but they will not come out. She pours more of the ammonia cleaner into the bowl, but the stains are still there. Finally, she reaches for a container of chlorine bleach, dumps some into the bowl, and leans over to scrub again.

This scenario underscores a vital element of chemical use in the housekeeping department: proper training in the safe and effective use of chemicals. Rita does not know that mixing ammonia and bleach will produce a deadly gas that will very probably result in her death.

Safety and security are two major responsibilities of hotel managers. Guests expect to sleep, meet, dine, and entertain in a facility that is safe and secure—and are entitled to reasonable care under law. Housekeeping personnel can help meet this guest expectation and, in some cases, make the difference in the property's safety and security system.

In a hospitality operation, **safety** refers to the actual conditions in a work environment. **Security** refers to the prevention of theft, fire, and other emergencies. This chapter will focus on safety and security needs of hospitality operations, the role that housekeeping plays in meeting those needs, a brief description of chemicals commonly used in housekeeping departments, what properties must do to comply with federal OSHA standards, and how safety and security issues affect housekeeping personnel.

Safety

The two hotel departments most prone to accidents and injuries are engineering and housekeeping. One basis for this frequency is the sheer labor-intensity of these two departments. In many operations, housekeeping and engineering employ more people than any other department. Another reason lays in the fact that working in housekeeping or engineering involves physical activity and equipment use—both of which increase the risk of accident and injury.

To reduce safety risks, the executive housekeeper must be aware of potential safety hazards and develop procedures to prevent accidents. Safety should be a top priority. Ongoing safety training programs help ensure that safe conditions are maintained in all work areas. To develop such programs, management must be aware of the laws that regulate the work environment—and more specifically, how those laws affect housekeeping personnel.

the Rooms
CHRONICLE®

Hotel Wisdom: A Baker's Dozen of Strategies for Safety and Security

The numbers 9-1-1 have evolved from the emergency response system to one that evokes a wide range of emotions, especially for citizens of the United States. Nine-Eleven today represents a vivid reminder of what can unexpectedly happen to us. The hurricane season of 2005, the fires that affected many western states, and the flooding in the northeast U.S. in early 2006 are all vivid examples of potential crises that can tax our resources.

In every one of these crisis situations, hotels were affected in some capacity, either as a victim of the devastation or a place of refuge for those individuals fleeing the afflicted areas. Therefore, worker and guest safety and security must be at the forefront of every hotel manager's list of priorities.

1. **Become aware of the real costs of safety.** The direct and insurance costs are obvious. Higher claims, especially if there is fault involved, can delay payments or cause extended periods of legal entanglement. Do not overlook the hidden costs of lost productivity, overtime to cover absence of an injured employee, inefficiencies in service, and the loss of guests to other hotels that will require expensive marketing to regain lost market share. This list can be very extensive and expensive.

2. **Define safety through control of safe practices and elimination of workplace hazards.** Your insurance carrier will assist you in this effort—they want you to provide safe environments for both guests and employees.

3. **When hiring, consider a Job Safety Analysis.** A Job Safety Analysis is a method that can be used to identify, analyze and record:
   - The steps involved in performing a specific job.
   - The existing or potential safety and health hazards associated with each step.
   - The recommended action(s)/procedures(s) that will eliminate or reduce these hazards and the risk of a workplace injury or illness.

   Additionally, this process is of special value when interviewing an applicant with a disability, as it becomes clear what is required on the job and what capabilities the person with disabilities must bring to the task.

4. **Remember the cost affiliated with Worker's Compensation.** Workers' Compensation hearings before an administrative judge usually require legal representation. These and court fees become additional factors that must be assumed by the lodging establishment.

5. **Always strive to maintain a property that will present minimal hazards to the public and guests.** Constant awareness by staff to those conditions that might contribute to an accident, with immediate mitigation of such circumstances, is essential. Given the litigious nature of today's society, many courts and juries tend to look unfavorably upon business operators that fail to exercise reasonable care to foresee and eliminate potential hazards. If management becomes aware of a hazard on the property that it controls, they must do one or more of the following:

(continued)

- Fix the hazard
- Warn others about the hazard
- Restrict access to the hazard thus preventing individuals from becoming injured

Failure to respond appropriately invites both injury and potential legal action.

6. **Create and actively sponsor a hotel Safety Committee.** An effective and involved Safety Committee representing staff, supervisory personnel, and management can make a real difference in anticipating and preventing potentially dangerous situations, and can also help the hotel mount an affirmative defense in the event of a lawsuit if the hotel can demonstrate reasonable care was undertaken.

7. **Maintain the proper types of Workers' Compensation, general liability and employee liability insurance.** Workers' Compensation is experience-rated, thus management can directly influence and control the premium costs through an effective accident prevention program. Similarly, general liability and employee liability coverage will provide the same dimension in incidents involving guests and the public or injuries received as a result of actions by hotel employees. While every state requires employers to provide some variation of Worker's Compensation, liability insurance is generally not mandated for all businesses. However, it is still a business necessity and should be secured in appropriate levels and limits.

8. **Train, train, train.** Hotels expend thousands of dollars on fire-safety and life safety systems, first-aid supplies, and emergency communication equipment. But are the majority of employees aware of, or even trained to use these items, or know how to respond in an emergency? At a minimum, all employees should be trained on fire safety and evacuation procedures, bloodborne pathogen response, and first aid and CPR/AED procedures. With this kind of training there will be a person ready to respond in most situations.

9. **Establish and practice preventive maintenance.** Establish an on-going and documented safety and inspection protocol throughout the lodging establishment. In coordination with the hotel's safety committee, typical activities will likely include both scheduled and impromptu walk-through inspections, fire drills and practice evacuations, first-responder training, and crisis management preparation.

10. **Certify staff.** Certifications in Certified Safety Professional (CSP) are available through the American Society of Safety Engineers (ASSE), as well as certified American Red Cross First Aid and CPR trainee. Certification designations show others that an employee has been trained to an industry standard and recognizes that employee for their experience and sacrifice. Certifications are also a great employee motivator. Consider rewarding personnel who achieve various designations with additional perks such as a small pay increase or an additional day off with pay.

(continued)

(continued)

11. **Make safety practices visible and important.** Recognition programs for safety excellence by individual, department, or property in a hotel organization pay for themselves in terms of dollars and appreciation by guests and staff.

12. **Keep current.** Keeping involved with the Loss Prevention Committee of the AH&LA; the Retail, Services and Logistics Section of the National Safety Council; or the Hospitality Branch of the American Society of Safety Engineers is a measurable way of remaining alert. A continuing awareness of and compliance with the Occupational Safety and Health Act mandates (OSHA) is essential.

13. **Ask your teams in every area for input.** Your staff, supervisors and managers should be encouraged to make suggestions to the Safety Committee through a formal suggestion program that ideally includes rewards for great ideas. Again, safety IS everyone's job!

Source: John Hogan, P.h.D., CHA, MHS, CHE, *The Rooms Chronicle*®, Volume 15, Number 3, pp. 6–7. For subscription information, please call 866-READ-TRC.

Insurance and Liability Concerns

An unsafe work environment can be costly from medical, legal, and productivity standpoints. Many work-related accidents result in loss of work. In addition, an employee injured on the job may require medical care. In some cases, the medical care can be extensive and expensive.

A chronic pattern of employee accidents will generally result in increasing costs for liability and medical insurance. A track record of unsafe work conditions can also result in the hotel being fined or sued. Liability insurance rates are high enough without being compounded by lawsuits by injured employees and guests. Overall **workers' compensation** rates may also increase if many workers' compensation claims are made over a period of time. All these charges add up. In other words, poor safety habits can cost a very substantial amount of money over time.

Employee Morale and Management Concerns

Unsafe working conditions have a negative effect on employee morale. If employees are preoccupied with hazardous conditions in the workplace, they will not be able to perform to the best of their ability. For the most part, it is difficult to motivate employees until the unsafe conditions are corrected.

One of management's top concerns should be for the health and welfare of employees. Employees are one of the most important assets a hotel has. If managers want employees to provide quality service, they must treat employees fairly and with respect. Respect for an employee's right to work in a safe environment is a good place to begin.

the Rooms
CHRONICLE®

When It Comes to Liability, It's Not Who You Know—It's Whether You Know

Hotel owners and managers may be liable to their guests for injuries caused by the condition of their property. This is true even if the hotel has no actual notice of the defective condition that caused the injury. In such cases, a guest who files a lawsuit may prevail against the hotel if he or she can show that the hotel had "constructive notice" of the condition causing the injury.

Constructive notice is a legal concept that can be every bit as costly to a hotel property as actual notice. A property in Louisiana was found to have had constructive notice of water on the floor of their lobby where a guest slipped and fell. A verdict was issued against the hotel for $930,000. A resort in New York was ordered to pay $275,000 to a guest who slipped on food on the floor of a club within the hotel.

What is constructive notice?

Constructive notice exists where a property may not have actual notice that a potentially dangerous condition exists but circumstances are present to infer that the property "should have known" of the condition. In a case against Trump Castle Associates, constructive notice was defined to occur when a defect was visible and apparent and it existed for a sufficient length of time prior to the incident to allow hotel employees to discover and remedy it. The evidence showed that puddles of water formed on a marble floor in an area where an ice machine was located. The puddles were evident at the scene after the accident. Circumstantial evidence including the size of the puddles and the size of the partially melted ice cubes in relation to those of the ice machine helped to determine whether the defect existed for a substantial period of time. In this case, the evidence was sufficient to support the existence of constructive notice.

Once a defect becomes known, or should become known to the hotel, employees should be vigilant to remedy the situation. Implementing preventive strategies such as conducting systematic inspections, having housekeeping or maintenance personnel watch for and report defects, promptly reviewing all incident reports, and just using common sense can help a property be proactive to prevent accidents involving constructive notice issues. Bear in mind that temporary seasonal changes and undesirable weather conditions should be anticipated, and not treated as an unexpected surprise. Place walk-off mats and monitor property entrances and exits during rainy and snowy conditions. Additionally, use warning signs such as yellow "slippery when wet" to serve constructive notice to guests and passers-by about impending threats.

What are the prime areas for constructive notice defects?

The manager of any property could no doubt conduct an audit of his or her property and identify problem areas for potential slip and fall situations or other constructive notice issues. As a guide, however, a review of past cases can assist in this process. The most common areas of concern can typically be categorized as follows:

(continued)

the Rooms CHRONICLE®

(continued)

- Lobby areas, especially those adjacent to outdoor areas
- Vending and ice machine locations
- Hallways, corridors, and stairwells, especially where carpeting and other floor covering is used
- Sidewalks, driveways, and parking lots
- Areas where food and drink are served
- Condition and placement of chairs, tables, and other furniture
- Condition and placement of recreation, fitness, and pool equipment

How to ensure that you know?

The one thing that any property can and should do to avoid a constructive notice issue is to implement a policy of systematic inspections with detailed recordkeeping, focusing on the areas identified above. Then, by encouraging employees to be attentive to and report potentially dangerous conditions or to respond to conditions that are reported, most defects should be detected. All that is left to do is to remedy the situation.

Source: Michael Gentile, J.D., *The Rooms Chronicle*®, Volume 13, Number 4, p. 4. For subscription information, please call 866-READ-TRC.

Potentially Hazardous Conditions

Managers and employees must work together to keep *all* job functions—no matter how routine or difficult—from becoming hazardous. The key is to identify a hazardous condition before it threatens employees, guests, and the property. Managers must train employees to recognize potentially hazardous conditions and to take appropriate corrective action. An alert and careful employee can be a property's best defense.

Wet floors and slippery walkways are accidents waiting to happen. Cluttered floors or cleaning equipment left out and in the way are invitations for injury. Improper lifting techniques and lifting or moving too much at once can threaten employee health. Such hazards result in the most common forms of employee injury in housekeeping departments: sprains, strains, and falls.

Accidents and injuries do not have to occur. By following three simple rules, employees can contribute to a safe, accident-free work environment.

1. **Take adequate time.** No job is so urgent that it must be done in an unsafe, hurried manner.

2. **Correct unsafe conditions immediately.** If you cannot correct an unsafe or hazardous condition yourself, report it at once to your supervisor.

3. **Do it safely the first time.** Every employee must do his or her job in a safe and correct manner. This is the best way to prevent accidents.

the Rooms
CHRONICLE®

Return to Work Is Goal for Injured Employees

Accidents will happen. Despite the best trainers, the best performers and the best supervision, sooner or later an employee is injured in the workplace. In the United States, if employees are unable to work due to the injuries, they can receive worker's compensation pay in lieu of their regular paycheck. But because worker's compensation pay affects the hotel's insurance rate, it is in the best interest of the employer and the employee to arrange a return to work as soon as medically advisable. Here are some important tips on handling employees with injuries.

Handle the accident

The most important thing at the time of the accident is to take care of the employee: provide first aid, arrange emergency care, provide transportation, notify family members, and investigate the facts. Be sure to determine the root cause of the accident and determine whether any pre-existing injury or medical problem may have caused or contributed to the accident. Injuries that are not the responsibility of the employer are not compensable under Federal and State worker's comp statutes.

Although most states are governed by federal law, some state regulations apply because they exceed federal mandates. Hotel managers should obtain from their state department of labor a new copy of regulations every two years.

Return to work instructions

After the employee has been treated, the doctor writes a Work Ability Report for the employer and instructs the employee about return to work information and possible restrictions to duties or hours worked.

An employer's goal should be to have the employee return to work as soon as feasible. Often, though, employees are restricted from performing some job tasks normally included in their job descriptions. When this occurs, it is the manager's responsibility to find transitional job tasks for the injured employees. For instance, if a front desk agent breaks a leg, the doctor's instructions may specify that the employee should not be required to stand. Substitute work that can be accomplished from a sitting position may be arranged. Later, perhaps a stool will be used behind the front desk to enable the employee to resume his or her full job. The extent of employee injuries must be considered when choosing transitional work, as well as the size and staffing levels of the hotel.

Often the restriction involves the amount of time an employee can work. Perhaps an employee has been told to work less than full-time. In any case, if the employer can arrange even ten hours per week, it benefits both the employee and the hotel to have a transitional arrangement.

Potential temporary work assignments

One important consideration in designing modified work assignments is the fairness that must be shown. One employee cannot be assigned easy work while another is assigned more distasteful duties. Plaintiff attorneys and the EEOC can use inconsistencies against the hotel. Second, whatever tasks are assigned should not displace another uninjured employee who normally performs those tasks.

(continued)

C the Rooms HRONICLE®

(continued)

Large hotels seldom have difficulty in finding temporary work assignments. Since there are few rules requiring the injured employee to do something within their specialty, a variety of assignments can be found. Some states, however, require the modified job to fit within pre-injury hours and days off.

Managers must remember that the restrictions in the beginning of the employee's recovery may be so severe no transitional work is available. In this case, the employer should stay in touch with the employee and institute work assignments as soon as the employee is able.

Some employees do not cooperate with assignment of temporary duties. In this case, managers should document any job refused as it may result in a loss of the employee's worker's compensation reimbursement.

Source: Mary Friedman, *The Rooms Chronicle*®, Volume 9, Number 6, pp. 4–5. For subscription information, please call 866-READ-TRC.

All lodging properties should have a list of safety rules. These guidelines should be part of a housekeeping safety plan to encourage employees to develop and practice safe work habits. Exhibit 1 shows a sample list of safety rules for housekeeping areas.

On any given day, housekeeping employees may lift heavy objects, climb ladders, operate machinery, and use dangerous cleaning chemicals—all of which represent hazardous conditions. The following sections provide safety tips for completing these routine activities safely and efficiently.

Lifting. Housekeeping tasks often involve lifting heavy objects. Employees may also be required to move furniture in order to complete a thorough cleaning task.

Incorrectly lifting heavy objects such as bags, boxes, and containers may result in strained or pulled muscles and back injury. In turn, these injuries can result in loss of work and long-term pain and suffering. Employees can also incur cuts and scratches when lifting trash or dirty linens that contain pointy objects or broken glass. In all instances, employees should know what conditions to look for and the special precautions to take. Exhibit 2 outlines safe lifting techniques for housekeeping personnel.

Employees should also be careful when doing housekeeping tasks such as opening windows. An attendant should never hit or tug on the window frame if a window sticks or will not open easily. Improperly pushing or pulling a stubborn window may result in a back injury or a cut from broken glass. If a window is stuck, the attendant should call for assistance. Engineering can usually open a window after applying a lubricant or fixing the window frame. Room attendants should also be cautioned against improperly pulling or tugging on heavy items such as room attendant carts and bundles of laundry. Like lifting, these actions can often result in injury.

Ladders. Ladders can be used when cleaning areas on or near the ceiling or for such tasks as changing light bulbs. When selecting a ladder for a particular cleaning

Exhibit 1   Sample Safety Rules List for a Lodging Operation

Rooms and Housekeeping Area: Safety Rules

- See General Safety Rules. (Section I)
- Keep glass out of linens.
- Be alert for cracked glasses that are wrapped.
- Empty razor containers before they become full.
- Keep cords out of pathways.
- Keep bed covers off the floors.
- Never smoke on the elevators.
- Place ashtrays on dressers, not beside beds where guests might be encouraged to smoke in bed.
- Do not overcrowd elevators.
- Use caution when pulling carts on and off elevators.
- Use the correct cleaning equipment for the job.
- Do not leave room-service trays in guest hallways.
- Walk on the right side of corridors.
- Carry pointed objects with the sharp end down and away from yourself.
- Never use a chair or box as a substitute for a ladder.
- Put broken glass and metal waste in the proper containers.
- Correct tripping and slipping hazards immediately.
- Use handrails on stairways.
- Report defective wiring, plugs, and uninspected appliances to your supervisor immediately.
- Check the cord and plug of any electrical appliance before plugging in. If there is a break or fray, or if sparks fly, *do not* try to plug it in. Return the appliance to the electric shop and secure a replacement.
- Look for broken glass before kneeling on carpeting or bathroom tile. If glass is present, sweep it up with broom and then use a portable vacuum. *Never* handle glass with bare hands.
- Dispose of broken glass in the "Broken Glass Containers" in the service halls.
- All ashtrays should be emptied in toilets, not in waste cans.
- Report any evidence of careless smoking in guestrooms, e.g., burnt carpets or bedspreads, burnt matches on floors, etc.
- Do not use bare hands to pull trash out of cans, as there may be broken glass or razor blades present.
- Be careful in the placement of luggage in public areas and the baggage room.
- Never attempt to carry more luggage than you can handle safely.
- Pick up any foreign objects on stairs or floors.
- Wait until incoming cars have stopped at the curb before attempting to open the door.
- Be sure that passengers' hands and feet are clear of the door frame before closing automobile doors.
- Know the location of wheelchairs and first aid equipment.
- Know the procedures for dealing with guest injuries and illnesses.

Courtesy of the Hotel duPont, Wilmington, Delaware

Exhibit 2   Guidelines for Safe Lifting

1. Inspect the object before lifting. Do not lift any item that you cannot get your arms around or that you cannot see over when carrying.
2. Look for any protrusions, especially when lifting trash or bundles of linen. Quite often, these items can contain pointy objects or broken glass. Exercise special care to avoid injury.
3. When lifting, place one foot near the object and the other slightly back and apart. Keep well balanced.
4. Keep the back and head of your body straight. Because the back muscles are generally weaker than the leg muscles, do not use the back muscles to lift the object.
5. Bend slightly at the knees and hips but do not stoop.
6. Use both hands and grasp the object using the entire hand.
7. Lift with the leg muscles.
8. Keep the object close to the body. Avoid twisting your body.
9. If the object feels too heavy or awkward to hold, or if you do not have a clear view over the object, set it down.
10. When setting an object down do not use your back muscles. Use the leg muscles and follow the procedures used to lift objects.

job, inspect its condition, height, and footing. Check the ladder for stability and examine crosspieces for sturdiness. If the ladder is broken or defective, do not use it. Rather, tag the ladder, place it out of service, and report it to the appropriate housekeeping supervisor or the engineering department.

Ladders come in many types. Ladders range from small step stools to 40-foot extension ladders and are usually constructed of wood, fiberglass, aluminum or another metal. A metal ladder should never be used when working near or on electrical equipment. Ladders with rubber footings should be used on tile floors or in kitchen areas to prevent slipping. In all instances, the floor should be dry and clean.

A ladder must be high enough so that an attendant can stand on it and do the job without overreaching. Never stand on the top step of a ladder. If the area cannot be reached while standing on the step below the top step, the ladder is too short for the job. Extension ladders should be placed so the footing is at least one fourth of the ladder length away from the wall. For example, if the ladder is twelve feet tall, the footing should be three feet away from the wall. Never place a ladder against a window or an uneven surface. When possible, have another employee stabilize the ladder while you are aloft by bracing the footing with his or her feet and steadying the ladder with his or her hands.

Before climbing, test the ladder for stability; it should be well balanced and secure against the wall and floor. Always be sure to face a ladder when climbing, and have clean and dry hands and feet. Do not hold any items or tools that may prevent the use of one or both hands. Mark the area underneath the ladder with caution signs so that guests or employees do not walk under the ladder. Walking under a ladder may be considered unlucky by the superstitious, but it is also a very unsafe practice.

the Rooms
CHRONICLE®

Back Injuries Remain the Nation's Number One Workplace Safety Problem

Preventing back injuries is a major workplace safety challenge in any industry. The lodging industry is no exception, especially in housekeeping departments. On-premise laundry workers who load and unload heavy loads of linens, housemen who transport soiled and freshly laundered linens or trash, and room attendants who flip mattresses on a regular basis are all prime candidates for a lower back injury.

The extent of the problem

According to the Bureau of Labor Statistics (BLS), more than one million workers in the United States suffer back injuries each year, with back injuries accounting for one of every five workplace injuries or illnesses. One-fourth of all compensation indemnity claims involve back injuries, costing industry billions of dollars on top of the pain and suffering borne by employees. In 2003, nonfatal injuries to leisure and hospitality workers accounted for 9.7 percent of all nonfatal workplace injuries. This corresponds to 45,300 reported cases of hotel workplace injury or illness and resulted in 24,100 cases of missed days from work and 21,200 cases where the employee was assigned to restricted duty or temporarily transferred to another position. In the U.S. lodging industry for 2003, 6.7 percent of the workforce had some recorded nonfatal workplace-related injury or illness. By far, the majority of these injuries were back injuries.

Lower back injuries abound

Muscular-skeletal injuries of the back are primarily brought on through lifting, placing, carrying, holding and lowering objects and materials in the workplace. The BLS survey shows that four out of five of these injuries were to the lower back, and that three out of four occurred while the employee was lifting. No approach has been found for totally eliminating back injuries caused by lifting, though it is felt that a substantial portion can be prevented by an effective control program and ergonomic design of work tasks.

Back injury prevention techniques

Executive housekeepers should take reasonable precautions to minimize opportunities for back-related injuries to their employees. These steps include:

- Require all employees to follow safe lifting procedures.
- Reeducate employees about safe lifting techniques on a periodic basis.
- Encourage employees to work in teams to lift, move, or flip heavy or bulky materials.
- Have employees utilize carts, hand trucks, winches, and laundry slings to transport or move heavy loads.
- Require employees who frequently move or lift heavy loads to wear back brace supports.
- Keep track of all on-the-job injuries to discern injury patterns or workplace practices that cause injuries.

(continued)

C the Rooms HRONICLE®

(continued)

- Reward personnel with a party or other recognition if the housekeeping or laundry department completes six months without an on-the-job injury.

- Enforce compliance of safe lifting habits through supervisor observations and implementation of progressive discipline

Conclusion

All employees are required to lift items and materials of varying weights, shapes, and sizes. If employees follow proper lifting techniques, the risk of on-the-job lower back injuries can be avoided or minimized. Once an employee's back has been injured, typical recovery may require light duty, bed rest, physical therapy, or surgery. Each of these treatments bears a cost to the employer and results in lost time and productivity for the housekeeping department, as other employees may be forced to work overtime or pick up the slack.

Once an employee incurs a back injury, it will become much easier for the back to suffer re-injury, even after initial healing. The general train of thought is that no one ever fully recovers from a back injury one-hundred percent. Rather, employees learn to live with discomfort, a reduced range of motion, and/or a dependency on pain killers or muscle relaxants. Proactive and preventive measures to prevent back injury are in the best interest of the employees, the housekeeping department, and management and ownership.

Source: *The Rooms Chronicle®*, Volume 13, Number 1, p.6.
For subscription information, please call 866-READ-TRC.

Machinery. Employees should be authorized and trained in the use of machinery and equipment before operating it. Most equipment, machines, and power tools come with instructions. Some employees may need additional training and supervised practice before operating equipment and machinery on the job by themselves.

Many power tools and other machinery are equipped with protective guards or shields. These safety guards should not be removed. Employees may also be required to wear protective eye goggles or gloves. All protective gear should be worn per instructions.

Equipment and machinery should never be left unattended while it is in use. When not in use, all tools and equipment should be turned off and stored in the proper place. Never use a piece of equipment or machinery that is not operating correctly. Contact the appropriate supervisor or the engineering department to have it repaired as soon as possible.

Electrical Equipment. Extra care must be taken when operating electrical equipment. Even common housekeeping appliances such as vacuum cleaners can be harmful or deadly if operated improperly or in unsafe conditions. Electrical equipment and machinery used at a lodging property should be approved by the Underwriters Laboratories. The **Underwriters Laboratories** is an independent, non-profit organization that tests electrical equipment and devices. The purpose of such testing is to ensure that electrical equipment is free of defects that can cause fire or shocks. Approved equipment bears the initials "UL" in a circle on packaging, instructional material, or a tag. Most equipment purchased in a retail store or through a wholesale purveyor will meet the Underwriters Laboratories standard.

An employee should never operate electrical equipment when standing in water or when his or her hands or clothing are wet. It is also unsafe to operate electrical equipment near flammable liquids, chemicals, or vapors. Sparks from electrical equipment could start a fire.

Equipment that sparks, smokes, or flames should be turned off immediately. If it is possible and safe to do so, the equipment should be unplugged. In no instance should an attendant attempt to restart the equipment. The malfunction should be reported to the appropriate housekeeping supervisor or the engineering department.

Equipment wires and connections should be checked periodically. Equipment with loose connections or exposed wires should not be used. An appliance should never be unplugged by pulling or yanking the cord. This will loosen the connection between the cord and plug and cause sparks and short circuits. Equipment should be unplugged by grasping the plug and pulling it gently away from the outlet.

When using electrical equipment, the cord should be kept out of traffic areas such as the centers of hallways or doorways. This is not always possible, particularly with such tasks as vacuuming corridors. In such situations, keep the cord close to the wall and post caution signs in the work area. If the appliance will be stationary and in use for a lengthy period, tape the cord to the floor and place caution signs over the taped cord.

Extension cords are sometimes required—particularly when an electrical outlet is not located near the work area. Extension cords should be inspected for exposed wire before use, just like any other electrical cord. There are many types of extension cords; not all are acceptable for use in a hospitality operation. The local fire department can pinpoint which types of cords meet the local, state, or federal fire codes and regulations.

When cleaning guestrooms, room attendants should check electrical lamps, appliances, and other fixtures for frayed wires, loose connections, and loose plugs. Exposed electrical wire may result in shock, injury, or even death when it is touched. Outlets and switch covers should be checked to ensure that they are covered properly and not cracked or broken. If any of these conditions are found, the room attendant should not attempt to fix them. Rather, potential problems should be reported to the appropriate housekeeping supervisor or to engineering.

Chemicals. Many housekeeping employees are exposed to dangerous chemicals in their daily work routines. These chemicals are powerful cleaners, and, when they are used properly with appropriate protective gear, they are relatively harmless. However, when used improperly, these same helpful chemicals can cause nausea, vomiting, skin rashes, cancer, blindness, and even death.

Chemicals are used to clean all areas of a lodging property, including bathrooms, kitchens, and floors. Potentially hazardous chemicals are also used to kill insects and rodents. Some housekeeping situations require employees to handle toxic substances to unstop clogs in toilets and other plumbing fixtures. Often, the use of such hazardous and toxic chemicals cannot be avoided.

Continual training in chemical safety is necessary for two reasons. First, misused chemicals can cause serious injury in a short period. Second, new employees—especially in properties with high employee turnover—need to be trained immediately.

Repetitive-Motion Injuries. Room attendants are at risk for suffering from repetitive-motion injuries. This has become an increasing concern as hotels have put in larger beds, more pillows, triple-sheeting, and heavier comforters. A Canadian study discovered that room attendants change body positions every three seconds, or about 8,000 times per shift. In November of 2007, a Los Angeles hotel was cited for violating the state's repetitive-motion rules. They were fined $14,000 for not following the same policies that other hotels in their chain had adopted. Employees at the property said that the hotel kept putting more things in the room that they had to clean but never reduced the number of rooms that they had to clean, causing them to incur various injuries such as tendinitis.

The primary risks for repetitive-motion injury are heavy workloads and forceful upper-limb motions. Ways to reduce the chance of injury include:

- Providing training materials in Spanish and English.

- Reducing the number of rooms each room attendant has to clean.

- Assigning more than one person to help lift heavy objects and cleaning equipment.

- Ensuring that employees break up tasks with rest time to prevent injury.

- Rotating cleaning duties—making beds, cleaning bathrooms, vacuuming— among two or three room attendants. (Have each room attendant do something different in each rotation.)

- Using team cleaning.

- Training employees on how to lift and move items properly.

- Training employees on ways to reduce bending.

- Purchasing easier-to-use vacuum cleaners that are lighter and vibrate less than standard models, have ergonomic handles, are self-propelled, and adjust to the room attendant's height.

Job Safety Analysis

Safety information is often best communicated through orientation and ongoing training. The design and use of a housekeeping safety manual is also an excellent communication vehicle. This manual should detail the different housekeeping jobs and instruct employees on the safe and proper way to perform each job. The first step in designing such a manual is to perform a job safety analysis.

A **job safety analysis** is a detailed report that lists every job function performed by all employees in a housekeeping department. The job list provides the basis for analyzing the potential hazards of a particular housekeeping position. The format for each analysis can parallel that of job breakdowns, with safety tips and potential hazards being cited.

For example, a task list for a room attendant may include the tasks of vacuuming, cleaning bathrooms, stocking room attendant carts, and emptying trash. Each task is then further broken down into a list of steps. The steps for vacuuming a guestroom may be:

1. Check the vacuum cleaner for safety.

2. Remove dirt from room corners and carpet edges.

3. Plug the vacuum into the outlet nearest to the guestroom door.

4. Vacuum all areas.

5. Unplug the vacuum, wind the cord correctly, and return the vacuum to the housekeeping cart.

For each step, a brief explanation should be written that describes a safe and standard method for performing that step. The how-to portion for step one, "Check the vacuum cleaner for safety," could be:

1. Before vacuuming the first room of the day, check to make sure the vacuum cleaner bag is empty.

2. Replace or empty the vacuum cleaner bag if it is full.

3. Immediately remove knots and tangles from vacuum cords, since they can cause electrical short circuits.

4. Immediately turn off equipment that sparks, smokes, or flames.

5. Take vacuum cleaners that need repair to the housekeeping department.

Finally, the safety tips section of the analysis lists any hazards that an employee may encounter when performing a particular job step. For example, the safety points that could be listed when checking the vacuum might be:

1. Safety must be a top concern at all times. If anything about your equipment looks unsafe, report it to your supervisor and have it repaired before you use it.

2. Do not use the vacuum if the cord is damaged. You could be hurt, or a short circuit could start a fire. Be careful not to trip on the vacuum cleaner cord.

3. Never use electrical equipment, such as your vacuum cleaner, when standing in water or when your hands or clothes are wet.

A complete job safety analysis should include all housekeeping jobs and the tasks involved. The analysis should be produced in booklet form; each employee should receive the sections that focus on the various tasks he or she will perform while working at the property.

It is not enough just to give the employee the analysis and hope that it gets read. Housekeeping managers should demonstrate and explain each task. At the end of the training period, the employee should sign a statement that he or she

Exhibit 3   Sample Safety Philosophy Statement

Hotel duPont Safety Philosophy

Safety is the number-one priority of all employees at the Hotel duPont. We share the duPont Company's philosophy that all injuries and incidents can be eliminated through an effective safety program. At the Hotel, our safety program is very much employee oriented, maximum employee participation is the key ingredient to its success. Our employees are taught that safety is a way of life, not something left at work, but carried home to their families.

Safety in the Hotel duPont does take on several meanings. When we talk about our safety programs, we may refer to any of the following:

- Employee Work Practices
- Off-the-Job Safety
- Life Safety
- Equipment Safety
- Safety Administration
- Food Sanitation
- Security
- Injury Prevention

These areas, when combined, form the safety philosophy of the Hotel duPont.

Courtesy of the Hotel duPont, Wilmington, Delaware

understands the job safety analysis and rules. The statement should include the safety and disciplinary consequences of not abiding by the job safety analysis guidelines.

Safety Training

Safety training begins the first day of the job. Housekeeping employee orientation must include an introduction to property safety rules and regulations. Employees must know what is expected of them in the area of safety in order to perform their jobs more safely.

A good safety policy is written with the employee in mind; it states how safety benefits the employee and the company. This statement should be a general safety philosophy that covers the entire property—not just housekeeping. Exhibit 3 shows the safety philosophy presented by one property during employee orientation.

Specific safety rules and procedures should also be presented at orientation. Orientation is a good opportunity to hand out any written safety information. This

the Rooms
CHRONICLE®

An Innovative Method to Connect With Hotel Employees Regarding Workplace Safety

It is no mystery that hotels are employment venues where all staff must exercise vigilant care to protect themselves and others from injury on the job. Given the routine nature of many positions, employees can lose their vigilance and become complacent to workplace safety dangers. Also, the lodging industry offers employment to individuals from many different nations and cultures who speak a variety of languages. Management often struggles with finding a means by which to effectively and repeatedly communicate the need for attention to workplace safety among its employees. Finding and employing an effective communications medium that all employees will recognize or can readily identify with has been made easier though.

In partnership with 20th Century Fox, Safetyworld/Owen Media, has created a safety awareness system that features Homer Simpson and the Simpsons characters. According to various sources, *The Simpsons* has been the #1 television show in the world with more than 13 billion episodes watched annually. In its 17th prime time season in 2007, the syndicated show has been translated into more than 45 languages and is shown in more than 150 countries.

Owen Media developed a comprehensive workplace safety communications program that employees can identify with and that will leave a lasting impression. The goal is to help employees remember their safety training, a key factor in reducing the frequency of injuries. This unique approach includes *Safety Meeting Quiz Cards* that use OSHA awareness content with a little humor provided by The Simpsons to capture employee attention. Other signature safety materials include matching Simpsons *Safety Posters* for employee entrances and high traffic areas and cafeteria-styled *Table Tents* to reinforce the monthly safety meeting.

Department managers hand out the safety meeting cards. After the five-minute safety meeting outline script is read, employees scratch off the correct answers from their safety quiz cards. Often, managers will then raffle off some of the Simpsons posters, which are all first editions. Other posters and table tents continue to reinforce the safety message throughout the hotel because of their bright colors, recognizable characters, and visual appeal.

According to Brian Krause, district manager for Owen Media, their *Inescapable Messaging* program has been successfully rolled out to multiple Hilton, Marriott, and Loews hotels. To review The Simpsons program online, go to www.safetyworld.com and click on *Topic Library*.

Source: *The Rooms Chronicle®*, Volume 15, Number 2, p. 16.
For subscription information, please call 866-READ-TRC.

information may be part of an orientation packet or may be a separate booklet or presented on video or online. In some employee orientation booklets, each area has a space next to it where the employee is to put his or her initials and the date. This reinforces the importance of these rules and ensures that the employee receives and understands the information.

Safety training does not end at orientation. At least once a month, every employee should participate in a safety education program. These sessions can be used to discuss new safety rules and the proper use of new equipment. Periodic safety education programs should also serve as refresher sessions for both new and seasoned employees. Familiar safety procedures should be reviewed and refined.

Early on in the training process—usually on the first or second day of the job—the employee should learn about specific safety conditions mandated by law—particularly those concerned with the use of hazardous chemicals. The following section provides an overview of chemical safety regulations.

Common Housekeeping Chemicals

Water

Water is an essential chemical in most cleaning solutions. Ironically, it can also be the trickiest to use because tap water is not the same from town to town, from state to state, or from country to country. Water absorbs minerals that affect its ability to clean or to react with cleaning agents.

Some common water minerals include calcium, iron, sulfur, and phosphates. Calcium can inhibit a detergent's cleaning ability, requiring more detergents to be added for cleaning jobs. Iron and sulfur can cause discoloration; sulfur also causes a "rotten egg" odor. Phosphates can actually enhance the cleaning power of some detergents so that less detergent is necessary.

Bathroom Cleaners

Room attendants sometimes use ammonia-based or chlorine-based cleaning compounds to clean guestroom bathrooms. It is important to know that these common cleaning chemicals should not be used together. *Ammonia should never be mixed with chlorine-, fluoride-, or bromine-based chemical cleaners.* When these chemicals are combined, they form a highly toxic gas. For example, when ammonia and chlorine are mixed in water, deadly phosgene gas is formed.

If possible, the housekeeping departments should purchase and use *either* ammonia-based cleaners *or* chlorine-, fluoride-, or bromine-based cleaners. By supplying room attendants with only one or the other, the risk of mixing the chemicals is almost eliminated. However, sometimes this is impossible due to the variety of surfaces that room attendants need to clean. Therefore, training and employee awareness is the best defense against potential chemical hazards.

All-Purpose Cleaners

There are a number of all-purpose cleaners on the market today. As their name suggests, they can be used to wash walls, scrub floors, clean tubs and showers, and even wash windows and mirrors. All-purpose cleaners are generally concentrated and can be diluted with water to adapt to different cleaning needs. Some all-purpose cleaners contain additives which limit their uses. A few of the more common additives are discussed in the following sections.

Abrasives. Abrasives are gritty substances used to remove heavy soils and polishes. Abrasives can be used safely on surfaces that will not show scratch marks. However, it can damage softer surfaces, such as marble or fiberglass. Most experts warn properties to avoid abrasives that could mar porcelain and synthetic surfaces.

Acids. Weak citric acids and vinegar can be used to clean glass, bronze, and stainless steel.

Alkalies. Like those used in the laundry, alkalies or bases in cleaning agents boost the cleaning ability of detergents. They also have disinfecting powers. Alkalies in all-purpose cleaners typically have a pH between 8 and 9.5. The **pH scale** measures the acidity or alkalinity of a substance compared to water. A pH of 7 is neutral. Acids have pHs of less than 7 to 0, which is the most acidic. Alkalies have values of more than 7 to 14, which is the most alkaline.

Degreasers. Degreasers (also called emulsifiers or stabilizers) are products that act on a variety of greases and soils. Solvents have many degreasing capabilities.

Delimers. Delimers remove mineral deposits that can dull, scale, and/or discolor surfaces.

Deodorizers. Deodorizers or room fresheners are designed to conceal the smell of cleaners in the room. Some fresheners may leave a film on surfaces in the guestroom and should be avoided. Fresheners can become overpowering if used every day. Also, many powder fresheners contain cornstarch, which attracts insects.

Disinfectants. Disinfectants kill bacteria, molds, and mildew. Cleaners with disinfectants are usually expensive. The added expense is often unnecessary, since not every surface needs to be disinfected. A good all-purpose cleaner used with proper cleaning, rinsing, and drying procedures is usually sufficient for lodging operations.

Fiberglass Cleaners. Many newer tub/shower units are made of fiberglass. Special cleaners are available to clean fiberglass without scratching the surfaces.

Metal Cleaners. Some oil-based metal cleaners remove soils but leave a thin, protective coating on the surface of the metal. This protective coating often picks up fingerprints. When transferred to clothing, it can damage many fabrics. Water-based metal cleaners avoid these problems and do a good job.

Wetting Agents. Wetting agents break down the surface tension of the water and allow water to get behind the dirt to lift it off the surface.

Safety Equipment for Using Chemicals

Housekeeping employees may use chemicals that require wearing protective gear. Personal protective gear may be used for covering the eyes, face, head, hands, and, in some cases, the entire body. Protective gear should be worn when using hazardous or toxic chemicals. It should also be worn when performing duties and using equipment that may result in injury from flying objects.

Gloves, goggles, or face shields may be required when diluting chemicals for cleaning purposes or when mixing chemicals for treating swimming pools. The chemical manufacturer must specify what type of personal protective equipment is needed when using the product.

When cleaning overhead areas such as ceiling vents, goggles and dust/mist respirators may be needed. Dust/mist respirators may also be used when cleaning very dusty areas. These respirators fit over the employee's mouth and nose and prevent dust and other small airborne particles from being inhaled.

OSHA Regulations

The federal government regulates work areas and businesses with respect to safety. The **Occupational Safety and Health Act** (OSHA) was enacted in 1970 to protect the worker at the workplace. OSHA regulations are quite extensive and mandate safety regulations and practices for many industries—including hospitality.[1]

OSHA standards cover a variety of areas that concern housekeeping employees. Regulations focus on the areas where employees work, materials used on the job, and other safety issues. OSHA standards are primarily designed to protect the employee—not the guest. However, some OSHA standards cover areas where guest safety may be a concern.

The following sections discuss only a portion of the OSHA regulations that pertain to hospitality operations. For a more detailed review of the standards, managers should contact local OSHA or U.S. Department of Labor offices or visit the OSHA website: www.osha.gov.

Work Areas

OSHA standards cover such areas as hallways, storerooms, and service areas. These standards require that work areas be kept clean, neat, and sanitary. Standards also require that hallways, passageways, and stairways have railings. Any stairway with four or more steps must have at least one railing.

OSHA also covers portable ladders used in such areas. Regulations state that the ladders must be of good construction and cannot have inappropriate additions. When in need of repair, ladders should be tagged properly. Regulations also cover scaffolds, mobile ladders, and towers.

Means of Egress

OSHA standards require that exits be clearly marked. The code details both the size and level of illumination of the sign. The exits and paths to the exits should not be visually or physically blocked. Exit doors should never be locked in such a way that employees or guests could not escape from a fire. The routes to the exits must also be marked so that an escape path can be easily followed.

The standards dictate the maximum occupancy level of individual rooms and the building, based on the number of exits, available fire protection, and building construction. OSHA standards should be referenced for more specific information.

All properties must have written emergency escape plans. Emergency escape routes and procedures must be clearly indicated. The plan should specify employee duties and placement within the facility during an emergency. These plans should enable management to evacuate the property safely and account for all employees during and after an emergency. Written procedures should be specified for the preferred means of reporting emergencies and fires. Plans must also establish rescue and medical duties for employees or local services.

OSHA also requires a list of the job titles or people who can be contacted for further information or explanation of duties under the emergency plan. The executive housekeeper and housekeeping supervisory staff may be included on this list.

Sanitation

OSHA standards are quite particular concerning sanitation. Waste disposal, employee washing facilities, and food and beverage consumption are among the areas addressed.

Waste Disposal. OSHA specifies that all waste containers be leakproof and have a tight-fitting cover. The waste containers must be maintained in a sanitary condition. The removal of all waste must be done without creating a menace or hazard to public health. Waste should be removed often or on a timely basis.

Washing Facilities and Showers. OSHA stipulates that washing facilities be kept clean and each bathroom be equipped with hot and cold running water. Hand soap or cleaner must be provided. Hand towels, paper towels, or warm air dryers should also be conveniently located for employee use. OSHA standards even dictate the number of toilets a lodging property must have based on the number and sex of employees.

If employees are required to shower before, during, or after their shift, the employer must provide the same items as required in the washing facilities. Individual towels must also be provided. OSHA standards require one shower for every ten employees of the same sex.

Food and Beverage Consumption. OSHA forbids the consumption of food and beverages in washroom areas. OSHA also stipulates that no food or beverages be consumed in areas such as storage rooms that contain hazardous or toxic chemicals.

If an operation provides employee meals, OSHA standards state that the food must be wholesome and not spoiled. Food must be prepared, served, and stored in a sanitary way so as to avoid contamination.

Also, it is important that glasses in hotel guestrooms be removed for washing and sanitizing through a dishwasher. It is a violation of public health codes to rinse glasses out in a guestroom sink. Clean, sanitized glasses should be placed in the guestroom every day.

Signs and Tags

OSHA standards require special signs for safety reasons. Three different types of signs are needed by the housekeeping department: danger, caution, and safety instruction. Accident prevention tags are also used to alert employees to potentially hazardous conditions.

Danger Signs. Danger signs are used only in areas where there is an immediate hazard. These signs indicate immediate danger and the necessity of special precautions. An appropriate use of danger signs would be in an area where a caustic cleaning liquid had been spilled. OSHA standards dictate that the colors of a danger sign be red, black, and white.

Caution Signs. Caution signs are used to warn against a potential hazard. A wet floor caused by water spillage or mopping would be a reason to use a caution sign. Caution signs should be stored near buckets and mops for easy access. Caution signs are yellow and black.

Safety Instruction Signs. Safety instruction signs are green and white, or black and white. They are used when general instructions need to be given in a certain area. For example, these signs may be used to instruct employees not to eat, drink, or smoke in a storage area.

Accident Prevention Tags. Accident prevention tags are a temporary means of alerting employees to a hazardous condition or defective equipment. One sample use of this type of tag would be to place it on a vacuum cleaner that has a frayed cord. The tag should read "Do not start," "Defective Equipment," or "Out-of-Service." This type of tag is not meant to be a complete warning, but only a temporary solution to a potential safety hazard. The tags should be red with white or grey letters. Accident prevention tags should be kept near electrical power equipment, ladders, and other housekeeping tools.

First Aid

OSHA stipulates that the employer provide employees with readily accessible medical personnel. Some properties have a house doctor or a nurse's station. In the absence of medical staff, the employer should indicate a local medical facility or doctor who can handle on-the-job injuries.

First aid supplies approved by a consulting physician should be stocked and readily available. If an employee works with corrosive materials, suitable facilities should be available to drench or flush eyes, face, and body in case of an accident. Caustic and corrosive cleaning solutions are generally used in kitchens to clean filters, exhaust hoods, and grills.

Bloodborne Pathogens

To protect employees from the risk of infectious disease, including hepatitis B and human immunodeficiency virus (HIV), OSHA requires that employers follow the Bloodborne Pathogens Standards. To this end, they publish a guide specifying what must be done in a "fill-in-the-blank" outline easily adaptable to each hotel.

A central component of a hotel's efforts should be the development of an Exposure Control Plan (ECP) tailored to the work site. Following are the key points of the Bloodborne Pathogens Standards. The guide provided by OSHA provides samples of these statements:

- Employers are required to write a statement of their determination to provide a safe and healthful work environment for the entire staff by implementing an ECP.

- Employers must designate in writing which employees are responsible for the implementation and administration of various ECP elements.

- Employers must determine for each job position what potential exists for exposure to blood or other infectious materials. This must be written and should include the specific tasks and procedures that may cause the employee to be exposed.

- Employers must determine a plan to control the exposure employees may incur and must state the training and procedures that will be implemented. This might include providing protective equipment, writing training programs for what to do if needles are found in a guestroom, how to handle bloody linens, etc.

OSHA Inspection

Housekeeping managers should be aware that OSHA compliance officers have the authority to inspect a property. These inspections are often done without any advance notice. An inspection may be refused, but the compliance officer may return with a court-approved warrant and inspect the property. It is usually best to allow a compliance officer to inspect the property once they have shown proper identification.

Compliance officers may wish to inspect the property, equipment, and records. In addition to OSHA records, the officer may want to see that the OSHA poster is prominently displayed. The inspection can also include safety committee reports, environmental sampling, and private discussion with individual employees. A management representative—perhaps the executive housekeeper—should accompany the officer during the inspection.

OSHA's Hazard Communication Standard

OSHA is a broad set of rules that protects workers in all trades and professions from a variety of unsafe working conditions. The federal government often revises or expands these regulations and notifies employers when they must comply with new rules.

OSHA regulations require hotel employers to inform workers about the risks posed by chemicals they may use to do their jobs. The rule also requires that employers provide training in the safe use of these chemicals. This regulation is called the **Hazard Communication** (often shortened to **HazComm**) **Standard**. Compliance with the regulations offers some real benefits for the property. One survey revealed that 9.7 percent of all employees in the lodging industry sustain some on-the-job injury. It is estimated that if the HazComm program prevents just one of these accidents, the cost of the program is recovered.[2]

Moreover, failure to comply with OSHA's Hazard Communication Standard can be expensive. Fines may be $1,000 for each violation, and every uninformed employee represents a potential violation. OSHA now conducts a review of a property's HazComm compliance with every inspection. In addition, states may have chemical safety laws that are as stringent as or more stringent than OSHA's.

OSHA requires that hotels take five steps to comply with the HazComm Standard. Hotels must:

1. Read the standard.

2. List the hazardous chemicals used at the property. This includes doing a physical inventory of chemicals used, checking with the purchasing department to make sure the list is complete, setting up a file on hazardous chemicals, and developing procedures for keeping the file current.

3. Obtain **material safety data sheets (MSDSs)** from the suppliers of the chemicals used at the property, and make them available to employees.

4. Make sure all chemical containers are properly labeled.

5. Develop and implement a hazard communication program that explains MSDS information and labeling procedures to employees and informs them about hazards and protective measures.

Listing Hazardous Chemicals

Properties may assign one person to inventory all the chemicals used by the property, or department heads may be responsible for inventorying chemicals used in their specific areas. Exhibit 4 shows the inventory sheet provided by OSHA that can be used to compile a list of hazardous chemicals.

The name of each chemical that appears on the MSDS and on the label should be included on the inventory form. The common or trade name for the chemical can also be included. Some substances on a list of hazardous chemicals used in the housekeeping department might be:

- Substances in aerosol containers.
- Caustics such as laundry alkali.
- Cleansers and polishes.
- Degreasing agents (emulsifiers) used in the laundry.
- Detergents.
- Flammable materials such as cleaners and polishes.
- Fungicides and mildewcides used on carpets or in the laundry.
- Floor sealers, strippers, and polishes.
- Pesticides.

Solutions and chemicals that come from manufacturers are not the only substances that should be listed. Any hazardous substance produced by certain tasks should also be included.

The MSDS will indicate whether a chemical is hazardous. To determine whether a chemical is hazardous, look for words such as "caution," "warning," "danger," "combustible," "flammable," or "corrosive" on the label.

If an MSDS for a particular chemical is not available, or if the MSDS does not indicate whether the chemical belongs on the list, OSHA recommends treating the substance as if it were a hazardous chemical.

Exhibit 4   Form for Listing Hazardous Chemicals and Indexing MSDSs

**List of Hazardous Chemicals
and
Index of MSDSs**

Hazardous Chemicals	Operation/Area Used (Optional)	MSDSs on File

Some chemicals are exempt from the HazComm Standard. For example, rubbing alcohol in a first aid station would be exempt from the standard because it is intended for personal use by employees. Also, common consumer products such as general lubricating oil would be exempt from the HazComm Standard if intended for personal and infrequent use.

The list of hazardous chemicals will be part of the property's hazard communication program. The list must be available to employees whenever they wish to see it, and a procedure for keeping the list up to date must be in place.

Obtaining MSDSs from Chemical Suppliers

Once the inventory of hazardous materials is completed, the person in charge of the inventory should check to see if MSDSs are on file for each of the materials listed. If the property has an MSDS for a chemical, the person in charge of the inventory can put a check in the last column of the inventory sheet presented in Exhibit 4. If there is no MSDS for the chemical, the property must contact the chemical manufacturer to obtain one. Many MSDSs are available online.

All MSDSs should be examined carefully to make sure they are complete and clearly written. If data on MSDSs provide an insufficient basis for training employees on the chemical's hazards, the person in charge of the inventory should contact the manufacturer for additional information or clarification.

MSDSs can be filed by hazard, ingredients, or work areas—whatever way will make it easy for employees to find MSDSs in case of emergencies. MSDSs must be available during *all* work shifts. They should not be stored in areas that will be locked during the afternoon or evening shifts.

Many chemical manufacturers use the MSDS form developed by OSHA. A copy of the form is presented in Exhibit 5. Some manufacturers develop their own forms for MSDSs. A sample manufacturer's MSDS is shown in the appendix. When appropriate, manufacturers' MSDSs must include the following information:

- Chemical identity

- Hazardous ingredients

- Physical and chemical characteristics

- Fire and explosion hazard data

- Reactivity data

- Health hazards

- Precautions for safe handling and use

- Control measures

Chemical Identity. OSHA requires that manufacturers list the chemical and common name(s) for the substance. The form must also include the manufacturer's name and address and a telephone number so information can be obtained in case of an emergency.

Hazardous Ingredients. The manufacturer must list certain hazardous substances in the chemical.

Physical and Chemical Characteristics. The physical and chemical properties of the chemical can help workers identify the chemical by sight or smell. This increases workers' understanding of the chemical's behavior and alerts them to take necessary precautions.

Fire and Explosion Hazard Data. Knowing if and under what circumstances the chemical could catch fire and/or explode is extremely important when training employees to handle chemical emergencies. OSHA requires manufacturers to recommend fire-fighting procedures and the substance (extinguishing media) to be used to extinguish the fire. The manufacturer must also note any unusual fire or explosion hazards.

Reactivity Data. The chemical manufacturer must provide information about the chemical's stability. A stable chemical is one that will not burn, vaporize, explode, or react in some other way under normal conditions. The MSDS should describe

Exhibit 5   Sample Material Safety Data Sheet—OSHA

Material Safety Data Sheet	**U.S. Department of Labor**
May be used to comply with OSHA's Hazard Communication Standard, 29 CFR 1910.1200. Standard must be consulted for specific requirements.	Occupational Safety and Health Administration (Non-Mandatory Form) Form Approved OMB No. 1218-0072

IDENTITY *(As Used on Label and List)*	Note: *Blank spaces are not permitted. If any item is not applicable, or no information is available, the space must be marked to indicate that.*

Section I

Manufacturer's Name	Emergency Telephone Number
Address *(Number, Street, City, State, and ZIP Code)*	Telephone Number for Information
	Date Prepared
	Signature of Preparer *(optional)*

Section II — Hazardous Ingredients/Identity Information

Hazardous Components (Specific Chemical Identity; Common Name(s))	OSHA PEL	ACGIH TLV	Other Limits Recommended	% *(optional)*

Section III — Physical/Chemical Characteristics

Boiling Point	Specific Gravity (H_2O = 1)
Vapor Pressure (mm Hg.)	Melting Point
Vapor Density (AIR = 1)	Evaporation Rate (Butyl Acetate = 1)
Solubility in Water	
Appearance and Odor	

Section IV — Fire and Explosion Hazard Data

Flash Point (Method Used)	Flammable Limits	LEL	UEL
Extinguishing Media			
Special Fire Fighting Procedures			
Unusual Fire and Explosion Hazards			

(Reproduce locally)	OSHA 174, Sept. 1985

(continued)

Exhibit 5 *(continued)*

Section V — Reactivity Data

Stability	Unstable		Conditions to Avoid
	Stable		

Incompatibility (*Materials to Avoid*)

Hazardous Decomposition or Byproducts

Hazardous Polymerization	May Occur		Conditions to Avoid
	Will Not Occur		

Section VI — Health Hazard Data

Route(s) of Entry: Inhalation?   Skin?   Ingestion?

Health Hazards (*Acute and Chronic*)

Carcinogenicity: NTP?   IARC Monographs?   OSHA Regulated?

Signs and Symptoms of Exposure

Medical Conditions
Generally Aggravated by Exposure

Emergency and First Aid Procedures

Section VII — Precautions for Safe Handling and Use

Steps to Be Taken in Case Material Is Released or Spilled

Waste Disposal Method

Precautions to Be Taken in Handling and Storing

Other Precautions

Section VIII — Control Measures

Respiratory Protection (*Specify Type*)

Ventilation	Local Exhaust		Special
	Mechanical (*General*)		Other

Protective Gloves	Eye Protection

Other Protective Clothing or Equipment

Work/Hygienic Practices

the circumstances under which the chemical could become unstable. Temperature extremes or vibrations, for example, could cause some chemicals to ignite.

Health Hazards. How the chemical could enter the body (routes of entry) and its **acute** and **chronic hazards** must be listed on the MSDS. Acute hazards are those which could affect the user immediately; chronic hazards are those that could affect the user over repeated, long-term use of the chemical. In addition, the manufacturer must list whether the chemical is a carcinogen according to the National Toxicity Program (NTP), the International Agency for Research on Cancer (IARC), or OSHA; whether it will aggravate any other medical conditions; and what emergency and first aid procedures should be taken if dangerous exposure to the chemical occurs.

Precautions for Safe Handling and Use. Chemical manufacturers must provide advice on handling, storing, and disposing of chemicals. Information on the proper handling of spills must also be included.

Control Measures. How to use the chemical safely must be outlined. Manufacturers may recommend that users wear protective gloves, goggles or clothing or that they use other personal protective equipment. A section on good work/hygiene practices must also be included.

Labeling All Chemical Containers

Chemical manufacturers, in addition to providing MSDSs, must provide proper labels for chemicals. OSHA requires employers to check these labels for completeness and accuracy. The label must contain the name of the chemical, hazard warnings, and the manufacturer's name and address. If no label is provided, the employer must prepare a label from the MSDS or ask the manufacturer to provide one.

The point of the labeling requirement in the HazComm regulations is to provide an "early warning system" for users of the chemical. Labels must note the chemical's physical and health hazards *during normal use* in order to comply with OSHA regulations. (It is nearly impossible to list all the hazards that could occur during accidents or improper use.) For example, the label may not simply state, "avoid inhalation." It must explain what effects inhaling the chemical could have. However, if the label is too detailed, employees may not see important cautions.

To make the label quick to read and easy to comprehend, some properties use a labeling system with color, letter, and number codes. For example, a red label might indicate that the chemical poses a physical hazard; the letter F might indicate that the chemical is flammable; and the number four (on a scale of one to four) might indicate that the hazard is relatively severe. Employees must be trained to read and understand whatever labeling system is used at the property.

The OSHA labeling provision also requires employers to ensure that employees properly label containers into which they pour chemicals. In some states, the portable containers into which chemicals are poured for immediate use *by the person pouring them* do not need to be labeled. Other states require labeling of all portable containers. Labeling requirements should be ascertained on a state-by-state basis.

Developing a Written Hazard Communication Program

HazComm training requirements apply only to employees who must use chemicals in the course of their jobs. Front desk agents, bellpersons, accounting clerks, and others who do not routinely use chemicals do not have to be trained.

Lectures, films, and videotapes can all be part of employee training. However, training must provide time for questions and discussions and help employees apply what they learn. The U.S. Department of Labor supplies training materials at www.osha.gov. It also offers several publications including a Hazard Communication Compliance Kit which can be purchased from the website or by calling the U.S. Government Printing Office at (202) 512-1800.

There are many successful Hazard Communication Programs at hotels around the country.

Security

Providing security in a hospitality operation is the broad task of protecting both people and assets. Security efforts may involve guestroom security, key control, perimeter control, and more. Each lodging property is different and has unique security needs.

Security should be recognized as and used as a management tool. Whether the property requires a large security staff or the hotel's manager-on-duty serves as the sole security officer, the security role should be clearly defined and implemented. In the development of security guidelines, all members of the property's management and supervisory team should be involved.

The information presented here is intended only as an introduction to security. Only those elements relevant to housekeeping are included. Hotel management should consult legal counsel to ensure that the property is in compliance with applicable laws.[3]

Security Committees

Some properties develop and refine security guidelines through a committee process. The **security committee** should consist of key management personnel—including department heads. Supervisors and selected hourly employees can also contribute important security information and add to the committee's effectiveness.

Among the major agenda items for the security committee are the development of a security handbook and the design of training and awareness programs. These materials and programs should cover guestroom security, key control, lighting, emergency procedures, and security records. Once developed, these materials and programs should be continually updated and revised by the committee to meet the changing needs of the property.

The committee should meet once a month to monitor the property's security plan and programs. Other committee responsibilities generally include:

- Monitoring and analyzing recurring security problems and suggesting solutions for them.

the Rooms
CHRONICLE®

Security Tips for Housekeeping Staff

1. Wear master keys around your waist or attached to a belt or pocket to ensure that keys are not inadvertently left on the cart or in a room.

2. Don't open rooms for guests. Ask for identification and call the front desk or hotel security to advise them of the situation.

3. If jewelry, cash, guns, or blood are seen in a guestroom, back out of the room and call a supervisor.

4. Report burned-out lights, broken window locks, low batteries, and other security issues to maintenance.

5. Keep storage areas, closets, and chutes locked at all times.

6. Have clear and thorough safety and security instructions readily accessible in the guestrooms.

7. Do not leave confidential guest information (such as rooming lists containing names and room numbers) in public view or on top of the cart.

Source: *The Rooms Chronicle®*, Volume 1, Number 3, p. 8.
For subscription information, call 866-READ-TRC.

• Maintaining records of such incidents as theft, vandalism, and on-site violence.

• Conducting spot security audits and property inspections.

• Investigating security incidents.

Last but not least, the security committee should maintain open lines of communication with the local police department. The local police can be a good source of ideas on security training and basic property security.

Suspicious Activities

A lodging property, although open to the public, is private property. Hotel operations have a responsibility to monitor and, when appropriate, to control the activities of persons on the premises. Along these lines, a property should establish a policy on how to approach and handle unauthorized persons.

The individuals allowed in guestroom areas are guests, their visitors, and on-duty employees who are performing their jobs in the authorized area. Hotel housekeeping employees can be part of an effective security force—particularly in guestroom areas. The housekeeping staff should be trained to spot suspicious activities and unauthorized or undesirable persons. If an individual is seen loitering, checking doors, knocking on doors, or looking nervous, he or she should be considered suspicious and approached.

Unauthorized or undesirable persons should be approached with caution. If an employee feels threatened or in danger, he or she should not approach the person but rather should go to a secure area such as a storage room or unoccupied guestroom, lock the door, and call the front desk or security.

If the employee does approach such an individual, he or she should do so politely. The attendant should ask the person if he or she can be of assistance, but avoid getting into a long conversation. If the individual claims to be a guest, the attendant should ask to see a room key. If the person says that he or she is not a guest, or does not have a room key, the attendant should explain the hotel policy and direct the individual to the front desk. The attendant should then watch to see whether that person proceeds to the directed area and then call the front desk or security.

Employees themselves can present similar security problems. Employees who are not in their designated work area should be stopped and asked if they need help. Depending on the individual's response and manner, he or she should be reported to security or the housekeeping supervisor.

Friends and visitors of employees should not be allowed in guestroom areas or employee locker rooms. Hotel management should choose a designated area where friends and visitors may wait to meet the employee. This policy also helps reduce the potential for theft.

Meth Labs

Methamphetamine labs are a very specific problem many hotels are dealing with. People wanting to manufacture the illegal drug will choose to set up shop in hotel rooms because it is too dangerous to do so in their own homes. They will use such equipment as the hotel coffee maker to cook the volatile substance, creating a danger to guests who stay in the room after them.

Highly toxic gases escape during the manufacture of methamphetamine. Once a meth lab is discovered, it can cost a property anywhere from $2,000 to $20,000 to clean up. Any room attendant discovering the remains of a lab should immediately contact security, because a Hazmat team will be needed to clean it up. Guidelines for cleaning up a meth lab are legislated at both the local and national level and need to be followed very carefully for the safety of employees and guests.

Room attendants have identified the makings of meth labs in the past by identifying the presence of such items as lye, drain cleaner, hydrochloric acid, red phosphorus, lithium metal, ether, ammonia, benzene, and pseudoephedrine. Other signs of a meth lab can include:

- Strong odors similar to fingernail polish, cat urine, or ammonia.

- Iodine- or chemical-stained fixtures in the bathroom.

- Propane tanks with blued fittings.

- Excessive trash that includes large amounts of discarded containers or packaging for cold medicine containing ephedrine/pseudoephedrine, drain cleaner, antifreeze, denatured alcohol, lantern fuel, and red-stained coffee filters.

- Bottles or jars with glass tubing.

Theft

It is impossible to eliminate all employee and guest theft in a hospitality operation. However, management can reduce the volume of furniture, fixtures, equipment, and soft goods stolen from a property by reducing the opportunities to steal. Opportunities present themselves as unlocked doors, lack of inventory control, and plain carelessness.

Guest Theft. Unfortunately, guest theft is all too common in hotels. Some guest theft is considered a form of marketing; other guest theft is not. Most hotels assume that guests will take items that prominently display the hotel logo such as matches, pens, shampoo, ashtrays, and sewing kits. For the most part, these items are provided for the guest's convenience and are actually a form of advertising used by the hotel. However, towels, bathrobes, trash bins, and pictures are not part of the marketing strategy and are not meant to be taken by guests. When these items turn up missing, it can add up to a large expense for a hospitality operation.

To reduce the theft of these items, some properties keep count of the number of towels placed in the room. When the guest requests additional towels, it is noted at the front desk. The room attendant, too, notes how many towels are in the room when cleaning the next day. The room attendant's ability to spot missing items may allow the hotel time to charge the guest for items that have been taken.

As another strategy, some hotels place items such as towels, bathrobes, and leather stationery folders on sale in their gift shops. This may reduce the likelihood of theft since guests have the option of purchasing these items. Also, having these items on sale helps set a standard price that can be levied against guests for a missing item. Other helpful ideas to reduce guest theft are:

- *Use as few monogrammed items as possible.* Most guests are looking for a souvenir when taking towels or bathrobes and are not really looking to steal. The use of fewer items with logos reduces temptation.

- *Keep storage rooms closed and locked.* Do not allow guests to take any items from storage rooms. Also, amenities stored on carts should be stocked in a secure place or in a locked compartment. Guests walking in the hallway could very easily take home a year's supply of shampoo and soap in a matter of minutes if items were stored on top of the cart.

- *Affix or bolt guestroom items and fixtures to appropriate surfaces.* If it is not nailed, glued, bolted, or anchored to the wall—and it is small enough to fit in a suitcase—it is a prime target for guest theft. The easier an item is to remove, the more likely it is that it will be removed. All pictures, mirrors, and wall decorations should be discreetly affixed to the wall. Lamps should be too large to fit easily into a suitcase or bag. Expensive items such as televisions should be bolted and equipped with an alarm that alerts the front desk or security if an attempt is made to remove the item. It is also a good practice to record serial numbers of items such as TV sets, and to etch the hotel name in a discreet spot on the surface.

Many luxury properties do not secure items such as alarm clocks, television remote controls, or books in order to preserve a certain image. This does not mean they do not have a problem with theft. These hotels, however, usually charge a high enough rate to compensate for stolen items. Despite this fact, room attendants should still inventory items when cleaning, and notify the front desk, security, or the appropriate supervisor or department of any missing items.

- *Secure windows.* The closer the guestroom is to the parking area, the easier it is to remove an item from a room. A classic hotel legend is the 75-pound wood-framed mirror that was removed through the back window of a first floor guestroom. The mirror was too large and too heavy to be walked out the front lobby door but was easily removed without notice through the guestroom window into a car. The moral is to secure all first floor windows—and sliding glass doors—so that they cannot be opened all the way. Whenever possible, limit the number of entrances and exits guests may use to get to their room.

Non-Guest Theft. As travelers begin bringing increasingly expensive items to the hotel, in particular technology gadgets and tools, they have been the target of thieves who find ways to enter the hotel and steal property. Housekeeping employees must be vigilant about noticing suspicious people and not allowing unauthorized access to guestrooms. Nor should guestroom doors ever be propped open while unattended.

Laptop computer thefts have been a particular concern to hotels as laptop theft rings have made hotels a primary target. Thieves will attempt to walk into rooms where a room attendant is cleaning, assuming that they won't be asked for identification. They'll also enter meeting rooms where laptops are too often left unattended. Computer theft accounts for $1 billion in losses each year. When a guest's laptop is stolen, he or she may seek compensation for not just the replacement cost of the computer, but also for lost documents, data, and productivity.

Many hotels have installed in-room guest safes that are large enough to accommodate most laptops and where guests can secure other valuables such as money, jewelry, passports, and personal electronic items such as DVD players, personal digital assistants, MP3 players, and cell phones. This can help reduce some of a property's liability.

Employee Theft. It is up to management to set the standards for reducing employee theft—and to act as a good example. A manager who takes hotel steaks home to barbecue will not be effective when asking employees not to steal food, linen, and other hotel property. Management should also detail explicit regulations concerning employee theft. The employee handbook should spell out the consequences of stealing hotel property. If the rules state that employees who are caught stealing will be prosecuted and fired then the hotel should follow through. It is important that management not discriminate against any employees when enforcing these rules.

Managers should screen applicants before making a job offer. A thorough background check should be conducted, including a check for any criminal convictions. Before asking any questions or making any inquiries, check local, state, and federal laws to ensure that the selected screening techniques are not illegal.

Good inventory control procedures can also help control theft. Detailed records that note any unusual or unexplained fluctuations should be kept for all items in stock. At one hotel, for example, it was noted that a consistent amount of toilet paper came up missing each month. Through strict and diligent inventory control, it was discovered that a housekeeping employee took a case of toilet paper each delivery day and sold it by the roll to fellow employees in the hotel parking lot.

It is a good practice to conduct a monthly inventory of all housekeeping supplies, including toilet paper, amenities, and linens. If the items in storage do not match the usage rate, or if too little stock is on the shelves, it may be an indication of employee theft. Employees should be aware of the results of monthly inventories—especially when shortages are discovered.

In addition to keeping records of items in stock, records should be kept of stolen or missing items—including those from guestrooms. The record should include the name of the room attendant and those of any other hotel employees who had access to the room. For example, if a room service employee delivers a meal, that employee's name should be entered into the log. Such detailed recordkeeping over time will make it easier for management or security to discern if patterns of theft or collusion exist among specific employees.

Keep all storeroom doors locked. Storerooms should be equipped with automatic closing and locking devices. Locks on storerooms should be changed periodically to reduce the opportunity for theft.

If the property's design permits, management should designate employee entrances and exits. These entrances should be well lighted, adequately secured, and provided with round-the-clock security. Employee entrances may include a security staff office that monitors arriving and departing employees.

Employees should know what items they may bring onto or remove from the property. Management may establish a claim-check system for bringing items onto the premises and a parcel-pass system for taking items off the premises. If an employee has permission to remove hotel property, he or she should be issued a signed permit from the supervisor or an appropriate manager before doing so.

Restricting employee parking to a carefully selected area can also help control losses. Keeping the area well lighted reduces the temptation to steal and also makes the lot safer for employees who leave work after dark. The employee parking area should not be so close to the building that it allows employees to easily and quickly transfer stolen property to their cars.

If the hotel is large or has a very high turnover rate, employees are less likely to know their fellow workers. In such cases, identification badges may be required to prevent strangers who pose as employees from gaining admittance to the property.

Bomb Threats

Housekeeping procedures for handling bomb threats should be part of the property's security manual. Housekeeping's role usually consists of helping in the search for any suspicious objects that could be bombs.

Where and how the search is conducted will depend on the way the property received the bomb threat. Information from the caller or letter may give clues as to where personnel should search and as to what type of bomb or object to look for. Searches often include stairways, closets, ashtrays, trash containers, elevators, exit areas, and window sills. It may be helpful to use a flashlight to inspect areas with little light.

Search-team employees look for objects that are normally not found in an area. Housekeeping personnel have an advantage since their daily routines promote familiarity with many hotel areas. If a suspicious-looking object is found, it should not be touched or moved; and do not touch anything else in the immediate area including light switches. Notify the person in charge of the search team or an appropriate supervisor immediately. Notification is best done face-to-face or over the telephone. Avoid using radios, walkie-talkies, or cell phones. Some bombs are sensitive to these transmission waves and may detonate.

If nothing is found after completing the search, the teams should regroup in a designated area. An all-clear signal should be given after all search procedures have been performed and management is satisfied that the guests, employees, and property are not under any real threat.

Quite often, guests are not notified when bomb threats are received. This is because many bomb threats are just that—threats. However, bomb threat emergency procedures should still be followed just in case it is a real emergency. Generally, these procedures do not include notifying guests until a search is completed. If a guest does ask an employee what he or she is doing during a search, the employee should respond in a way that does not arouse unnecessary suspicion or fear.

The safety and security manual should include evacuation plans in case a bomb should actually be found or explode on the premises. It should also include provisions for emergency medical services. If the bomb explodes, housekeeping employees should follow procedures to assist in rescue efforts. The local police should be notified of all bomb threats. If police respond to such calls, the hotel should follow the directions laid out by police personnel.

Exhibit 6 describes Operation Nexus, a plan that the New York City Police Department put into place to help prevent terrorist attacks.

Fires

Fires are grouped into four classifications based on the different materials of combustion. Class A fires involve wood and paper products. Class B fires involve flammable liquid, grease, and gasoline. Class C fires are electrical in nature. Class D fires ignite by combustible metals and do not usually occur in hospitality operations.

Many hotel fires are fueled by a combination of combustibles. It is very possible that a fire started by Class A combustibles will grow to include Class B and C materials.

Fires start for many reasons. Some fires are caused by an accident or mechanical malfunctions. Others are the result of arson. In the 1980s, several fires occurred in the lodging industry that involved fatalities. The causes of two of the worst fires were traced to electrical malfunction and arson.

Fire Detection Systems. Because of the tragedy and implications of hotel fires, state and federal legislation has been passed that places more fire safety requirements on hotel operations. These requirements include the installation of smoke detectors, suppression systems, and alarms.

Exhibit 6 Operation Nexus

The New York City Police Department's (NYPD) Operation Nexus is a broad network of business and enterprises joined in an effort to prevent terrorist attacks. This network includes 25,000 firms and is being joined by nationwide business, professional, and trade associations (including the American Hotel & Lodging Association) that have agreed to transmit this Operation Nexus "Best Practices" message to their members.

Operation Nexus is driven by the NYPD's belief that individuals seeking to commit acts of terrorism may portray themselves as legitimate customers in order to purchase or lease certain materials or equipment, or to undergo certain formal training to acquire important skills or licenses. There is also a concern that these individuals may simply steal certain types of vehicles, equipment, or materials in the inventory of legitimate businesses. Whatever the method, once appropriated, these items could then be used to facilitate a terrorist plot.

Through Operation Nexus, the NYPD actively encourages business owners, operators, and their employees to apply their particular business and industry knowledge and experience against each customer transaction or encounter to discern anything unusual or suspicious that might indicate a link to terrorism. Such instances should be reported to local or federal authorities.

With these goals in mind, the NYPD requests the following list of suspicious activities, though not all inclusive, be considered as part of "Best Practices" counterterrorism guidelines for notifying law enforcement authorities:

- Last-minute, walk-in registrants, the day before a major event (e.g., New Year's Eve).
- Guests who deny access to the housekeeping staff to perform routine room cleaning duties over a period of several consecutive days.
- Guests who permit housekeeping staff to enter rooms, but who unusually supervise or rigorously monitor their actions.
- Evidence that room occupants have intentionally changed their physical appearance (e.g., shaving/close cropping of hair, hair dyes, large amounts of shaving cream, razors). Requests for staff to clear clogged drains due to large amounts of hair.
- Identification offered for room reservations based on documents of questionable authenticity (e.g., misspellings on "official" papers, altered photos, P.O. Box addresses, no telephone numbers).
- Payment with a large sum of cash instead of a credit card to cover an expensive lodging bill (or any other unusual registration and reservation information).
- Room phone bills for overseas phone calls.
- Reports of the thefts of guests' luggage or baggage containing sensitive documents such as passports/visas and other forms of identification.
- An unusual number of visitors admitted by a guest; persons loitering on guest floors.
- Unusual or excessive luggage, containers, tools, wires, etc. Discarded luggage by guests.
- A guest who arrives with luggage that is seemingly empty.

(continued)

Exhibit 6   *(continued)*

- Possession of very expensive photographic/surveillance equipment, binoculars or other equipment not typically carried by guests or tourists (e.g., night-vision goggles, military binoculars).
- Possession of unauthorized uniforms (airport, postal, police, military).
- Unusual odors or substances unknown to you; oil-based stains or other flammable material.
- A request at check-in for a specific room because of its view of another city building or other location that could be considered a potential target of terrorism.
- Delivery of a suspicious parcel (e.g., unusual weight/balance; protruding wires; greasy marks on the wrapping or envelope; unusual smell; delivered by hand by an unknown source, etc.).
- Loitering in the hotel lobby for an unusual period of time.
- Suspicious person(s) loitering near HVAC system vents, intakes, equipment, etc.

Source: AH&LA website.

Smoke detectors. Smoke detectors are commonly found in hotel rooms. Some are battery operated and function independently from the hotel alarm system. Other smoke detectors are hard wired. When one goes off, an alarm sounds not only in the room or immediate area, but at a control panel located at the front desk or engineering office.

Smoke detectors are set off by sensing smoke. There are two types of detectors: photoelectric and ionization. Photoelectric detectors activate when smoke interferes with or blocks off a beam of light located inside the detector. Ionization smoke detectors also activate when they sense smoke. However, the alarm sounds when the detector senses a shift in electrical conductivity between two plates.[4]

Smoke detectors can become activated when a fire is not present. Steam from very long and hot showers or smoke from a guest's cigarette can sometimes inadvertently activate these alarms.

Fire suppression systems. Fire suppression systems include sprinklers that extinguish a fire with water. Sprinklers are generally triggered by heat—not smoke. Therefore, if a smoke detector sounds an alarm, it does not necessarily mean that the sprinkler system will go off. Sprinkler heads are usually located near or on the ceiling in guestrooms, housekeeping storage closets, and laundry rooms, as well as in other public areas. Since sprinkler heads extend several inches from the ceiling or wall, employees must be careful when cleaning around them. If a head is broken or knocked during cleaning, it could set off the fire alarm and send hundreds of gallons of water into the area.

Pull stations. Alarms can be set off by smoke detectors, heat detectors, sprinkler systems, and pull stations. Pull stations are located in public areas such as lobbies and corridors and near elevators and exits. These stations are usually red and require someone to break a glass panel or pull a lever to turn on a fire alarm. Employees should know the locations of pull stations and how to sound the fire alarm should they spot a fire or see smoke.

Fire Safety Training. Housekeeping staff may be involved with the evacuation of guests and other employees in the case of a fire. In some instances, housekeeping staff may be required to search guestrooms in areas of the hotel that the fire has not reached to ensure that all guests have left the property. Training is important in any fire safety program so employees know how to respond calmly and professionally in an actual emergency.

Fire safety training should also provide instruction on reporting a fire and on what to do if a fire is spotted. The training program should include emergency escape procedures and outline duties for housekeeping staff involved in helping evacuate guests. The training should also describe a method of accounting for all employees after emergency evacuation has taken place. This can be accomplished by instructing all employees to meet at a designated area outside the hotel.

Since most deaths and injuries from a fire are a result of smoke and toxic fumes—not the flames—employees should be shown how to escape a smoke-filled hallway or room. When trying to leave a smoke-filled room, the employee should stay close to the floor and cover his or her mouth and nose with a wet towel. Employees should be instructed never to use an elevator in a fire and always to leave the property by using the fire escape or stairway.

Employees should be instructed on how to put out a small fire that is confined to a trash can or limited area. Different portable fire extinguishers will do the job for different types of fires. Exhibit 7 lists approved types of fire extinguishers. Most hotel properties have type ABC extinguishers; these can be used on most types of fires encountered in a lodging operation. Employees should be told where fire extinguishers are located and be trained in how to use them.

OSHA mandates standards for fire safety training with respect to emergency and fire prevention plans. Any employee training above and beyond OSHA and local fire and safety laws can benefit the hotel in more than one way. For one, it provides a safer environment for hotel employees. Secondly, it can be used as a selling point by the hotel since well-trained employees provide a higher level of safety for guests. Thirdly, fire safety training can be used by a hotel that has experienced a fire as an added legal defense. Training employees can demonstrate that hotel management took precautions with respect to fire safety and was not negligent.[5]

Flame-Resistant Materials. Fires need fuel to burn. In a hotel, fuel for a fire can include beds, linens, draperies, carpeting, and cleaning chemicals. As part of a comprehensive fire protection program, properties should purchase and use fire-resistant fabrics and materials whenever possible. Fire-resistant materials are rated with flame spread ratings. A zero flame spread is the lowest. Local, state, and federal codes may dictate the minimum fire-resistant ratings for each material. The local fire department may also provide information regarding flame-retardant fabrics and material.

Key Control

Proper key control procedures are important for guest security and privacy. **Key control** also protects the property by reducing the possibility of guest and property theft. Housekeeping is primarily concerned with four categories of keys: emergency, master, storeroom, and guestroom.

Exhibit 7   Types of Fire Extinguishers

Extinguisher Classifications †	A		AB	BC				ABC		
Extinguishing Agent	Water Types (includes antifreeze)		AFFF Foam and FFFP	Carbon Dioxide	Dry Chemical Types Purple K Super K Monnex Potassium Bicarb. Urea based		Halogenated Types 1211 1301 1211/1301	Multipurpose Dry Chemical		Halogenated Types 1211 1211/1301
Discharge Method	Stored Pressure	Pump Tank	Stored Pressure	Self Expelling	Stored Pressure	Cartridge Operated	Stored Pressure	Stored Pressure	Cartridge Operated	Stored Pressure
Sizes Available	2½ Gal.	2½-5 Gal.	2½ Gal. (33 Gal.)	5-20 lb. (50-100 lb.)	2½-30 lb. (50-350 lb.)	4-30 lb. (125-350 lb.)	1-5 lb.	2½-20 lb. (50-350 lb.)	5-30 lb. (125-350 lb.)	5½-22 lb. (50-150 lb.)
Horizontal Range (Approx.)	30-40 ft.	30-40 ft.	10-25 ft. (30 ft.)	3-8 ft. (3-10 ft.)	10-15 ft. (15-45 ft.)	10-20 ft. (15-45 ft.)	10-16 ft.	10-15 ft. (15-45 ft.)	10-20 ft. (15-45 ft.)	9-16 ft. (20-35 ft.)
Discharge Time (Approx.)	1 Min.	1-3 Min.	50-65 Sec. (1 Min.)	8-15 Sec. (10-30 Sec.)	8-25 Sec. (25-60 Sec.)	8-25 Sec. (25-60 Sec.)		8-25 Sec. (20-60 Sec.)	8-25 Sec. (25-60 Sec.)	10-18 Sec. (30-45 Sec.)
Operating Precautions and Agent Limitations	Conductor of electricity. Needs protection from freezing. (except antifreeze). Use on flammable liquids and grease will spread fire.		Conductor of electricity. Needs protection from freezing. Not effective on water-soluble flammable liquids such as alcohol, unless otherwise stated on nameplate. AFFF not effective on pressurized flammable liquid/gas fires.	Smothering occurs in high concentrations. Avoid contact with discharge horn. Limited effectiveness under windy conditions. Severely reduced effectiveness at sub-zero (F) temperatures.	Extensive cleanup, particularly on delicate electronic equipment. Obscures visibility in confined spaces.		Avoid high concentrations and unnecessary use.	Extensive cleanup. Damages electronic equipment. Obscures visibility in confined spaces. Limited penetrating ability on deep-seated Class A fires.		Avoid high concentrations and unnecessary use.

NOTE: Protection required below 40°F and above 120°F.

NOTE: Only dry chemical types are effective on pressurized flammable gases and liquids; for deep fat fryers, multipurpose ABC dry chemicals are not acceptable.

Notes: Figures in parentheses refer to wheeled units.
†Class D information is not shown.

Source: Adapted from the National Association of Fire Equipment Distributors, "Selection Guide to Portable Fire Extinguishers," Chicago, Illinois, copyright 1988. Used with permission.

Types of Keys. Emergency keys open all doors in the property—even those that guests have double-locked. These keys should be kept in a secure place such as the hotel safe or in the security office. Some properties also keep an emergency key off the premises. Distribution and use should occur only in emergency situations such as a fire or when a guest or employee is locked inside a room and needs immediate assistance. Most housekeeping personnel do not use emergency keys on a day-to-day basis.

Master keys also open more than one guestroom. Master keys are separated into three levels of access. The highest level is the grand master. This key opens every hotel room and, many times, all housekeeping storage rooms. If the guest has engaged the dead bolt, master keys will not open the door. Master keys can be used in emergency situations when it is vital for an employee to enter some or all areas of a hotel. Master keys are stored and issued at the security office or kept at the front desk for such purposes.

The next level of master key is the section master. This type of master key opens rooms in one area of a hotel. A housekeeping supervisor may be issued more than one key of this type because he or she may be required to inspect the work of room attendants in various sections of the hotel.

The lowest level of master key is the floor key. Generally, a room attendant is given this key to open the rooms he or she is assigned to clean on that floor. If the employee has rooms to clean on more than one floor or area, he or she may need more than one floor key. Floor keys typically open the housekeeping storeroom for that floor—unless the room is specially keyed or is accessed by another master key.

Guestroom keys are those keys distributed to guests. This type of key opens a single guestroom and, in some cases, other locked areas such as the swimming pool, exercise room, business center, or various exterior entrances to the hotel. When not in use, guestroom keys are stored at and issued by the front desk.

Key Control Procedures. A log should be used to monitor the distribution of master keys. This log should include the date, time, and the signature of the person who signed out a particular key as well as the signature of a witness or issuing manager or security officer. In larger properties, the linen room attendant distributes and secures the keys for the room attendants. At smaller properties, the executive housekeeper or the front desk may assume this function.

Employees issued keys should keep the keys on their persons at all times. Key belts, wristbands, or neck chains are recommended devices for keeping track of master keys. Master keys should never be left on top of a housekeeping cart, in a guestroom, or in an unsecured area. An employee should never loan the key to a guest or to another employee. The room attendant who signed for the master key is the employee who is responsible for it, and it should never leave the property. Finally, a room attendant should never use a master key to open a room for a guest. If a guest asks an employee to unlock a room, the employee should politely explain the hotel's policy and direct the guest to the front desk.

Room attendants are also responsible for retrieving guestroom keys if the guest leaves the key in the room. Many hotels provide key lockboxes on the room attendants' carts to store guestroom keys. If no lockbox is available, room keys should be kept in a secured area—not on top of the cart—until returned to the

the Rooms
CHRONICLE®

Ask Gail—It is amazing what some guests leave behind when they check out!

Dear Gail:

What are the most common items left behind in hotel rooms by guests? I ask this because it seems that our housekeepers continue to find various items of odd and unusual nature.

Vanessa J.
Fresno, CA

Dear Vanessa,

Our TRC researchers spoke with a number of our housekeeping contacts in the field and did a little research on this topic. At one time, the most recurring items were clothing. Typically, it was stray socks under the bed or caught between the bed linens, nightgowns left hanging on the back of the bathroom door, or damp bathing suits left hung to dry in the bathtub, but obscured by a shower curtain.

In today's world of technologically dependant travelers, it seems that the most predominant items left behind are cell phone charging cords and electrical power cords for laptop computers. These items are easy for guests to miss as frequently the cords are plugged into an electrical outlet behind or underneath a desk or nightstand.

Of course, today's guests still leave behind the occasional contact lenses, eyeglasses, personal toiletries, errant clothing, and half-eaten pizzas. Certainly, one can assume that the pizzas were intended to be disposed of. One executive housekeeper reported finding a boa constrictor snake lurking under the bed. Yes, it was a pet left by a guest by mistake. Another reported that a family forgot to check out with their dog. I suppose when guests start leaving their children behind, then we should really be concerned ... or at least charge their credit card for another night's stay!

Source: *The Rooms Chronicle®*, Volume 13, Number 2, p. 7.
For subscription information, please call 866-READ-TRC.

front desk. If a room attendant finds a room key in the hallway or public area, the front desk should be notified immediately. The key should be returned to the front desk or placed in the lockbox.

Door Locking Systems. Most hotels use an electronic locking system or card key system for guest doors and storerooms. This type of room-locking mechanism uses special door locks and customized plastic cards that act as keys to unlock the doors. Electronic card keys look like credit cards and have magnetic strips, whereas mechanical card locks utilize plastic cards with holes punched in them. A key encoding machine at the front desk activates the next sequential code on each electronic card key to unlock doors. Each door lock is programmed to recognize a sequence of over a million codes, thus making the previous code obsolete once a new electronic key is coded and introduced into the lock. A single electronic card key can be coded to permit a room attendant access to multiple specific rooms.

the Rooms
CHRONICLE®

Hotel Liability for Guests' Personal Property Can Be Enormous

An age-old problem for the hospitality industry is the protection of personal property of hotel guests. Traditionally, guest property consisted of clothing, luggage, money, jewelry, and vacation items. Today, hotel guests are likely to have with them such items as laptop computers, cell phones, various electronic devices and perhaps inventory for the traveling salesperson. These items can be worth thousands of dollars, possibly exposing the hotel to extensive liability for their loss.

It becomes incumbent upon property managers to be aware of their responsibilities when it comes to the preservation of personal property for their guests.

Bailment. The legal theory of *bailment* is one that is defined as the delivery of an item of tangible personal property for some purpose with the express or implied understanding that the person receiving the property shall return it in the same or similar condition to which it was received when the purpose has been completed. Essentially, it is entrusting personal property to the hotel for temporary safekeeping. In a hotel setting, this would include items guests placed in safes or safety deposit boxes, luggage storage, valet parking, and valet laundry services. The application of law is somewhat different if the bailment created is expressed or implied.

Theories of liability. Management's responsibility for a guest's lost or missing property only applies when the property was within the walls of the hotel or was in the care or charge of the innkeeper. *Common law liability* states that the hotel is in essence an insurer and is responsible for the loss, unless it can show the guest was negligent, or an act of god or an act of a common or public enemy caused the loss. *Statutory liability*, sometimes referred to as a limiting liability statute, has been created in most jurisdictions to limit common law liability for hotels. All 50 U.S. states have passed legislation designed to limit an innkeeper's liability for guests' personal property. However, to receive the protection of the limiting liability statute, management must do the following:

- Provide safes that withstand fire and theft, either in rooms or in a central location.
- Post notices that safes are available for guest use.
- Post notices of that state's maximum monetary limit of liability.
- Require guests to declare the value of goods at the time of surrender if the state's statutory limit is to be exceeded.

The next step is an analysis of the type of bailment created to determine responsibility for the lost property. If a hotel provides a safe or some other service to keep or store guest property, an expressed bailment is created. When property is given by the guest to the hotel management and both parties receive some benefit (such as a tip to the bell attendant and safekeeping for the guest), this may be referred to as mutual-benefit bailment. In these cases, the hotel is required to exercise ordinary care over the property. This may even extend to periods of time when the hotel holds property for non-guests or former guests, such as when luggage is stored before check-in or after check-out.

(continued)

the Rooms
CHRONICLE®

(continued)

Lost and found items. In lost and found situations, a case of constructive bailment has been created. Though the hotel comes into lawful possession of the property by means other than a mutual agreement, it is still treated as the property of the guest. Hence, bailment has automatically been created through a default process the moment an employee finds lost or mislaid guest property. The hotel now has the responsibility to return the property to its rightful owner to complete the bailment. To comply, hotel management should take the following steps:

- Review the lost and found laws for their state.
- Require employees and staff to immediately turn in lost property to the hotel's lost and found department.
- Keep a log of such found property.
- Make reasonable, documented efforts to find the owner, especially for items of significant value.
- Safeguard and hold the personal property for the length of time prescribed by the state's statute of limitations for lost or mislaid property.
- Ascertain the identity of the purported owner by requiring proof of ownership or identification of lost items before returning found property.
- If the original owner cannot be found, dispose of the property in accordance with written procedures and the laws of the jurisdiction.

Lost property can be a tricky issue. Is the property truly lost or was it left behind to be discarded? Is there a financial or sentimental value to the property? What efforts must be made to find the owner? Management should err on the side of caution and assume that the property is in fact lost, then follow the steps outlined above.

Source: Michael Gentile, J.D., *The Rooms Chronicle®*, Volume 12, Number 5, pp. 14–15. For subscription information, please call 866-READ-TRC.

Electronic door locks provide hotels with increased security and are so popular that some experts believe that hotels without them will face an increasingly difficult time purchasing insurance. Electronic key systems automatically generate logs of who has entered the room and when. This has protected many guestroom attendants who were accused of theft.

Electronic locking systems can also be used to determine the status of a guestroom. Some properties have that status communicated to the energy management system so that temperature controls can be activated.

In contrast, mechanical card locks, which are technologically less sophisticated, must be rekeyed manually directly at the guestroom door after each guest departs or when a guest loses their room key.

Lost and Found

Many times, the housekeeping department handles the lost-and-found function. Lost-and-found items should be stored in an area that is secure and has limited access. One employee per shift should be assigned to handle the lost and found as part of his or her job.

In large hotels, the linen room attendant may handle the lost-and-found procedures. In smaller properties, the task may be delegated to the executive housekeeper or front desk personnel. When an employee finds an item left behind by a guest, he or she should immediately turn it over to the lost and found. In no instance should lost and found items be left in an unsecured spot such as on top of a room attendant cart.

Items should be tagged, logged, and secured after they have been turned over to the lost and found. Tags may be numbered and used to identify the item. A log should be used to record the date, time, where the item was found, and by whom. The log should also have space to record if and when the item was recovered by its owner.

If the housekeeping department is primarily responsible for a hotel's lost and found function, it is important that housekeeping staff deliver the log to the front desk during hours when the housekeeping office may be closed. This will enable the hotel to respond more quickly to after-hours inquiries about lost and misplaced items.

All lost-and-found property should be kept for at least 90 days. If items are not claimed after 90 days, it is up to management to decide how to dispose of the items properly. Many hotels donate unclaimed lost-and-found items to local charities. It is important to ensure that the lost-and-found policy of the hotel complies with local and state laws.

Guestroom Cleaning

Security in guestroom areas is important to maintain for the safety of the guests and employees. Room attendants should respect guest property and should not open guest luggage or packages or snoop in dresser drawers or closets. Some hotels even have a policy that forbids room attendants to move guest property. In these instances, room attendants are instructed to clean around guest objects.

Since guests sometimes hide valuables and belongings in pillowcases or between mattresses, room attendants must be extra careful when removing linens. Other favorite hiding places for guest valuables include the top of closets and under lamps.

If room attendants notice any of the following while cleaning, they should immediately contact their supervisor, security, or the front desk:

- Guns or weapons of any kind
- Controlled substances or drugs
- Unauthorized cooking appliances or unsafe electrical appliances
- Foul odors
- Unauthorized pets
- Ill guests
- Large amounts of cash or valuable jewelry

When cleaning, the room attendant should always keep the door closed (unless property policy dictates otherwise) and the housekeeping cart rolled in front of the entrance to block access from the outside. If a guest wants to enter the room while the attendant is cleaning, the attendant should politely ask the guest his or her name and ask to see a room key. It is imperative that the room attendant insert the key into the door lock to ensure that the room being cleaned is that guest's room. If the guest does not have a key or the key fails to unlock the door, the attendant should tell him or her to contact the front desk. A guest should never be allowed to enter a room just to look around. Again, the attendant should explain that this is the hotel's policy and is enforced for the guest's safety and security.

A room should never be left unattended with the door open. If an employee must leave the room while cleaning, he or she should lock the door on the way out. This procedure should be followed even if the employee is out of the room for only a few minutes.

After cleaning the room, all windows and sliding glass doors should be locked. The guestroom door should also be checked to see that it is locked.

Unfortunately, guests often accuse the room attendant if an item comes up missing from the guestroom. This is just one more reason for room attendants to be considerate of guest property and to protect the guest's room from any possible theft. For the most part, an employee who is alert and careful can contribute to the overall safety and security of the operation—and to a guest's safe and trouble-free stay.

 Endnotes ——————————————————————————————————

1. This discussion on OSHA is adapted from Raymond C. Ellis Jr. and David M. Stipanuk, *Security and Loss Prevention Management* (Lansing, Mich.: American Hotel & Lodging Educational Institute, 1999), Appendix.

2. "Is Your Hotel a Hazard?", *Lodging Hospitality*, October 1988, p. 228.

3. This discussion is adapted from Ellis, Jr. and Stipanuk, Security and Loss Prevention Management. The information provided is in no way to be construed as a recommendation by the American Hotel & Lodging Educational Institute or the AH&LA of any industry standard, or as a recommendation of any kind, to be adopted by or binding upon any member of the hospitality industry.

4. Brian Ledeboer and A.H. Petersen Jr., "Detect, Control Fires Before They Become Infernos," *Power*, June 1988, p. 27.

5. Walter Orey, "Full Fire Protection Requires Diligence," *Hotel and Motel Management*, January 12, 1987, p. 32.

 **Key Terms** ——————————————————————————————————

acute hazard—Something that could cause immediate harm. For example, a chemical that could cause burns on contact with the skin is an acute hazard.

chronic hazard—Something that could cause harm over a long period; for example, a chemical that could cause cancer or organ damage with repeated use over a long period.

emergency key—A key that opens all guestroom doors, even when they are double locked.

guestroom key—A key that opens a single guestroom door if it is not double locked.

HazComm Standard—Hazard Communication Standard; OSHA's regulation requiring employers to inform employees about possible hazards related to chemicals they use on the job.

job safety analysis—A detailed report that lists every job task performed by all housekeeping employees. Each job task is further broken down into a list of steps. These steps are accompanied by tips and instructions on how to perform each step safely.

key control—The process of reducing guest and property theft and other security-related incidents by carefully monitoring and tracking the use of keys at a hospitality operation.

master key—A key that opens all guestroom doors that are not double locked.

MSDS (material safety data sheet)—A form that is supplied by the chemical's manufacturer containing information about a chemical.

OSHA (Occupational Safety and Health Act)—A broad set of rules that protects workers in all trades and professions from a variety of unsafe working conditions.

pH scale—A scale that measures the acidity or alkalinity of a substance; according to the scale, a pH of 7 is neutral; acids have values of less than 7 to 0; and alkalies have values of more than 7 to 14.

safety—A condition in which persons are safe from injury, hurt, or loss while present in the workplace.

security—The prevention of theft, fire, and other emergency situations in the workplace.

security committee—A committee consisting of key management personnel and selected employees that develops and monitors a property's security plans and programs.

Underwriters Laboratories—An independent, nonprofit organization that tests electrical equipment and devices to ensure that the equipment is free of defects that could cause fire or shock.

workers' compensation—Insurance that reimburses an employer for damages that must be paid to an employee for an injury occurring in the course of his or her employment.

Review Questions

1. What three simple steps can employees take to prevent accidents and injuries?
2. Why is it necessary to establish a continual training program for cleaning chemical safety?

3. What are some common chemicals used by housekeeping staff? What functions do each of these chemicals perform?

4. What types of safety equipment are available for employees to use when handling chemicals?

5. What is the purpose of the Occupational Safety and Health Act? Name three areas in a hospitality operation that are covered by OSHA regulations.

6. Compare the primary uses of danger, caution, and safety instruction signs.

7. How does OSHA's HazComm Standard benefit employers and employees alike?

8. Where do material safety data sheets (MSDSs) come from, and what kinds of information do they contain?

9. What are OSHA's requirements for chemical container labeling? Why is it important to label chemical containers?

10. What are three ways that a property can reduce the incidence of guest theft? Of employee theft?

11. What three fire-detection systems are required in hotel operations?

12. What part does housekeeping play in a property's key-control efforts?

13. What four conditions or items should a room attendant report to his or her supervisor or to security if they are spotted during guestroom cleaning?

 ## Internet Sites

For more information, visit the following Internet sites. Remember that Internet addresses can change without notice. If the site is no longer there, you can use a search engine to look for additional sites.

Allied Safe and Vault
www.alliedsafe.com

Carneill Solutions (Door Sentry)
www.carneillsolutions.com/
index.htm

HazCom safety training
http://www.osha-safety-training.net/
HOT/hotel.html

OSHA
www.osha.gov

 ## Case Study

The Case of the Missing Earrings

The Quick Stop Motel was a small property with a limited staff. It was the first hotel built in the city when the expressway came through 40 years earlier.

Juanita looked up and smiled as a guest came toward her cart. "Good afternoon, Mr. Tills."

"I bet you think it's a good afternoon," Mr. Tills snarled at her. "Best afternoon of your life, eh?"

"Sir?" Juanita queried, looking bewildered.

"Oh, the very picture of innocence!" he said sarcastically. "I suppose you don't know anything about my wife's earrings."

Juanita's eyes got wide and she shook her head slowly. "Sir, I don't know what you're talking about."

"The earrings you stole from my wife. She left them in the room after she took them off last night, and this afternoon they were gone—after *you'd* cleaned the room. If you fork them over right now, *maybe* I won't tell your supervisor."

Juanita continued to shake her head, "Sir, I do not steal things! I am not a thief!"

"Then would you care to tell me where they are? Surely you're not so obtuse that you would vacuum up a pair of $1,000 diamond earrings!"

"Sir, no, I ..."

"Forget it," Mr. Tills snapped at her. "I'll just go to the front desk, and you can be sure if I don't get them back, I'll have the $1,000 out of your paycheck!"

Mr. Tills turned and stomped off to the front desk, leaving a distraught Juanita, who immediately abandoned her cart and headed straight for the housekeeping offices. She entered the stock room where Cindy, the executive housekeeper, was going over inventory with the assistant executive housekeeper, Chandis.

"Miss Volk, a guest just accused me of being a thief," Juanita burst out.

Cindy set her clipboard down. Juanita seemed on the verge of either crying or screaming. Cindy wished once again that the hotel had security officers who could handle this situation. She motioned to Chandis to follow her and gently said, "Juanita, let's go sit in my office and you can tell me what happened."

The three quickly retreated to the executive housekeeper's office where Cindy sat down beside Juanita, and Chandis moved to the chair behind Cindy's desk.

"OK, Juanita, you seem very upset. What happened?" Cindy asked.

"Mr. Tills said I stole his wife's earrings and he was going to have $1,000 held out of my paycheck. How am I supposed to feed my family if I have to pay him $1,000? It'll take months to pay him back! And it's not fair! I didn't take anything; you know I wouldn't take anything, Miss Volk. I've worked for this hotel for 20 years and no one has ever called me a thief! I don't have to put up with this, Miss Volk. I'll quit before I will put up with this!"

Cindy picked up a notepad, "I understand you're angry, Juanita. I would be upset too if someone accused me of theft. So, Mr. Tills claims his wife's $1,000 earrings are missing?"

Juanita nodded, "Of course I'm angry—everyone's going to hear about this and say that I'm a thief."

"Well, I'm not going to call you a thief, Juanita. Take a deep breath, and let me ask you some questions so we can try to sort this out. Did you clean the Tillses' room this morning?"

"Yes, but I didn't even see any earrings!"

"So, the earrings weren't there when you cleaned the room?"

"How should I know? I didn't go through her purse or their suitcases."

"What time did you clean the room?"

"It was around 9:30 A.M. I saw the Tillses leave for breakfast and wanted to get their room clean for them before they returned."

"Did you notice any unusual activity around the guestroom? Did anyone else enter the room or try the door?"

"I'm not sure," Juanita answered. "But Evans was working the rooms across the hall; he might have seen something. I only cleaned the poolside rooms on that floor. There was a basketball team checking into rooms down the hall."

"OK. When you cleaned the room, did you move their suitcases or open up the drawers?"

"Let me try to remember," Juanita said, closing her eyes. "It was my second room. They had a makeup bag on the bed that I moved to the nightstand so I could make the bed." Juanita opened her eyes again, "I didn't open the drawers—I never do in stayover rooms. You told us not to."

Just as Cindy was about to ask another question, the phone rang. Chandis picked it up quickly to minimize the interruption, but then handed the phone to Cindy. "Cindy, it's Mark at the front desk. He says he needs to talk to you immediately."

"Excuse me for a moment, Juanita. I'll make this short," Cindy apologized, taking the phone from Chandis. "Good morning, Mark, what can I do for you?"

"Cindy, I have a hotel guest, Mr. Tills, here. He tells me that one of your room attendants stole his wife's earrings."

Cindy sighed and looked over at Juanita, whose distress was slowly turning to indignation. "I'm aware of the situation, Mark. What did the guest tell you?"

"Mr. Tills's wife took her earrings off last night and placed them in the unused ashtray inside the dresser drawer. She went to put them on this afternoon and they were gone. Mr. Tills is convinced that the room attendant took them. Would you like the description he gave me of the room attendant?"

"That won't be necessary, Mark. I have Juanita here in my office. Mr. Tills spoke with her this morning," Cindy said, wishing to head off any disparaging description that the angry guest may have given. Juanita began muttering about the guest's method of "speaking with her" as Cindy continued her conversation with the front desk agent. "Mark, is Mr. Tills still standing there?"

"Yes, he is," Mark replied.

"OK. I'll be right out. Ask him to sit down in one of the offices so I can talk to him away from the lobby."

"I'll tell him, Cindy. Thanks," Mark said and promptly hung up.

"Juanita, take a few moments to calm down if you need to, then go finish your rooms. I'm going to talk to Mr. Tills, and I'll let you know by the end of the day what has happened."

Discussion Question

1. What steps should Cindy take to investigate the situation?

The following industry experts helped generate and develop this case: Gail Edwards, CHHE, St. Louis, Missouri; Mary Friedman, Edina, Minnesota; and Aleta Nitschke, CHA, founder of *The Rooms Chronicle*®, Garfield, Minnesota.

Task Breakdowns: Safety and Security

The procedures presented in this section are for illustrative purposes only and should not be construed as recommendations or standards. While these procedures are typical, readers should keep in mind that each property has its own procedures, equipment specifications, and policies regarding protective gear which are designed to fit individual needs.

Respond Appropriately to Theft and Vandalism

Materials needed: local theft policies, tape to cordon off area, the room/space inventory sheet, the furniture inventory sheet, project identification program lists, local vandalism policies, a pen, paper, and the passdown log or duty log, camera, incident report form.

STEPS	HOW-TO'S
1. Establish or review local policies for handling front desk holdups or theft of guest and employee possessions.	
2. Respond to reports of theft.	❑ Notify your supervisor. ❑ Follow local procedures. ❑ The steps to follow to respond to reported theft vary among properties. ❑ Notify the security department and police department (if appropriate).
3. Secure the crime scene if appropriate.	❑ Lock down or cordon off the area of the crime scene. ❑ Do not touch any potential evidence. ❑ Monitor all access to the crime scene to prevent access by unauthorized access. ❑ Await police arrival (if notified).
4. Make a list of stolen items.	❑ Ask employees or guests what is missing. ❑ Search surrounding areas for missing items.
5. Check if stolen items were marked with serial numbers.	❑ Check the furniture inventory sheet and the room inventory sheet for items owned by the property.
6. Escort security personnel to the scene of the theft.	
7. Review local policies for handling vandalism.	

Respond Appropriately to Theft and Vandalism (continued)

STEPS	HOW-TO'S

8. Look for signs of vandalism.	❑ Look for:
	   • Broken windows
	   • Graffiti on walls
	   • Punctured tires
	   • Damaged fire equipment
	
	❑ Report signs of vandalism to your supervisor.

9. Investigate incidents of vandalism.	❑ Photograph vandalized property for incident report.
	
	❑ Question guests and employees to gather information about the incident.
	
	❑ Try to find out:
	   • Who did it
	   • If perimeter patrols are too infrequent
	   • If there is a disgruntled past or present guest or employee who has a reason for causing damage.

10. Make sure vandalism damages are repaired or removed immediately.	

11. Make an appropriate entry in the log book immediately after an incident of vandalism occurs. Complete a detailed Incident Report form	❑ Include the following information:
	   • Who was involved
	   • What happened
	   • Where it happened
	   • Actions taken to respond
	   • Any other important details
	
	❑ Write all information in ink.
	
	❑ Sign your initials by the entry.
	
	❑ Sign your name on the Incident Report form.

Respond Appropriately to Suspicious People

Materials needed: a pen and the passdown log or duty log.

STEPS	HOW-TO'S
1. Watch for people who seem suspicious or out-of-place.	❑ Look for people who: • Seem nervous or apprehensive • Glance back repeatedly • Wait in the same place for a long time • Are in an area you don't normally see people in • Are in an area at the wrong time • Act like they don't want to be noticed • Try to get into restricted areas • Are unaccompanied
2. Approach suspicious people.	❑ Approach suspicious people only if you feel safe doing so. If you don't feel safe, get help from security or another employee. ❑ Approach the person and identify yourself. Remain calm and courteous. Don't threaten the person. ❑ Ask if you may help the person. Ask if he or she is a guest. If he or she claims to be a guest, ask to see a room key. ❑ If the person is not a guest, explain your property's policy and direct the person to the front desk. ❑ If the person is not authorized to be in the area, explain that the area is restricted. Politely ask the person to leave the area or the property. ❑ If the person is an employee who is not authorized to be in a particular area, ask if he or she needs help. Remind the person that the area is restricted, and make sure he or she leaves the area.

Respond Appropriately to Suspicious People *(continued)*

STEPS	HOW-TO'S
3. Escort unauthorized people from restricted areas.	❑ Walk with unauthorized people to an exit. ❑ Avoid touching them. ❑ If they refuse to leave, call the appropriate personnel. ❑ Monitor the exit until the unauthorized people de-part hotel grounds.
4. Ensure that the area is properly secured to keep others from unauthorized entry.	
5. Report suspicious people.	❑ Report suspicious people to the front desk. ❑ Make an entry in the logbook. Include all relevant details about the incident.

Respond Appropriately to Fires

Materials needed: the facility's emergency procedures, a fire alarm, a telephone or radio, the occupancy report, a fire extinguisher, master keys, house count report and rooming lists, a pen, the duty log, and the passdown log.

STEPS	HOW-TO'S
1. Ask your supervisor to review with you the property's emergency procedures.	
2. Sound an alarm if you see smoke or flames.	❑ Go to the nearest fire alarm pull station and pull the alarm. ❑ Give verbal alarms if appropriate.
3. Use a phone or radio to notify the front desk, the fire department, and other appropriate employees.	❑ The front desk may notify appropriate personnel. Fire alarms may automatically alert fire departments. Make sure you know whether your property's alarms do this.
4. Try to put out small fires.	❑ Try to put out fires only if it's safe, you feel comfortable doing so, and you have received proper extinguisher training. ❑ The steps to put out small fires vary among properties.
5. Evacuate the area.	❑ Remove any obstacles such as housekeeping carts from egress routes. Store then In a closet or guestroom. ❑ Evacuate danger areas according to your property's policies. Evacuation routes should be clearly posted in each room and on every floor.
6. Prevent fires from spreading.	❑ Close doors and windows and turn off electrical equipment if time permits and there's no danger. ❑ Do not lock doors.

Respond Appropriately to Fires (continued)

STEPS	HOW-TO'S
7. Go to your assigned area or marshalling point.	❑ Stay a safe distance from the building. ❑ Get an immediate headcount by category of guests, employees, and visitors to the property.
8. Follow the instructions of emergency personnel.	
9. Give a set of master keys or emergency keys as well as the house count and rooming lists to the fire captain. Identify which occupied guestroom may contain disabled guests.	

Respond Appropriately to Medical Emergencies

Materials needed: a telephone, a first aid kit, a pen, and the passdown log or duty log.

STEPS	HOW-TO'S
1. Quickly evaluate the situation.	❑ Find out what the problem is. Determine if the person is injured or sick.
	❑ Try to identify important symptoms, but don't take too long analyzing every detail.
	❑ If the victim's condition involves spilled blood or other body fluids, use protective equipment. Avoid direct contact with body fluids.
2. Send for emergency medical help immediately.	❑ Call 911 or another local emergency number as appropriate.
	❑ The personnel to call when someone needs first aid vary among properties.
	❑ Give your exact location and as many details as possible about the emergency.
3. Help the injured person while waiting for medical help to arrive.	❑ Tell the person that help will arrive soon.
	❑ Keep the person calm by: • Speaking quietly • Using a caring tone of voice • Treating him or her with respect
	❑ Make the victim as comfortable as possible.
	❑ Keep the victim still. Don't try to move him or her unless it's dangerous to stay in the area.
	❑ Ask if he or she has a relative or friend who should be called.
	❑ Try to find out what happened if possible. Details given by the victim could help medical personnel treat him or her.
	❑ Keep bystanders away from the scene.

Respond Appropriately to Medical Emergencies (continued)

STEPS	HOW-TO'S
	❑ Check for medical alert tags or bracelets.
4. Provide basic first aid, if appropriate.	❑ Start first aid at once if you are trained. Only people who have been trained should give first aid such as cardiopulmonary resuscitation (CPR) automated external defibrillator (AED) assistance, or the Heimlich Maneuver. Trying to perform first aid procedures without training can cause more harm than good. Only provide first aid to stop bleeding, to maintain the victim's breathing, or if the victim is in shock.
	❑ The location of first aid kits varies among properties.
5. Give details of the situation when medical personnel arrive.	
6. Provide support to medical personnel as needed.	
7. Make an entry in the logbook as soon as possible after the incident.	❑ Include all important details.
	❑ Write all information in ink.
	❑ Sign your initials by the entry.

Respond Appropriately to Natural Disasters

Materials needed: emergency plans for natural disasters, weather reports, emergency supplies, foul-weather gear, and flood-control equipment.

STEPS	HOW-TO'S
1. Know where to find emergency plans for each type of natural disaster.	❑ The location of emergency plans varies among properties.
2. Prepare to follow emergency procedures whenever storms are expected.	❑ Find out when it is necessary to notify guests and employees of potential danger.
	❑ Follow local procedures regarding weather alerts and storm warnings.
3. Carry out your assigned responsibilities.	❑ Follow directions given by your supervisor or local emergency authorities.
	❑ Stay calm.
	❑ Assigned responsibilities vary among properties. During storm warnings, your responsibilities may include: • Putting storm shutters on windows to protect guests from flying glass or other objects. • Bringing mobile objects such as chairs, trash cans, and tables inside during high winds. • Using tape or caulking to seal doors and windows.

Respond Appropriately to Natural Disasters *(continued)*

STEPS	HOW-TO'S
4. Know where emergency supplies are kept, when to get them, and how to use them.	❑ The location of emergency supplies varies among properties. ❑ Emergency supplies may include: • Waterproof flashlights and batteries • Food and water supplies • First aid kit and medical equipment • Sandbags • Tools Planning for emergencies helps you: • Protect guests and employees • Protect property assets • React more quickly after a natural disaster ❑ Inspect portable radios to make sure they are working. ❑ Make sure emergency lights are in good working order. ❑ Collect any needed equipment.
5. Secure in weather-tight areas money, important documents, and other valuable assets.	❑ The place to store money, important documents, and other valuable assets varies among properties.
6. Secure all hazardous materials.	❑ Shut off gas valves throughout the property if necessary. ❑ The hazardous materials to secure vary among properties. ❑ The steps to secure hazardous materials vary among properties.
7. Respond to floods.	❑ Call maintenance whenever there is flooding in the facility.

(continued)

Respond Appropriately to Natural Disasters (continued)

STEPS	HOW-TO'S
	❑ Work with other departments to: • Issue foul-weather gear as appropriate. • Set up a large flood-control pump at first warning • Prepare flood-control equipment. • Install any additional sump pumps. • Clear from low-lying areas any objects that might get lost or damaged, or might clog a sump pump. • Erect flood control barriers when the water reaches barrier stages. • Place sandbags in appropriate locations. ❑ Flood-control equipment varies among properties.
8. Respond to earthquakes.	❑ Turn off gas and water valves throughout the property. Do not turn off the water valve for the fire sprinkler system.
9. Evacuate employees and guests if appropriate.	❑ Keep guests informed of the storm's progress. ❑ Tell guests and employees any deadlines for leaving the property, where they should go, and how much time there is before the storm is expected to hit. ❑ Make sure everyone has taken shelter in designated safe areas. ❑ Keep people in shelters until the danger has passed.

Respond Appropriately to Utility Failures

Materials needed: a telephone or radio, an elevator phone or intercom system, an elevator key, and "out of order" signs.

STEPS	HOW-TO'S
1. Contact the appropriate personnel.	❑ The personnel to contact in a utility failure vary among properties. You may need to contact the front desk, the fire department, or the maintenance department, depending on the type of failure and your property's policies. ❑ If phones aren't working, use a radio or alert contacts in person.
2. Explain the situation to contacts.	❑ Give contacts the following information: • Your name and phone number • Location of the problem • Type of utility failure • Description of the situation
3. Respond to power failures.	❑ Alert appropriate personnel. ❑ Report equipment malfunctions or other potential causes. ❑ Go to the front desk. ❑ Proceed quickly but safely. ❑ Help individuals trying to move around in the dark. Direct them to their rooms, the lobby, or an evacuation area. ❑ Notify guests regarding the problem. Ask them to remain in their rooms unless it is absolutely necessary for them to leave. ❑ Remind guests that using matches, candles, etc. for light is a fire hazard. ❑ Turn off or unplug electrical equipment, and secure valuable assets. ❑ Follow your property's procedures for responding to power failures.

(continued)

Respond Appropriately to Utility Failures (continued)

STEPS	HOW-TO'S
5. Respond to elevator malfunctions.	❏ Find out what floors the elevator is trapped between.
	❏ Use the elevator's phone or intercom system to communicate with anyone trapped inside the car. If the phone or intercom doesn't work, call to the elevator through the elevator shaft. Do not enter the elevator shaft.
	❏ Reassure passengers of their safety.
	❏ Ask passengers what happened. Ask for details that could help maintenance personnel or the elevator company fix the elevator.
	❏ Tell passengers what is being done to fix the problem, and ask them to remain calm.
	❏ Don't try to evacuate passengers from the car. Leave evacuation for the fire department or the elevator company.
	❏ Call the maintenance department and describe the situation. Keep passengers updated on what's being done and how long it may take.
	❏ Prevent people from using the elevator until it has been checked and repaired. If possible, lock the elevator and post "out of order" signs.
6. Respond to other utility failures.	❏ The steps to respond to boiler failures, air conditioning failures, and telephone system failures vary among properties.

Handle Hazardous Materials

Materials needed: *Material Safety Data Sheets, gloves, safety goggles, markers, labels, respirators, leak-proof containers, a typewriter, and personal protective equipment.*

STEPS	HOW-TO'S
1. Find and read Material Safety Data Sheets (MSDSs).	❑ Where MSDSs are kept varies among properties.
2. Use cleaning chemicals safely.	❑ Wear gloves, safety goggles and other personnel protective equipment when using cleaning chemicals.
	❑ Follow directions for using and storing chemicals.
	❑ Clearly mark all spray bottles with proper labels.
	❑ Do not change spray heads.
	❑ Wear respirators when cleaning overhead areas or very dusty areas.
3. Never mix two chemicals together.	
4. Water down chemicals only in storage rooms or in back-of-house areas.	
5. Put hazardous materials in leak-proof containers with tight-fitting lids and dispose of them properly.	
6. Properly label all chemical containers.	❑ Write or type on the label the name of the chemical, hazard warnings, and the manufacturer's name and address.
	❑ Include the chemical's physical and health hazards during normal use.

(continued)

Handle Hazardous Materials *(continued)*

STEPS	HOW-TO'S
7. Immediately report hazardous material spills.	❑ The person to report hazardous material spills to vary among properties. ❑ Provide contacts with the following information: • Your name and phone number • Location of the spill (building, floor, etc.) • Date and time the spill occurred • Material spilled • Characteristics of material (ignitable, corrosive, toxic, etc.) • Quantity spilled • Source and cause of the spill • Anticipated movement of the spill and action taken • Possible hazards to human health and the environment • Extent of injuries, if any
8. Evacuate guests and employees from dangerous areas.	
9. Contain hazardous spills.	❑ Only contain hazardous spills if you are trained to do so and it is safe to do so. ❑ Follow the procedures taught in your training. ❑ Wear and use appropriate personal protective equipment.

Chapter Appendix

Material Safety Data Sheet

CLORCLEAN LIQUID PLUS

Section 1. Chemical product and company identification

Trade name	: CLORCLEAN LIQUID PLUS
Product use	: Cleaning solutions.
Supplier	: Ecolab Food and Beverage
	5105 Tomken Road
	Mississauga ON L4W 2X5
	1-800-352-5326
Code	: 911271
Date of issue	: **26-August-2005**

EMERGENCY HEALTH INFORMATION: 1-800-328-0026
Outside United States and Canada CALL 1-651-222-5352 (in USA)

Section 2. Composition, Information on Ingredients

Name	CAS number	% by weight
potassium hydroxide	1310-58-3	10 - 30
phosphoric acid, tripotassium salt	7778-53-2	7 - 13
polyphosphoric acids, potassium salts	68956-75-2	1 - 5
Sodiumhypochlorite	7681-52-9	1 - 5
silicic acid (h2sio3), dipotassium salt	10006-28-7	1 - 5

Section 3. Hazards identification

Physical state	: Liquid. (Liquid.)
Emergency overview	: DANGER!
	CAUSES RESPIRATORY TRACT, EYE AND SKIN BURNS. HARMFUL IF SWALLOWED.
	Do not get in eyes, on skin or clothing. Do not breathe vapour or mist. Keep container closed. Use only with adequate ventilation. Wash thoroughly after handling.
Routes of entry	: Skin contact, Eye contact, Inhalation, Ingestion

Potential acute health effects

Eyes	: Corrosive to eyes.
Skin	: Corrosive to the skin.
Inhalation	: Corrosive to the respiratory system.
Ingestion	: Harmful if swallowed. Causes burns to mouth, throat and stomach.

See toxicological Information (section 11)

Section 4. First aid measures

Eye contact	: In case of contact, immediately flush eyes with cool running water. Remove contact lenses and continue flushing with plenty of water for at least 15 minutes. Obtain medical attention immediately.
Skin Contact	: In case of contact, immediately flush skin copiously with water for at least 15 minutes while removing contaminated clothing and shoes. Wash clothing before reuse. Clean shoes thoroughly before reuse. Obtain medical attention immediately.
Inhalation	: If inhaled, remove to fresh air. If not breathing, give artificial respiration. If breathing is difficult, give oxygen. Obtain medical attention immediately.
Ingestion	: Rinse mouth; then drink one or two large glasses of water. Do not induce vomiting. Never give anything by mouth to an unconscious person. Obtain medical attention immediately.

Section 5. Fire fighting measures

Auto-ignition temperature	:	Not available.
Flash point	:	> 100°C
Flammable limits		
Upper:		Not available.
Lower:		Not available.
Products of combustion	:	These products are halogenated compounds, hydrogen chloride.
Fire-fighting media and instructions	:	Use an extinguishing agent suitable for surrounding fires.
		Dike area of fire to prevent product run-off.
		No specific hazard.
Special protective equipment for fire-fighters	:	Fire fighters should wear appropriate protective equipment and self-contained breathing apparatus (SCBA) with a full face-piece operated in positive pressure mode.

Risks of explosion of the product in presence of mechanical impact: Not available.

Risks of explosion of the product in presence of static discharge: Not available.

Section 6. Accidental release measures

Personal Precautions	:	Ventilate area of leak or spill. Do not touch damaged containers or spilled material unless wearing appropriate protective equipment (Section 8). Stop leak if without risk. Prevent entry into sewers, water courses, basements or confined areas.
Environmental precautions	:	Avoid dispersal of spilled material and runoff and contact with soil, waterways, drains and sewers.
Methods for cleaning up	:	If emergency personnel are unavailable, contain spilled material. For small spills add absorbent (soil may be used in the absence of other suitable materials) scoop up material and place in a sealed, liquid-proof container for disposal. For large spills dike spilled material or otherwise contain material to ensure runoff does not reach a waterway. Place spilled material in an appropriate container for disposal.--

Section 7. Handling and storage

Handling	:	Do not ingest. Do not get in eyes, on skin or on clothing. Keep container closed. Use only with adequate ventilation. Do not breathe vapour or mist. Wash thoroughly after handling.
Storage	:	Keep out of the reach of children. Keep container tightly closed. Keep container in a cool, well-ventilated area.
		Store between 40 and -25°C

Section 8. Exposure Controls, Personal Protection

Engineering controls	:	Provide exhaust ventilation or other engineering controls to keep the airborne concentrations of vapours below their respective occupational exposure limits. Ensure that eyewash stations and safety showers are close to the workstation location.

Personal protection

Eyes	:	Use chemical splash goggles. For continued or severe exposure wear a face shield over the goggles.
Hands	:	Use chemical resistant, impervious gloves.
Skin	:	Use synthetic apron, other protective equipment as necessary to prevent skin contact.
Respiratory	:	Use a properly fitted, air-purifying or air-fed respirator complying with an approved standard if a risk assessment indicates this is necessary. Respirator selection must be based on known or anticipated exposure levels, the hazards of the product and the safe working limits of the selected respirator.

Name	Exposure limits
potassium hydroxide	**ACGIH TLV (United States, 1/2004).**
	CEIL: 2 mg/m^3 Form: All forms

Section 9. Physical and chemical properties

Physical state	:	Liquid. (Liquid.)
Colour	:	Yellow. (Light.)
Odour	:	chlorine
pH	:	12 (100%)
Boiling/condensation point	:	Not available.
Melting/freezing point	:	Not available.
Specific gravity	:	1.331 (Water = 1)
Vapour pressure	:	Not applicable.
Vapour density	:	Not available.
Odour threshold	:	Not available.
Evaporation rate	:	Not available.
LogK$_{ow}$	:	Not available.

Section 10. Stability and reactivity

Stability	:	The product is stable.
Conditions of instability	:	Not available.
Reactivity	:	Extremely reactive or incompatible with acids.
		Slightly reactive to reactive with metals.
		Mixing this product with acid or ammonia releases chlorine gas.
Incompatibility with various substances	:	Not available.
Hazardous Decomposition Products	:	These products are halogenated compounds, hydrogen chloride, chlorine.

Section 11. Toxicological information

Potential acute health effects

Eyes	:	Corrosive to eyes.
Skin	:	Corrosive to the skin.
Inhalation	:	Corrosive to the respiratory system.
Ingestion	:	Harmful if swallowed. Causes burns to mouth, throat and stomach.
Irritancy of Product	:	Hazardous by WHMIS criteria.

Potential chronic health effects

Carcinogenic effects	:	No known significant effects or critical hazards.
Mutagenic effects	:	No known significant effects or critical hazards.
Teratogenic effects	:	No known significant effects or critical hazards.
Reproductive effects	:	No known significant effects or critical hazards.
Sensitization to Product	:	No known significant effects or critical hazards.
Synergistic Products (Toxicologically)	:	Not available.

Toxicity data

Ingredient name	Test	Result	Route	Species
Potassium hydroxide	LD50	273 mg/kg	Oral	Rat
phosphoric acid, tripotassium	LD50	>4640 mg/kg	Dermal	Rabbit
salt	LDLo	4640 mg/kg	Oral	Rat
sodium hypochlorite	LD50	5800 mg/kg	Oral	Mouse

Target organs : Contains material which causes damage to the following organs: lungs, upper respiratory tract, skin, eye, lens or cornea.

Section 12. Ecological information

Ecotoxicity data

Ingredient name	Species	Period	Result
Sodiumhypochlorite	Daphnia magna (EC50)	48 hour(s)	0.04 mg/l
	Daphnia magna (EC50)	48 hour(s)	0.17 mg/l
	Daphnia magna (EC50)	48 hour(s)	1.57 mg/l
	Oncorhynchus mykiss (LC50)	96 hour(s)	0.059 mg/l
	Oncorhynchus mykiss (LC50)	96 hour(s)	0.09 mg/l
	Oncorhynchus mykiss (LC50)	96 hour(s)	0.2 mg/l

Products of degradation   : These products are halogenated compounds, phosphates. Some metallic oxides.

Section 13. Disposal considerations

Waste disposal   : The generation of waste should be avoided or minimised wherever possible. Avoid dispersal of spilled material and runoff and contact with soil, waterways, drains and sewers. Disposal of this product, solutions and any by-products should at all times comply with the requirements of environmental protection and waste disposal legislation and any regional local authority requirements.

Consult your local or regional authorities.

Section 14. Transport information

Regulatory information	UN number	Proper shipping name	Class	Packing group	Additional Information
TDG Classification	UN1719	CAUSTIC ALKALI LIQUID, N.O.S. (potassium hydroxide, Sodium hypochlorite)	8	II	**Passenger Carrying Road or Rail Index** 1 **Special provisions** 16

APPLIES ONLY DURING ROAD TRANSPORT
Any variation of the shipping description based on the packaging is not addressed.

Section 15. Regulatory information

WHMIS   : Class E: Corrosive material.

This product has been classified in accordance with the hazard criteria of the *Controlled Products Regulations* and the MSDS contains all the information required by the *Controlled Products Regulations*.

Section 16. Other information

Date of issue	: **26-August-2005.**
Responsible name	: **Regulatory Affairs**
Date of previous issue	: **11-January-2005.**

Notice to reader

The above information is believed to be correct with respect to the formula used to manufacture the product in the country of origin. As data, standards, and regulations change, and conditions of use and handling are beyond our control, NO WARRANTY, EXPRESS OR IMPLIED, IS MADE AS TO THE COMPLETENESS OR CONTINUING ACCURACY OF THIS INFORMATION.

Chapter 8 Outline

Competencies

1. List factors to consider when planning an on-premises laundry operation for a hotel. (pp. 319–325)

2. Outline the steps involved in processing linens as they flow through an on-premises laundry operation. (pp. 326–340)

3. Identify the various types of machines and equipment that might be found in a hotel's on-premises laundry operation. (pp. 340–346)

4. Summarize valet service (guest laundry) issues. (pp. 346–349)

5. Describe effective staffing and scheduling practices for on-premises laundry operations. (pp. 349–353)

Managing an On-Premises Laundry

DOING THE LAUNDRY at home or at the laundromat may not be everyone's favorite chore, but it is not a difficult one. Once or twice a week, it is necessary to sort a basket of wash, select a detergent and the proper washer setting, and then dry and fold the items. But imagine doing laundry every day by the truckload, and one begins to have an idea of the scope of a lodging property's laundry. Add to the sheer volume of wash the responsibilities of making it look, smell, and feel good and getting it to the right place at the right time. Then consider that linen (sheets, towels, tablecloths, and other items) is a housekeeping department's second-largest expense, and one will understand why good laundry management is essential to the success of a lodging operation.

Some hotels do not operate on-premises laundries. These properties contract with an outside laundry service that provides them with clean linen on a scheduled basis. The linen supply may be owned by the hotel or rented from the laundry service.

Since the recent trend has been for hotels to operate an on-premises laundry (OPL), this chapter focuses on OPL management. The topics covered include planning the physical layout of the OPL, procedures for laundering various fabrics, the flow of linens through the OPL, typical machines and equipment, and staffing considerations.

Planning the OPL

The best OPL is the one tailored to the needs of the hotel it serves. If possible, representatives from areas of the hotel affected by the laundry operation should be involved in the planning stages of the OPL. Some of the important planning considerations follow:

- What is the maximum amount of laundry (output) the OPL will be expected to handle? Output is generally measured in pounds. The number of pounds should be related to the occupancy levels in guestrooms and the number of covers in food and beverage outlets. The OPL should be designed to handle maximum output for peak business periods.

- How much space should be devoted to the OPL? Laundry needs, amount of equipment, and the amount of linen to be kept on-hand in storage will determine space needs. Many properties allocate extra space in case of growth.

- How much equipment should be purchased? The output levels will determine the amount of equipment necessary to handle the hotel's laundry needs. The type of linens the hotel uses usually determines what kind of equipment is necessary. Energy and water conservation concerns may also affect equipment decisions.

- Will there be valet service? Valet service will require dry-cleaning equipment and separate work areas for valet staff.

The size of the property and type of service offered are other important planning considerations. Laundry needs in small properties (under 150 rooms) vary considerably. A very small operation offering economy services may devote between 400 and 800 square feet of space to the OPL. A property offering mid-market service with a food & beverage operation may require between 1,500 and 2,000 square feet for the OPL. On average, a small property's OPL processes about 400,000 pounds of laundry per year. It contains washer/extractors and drying machines. Small properties frequently rely on no-iron linens to reduce finishing time. However, no-iron linens lose their wrinkle-free characteristics after numerous washings. A small **flatwork ironer** is often needed to keep these linens looking good.

Medium-sized properties (150 to 299 rooms) may offer economy to luxury services. Properties with food & beverage outlets generally require more linens than hotels offering limited or mid-market services without food & beverage operations. Up to 1.5 million pounds of laundry per year may flow through a medium-sized property's OPL. OPL space varies from 2,000 or 3,000 square feet to as many as 6,500 to 7,000 square feet. That space may accommodate flatwork ironers with folding capabilities, steam tunnels or cabinets, and valet service equipment.

Large properties (300 rooms or more) may devote from 8,000 to 18,000 square feet to the OPL and handle as much as 8.5 million pounds of laundry per year. Large OPLs use more sophisticated equipment than smaller OPLs.

Laundering Linens

The marketplace offers more fabrics to choose from than ever before. The choice of fabric is also more important than ever before because it directly affects the costs of operating the OPL.

The synthetic fabrics introduced in the 1960s led to the development of no-iron sheets. Because these sheets eliminated or reduced the need for ironing, many properties were able to switch from an outside laundry service to an OPL. Moreover, properties that used the no-iron linens discovered these linens to be more durable than all-cotton linens. This durability cut down the rate at which the linens had to be replaced (and still does).

Today's fabrics range from all-natural fibers (wool and cotton, for example) to a variety of synthetics (such as polyester and nylon). For most properties, the fabric of choice is a polyester/cotton blend (sometimes called **polycotton**) because it requires less care than all-natural fabric yet offers most of its comfort.

Ten Key Tips for In-House Laundry

Here's a quick list of ten things to help in-house laundry operations be more efficient:

1. Load machines to manufacturer's recommendation. Use scale cart.
2. Secure the laundry area.
3. Prevent employee abuse of linen. Managers should walk the movement cycle.
4. Schedule labor in sync with equipment and demand.
5. Operate with a good preventive maintenance plan.
6. Rotate positions. All laundry employees work all laundry positions.
7. Obtain cooperation throughout the hotel so all used linens come to the laundry every night.
8. Maintain par stocks.
9. Maintain a stain treatment plan.
10. Provide ongoing training, including chemical training.

Source: *The Rooms Chronicle*®, Volume 10, Number 6, p. 5.
For subscription information, call 866-READ-TRC.

However, no-iron linens do not totally fulfill the basic functions guests have learned to expect with 100 percent cotton linens. For example, polyester napkins are not as absorbent as 100 percent cotton napkins. Polycottons also pick up and retain stains more easily, because the cotton absorbs the stain and the polyester traps it in the fabric. Furthermore, the resins that keep no-iron fabrics from wrinkling tend to break down and are washed out at high temperatures. The resins also retain chlorine from bleach, which weakens the fabric.

No matter what linens the property decides to buy, it is important to make certain that all items needing laundering include thorough instructions for care from the vendor. The following sections discuss some of the most popular fabrics used in hospitality operations. Exhibit 1 contains a summary of general care instructions for the fabrics listed here.

Cotton. Cotton is strong and actually becomes stronger when wet. It is very absorbent and can be starched, which makes it especially good for napkins and tablecloths. It can also be washed and ironed at high temperatures. Some shrinkage (from 5 percent to 15 percent in its first washings) does occur. Cotton fabrics have a lower color-retention capability than polyester fabrics.

Mineral acids are hard on cotton fibers. These acids form when microscopic mineral particles (called ions) mix with oxygen. Ions are found naturally in many water supplies. Mineral acid damage underscores the need for a source of good water in the OPL.

Wool. Once the fabric of choice for blankets, wool has fallen out of favor in many commercial operations because it is not as durable as some synthetic materials and

Exhibit 1   General Care of Linen Fabrics

Fiber Group	Cleaning Method	Water Temperature	Chlorine Bleach	Dryer Temperature	Iron Temperature	Special Storage
Acrylic	launder	warm	yes	warm	medium	none
Cotton	launder	hot	yes	hot	high	store dry
Polycotton	launder	hot	yes	warm	medium	none
Nylon	launder	hot	yes	warm	low	none
Polyester	launder	hot	yes	warm	low	none
Wool	dry-clean	warm	no	warm	medium with steam	protect from moths; do not store in plastic bags

Fabric combinations should always be cared for by following the manufacturer's recommendations.

can be irritating to the touch. Wool is one of the weakest fibers and becomes even weaker when wet. It also shrinks and mats relatively easily. For this reason, many heavy-duty cleanings will break down the fibers of a wool blanket very quickly. Wool does resist soiling better than some other common fabric materials and is very absorbent.

Acrylic. Acrylic is lightweight and does not shrink. Its strength is similar to cotton's, but it decreases when wet. Because it holds moisture on its surface, acrylic is fairly slow-drying.

Polyester. Polyester is one of the strongest common fibers and does not lose its strength when wet. It dries quickly, is wrinkle-resistant, and does not soil easily. Polyester tends to break down at higher drying and ironing temperatures. Polyesters and polyester blends are good choices for uniforms, aprons, and other garments. They are less effective as napery (table linens).

Nylon. Nylon is very strong when wet or dry. It is also easy to wash and quick to dry. Nylon, however, is sensitive to heat.

Blends. Many properties use linens made of cotton/polyester blends. These gain strength with initial washings. Their characteristics depend on the amount and types of fibers blended. Blends can be damaged by high wash temperatures—those greater than 180°F [83°C]—or high dryer temperatures—those greater than 165°F [74°C].

Sort through the Laundry Room to Find Big Energy Savings

The laundry area of the hotel is an extremely energy-intensive area, consuming five times more energy than most other areas of the hotel. There are a number of ways to reduce consumption without adversely affecting the laundry operation.

The laundry-drying system is the most energy-intensive area of the laundry. A typical laundry may have four gas dryers that each consumes up to 200,000 BTUs (British thermal units) per hour. That means those

Reducing Expenses in Laundry Operations

Are dollars being needlessly wasted in the laundry? To evaluate and improve operations within this critical area, consider the following suggestions:

- Ask the chemical company to review the time and formula cards for the laundry equipment. Ensure that lengths of cycles, temperatures of water, and amounts of chemicals are correct for the most efficient operation.

- Operate with minimum chemical inventory to limit dollars sitting on storeroom shelves.

- Use automatic chemical-dispensing equipment, ensuring more accurate measurements and limiting hazards related to employee handling of chemicals.

- Put equipment on a preventive maintenance schedule to avoid costly and disruptive breakdowns.

- Buy equipment that will help eliminate accidents, such as spring-loaded lifters in laundry carts that reduce bending and ease lifting.

- Provide goggles, gloves, back braces, and proper shoes as necessary.

- Keep lint traps clean. This not only facilitates faster drying times, but, more important, eliminates a fire hazard.

- Devise an employee schedule that provides ready linen in a timely fashion. Keep in mind that running equipment at off-peak hours will save on energy bills as well as limit hot water usage during peak guest demand. Also, properties that run the laundry in the evening get the advantage of having housekeeping open during hours when most guests are on the property.

- Conduct ongoing training in handling chemicals and linens. Meeting OSHA standards for handling bloodborne pathogens and other dangerous substances is essential. In addition, provide Material Safety Data Sheet training for each chemical used.

- Cross-train laundry employees in all tasks so that job rotation during the shift will reduce the possibility of strained and pulled muscles and so that the number of employees needed can be minimized.

- Use creative scheduling as an employee perk. For example, allow four-day weeks, half days, or closing on weekends.

- Provide training for all food and beverage personnel to limit linen abuse in restaurant operations.

- Take accurate monthly or quarterly inventories and maintain a minimum of three pars of linen at all times. It is standard to have one par in the guestrooms, one par being washed and dried, and one par in motion between the laundry and guestrooms.

(continued)

the Rooms CHRONICLE®

(continued)

- Review the transport of linen to ensure that items are not getting soiled on the way to the laundry (wheels running over them, people stepping on them, concrete stains, etc.).

- Keep linen moving. Dirty linens waiting to be washed can mold, washed linens waiting to be dried can mildew, and dried linens waiting to be folded can get wrinkles set in them that can't be removed without ironing or reprocessing.

Remember that chemical companies are willing to review the five important functions (time, temperature, mechanical action, chemical action, and procedures) to ensure that the laundry operation gets good results. These important suppliers are also helpful in assisting with employee training.

Source: Gail Edwards, CHHE, *The Rooms Chronicle®*, Volume 2, Number 6, p. 5. For subscription information, call 866-READ-TRC.

four dryers running for just one hour use about the same amount of energy required to heat eight typical homes for an entire winter.

First, put the dryers on an exterior wall in a corner of the laundry room to allow construction of a plenum to enclose the dryers on the top and sides. This will contain the heat in and around the equipment and provide a simple form of heat recovery, as intake air will be slightly heated by radiant heat as it enters dryers.

The dryer plenum is also the area through which outside air is provided to the dryers for gas combustion. It is extremely important that the combustion air opening be sized properly. There should be approximately one-half square inch of free-air opening for every 5,000 BTUs of dryer gas-energy input. Verify this information with local codes. Typically, combustion air openings are 400 percent larger than necessary, allowing cold, outside air to be introduced into the dryer plenum, reducing efficiency significantly.

Also, consider installing automatic dampers to close off outside air when dryers are turned off.

Request that the chief engineer check the dryer flame several times per year. The flame, when viewed from the rear of the dryer, should be somewhat bluish with a firm shape. If the flame is somewhat yellow and lazy looking, it is operating inefficiently. This can be caused by dirt and lint in the burner area or components in the gas that build up in the dryer burner. The dryer burner should be disassembled and thoroughly cleaned at least once per year with a small drill bit and wire brush.

Most new dryers include solid-state electronic ignitions as standard equipment. If the hotel's dryers are old, request that the local gas company replace the standing pilots with electronic ignitions.

Remember that most fire codes require the dryer area and plenums to be clean and clear, for obvious safety reasons. Also, consult the laundry operation manual for information on all proper techniques for laundry drying.

Laundry Lighting. A well-lighted laundry area that provides in excess of 50 footcandles will improve employee efficiency. Lighting in most laundries consists of old-style, standard, fluorescent fixtures that are either 4 or 8 feet long. The federal Energy Policy and Conservation Act specifies that this type of lighting be replaced with new, energy-efficient "T-8" fluorescent lights. These energy-efficient lights use an electronic ballast that reduces energy consumption for lighting by about 20 percent. Contact a local electrical supplier to implement this suggestion. Also, request that all exit signs be replaced with new, energy-efficient, two-watt-type LED exit lights.

Laundry areas are often unoccupied and thus are a very good application for a lighting motion sensor, which automatically turns off lights whenever people leave the area.

If the laundry is a small area, it may be more practical to use a light-switch motion sensor. These are easy to install, and they fit directly into the existing light switch. These devices will also turn off lights automatically when the area is unoccupied.

Water Heating and Temperature. Many recent audits of limited-service hotels have observed that one water system serves the laundry and the guestrooms. Because both the laundry and kitchen require water temperatures to be 140°F [60°C], the hotel is forced to maintain that temperature for guestrooms as well. However, not only is this expensive, it is unsafe. Both OSHA and the American Hotel & Lodging Association recommend domestic hot-water temperatures of 115 to 120°F [46°C to 49°C] in the guestrooms. It is highly recommended that these hotels install a second water-heating system for the laundry and kitchen and set temperatures correctly for each area.

Miscellaneous Energy Tips. A good maintenance program is crucial to an energy-efficient laundry. For example, a dripping faucet in the laundry can cost more than $100 a year in lost water and sewer charges. A leaking steam trap reduces system efficiency by wasting steam and the chemicals to treat the steam. These are typical items that the engineering department should document well and should include in a thorough preventive maintenance program.

A laundry operation manual will provide detailed information on how to operate equipment efficiently. Proper-sized loads will head the list. If the hotel has occasional small loads, it may be wise to install a small residential-style washer and dryer in the laundry.

There are special utility rates available to hotels that encourage the use of energy at night. Especially if the hotel has an all-electric laundry, it may be advantageous to set up a nighttime laundry operation. In all cases, when the laundry is through for the day, be sure to turn off all the equipment and set back the heating and ventilation equipment.[1]

The Flow of Linens through the OPL

Every laundry uses a basic cycle of operation. This cycle includes the following steps:

- Collecting soiled linens
- Transporting soiled linens to the laundry
- Sorting
- Loading
- Washing
- Extracting
- Drying
- Finishing
- Folding
- Storing
- Transferring linens to use areas

Exhibit 2 diagrams an abbreviated version of this process. Executive housekeepers or laundry managers should develop procedures for each of these steps to prevent resoiling of clean linens, extend the life of the linens, and keep the OPL efficient and cost-effective.

Collecting Soiled Linens

Room attendants cleaning guestrooms should strip linens from beds and bath areas and put them directly into the soiled-linen bags attached to the housekeeping cart. Items should never be piled on the floor where they can be walked on and soiled further or damaged. Putting the linens directly into soiled-linen bags prevents room attendants from using towels, sheets, napkins, or other items to blot spills or wipe smudges. *Staff should never use linens for any cleaning purposes.* Misuse of linens can permanently damage items—which can lead to higher replacement costs.

In some properties, room attendants follow procedures for presorting soiled linens. This may simply mean tying a knot in one corner of a heavily soiled item to help laundry workers sort it more easily. Room attendants may also sort linens by soil type and put them into specially marked plastic bags. Some hotels give room attendants a spray bottle of stain-release agent to treat a stain as they place the stained linen on the cart. In food & beverage outlets, buspersons gather soiled linens when tables are cleared. Because tableware can easily get gathered up with linens and thrown into the soiled-linen hamper, buspersons should be cautioned to carefully remove all items from tables. Some tableware metals can permanently stain linens. Buspersons should shake napkins and tablecloths over a waste receptacle to remove crumbs and food as soon as possible after the table is cleared. Linens can then be placed in soiled-linen hampers for delivery to the laundry.

Exhibit 2   The Flow of Laundry through the OPL

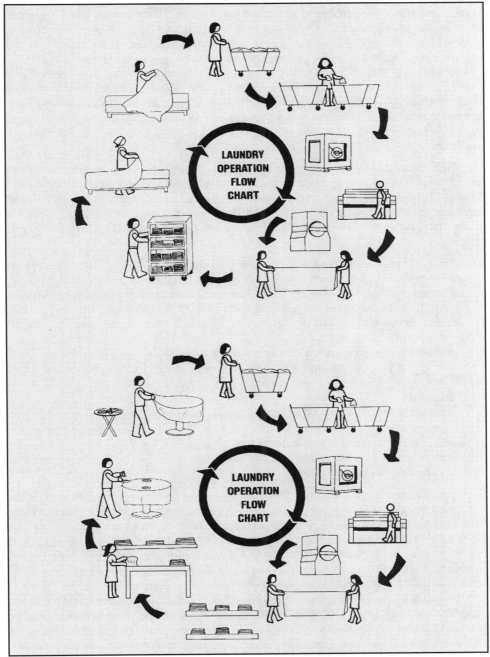

Source: "On Premises Laundry Procedures in Hotels, Motels, Healthcare Facilities, and Restaurants" (pamphlet) (St. Paul, Minn.: Ecolab, Institutional Products Division), undated.

Transporting Soiled Linens to the Laundry

Linens are either hand-carried or carted to the OPL. Employees who are hand-carrying linens should be careful not to allow items to drag on the floor, further soiling them. Dragging linens can also create safety hazards for staff who could trip over trailing items. Some properties use linen chutes to transport linens.

Linen carts should be free of protrusions that could snag or tear items. Carts should move easily, and staff should be able to load and unload linens without undue bending and stretching. Workers should be careful not to snag linens against the cart or the chute, causing tiny rips.

Sorting

The OPL should contain a sorting area large enough to store a day's worth of laundry without slowing down other activities in the OPL. Soiled linens should be sorted by the degree of soiling and by the type of fabric. Both types of sorting help prevent unnecessary wear and damage to linens. *Cleaning rags should always be separated and washed by themselves; never washed with linen that guests will use.*

Sorting by Degree of Soiling. When sorting by degree of soiling, laundry workers divide linens into three categories: lightly, moderately, and heavily soiled. Heavily soiled items require heavy-duty wash formulas and longer wash time. Moderately or lightly soiled linens are washed with gentler formulas and in fewer cycles. (Sheets are usually classified as lightly soiled, while pillowcases are considered moderately soiled.)

Without sorting by soil, all linens would have to be washed in heavy-duty formula. Lightly soiled items would be overprocessed, leading to unnecessary wear. Sorting by soil also saves repeated washings of items to remove stubborn soils and stains.

Sorting, of course, can lead to partial loads of laundry. Doing too many partial loads wastes energy and water. However, if heavily soiled fabrics are not washed promptly, stains could set and ruin the item. Some OPLs solve this problem by providing several sizes of washers so that smaller loads can be washed promptly without wasting water and energy.

Sorting by Linen Type. Different fibers, weaves, and colors require different cleaning formulas and washing methods. Sorting linens by type ensures that the right temperature and formulas are used on similar fabrics. Wool and loosely woven fabrics, for example, require a mild formula and gentle agitation. Colors should not be washed with chlorine bleach. New colored linens should be washed separately the first few times to avoid dying other fabrics. Some special items such as aprons should be washed in nylon bags to prevent tangling.

Some OPLs purchase different washers for different fabrics. For example, if the property has only a few all-cotton items that must be washed in hot water, smaller washers may be designated for cottons. This can save energy and water costs.

Sorting by linen type includes sorting categories such as blankets, bedspreads, restaurant linen, and terry. All terry items can be kept in one group since they receive the same finishing process. Restaurant linens probably have stains on each piece.

the Rooms CHRONICLE®

Linen Chutes Save Time and Effort But Must Always Be Secured

A properly installed and well-maintained linen chute is a wonderful thing. Many steps, including excessive lifting and bending, are saved by dropping linen from the floor above to the discharge area at the end of the linen chute. Some chutes discharge directly into the hotel's on-premise laundry.

Like most wonderful things, linen chutes are frequently abused and misused. Each opening of a linen chute should have a fire rated, self-closing and self-latching door. The chute doors should either be locked when not in use or kept secured in housekeeping closets behind locked doors. There have been several incidents where inebriated hotel guests and adventure-seeking visitors have decided to slide down a hotel's laundry chute. Since the installation of most laundry chutes is vertical, the slide instantly becomes a fall, at a minimum of around ten feet, maybe several hundred feet; unpleasant at best, deadly at worst case.

People have also been known to drop foreign objects such as bowling balls, room service trays or cigarettes down open laundry chutes. This could potentially be deadly to a laundry worker. It is best to keep laundry chute doors on guestroom floors closed and locked when not attended.

The door should be fire rated because a linen chute works like a chimney if a fire occurs in the discharge area and the discharge door does not close and latch. Smoke and possibly fire will exit at each opening up the chute that is not closed and latched. During a fire in the discharge area, the most important door is the one at the bottom of the chute. These doors should be held open by a chain, cable, or similar apparatus which includes a fusible link between an attachment point on the chute door and an attachment point on the wall or some other structure member strong enough to support the door. Perilously, doors are often held open by wire from coat hangers. They should be held open with fusible links. Fusible links are typically constructed with two pieces of ferrous metal joined by solder. The solder softens or melts when heated, releasing the door. Fusible links also break when there is no fire because they are overloaded.

It is a little known fact that fusible links have a load rating. These vary from two pounds to forty pounds. Too often, a ten-pound rated link is used to hold open a twenty-pound door. It works initially, but soon fails. There is apparently no time delay factor related to the load rating, so it is best to install a forty-pound rated fusible link to assure reliability in operation. There should also be self-latching locks on the discharge, so the discharge door latches securely when released.

Keeping the doors secured and working correctly takes care of many of the issues associated with a linen chute, allowing huge amounts of linens to be delivered to the laundry quickly. Before laundry employees handle soiled linens from the chute, they should don personal protective equipment. In this case, puncture resistant gloves and a moisture-resistant apron. Leather gloves could be penetrated by a syringe, but will likely resist the needle sufficiently to prevent an injury. An apron will help keep any contaminants on the linen off the laundry attendant's clothing.

Finally, engineering personnel should check each linen chute on a monthly basis to ensure the doors close and latch properly.

Source: Jesse Denton, *The Rooms Chronicle*®, Volume 14, Number 5, pp. 1–2.
For subscription information, please call 866-READ-TRC.

C the Rooms
HRONICLE®

Handle Grease Rags and Lint with Special Care

High turnover of employees in the hotel industry creates a tremendous liability in the operation of the laundry because training doesn't always keep pace with turnover. A single employee's lack of training can cause the hotel to go up in flames.

While all hotel laundries are prone to fires caused by lint in the dryer filters igniting, it is the hotel with a kitchen that is particularly susceptible to fires. Why? Highly combustible kitchen greasy rags require special care in washing.

Many hotels use old guest towels and washcloths to clean up in the kitchen. When these rags become greasy, the danger begins. Greasy rags can catch on fire while just sitting in a bag waiting to be laundered.

The danger can continue after they have been washed if they are placed in a dryer before the grease has been totally removed. Spontaneous combustion is the culprit and can strike any laundry operation where employees have not been trained. The best deterrent is to use disposable rages or rented rags for grease clean-up, but many hotels prefer to process the rags in-house.

To avoid a fire in the laundry, managers should include these procedures in employee training:

Clean the lint filters regularly. Lint filters in dryers must be cleaned three to four times daily. No exceptions. Put up a sheet to log when the lint screen was cleaned and who cleaned it.

Process greasy rags with care.

1. Deliver a 5-gallon bucket (half full of a degreaser solution) to the kitchen.
2. Train kitchen employees to make a judgment about whether a greasy rag is cleanable or whether it should be thrown away. Some rags cannot be effectively cleaned no matter what process is used.
3. Train kitchen employees to place dirty rags in the bucket of degreaser solution. This serves two purposes: the rags cannot catch on fire while under water, and they are being presoaked while waiting to be laundered.
4. Wash the greasy rags as a separate wash load on a special card that includes special temperatures, extra chemicals, and extra rinses.
5. Clean the dryer lint filter before loading the dryer with the rags. This will ensure maximum airflow.
6. Run a cool-down cycle after the heat cycle to remove all heat from the rags.
7. Remove rags promptly from the dryer when the cool cycle is complete and store the rags in a covered metal container. If there is enough residual heat and grease left in the rags to start a fire, the available oxygen in the metal container will quickly be used and the fire will be smothered. Metal-covered containers are easy to purchase and cost much less to replace than a dryer.
8. Deliver rags to the kitchen in a metal-closed container. There have been may fires documented that began in a stack of "clean" greasy rags stuffed in a drawer or bag waiting to be used.

These simple procedures should be etched in stone for laundry and kitchen employees.

Source: Jesse Denton, *The Rooms Chronicle®*, Volume 8, Number 3, p. 8.
For subscription information, please call 866-READ-TRC.

Loading

Washing machines work best when optimally loaded. Washers are rated for poundage—that is, 50-pound washers, 35-pound washers, and so on. This weight refers to the clean, dry weight of linen or CDW. Since bed linen is generally dry when dirty, a 50-pound washer should be loaded with 50 pounds of sheets. But terry cloth is generally wet when dirty and could weigh as much as 40 percent more when wet. To get a full load of terry, employees would have to load approximately 70 pounds of wet terry to meet the 50 pound CDW guideline. Most manufacturers advise users to stuff the washer until there is room only to push in a hand's width on top of the load.

Loading improperly can cost significant dollars. For instance, if there were 500 towels to process each day in a 50-pound washer, a user could load 7 loads of 71 pounds, or 10 loads of 50 pounds. Assuming that each load costs $1.00 for chemicals, loading the machine to the maximum would save $3.00 per day or $1,095 per year just on chemicals. When the extra labor to handle loading and unloading three more loads is computed, and the time and energy costs of these wasteful loads is added, it becomes clear that loading properly can save a significant amount of money.[2]

Washing

After linens are sorted, laundry workers collect batches of laundry and deliver them to the washers. Linens should be weighed before they are put into the washer to ensure that washers are not overloaded. Weighing is also important for measuring OPL output.

Laundry workers at some hotels pretreat soiled linens before washing them. However, pretreating laundry takes a great deal of time and can increase labor costs dramatically. As a result, most OPLs rely on the chemicals used in the washer to clean linens.

Today's modern washing equipment can overwhelm an inexperienced worker used to doing laundry on a wash-rinse-spin machine at home. OPL washing equipment requires workers to choose from as many as ten cycles and from a range of detergents, soaps, and fabric conditioners. Asking five basic questions makes these choices less confusing and helps determine the proper procedure for doing a particular batch of laundry. The five questions follow:

- How much *time* will it take to wash any given item properly? Linens that are heavily soiled will take more time to wash; lightly soiled linens will take less time. Improperly regulating the time it takes to wash linens will result in a poor wash or unnecessary wear on fabric. It can also waste energy and water.

- At what *temperature* should the water be in order to get items clean? In general, laundry workers should "think low," choosing the lowest possible temperature to do the job in order to save energy. However, some detergents and chemicals work properly only in hot water, and some types of soils require higher temperatures. For example, the water temperature for washing oily soils should be 180°F to 190°F [83°C to 88°C]; for moderate to heavy soils, at least 160°F [72°C]. Kitchen rags and linens should be washed at 140°F [60°C].

- How much *agitation* is needed to loosen soils? Agitation is the "scrubbing" action of the machine. Too little agitation—which is frequently caused by overloaded washers—leads to inadequate washing. Overloading also causes unnecessary wear and tear on equipment. Too much agitation can cause fabric damage.

- What *chemicals* will do the best job on particular soils and fabric types? Chemicals may include detergents, bleaches, softeners, and so forth.

- What *procedures* are used to facilitate washing? Different cycles should be chosen for different kinds of linen. For example, extraction time for terry cloth should be longer than extraction time for sheets.

The type of soil and fabric will dictate wash time, temperature, degree of agitation, which chemicals to use, and what procedures to follow. Each of these elements affects the others. For example, using too much detergent for the water level will create too many suds; too many suds will impede the agitator. Exhibit 3 offers an overview of common washing problems, their causes, and some solutions.

Usually, time, temperature, and mechanical action are preset by supervisors in the laundry room. Equipment salespeople can also help with presetting.

Wash Cycles. The typical wash process consists of as many as nine steps:

1. **Flush (1.5 to 3 minutes)—Flushes** dissolve and dilute water-soluble soils to reduce the soil load for the upcoming suds step. Items are generally flushed at medium temperatures at high water levels.

2. **Break (4 to 10 minutes, optional)—**A high-alkaline **break** (soil-loosening) product is added, which may be followed by additional flushes. The break cycle is usually at medium temperature and a low water level.

3. **Suds (5 to 8 minutes)—**This is the actual wash cycle to which detergent is added. Items are agitated in hot water at low water levels.

4. **Carryover suds or intermediate rinse (2 to 5 minutes)—**This rinse cycle removes soil and alkalinity to help bleach work more effectively. This cycle rinses linens at the same temperature as the suds cycle.

5. **Bleach (5 to 8 minutes)—**Bleach is added to this hot-water, low-water-level cycle. Bleach kills bacteria, whitens fabrics, and removes stains.

6. **Rinse (1.5 to 3 minutes)—**Two or more rinses at medium temperatures and high water levels are used to remove detergent and soil from the linens.

7. **Intermediate extract (1.5 to 2 minutes, optional)—**This high-speed spin removes detergent and soil from linens, usually after the first rinse step. This cycle should not be used after a suds step, because it could drive soils back into the fabric. It should not be used on no-iron linens unless the temperature of the wash is below 120°F [49°C].

8. **Sour/softener or starch/sizing (3 to 5 minutes)—**Softeners and **sours** are added to condition fabric. The cycle runs at medium temperature and at low water levels. Starches are added to stiffen cotton fabrics; **sizing** is added for polyester blends. Starching/sizing replaces the sour/softener step.

Exhibit 3 Common Laundry Problems

Problem	Cause	Solution
Graying	Too little detergent	Increase amount of detergent; add bleach.
	Wash cycle temperature too low	Increase temperature.
	Poor sorting; transfer of soiling occurs	Rewash with increased detergent at hottest possible temperature. Use bleach suitable for fabric. Implement proper sorting procedures.
	Color "bleeding"	Do not dry. Rewash with detergent and bleach. Sort more carefully by color. Launder new colored fabrics separately the first few times.
Yellowing	Insufficient detergent	Increase the amount of detergent or use an *enzyme* product or bleach.
	Wash cycle temperature too low	Increase wash temperature.
	Use of chlorine bleach on wool, silk, or spandex items	Yellowed items cannot be restored. Avoid chlorine bleach on such items in the future.
Rust stains	Iron and/or manganese in water supply, pipes, or water heater	Rewash clothes with a commercial rust-removing product; *do not use chlorine bleach.* To prevent further staining, use a water softener to neutralize iron/manganese in water supply. If iron is in pipes, run the hot water for a few minutes to clear the line. Drain water heaters occasionally to remove rust buildup.
Blue stains	Blue coloring in detergent or fabric softener fails to disperse properly	For detergent stains, soak items in a plastic sink or container for an hour in a solution of 1 part white vinegar per 4 parts water. For softener stains, rub fabric with bar soap and wash. To prevent stains, add detergents to the washer before clothes, then start washer to ensure better mixing of detergent. Dilute fabric softener before adding to wash.
Poor soil removal	Too little detergent	Increase amount.
	Wash temperature too low	Increase temperature.
	Overloading washer	Wash fewer items per load, sort properly, and use the proper amount of detergent and water temperature.
Greasy or oily stains	Too little detergent	Treat with prewash stain remover or liquid laundry detergent; increase amount of detergent.
	Wash temperature too low	Wash in higher temperature.
	Undiluted fabric softener has come into contact with fabric	Rub fabric with bar soap and wash; dilute fabric softener before adding to cycle.
	Dryer-added softener	Rub fabric with bar soap and wash. Avoid too small a load, improper dryer setting, too hot dryer.
Residue of powder (especially noticeable on dark or bright colors)	Undissolved detergent	Add detergent to the washer before clothes, then start washer.
	Nonphosphate granular detergent combines with water minerals and forms residue	Remove stain by mixing 1 cup of white vinegar with 1 gallon of warm water. Soak in a plastic container or sink and rinse. To prevent residue, switch to a liquid detergent.

(continued)

Exhibit 3   *(continued)*

Problem	Cause	Solution
Stiff, faded, or abraded fabrics	Nonphosphate granular detergent combines with water minerals and forms residue	Remove stain by mixing 1 cup of white vinegar with 1 gallon of warm water. Soak in a plastic container or sink and rinse. To prevent residue, switch to a liquid detergent.
Lint	Improper sorting (mixing *napped* fabrics with others)	Dry items and pat with masking or transparent tape, rewash and use fabric softener in final rinse. Prevent problems by sorting more carefully.
	Tissue in apron or uniform pockets	Check pockets before laundering.
	Overloading washer or dryer	Wash and dry fewer items.
	Insufficient detergent	Increase amount of detergent.
	Clogged washer lint filter or dryer lint screen	Clean filters and screens after use; rewash items.
	Overdrying causes static electricity which attracts lint	Rewash items using fabric softener; remove items from dryers when they are slightly damp.
Holes, tears, or snags	Incorrect use of chlorine bleach	Always use a bleach dispenser and dilute bleach with 4 parts water; never pour directly on linens.
	Unfastened zippers, hooks, or belt buckles	Fasten zippers, hooks and eyes, and belt buckles before washing.
	Burrs in washer	Inspect washer on a weekly basis and repair as necessary.
	Washer overload	Avoid overloading.
Color fading	Unstable dye	Test items for colorfastness before washing; wash new items separately.
	Water temperature too hot	Use cooler water.
	Improper use of bleach	Test item for colorfastness; use oxygen bleach.
	Undiluted bleach poured on fabric	Dilute bleach.
Wrinkling	Failure to use correct cycle	Use permanent-press cycle; and cooler temperatures in wash; remove items promptly from dryers and fold immediately.
	Washer/dryer overloading	Do not overload.
	Overdrying	Put items back in the dryer on permanent-press cycle for 15 to 20 minutes; heat and cool-down time will remove wrinkles. Remove all items promptly.
Shrinking	Overdrying	Reduce drying time and remove items while damp; remove knits (especially cotton) while slightly damp and stretch back into shape; dry flat.
	Residual shrinking	Allow for some shrinking when purchasing items.
	Agitation of wool items	Lower agitation in wash/rinse cycles; regular spinning will not promote shrinkage.
Pilling	Synthetics pill naturally with wear	Prevent unnecessary wear by using fabric softener and spray starch or fabric finish.

Source: Edwin B. Feldman, P.E., ed., *Programmed Cleaning Guide for the Environmental Sanitarian* (New York: The Soap and Detergent Association), pp. 163–168.

9. **Extract (2 to 12 minutes)**—A high-speed spin removes most of the moisture from the linens. The length of the spin depends on fabric type, extractor capacity, and extractor speed.

Many OPLs are now choosing washers with cold-water options. Cold-water washes with synthetic bactericidal detergents can do the following:

- Remove stains that hot water will set

- Preserve the wrinkle-free characteristics of no-iron fabric and absorbency of towels

- Save energy costs

Chemicals. Hotel and other commercial OPLs use many more chemicals to wash linens than people use in their washers at home. The hotel laundry "fine-tunes" its chemicals to ensure an effective wash that leaves linens looking as close to new as possible. In general, a laundry's chemical needs depend mainly on the types of linens it uses and the soiling conditions encountered. In addition, hotel OPLs use more **alkali** to enhance the detergent's cleaning power. Alkali, however, is abrasive and must be neutralized with other chemicals.

Generally, it is a good idea to deal with more than one chemical vendor. This ensures that you obtain good advice on chemical usage along with updates on new technology. However, juggling several vendors at the same time may not be the most effective use of the executive housekeeper's time. Some executive housekeepers accept bids from chemical vendors and select one vendor as the sole supplier for the upcoming year. This system works well as long as the vendor selected is keenly aware that if the property's needs are not met, another vendor stands ready to do the job.

The following list provides a brief description of the major categories of chemicals used in laundry operations.

Water. Although not always recognized as such, water is the major chemical used in the laundry process. Two to five gallons of water are used for every pound of dry laundry. Water that is perfectly safe to drink may not be suitable for washing linens. Certain minerals, for example, can stain or wear linens. Other substances can cause odors or "hard" water that hampers sudsing. Many of these substances can also clog pipes and machinery. Fortunately, other chemicals can be added to water to help it clean better. Many OPL operators recommend testing the laundry's water supply to identify potential problems.

Detergents. The term "detergent" is actually a catchall word for a number of cleaning agents. **Synthetic detergents** are especially effective on oil and grease. Synthetic detergents often contain **surfactants**. These are chemicals that aid soil removal and act as antibacterial agents and fabric softeners. **Builders** or alkalies are often added to synthetic detergents to soften water and remove oils and grease. **Soaps** are another kind of detergent. Neutral or pure soaps contain no alkalies; built soaps do. Built soaps are generally used on heavily soiled fabrics; pure soaps are reserved for more lightly soiled items. Hard water reduces a soap's cleaning ability and also leaves a "scum" on fabrics that causes graying, stiffness, and odor. Soaps are destroyed by sours.

the Rooms CHRONICLE®

Tips for Handling Linens in the Laundry

Do not overdry permanent-press items.

The secret to these "no-iron" linens is to avoid excessive spin cycles and limit the drying time. If linens are removed from the dryer just slightly damp, but warm, and folded immediately, they will continue drying (and press themselves) while resting on the shelf overnight.

Allow permanent press to rest.

Permanent-press linen that is allowed to rest for 24 hours between uses has a longer life than that which is taken immediately from the dryer to a bed.

Do not overdry terry cloth.

The chlorine used to keep these materials white is activated with heat during the drying process, and overdrying will actually destroy the cotton fibers and shorten the life of the towel.

Set up a program for linen recovery.

Remove a stained piece immediately for treatment. This should happen both in the laundry, as workers observe the linen, and in the operational areas. Room attendants should designate torn or stained linen by tying a knot in the corner or placing the piece in a separate pillowcase. Food & beverage workers should have a special box or bin in which to set aside stained and torn linen. Sorting out reject linen before it is sent back into circulation, only to be discarded, sorted, washed, and dried again, will save labor dollars in all areas.

Keep an abundance of rags.

Make rags available to all workers so that good linen is not ruined by misuse.

Apportion linen equally.

Even distribution of linen among room attendants ensures that all have the tools to complete their assignments. Stocking linen storage closets with a maximum/minimum par level for the bed types in that area can make this easy. Overstocking closets or carts will lead to mixed-up, thrown-around linen which then must make a trip back to be washed before it can be used.

Study workers' movements.

Observe the activity in the laundry and retrain workers for more efficient motion. Ask the question: "What is the minimum number of times this pillowcase has to be touched while it is being processed?" Rearrange tables and carts to best accommodate the motions.

Eliminate fussing from folding.

For example, pick up the towel, lay it down, and fold over one part all in *one* motion. After the first part is laid over, it is not necessary to "fuss" by smoothing it or touching it again. Simply move on to making the second fold. Streamlining motions in the folding process will save time.

(continued)

Keep terry folds simple.

Since terry cloth items usually are specially folded while being placed in the guest-room, laundry workers should not be concerned about perfectly folding each towel. Devise a simple fold that will fit well on a room attendant's cart, and leave the final folding to the room attendant.

Make bed packets of linen.

Consider folding two sheets together, adding pillowcases and creating a packet which the room attendant can easily pull off a shelf to use: one packet per bed. This allows the room attendant to open and spread both sheets together instead of each sheet separately. For properties without a sheet ironer or folder, it cuts folding time in half.

Source: Gail Edwards, CHHE, *The Rooms Chronicle*®, Volume 3, Number 1, p. 5. For subscription information, please call 866-READ-TRC.

Fabric (optical) brighteners. Brighteners keep fabrics looking new and colors close to their original shade. These chemicals are often premixed with detergents and soaps.

Bleaches. Bleaches cause strong chemical reactions that, if not carefully controlled, can damage fabrics. Used properly, bleaches help remove stains, kill bacteria, and whiten fabrics.

There are two kinds of bleaches: chlorine and oxygen. Chlorine bleach can be used with any washable, natural, colorfast fiber. Chlorine bleach is safe for some synthetics and destroys others. All synthetics should therefore be tested before chlorine bleach is used. Oxygen bleach is milder than chlorine bleach and is generally safe for most washable fabrics. Oxygen bleach works best in hot water and on organic stains. Oxygen bleach should never be used with chlorine bleaches as they will neutralize each other.

A bleach's pH (degree of acidity or alkalinity) and water temperature must be controlled carefully to prevent fabric damage. Dry bleaches contain buffers that control pH, but they are more expensive than the liquid variety.

Alkalies. Alkalies or alkaline builders help detergents lather better and keep stains suspended in the wash water after they have been loosened and lifted from the fabric. Alkalies also help neutralize acidic stains (most stains are acidic), making the detergent more effective.

Antichlors. Antichlors are sometimes used in rinsing to ensure that all the chlorine in the bleach has been removed. Polyester fibers retain chlorine and for this reason are typically treated with antichlors when chlorine bleach is used.

Mildewcides. Mildewcides prevent the growth of bacteria and fungus on linens for up to 30 days. Both of these types of microorganisms can cause permanent stains that ruin linens. Moisture makes a good breeding ground for mildew growth. Therefore, soiled damp linen should be washed promptly and not allowed

Exhibit 4   Common Finishing Problems

Problem	Cause	Solution
Wrinkling (synthetics)	Washing/drying temperatures too high, causing breakdown of no-iron characteristics	Reduce heat.
	Insufficient cool-down in dryer	Turn heat down during the last few minutes of drying time; remove linens before they are bone-dry.
Glazed or fused fibers (synthetics)	Dryer heat is too high	Lower heat (140°F to 145°F; 60°C to 63°C); heat over 160°F (71°C) is too high.
Loss of absorbency	Washing/drying temperatures too high	Reduce heat.
	Too much fabric softener	Use less softener.

to sit in carts for long periods. Clean linens should be dried and/or ironed as they are removed from washers or extractors.

Sours. Sours are basically mild acids used to neutralize any residual alkalinity in fabrics after washing and rinsing. Detergents and bleaches contain alkali, and any residual alkali can damage fibers and cause yellowing and fading. In addition, residual alkalies can cause skin irritation and leave odors.

Fabric softeners. Softeners make fabrics more supple and easier to finish. Softeners are added with sours in the final wash cycle. They can reduce flatwork ironing, speed up extraction, reduce drying time, and reduce static electricity in the fabric. Too much softener can decrease a fabric's absorbency.

Starches. Starches give linens a crisp appearance that stands up during the items' use. If they are used, starches should be added in the final step in the washing process.

Extracting

Extracting removes excess moisture from laundered items through a high-speed spin. This step is important because it reduces the weight of the laundry and makes it easier for workers to lift the laundry and move it to dryers. Extracting also reduces drying time. Most washing machines now have extracting capabilities.

Finishing

Finishing gives the linens a crisp, wrinkle-free appearance. Finishing may require only drying or may include ironing. Linens should be sorted by fabric type before they are dried. Steam cabinets or tunnels are often used to dry blends because they give these fabrics a finished, wrinkle-free look. Some common finishing problems and their solutions are outlined in Exhibit 4.

Drying. Items that are dried generally include towels, washcloths, and some no-iron items. Drying times and temperatures vary considerably for various types of linens. In every case, however, drying should be followed by a cool-down tumbling period to prevent the hot linens from being damaged or wrinkled by rapid cooling and handling. After drying, linens should be removed immediately for folding. If folding is delayed, wrinkles will set in.

Dryers should never be prewarmed or run when empty. This can lead to "hot spots," which can damage fabric or cause fires. It also wastes energy.

Dry all fabrics according to manufacturers' recommendations or until moisture is completely removed. Determining correct drying times depends on the following:

- Type of dryer

- Amount of water left in the goods after washing

- Time of year (temperature of the dryer-intake air)

- Temperature of the linen when it is removed from the washer

It is best to conduct a test with the laundry and write procedures specific to the hotel that allow linens to dry without overdrying.

Sheets and pillowcases, if they will be hand-folded, need proper handling to minimize wrinkling. Linens should be taken from the washer/extractor immediately and loaded into the dryer.

Remember that dryers are rated for clean, dry weight (CDW), so that a 100-pound dryer will handle 100 pounds of clean, dry linen. Since linens are always wet when loaded into the dryer, allow for this difference. If the hotel has 100-pound washers and 100-pound dryers, the same load can be moved directly from a washer to a dryer. However, when the washer is rated for 100 pounds CDW and the dryer for 150 pounds CDW, the dryer will hold one and a half loads of wash.

Always load dryers to capacity. Drying time is not a function of the percentage of linen loaded. In other words, a dryer may complete a full load in 45 minutes, but it may take 35 minutes for half a load. Energy costs can skyrocket with careless use of dryers.

Permanent-press linens require a cool-down period after drying. Many times, employees keep turning the dryer control to continue the tumbling until they have time to fold the linen. But when dry linens tumble, the fibers are broken by hitting the sides of the dryer. This severely shortens the life of the linen and wastes energy. Remove linens from the dryer immediately upon the cycle's end.

Common problems encountered with dryers include clogged lint traps, gas flames out of adjustment, and broken thermostat controls. Slow drying times and smelly or scorched linens result from lack of attention to these items.[3]

Ironing. Sheets, pillowcases, tablecloths, and slightly damp napkins go directly to flatwork irons. Ironers vary in size and degree of automation. Uniforms are generally pressed in special ironing equipment. Steam tunnels are being used more often than ironers for removing wrinkles from polyester blend uniforms.

Folding

Since some properties still do a lot of folding manually, folding usually sets the pace for the linen room. Washing and drying items faster than they can be folded leads to unnecessary wrinkling and resoiling.

Not all laundry rooms have an ironer to process linens. In this situation, the permanent-press linen should be removed from the dryer immediately after the cool-down phase has ended. If linens are folded immediately and stacked to a minimum of 12 inches for 12 hours, a very good result can be obtained. Linens will have a smooth appearance with proper creases.

Folding personnel must also inspect linens, storing those that are to be reused and rejecting stained, torn, or otherwise unsuitable items. This inspection may increase folding time. Folding and storing should be done well away from the soiled linen area to avoid resoiling clean laundry.

Laundry employees should be encouraged to make folds that are quick and easy. Their only concern should be getting the item folded and moved to storage or the guestroom. The final, fancy folding of terry cloth is done by the room attendant when placing the item in the room.[4]

Storing

After folding, the items are postsorted and stacked. Postsorting separates any linen types and sizes that were missed in presorting. There should be enough storage room for at least one par. Finished items should be allowed to "rest" on shelves for 24 hours after laundering, because many types of linens are more easily damaged right after washing. Once linens are on shelves, yellowing and fading can be spotted quickly.

Transferring Linens to Use Areas

Linens are usually transferred to their use areas via carts. Carts should be cleaned at least once daily and more often if necessary. Transferring linens just before use and covering carts can help prevent resoiling. It is a good idea to use separate carts for soiled and clean linens to avoid accidental soiling.

Machines and Equipment

OPL machinery is a major investment in itself and affects the life span of another major investment—linens. The choice of OPL machines and equipment could mean the difference between a financially successful and a disastrous OPL. Machines with insufficient capacity, for example, result in damaged linens, unsatisfactory cleaning performance, excessive energy and water costs, or increased maintenance costs. Improperly maintained equipment can also lead to higher linen and equipment costs.

Most laundry equipment manufacturers offer free estimates of the type and amount of equipment needed, based on how many pounds of linen the operation must process in a day. The following discussion offers some basic information about the types of equipment available for OPLs.

Washing Machines

Most washers are made of stainless steel. They are sized by their capacity (that is, the number of pounds of linen they can handle in a single load). Sizes vary from 25- to 1,200-pound capacities. A large-capacity washer in a hotel laundry may not resemble a conventional washer designed for home use. Some machines have separate "pockets" which hold several large loads at a time. Some washers, called **tunnel washers**, have several chambers; each chamber is used for a particular wash cycle. As soon as the first cycle is finished on the first load of laundry, the wash moves into the second chamber. The laundry attendant can then load the first chamber with the next batch.

Washers consist of a motor, inside and outside shells, and a casing. The outside shell is stationary and holds the wash water. The inside shell holds the laundry and is perforated to allow water for various cycles to flow in and out.

In the past decade, most washers have been designed so that the perforations are turned away from the articles to be washed. Perforations on older equipment, however, may protrude and cause excess wear and tear on linens. This can reduce the useful life of linens by up to 50 percent. Even in a medium-sized OPL, older machines can cause enough fabric damage to pay for a new washer in about one year.

The washer's motor rotates either the perforated inner shell (on washwheel washers) or an agitator (agitator washers). The rotating shell or agitator helps the detergent break up soils on fabrics in the wash cycle and remove detergents and other chemicals during the rinse cycles.

Most newer washers have automatic detergent and solution dispensing capabilities. These washers are programmed electronically—either at the factory or in the OPL—to dispense solutions. Other washers require an operator to add detergent and solutions manually. Machines that require manual dispensing usually have fewer **ports** or **hoppers** (openings through which detergents can be poured). Equipment should have at least five ports—two for detergents and one each for bleach, sour, and softener. Chemicals that are simply dumped onto the linens can severely damage them. To ensure proper mixing, many commercial systems are automated.

Whether added automatically or manually, solutions must be added in the right amounts and at the right times. As increasingly sophisticated chemicals are developed to improve the quality of the wash at a lower cost, measuring solutions and adding them at the right times becomes increasingly important.

While many automated machines are more economical to operate than washers requiring manual dispensing, they can also cause problems if improperly used. Allowing detergent salespeople to tinker with automated machines to "improve" the quality of the wash can, in fact, decrease the quality of the machine's performance. Having the manufacturer's representative check the machine periodically is probably the surest way to get the most out of the machine.

Microprocessors—one of the latest innovations in washers—allow greater control over the washer's functions than more conventional automatic models. For example, water temperature can be regulated more exactly. Microprocessors also allow operators more ease and flexibility in programming combinations of detergents and solutions for specific fabric types and soil levels.

Another new innovation is the reuse washer. This machine can save energy, sewage, water, and chemical costs. A water reuse washer is equipped with insulated storage tanks. Water that can be reused is siphoned into the tanks to maintain the proper temperature and then released into the proper cycle of the next batch of laundry. Control panels allow laundry operators to make adjustments in the water to be reused to account for soil conditions, water hardness, and fabric type. The control also automatically saves reusable water and discharges water that cannot be reused.

Hotels in extremely dry climates are beginning to use OPL wastewater to irrigate lawns and gardens. Some treatment is needed to neutralize phosphates and other chemicals before the water can be used on plants. Special care also must be taken to ensure that recycled water is not accidentally used for drinking. Many properties, for example, color used water with a harmless vegetable dye to avoid mix-ups.

Most washers have extraction capabilities. The motor spins the inside shell rapidly to remove most excess water after washing is completed. If the washer cannot remove this water, a separate extractor must be used. Extractors are available in centrifugal, hydraulic, and pressure types.

Many washers offer high-speed extraction capabilities. These machines are often sold and purchased as time savers. In addition, they often offer substantial energy savings because they reduce drying time.

High-speed extraction requires that a machine be able to handle many times its capacity weight during the extraction cycle. For example, machines in hotel OPLs typically handle 70 to 300 pounds of dry laundry. Add to that load the weight of the water and the force of the spin, and the machine may be handling up to half a ton of real weight. Washers with high-speed extractors should be mounted on special soft mount pads and then bolted onto the floor. The soft mount pads act like shock absorbers and ensure that the machine will not loosen from its foundation.

Washers and dryers should also be designed to prevent burns and bruises. Most machines built after 1980 have well-insulated bodies and glass on doors to keep heat from escaping. The insulation also protects employees from burns.

Washing machines do break down; when one is out of operation, the hotel is faced with a series of expensive problems. For one, a broken machine may idle many of the hotel's housekeeping staff—which means wasted labor. Second, a broken machine may hamper the flow of linen and the makeup of guestrooms—which means lost sales. Finally, a breakdown means that the OPL will later be overworked—which translates into overtime expenses.

Three rules help reduce breakdown time. First, buy only strong, industrial equipment from a trustworthy supplier. Before making a purchase decision, spend sufficient time reading sales literature to identify the brands and models of machines appropriate for the hotel's laundry operation. For example, machine specifications should list the weight of the machines. In general, heavier machines are more durable because an inner frame supports the cylinders and puts less stress on the body of the machine. Second, read, thoroughly understand, and follow the equipment's maintenance requirements. More than 90 percent of all machine failures can be prevented by following the manufacturer's maintenance recommendations. Finally, consider buying extended warranties on the equipment. Usually, this cost is less than that incurred by equipment failure. More important, the warranty forces the manufacturer's local representative to maintain a vested interest in keeping equipment operating properly.

Drying Machines

Dryers remove moisture from articles by tumbling them in a rotating cylinder through which heated air passes. Air is heated by gas, electricity, or steam. The airflow must be unrestricted to ensure the dryer's energy efficiency.

Like washers, dryers must be maintained properly. As dryers get older, they frequently receive less maintenance even though they require more. This means they waste more energy. Laundries are usually designed with greater drying capacity than washing capacity because it takes one and a half to two times longer to dry laundry than to wash it. As a result, work can continue relatively smoothly for a short time if a dryer breaks down. However, it is easier to keep dryers properly maintained in the first place than it is to work around broken machinery. Dirt or lint clogging the air supply to the dryer is the most frequent problem. Cleaning air vents twice daily can help eliminate this.

The Occupational Safety and Health Act (OSHA) requires that lint levels in the air be controlled in institutional laundries. Most dryers are equipped with a system of ducts which eject lint into containers and minimize air contamination. Ducts should be checked regularly for leaks, and containers should be emptied regularly.

Steam Cabinets and Tunnels

Steam cabinets or **tunnels** effectively eliminate wrinkles from heavy linens such as blankets, bedspreads, and curtains. A steam cabinet is simply a box in which articles are hung and steamed to remove wrinkles. A steam tunnel actually moves articles on hangers through a tunnel, steaming them and removing the wrinkles as they move through.

Steam cabinets—and tunnels to a lesser extent—can disrupt the flow of laundry through the OPL, because they are time-consuming to operate. They also require a worker to load and unload the tunnel or cabinet, which increases the OPL's labor costs. As a result, only very large hotels with valet service or hotels that do frequent loads of curtains, bedspreads, and blankets find steam tunnels cost-effective. Most hotels that use no-iron linens do not require steam cabinets.

Flatwork Ironers and Pressing Machines

Flatwork ironers and pressing machines are similar, except that ironers roll over the material while presses flatten it. Also, items can be fed into ironers but must be placed on the presses manually. Either process is time-consuming and thus used only for items that require ironing. Some ironers also fold the flatwork automatically.

It is important for proper iron operation and maintenance that material arrives in the proper condition from the finishing process. For example, dirt left on linens because of improper rinsing in the wash process can shorten ironer life. Too much sour left in the linens can cause them to roll during ironing, and too much alkali can cause linens to turn brown. Moisture extraction must be controlled, too. Linens should be moist before going into the ironer. Linens that are too dry will cause static electricity to build up on the ironer. On the other hand, linens that are too wet will be difficult to feed into the ironer.

It should be noted that older no-iron linens frequently have to be ironed. In reality, no-iron linens have two distinct lives. Initially, their performance is that of a true, no-iron fabric. However, this condition usually lasts less than half the article's total useful life. Over time, the crispness of no-iron linens is reduced because repeated washings break down the fabric. Because linens are so expensive, many OPLs have discovered that buying an ironer is cheaper than buying new linens.

Folding Machines

For large hotels folding machines are available that virtually eliminate tumble drying and hand folding. These space-saving units dry, iron, fold, and often crossfold and stack flatwork. Some have microprocessor controls that determine fold points and trigger other related functions.

For smaller properties, the term "folding machine" is actually a misnomer. These hotels typically employ a machine known as an "extra hand" folding machine that does not actually fold the laundry, but holds one end of the linen item so that staff can fold it more easily. This non-automated folding machine acts as a passive partner, providing the worker with an extra "hand" designed to help boost productivity and decrease folding time.

Rolling/Holding Equipment

Rolling and holding equipment is used for linen handling. Carts are used in most laundries to move linens and to hold them after they have been sorted for washing, drying, and finishing. Carts must be kept orderly so that staff can move freely through the OPL. They must also be carefully marked so that carts for clean linens are not mixed up with those used for soiled items.

Very large OPLs may have an overhead system of tracks to which laundry bags can be attached to hold linen ready to be sorted, washed, dried, or finished. Overhead systems may be semi-automated or fully automated, depending on the size of the OPL.

Automated overhead systems have a number of advantages. First, they allow laundry to move in an orderly manner throughout the OPL. Second, one person can move all the carts simultaneously instead of many people having to move carts to and from washers, dryers, extractors, ironers, and other equipment on the OPL floor. This can represent considerable labor cost savings for large OPLs. Finally, overhead systems also provide extra storage space in case one step in the laundry process gets backed up, preventing a disorderly pileup of carts on the OPL floor.

Very sophisticated OPLs have automated equipment that will move soiled laundry to the machines. These systems include conveyors, overhead monorails, and pneumatic tubes.

Even though a sophisticated linen-handling system may require a large initial cash investment, it could pay for itself very quickly in labor savings. The larger the operation, the more desirable an automated system becomes.

Regardless of the type of system used within the hotel's laundry, one should observe a few basic guidelines. First, transport devices should not have sharp corners or other parts that could tear linens. Second, they should be easy to use. They should not require workers to bend excessively or repeatedly to remove items from the bottom of a cart. Carrying should be avoided as a means of linen transportation. Third, make certain there is adequate headroom and floor space for personnel traffic. Make sure carts can fit comfortably through doorways. Holding space should be situated so that workers do not have to reach high or far back on shelves.

Preventive Maintenance

A detailed, strictly observed preventive maintenance program is essential to the efficient operation of an OPL. Lost productivity and expensive repairs easily justify the costs of these programs. The program should include a record of repairs or maintenance procedures and the total cost of each. Manufacturers usually provide literature about their equipment, but they should also offer instructions for making and keeping good maintenance records. This data will identify troublesome units that may have more serious problems. When the total cost of the repairs and maintenance begins to approach the cost of the machine itself, the property should consider replacing it.

Typical examples of daily maintenance procedures include checking safety devices; turning on steam, water, and air valves; checking ironer roll pressure; and cleaning dryer lint screens.

Maintaining water and energy efficiency is an important aspect of preventive maintenance, as is reducing repair and downtime costs. Leaking valves, damaged insulation, and constricted gas, air, and water paths can be quite costly. Keep accurate records of utility use to identify such problems. Periodically, check water levels in washers. Too much water results in decreased agitation and poor cleaning. Not enough water causes excessive mechanical action that can damage fabrics.

Even for properties that develop and strictly adhere to an extensive preventive maintenance program, unexpected breakdowns or repair delays can occur. For this reason, many hotels develop a contingency plan to help cope with unforeseen emergencies. A contingency plan should include an estimate of how long the stock of clean linen will last and at what point an outside laundry will need to be called. Having a number of outside laundry contacts will allow any laundry supervisor to have soiled linen cleaned in time to meet the hotel's needs. Some hotels form an emergency laundry network so that they can help each other out in the event of OPL emergencies.

Staff Training

Manufacturers and distributors can often help train employees to use machinery properly. They can also provide safety instructions and updates that can help the executive housekeeper or laundry supervisor develop good safety procedures. In general, staff should be trained to inspect all equipment daily before start-up and to treat all equipment with care.

Once safety procedures are established, the executive housekeeper or laundry supervisor must ensure that employees follow them. Such measures as unannounced fire drills, displayed charts outlining safety procedures, quarterly safety meetings, and monthly reviews of and follow-up on all work-related accidents can be good ways to ensure that safety procedures are followed. The executive housekeeper or laundry supervisor should periodically review procedures with all employees individually. This keeps long-term employees alert, reinforces prior training, and orients new personnel to the proper use of equipment and supplies. Periodic retraining procedures are an important part of any safety program.

More and more workers, especially in service occupations, do not read or speak English. This poses problems for training in general, but is especially critical in the area of safety training. Safety procedures printed in languages besides English should be available if needed. Whenever possible, briefings or safety lectures should be presented by bilingual staff members. Some properties help bridge the communication gap by assigning bilingual "buddies" to workers not proficient in English so that safety procedures can be communicated to those workers.

Valet Service

Valet service means that a hotel will take care of guest laundry needs. Valet service can be handled in two ways. The hotel may contract with an outside laundry or dry-cleaning operation to take care of guest needs; or, the hotel may have its own valet service equipment and staff on the premises. Whether contracted or on-premises, valet service is typically classified as either "same-day" or "overnight." Same-day service means that laundry is sent out in the morning and arrives back in the guest's room by evening. Overnight service means that laundry is sent out in the evening and returned by morning.

Contract Valet Service

Hotels that use outside contractors should operate under a formal agreement that specifies exactly what services the outside laundry or dry-cleaning operation will provide. Some hotels provide and ask the contractor to use special bags and boxes for laundry stamped with the hotel's name and/or logo. The agreement should also state when laundry will be picked up and returned.

Bell service staff or room attendants may deliver clean laundry to guestrooms. In small properties, the front desk may activate the message light on the guest's telephone. When the guest reports for the message, the laundry is delivered.

On-Premises Valet Service

Hotels that provide on-premises valet service cite four major advantages to their operation. They say that it is often quicker and promotes more goodwill with guests than contracting with an outside operation. Furthermore, the dry-cleaning equipment required by a valet service allows the OPL to handle employee uniforms as well as special linen items. Most important, however, is the revenue the valet service generates. An efficient valet service helps defray the overall OPL costs. In fact, the decision to operate on-premises valet service often rests solely on whether it will turn a profit.

Offering valet service requires the housekeeping department virtually to set up its own laundry business. It must do the following:

- Set times for laundry pickup and delivery.

- Determine how laundry will be delivered to guestrooms.

- Figure bills to be attached to clean laundry (though the hotel's controller usually sets the price rates).

- Determine the final hotel liability policy in accordance with state and local laws.

- Handle lost and damaged items.

- Field guest comments and complaints.

Whether or not the hotel can provide on-premises valet service often depends upon the amount of space in the OPL. Valet staff will need their own workspace for sorting, tagging, pretreating spots, washing, drying, and finishing. Extra space will be needed for equipment. Valet staff also need to be specially trained. Often, a valet supervisor is responsible for training and overseeing valet attendants.

Some hotels have a valet extension number that guests can call to get laundry pickup. Soiled laundry is collected by a valet staff runner, who returns it to the valet service area of the laundry room. There, valet staff tag, sort, and pretreat (if necessary) each item. Some valet services include minor mending jobs such as sewing on a button. When laundry is finished, properly packaged, and ticketed with a bill, the runner returns items to guestrooms.

Accepting Outside Laundry

As hotel operations look for ways to increase their revenue and profits, some hotel laundries have turned their operations into revenue producers. It is an idea that is meant to help bring in additional revenue and to offer consistent full-time employment to the laundry staff regardless of hotel occupancy levels.

Laundry expense is one of those "cost of doing business" factors associated with running a hotel. Hotel managers who bring in outside laundry are able to increase their profits and the hotel's bottom line. Bill Cummings, the executive facility services manager and laundry general manager of the Grove Park Inn Resort & Spa in Asheville, North Carolina, said they were able to reduce their laundry expenses by more than 50 percent.

The concept of using hotel equipment to wash other companies' laundry is not a new concept. However, it isn't a simple one and requires a systematic approach.

A hotel's on-premises laundry operation must be large enough to handle outside sourced linen. The ability to do this will be contingent on physical capacity, current laundry use, equipment available, laundry-staffing levels, internal hotel needs, and time availability.

Equipment. Depending on the hotel's laundry equipment and product mix, as well as their efficiency ratings, productivity could range quite a bit. How many loads can each machine do per hour? The productivity output will vary depending on its load capacity.

Hours. What days and hours does the hotel laundry normally operate? Given the equipment output and current staffing levels, can capacity be added? Or will it be necessary to expand the laundry's hours of operations? If so, will this entail additional personnel and labor costs? When is maintenance performed? Can maintenance be performed at other times so as not to interfere with laundry production? Can the hotel take advantage of less expensive energy costs by operating the on-premises laundry during non-peak hours?

Staffing. Once the required facility hours have been determined, it is necessary to determine how to staff it. A manager must decide whether it is feasible to have full production during all open hours or whether it might make more sense to handle specialty items during some periods. Laundry personnel might sort and wash during non-peak hours and complete finishing during peak hours. Some properties offer pay rate differentials for non-peak hours. The operation must also determine whether additional supervisory and maintenance personnel will be needed.

Facility Space/Product Flow. Next, determine whether the hotel laundry has the physical space to handle the additional volume. Consider that for every 300 to 400 pounds of terry, the laundry will require an additional transport cart (if using the standard exchange carts). Each cart takes up roughly 9.5 square feet of floor space. Since sheets and table linens are denser and require less space, each cart will need approximately 9.5 square feet for every 800 to 1,000 pounds of these items. If the facility adds laundry volume, where will it stage the dirty linen to be sorted and the clean linen to be delivered? If the hotel laundry will be processing healthcare linens, is the facility set up for containment and does it comply with regulations as specified by the Joint Commission on Accreditation of Healthcare Organizations? If the facility will be processing healthcare product, its accreditations will be contingent on the laundry passing regulatory inspections.

Transport. Once the hotel has decided to accept and process contract linens, transportation issues to and from the laundry facility must be resolved. How will the linens get to and from the customers' sites to the hotel? If customers are dropping off and picking up their orders, does their liability insurance protect or indemnify the hotel when doing so? If the hotel handles or oversees pickup and delivery, does the hotel's insurance protect all parties? The hotel will also have to determine what vehicles laundry personnel will use for pickup and delivery. Drivers will have to be trained in handling roadside emergencies and have the proper licensing.

Administrative. Management has several logistical responsibilities in serving a customer. It begins by preparing for all contingencies. This includes setting up a complaint system, determining charges (the most common method is by the pound), establishing weighing systems (who does it, wet weight or dry weight, who verifies weights), handling rush orders, processing invoices and payments, executing contracts, and ensuring that the primary operation of servicing the hotel is not disrupted.

There are several variations on how to handle sourced laundry. Three primary ways of handling laundry are:

- Linen leasing: the laundry owns the product and is responsible for inventory.

- Linen loanership: programs where the inventory gradually shifts ownership from the laundry to the customer.

- Service only: the customer owns the linens and the laundry merely cleans and delivers them.[5]

Staffing Considerations

Proper staffing is critical to the efficiency of the OPL. Labor costs—the number-one expense in any hotel operation today—must be carefully controlled in order for the OPL to remain cost-effective. Scheduling too many employees can severely cut into the hotel's profits. Having too few employees can also eat up profits in overtime pay and inefficiency that could ultimately affect guests and result in lost business.

Staff Scheduling

To efficiently schedule the laundry staff, executive housekeepers or laundry managers must be able to forecast the hotel's daily linen needs three or four weeks in advance.

Forecasting Linen Needs. The first step in forecasting the hotel's daily linen needs is to review past records and determine the average number of pounds of linen used per occupied room and per dining-room cover. The second step is to obtain occupancy forecasts from the rooms division and cover forecasts from the food & beverage division. These forecasts should include special events that will affect the hotel's linen needs. These events might be an unusual number of banquets and parties, economic circumstances that keep occupancy high or low, construction projects around the hotel, conventions, and so on.

Multiplying the number of expected occupants (or covers) by the average number of pounds of linen used per occupied room (or cover) yields the total number of pounds of linen that the laundry will have to process the next day.

Scheduling Staff. Once the daily needs for the schedule period are known, one more thing must be determined: how many workers will it take to handle the load? By keeping productivity records over a period of time, laundry supervisors should be able to develop some ratios that will help them determine the number of staff needed to process various amounts of linen.

Along with these ratios, it will be necessary to set minimum and maximum staff levels for the OPL. For example, two people in the OPL may not be able to keep the laundry moving through the sorting, washing, drying, finishing, and folding stages smoothly—no matter how light the linen demand. By the same token, the OPL may be too small to allow more than a certain number of workers to work efficiently together at the same time.

When a hotel needs more people than its OPL can handle comfortably in one shift, it can schedule two or three equally staffed shifts—or it can schedule one or two shifts with the maximum number of workers and another shift with just enough workers to meet the remainder of the linen demand. If the laundry finds itself unable to meet the hotel's demands with three fully staffed shifts, a bigger OPL is needed.

Many managers prefer to schedule two or three equally staffed shifts instead of one or two full shifts and another partially staffed shift. They say that the full shifts tend to overload machines and partial shifts underload them, causing unnecessary wear and tear on machines and inefficient energy use. Some managers reason, too, that it is more efficient to run a full staff some days and close down on others than it is to operate with a partial staff. Union rules (if applicable) may, however, dictate the way the OPL is staffed.

Other Staffing Considerations. Besides determining laundry needs and the number of workers needed to fulfill those needs, there are other staffing considerations.

Many properties cross-train laundry personnel so that each worker can do every job in the OPL. Cross-training allows for some job variation and lets workers cover for one another during vacations, illnesses, or other leaves. While the laundry supervisor or executive housekeeper is in charge of training employees, each area of the OPL—sorting, washing, finishing, etc.—may have a team leader who supervises the workers in that area. Workers are often rotated to different areas on a regular basis and work with different staff members as well.

Another important item to consider is when to schedule shifts. If the laundry is not located in the basement of the hotel or in a separate building, for example, it probably should not operate at night when guests could be disturbed.

Whether to stagger schedules is another consideration. There are some advantages to having one or two workers begin their shift early and then bringing in other workers at intervals of two or three hours. Shift staggering can provide full staffing in the middle of the day when the laundry load is heaviest.

Job Lists and Performance Standards

Besides determining the proper number of workers for the laundry, the executive housekeeper or laundry supervisor develops the job lists and performance standards for various positions in the OPL. Exhibits 5 through 9 present sample job lists for various positions in the OPL.

Exhibit 5 Sample Job List: Washer

Reports to: Head washer
Tasks:

1. Sort linens and uniforms.
2. Pretreat and/or rewash heavily soiled items.
3. Load, use, and unload washers.
4. Clean and maintain work areas.
5. Inform the head washer about all matters pertaining to the washroom.

Exhibit 6 Sample Job List: Laundry Attendant

Reports to: Laundry manager
Tasks:

1. Load, use and unload dryers.
2. Iron linens using a mechanical flatwork ironer.
3. Use mechanical linen-folding equipment.
4. Fold linens by hand.
5. Iron linens by hand.
6. Mend and sew linens and/or uniforms.
7. Clean and maintain work areas.
8. Inform the laundry manager about any malfunctions on finishing equipment or problems with safety mechanisms.

Exhibit 7 Sample Job List: Linen Distribution Attendant

Reports to: Laundry manager
Tasks:

1. Use mechanical linen-folding equipment.
2. Fold linens by hand.
3. Fill banquet and restaurant requisitions.
4. Deliver guest service supplies to guestrooms.
5. Process contract-cleaned linens and uniforms.
6. Issue and receive employee uniforms.
7. Restock housekeeping closets and carts.
8. Provide towel service to recreation areas.
9. Clean and maintain work areas.

As soon as the equipment is installed in any OPL, performance standards should be developed for all activities, and employees should be thoroughly trained. The equipment supplier can often provide information that can be used to develop performance standards and help train employees. Proper training and

Exhibit 8   Sample Job List: Head Washer

Reports to: Laundry manager
Tasks:

1. Supervise all personnel in the washing and sorting areas of the OPL.
2. Make reports about all washing and sorting activities to the laundry manager.
3. Oversee:
   - Sorting and washing procedures
   - Filling linen needs for guestrooms and food and beverage outlets
   - Maintaining adequate supplies of clean uniforms
   - Setting formulas and cycles for types of linen and types of soils
4. Make sure all workers assigned to a shift are present.
5. Make sure staff keep areas and equipment clean and neat.
6. Maintain employee performance and machine performance records.
7. Check supply levels.

Exhibit 9   Sample Job List: Laundry Supervisor

Reports to: Executive Housekeeper
Tasks:

1. Record laundry costs.
2. Make reports and recommendations when requested.
3. Oversee the preventive-maintenance program.
4. Approve distribution of linens to guestrooms and food and beverage areas.
5. Direct all OPL staff.
6. Prepare the OPL budget with the Executive Housekeeper.
7. Hire and train new OPL employees.
8. Develop methods for increasing OPL efficiency.
9. Coordinate all maintenance and repairs of machinery.
10. Supervise the OPL safety program.
11. Evaluate OPL staff performance.

performance standards become more vital to efficient OPL operation as machinery becomes more complicated.

Typical laundry-room performance standards might cover, for example, the steps an employee should take in loading a particular machine. This might include a chart showing the number of sheets, pillowcases, towels, or other items that constitute a load; an explanation of the use of a linen scale for weighing loads; the steps for checking the safety of a load before washing it; and the proper way to close and secure the washer door.

Other performance standards particularly suited to laundry operations are preventive-maintenance procedures (see the section on preventive maintenance in this chapter), linen-handling procedures, inventory control procedures, time card control, chemical-handling procedures, and linen-sorting procedures.

Endnotes

1. Source: Phil Sprague, *The Rooms Chronicle®*, Volume 3, Number 6, p. 13. For subscription information, call 866-READ-TRC.

2. Source: Mary Friedman, *The Rooms Chronicle®*, Volume 4, Number 1, p. 4. For subscription information, call 866-READ-TRC.

3. Source: Mary Friedman, *The Rooms Chronicle®*, Volume 4, Number 2, p. 4. For subscription information, call 866-READ-TRC.

4. Friedman, Volume 4, Number 2, p. 4.

5. Source: Bill Cummings, CRDE, CHHE, CLLM, CFT, *The Rooms Chronicle®*, Volume 14, Number 4, pp. 4–5. For subscription information, call 866-READ-TRC.

 # Key Terms

alkalies—Laundry chemicals that help detergents lather better and keep stains suspended in the wash water after they have been loosened and lifted from the fabric. Alkalies also help neutralize acidic stains (most stains are acidic), making the detergent more effective.

antichlors—Laundry chemicals that are sometimes used at the rinse point in the wash cycle to ensure that all the chlorine in the bleach has been removed.

bleach—There are two kinds of bleaches: *chlorine* and *oxygen*. Chlorine bleach can be used with any washable, natural, colorfast fiber. Oxygen bleach is milder than chlorine bleach and is generally safe for most washable fabrics. Oxygen bleach should never be used with chlorine bleach, as they will neutralize each other.

break—This is the point in the laundry wash cycle at which a high-alkaline, soil-loosening product is added. The break cycle is usually at medium temperature and low water level.

builders—Builders or alkalies are laundry chemicals that are often added to synthetic detergents to soften water and remove oils and grease.

fabric (or optical) brighteners—Fabric (or optical) brighteners are laundry chemicals that keep fabrics looking new and colors close to their original shade. These chemicals are often premixed with detergents and soaps.

flatwork ironer—Flatwork ironers are similar to pressing machines, except that ironers roll over the material while presses flatten it. Some ironers also fold the flatwork automatically.

flushes—Steps in the wash cycle that dissolve and dilute water-soluble soils to reduce the soil load for the upcoming suds step. Items are generally flushed at medium temperatures at high water levels.

hoppers—Openings in washing machines through which detergents can be poured. Also called ports.

mildewcides—Laundry chemicals added to the wash cycle to prevent the growth of bacteria and fungus on linens for up to 30 days.

polycotton—A polyester/cotton blend.

ports—Openings into washing machines through which detergents can be poured. Also called hoppers.

sizing—Laundry chemicals added to the wash cycle to stiffen polyester blends.

soap—A kind of detergent. Neutral or pure soaps contain no alkalies; built soaps do. Built soaps are generally used on heavily soiled fabrics; pure soaps are reserved for more-lightly soiled items. Soaps are destroyed by sours.

sours—Mild acids used to neutralize residual alkalinity in fabrics after washing and rinsing.

steam cabinet—A box in which articles are hung and steamed to remove wrinkles. Steam cabinets are typically used to remove wrinkles from heavy linens such as blankets, bedspreads, and curtains.

steam tunnel—A piece of laundry equipment that moves articles on hangers through a tunnel, steaming them and removing the wrinkles as they move through.

surfactants—Synthetic detergents often contain surfactants, chemicals that aid soil removal and act as antibacterial agents and fabric softeners.

synthetic detergents—Synthetic detergents are especially effective on oil and grease. Builders or alkalies are often added to synthetic detergents to soften water and remove oils and grease.

tunnel washer—A long, sequential laundry machine that operates continuously, processing each stage of the wash/rinse cycle and extracting in another section of the machine.

Review Questions

1. What factors must be taken into account when laundering various types of linen fabrics?

2. What are the steps in the flow of linens through an OPL?

3. What are two ways in which soiled linens can be sorted before washing? Why are both sorting procedures important?

4. What are the nine steps of the typical wash cycle?

5. What is the function of the various chemicals used in the wash process?

6. What are the basic types of laundry equipment used in an OPL?

7. Why is a preventive-maintenance program important to the operation of an OPL?

8. What kinds of equipment and personnel are necessary for an OPL to provide on-premises valet service?

9. How are linen needs forecasted?

10. What factors must be considered when scheduling OPL staff?

Internet Sites

For more information, visit the following Internet sites. Remember that Internet addresses can change without notice. If the site is no longer there, you can use a search engine to look for additional sites.

Continental Girbau
www.continentalgirbau.com

Ecolab
www.ecolab.com

G.A. Braun, Inc.
www.gabraun.com

Laundry Today
www.laundrytoday.com

Maytag Commercial Laundry
www.maytagcommerciallaundry.com/home.jsp

Case Study

Penny Wise and Pound Foolish with Linens

Penny Wise is the executive housekeeper at the Sweetrest Hotel, a 500-room property. In October, Penny put together the housekeeping budget for the next year, requesting $90,000 for linens. She based this number on last year's linen use and projected occupancy for next year, with a six percent increase thrown in to allow for cost increases.

Scott Pound is the hotel's controller. When he reviewed Penny's budget in November, he agreed with most of her numbers, but he decided to cut the linen line item to $70,000, a reduction of $20,000. His reasoning? He had to make cuts in the budget to meet next year's profit goal, and linens was an area he felt he could trim. The general manager approved the cut in linens.

When Penny received the approved budget in late December, she was disappointed but not surprised to see the money for replacement linen reduced for next year. Hotel managers throughout the industry are notoriously stingy with linen. As one general manager said to her years ago, "Why should I buy you more? You'll just use it." She could never get him to see that housekeeping would use the additional linen because it was truly needed, not because housekeeping wanted to be wasteful or have an unnecessary cushion.

Although she was almost certain it wouldn't do any good, Penny wrote Scott a memo that explained why she set the linen budget at $90,000 and why cutting it to $70,000 almost certainly invited a late-year disaster. In the memo, she pointed out some of the problems the hotel might experience if a linen shortage occurred. She concluded the memo by suggesting that her original request of $90,000 might even be too low, depending on which groups the hotel attracted next year. Certain groups are harder on linens than others. For example, groups that bring children along are especially hard on linens (sometimes Penny suspects the little tykes snack on washcloths and bath towels!).

After reading Penny's memo, Scott called her and said he appreciated her concerns, but felt the hotel could survive on a $70,000 linen allowance. "Maybe when we're putting the budget together next year we'll take another look and beef up the budget line for linens."

Penny had heard "maybe next year" so often regarding linens that she didn't get angry about it anymore. She just said OK and quietly hoped the hotel could squeak through one more year without linen becoming a major problem.

The hotel purchased linens at the beginning of each quarter, and Penny made her regular linen purchase in January. Month after month this year, business was even better than expected; by July, Penny discovered that, to maintain linen par levels, she would have to spend money earmarked for both third and fourth quarters to get enough washcloths, bath towels, sheets, and so on. She spent the money and crossed her fingers; maybe business would slow down in the fourth quarter. As a precaution, however, she sent a memo to Scott explaining that she had just spent the last dollar earmarked for linens that year, and it was only July—a linen shortage was likely. Scott sent an e-mail message to the general manager, suggesting that guestroom linen par levels be reduced from four bath towels to three, and from three washcloths to two. The general manager approved the suggestion and Scott passed the word to Penny.

The hotel experienced record guestroom sales in August, September, and October. Occupancy was 15 percent over projected budget levels. Penny knew it was only a question of time before something had to give.

At the end of October, the marketing department announced some major last-minute sales; it had just booked a big church group, two college hockey teams, and a beautician convention for November. Considering the groups already booked, this meant all occupancy records for November would be broken.

By mid-November, the housekeeping department resembled a war zone. Every day was more hectic than the one before. Scheduling room attendants was a nightmare, and everyone in the laundry room was working overtime. Penny couldn't walk anywhere in the hotel without being accosted by angry guests wanting more towels or frustrated room attendants wanting more linens. The volume of guest comment cards skyrocketed as guests competed to see how colorfully they could gripe about the linen shortage. Front desk phones never stopped ringing, and the hotel staff never stopped scurrying, rushing stacks of towels still hot from the dryers to whichever room attendant complained the loudest. Each morning Penny anxiously scanned the occupancy projections for December, silently praying that at least one group—the Eastern Region Cosmetics Association or the American Academy of Podiatrists or, better yet, the National Family Council—would cancel its meeting. But day after day, the news was "terrible"; no one canceled, and December's business still looked great.

By Thanksgiving, guest complaints got so bad that the general manager called a meeting of the hotel's senior staff. "What's going on here?" he fumed. "Business has never been better, yet we seem to be falling apart. If I hear one more person whine about bath towels, I'll scream. Does anyone have any ideas about how we can get out of this mess?"

Discussion Questions

1. Do you think the hotel really saved $20,000 by reducing the linen budget line? Why or why not?

2. What short-term solutions can Penny suggest? What long-term solutions?

Case Study

Airing the Dirty Laundry

Rose, the hotel's controller, shook her head as she reviewed the amount of linen loss at her hotel, which had been increasing monthly. Ian O'Toole, the general manager, had asked Rose to respond to these losses. Anita, the executive housekeeper, told Rose she's aware of the problems, but she and Adrian, the laundry manager, have not been able to get Chef Franz or Shari, the dining room manager, to listen to the laundry's concerns.

The property where Rose worked previously had a linen committee to help resolve linen problems. Rose decided to call Mr. O'Toole and convince him to convene a linen committee including the laundry manager, the controller, the chef, the executive housekeeper, the banquet captain, and the food and beverage manager.

It took Rose very little effort to convince the general manager that a linen committee was a good idea—she merely showed him the rising linen costs and offered the possibility that such a committee could bring costs down.

The linen committee's first meeting was held a month before the annual budget meetings. Mr. O'Toole opened the meeting: "As you all know, linen is one of the major line items in our budget, one that is constantly growing. It is my hope that, by working together, we can find ways to bring these costs down."

"I'm not sure why I'm here," Shari said. "My people are much too busy serving guests to worry about whether the napkins are getting too dirty."

"Or even to make sure the napkins get down to the laundry," Adrian muttered.

"It is my hope," the general manager said in a louder voice, "that we will work *together*, because we all have linen abuse in our areas and can all contribute to lowering our linen expenses. I'd like Rose to begin by explaining some of the problems that contribute to our large linen loss."

"Glad to," Rose said, taking the floor. She began ticking off on her fingers sources of what she described as linen abuse:

1. Room attendants used washcloths as rags.

2. Laundry workers ran carts over dirty linen on concrete floors.

3. Laundry workers used too many chemicals, too much heat, or too much ironing on linen.

4. Dining room employees and public space cleaners used linen napkins to clean out ashtrays.

5. Banquet employees wrapped ashtrays, silverware, or broken glassware in linens.

6. Cutlery used food and beverage napkins as pot holders and rags.

7. Banquet servers wrapped all the linen in tablecloths and then dragged the bundles down the service hallways, leaving the linen torn and permanently concrete stained.

8. The chef sent one of his cooks to wash grease rags after hours; the cook put the rags in the dryer, igniting a small fire.

9. Dining room staff members packed their linen in plastic bags and dumped the bags outside the laundry rather than using laundry carts. Several times, the bags of linen were found in the outside trash bin.

"Hold on," Chef Franz interrupted. "My cooks use the linen because they don't have enough rags. If the housekeeping department wouldn't hoard all the reject linen, we'd have enough rags. Surely, you don't expect my cooks to burn themselves just because there are no rags handy?"

"And again, my wait staff is much too busy serving guests to spend time carting linens back and forth to laundry," Shari said.

"Things would be much better if they would put the linens in carts instead of in garbage bags," Adrian protested. "We make sure you have two carts daily for linens. If you could just get your employees to throw the linen into the carts instead of into the garbage, it would save us a lot of linen."

"Shari, it shouldn't be that hard to get your wait staff to use carts. It is completely unacceptable to have bags of linen thrown out. However, Chef Franz is right," Mr. O'Toole said. "The cooks can't risk injuring themselves, but using the table linen for rags is an inappropriate, expensive way to go."

"*Very* expensive," said Rose. "Let me show you just *how* expensive." Rose passed out a spreadsheet and graph that clearly demonstrated how much linen abuse was costing the hotel. She also displayed an expensive banquet tablecloth with an oil stain on it and pictures of linens and trash in the same laundry cart. The committee grew silent.

Finally, Chef Franz huffed, "This is all well and good, but do you want me to serve those 1,000-person banquets, or do you want me to police linen use?"

Discussion Question

1. List several ways to reduce the linen abuses listed by the controller. Be sure to consider the labor concerns raised by Shari and Chef Franz.

The following industry experts helped generate and develop these cases: Gail Edwards, CHHE, St. Louis, Missouri; Mary Friedman, Edina, Minnesota; and Aleta Nitschke, CHA, founder of *The Rooms Chronicle®*, Garfield, Minnesota.

Task Breakdowns: Laundry

The procedures presented in this section are for illustrative purposes only and should not be construed as recommendations or standards. While these procedures are typical, readers should keep in mind that each property has its own procedures, equipment specifications, and policies regarding protective gear which are designed to fit individual needs.

Sort Linens and Uniforms

Materials needed: *Heavy latex utility gloves and laundry carts for soiled linens and uniforms.*

STEPS	HOW-TO'S
1 Follow safety precautions when sorting laundry.	❑ Wear heavy latex utility gloves. ❑ Be careful to avoid cuts from broken glass in table linens. ❑ Do not handle linens or uniforms soiled with bodily fluids. Notify your supervisor.
2. Look for and remove items from soiled laundry as you sort it.	❑ Remove pens, pencils, corkscrews, change, paper, etc. from uniform pockets. ❑ Remove employee name tags, employee service pins, promotional buttons, etc. that are attached to the garments. ❑ Remove food scraps, silverware, glasses, china, wine corks, etc. from table linens before washing.
3. Sort linens according to the degree of soiling.	❑ Separate lightly soiled, moderately soiled, and heavily soiled linens. Heavily soiled linens require heavier-duty wash formulas and longer wash times than moderately or lightly soiled items.
4. Sort linens according to use and fabric type.	❑ Sort linens into the following groups: • Sheets • Pillowcases • Bath towels • Hand towels • Beach/pool towels • Washcloths • Bath mats • Shower curtains and liners • Blankets and mattress pads • White tablecloths • White linen napkins • Pastel tablecloths • Pastel linen napkins • Dark tablecloths (sorted by color) • Dark napkins (sorted by color)

Sort Linens and Uniforms (continued)

STEPS	HOW-TO'S
	• Housekeeping cleaning cloths • Buffer pads (wash alone, don't dry) • Kitchen cleaning cloths ❏ Separate cleaning cloths from guest linens. ❏ Separate greasy cloths, which are fire hazards, from other cleaning cloths. ❏ Separate table linens from other linens. ❏ Separate red and burgundy linens from other items.
5. Sort uniforms according to department.	❏ Put the same color shirts together, the same color skirts together, the same color pants together, etc.
6. Place sorted laundry in the correct laundry carts.	

Load, Use, and Unload Washers

Materials needed: Laundry scales, a laundry production log, washers, nylon mesh bags, laundry chemicals, and laundry carts.

STEPS	HOW-TO'S
1 Prepare loads of laundry.	❑ The correct weight of each load varies among properties. Some lodging properties determine load size by counting out a specific number of items or use scales to weigh the soiled items. ❑ Do not put too many or too few items in a load. Overloaded washers will not get linens clean. Partially full washers waste water and chemicals.
2. Organize your work.	❑ Follow the laundry production log to determine the order in which to wash loads. The laundry production log is used to track productivity. You may need to record the loads you wash on the log. ❑ Wash heavily soiled linens first so that stains will not set and ruin the items. ❑ Stagger the starting times of washers at least two to five minutes apart. Staggering start times: • Aids in a smooth and constant work flow • Does not use up the water supply • Does not cause electrical overloads • Prevents flooding and clogged drains from machines draining at the same time ❑ Schedule loads to meet the production demands of other departments. ❑ Keep enough flatwork, such as tablecloths and sheets, washed to allow continuous operation of the ironer. ❑ Wash towels when there is enough flatwork on hand to keep the ironer busy.

Load, Use, and Unload Washers *(continued)*

STEPS	HOW-TO'S
3. Be aware of special considerations.	❑ Wash new colored linens separately the first few times to avoid dyeing other fabrics.
	❑ Wash dark-colored fabrics at lower temperatures to prevent fading. Uniforms will often have more than one color of fabric within a single garment and will require a cold-water wash to prevent fading of darker colors onto lighter colors.
	❑ Do not wash colors with chlorine bleach. Use only approved chemicals in washers.
	❑ Place delicate items, items with decorative buttons, and items with strings (such as aprons) in nylon mesh bags to prevent damage or tangling.
4. Load washers.	❑ Fill washers from front to back and from side to side. Filling washers this way will allow room for the laundry to fall into the wash solution.
	❑ Leave a three- to four-inch gap at the top of the washer.
	❑ Only put one load in each washer; never over- or underload washers.
5. Calculate wash formulas.	❑ Follow your supervisor's instructions or the instructions on the tag in each type of garment. The type of soil and fabric will determine the wash formula.
	❑ Find out the following: • *Time*—How much time will be needed to wash the laundry you have loaded? • *Temperature*—What temperature should the water be in order to get the items clean? • *Agitation*—How much agitation is needed to loosen the soil in these fabrics?

(continued)

Load, Use, and Unload Washers *(continued)*

STEPS	HOW-TO'S
	• *Chemicals*—What chemicals will do the best job on the particular soil and fabric types?
	❑ Wash formulas for different types of loads vary among properties.
	❑ Certain washers may be set aside for certain fabrics. If so, find out which washers to use for each fabric type and soil condition.
	❑ Do not wash colors with chlorine bleach. Use only approved chemicals in washers.
6. Set the controls on the machine according to fabric type.	❑ The steps to set controls for each fabric type vary among properties.
	❑ Do not turn on the washers and leave them running unattended.
7. Unload washers.	❑ Remove wet laundry promptly from washers to prevent wrinkles. If laundry is very wet at the end of the cycle, more extraction time may be needed. Otherwise, extra drying time will be needed, which is more costly than extraction.
	❑ Don't wrestle with heavy laundry. Remove a few pieces at a time from the top of the load.
	❑ Shake out the linens as you remove them to prevent twisting and wrinkling.
	❑ Place wet linens in carts for clean laundry until you place the linens in the dryers. If empty dryers are nearby, put the wet laundry directly in the dryers.

Load, Use, and Unload Dryers

Materials needed: *Broom, small plastic bag, dryers, laundry scales, laundry carts, hangers, and nylon mesh bags.*

STEPS	HOW-TO'S
1. Check dryers for correct temperatures.	❑ Follow posted dryer times or temperatures, or ask your supervisor for correct times and temperatures for different items.
2. Clean lint from filters at least twice a day to prevent fires.	❑ Remove the panels in front of the filters. ❑ Use a broom to sweep the lint from the filters into a small plastic bag. ❑ Close the bag and throw it away. Close the panel. ❑ Clean lint filters each time you fill a dryer.
3. Load dryers.	❑ Follow your supervisor's or the equipment manufacturer's loading instructions. Loading dryers correctly prevents wasted energy. ❑ Load dryers by weight or piece count. Overloading increases the drying time and wrinkling. Underloading wastes energy. ❑ Keep the linens sorted according to fabric type as they were sorted for washing.
4. Set time, temperature, and cool-down time.	❑ Know the drying times and temperatures for each fabric. ❑ Always let pillowcases and sheets run through a cool-down cycle of three to five minutes to reduce wrinkles and save the permanent press features of the fabric. The cool-down cycle also will reduce the chance of burns. ❑ Run table linens through a three- to five-minute cool-down cycle in the dryer before folding.

(continued)

STEPS	**HOW-TO'S**

Load, Use, and Unload Dryers (continued)

STEPS	**HOW-TO'S**
5. Dry items.	❑ Dry uniforms with polyester fibers on medium heat to prevent damage to the fabric.
	❑ Dry delicate items, items with strings, and items with decorative buttons in nylon mesh bags to prevent damage and tangling.
	❑ Make sure drying is followed by a cool-down tumbling period to prevent the hot linens from being damaged or wrinkled by rapid cooling and handling.
6. Remove items from dryers.	❑ Avoid burns from hot dryer surfaces.
	❑ Hang uniforms as you remove them from the dryer, even if they will be ironed.
	❑ Avoid dropping clean linens on the floor. If you drop clean linens on the floor, put them with soiled linens to be rewashed.
	❑ Do not let dryers run after the laundry has closed.
	❑ Do not leave linens in the dryers overnight. Running dryers after closing time and leaving linens in dryers are serious fire hazards.

Chapter 9 Outline

Competencies

1. Identify procedures room attendants typically follow when reporting to work and preparing to clean guestrooms. (pp. 369–375)

2. Describe the procedures typically followed by room attendants when cleaning guestrooms. (pp. 375–391)

3. Explain the function of a guestroom inspection program. (pp. 391–394)

4. Distinguish routine guestroom cleaning from deep cleaning functions. (pp. 395–400)

5. Describe what hospitality properties are doing to provide allergen-free guestrooms. (pp. 400–401)

6. Identify typical procedures room attendants follow when providing turndown service for guests. (p. 402)

Guestroom Cleaning

No OTHER FEATURE OR SERVICE provided by a property will impress the guest more than a spotlessly clean and comfortable guestroom. The condition of the guestroom conveys a critical message to guests. It shows the care that the property puts into creating a clean, safe, and pleasant environment for its guests. This places a big responsibility on the housekeeping department. After all, the guestroom is the main product that a property sells. Housekeeping plays a greater role than any other department in ensuring that this product meets the standards that guests need and expect.

To maintain the standards that keep guests coming back, room attendants must follow a series of detailed procedures for guestroom cleaning. A systematic approach can save time and energy—and reduce frustration. In this respect, room cleaning procedures not only deliver quality to the guest, but ensure efficiency and satisfaction for the employee performing the task.

The sequence of room cleaning consists of preparatory steps, actual cleaning tasks, and a final check. Room inspections are also an integral part of the overall process of guestroom cleaning. In some properties, the responsibilities of room attendants extend to providing special services and amenities. Regardless of the range of services, a room attendant should recognize the value and logic behind the organization of cleaning activities. Adhering to a careful routine can save time and ensure a professional job.

Preparing to Clean

In most properties, the room attendant's workday begins in the **linen room**. The linen room is often considered the headquarters of the housekeeping department. It is here that the employee reports to work; receives room assignments, room status reports, and keys; and checks out at the end of his or her shift. Here, too, the room attendant prepares for the workday by assembling and organizing the supplies that are necessary for cleaning.

Assembling Supplies

Like most craft workers, a room attendant requires a special set of tools to do his or her job. For the professional room attendant, these tools come in the form of the various cleaning supplies and equipment, linens, room accessories, and **amenities** that are necessary for preparing a guest's room.

In a sense, the **room attendant's cart** is like a giant tool box stocked with everything necessary to do an effective job. Just as a carpenter would avoid going on-site

the Rooms CHRONICLE®

Ask Gail—Start of Day

Dear Gail:

Any tips to help avoid mass confusion in housekeeping in the morning when everyone is trying to sign in? What a mess with room attendants waiting for keys, grabbing rags, and fighting over spray bottles.

D.B., Boston, MA

Dear D.B.:

It's easy to start the day if you are prepared before the rush. Fill the bottles and restock carts or caddies in the evening so that a room attendant does not have to search for supplies.

Have assignment papers written and laid out on the desk with the necessary keys on top of each paper. Room attendants should form a line to be handled one at a time. The room attendant signs in (or punches in), signs the key control log, receives the keys and assignment, and moves on to another window or counter to pick up the supply caddy.

Smaller properties put the assignment sheet and keys in the caddy to simplify handing out equipment. Larger properties stagger the start times so that labor hours are not wasted by employees waiting to begin. For example, at an 800-room property, three groups can be started 15 minutes apart.

Source: Gail Edwards, CHHE, *The Rooms Chronicle®*, Volume 2, Number 4, p. 9. For subscription information, please call 866-READ-TRC.

with an inadequate supply of wood and nails, so would a room attendant avoid going to an assigned room with an inadequate supply of cleaning items.

A well-organized and well-stocked cart is key to efficiency. It enables the room attendant to avoid wasting time looking for a cleaning item or making trips back to the linen room for more supplies. The specific amounts of items loaded onto a cart will vary according to the types of rooms being cleaned, the amenities offered by the property, and, of course, the size of the cart itself. A room attendant's cart is generally spacious enough to carry all the supplies needed for a half-day's room assignments.

Stocking the Cart. Carts are typically stored in the linen room along with the housekeeping supplies. In large properties, supplies are often centralized in a particular area and issued to room attendants each morning. Most carts have three shelves—the lower two for linen and the top for supplies. It is just as important not to overstock a cart as it is not to understock. Overstocking increases the risk that some items will be damaged, soiled, or stolen in the course of cleaning. Items typically found on a room attendant's cart include the following:

- Clean sheets, pillowcases, and mattress pads
- Clean towels and washcloths
- Clean bath mats
- Toilet and facial tissue
- Fresh drinking glasses
- Soap bars

In most cases, all the cleaning supplies for the guestroom and bathroom are positioned in a **hand caddy** on top of the cart. This way, the room attendant does not have to bring the entire cart into the room in order to have easy access to supplies. Items conveniently stocked in the caddy may include:

- All-purpose cleaner
- Window and glass cleaner in a spray bottle
- Bowl brush
- Dusting solution
- Cloths and sponges
- Rubber gloves

A laundry bag for dirty linens is usually found at one end of the cart and a trash bag is at the other. A broom and vacuum are also positioned on either end of the cart for easy access. For safety and security reasons, personal items and room keys should not be stored on the cart.

Exhibit 1 illustrates one efficient stocking arrangement for a room attendant's cart. In all cases, carts should be stocked according to a property's specifications. Room attendants must also be sure to stock the proper eye, hand, and face protection. Each property should inform room attendants of its policies regarding the use of such personal protective equipment and for handling cleaning chemicals.

Alternative Carts. Some hotels now use an integrated transporting and storing system as an alternative to the traditional room attendant cart. The equipment is modular in design and consists of various containers, caddies, and shelves that can be easily removed and arranged within a larger service cart. These components are loaded to convenient levels to allow for the efficient movement of linens and supplies when servicing guestrooms. Like a boxcar, a separate, detachable component accompanies the main unit and is used to catch trash and soiled linen.

These carts are furniture-grade in appearance and can be secured with a locking tambour door. Given these unobtrusive features, some properties preload carts and deliver them directly to guestroom floors for pickup by the room attendants. Among other advantages, these carts are lightweight and easy to clean.[1]

Room Assignments

After assembling supplies, the room attendant is ready to begin cleaning guestrooms. The order in which he or she cleans rooms will be determined by the room status report.

Exhibit 1   Sample Stocking Arrangement for Room Attendant's Cart

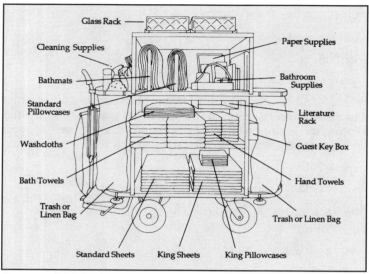

Glass Rack

Cleaning Supplies

Paper Supplies

Bathmats

Bathroom Supplies

Standard Pillowcases

Literature Rack

Washcloths

Guest Key Box

Bath Towels

Hand Towels

Trash or Linen Bag

Trash or Linen Bag

Standard Sheets   King Sheets   King Pillowcases

Courtesy of Holiday Inn Worldwide

The **room status report** (sometimes called the housekeeping report) provides information on the occupancy or condition of the property's rooms on a daily basis. It is generated through two-way communications between the front office and the housekeeping department. For example, when a guest checks out, the front desk notifies housekeeping by phone or through a computer system. In turn, once a room is clean and back in order, the flow of information is reversed so the front office will know the room is again ready for sale.

The room status report is generally easy to read and uses simple codes to indicate room status. There are several categories of room status, but, for the most part, a room attendant's cleaning schedule will be determined by these three:

Check-out: A room from which the guest has already checked out
Stayover: A room in which the guest is scheduled to stay again
Due out: A room from which a guest is due to check out later that day

Another designation commonly used is early makeup. This refers to rooms for which a guest has reserved an early check-in time or to a request for a room to be cleaned as soon as possible. Abbreviations used to indicate these categories on the room status report will vary from property to property.

Room assignments are typically printed from the rooms module of the property management system. Room assignments are generally listed according to room number and room status on a standardized form. The number of rooms assigned to a room attendant is based upon the property's work standards for specific types of rooms and cleaning tasks. The room attendant uses the assignment sheet to prioritize the workday and to report the condition of each assigned room

Exhibit 2   Sample Room Assignment Sheet

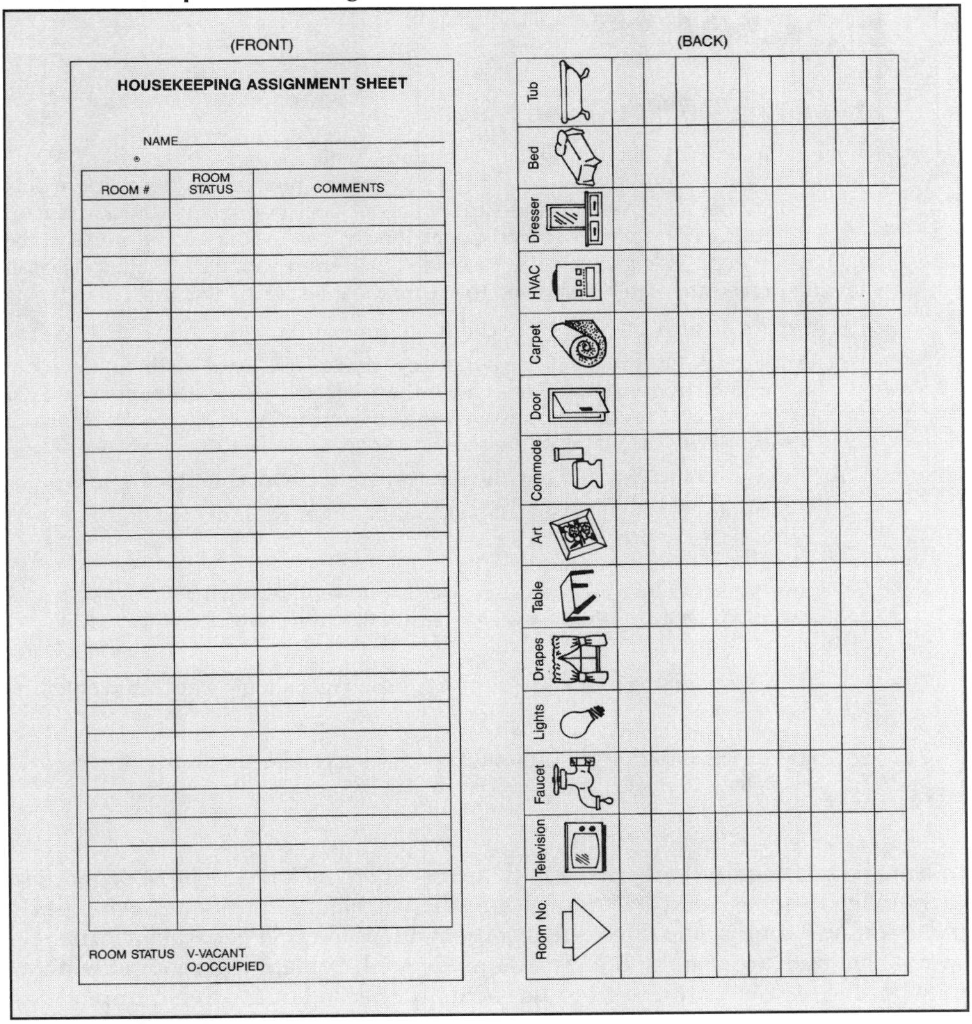

(FRONT)

HOUSEKEEPING ASSIGNMENT SHEET

NAME_____

ROOM #	ROOM STATUS	COMMENTS

ROOM STATUS   V-VACANT
              O-OCCUPIED

(BACK)

Tub
Bed
Dresser
HVAC
Carpet
Door
Commode
Art
Table
Drapes
Lights
Faucet
Television
Room No.

Courtesy of Holiday Inn Worldwide

at the end of the shift. In the sample form illustrated in Exhibit 2, room attendants are provided space to make written comments on each room and to indicate room items needing repair. Some properties have replaced room assignment sheets with handheld devices that enable the room attendant to access the hotel's property management system.

After reviewing the assignment sheet, a room attendant will have a sense of where he or she should begin cleaning. For the most part, the order in which rooms are cleaned is the order that best serves guests. Check-outs are usually done first so the front office can sell the rooms as guests arrive. The exceptions to this

Honoring Do Not Disturb Signs

Imagine a Do Not Disturb (DND) card upon which a guest has written "THIS MEANS YOU!" Finding this at one hotel prompted a meeting with a quick review about just what a Do Not Disturb card means. It does not mean "Knock, please," or "Hide the sign on your cart and knock loudly," or "Make a lot of noise in the hall by my door." It *does* mean, "Please don't bother me, come back later." The following procedures can be followed to assure the guest's privacy:

1. Do not disturb a DND before check-out time.
2. After check-out time, notify a supervisor that a DND card is still on the room door. The supervisor will telephone the room to inquire if the guest would like service. If there is no answer, the supervisor will check with the front desk to verify the status of the room.
3. If the guest has checked out, the room attendant may enter the room.
4. If the guest is staying over, a note should be slipped under the door:

Dear Guest:

To honor your Do Not Disturb sign, we did not enter your room today. If you require fresh towels or other services, please call extension xxx.

Thank you.

5. If the status of the room is in question, a manager should knock and enter the room.

Source: Mary Friedman, *The Rooms Chronicle®*, Volume 2, Number 3, p. 4. For subscription information, please call 866-READ-TRC.

---

rule are rooms needing early makeup or are occupied by VIPs. In most properties, early-makeup rooms and VIP rooms are cleaned before check-outs. After early makeups, VIP rooms, and check-outs, a room attendant will generally clean stay-overs. Due outs are usually the last rooms cleaned. Sometimes, room attendants may be able to wait until the guest has actually checked out to avoid duplication of efforts.

In all cases, the room attendant should avoid disturbing the guest. A Do Not Disturb sign clearly indicates that the room attendant should check back on the room later in the shift. Other rooms that room attendants must delay servicing include rooms that the guest has double-locked from the inside. Many properties have room attendants leave a card on the door which indicates that attempts at service have been made. These cards may also offer fresh towels or service later in the evening. Usually, a room attendant will report such rooms to the housekeeping manager on duty if he or she is unable to service the room by 2:00 or 3:00 P.M.

When a guest refuses service, a floor supervisor or other management person should call to arrange a convenient time for cleaning. Such calls are also made to check that the guest is not experiencing a situation that requires intervention, such

Exhibit 3   Sample Room Attendant Task List

1. Use your room assignment sheet.
2. Get guest amenities for assigned rooms.
3. Get cleaning supplies for assigned rooms.
4. Keep your cart and work areas organized.
5. Enter the guestroom.
6. Prepare the guestroom for cleaning.
7. Begin to clean the bathroom.
8. Clean the tub and shower area.
9. Clean the toilet.
10. Clean the sink and vanity.
11. Clean the bathroom floor.
12. Finish cleaning the bathroom.
13. Clean the guestroom closet.
14. Make the bed.
15. Dust the guestroom.
16. Replenish supplies and amenities.
17. Clean windows, tracks, and sills.
18. Put finishing touches on the guestroom.
19. Vacuum the guestroom and report room status.
20. Exit the guestroom.
21. Correct cleaning problems found during inspection.
22. Complete end-of-shift duties.
23. Rotate and flip mattresses.
24. Set up or remove special guest service equipment.
25. Clean multi-room guest suites.
26. Provide evening turndown service.

The order of tasks may vary among properties.

as a serious illness or accident. Upon contacting the guest, the floor supervisor or manager should also ask the guest if he or she would like fresh towels and amenities. In many hotels, the guest is asked to initial the supervisor's report to indicate that he or she refused service. Under no circumstances should a room remain unserviced for more than two days without the approval of the general manager.

Cleaning the Guestroom

Room attendants must follow a system to consistently produce spotlessly clean guestrooms. A systematic plan saves time and can prevent the room attendant from overlooking a cleaning task—or even from cleaning an area twice.

To be most effective, guestroom cleaning should follow a logical progression from actually entering the guestroom to the final check and departure. Exhibit 3 shows a list of all tasks room attendants might perform at a property from the time they arrive until the time they leave. The easiest and most direct manner to explain these guestroom cleaning tasks is from the perspective of the room attendant.

Entering the Guestroom

Guestroom cleaning begins the moment the room attendant approaches the guest-room door. It is important to follow certain procedures when entering the guestroom that show respect for the guest's privacy.

When approaching a guestroom, first observe whether the guest has placed a Do Not Disturb sign on the knob. Also, be sure to check that the door is not double-locked from the inside. If either condition exists, respect the guest's wishes and return later to clean the room. If this is not the case, knock on the door and announce "Housekeeping." Never use a key to knock since it can damage the surface of the door. If a guest answers, introduce yourself and ask what time would be convenient to clean the room. Note that time on your status sheet or schedule. If no answer is heard, wait a moment, knock again, and repeat "Housekeeping." If there is still no answer, open the door slightly and repeat "Housekeeping." If the guest does not respond after this third announcement, you can be fairly certain that the room is empty and can begin to enter.

However, just because a guest doesn't answer doesn't always guarantee that a guest is not in the room. Sometimes the guest may be sleeping or in the bathroom. If this is the case, you should leave quietly and close the door. Should the guest be awake, excuse yourself, explain that you can come back later, discreetly close the door, and proceed to the next room.

In many properties, a room attendant may use a handheld device or room telephone to interface with the hotel's property management system. By entering an employee identification code, room number (not always necessary), and a housekeeping status code number, a room attendant may update a guestroom's current status. The system may automatically log the time of the call.

When you do finally enter, position your cart in front of the open door with the open section facing the room. Doing so serves three purposes: it gives you easy access to your supplies, blocks the entrance to intruders, and, in the case of stay-overs, alerts returning guests of your presence. If the guest does return while you are cleaning, offer to finish your work later. Also, make sure that it is, in fact, the guest's room, by checking his or her room key. This is done for security purposes to prevent unauthorized persons from entering the room.

Many hotels now require that room attendants close the guestroom door while inside servicing the room and to place a doorknob hangtag or magnet on the door advising that the housekeeper is inside the room. This procedure has been implemented to provide a more secure environment for room attendants who often work alone and to keep outsiders from seeing any guest possessions that may remain in a stayover room.

Beginning Tasks

Most room attendants begin their system of cleaning by airing out and tidying up the guestroom. After entering the room, turn on all the lights. This makes the room more cheerful, helps you see what you are doing, and allows you to check for light bulbs that need to be replaced. Draw back the draperies and check the cords and hooks for any damage. Open the windows so the room can air out while you are cleaning. Check the air conditioning and heater to make sure they are working

Open or Close the Door during Guestroom Cleaning?

Old Habits Are Hard to Break

Traditionally, hotels have trained room attendants to place the housekeeping cart as close to the open guestroom door as possible and keep the door open while cleaning a room. The industry thinking for years has been that keeping the door open during cleaning improves the safety of both the room attendant and the guest's personal belongings. The industry has insisted that with the guestroom door open, the cries of a room attendant could easily be heard if he or she were attacked. The industry has also whispered for years that keeping the door open during cleaning would reduce the likelihood of staff pilfering guest belongings.

Like other age-old traditions in the hotel industry, it may be time to rethink the policy of open-door guestroom cleaning.

Protecting Guest Belongings

A hotel that has a policy of cleaning rooms with the doors open usually includes the following instructions in training programs:

- The room attendant should request to see the guestroom key of any individual entering the room while he or she is cleaning.
- The room attendant should then verify that the key unlocks the guestroom door.
- The room attendant may also request the individual's name to verify with the front desk that the individual is assigned to the room.

These things should happen, but unfortunately, sometimes don't. The hotel teaches staff during customer service training that the customer is always right. This training causes some staff members to avoid confronting the guest to verify his or her right to be in the room. Also, employees in some hotels are not comfortable communicating with guests in English. The result in either case is that individuals can convince the room attendant to allow them to take articles from the room or to leave the room to finish cleaning it later.

Protecting Room Attendants

Pulling the cart across the entry to the guestroom does not adequately protect the room attendant. He or she might be scrubbing a tub with water running and the bathroom door nearly closed, or vacuuming across the room with her or his back to the door. There are many situations during which a room attendant would not notice that someone had moved the cart to enter the room. In fact, the intruder could enter, close the door, and abuse the room attendant before anyone would notice the closed door.

Close the Door

To prevent this type of incident and increase the security of the room attendants, many companies have recommended that room attendants close doors when they clean. With this policy, anyone entering the room must have a valid guestroom key, thus eliminating the need for the room attendant to question or confront the

(continued)

the Rooms CHRONICLE®

(continued)

guest. When cleaning the room with the door closed, the room attendant is actually better protected since the room is not open to people walking down the corridor who might enter the room with ill intentions.

Does closing the door mean that a room attendant might be locked in with a guest who intends to harm him or her? Hotels that have implemented this policy teach room attendants to prop the guestroom door open if the guest is in the room when servicing starts or if the guest enters during servicing. By leaving the door open when the guest is present, the room attendant avoids the awkwardness and potential danger of being in the closed room with the guest.

Changes to age-old, established practices are hard to make. Requiring room attendants to keep the guestroom door open, however, will pay benefits to the hotel industry by giving better protection to the guests, their belongings, and the housekeeping staff.

Source: Wendell H. Couch, *The Rooms Chronicle®*, Volume 3, Number 3, p. 12. For subscription information, please call 866-READ-TRC.

properly and are set according to property standards. Some properties require that the temperature be left where the guests set it in a stayover room.

Next, take a good look at the condition of the room. Make note of any damaged or missing items such as linens or wastebaskets. If anything of value is gone or if something needs repair, notify your supervisor.

Remove or replace dirty ashtrays (if it is a smoking room) and glasses. Always make sure that cigarettes are fully extinguished before dumping them in the appropriate container. As you replace the ashtrays, be sure to replenish matches. Collect any service trays, dishes, bottles, or cans that might be scattered around the room. Follow your property's procedures for taking care of these items properly. Some properties have room attendants set these items neatly in the hallway and call room service for pickup. Empty the trash and replace any wastebasket liners. In stayover rooms, straighten any newspapers and magazines. Never throw out anything in a stayover room unless it is in the wastebasket. In rooms where the guest has checked out, visually scan the room and check the dresser drawers for personal items that may have been left behind. Report these items to your supervisor, or hand them in to the lost and found, depending on the hotel's policy.

Making the Bed

Making the bed is the next task completed in guestroom cleaning. It is important to start cleaning here—especially in stayover rooms. If the guest returns while the room is being cleaned, the freshly made bed will give the room a neat appearance—even if other areas have not been touched. In check-out rooms, some properties recommend stripping the bed shortly after entering and remaking it near the end of the cleaning. This will allow the bed to air out.

the Rooms
CHRONICLE®

To Increase Efficiency, Limit Trips to the Cart

The best room attendants have developed a system to clean their rooms. Whether or not they have been formally trained, veteran cleaners work out a routine which they use in each room.

One of the secrets of being an excellent executive housekeeper is to help every room attendant learn a system which will save both steps and time.

Although there are disputes about the correct order of cleaning, the most important factor is to limit the number of trips to the cart. This is a list which has been successful in many hotels. Note that there are only four trips to the cart.

1 Set the vacuum cleaner inside the door. Enter the room carrying cleaning supplies. Circle around the room turning on lights, collecting trash, opening drawers and drapes, and checking supplies. Return to the cart to empty the trash. Set empty wastebaskets near the bathroom door to be washed.

2. Carry in replacement supplies. Strip the bed(s), collect dirty linen from the bathroom, and return to the cart with all dirty linen.

3. Carry in the clean linen. Clean the bathroom and place clean terries. Make the beds. Move around the room in a circular pattern to dust, clean mirrors, and straighten supplies. Return the cleaning supplies to the cart.

4. Carry in supplies that may have been forgotten on earlier trips. Vacuum beginning at the farthest point from the entry door. Close the drapes, set the HVAC, and turn out the lights while vacuuming back toward the cart. Give the room one last look. Close and lock the door. Write up the room status and any maintenance problems.

Suites, kitchenettes, and other special situations require more creativity to streamline the process, but the goal should always be to save steps. Buy caddies and other tools which will make it easy to move cleaning supplies and amenities from the cart to the room. Choose uniforms or aprons that have big, usable pockets. Organize the room's paper supplies into a notebook which the cleaner can simply replace. Notebooks can be refilled after hours in the housekeeping office by other employees.

The best way to help room attendants understand wasted steps is to have them pretend that they have wet paint on the bottoms of their shoes. How many footsteps would be on the floor after they finished a room? They need enough to do the job, but not make too many.

Source: Gail Edwards, CHHE, *The Rooms Chronicle®*, Volume 2, Number 4, p. 5.
For subscription information, please call 866-READ-TRC.

To begin, the room attendant should remove any guest personal items from the bed and place them aside. Then remove any bedding items that will not be replaced (for instance, pillows or bedspread) and put them on a chair to keep them clean and free from dust and dirt. If any of these items are dirty—or have any holes or tears—they must be replaced. All dirty linen should be stripped.

Exhibit 4   Step-by-Step Approach to Mitering

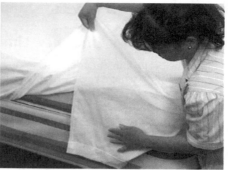

Step 1   Begin with the sheet hanging loosely over the corner. Tuck in the sheet along the foot of the bed, right up to the corner.

Step 2   Take the loose end of the sheet, about one foot from the corner, and pull it straight out, forming a flap.

Step 3   Pull up the flap so it is flat and wrinkle-free.

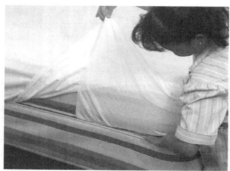

Step 4   Tuck in the free part at the corner, making sure it is snug.

Step 5   Pull the flap out toward you and down over the side of the bed.

Step 6   Tuck in the flap and make sure the corner is smooth and snug.

The room attendant should then check the mattress pad and the mattress and notify a supervisor if the mattress shows any stains, burns, or damage. If the mattress pad needs changing, the old pad should be removed with a fresh one placed on the bed so it unfolds right-side up. The pad should be spread evenly over the center of the bed and with wrinkles smoothed.

The most efficient way of making a bed is to completely finish one side before beginning on the next. This system saves time walking back and forth around the bed. A room attendant would begin by placing the bottom sheet on the mattress and mitering that sheet in the upper-left-hand corner of the bed. **Mitering** is a simple way to make a smooth, neat, professional corner. A step-by-step method for mitering a corner is illustrated in Exhibit 4. Next, the room attendant would move to the foot of the bed—still on the left-hand side—and miter that corner of the sheet. Many properties use fitted sheets rather than flat sheets for the bottom. A fitted sheet is easy for room attendants to place as it does not require mitering.

The next step in bedmaking may be different from one property to another depending upon the hotel's standards. Traditionally, every hotel bed contained two sheets, a blanket, and a bedspread. However, it is now common for hotels to vary from this tradition. The bed might contain only a bottom sheet and a comforter (encased in a duvet cover), or perhaps a bottom and top sheet with the comforter/duvet cover. In some cases, hotels place a bottom sheet, a top sheet, a comforter or blanket, and then a third sheet on top of the comforter. Using a third sheet to protect the comforter/blanket is known as "triple-sheeting."

To make up the traditional bed, the room attendant places a fresh top sheet (wrong-side up) on the bottom sheet. Then, the blanket is added on top of the sheet. At the head of the bed, the top sheet is turned back over the blanket about six inches. The linens should be smoothed so the surface appears even and without wrinkles. The top sheet and blanket should be mitered at the bottom, left-hand corner of the bed. (Many executive housekeepers instruct room attendants to also tuck the linens in along the side of the bed.) Then, working clockwise, the room attendant walks to the other side of the bed, miters the bottom sheet at the right foot of the bed, followed by the top sheet and blanket. Moving down the right-hand side of the bed the employee miters the bottom sheet in the top-right corner and folds the top sheet over the blanket so it is even with the left-hand side. Finally, the blanket and top sheet are neatly tucked in along the sides and at the foot of the bed.

For this traditional bed, the bedspread is centered evenly, and folded down from the head of the bed, leaving enough room to cover the pillows. The pillows are fluffed and pillowcases added. For sanitary reasons, employees should never hold the pillow under their chins or with their teeth. Many executive housekeepers instruct their staff to tuck the loose ends of the pillowcase into the pillow for a neat appearance. The employee should position the pillows at the head of the bed with the tucked ends facing the center and the tucked flaps facing down on the underside. The bedspread should be pulled over the pillows and tucked under. If hotels offer extra pillows for each bed, they stand them against the headboard on top of the bedspread rather than under.

When a hotel's standards vary from the traditional style by substituting comforters for bedspreads and blankets, employees are trained to make the bed with triple sheeting or duvet covers. Special care should be devoted to instruct employees in the most efficient ways to remove and install duvet covers.

It is equally important to teach the details of triple sheeting as the inclusion of a third sheet can pose some unique challenges. The triple-sheeting process has slowed some room attendants by five to ten minutes per room. When hotels fail to change the allotted time maximum for cleaning rooms, room attendants can end up feeling frustrated and have difficulty adjusting to the new performance standards. Also, with a triple-sheet system, it is unlikely a room attendant will be able to use the one-sided bed making system. See Exhibit 5 for a step-by-step guide to making a double-sheeted and triple-sheeted bed. One solution is to

Exhibit 5   Steps to Making a Bed

Traditional steps to making a double-sheeted bed:
1. The fitted or a flat sheet goes on first.
2. A flat sheet goes on next.
3. The blanket goes on third.
4. The comforter is placed on top and pulled down halfway.
5. The pillows are placed on the bed.
6. The comforter is pulled over the pillows.

However, when the bed needs to be triple-sheeted, this adds a few more steps:
1. The fitted or a flat sheet goes on first.
2. A flat sheet goes on next.
3. The blanket goes on third.
4. Another flat sheet goes over the blanket.
5. The comforter is placed on top and pulled down halfway.

From here, there are two approaches one can take:
6. The pillows are placed on the bed.
7. The comforter is pulled over the pillows

OR

6. Fold back one corner of the middle sheet, blanket, and top sheet 12 to 15 inches diagonally fro the top of the bed.
7. Hold the bottom corner of the diagonal fold. Fold it up so that it is parallel to the edge of the bed.
8. Tuck the ends neatly under the diagonal fold.
9. Tuck the sheets and blanket under the mattress.
10. Straighten the end of the fold on the other side of the bed.
11. Pull the turned down bedspread (with liner exposed) up to the point that the turned down edge of the bedspread meets the diagonal fold.
12. Fold a piece of the bedspread back up toward the pillow to hide the lining.
13. Stand the pillows up, leaning them against the headboard across the bed.

The latter method, while more time consuming and labor intensive, better presents the extra effort taken to triple-sheet the bed for the guests' extra comfort and cleanliness.

Source: Elizabeth Kozlowski, *The Rooms Chronicle*®, Volume 13, Number 2, p. 3.
For subscription information, please call 866-READ-TRC.

use team cleaning so everyone can help each other get the rooms done faster.

Despite the challenges posed, triple-sheeting or the use of duvet covers is a more sanitary way of preparing the room for the guest. It is very difficult for any hotel to wash all of the guestroom blankets on a regular basis. Many hotels wash their blankets only quarterly. With the triple-sheet standard to provide somewhat of an extra separation between the

the Rooms
CHRONICLE®

Pillow Menu: Great Amenity, Low Cost

As if the luxurious foam-core, down-surrounded pillows on the bed are not enough, more pampering is just a phone call away. At the Benjamin, a luxury boutique-style hotel in Manhattan, guests are provided with a complete menu of pillow options. The Sound Sleep Pillow Menu is printed on a small laminated card placed on the bedside stand at turndown each evening. By dialing the noted extension, guests can order any of the following pillow types, provided at no charge:

- **Down.** Classic favorite with medium firmness. Available in standard and king sizes.
- **Upper Body.** Candy cane-shaped pillow for head and upper back support.
- **Buckwheat.** Buckwheat hulls conform to the head and neck for maximum support and stress reduction.
- **Water-Filled.** Positions head and neck naturally for instant relief from headaches and neck pain. Vinyl cushion fills with warm or cold water, adjusting firmness and support.
- **Jelly Neckroll.** Therapeutic moldable gel core conforms to the head and neck. Removable core can be heated or chilled.
- **Satin Beauty.** Soft foam designed to reduce pressure on facial bones. Silky satin cover helps maintain hairstyles overnight.
- **Hypo-Allergenic.** Relieves sneezing, morning headaches, sinus congestion and other symptoms associated with allergies to feathers, fibers, and dust.
- **Snore-No-More.** Reduces snoring to promote a deeper, more restful sleep by elevating the chin from the chest, keeping the airway open.
- **5-foot Body Cushion.** Aligns the spine for better sleeping posture while reducing neck, back, and joint pain. Perfect for pregnancy or recovering from surgery.
- **Swedish Memory.** Unique self-molding characteristics help to relieve pressure. Reacts to body temperature keeping sleepers cool in the summer and warm in the winter.
- **Magnetic Therapy.** Reduces swelling and discomfort, relieves insomnia and fatigue, soothes tense muscles and aching joints and improves skin tone by stimulating circulation.

The Benjamin, located on a busy Manhattan street and not far from a fire station, really endeavors to help their guests' sleep well. In addition to a complete selection of pillows, guests may request a white noise machine from the Sound Sleep Pillow menu as well as other bedtime amenities.

Hotel Manager John Moser reports an excellent guest response to the pillow menu. "Approximately 30 percent of our guests actually request one of our specialty pillows," he says.

When asked about the costs of maintaining such a program, he replied, "The costs, other than the original purchase and replacement expense, are minimal. We had storage space available and we already staffed for round-the-clock guestroom deliveries." The positive impact on guest perceptions of the hotel, however, is very strong.

Source: *The Rooms Chronicle®*, Volume 10, Issue 1, p. 7.
For subscription information, please call 866-READ-TRC.

Room attendants need different cloths for general washing, toilet cleaning, and drying. Color coding rags can help avoid confusion.

guest and the blanket, the guests' minds are more at ease and blankets/comforters tend not to soil quite as rapidly.[2]

Cleaning the Bathroom

A clean bathroom is important for more than simply appearance. Health and safety considerations on the local, state, and federal levels necessitate that the room attendant take extra care when scrubbing, rinsing, and drying bathroom surfaces.

Bathrooms are usually cleaned in the following sequence: shower area, vanity and sink, toilet, walls and fixtures, and floor. Like most cleaning tasks, it is important to work from top to bottom to avoid spotting or dirtying areas already cleaned. The necessary cleaning equipment should be conveniently stocked in the hand caddy. Cleaning items usually consist of an approved all-purpose cleaner for bathroom surfaces; cloths and sponges; glass and mirror cleaner; rubber gloves; and protective eye covering. Some properties also use an odorless disinfectant. Do not use a guest towel for cleaning.

Begin by turning on a fan or opening a window to provide ventilation to the area. For personal safety, never stand on the edge of the tub when cleaning. As you wash and wipe the tub or shower walls, continually check their condition so you can report any needed repairs to your supervisor. If the tub has a drain trap, be sure to check it for hair. After cleaning the tub itself, clean the shower head and tub fixtures. Make sure to leave the shower head aimed in the correct position. To

Ask Gail—Bathroom Cleaning

Dear Gail:

I have just taken charge of a 300-room property with severe mildew problems on the shower walls. What can we do?

T.W., Sacramento, Calif.

Dear T.W.:

When I see rooms like that, I just feel like blowing the darned things up. But since we can't do that, here's a procedure which works for me. First, find a good antibacterial chemical that will not damage your fixtures or tile. A mixture of one-to-one household bleach and water works well. Apply it to the walls with a spray bottle. Let this stand for approximately ten minutes. Scrub the walls well with a nylon bristle brush. Be sure to include the grouting. Rinse, then dry the area thoroughly. Repeat this effort twice more to completely remove the mildew and stain.

Dear Gail:

What do I use to clean the chrome in the shower? We have about scrubbed all the chrome plating off.

D.F., Quinault, WA

Dear D.F.:

Since chrome is just plated-over metal, it must be cared for gently. Chemicals (especially chlorine) can etch it, and hard water can also cause damage. The recommended care is to use a mild detergent and then dry the fixture with a soft cloth. If that doesn't work, it may help to rub the chrome with baking soda sprinkled on a wet sponge. White vinegar or toothpaste may also be used, but be sure to rinse and then dry the fixture with a soft cloth. If the chrome is already worn, there are only two choices: replace the fixture; or, if it is a quality, irreplaceable fixture, remove it and have it refurbished.

Dear Gail:

After recently regrouting and caulking some of our bathtubs, we noticed they had quickly started to turn yellow. What can we do?

D.H., Chester, VA

Dear D.H.:

If the regrouting is turning yellow, it may be that the product used contains some plaster. Be sure to use 100 percent cement-based grouting. If the caulking turns color again, it may be a product problem. Don't try to save money by buying cheap caulking. Buy the best—some even contain mildew resistor, and some carry a 50-year product guarantee. If a change of product doesn't do the trick, then check the water for hardness and mineral content. It could be some combination of water and chemicals. And as a last resort, check the room attendant's cleaning products. Perhaps a chemical mix here is prompting the yellow color.

(continued)

(continued)

Dear Gail:

Can you help us with keeping our marble shower clean?

An Interested Reader

Dear Reader:

Beautiful to look at, difficult to clean. Most housekeepers do not thank hotel designers who put marble in certain places. A shower is one of those places. Marble is very porous, and very soft. It is easily scratched and easily stained. If you study how the people of India keep their wonderful marble clean, you'll find they polish it with another piece of stone. This, however, is too labor-intensive. Helpful advice from another executive housekeeper is as follows: "to clean your shower, use a neutral cleaning solution made specifically for marble. Then polish with a special marble polish. Avoid abrasive cleaners, and avoid sealing the walls."

Dear Gail:

We're looking for an easy way to clean the abrasive circles which are etched in the bottoms of our bathtubs. The dirt collects in the roughness making it look grey or black, and we can't seem to get them white again.

J.K., Seattle, WA

Dear J.K.:

This idea has worked like magic for us. Wash the tub and rinse it well. Run enough HOT water to cover the dots or strips on the bottom of the tub. Add one-half to one cup of automatic dishwasher powder and agitate the water. Let it stand for an hour. Use a nylon bristle brush and scrub the tub well. Drain, rinse, and dry. You should have a clean, white tub which is easily maintained by daily use of a brush.

Source: Gail Edwards, CHHE, *The Rooms Chronicle*®, Volume 1, Number 2, p. 9; Volume 2, Number 2, p. 9; Volume 4, Number 1, p. 11; Volume 4, Number 1, p. 11; and Gail Edwards, CHHE, Volume 2, Number 4, p. 9.
For subscription information, please call 866-READ-TRC.

prevent spotting and add sparkle, immediately wipe and polish the fixtures with a dry cloth. Also, clean the shower curtain or shower door. Pay special attention to the bottom, where mildew may accumulate. Always reposition the door or curtain when you are finished cleaning.

You should exercise the same exacting care when cleaning the vanity and mirror as you do when cleaning the shower area. Clean the countertop and basin, making sure that you remove any hair from the sink stopper and drain. Wipe up any spillage or spots from toothpaste or soap. Rinse and polish the chrome fixtures so they shine. Finish the vanity area by cleaning the mirror with glass cleaner.

Next, clean the toilet bowl and exterior surfaces. Some cleaning procedures recommend applying an all-purpose cleaner before any other cleaning task. This way, the cleaner has time to stand while you clean other bathroom areas.

All-purpose cleaners are preferable to acid bowl cleaners for use on a daily basis. When used consistently, acid bowl cleaners can destroy bathroom surfaces. These cleaners also present hazards to employees who use them, most noticeably in terms of causing skin irritation. Most properties use bowl cleaners once or twice a year in deep-cleaning programs—and then only under strict supervision.

Regardless of the method followed, flush the toilet to remove any residue and apply the cleaner around and under the lip of the bowl. Clean the exterior of the bowl, working down the sides to the base. Scrub the inside of the toilet with the brush around the insides and under the lip—then flush it again. Use a cloth damp with cleaning solution to clean the top of the seat, the lid, and the sides of the tank.

Towels, washcloths, bath mats, toilet and facial tissue, and guest amenities should be replenished according to property standards. Spot-clean for fingerprints and other obvious smudges on the walls, especially around light fixtures and electrical outlets. Wipe down the walls and clean both sides of the bathroom door. Starting with the far corner of the bathroom and working back toward the door, mop or wipe down the floor—including the baseboards. Then, gather your things and make your final check of the bathroom. Stop for a moment and visually scan all surfaces from the ceiling to the fixtures to the floor. Check that you've left the bathroom in the best possible condition before turning out the lights.

Several housekeeping executives had reported that it can be difficult to convince room attendants to get on their hands and knees to clean the bathroom floor. Many would either refuse or would use their foot as a makeshift broom handle on the rag. To combat this, some properties tried using small mops with replaceable mop heads. However, this wasn't always effective because the mops would collect hair and rust out very quickly. Also, buckets and mops can be unsanitary and unsightly. One solution proposed is the use of microfiber mops. They are lightweight, easy to use and can reduce the time and energy spent maintaining all types of flooring surfaces. Because of how they are constructed, room attendants typically won't need to presweep. The microfiber cloths can be rewashed for several uses and are usually held onto the mop by spring-loaded hinges.[3]

Dusting

Like bed-making, the task of dusting requires a systematic and orderly approach for efficiency and ease. Some room attendants start dusting items at the door and work clockwise around the room. This reduces the chance of overlooking a spot. In all cases, begin with the highest surfaces so that dust doesn't fall on the items you have already cleaned. If your property uses a dusting solution, spray a small amount into the dust cloth. Never spray dusting solution directly onto an object since it can stain or cause stickiness.

The items needing dusting and their location will vary from property to property. As a general rule, the following should be dusted and/or polished:

- Picture frames
- Mirrors

- Headboards
- Lamps, shades, and light bulbs
- Bedside tables
- Telephone
- Windowsills
- Window and sliding-glass door tracks (if applicable)
- Dresser—including inside the drawers
- Television and stand
- Chairs
- Closet shelves, hooks, and clothes rod
- Top of doors, knobs, and sides
- Air conditioning and heating units, fans, or vents

You should also clean all mirrors and glass surfaces in the room using glass cleaner or water—including the front of the television set. When you clean the set, turn it on for a moment to make sure it works properly. Use a damp sponge followed by a clean cloth to clean mirrors. Glass cleaner may leave streaks. Some properties also use a special cleaner or disinfectant for telephone surfaces. As you dust your way around the room, note any bedroom supplies and amenities which may be needed and replenish them per your property's specifications. Finally, check the walls for spots and marks and remove any smudges with a damp cloth and all-purpose cleaning solution.

Vacuuming

Before vacuuming, loosen dirt around baseboards with a broom or rag so it is easier to pick up. Run the vacuum over all exposed areas of the carpet that you can reach, including under the tables and chairs and in the closet. Don't worry about inaccessible areas such as under the bed or dresser. Since cleaning these areas requires moving or lifting heavy furniture, most properties vacuum these areas on a special-project basis. However, it is your responsibility to check under beds and furniture for guest belongings or for any debris which must be removed.

You should start at the farthest end of the room and vacuum your way back—just as you did when you wiped down the bathroom floor. As you vacuum, be careful not to bump the furniture. Some properties recommend closing windows and draperies and turning off lights as you work your way back to the door. Working in this fashion saves steps. It also eliminates the need to walk back across the floor after it has been vacuumed, thus preventing the footprints and tracks that can appear in certain types of carpet.

Final Check

The final check is a critical step in guestroom cleaning. It makes the difference between just cleaning the room and doing a professional job.

Preparing a Room for Nonsmokers

To change a room where smoking has occurred into a fresh, clean room for use as a nonsmoking room, the following procedures may be helpful:

- Wash down the walls.
- Change the filters in HVAC units.
- Clean the bathroom vents.
- Remove the drapes, wash sheers, dry-clean black-outs.
- Remove the furniture and deep-clean the entire carpet.
- Deep-clean the upholstered furniture.
- Wash wooden furniture with oil soap.
- Wash laminate furniture with all-purpose soap.
- Remove all lampshades. Vacuum or wash them if possible; replace them if necessary.
- Check the condition of the mattress and bedspring. If they smell of smoke, either replace them or cover them with zip-on plastic covers.
- Wash all pillows, mattress pads, and blankets.
- Wash or dry-clean the bedspreads.
- Wash the shower curtains and bath rugs.

This process can be very costly and labor intensive. Since one guest smoking in the room for just one evening can destroy all these special preparations, extra care should be taken to keep the rooms smoke-free.

Source: Mary Friedman, *The Rooms Chronicle*®, Volume 3, Number 2, p. 9.
For subscription information, call 866-READ-TRC.

After reloading your vacuum and cleaning supplies on your cart, take a few moments to give the room a careful look from the guest's perspective. Start at one point in the room and scan it in a circular fashion from one corner to the next until you have visually inspected each item. By doing so, you may discover something you overlooked or that was difficult to spot on the first cleaning.

Make sure that all the furnishings are back in their proper places. Look for little things like crooked lampshades or lampshades with their seams showing. Smell the air for any unusual odors. If you detect any unpleasant smells, report them to your supervisor. Spray air freshener if needed. Remember that your last look is the guest's first impression. When you are satisfied that the guestroom is neat and thoroughly cleaned, turn off the lights, close the door, and check to see

the Rooms CHRONICLE®

Remembering to Clean Those Often-Missed Spots in Guestrooms

There is no doubt that guests insist upon clean guestrooms during their hotel stay. Research continually proves this, guest advocacy groups keep preaching this, and even hotel managers check for evidence of cleanliness when they arrive in their guestrooms as part of their vacations or business trips. The most common places guests initially check for cleanliness are the bathtub, toilet and sink, the bed linens, and the mirror and counter surfaces.

There are certain areas that room attendants frequently miss when servicing a guestroom and housekeeping managers need to be vigilant about checking them.

Too often it seems that room attendants fail to dust the guestroom from top to bottom. Synthetic and feather dusters are fine for high areas and for lamps, but a diaper-style cloth dampened with water works well for most hard surfaces other than glass. Damp cloths pick up the dust instead of spreading it onto another surface. To prevent injury, a room attendant should never use a damp cloth to dust light bulbs, lamp shades, or televisions; use a feather duster only after turning off the appliance.

All dusting should be done starting with the highest surfaces and working down after the guestroom has been serviced. Don't forget to dust exposed pipes under the bathroom sink, as this is another area that is often overlooked. Finally, the room attendant should vacuum the guestroom carpet starting at the farthest edge and working her way out the guestroom door.

There are four other cleaning tasks that many room attendants fail to properly complete. First, the ice bucket should be emptied and rinsed if it has been used. Always replace with a fresh plastic liner; never leave a used ice bucket liner for the guest to reuse.

Next, if the guestroom is so equipped, unplug and thoroughly clean the coffee pot and rinse out its water reservoir. Pull the coffee maker from the corner of the counter or table and clean under and behind where it sits. Unfortunately, some in-room coffeemakers are prone to overflow if they get too hot. But many room attendants do not realize this and fail to ever pull the coffeemaker away from the spot it occupies on a counter. Hence, they never clean under or behind it.

This same rationale applies to amenity baskets and trays typically found on bathroom vanities. It is easy for water, soap, and other oversprays to leach underneath and discolor countertop surfaces if left unchecked.

Finally, in-room microwaves and refrigerators (including the icebox section) should be cleaned thoroughly both inside and out with every room turn. No one wants to open the door to these appliances and find remnants of the previous guests' stay staring them in the face.

Hot tip: train room attendants to pull open the draperies, turn on all lights, lamps, and televisions, and to turn off the alarm mode of any alarm clocks after they enter a guestroom. This will allow them to inspect for any window damage, ensure that no bulbs are burnt out or lamps are unplugged, and prevent an unoccupied room's alarm clock from waking others in the middle of the night.

Source: Gail Edwards, CHHE, *The Rooms Chronicle*®, Volume 13, Number 4, p. 5. For subscription information, call 866-READ-TRC.

that it is locked. Note the condition and status of the room on your assignment sheet, and proceed to the next room on your schedule.

The room attendant may, instead of marking a room assignment sheet, use a handheld device or room telephone interface to notify the property management system that the room is now ready for inspection. The system may automatically log the time of the call. The log of room attendants' times in and out enables the rooms management module to determine room attendant productivity rates.

Personal Touches. Some executive housekeepers encourage their room attendants to add personal touches to the guestrooms of stayover guests. These include providing more inviting atmosphere for the guests by lining up their footwear along the baseboard, reassembling messy newspapers and placing them on the guestroom desk, aligning personal toiletry and grooming items on the bathroom counter and restoring irons and ironing boards left out by guests.[4]

Inspection

Guestroom inspection ensures that the desired results of an established cleaning system are consistently achieved. The purpose of a **room inspection** is to catch any problems that may have been overlooked during cleaning before the guest does. A well-conducted and diplomatic inspection program can also motivate employees. Most room attendants take pride in their work and enjoy having the opportunity to show it off to others. Quality cleaning jobs should be noted during inspections and the appropriate personnel recognized.

Inspection programs can take many forms. In some properties, rooms are spot-checked randomly; in others, every room is checked daily. Inspections should be conducted by personnel on the supervisory level such as a floor or shift supervisor, section supervisor, executive housekeeper, or even a manager from outside the housekeeping department. Each inspector is usually responsible for a certain number of rooms and should be aware of the current status of each room he or she is assigned. As a general rule, check-out rooms are inspected soon after room attendants report that they have been cleaned. Rooms that are occupied or have refused service are inspected on varying schedules. For these rooms, the executive housekeeper or inspector will contact the guest to arrange a convenient time for guestroom cleaning and/or inspection. Vacant rooms should also be inspected on a varying schedule based on the number of days the room remains empty between sales.

Room inspections not only help identify ordinary problems with cleaning but also help identify areas in the room needing deep cleaning or maintenance. A room inspection report should be completed which notes such items as the condition of furniture, fixtures, and equipment; the appearance of the ceiling and walls; the condition of the carpet and other floor coverings; and the cleanliness of window interiors and exteriors. Exhibit 6 shows a sample inspection form. Depending on the property's policies and procedures, the inspector may also be responsible for filling out any work orders or maintenance requests that are needed.

An inspection program is never any better than the follow-up that is given to an identified problem. Each situation noted on the inspection report or maintenance request should be initialed by the manager who is directly responsible

Exhibit 6   Sample Room Inspection Report

Room Inspection Report

ROOM NO._____

TYPE_____   DATE INSPECTED_____

CONDITION: ☐ EXCELLENT   ☐ ACCEPTABLE   ☐ UNACCEPTABLE

	BEDROOM	CONDITION		BATHROOM	CONDITION
1	Doors, locks, chains, stops		21	Doors	
2	Lights, switches, plates		22	Lights, switches, plates	
3	Ceiling		23	Walls	
4	Walls		24	Tile	
5	Woodwork		25	Ceiling	
6	Drapes and hardware		26	Mirror	
7	Windows		27	Tub, caulking, grab bars	
8	Heating/air conditioning setting		28	Shower head and curtain	
9	Phone		29	Bath mat	
10	TV and radio		30	Vanity	
11	Headboards		31	Fixtures/faucets/drains	
12	Spreads, bedding, mattress		32	Toilet: flush/seat	
13	Dressers, nightstand		33	Towels: facial/hand/bath	
14	Promotional material		34	Tissue: toilet/facial	
15	Lamps, shades, bulbs		35	Soap	
16	Chairs, sofa		36	Amenities	
17	Carpet		37	Exhaust vent	
18	Pictures and mirrors				
19	Dusting				
20	Closet				

OTHER_____

_____

_____

_____

_____

INSPECTED BY:_____

(Signature)

for that area. As a general rule, this should occur no later than 24 hours after the inspection.

Inspection Program Technology

Bar Codes. A technology that has significantly affected the retail trade promises to lend the same ease and efficiency to the hospitality industry over the next several years. Just as bar code technology saves time and ensures accuracy in countless checkout lanes, so can it save time and ensure accuracy in a hospitality inspection program. A **bar code** is the group of printed and variously patterned bars, spaces, and numerals that appears on the packaging of almost every retail item. These codes are designed to be scanned and read into a computer system as identification for the objects they label.

For a hotel, instead of storing price and inventory information, bar codes can be used to store room inspection data. Inspectors or maintenance personnel would gather and record room status information by scanning bar codes with a special device about the size of a credit card—rather than recording information onto

Exhibit 7 Sample Inspection Forms Using Bar Code Technology

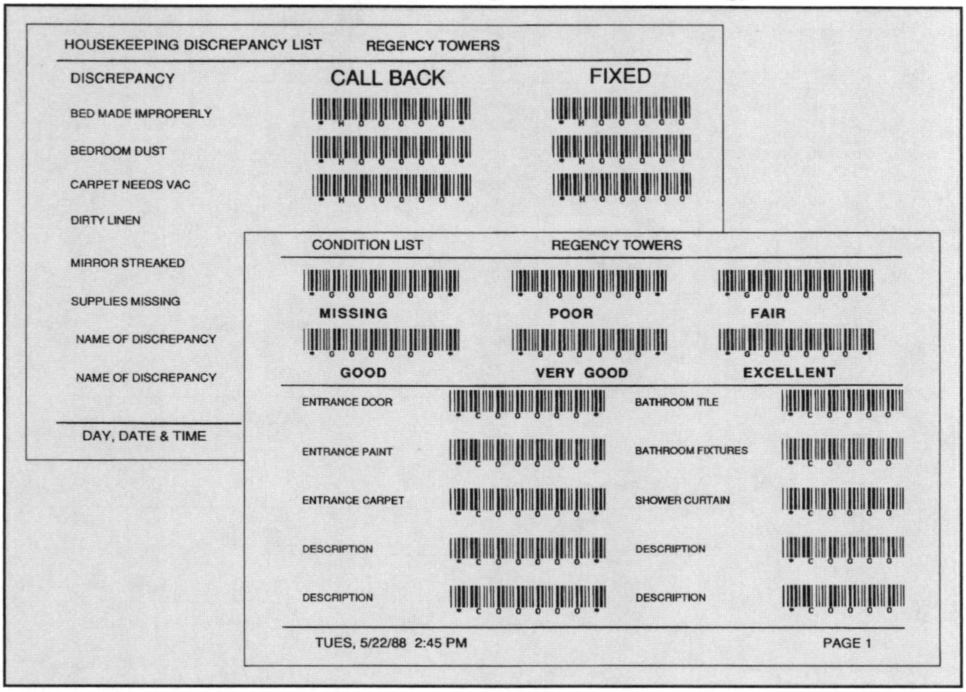

HOUSEKEEPING DISCREPANCY LIST REGENCY TOWERS

DISCREPANCY	CALL BACK	FIXED
BED MADE IMPROPERLY		
BEDROOM DUST		
CARPET NEEDS VAC		
DIRTY LINEN		
MIRROR STREAKED		
SUPPLIES MISSING		
NAME OF DISCREPANCY		
NAME OF DISCREPANCY		

DAY, DATE & TIME

CONDITION LIST REGENCY TOWERS

MISSING	POOR	FAIR
GOOD	VERY GOOD	EXCELLENT

ENTRANCE DOOR	BATHROOM TILE
ENTRANCE PAINT	BATHROOM FIXTURES
ENTRANCE CARPET	SHOWER CURTAIN
DESCRIPTION	DESCRIPTION
DESCRIPTION	DESCRIPTION

TUES, 5/22/88 2:45 PM PAGE 1

Courtesy of Bar Code Technology, Eastham, Massachusetts

forms. This information would later be read by a computer and compiled into various reports to track housekeeping and maintenance activities.

In a property using a bar code inspection system, each guestroom is identified with a small, permanently mounted bar code tag. The tag is placed in a discreet spot, such as on the door frame. The inspector or maintenance person is equipped with a bar code reader and a set of cards that list items or conditions that need to be inspected, attended to, or repaired. Like the guestroom itself, each of these items would have a corresponding bar code. Exhibit 7 shows sample discrepancy and condition lists that can be customized to fit the needs of individual properties.

Upon entering the room, the inspector scans the room's bar code tag. This automatically records the room number, time, and date in the bar code scanner. The condition of each inspected item is noted by scanning the appropriate bar code or combination of bar codes on the inspection cards. For example, if the bed is improperly made, the inspector would scan the "call back" bar code next to that item—indicating that the room attendant needs to redo the bed. At the end of the visit, the inspector "scans out" by scanning the room bar code a second time.

The information stored on the scanner can be retrieved by inserting the card into a special reader attached to a computer system. Depending on the program and property needs, the information can be presented in a summary or report

Exhibit 8   Sample Inspection Report Generated through a Bar Code System

Location	Time In	Time Out	Time Spent	Cleaner	Housekeeping	Fixed	Call Back	Maintenance	Ticket #
101	9:00 AM	9:15 AM	0:15	Smith, Nancy					
103	9:20 AM	9:30 AM	0:10	Smith, Nancy	Heat On	•			
102	9:40 AM	10:00 AM	0:20	Hall, Judy				Faucet Washer	300025
105	10:05 AM	10:30 AM	0:25	Smith, Nancy					
Break	10:40 AM	10:55 AM	0:15						
106	11:00 AM	11:17 AM	0:17	Hall, Judy	Dust	•			
					No Comment Card	•			
107	11:25 AM	11:45 AM	0:20	Smith, Nancy					
Lunch	12:00 PM	1:00 PM	1:00						
108	1:10 PM	1:16 PM	0:06	Hall, Judy					
110	1:25 PM	1:45 PM	0:20	Hall, Judy					
112	1:50 PM	2:05 PM	0:15	Hall, Judy					
111	2:10 PM	2:28 PM	0:18	Smith, Nancy	Heat On	•			
113	2:32 PM	2:55 PM	0:23	Smith, Nancy					
115	3:00 PM	3:15 PM	0:15	Smith, Nancy					
114	3:22 PM	3:35 PM	0:13	Hall, Judy	Guest Supplies		10001	Bathroom Tile Loose	300026
116	3:40 PM	4:05 PM	0:25	Hall, Judy					
118	4:10 PM	4:22 PM	0:12	Hall, Judy					
120	4:25 PM	4:30 PM	0:05	Hall, Judy	Bathroom Tile		10002		
119	4:35 PM	4:50 PM	0:15	Smith, Nancy					

SUMMARY

Number Rooms	Total Time	Inspect Time	Percent Inspect	Maintenance Problems
17	6:45	5:49	87%	2

	# Rooms	Cleaner	# Problems	# Fixed	# Callbacks
	8	Smith, Nancy	2	2	
	9	Hall, Judy	4	2	2

Inspector Report: Jones, Ann   The Regency Towers   4/6/

Monday, 4/11/   4:45 PM   PAGE 1

Courtesy of Bar Code Technology, Eastham, Massachusetts

format that provides management with an overview of the condition of each inspected room. Exhibit 8 shows one type of inspector report generated through a bar code system.

Bar code technology lends itself to a great deal of flexibility and can be customized to meet the specific needs and procedures of any property. Some properties coordinate bar code inspection programs with maintenance and engineering activities; others adapt the technology for such purposes as equipment tracking and security inspections. The information gathered and compiled can be as detailed or simple as required.

RFID Technology. An RFID system consists of three components: a transponder (tag), an integrated RF circuit and antenna, and a transceiver (reader). Basically, a transceiver transmits radio frequencies to, and receives them from, a transponder via antenna relay. The transceiver then transfers data to a processing device. It offers a wireless and automated process to collect information throughout the hotel. In the housekeeping department, RFID tags can be used to set housekeeping status. They can also allow supervisors to confirm their inspections directly to the property management system. They can also report out of order rooms or "do not disturb" requests to the property management system.

Deep Cleaning

Routine cleaning can maintain a guestroom's fresh and spotless appearance for a period of time, but after awhile, a room will need **deep cleaning**. Because of the thoroughness involved, deep cleaning requires special scheduling. In some properties, deep cleaning is done by room attendants on a special project basis. For instance, room attendants might clean the carpet corners of every room they clean that day. Some schedule one room to deep clean each day per room attendant as part of the daily assignment. Other hotels use deep cleaning teams in which each employee does a particular deep cleaning task for a section of rooms.

Deep cleaning is the process of taking a room out of a hotel's salable inventory and thoroughly cleaning it to more exacting standards than is normally performed during the daily housekeeping maintenance.

Most guestrooms are deep-cleaned between two and four times a year depending on the occupancy level of the hotel. Because higher occupancy results in more wear and tear on the furniture, fixtures, equipment, and infrastructure of the hotel's guestrooms, a hotel that experiences higher occupancy will need to deep clean its guestrooms on a more frequent basis than a lodging facility with lower overall occupancy.

Preventive maintenance: In a sense, deep cleaning is really the combined process of repair and preventive maintenance. The deep cleaning process permits hotel personnel to spend longer (typically a total of 4-6 hours) than the usual 30 minutes inside a vacant guestroom in order to thoroughly clean all surfaces from top to bottom, repair or replace any worn or damaged items, and sanitize the guestroom to a much higher degree than is obtained through daily housekeeping maintenance. By doing this, the service life of the carpeting, wallcoverings, draperies, furniture, and fixtures will be extended significantly.

Consider it the equivalent of an oil change and a tune-up for an automobile. If one doesn't change the oil frequently and properly maintain their car through preventive maintenance, the vehicle is destined for a shorter life than if it were maintained at proper intervals. Hotel renovations and retrofits are extremely costly; therefore, it is the duty of every manager to extract the highest rate of return from the hotel's investment in its furnishings, fixtures, and equipment in guestrooms. A higher rate of return results in higher profitability to the hotel and a better return on the hotel owners' investment.

Guests expect clean accommodations: Equally significant, is the issue of hygiene. Today's hotel guests demand guestrooms that are sanitary, well-maintained, and free of obvious defects. Multiple studies have discovered that perceived cleanliness is the number one factor for men and the number two factor for women in determining which hotel they will choose. Recent exposés on guestroom cleanliness by newspapers, television magazines, and investigative journalists as well as lawsuits pertaining to bedbug injuries have brought the cleanliness issue to the forefront of travelers' minds. And, the multitude of online travel blogs makes it

C the Rooms HRONICLE®

Ten steps to guestroom deep cleaning will maintain your hotel investment and prolong its earning potential

Deep cleaning usually entails completing ten task areas. The actual number of tasks may vary depending upon the brand's standards or an individual property's need.

The first issue that must be determined is whether the guestroom carpet will be shampooed or merely spot treated. If the entire carpet will be shampooed, this must be the last task performed and it will necessitate removing all the furniture from the guestroom. The furniture should only be returned to the guestroom once the carpet dries thoroughly. Otherwise, begin with Task 1. Once this question has been addressed, begin the ten tasks.

Task 1. High dusting.

Use a dust wand with long handle to reach all the high areas of the guestroom. A step ladder will also help to reach high corners and intricate areas. Make sure to reposition the ladder frequently rather than overreaching. Don't forget to dust smoke detectors and sprinklers, but use caution so as not to break the heat vial on the sprinkler heads and engage the sprinkler system. Dust light diffusers, air vent grates, the top of entertainment hutches or armoires and above door jams. If necessary, clean these areas with a damp rag. It may also be necessary to temporarily remove vent grates to thoroughly clean the dust buildup from them.

Task 2. Clean lights.

Remove glass or plastic globes from wall mounted sconces and ceiling mounted lights. Wipe dust, dead insects, and other contaminants from the globes with a rag and glass cleaner. Remove shades from floor and table lamps. Vacuum fabric shades with a crevice tool. Wipe plastic shades clean with a damp rag. Use a dry rag or dust wand to dust the light bulbs. Never spray cleaner directly on a light bulb, shade or lamp that is plugged into an electrical outlet. Don't forget to clean the lights in the bathroom. This may require lifting the plastic light diffuser from the fixture.

Task 3. Clean window areas.

Always use a stepladder to remove draperies and sheers from their curtain rods or tracks. Dry-clean fabric draperies; wipe vinyl draperies clean with an all-purpose cleaner and clean rag. Launder window sheers in a mild detergent. Inspect drapery hook and tracks for damage or dirt. Clean or repair as necessary. Using glass cleaner, wash the inside of the guestroom windows; clean the window frame and track. Ensure window locking mechanism engages properly. Vacuum the PTAC air conditioning unit grates. While this is being done, engineering personnel should replace or clean the PTAC filter and run a diagnostic check on the unit. Hang replacement or dry-cleaned draperies and laundered sheers.

Task 4. Service bed(s).

Strip the bed of its duvet cover or bedspread, all linens and blankets, and mattress pad. Inspect the top and all ends of the mattress for rips, stains, protruding springs, and sagging. Stand the mattress on its side against the wall. Remove dust

ruffles from box spring, if applicable. Inspect the box spring in a similar manner. Stand it on end against the mattress. Vacuum the carpet under the bed. Inspect the bed frame or platform for sturdiness. Wipe down the bedrails or platform. Remove the headboard from the wall and inspect both sides for contamination. Clean as needed. Ensure that it is securely put back in place. Rotate and replace the box spring onto the bed frame and reinstall dust ruffles. Following manufacturer's recommendations, rotate and/or flip the mattress. Vacuum the cording of the mattress with a crevice tool. Inspect pillows for stains and rips, replace if needed. Remake bed using laundered mattress pad, linens, blankets, and duvet/cover/bedspread.

Task 5. Wash walls, baseboard and doors.

Use all-purpose cleaner. Wear goggles and protective gloves. Spray all-purpose cleaner on sponge; do not spray directly on surfaces. Do not use excessive moisture. Work from the bottom up to avoid streaks. Dry with a clean rag. Don't forget to clean doorknobs, pictures, luggage racks, and closet racks. To clean light switch and electrical outlet covers unscrew them from the wall to avoid risk of electrical shock. Replace after cleaning. Don't forget to check the security of mirrors and pictures that are mounted on the walls. Check the door's viewfinder to make sure it is clean and operational. Ensure that the fire escape route map is properly posted on the backside of the guest door as well as the State's Innkeeper Statutes/Liability Notice.

Task 6. Clean furniture.

Vacuum furniture with upholstery tool. Be sure to turn cushions if they are upholstered on two sides. Use vacuum crevice tool in nooks to pick up loose debris in recessed areas. Inspect upholstery for stains and rips. Repair as needed. Use spot cleaner on upholstery as needed. Shampoo/extract upholstery if possible. Use oil-base cleaner or furniture polish on wood furniture. Use all-purpose cleaner on laminated furniture. Don't forget to clean the backs of furniture. Clean television remote control and telephone handsets with disinfectant; wipe other parts clean with all-purpose cleaner. Use all purpose cleaner to cleanse lamp bases. Clean the inside of credenza and nightstand drawers. Check drawer slides for smooth operation. Examine Bible and telephone directories for staining and ripped or missing pages. Replace as needed.

Task 7. Repair surfaces, furnishings, and equipment.

This is a job performed by Engineering or maintenance personnel. Concurrently, while the room is being deep cleaned by housekeeping personnel, an engineer will spot repair any guestroom items such as wallcoverings, painted surfaced, scratched or stained wooden furniture, etc. Items that cannot be repaired onsite will be removed from the guestroom and taken to the engineering shop for repair. It is important to note that after deep cleaning has concluded, a guestroom should not be placed back into salable inventory until all the guestroom items have been repaired or replaced.

Task 8. Replace shower curtain.

Remove bathroom shower curtain by standing on a stepladder or stepstool if it can't be reached easily. Do not stand on the toilet or edge of the bathtub. Remove

(continued)

(continued)

the curtain hooks from the rod. Clean the curtain hooks by soaking them in a pail of white vinegar or all-purpose cleaner to eliminate built up soap scum. Replace broken shower curtain hooks. Inspect curtain rod for rust and clean with all-purpose cleaner. Launder or replace shower curtain and rehang.

Task 9. Scrub floor tile and grout.

Employees should always wear goggles and protective gloves. Do not use steel wool, abrasives, or harsh chemicals on tile or grout. Instead, use a nylon bristle brush and general cleaner to clean floor tiles. Rinse with fresh water and dry with clean rags. Use a nylon bristle brush and disinfectant that is a little larger than a toothbrush to clean around the edge of the sink and toilet fixtures. Wipe dry.

Task 10. Carpets.

Vacuum carpets thoroughly including cleaning edges with crevice tool. Move furniture out of way to do this. Work clockwise around room. Shampoo/extract carpet and dry thoroughly. If the carpet will not be shampooed, use spot treatment cleaner to remove stains. Blot with clean white rags. Allow to dry.

   The purpose of deep cleaning is to prolong the life of the hotel's investment in its guestrooms. It is a labor intensive process that works best when two housekeeping employees work together simultaneously. Always use two employees when moving furniture and rotating mattresses. Train employees in proper lifting techniques and require that those who will lift heavy items wear back brace supports that will force them to bend at the knees at not at the waist. Finally, the experienced housekeeping manager will plan out their hotel's deep cleaning schedule well in advance in consultation with the Front Office Manager, Director of Sales and Chief Engineer to avoid these preventive maintenance efforts from occurring when the hotel will need every guestroom or might be committed to other manpower-intensive endeavors.

Source: *The Rooms Chronicle*®, Volume 15, Number 6, pp. 1, 3, 10–11.
For subscription information, please call 866-READ-TRC.

easier for guests to share their dissatisfaction with others who may read their highly critical and sometimes disparaging postings.

Frequency: Except during the highest occupancy periods, most hotels will deep clean 0.5 percent to 1.5 percent of their guestroom inventory on a daily basis. This means a 300-room hotel will deep clean an average of two to three guestrooms daily. In order to avoid disturbing guests, deep cleaning is normally scheduled to be performed on weekdays between the hours of 9 A.M. to 5 P.M.

   Generally, it is advisable to clean a small section of guestrooms in the same day as opposed to three or four rooms scattered throughout the hotel. This will minimize the need to move deep cleaning equipment and

the Rooms
CHRONICLE®

The "Quick Six" Inspection: For the Busy Manager to Stay in Touch

Looking for a quick way to determine whether a guestroom is top-to-bottom clean? Maybe there just isn't time to do a thorough inspection which includes every nook and cranny? Well, here's a "Quick Six" inspection that can be done in less than two minutes.

The "Quick Six" inspection focuses on things that are not easy for a room attendant to accomplish. When these things are cleaned correctly, it is a signal that the room attendant has paid attention to detail.

Open the guestroom door. Pause for a moment to observe the entire room. Is everything straight? Look at the bedspread, lampshades, chairs, and the pictures on the wall. If everything is straight and orderly, the inspection is off to a good start.

Take a deep whiff of the air. Smell good? Have all odors of staleness, smoke, or dampness been removed? Now begin the inspection.

1. Credenza

   Proceed to the area near the credenza or armoire. Check the carpet behind the credenza for dust, trash, or hotel promotional pieces. Since this piece of furniture is difficult to move, this area is often overlooked. If it's clean, so far, so good.

2. Nightstand

   There's generally an area between the nightstand and the bed where dust, food crumbs, toenail clippings, and cigarette butts fall. The bedspread hides this area when the bed is made, but when the guest turns back the spread, the accumulation is easy to see. Inspect this area to see if the carpet and wall around the nightstand have been cleaned.

3. Bed Linen

   While near the bed, examine the pillow. How does it look? Is the pillowcase clean and free of wrinkles? Free of hairs? How does it smell? Would a guest enjoy resting on it all night? How does the sheet look? Free of wrinkles? Neatly tucked in?

4. Vanity Wall

   Proceed to the bathroom. Check the wall near the wastebasket. This is generally to the right or left of the vanity. Because of the location of this wastebasket, the wall above the receptacle is often splashed with dirt, soap, or soda pop. It's an area that is difficult for a room attendant to notice, but it is often in plain view of a guest sitting on the toilet.

5. Shower Wall

   No one enjoys scrubbing a tub/shower wall. It's awkward and hard to reach, and cleaning it is sometimes an exercise in futility if the proper chemicals are not used. When a hand is rubbed across a clean tile wall, it sort of glides, maybe even squeaks. Across a dirty wall, a hand can feel the grime, and may show an accumulation of white soap residue. If it squeaks, great.

(continued)

(continued)

6. Toilet

Has the toilet been scrubbed? Take a cotton swab, dip it in the water and rub it under the rim of the toilet bowl. If the toilet hasn't been scrubbed, the cotton swab will show the nasty truth.

Now, what if these things aren't clean? Rather than raging and rolling heads, ask: What can we do to prevent this in the future? What kind of system will ensure this doesn't happen? What can I, as a manager, do to help get these rooms clean?

And, what if the room passes with flying colors? Reward the responsible employees—recognition, money, candy bars, personal letters, points, or time off with pay. People work well when managers care—when there is a sense of teamwork, a buzz of excitement, something to look forward to, an opportunity for recognition and reward. Taking two minutes for the "Quick Six" could have long-term benefits for the entire hotel.

Source: Gail Edwards, CHHE, *The Rooms Chronicle*®, Volume 3, Number, p. 5.
For subscription information, call 866-READ-TRC.

tools long distances and will concentrate any noise generated to a single guest floor or area of the property. Similarly, furniture and mattresses may be moved from one guestroom into an adjacent guestroom to shampoo carpets and perform wallpaper and paint touchups.[5]

Allergens and Allergies

As hospitality properties became more environmentally conscious, they also became aware of the need to accommodate the increasing number of guests who suffer from allergies and chemical sensitivities. Because allergies and sensitivities can exist on such a wide variety of items, preparing what has become known as "allergy-friendly" rooms creates a challenge for hospitality properties and, particularly, for housekeeping.

It's a movement still in its infancy, though the issue has been steadily gaining attention. The American Hotel & Lodging Association in 2004 found that only 17 percent of the properties it queried had air purifiers.

In 2005, the Survey Research Institute of Cornell University released a report on the results of a survey of hotel patrons regarding allergy-friendly facilities. It found that nearly one-third of them had allergy issues or traveled with family members who did. Eighty-three percent of those surveyed said they would prefer to stay in a hotel room that is specially treated to remove airborne allergens. Even those without allergies said they would prefer an allergy-friendly room. More than half of the respondents said they would be willing to pay a small premium for an allergy-friendly room and a like number said that they would be more likely to choose a hotel that had allergy-friendly rooms available.

The steps to make a room allergy friendly vary. Some techniques properties are using include:

- Installing air and water purifiers.

- Using green cleaning supplies.

- Providing special pillow encasements and mattress covers.

- Providing antimicrobial coatings.

- Removing nuts and chocolates from minibars.

- Eliminating the use of deodorizers.

- Reducing the amount of detergent used on bedding and using hotter water instead.

- Creating "feather-free" floors.

- Installing germicidal ultraviolet lights in air-conditioning units to keep cooling coils free of fungi.

- Installing charcoal-filtered shower heads.

Some properties have created special allergy-free rooms that are specially designed for allergy sufferers. These properties might remove carpeting and drapes from rooms, replacing them with hardwood floors and shutters and applying an anti-microbial coating on bathroom fixtures and doorknobs.

Other properties are designing allergy-free rooms or floors that they rent at a premium to guests. Costs to convert a room are high and the housekeeping staff must take extra measures to clean these rooms, resulting in higher labor costs. However, these rooms have proved popular and hotels are increasingly considering them as an option.

In 2007, the University of Buffalo decided to begin researching the air quality of allergy-friendly hotel rooms. While the research is still incomplete at this writing, early results showed that in treated rooms, breathable particle counts dropped by about 75 percent.

Hotels that do not have allergy-free rooms will still need to respond to requests from guests who suffer from allergies. Such requests may include:

- Hypoallergenic bedding.

- No pets in the room for 30 days prior.

- Non-smoking.

- Bedding that was washed in hot water with no detergents.

- A room cleaned without harsh chemicals.

- A room away from the swimming pool, beach, woods, or anywhere with a higher concentration of molds or pollens.

Some guests will even rent out a room the day before they arrive and ask that it be kept empty and that no chemicals are used in the room for the 24 hours before they arrive.

Turndown Service and Special Requests

As the name implies, **turndown service** involves turning down the guest bedsheets and freshening the guestroom for the evening. Some properties—particularly luxury hotels and resorts—have a shift of room attendants whose primary duty is to provide turndown service. This second shift is generally smaller than the day shift and services more rooms per hour. In some hotels, an employee on the turn-down shift might service 20 rooms per hour, depending on the tasks involved.

Procedures for turndown service include:

- Cleaning the bathroom and restocking it with fresh towels.
- Rotating or restocking amenities.
- Tidying the guestroom.
- Emptying wastebaskets.
- Folding back the bedspread, blanket, and top sheet or arranging the duvet.
- Fluffing the pillow.
- Drawing the drapes.

As an added touch, some properties have the room attendant leave a fresh blossom or a chocolate mint on the pillow to wish the guest "sweet dreams."

In addition to turndown service, housekeeping may be called upon to provide other types of special amenities. These items vary from property to property depending on the markets the operation attempts to reach and satisfy. There are several categories of amenities ranging from conveniences and services to luxuries. Among the items stocked and distributed by some housekeeping departments are a variety of pillow types, sewing kits, spot removers, soft music CD's, bottled water and other conveniences to make the guest's stay more pleasant.

To a great extent, the success of a property depends on the cleanliness, appearance, and ambience of its rooms. Maintaining standards for guestroom cleanliness is accomplished through the meticulous cleaning procedures employed by housekeeping personnel.

Endnotes

1. Robert Propst, *The New Back-of-the-House, Running the Smart Hotel* (Redmond, Wash.: The Propst Company, 1988).

2. Source: Elizabeth Kozlowski, *The Rooms Chronicle®*, Volume 13, Number 2, pp. 1–3. For subscription information, call 866-READ-TRC.

3. "Cleaning Bathroom Floors in Guestrooms...Are Microfiber Mops the Answer?" *The Rooms Chronicle®*, Volume 12, Number 1, p. 6. For subscription information, call 866-READ-TRC.

4. "Personal Touches Can Brighten a Guest Stay," *The Rooms Chronicle®*, Volume 11, Number 4, p. 4. For subscription information, call 866-READ-TRC.

5. Source: *The Rooms Chronicle®*, Volume 15, Number 6, pp. 1, 3, 10–11. For subscription information, call 866-READ-TRC.

 **Key Terms** ————————————————————————————

amenity—A service or item offered to guests or placed in guestrooms for convenience and comfort and at no extra cost.

bar code—A group of printed and variously patterned bars, spaces, and numerals that are designed to be scanned and read into a computer system as label identification for an object.

deep cleaning—Intensive or specialized cleaning undertaken in guestrooms or public areas. Often conducted according to a special schedule or on a special-project basis.

hand caddy—A portable container for storing and transporting cleaning supplies. Typically located on the top shelf of the room attendant's cart.

linen room—Area in a hospitality operation that is often considered the headquarters of the housekeeping department. This is the area where the employee typically reports to work; receives room assignments, room status reports, and keys; assembles and organizes cleaning supplies; and checks out at the end of his or her shift.

mitering—A method for contouring a sheet or blanket to fit the corner of a mattress in a smooth and neat manner. The results are sometimes referred to as "square corners" or "hospital corners."

room attendant's cart—A wheeled vehicle used by room attendants for transporting cleaning supplies, linen, and equipment needed to fulfill a block of cleaning assignments.

room inspection—A detailed process in which guestrooms are systematically checked for cleanliness and maintenance needs.

room status report—A report that allows the housekeeping department to identify the occupancy or condition of the property's rooms. Generated daily through a two-way communication between housekeeping and the front desk.

turndown service—A special service provided by the housekeeping department in which a room attendant enters the guestroom in the early evening to restock supplies, tidy the room, and turn down the guest bedsheets.

Review Questions ——————————————————————————

1. What are the advantages of taking a systematic approach to guestroom cleaning?

2. When stocking a cart, what items typically go on the bottom two shelves? On the top shelf? In the hand caddy?

3. After reviewing a room status report, what types of rooms should the room attendant clean first? Second?

4. How are rooms that refuse service (including those with a Do Not Disturb sign) typically handled?

5. What is the first *major* task a room attendant will do after entering a guest-room? Why?

6. Why is it important to work from the top down when cleaning items and surfaces?

7. Why is it important to make a final check after cleaning the guestroom? What are some of the conditions that a room attendant should look for?

8. What is the purpose of guestroom inspection? What benefits can employees derive from the process?

9. What are three ways that deep cleaning can be scheduled at a property?

 **Internet Sites** ————————————————————————

For more information, visit the following Internet sites. Remember that Internet addresses can change without notice. If the site is no longer there, you can use a search engine to look for additional sites.

American Hotel Register Company
www.americanhotel.com

Ecolab, Inc.
www.ecolab.com

Hotel Housekeepers
www.careerprospects.org/briefs/E-J/
Housekeeping.shtml

Task Breakdowns: Guestroom Cleaning

The procedures presented in this section are for illustrative purposes only and should not be construed as recommendations or standards. While these procedures are typical, readers should keep in mind that each property has its own procedures, equipment specifications, and policies regarding protective gear which are designed to fit individual needs.

Prepare the Guestroom for Cleaning

Materials needed: Stocked housekeeping cart, a room assignment sheet, a pen heavy latex utility gloves, a tissue, a plastic bag, and a biohazard sticker.

STEPS	HOW-TO'S
1. Set up supplies and equipment for cleaning the room.	❑ Place the vacuum cleaner inside the room by the door. ❑ Place the cleaning supply caddy on the floor outside the bathroom door.
2. Turn on lights and replace burned-out or missing light bulbs.	❑ Turn on the wall switch just inside the door. ❑ Turn on all lamps in the room. This will help you see what to clean. ❑ Replace burned-out or missing bulbs. Turn off the light before replacing the bulb. There should be light bulbs on your cart. ❑ Be careful when changing bulbs. They may break when screwed out of socket. Always use care to avoid cuts.
3. Check the television, remote control, and radio.	❑ Turn on the television using the remote control. Turn on the radio. ❑ After checking the television and radio, turn them off while cleaning.
4. Open drapes and check the rods, cords, or wands.	❑ If the drapes and sheers have a draw cord, always open them with this cord. Opening drapes or sheers without using the draw cord will damage the rod mechanism. ❑ If the rod or draw cord has been damaged, report the damage on your room assignment sheet. Your supervisor must schedule an engineering employee or a public space cleaner to repair the rod. ❑ If the drapes have no draw cord, pull the drapes and sheers back without pulling down on the fabric.

Prepare the Guestroom for Cleaning (continued)

STEPS	HOW-TO'S
5. Clean windows, tracks, and sills as needed using a window cleaner.	❑ See Task list, "Clean Windows, Tracks, and Sills."
6. Remove room service equipment.	❑ Gather all room service equipment and move it right outside the guestroom door. Make sure there are no guest items on the room service tray or cart.
	❑ If the equipment has not yet been removed when you finish the room, move it to a housekeeping closet or service area. Room service equipment creates a safety hazard in the guest corridor.
	❑ The steps to alert the room service staff about room service equipment vary among properties.
7. Strip the bed to allow it to air while you clean the bathroom.	❑ Remove any guest clothing from the bed and neatly lay it across the back of the chair.
	❑ Remove personal items from the bed and neatly place them on a chair.
	❑ Put on heavy latex utility gloves. Gloves will protect you from exposure to any body fluids in bed linens.
	❑ Place the bedcover, blanket, and pillows on a chair or table. Bedcovers, blankets, and pillows could get damaged if you put them on the floor—and you could trip over them. In addition, if guests see these items on the floor, they'll get a poor impression of the property.
	❑ Remove sheets and pillowcases and place them outside the bathroom.
	❑ Remove stained or torn mattress pads and place them outside the bathroom door.
	❑ Notify your supervisor of any stains or damage to the mattress.

(continued)

Prepare the Guestroom for Cleaning (continued)

STEPS	HOW-TO'S
	❑ Check between the mattress and box springs for items left behind by checked-out guests.
	❑ Follow your property's lost and found procedures if you find something.
8. Remove soiled linens from the bathroom and bedroom.	❑ Collect all terry that was handled by the guest. Be sure that no guest belongings are collected with the soiled terry or linens.
	❑ If a check-out room has a terry cloth robe, remove it.
	❑ Collect the soiled terry and bed linens and place them in the linen bag on your cart.
	❑ Do not use guest linens or terry for cleaning.
9. Use judgment to decide when to remove used guest amenities and drinking glasses from a stayover room.	❑ In a stayover room, leave a fresh bar of soap if needed according to the hotel's procedures.
	❑ Leave any mints from turndown service on the nightstand.
	❑ Use good judgment to remove drinking glasses. Guests might keep something in a glass (such as medicine) that they plan to drink later.
10. Collect trash, and empty ashtrays.	❑ Collect bathroom trash and place it in the bathroom wastebasket.
	❑ Collect bedroom trash, and place it in the bedroom wastebasket.
	❑ Collect recyclable items and place them in the correct container on your cart. At some properties, the following items are recycled: • Newspapers • Aluminum cans • Glass bottles
	❑ Do not throw away any guest property that may be wrapped in a tissue.

Prepare the Guestroom for Cleaning (continued)

STEPS	HOW-TO'S
	❑ In check-out rooms, open all drawers and closets to: • Remove trash • Remove articles left behind • Restock guest supplies • Arrange clothing hangers • Remove nonstandard hangers
11. Handle guest clothing and personal items strewn around the room.	❑ The steps to handle guest items strewn around the room vary among properties.
12. Remove trash.	❑ Empty the wastebaskets into the trash bag on your cart. Empty trash without reaching into it. Taking care when dumping the trash helps you avoid sharp objects such as broken glass or razor blades. ❑ Return the wastebaskets to the bedroom and bathroom.
13. Follow bloodborne pathogen safety procedures.	❑ Always carry dirty linens by the top. Never carry linens by placing your hands under them. You could be punctured by a needle if you carry linens from the bottom. ❑ Look for blood or body fluids on terry, and only pick it up while wearing gloves. ❑ Place contaminated linens and terry in a plastic bag, and label the bag with a biohazard sticker. A housekeeping supervisor will deliver this bag to the laundry.

Make the Bed

Materials needed: Mattress pad, clean linens, and a room assignment sheet.

STEPS	HOW-TO'S
1. Check the mattress pad, mattress, and box springs.	❑ Look at the mattress pad to see if it is stained, torn, or damaged. If it is not, straighten it and make sure the mattress and box spring are even. Adjust them if necessary. Whenever you adjust the mattress, lift with your legs, not your back to avoid injuries.
	❑ If the mattress pad is stained, torn, or damaged, remove it.
	❑ Look at the mattress and box springs to see if they are also stained, torn, or damaged. Tell your supervisor about any problems right away.
	❑ If the mattress and box springs are not stained or damaged, make sure the mattress and box springs are even. Adjust the mattress as needed.
	❑ Place a clean mattress pad on the mattress: • Lay the fresh pad on the bed • Unfold the pad right-side up and spread it evenly over the center of the bed • Smooth out wrinkles
	❑ Mattress pads are about the same size as the mattress. Different size pads are required for double and king-size beds. Be sure to get the correct size.
2. Center the bottom sheet on the mattress so that an equal amount of sheet hangs over each side the bed.	❑ Make sure you have the correct size sheets.
	❑ Do not use a stained or torn sheet. Follow the property's instructions for disposal of the item.

Make the Bed *(continued)*

STEPS	HOW-TO'S
3. Miter the bed corners.	❑ Tuck the bottom sheet along one side of the bed except for the corners.
	❑ Take the loose end of the sheet, about a foot from the corner at the head of the bed, and pull it straight out, forming a flap. Pull up the flap so it is flat.
	❑ Tuck in the free part at the corner.
	❑ Pull the flap out toward you and down over the side of the bed. Tuck the flap in.
	❑ Move to the corner at the foot of the bed on the same side of the bed, and repeat the procedure.
4. Put the top sheet on the bed.	❑ Center the top sheet on the bed with the hem-side up.
	❑ Position the sheet so that the top edge is at the top of the mattress.
5. If a comforter and duvet cover are used, follow the property's instructions for changing the linen.	
6. If a blanket is used, place it on the bed.	❑ Arrange the blanket so that its top edge is about one palm-length below the top of the sheet.
	❑ Fold the top edge of the sheet over the top edge of the blanket. Smooth the sheet and blanket. By folding the top sheet over the top edge of the blanket, guests may pull the blanket up around their neck without touching the blanket. This keeps the blanket cleaner and protects it from added wear.
	❑ Go to the foot of the bed. Tuck in the sheet and blanket smoothly.
	❑ Miter the corners of the blanket and sheet together at the foot of the bed. Do not tuck in the sides of the top sheet.
	❑ Working clockwise, walk to the other side of the bed. Miter the bottom sheet at the right foot of the bed, followed by the top sheet and blanket.

(continued)

Make the Bed *(continued)*

STEPS	HOW-TO'S
	❏ Move up the right-hand side of the bed and miter the bottom sheet in the top right corner.
	❏ Fold the top sheet over the blanket so that it is even with the left-hand side.
7. If triple sheeting is used, add the third sheet on top of the blanket.	
8. Put pillowcases on the pillows.	❏ Insert pillows into the pillowcases and tuck in the loose ends. Double beds often have two standard-size pillows. King-size beds have three standard-size pillows or two king-size pillows. Use your hands, not your chin or teeth, to put pillows into the pillowcases.
	❏ Place the pillows on the bed with the tucked edges facing the center and the tucked flaps on the other side of the pillows.
9. If a bedspread is used, place it on top of the blanket.	❏ Position the bedspread on the bed with equal amounts hanging over both sides and the foot of the bed. Notify your supervisor if there are stains on or tears in the bedspread.
	❏ Smooth the bedspread over the pillows to the head of the bed.
	❏ Tuck the remainder of the bedspread under the front edge of the pillows.
	❏ Smooth the surface of the bed,
	❏ Check the bedspread for evenness on both sides at the foot of the bed.
10. Place menus or property materials on the bed.	❏ The menus and property materials placed on the bed vary among properties.
	❏ Sometimes important materials with information about fire exits or emergency procedures will be placed on pillows so that guests will be sure to see them.

Make the Bed *(continued)*

STEPS	HOW-TO'S
11. Make sofa beds.	❑ If instructed, make up the sofa bed.
	❑ Follow the same basic procedures for making a standard bed. Place the blanket and tuck it and the top sheets tightly at the foot, and then on both sides of the bed. Sheets may be larger than the sofa bed mattress and may require special care when tucking on all sides to give a smooth appearance.
	❑ Place the pillows neatly on the bed and check the overall appearance of the bed.
	❑ Procedures for leaving the sofa bed open or closed vary among properties.
	❑ If a guest requests the bed to be closed, remove the pillows, make the bed, then fold it into a sofa. In this case, place the pillows on the closet shelf or in a bottom dresser drawer.
12. Set up Murphy or Sico fold-up beds.	❑ Your room assignment sheet will indicate if the Murphy or Sico bed is to be set up. (A Murphy or Sico bed folds up into the wall and looks like a bookshelf when it is put away.) Be careful to avoid injury when opening Murphy or Sico fold-up beds. Make sure everything is out of the way before lowering the bed.
	❑ Open Murphy or Sico beds completely and then make them up like a sofa bed.
	❑ Fold up the bed.
	❑ Put clean pillowcases on the pillows and store them in the closet or in a bottom dresser drawer.

Begin to Clean the Bathroom

Materials needed: *Stocked housekeeping cart, a dry cloth or dry brush, and a broom or a feather duster.*

STEPS	HOW-TO'S
1. Soak the soiled ashtrays.	❑ Cover ashtrays with soapy water in the bathroom wastebasket. Handle ashtrays carefully to avoid breaking them. ❑ Place the wastebasket and ashtrays on the vanity by the sink to soak.
2. Clean vents.	❑ Remove all dirt and dust from vents using a dry cloth, small broom, or dry brush. If you need special equipment to do this job correctly, report this to your supervisor or the executive housekeeper. ❑ Do not leave streaks on the wall or ceiling around the vents.
3. Clean the ceiling.	❑ Use a feather duster or a dry cleaning cloth on a broom to remove hair, dust, lint, and cobwebs from the ceiling—especially the corners. ❑ Stand on the floor to clean. Do not climb on the toilet or the edge of the bathtub. Do not use chairs from the guestroom for cleaning the bathroom ceiling. Follow safe work practices when cleaning high places. Detailed cleaning is important, but your personal safety is more important. A public space cleaner will help you if you need a ladder to clean safely. Be careful when cleaning a rough-blown acoustical ceiling. Pieces of the ceiling could fall off.
4. Contact your supervisor for help if a cleaning problem requires immediate attention.	

Clean the Tub and Shower Area

Materials needed: A tissue, a scrub brush, a sponge, cleaning supplies, soap and dry cloths.

STEPS	HOW-TO'S
1. Scrub the tile and bath area.	❑ In a stayover room, clean around guests' belongings left in the bathtubs.
	❑ Place guest clothing left in the tub or shower area out of the way until you have finished cleaning, and then return it.
	❑ Remove hair from the tub or shower.
	❑ Use a soap and water solution and a scrub brush or sponge to scrub the grout, soap dish, fixtures, faucets, showerhead, shower towel rack, and tub.
	❑ Clean shower doors carefully with cleaning solution and a sponge. Clean the track with a brush.
2. Clean the shower curtain liner.	❑ Clean the liner with a cleaning solution and sponge. Scrub off soap buildup with a brush. Wipe down the edges and across the bottom of the liner.
	❑ Replace the shower curtain or liner if either is stained or damaged.
3. Scrub the tub and skid strips.	❑ Run about one inch of water into the tub. Add cleaning solution. scrub the strips as necessary with a scrub brush or sponge. Strips must remain white.
	❑ Spray the remainder of the tub with an all-purpose cleaner, and wipe down with a cleaning cloth. Remove all soap scum.

(continued)

Clean the Tub and Shower Area *(continued)*

STEPS	HOW-TO'S
4. Polish the fixtures with a dry cloth.	
5. Dry all tub and shower surfaces with a cloth.	
6. Arrange the shower curtain and liner.	❑ The arrangement of the shower curtain and liner varies among properties.

Clean the Toilet

Materials needed: Gloves, goggles, cleaning supplies, a damp sponge, a toilet bowl brush, dry cloths, a pen, and a room assignment sheet.

STEPS	HOW-TO'S
1. Put on protective gloves and goggles.	
2. Flush the toilet and make a note on your room assignment sheet if it does not flush and fill properly.	
3. Spray cleaning solution on the inside and outside of the toilet, the walls beside and behind the toilet, and under the vanity.	
4. Clean the area around the toilet.	❑ Wipe the walls around the toilet. ❑ Wipe the pipes leading to the toilet. ❑ Wipe the wall under the vanity and the drain pipe. ❑ Wipe the top, lid, seat, and outside of the toilet.
5. Clean the inside of the toilet.	❑ Use a toilet bowl brush to scrub the inside of the toilet bowl. Be sure to clean under the rim and the seat. ❑ Rinse the brush in the toilet when you are done and flush. This brush should only be used for cleaning the toilet.
6. Polish the toilet.	❑ Use a dry cloth to wipe the outside of the toilet. Polish the walls and pipes at the same time.

Clean the Sink and Vanity

Materials needed: A clean washcloth or hand towel, cleaning cloths, a stiff brush, and cleaning supplies.

STEPS	HOW-TO'S
1. Move guest toiletries when necessary.	❑ Clear a spot on the vanity. ❑ Place a clean washcloth or hand towel on that spot. ❑ Arrange the guest's toiletries on the hand towel.
2. Wipe the light fixture, towel racks, and other bathroom fixtures.	
3. Wash the ashtrays and wastebasket.	❑ Wash the ashtrays and wastebasket, rinse, and dry with a clean cloth. ❑ Set the clean ashtrays aside in the wastebasket.
4. Rinse your cleaning cloths as needed.	
5. Remove the sink stopper.	
6. Clean surface areas.	❑ Spray cleaning solution on the sink, stopper, overflow and main sink drains, fixtures (all sides), and vanity. ❑ Use a stiff brush to clean overflow holes in the sink. Dirt often collects in sink overflow drains. ❑ Using a damp cleaning cloth, wipe all the surfaces. ❑ Polish with a dry cloth to prevent water spots.
7. Replace the sink stopper.	

Clean the Bathroom Floor

Materials needed: A towel, small broom, cleaning cloths, and cleaning supplies.

STEPS	HOW-TO'S
1. Sweep out the bathroom floor with a small broom or vacuum. Spray the bathroom floor and baseboards with an all-purpose cleaning solution.	
2. Scrub away grime.	❑ Start with the farthest corner and work toward the door. Kneeling on a towel while you wash the floor will protect your knees and keep you from slipping.
	❑ Scrub the floor with a cleaning cloth.
	❑ Wipe baseboards as you go.
	❑ Pay special attention to the areas around the toilet, behind the door, and in corners.
3. Dry the floor with a clean cloth.	

Finish Cleaning the Bathroom

Materials needed: A damp sponge, dry, clean cloths, cleaning supplies, an ice bucket liner, a paper mat, glasses, glassware caps; clean towels and linens; facial tissues, toilet tissues, and guest bathroom amenities.

STEPS	HOW-TO'S
1. Clean mirrors in the bathroom and guestroom.	❑ Use a damp sponge with water only to wipe the mirror. Glass cleaner is not recommended for cleaning mirrors because it may leave streaks. ❑ Dry and polish the mirror with a dry cloth.
2. Clean the ice bucket and replace water glasses.	❑ Remove used glassware. Never wipe out glasses or covers and reuse them. Glassware must be washed and sanitized through a dishwasher to meet sanitation codes and ensure guest safety. ❑ Unless the bucket contains fresh ice, empty it into the sink. ❑ Throw the plastic bag liner into the trash bag on your cart. ❑ Clean and sanitize the bucket with an approved cleaner and a clean cloth. ❑ Put a new liner in the bucket. ❑ Wipe the tray and return the bucket. Replace the paper mat with a fresh one. ❑ Place clean glasses and glassware caps in the bathroom or the assigned location. To maintain sanitation, always handle clean glassware with care.
3. Pick up supplies from your cart and restock fresh bath towels and washcloths.	❑ Gather enough towels, washcloths, and bed linens from your cart to meet property standards. To work efficiently, you'll want to make every trip in and out of the room count. Picking up clean bed linens when you get the towels will save you a trip when you make the bed.

Finish Cleaning the Bathroom *(continued)*

STEPS	HOW-TO'S
	❏ Place clean bed linens on a chair near the bed until you need them. To keep fresh bed linens clean, never place them on the floor.
	❏ Return to the bathroom and place towels where they are needed.
	❏ The standard arrangement for placing towels varies among properties.
4. Restock paper bath supplies.	❏ Check the facial tissues in the box. If the tissue box is empty or nearly empty, replace it with a new box. Attention to details, such as the supply of facial or toilet tissue, is very important.
	❏ Replace the toilet tissue roll according to the property's guidelines.
	❏ Install the roll so that the paper feeds over the top away from the wall.
	❏ Form a VIP point on the lead sheet of toilet tissue.
	❏ According to the property's guidelines, leave a fresh roll of unwrapped toilet tissue in the spot your supervisor shows you.
5. Restock guest bathroom amenities as instructed by your supervisor.	
6. Return the clean bathroom wastebasket and ashtrays to their correct locations.	

Dust the Guestroom

Materials needed: Clean cloths, dusting materials, feather duster, a damp sponge, glass cleaner, disinfectant spray, a pen, and a room assignment sheet.

STEPS	HOW-TO'S
1. Prepare to dust by gathering materials as instructed by your supervisor.	
2. Follow a dusting system.	❑ Start at one side of the room and work your way around in a circle. ❑ Dust from the top down.
3. Dust all of the doors in the guestroom.	❑ Note on your room assignment sheet whether any guest room supplies are missing, and replace them before you report the room status. ❑ Use a dusting cloth to dust the inside and outside of each door, frame, and threshold.
4. Dust the walls and ceiling moldings.	❑ Use a feather duster for hard-to-reach areas, and remove dust and cobwebs from wall boards and ceiling corners.
5. Dust and polish mirrors.	❑ If mirrors have wooden frames, clean the frames with a cloth. ❑ Wipe the mirrors with a damp cloth followed by a dry cloth, using a sideways motion from top to bottom.

Dust the Guestroom (continued)

STEPS	HOW-TO'S
6. Dust and polish pictures.	❑ Wipe frames with a cloth. ❑ Clean and polish the glass on pictures.
7. Make sure drapes are dust and dirt free and are pinned and hung correctly.	
8. Dust and polish the dresser.	❑ Wipe the sides, front, edges, and top using a cloth. ❑ If the guest has checked out, open the drawers and wipe inside. ❑ Polish the sides, front, edges, and top with a clean cloth.
9. Dust the nightstands and beds.	❑ Start at the top of each nightstand and work down the sides to the legs and base, wiping with a cloth. ❑ Dust any exposed areas of the bed frame, including the headboard and footboard.
10. Clean and disinfect the telephone.	❑ Pick up the receiver and listen for the dial tone. ❑ Write any problems with the telephone on your room assignment sheet. ❑ Clean the telephone thoroughly. ❑ If required by the hotel's procedures, spray disinfectant on a cloth and wipe the mouthpiece and earphone.

(continued)

Dust the Guestroom (continued)

STEPS	HOW-TO'S
11. Dust tables, chairs, and lamps.	❑ Dust each table, beginning with the top surface and working down to the base and legs.
	❑ Dust wood and chrome surfaces on chairs, beginning at the top and working down to the legs.
	❑ Dust lamp shades, bulbs, and bases. Straighten shades and turn the seams toward the back.
12. Dust the television and stand.	❑ Dust the top and sides of the television set and its stand.
	❑ Clean the television screen with glass cleaner sprayed on a clean cloth. Only clean the screen when the television is off.
13. Set the air conditioner and heater controls.	❑ In an occupied room, leave the settings the way the guest had them.
	❑ The proper temperature setting for the air conditioner and heating controls in an unoccupied room varies among properties.
	❑ Ask your supervisor to show you how to set the controls

Vacuum the Guestroom and Report Room Status

Materials needed: *A small, stiff broom; a vacuum cleaner; a room assignment sheet; and a pen.*

STEPS	HOW-TO'S
1. Check the vacuum cleaner for safety.	❑ Safety must be a top concern at all times. If anything about your equipment looks unsafe, report it to your supervisor and have it repaired before you use it.
	❑ Do not use the vacuum if the cord is damaged. You could be hurt, or a short could start a fire. Be careful not to trip on the vacuum cleaner cord.
	❑ Before vacuuming the first room of the day, check to make sure the vacuum cleaner bag is empty.
	❑ Replace or empty the vacuum cleaner bag if it is full.
	❑ Immediately remove knots and tangles from vacuum cords since they can cause electrical shorts.
	❑ Immediately turn off equipment that sparks, smokes, or flames.
	❑ Never use electrical equipment, such as your vacuum cleaner, when standing in water or when your hands or clothes are wet.
	❑ Take vacuum cleaners that need repair to the housekeeping department.
2. Remove dirt from room corners and carpet edges.	❑ Use a small, stiff broom to brush dirt from room corners and carpet edges to a carpeted area that a vacuum can reach.
	❑ Push down on the broom and pull it toward you—away from the wall.
3. Plug the vacuum cleaner into the outlet nearest to the guestroom door.	

(continued)

Vacuum the Guestroom and Report Room Status (continued)	
STEPS	**HOW-TO'S**
4. Vacuum all areas.	❑ Begin vacuuming the room at the point farthest from the guestroom door. Use the vacuum cleaner only on carpeted surfaces. ❑ Work back toward the guestroom door. (In other words, vacuum over your footsteps.) ❑ Vacuum carpet edges slowly and carefully. ❑ Move chairs and tables, if necessary, to vacuum underneath them. When finished, put the furniture back in its proper location. ❑ Check under and behind the dressers, nightstands, and beds for trash and left-behind items. ❑ Turn off lamps and light switches as you pass them. ❑ Vacuum according to hotel procedures under the heavy items in the room, such as armoires, credenzas, beds, desks, and sofas. ❑ Vacuum under drapes, in front of the television, behind the doors, and in the closet. ❑ Vacuum the center of the room.
5. Unplug the vacuum, wind the cord correctly, and return the vacuum to your cart.	❑ Unplug the vacuum by grasping the plug (not the cord) and pulling it from the socket. ❑ The steps to wind the vacuum cord vary among properties.
6. Record information on your room assignment sheet.	
7. Tell the correct person or department that the room is clean.	❑ If the room is vacant, report its status to your supervisor or to the front desk. The front desk must know right away when vacant rooms are clean and ready for guests who are checking in, especially when the property is busy. ❑ The steps to report room status vary among properties.

Provide Evening Turndown Service

Materials needed: *A stocked housekeeping cart, a turndown assignment sheet, a pen, and special turndown amenities.*

STEPS	HOW-TO'S
1. Enter the guestroom.	❑ The turndown assignment sheet will tell you the rooms for which you will provide turndown service. ❑ Knock on the door and announce "Housekeeping" before entering the room. ❑ If the guest is in the room, inquire if there would be a convenient time to provide turndown. ❑ Prop the guestroom door open with a doorstop. ❑ Position your cart.
2. Remove guest items from the bed.	❑ Some properties do not allow you to move guest items.
3. Turn down the bed.	❑ Follow your supervisor's instructions for preparing the bed. ❑ At some properties, you may leave one terry bathrobe per adult guest neatly folded on the foot of the bed.
4. Place a turndown amenity in the appropriate location.	❑ Amenities will vary for each property and may be changed from time to time. ❑ Along with the amenity, you may also place a note or business card from the general manager or director of sales and marketing.

(continued)

Provide Evening Turndown Service *(continued)*

STEPS	HOW-TO'S
5. Tidy the sleeping room.	❑ Look around the room and straighten or tidy anything that is out of order. If a room is messy, it may require more extensive cleaning. ❑ Replace dirty ashtrays in smoking rooms. Restock matches. ❑ Replace dirty glasses. ❑ Collect any food service trays and dishes and move them to the service area in the corridor. Call room service and request that they be picked up. ❑ Empty the trash and replace the wastebasket liners. ❑ Vacuum if the room needs it.
6. Tidy the guest bathroom.	❑ Remove used terry from the bathroom. Restock with fresh terry. Your goal is to make the bathroom look as fresh as it did when it was completely cleaned earlier in the day. ❑ Straighten and wipe down the vanity area. Dry and polish the fixtures. ❑ Straighten and wipe down the tub area. Dry and polish the fixtures. ❑ Check the toilet tissue and facial tissue supply. Refill if necessary. ❑ Empty the trash and replace the liner.
7. Create a pleasant atmosphere in the guestroom.	❑ Close the drapes. ❑ Turn on the bedside lamp. ❑ Turn on the radio to a recommended easy-listening FM station. Adjust to a low volume. At your property, you may be told not to turn on the radio.

Provide Evening Turndown Service (continued)

STEPS	HOW-TO'S
	❑ Leave the thermostat set as the guest left it.
	❑ The room should appear comfortable and appealing when the guest returns at the end of his or her evening activities.
8. Double-check everything.	❑ Scan the guestroom, beginning at one point and working your way around. The appeal of the room may make a lasting impression that will result in repeat business.
	❑ Attend to any turndown task that you may have overlooked.
9. Exit and secure the room.	❑ Leave the room.
	❑ Lock the door.
	❑ Double-check to be sure the room door is locked. Protect the security and belongings of the guest by always making sure the door is locked.
10. Note on the turndown assignment sheet that the room has been completed.	

Competencies

1. Identify housekeeping's cleaning responsibilities in front-of-the-house areas of the hotel. (pp. 431–442)

2. Describe typical cleaning responsibilities of the housekeeping department in relation to food and beverage areas and banquet and meeting rooms. (pp. 442–443)

3. Describe housekeeping's responsibilities in relation to cleaning administrative offices, employee areas, and housekeeping department areas. (pp. 444–445)

4. Explain how the housekeeping department can respond to threats such as mold, mildew, and viruses. (pp. 446–449)

Public Area and Other Types of Cleaning

MOST PEOPLE—including guests—trust first impressions. In a hotel, a guest's first impression often revolves around what he or she sees and experiences in the property's public areas.

Public areas consist of a property's entrances, lobbies, corridors, elevators, restrooms, and health facilities. Other areas that the guest sees include dining areas, banquet and meeting rooms, spas, and sometimes, administration and sales offices. Some properties engineer public areas to convey a particular mood through such dramatic features as high ceilings, plant-laden balconies, mezzanines, decorative fabric panels, textured walls and floors, lighting, and ornate furniture and fixtures. But all levels of architecture and design aside, nothing can make or break an impression more than the cleanliness and condition of a property's public areas.

The condition of public or **front-of-the-house areas** makes a strong statement about the rest of the property. Spotless and well-kept public areas signal guests to expect the same level of care and attention in their guestrooms. They show, too, that the property most likely maintains the same standards of cleanliness for its "employees-only" areas—or for its rooms and corridors in the back of the house. To a large extent, the responsibility for cleaning public and other functional areas rests with the housekeeping department.

Front-of-the-House Areas

Establishing and maintaining housekeeping procedures for public areas is just as important as it is for guestrooms, but much less standardized. The housekeeping needs of public areas vary considerably among properties because of architectural differences, lobby space allocations, activities, and guest traffic. These and other factors also affect scheduling routines, requiring many of the cleaning tasks to be performed at night or on a special-project basis. Among the typical front-of-the-house areas that need daily—if not hourly—housekeeping attention are entrances, lobbies (including the front desk), corridors, elevators, public restrooms, swimming pools, exercise rooms, and spas.

Entrances

Hotel entrances demand stringent attention since they are among the most heavily trafficked areas in a property. Entrances must be kept clean both for aesthetic and for safety reasons.

The **frequency** of cleaning hotel entrances is largely contingent on the weather. Rainy and snowy days will require that these areas receive attention more often than days when the sun is shining. Salt and mud tracked in during the winter and spring also contribute to the deterioration of floor coverings and surfaces—particularly carpets.

Mats or runners placed both inside and outside hotel entrances can alleviate some of the headaches involved in keeping public space areas free of puddles, footprints, and outside dirt—and can protect guests from slips and falls. If properly positioned, these floor coverings can also protect the inside carpeting. Inclement weather will demand that runners and mats be frequently wet vacuumed or changed out. Because walk-off mats and runners have a tendency to shift across a smooth floor when subject to a high volume of foot traffic, an attendant should be assigned to see that the runners and mats are always laying flat and that the edges or corners have not curled thus creating a potential tripping hazard.

Regardless of weather conditions, hotel entrances should be monitored for cleanliness and safety throughout the day. Attendants should also frequently clean fingerprints and smudges from door surfaces—particularly glass areas. Even one set of fingerprints can spoil the appearance of an otherwise clean entranceway. Thorough vacuuming of entrance mats and cleaning of door surfaces, including door tracks, is conducted very early in the morning to avoid inconveniencing guests.

Lobbies

Lobbies require continual cleaning both because they are heavy-traffic areas and because they are the "gateways to the hotel." Many lobbies are a hub of activity where guests check in, socialize, relax, or, in the case of some properties, window-shop boutiques or specialty stores.

Since lobbies are such dynamic areas, properties generally schedule cleaning for the late-night and early-morning hours—meaning from 10:30 P.M. to 7:00 A.M. In this way, guests incur minimal inconvenience—and the staff can clean with little or no interference. Some cleaning tasks, however, must be performed during daylight hours to maintain lobby aesthetics. These tasks include emptying ashtrays and sand urns, picking up litter, attending to heavily trafficked floor areas, and straightening furniture.

Generally speaking, cleaning duties in the lobby can be performed once every hour, once every 24 hours, or once a week. In most properties, there are no hard and fast rules for how frequently a certain task should be performed. Some properties assign a lobby attendant to patrol the area and attend to cleaning activities as necessary. Activities usually assigned on an hourly or daily basis include the following:

- Emptying and wiping down wastebaskets
- Cleaning glass and window areas
- Wiping and dusting lobby telephones
- Cleaning drinking fountains
- Polishing railings
- Removing fingerprints or spots from walls
- Dusting furniture and table fixtures

the Rooms
CHRONICLE®

Consistent Public Space Cleaning through a Rotation Schedule

If you want to ensure that the hotel's public spaces are consistently clean, a useful tool is a rotational schedule. Such a schedule lists all the necessary tasks in an easy-to-follow, organized timetable. To begin this system, the staff went to the hotel's lobby with a clipboard and pen. Public space cleaners and managers together made a list of everything that required cleaning.

When all of the lobby tasks were listed, we moved on to other areas: dining rooms, restrooms, offices, hallways, and so on. When each area was complete, we gathered around a conference table to decide how often each task should be completed in order to keep the areas consistently clean. Tasks that had to be done hourly, daily, or frequently throughout the week were included in the normal job specification or description for public space cleaners. Tasks that had to be done weekly, monthly, or several times a year were included on the rotational schedule. For instance, dusting the furniture is done once a day and should be part of the daily routine. But rubbing the wood furniture with scratch-cover polish is only done twice a year and should be part of the rotation.

After all the decisions about timing were made, the rotational tasks were organized. This was like putting a giant jigsaw puzzle together. We tried to take into account the types of tasks, hotel occupancy patterns, and the available work hours. This can be done on a computer spreadsheet or on a large accountant's analysis pad.

Some hotels have special-project people who concentrate solely on the rotation tasks. Other hotels assign an hour or two of rotation work to each public space cleaner as part of his or her daily assignments. Our staff preferred the latter because each person wanted full responsibility for a given area of the hotel.

When the rotational schedule was complete, we posted it on a wall under a sheet of clear acrylic. When a day's tasks are completed, the cleaners cross them off with great satisfaction. If circumstances prevent a task from being completed, it is moved to another time. All these marks are made on the acrylic, which preserves our basic schedule for use year after year. We frequently revise our original timing of tasks as we get better about predicting wear and tear.

This proactive system keeps all of us so organized! Cleaners know well in advance what projects they will be doing, and guests always see us at our best.

Source: Gail Edwards, CHHE, *The Rooms Chronicle*®, Volume 2, Number 2, p. 5. For subscription information, call 866-READ-TRC.

- Polishing doorknobs and wiping surrounding areas
- Dusting and cleaning doorjambs and tracks
- Vacuuming the carpet
- Sweeping tile or hardwood floor areas
- Straightening furniture
- Emptying and cleaning ashtrays

Unique architectural design presents special cleaning considerations for housekeeping. (Courtesy of Marriott Marquis, Atlanta, Georgia)

Among the tasks typically assigned to public area attendants on a weekly basis are the following:

- Polishing wooden furniture
- Vacuuming upholstered furniture
- Vacuuming or cleaning drapes or window coverings
- Cleaning windowsills
- Dusting ceiling vents
- Dusting in high or hard-to-reach areas
- Cleaning carpet edges and baseboards

Some public area cleaning involves using a stepladder to reach high spots on walls, lighting fixtures, or decorative wall pieces. In all instances, employees should follow prescribed safety procedures when performing these cleaning tasks. Properties with unique architecture and interior design may hire outside contractors to attend to special cleaning needs on a periodic basis.

Front Desk

Like lobby cleaning, front desk cleaning must be scheduled during non-peak hours to avoid interrupting the flow of business. The front desk area should be cleaned with the same degree of attention as the lobby since it is such a pivotal area for shaping the guest experience. Although this area is technically part of the lobby, the front desk has its own set of cleaning needs and peculiarities.

Front desks vary in design. Some properties incorporate simple, straightforward designs into their decor while others opt for more elaborate fluted, curved, or grooved surfaces. The latter will generally take longer to clean than a more basic design since they may require special cleaning techniques and equipment. Whether rectangular or round, smooth or textured, every front desk needs the careful attention of the public area attendant to maintain a spotless appearance.

Vacuuming and emptying wastebaskets should be done both in front of and behind the desk. In some properties, housekeeping employees will also be responsible for wiping down and polishing front desk surfaces. Special care should be taken to remove fingerprints, smudges, and shoe and scuff marks, especially near the base of the desk. Any nicks, scratches, or other surface damage should be reported to the appropriate housekeeping supervisor. In all cases, public area attendants must never move any papers or other business-related items or touch or unplug equipment in the front desk area.

Corridors and Stairwells

Other sections of the hotel that most guests see before stepping foot into the guestroom are the public corridors or halls. In some properties, corridors are considered "guest space" and, therefore, become an extension of guestroom cleaning tasks.

A big part of corridor cleaning involves attending to the floor. In most cases, floors are covered with durable, attractive carpet designed for easy care and maintenance. Floors should be vacuumed at least once a day based on guest traffic and occupancy. Carpet shampooing is generally scheduled on a special-project basis—most likely during an off-season or a low-occupancy period.

Many properties recommend that, when cleaning baseboards, the attendant begin at one point in the corridor, work his or her way completely down one side of the hall, and then work back down the other side to his or her starting point. The attendant should also wipe down any trim around guestroom doors, paying special attention to fingerprints and smudges. Light fixtures should be dusted and any burned-out light bulbs replaced. Air supply vents and sprinklers should also be dusted and checked for proper functioning. Attendants should note the condition of emergency exit lights and report any damage to his or her supervisor.

Spot-cleaning the walls for smudges and fingerprints can be done much like baseboard cleaning, with the attendant working his or her way down alternate sides of the corridor. As a final step, the attendant should clean the front and back of the exit door, wipe any dirt and dust from its tracks, and check to see that it opens and closes properly.

Hotel stairwells are also considered "guest space" because they are often used by guests for travel between floors or to exit the building. Even if a stairwell is marked for emergency use only, housekeeping staff must keep it neat as it can represent the hotel's overall attention to cleaning detail. Walls, railings, light fixtures, steps, and signage must all be cleaned on a regular schedule based on the usage of the stairwell. In addition, each stairwell should be included on a daily schedule for an employee to check for litter or spills.

Ice/Vending Machine Areas. Some properties locate ice and vending machines in easy-to-find or low-traffic areas of guest corridors. These devices—and their surrounding areas—will require the attention of a public area attendant or house-person to ensure cleanliness and proper functioning.

Ice machines should be checked and cleaned daily. Before cleaning them, the attendant should make sure the unit functions correctly by checking the dispenser mechanism. Any clogs or other malfunction that cannot be readily corrected should be noted and reported. The attendant should also check for any water on the floor. Sometimes, when ice machines malfunction, melted ice leaks out and can cause floor damage. When cleaning the area, the attendant should remove any unmelted ice from the dispenser area and wipe the area dry. Exterior surfaces should be cleaned with the recommended cleaning solution and wiped dry. Particular attention should be paid to handles where fingerprints and smudges occur. Sometimes, housekeeping staff clean and sanitize actual mechanisms. If so, procedures should be designed according to the manufacturer's cleaning recommendations.

Vending machines can be either leased or owned by the hospitality operation. In either case, the public area attendant will usually be responsible for cleaning and dusting the exterior surfaces and checking mechanical functions. If the machine is owned by the hotel, the attendant should make a note of any items that need to be restocked and report them to his or her supervisor. Attendants may also be required to clean areas underneath and behind the machine. Such tasks are usually scheduled on a special-project basis since they require heavy lifting and moving.

Elevators

Elevators require frequent cleaning because of the volume of use. As with the lobby and front desk area, the best time to clean elevators is late at night or very early in the morning to avoid high-traffic periods.

Depending on interior design features, elevator surfaces may consist of metal, wood, carpet, vinyl, wallpaper, glass, mirrors, or a combination of materials. Each surface will require the public area attendant to follow a specific set of cleaning procedures to achieve the most effective results. In most instances, the attendant should clean from the top down to avoid resoiling areas already cleaned.

Among the problem cleaning areas in elevators are the sides near the floor. These areas are prime targets for scuff marks, scratches, or tears. Such damage should be noted and reported to the appropriate supervisor. Handrails should be polished to remove fingerprints, as should elevator controls and surrounding wall areas. When cleaning glass and mirrors, the attendant should step back and check the surface for streaks. Both the inside and outside of the elevator door should be wiped down, including the door tracks where dirt and dust collect.

Floor carpets are perhaps the most difficult to keep clean in elevators because of concentrated wear and tear. Some properties use standard vacuums to sweep elevator carpets while others supply attendants with high-powered, portable canister vacuums. In all instances, vacuuming should be completed quickly to lessen the time the elevator is out of service. Some properties carpet elevator floors with removable floor coverings. This way, the carpet can be removed for washing instead of being shampooed in place. A matching piece of carpet, of course, is carefully laid and secured while the dirty piece is being serviced.

Public Restrooms

Public restrooms are relatively constant from property to property. Some properties evoke a special atmosphere by decorating restrooms with ornate fixtures and mirrors, allocating lounge space filled with upholstered furniture and plants, and by providing conveniences such as hand blow dryers and changing tables.

Any special feature or convenience will require the property to devise an efficient cleaning procedure. To a large degree, the structure and size of a public restroom is determined by the service level of the property. Despite the features, the goal in cleaning any public washroom is to maintain a sanitary, safe, and attractive atmosphere for the visiting guest. This section will cover the most basic elements in public restroom cleaning.

At the very minimum, public restrooms should be cleaned twice daily: once in the morning and once in the evening. In some properties, more frequent cleanings are required to maintain a pleasant environment and to ensure proper sanitation and safety levels. Sometimes, these additional cleanings consist of "touch-up" cleanings every one or two hours—depending on the traffic.

The equipment needed for cleaning public restrooms is basically the same as that required for cleaning guest bathrooms: an approved all-purpose cleaner for bathroom surfaces; a bowl brush; cloths and sponges; water or an approved glass and mirror cleaner; rubber gloves; and protective eye covering. Some properties also use an odorless disinfectant. Attendants will also need a bucket, mop, and floor-cleaning chemicals.

Before entering the restroom, the attendant should check to see that the facility is vacant. If the attendant is cleaning a bathroom for members of the opposite sex, he or she should knock on the door, announce "housekeeping," and wait for a response. Generally, it is assumed safe to enter if a response is not heard after three announcements. When entering, the attendant should prop the door open and place an approved floor sign at the entrance, which indicates the restroom is being cleaned.

Many properties recommend applying the appropriate cleaner to toilets and urinals before attending to any other task. This way, the chemical has time to work while other areas are being cleaned. After applying the cleaner, trash containers should be emptied, wiped, and relined with new bags.

the Rooms
CHRONICLE

Are Public Restrooms Giving a Great First Impression?

Veteran cleaners explain how to inspect a public restroom: "Walk in the door. Look up to see if the ceiling vent is fuzz free, and look down to see if the floor drain is clean and polished." In two quick glances, our experts can determine whether the restroom receives regular, detailed care or only a passing touch-up.

Does this two-glance method really separate the clean from the not-so-clean? "Yes," veteran cleaners will say. "When the cleaning staff cares enough to reach up to vacuum the air vents or to get on hands and knees to polish the metal floor drain, you can be sure they have also cleaned the walls, floors, and fixtures." Keeping public restrooms clean and safe requires a strong combination of daily and regular cleaning.

Daily/Hourly Tasks. All public restrooms should be cleaned twice daily, inspected regularly, and touched up as necessary. A record should be kept of cleaning and inspection activities to limit the hotel's liability in case of a guest accident. For instance, if a guest slips, a log verifying that the hotel demonstrated reasonable care in keeping the floor dry would limit the hotel's exposure to a lawsuit. Records can be maintained using a log kept in the restroom. Some hotels post the log inside the towel dispenser or on the back of the entry door. Others keep a clipboard on the cleaner's cart and update a file in housekeeping after each day's inspection.

While working, employees must take care to keep cleaning supplies out of guests' view. Some hotels have special, shielded carts or use storage rooms near the restroom. When restrooms are closed for cleaning, it is courteous to guests to post signs indicating the locations of nearby restrooms.

Deep-Cleaning Tasks. Many tasks in the job of cleaning a public restroom require that the room be placed out of service for a few hours while it is deep cleaned. For instance, stripping the floor and resealing it may need to be done four times a year, depending on the traffic in the restroom. Men's restrooms often need the area around urinals redone more frequently, due to splashes of urine deteriorating the floor sealant.

Other projects might be: scrub the floor drains; wash all walls; clean all edges; remove ceiling vents and clean them; clean the light fixtures; scrub the trash receptacles; scrub the carpet; and wash the windows.

Reporting Maintenance Issues. It is extremely important that public restroom cleaners immediately report maintenance issues. Failure to repair drips, leaks, burned-out bulbs, broken locks, and other such things in a timely manner will cost the hotel precious profit.

Meeting Guest Expectations. The appearance of public restrooms is very important if a hotel is to have a favorable impact on guests. Always under the scrutiny of the public, the condition of these bathrooms makes a strong statement about the rest of the hotel. Customers who only visit the restaurant or bar or who only attend a meeting will draw conclusions about the condition of guestrooms based on their impressions of the public space.

Source: Gail Edwards, CHHE, *The Rooms Chronicle*®, Volume 4, Number 3, p. 5.
For subscription information, call 866-READ-TRC.

Basins and surrounding countertop areas should be cleaned next. Most attendants begin by spraying the sinks and vanity with a cleaning solution and wiping the area with a sponge or cloth. Drain traps should be checked for hair and other debris; faucets should be checked for drips. If there is any exposed piping, attendants should ensure the pipes are free of dust, dirt, and leaks. When cleaning the countertop area, the attendant should check for stains and damage as he or she wipes down the area. Fixtures should be wiped with cleaning solution and a damp rag and then polished. All sinks and surrounding countertops should be wiped dry with a clean cloth. Finally, mirrors should be wiped down with the recommended cleaning solution. Careful attention should be paid to leaving the mirror free of streaks and water spots.

Toilets and urinals should be cleaned using the bowl brush and a clean cloth. After swabbing the entire bowl or urinal, the attendant should flush the unit while rinsing the bowl brush in the fresh water. Outer areas of the fixture should be wiped with a damp cloth or sponge, working from the top to the base. As a final step, handles should be wiped and polished with a dry cloth.

Partitions are most efficiently cleaned using a spray bottle with cleaning solution and a damp cloth or sponge. Most attendants clean each stall panel separately, beginning in the right-top corner and working across and down with wide sweeping movements. Special attention should be paid to areas around door locks and paper dispensers to remove any smudges or fingerprints. An attendant should *never* stand on a toilet to clean high or hard-to-reach areas of partitions. Special cleaning tools with long or extendable handles are available for this purpose. After wiping surfaces clean, the attendant should look for scratches or other surface marks and make a note to report them to his or her supervisor.

Once partitions are clean, the attendant can begin to wipe down walls. Appropriate cleaning solutions will vary depending on whether surfaces are tiled, painted, or paneled. In each case, the attendant should work systematically, beginning at one point and cleaning his or her way back to the start. Any scuffs, nicks, or other damage to wall surfaces should be noted.

At this point, dispensers for toilet seat covers, toilet paper, tissue, paper towels, and soap should be restocked. A cleaning of each dispenser is usually performed when it is empty to avoid damaging or soiling the paper products. In most instances, a light dusting or simple polishing is appropriate to remove any surface marks or smudges.

Among the last steps in cleaning public washrooms is sweeping and mopping the floor. Beginning in the farthest corner from the entrance, the attendant should sweep all exposed floor areas and the baseboards. Doing so prepares the floor more fully for wet cleaning and removes loose dust and dirt that can muddy mop water. When mopping, it is important to use clean warm water and the appropriate amount of cleaning solution. Solution can be mixed in the water or applied directly onto the floor. As with sweeping, the attendant should begin mopping in the farthest corner and work his or her way back toward the entrance. Mopping around fixtures should be approached slowly and carefully to avoid splashing dirty water onto clean surfaces.

A second bucket of clear hot water should be prepared for rinsing. The attendant should rinse the mop, wring out the excess water, and mop the surfaces a second time. During this stage, it is important to rinse and wring the mop out frequently to ensure that the floor is thoroughly cleansed. Frequently wringing out the mop also prevents excess water on the floor since it functions, in a sense, as a "dry mop."

When the task is completed, the public area attendant should reassemble his or her supplies and make one final check. Any unusual or offensive odors could indicate an improperly functioning ventilation system. If the floor is still wet from mopping, an appropriate warning sign should be in place to alert guests until the floor is dry. As always, any condition requiring maintenance should be noted and reported to the appropriate supervisor.

Swimming Pool Areas

Swimming is perhaps the most popular of all recreational sports. Many properties—particularly resorts—cater to this interest by providing swimming facilities.

Pools can be either indoor or outdoor. Pool designs are as varied as hotel operations and range from very basic to very elaborate settings. Some pool areas include whirlpools and saunas. In most hotels, the daily care and maintenance of the pool, sauna, or whirlpool is the responsibility of the engineering or maintenance department. However, the housekeeping staff does "make the rounds" to attend to specific tasks within the pool area.

Among the pool-area duties usually appointed to housekeeping staff are:

- Collecting wet towels.

- Restocking towels.

- Emptying and cleaning trash receptacles.

- Emptying and cleaning ashtrays.

- Cleaning wall areas.

- Sweeping and mopping hard floor surfaces.

- Caring for any carpeted areas.

- Washing window or glass areas.

- Cleaning and straightening lounge furniture.

As with any public area, unsafe, unsanitary, or damaged conditions should be noted and reported to management staff.

Exercise Rooms

The rising interest in physical fitness and health has produced a long-term demand for health products and services. In response to this trend, many properties have made health facilities a part of their overall package.

Housekeeping's part in servicing these facilities will largely be determined by the size and scope of these areas and the equipment involved. Health and fitness services can range from simply a pool and a sauna to fully outfitted gymnasiums with a trained staff. Equipment for an exercise room might include universal gyms, cardiovascular equipment (such as treadmills, stair steppers, elliptical machines, and stationary bicycles), rowing machines, floor mats, barbells, and dumbbells. The design of these facilities often incorporates special flooring or hardwood surfaces, mirrors, and special light fixtures. Properties with more elaborate facilities provide locker rooms and shower areas.

The responsibility for maintaining exercise equipment typically rests with the hotel's engineering staff. Housekeeping personnel, however, will play a role in ensuring that these facilities meet the same standards of cleanliness that the guest enjoys in other public areas. For the most part, an attendant will be assigned on a daily basis to perform such tasks as:

- Dusting and sanitizing equipment.

- Cleaning mirrors and glass areas.

- Sweeping and mopping floors.

- Removing soiled linen.

- Restocking clean linen.

- Cleaning and straightening any furniture.

- Dusting light fixtures.

- Spot-cleaning walls.

For safety reasons, it is extremely important for attendants to note the general condition of the equipment and report any suspected malfunctions to their supervisor. Attendants may also be responsible for cleaning shower and locker areas and replenishing guest amenities.

Spas

Throughout the 1990s and 2000s, hotels have added spas at an ever-increasing rate. Once considered an amenity for the spouses of golfers, spas have become almost as necessary as a pool for higher-end lodging properties.

At some lodging properties, spa staff are responsible for cleaning spa areas. Between guests, spa staff is typically responsible for cleaning treatment rooms and changing the sheets and linens after each treatment.

More thorough cleaning is typically done each night after the spa closes as well as at scheduled intervals throughout the day. This may be done by the property's housekeeping department staff. The use of disinfectants are of particular importance for health reasons.

Most spas use a great deal of water, whether it is in pedicure stations, hydrotherapy equipment, hot tubs, showers, or baths. Bacteria is attracted to wet surfaces, so these surfaces in a spa need to receive thorough, regular cleaning and sanitizing. Water reservoirs also need careful cleaning and disinfecting.

Floors need regular cleaning with a damp sponge or a disposable mop using a detergent and a low-level disinfectant. Cloths and mops have to be changed frequently to avoid recontaminating surfaces. Other cleaning tasks in a spa include:

• Cleaning walls, blinds, and curtains with a detergent and disinfectant.

• Vacuuming carpets and upholstery.

• Cleaning toilets and sinks.

• Disinfecting hydrotherapy equipment.

• Cleaning and sanitizing locker room and shower areas.

• Cleaning and maintaining duct, fan, and air systems.

Other Functional Areas

Besides cleaning public areas such as lobbies and restrooms, housekeeping staff may be responsible for cleaning dining rooms, banquet and meeting rooms, administration and sales offices, employee areas, and housekeeping offices and work areas. In some of these areas, housekeeping staff will have limited responsibilities; in others, cleaning activities will be as elaborate as the area's counterpart in the front of the house.

Dining Rooms

Cleanliness in dining rooms is important not only for image, but for safety and sanitation reasons. Depending on the size and services of a hotel, the housekeeping department may be responsible for cleaning restaurant areas and/or areas adjacent to the lobby where breakfast is served.

In the restaurants, the dining room staff will be responsible for keeping the area presentable during operating hours. This includes cleaning tables, changing linens, attending to on-the-spot spills, and light vacuuming or sweeping. In most properties, housekeeping staff work on an after-hour basis nightly, weekly, or monthly to accomplish more thorough cleaning.

In breakfast rooms adjacent to lobbies, the housekeeping staff may play a more direct role. Often it is a public space employee who serves as the breakfast room attendant to set up the room, act as a greeter, serve the food, and clean up at the conclusion of the breakfast.

Cleaning tasks associated with dining room and breakfast room areas include:

• Vacuuming (often moving furniture to ensure best results).

• Spot cleaning and shampooing carpet as needed.

• Wiping down counters, host station, food/beverage dispensers.

• Spot-cleaning walls.

• Wiping windowsills.

• Dusting and polishing furniture.

- Cleaning upholstery.

- Attending to light fixtures.

Many properties establish schedules that designate when certain cleaning tasks should be performed.

Banquet and Meeting Rooms

As with dining areas, banquet and meeting rooms are often cleaned by another department—in this case, the banquet or conference services staff—with house-keeping's assistance. All meeting rooms should be cleaned immediately after a function. Nothing is more unappealing to passing guests or prospective clients than viewing a meeting room that displays the unsightly evidence of the previous night's festivities. Furthermore, stains that are allowed to set in carpeting or other furnishings can become nearly impossible to remove the next day.

In some properties, housekeeping staff will be responsible for cleaning chairs, tables, furniture, and wall and floor areas after all special meeting and food service items have been removed. When cleaning furnishings, special attention should be given to removing food particles and stains from upholstered surfaces. Attendants should note the condition of each piece of furniture and report any damage or stains to the appropriate supervisor. Carpet care involves thorough vacuuming, stain removal, and shampooing on a frequent basis. In addition, attendants may have special cleaning tasks depending on the design and function of the room. Sometimes, too, the services of outside contractors may be needed—particularly for cleaning high ceilings and ornate lighting fixtures such as chandeliers.

Administration and Sales Offices

The design of most properties include office areas for conducting various administrative and sales activities. Depending on size and service level, the operation may contain administrative offices for the management of all divisions (such as human resources, rooms, food & beverage, marketing and sales, etc.)—plus areas for supporting staff. Although technically considered back-of-the-house areas, administrative and sales offices periodically host important interactions between property staff and outside clients, vendors, business associates, and prospective employees.

To ensure that these areas look their best at all times, the housekeeping staff is called upon to maintain their overall cleanliness and appearance. The scope of the tasks will vary from property to property. For the most part, attendants will dust, empty wastebaskets, spot-clean wall areas, and sweep or vacuum on a nightly basis. Other tasks such as washing windows are scheduled on a weekly or monthly basis. Deep-cleaning tasks that require moving furniture are typically scheduled during low-volume business periods to minimize disruption. While doing any cleaning task in these areas, housekeeping attendants should avoid moving or rearranging any items on desks or work surfaces—particularly computers, business papers, and folders.

Employee Areas

Employee areas in the back of the house often constitute as much space—if not more—as front-of-the-house areas. Although technically "closed" to the guest, these areas deserve the same level of cleaning attention that public areas do. A property that ensures that employees have a safe, clean, and pleasant environment in which to work, eat, take breaks, and go to the bathroom will gain the respect and loyalty of those employees. In the long run, this will invariably show in the quality of products and services provided by employees.

Although each employee does his or her part in maintaining the neatness of the **back-of-the-house areas**, the responsibility for heavy-duty cleaning tasks rests with the housekeeping staff. Housekeeping attendants will see that employee areas are free of dirt, grime, and dust by adhering to a cleaning schedule that is as carefully devised as that for cleaning the front of the house. Typical areas for which housekeeping will be responsible include service corridors and elevators, employee dining areas, employee washrooms and locker rooms, loading docks, and storage areas. In properties with food service outlets, housekeeping may also be responsible for some limited tasks in kitchen areas such as maintaining floor, wall, and ceiling surfaces.

Back-of-the-house areas are generally designed to withstand more wear and tear than areas open to guests—which reflects their function. Floors may consist of such stain-resistant materials as tile; painted concrete; or flat, tightly woven carpets. Walls and ceilings, too, will usually be smooth in texture and void of complicated angles or hard-to-reach areas. Even though procedures for back-of-the-house cleaning resemble front-of-the-house practices, attendants may enjoy a less complicated routine since surfaces tend to be smoother and furniture and fixtures less ornate. Often, too, these areas lend themselves to cleaning with heavy-duty equipment which can speed cleaning tasks.

Housekeeping Areas

Housekeeping areas should be spotless since they represent the headquarters of the property's professional cleaning staff. The size and composition of these areas is dependent on the size and service level of the property itself. Typically, housekeeping operations emanate from three basic areas: the housekeeping office, the laundry, and the linen room.

Like any administrative office, the housekeeping office should be cleaned and maintained to the same standards as a public area. Floors should be swept, mopped, and vacuumed; walls spot-cleaned; and wastebaskets cleaned and emptied. Baseboards should be free of dust and dirt; windows free of grime and streaks; and furniture free of dust.

The same applies to the laundry area. In addition, special care should be taken to keep the exterior surfaces of machines clean to prevent resoiling linen. The inside drums of washers, dryers, and extractors should be wiped down between cycles; buildup on lint filters and in detergent areas should also be removed. Distinct areas should be maintained for processing dirty and clean laundry items. Folding tables, irons, clips, hangers, and other laundry aids should also be frequently wiped and cleaned to prevent the contamination of freshly laundered

the Rooms CHRONICLE®

Public, Employee Spaces Need Spring Cleaning

Mention the word "spring" to executive housekeepers and they automatically add the word "clean." Spring and clean are two words that just go together for managers who focus on the housekeeping side of hotels. The words provoke vivid images. Say "spring clean" and thoughts pop up of airing it out, washing it down, cleaning it up, and throwing it out. Dreams prevail of having everything fresh and organized. But how can a manager change this dream into reality? How can spring cleaning really happen?

Most year-round hotels do not have budgets for extra spring-cleaning hours. Their budgets are strictly based on productivity measures attached to rooms rented. Also hotels are supposed to look their best all the time.

Still, there are some projects that need to be done only annually or biannually. Think chandeliers. Think pool furniture. Then think about projects that seem to get shoved aside because there is never enough time: Like cleaning out linen discards. Like equipment inventories. Like organizing uniforms.

The public and employee spaces of hotels need spring cleaning. Whether the housekeeping department accomplishes the work in the spring or at another time of the year, the work must be done. Here's how:

- Prepare the project list and prioritize tasks.

- Work within the budget.

- If the project involves another department, schedule a realistic time period for cleaning.

- Get in the mood. Prepare the staff, make it fun, and get the work done.

- Going forward, ensure more of the projects are included in routine task schedules so that next year's spring-cleaning list will not be so long.

With a good plan in place and a spring-cleaning mindset, it is possible to create a perfect hotel and achieve the goals of the housekeeping manager. Whether the clean-up and clean-out is accomplished in a day or a month or over the course of a year, spring cleaning is necessary.

Source: Mary Friedman, *The Rooms Chronicle®*, Volume 11, Number 1, pp. 4–5. For subscription information, please call 866-READ-TRC.

linens. Finally, all shelves and storage areas should be periodically wiped and dusted. Any laundry supplies should be straightened and tidied for easy access and inventory purposes.

Linen rooms also contain rows of supply shelves, which require frequent cleaning and dusting. It is extremely important to keep these areas well-organized—both for efficiency and for maintaining accurate inventories. Cleanliness, too, is critical since the property's laundered sheets, pillowcases, blankets, towels and washcloths, and food service linens are stored in this area. In addition to cleaning floors and walls, routine tasks in the linen room may include dusting shelves, straightening supplies, and positioning room attendant carts for ease in restocking.

Special Concerns

Depending on the property's design and architectural features, housekeeping may be assigned projects that involve complicated cleaning techniques, special equipment, and team efforts. Special projects might include cleaning certain weaves and types of carpet, ornate light fixtures such as chandeliers, staircases and handrails, interior fountains, windows and window coverings, and other decorative features such as wall hangings. Most special cleaning projects require a great deal of expertise and planning in terms of assembling supplies and equipment.

Some projects may require that the hotel contracts with an outside company that possesses the expertise and/or equipment in order to complete a project. These projects typically include exterior window washing for multi-level hotels, cleaning of large or expensive chandeliers, and air duct and exhaust vent cleaning.

The procedures section of this chapter provides sample guidelines for cleaning the more standard public areas.

Mold and Mildew

Molds and mildew are potential concerns for housekeepers. Essentially they are fungi that grow on the surfaces of objects, within pores, and in deteriorated materials. They can cause discoloration and odor problems, deteriorate building materials, and lead to allergic reactions in guests and employees, as well as other health problems. Mold thrives when four conditions are present:

- Temperatures between 40° and 100°F [4° to 38°C].

- Nutrients such as furnishings and building materials.

- Spores (which are present everywhere).

- Moisture (relative humidity) of greater than 70 percent.[1]

Mold problems in hotels experienced a sharp upswing in the 1990s, with four-star hotels being hit even harder than three-star hotels. In Honolulu, Hilton opened a new tower at one of its resorts in April 2001. They had to close it by July 2002 because of mold problems. It required 14 months and $55 million to eradicate the mold and reopen the tower.

Most of the responsibilities for preventing mold fall to the engineering department and those who design the hotel. However, housekeeping also contributes to the battle against mold. Public space cleaners who travel throughout the hotel should be on the lookout for condensation and wet spots. They need to fix the source of moisture problems as soon as possible. Any wet or damp spots should be cleaned and dried within 48 hours. Any signs of mold should also be reported immediately to engineering and management.

Viruses

In June of 2007, *Lodging* Magazine reported that hotels have been hit with outbreaks of norovirus, a highly contagious gastrointestinal illness that causes vomiting and diarrhea. Guests are often contagious for days before any symptoms of the

the Rooms CHRONICLE®

Preventing Mold and Mildew Growth Presents Unique Challenges

Aside from unattractive stains, foul odors, and expensive repairs, mold and mildew growth presents the possibility of serious health problems. According to the United States Environmental Protection Agency (EPA), mold growth produces allergens, irritants, and in some instances toxic substances. Mold can also irritate eyes, skin, nose, throat, and lungs for both those who are allergic to mold, and those who have no known allergy to mold.

Housekeepers, maintenance engineers and general managers all need to be aware of the signs associated with mold and mildew growth in order to ensure a completely comfortable stay for all guests. Since mold and mildew grow where moisture is present, the most common area to see signs of mold and mildew growth is in the bathroom. Common signs include discoloration of surfaces exposed to high moisture content, a musty and moldy smelling odor, higher than average complaints of illness, and a slimy texture.

Extensive use of bathroom appliances allows for moisture and humidity—crucial elements to promote the growth of mold and mildew—to build up in the bathroom and guestroom. While limiting the number of showers a guest can take is not wise and impractical, there are other ways to prevent mold and mildew growth, and to repair existing damage.

Keeping it dry

Although the EPA states that mold and mold spores cannot be eliminated completely, there are steps that housekeepers can take to reduce the likelihood of mold growth. The easiest preventative step is to make sure all items are dry. Check to make sure there isn't excessive water near the bathtub or shower, that waste baskets are free of liquids, that there are no signs of water damage on the ceiling or walls, and that carpeted areas near the bathroom and guestroom windows are dry. Also, make sure housekeepers regularly check windows and pipes for leaks. If leaks or excessive moisture are present, notify engineering immediately.

Another step in the prevention of mold and mildew growth is keeping a close eye on absorbent and porous items. Again, check carpeted areas for signs of water damage. In addition, cloth and plastic shower curtains have a high potential for mold growth since they are exposed to moisture constantly. Cloth curtains are very absorbent and tend to dry slowly; plastic curtains can fold over to prevent moist areas from drying properly.

Housekeepers should constantly check to see that shower curtains are drying thoroughly and are not showing any signs of mold or mildew growth. If mold and mildew growth is present, housekeepers can either replace existing curtains with new ones, or they can bleach the curtains. Bleaching will help to kill and remove mold, as well as brighten shower curtains.

Other items that are especially porous yet overlooked are bathroom counters, showers, and bathtubs. Porous materials used for countertops allow for moisture and humidity to seep deep into surfaces, offering ideal conditions for mold to

(continued)

grow. Likewise, porous tiles used for the shower and bathtub area provide exceptional opportunities for mold growth, especially since they are constantly exposed to high humidity. In addition to porous tiles, the shower and bathtub areas usually have grout between the tiles. These surfaces are annoying to clean efficiently and are therefore perfect areas for mold growth.

To prevent mold and mildew from growing on these surfaces, use cleaning sprays and tools specifically designed to eliminate mold spores and destroy mold that is already growing. Also, make sure that during the deep cleaning process housekeepers pay close attention to corners, grout, and the shower, tub, and counter for signs of mold growth.

An essential step to prevent mold and moisture damage in guest bathrooms is to install exhaust fans or moisture vents. Without these ventilation outlets, humidity will be trapped in the bathroom until the door is open, thus subjecting every surface in the bath to unwanted moisture buildup.

Bathroom ceilings

Don't forget to pay close attention to the ceiling in the guest bath, especially around the shower/bathtub area. The steam associated with long, hot showers as well as humidity's propensity to rise probably makes the bathroom ceiling the most fertile surface for mold and mildew growth. Given that most guests close the door when using the bathroom or showering, it is very easy for steam to become trapped in the confined room. Since most guestroom ceilings are painted with flat paint, there is little barrier to prevent the excessive moisture from being absorbed by the ceiling substrate.

To create a vapor barrier on ceilings and other painted surfaces, semi-gloss or high gloss enamel paint should be used. Alternatively, various companies offer a mold and mildew-proof paint specifically formulated for commercial bathrooms. The latex paint comes available in eggshell, satin and semi-gloss sheen and is highly resistant to peeling and blistering.

Mold remediation

Besides removing water damaged carpets and counter tops, there are other, less expensive, methods to remove mold. If the damage and mold growth is not too extensive, less than ten square feet, the housekeeping department will be able to take care of the situation. Make sure housekeepers use special solutions designed to kill and remove mold and that won't cause further damages to the surfaces on which the mold is growing on. However, if mold growth and damage is widespread, then mold remediation professionals need to be called in. The EPA recommends hiring a contractor or cleaner that has experience in the killing and removal of mold.

Mold and mildew growth should not be taken lightly. This is a serious problem that can cause considerable, and expensive, problems for hotels. Although the costs for replacing and fixing items that are damaged by mold can be costly, the main concern for hotels should be the health of guests and employees. Proper steps need to be taken to assure that mold growth is kept to an absolute minimum. Existing mold growth needs to be removed in order to eliminate dangerous health risks.

(continued)

For more information about indoor air quality and mold, visit the EPA's website at http://www.epa.gov/mold/. Additionally, the EPA has published a free online booklet titled, "Mold Remediation in Schools and Commercial Buildings." This publication presents guidelines for the remediation/cleanup of mold and moisture problems in commercial buildings, including hotels. It has been designed primarily for building managers, plant engineers, and others who are responsible for commercial building maintenance. Using this document, individuals with little or no experience with mold remediation should be able to make a reasonable judgment as to whether their mold situation can be handled in-house. The publication can be viewed and downloaded at: http://www.epa.gov/mold/mold_remediation.html

Source: Natalka A. Gluszko, *The Rooms Chronicle®*, Volume 13, Number 2, pp. 8–9. For subscription information, call 866-READ-TRC.

illness appear. Two Washington hotels ended up shutting down for several days due to norovirus contamination. To eliminate the highly contagious virus—a virus that could cling to elevator buttons—each hotel sanitized every room. A medical service laundry was hired to clean the linens. All hard surfaces in the hotel that were seven feet tall or lower were cleaned with sanitizers, and harsh chemicals were sprayed on all soft surfaces. Airborne chemicals were released into some areas, forcing everyone to evacuate the premises for 24 hours. To prevent future outbreaks, the hotel had to switch to cleaning chemicals with disinfectants. Public health experts say that it is now necessary for housekeeping staff to receive special training on cleaning hard surfaces. Likewise, housekeeping staff should be on the lookout for signs of illness such as vomiting or fecal matter. These are signs that an area should be disinfected.

Endnote

1. U.S. Environmental Protection Agency, *Building Air Quality: A Guide for Building Owners and Facility Managers*, December 1991, p. 141.

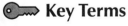 **Key Terms**

back-of-the-house areas—The functional areas of the hotel in which employees have little or no guest contact, such as engineering and maintenance.

frequency—How often each item on an area inventory list needs to be cleaned or maintained.

front-of-the-house areas—The functional areas of the hotel in which employees have extensive guest contact, such as food and beverage facilities and the front office.

Review Questions

1. What message does a spotless and well-kept public area convey to guests?

2. Why do the housekeeping needs of public areas vary considerably from property to property?

3. Name cleaning activities that are generally performed every 24 hours in a lobby area.

4. What is the minimum number of times that public washrooms should be cleaned each day?

5. What is the first cleaning task many properties recommend that the public area attendant do after he or she enters a public washroom? Why?

6. Name duties usually assigned to housekeeping staff in swimming pool areas.

7. In hotels with fitness facilities, which department generally has the responsibility for maintaining the proper functioning of exercise equipment?

8. Name cleaning tasks that housekeeping may perform in dining areas.

9. Why is it important to maintain the same standards of cleanliness for back-of-the-house areas and for front-of-the-house areas?

10. What are some of the special tasks involved in cleaning housekeeping areas? Why are they important?

Internet Sites

For more information, visit the following Internet sites. Remember that Internet addresses can change without notice. If the site is no longer there, you can use a search engine to look for additional sites.

Ecolab
www.ecolab.com

Environmental Protection Agency
www.epa.gov/mold

Grainger WW
www.grainger.com

Jani-King Housekeeping Services
www.janiking.com

Stuart Dean Co., Inc.
www.stuartdean.com

Task Breakdowns: Public Area and Other Types of Cleaning

The procedures presented in this section are for illustrative purposes only and should not be construed as recommendations or standards. While these procedures are typical, readers should keep in mind that each property has its own procedures, equipment specifications, and policies regarding protective gear which are designed to fit individual needs.

Clean Elevators

Materials needed: *Stocked public-space cleaning cart, an elevator key, a vacuum cleaner with attachments, a stepladder, and a small brush or broom.*

STEPS	HOW-TO'S
1. Take the elevator out of service.	❏ The steps to place an elevator out of service vary among properties. ❏ The elevator will stay on one floor and the door will stay open until you place the elevator back in service.
2. Dust the ceiling and lights.	❏ Use a stepladder to reach the ceiling. Don't climb higher than the second step from the top. ❏ Wipe the ceiling and lights with a cleaning cloth. ❏ Move the stepladder as necessary to clean the entire ceiling.
3. Dust all surfaces with a dust cloth or a damp cloth followed by a clean, dry cloth.	
4. Vacuum carpeted elevators.	❏ Report loose or ripped carpeting to your supervisor and note it on your assignment sheet.
5. Clean hard floors in elevators.	
6. Clean the door tracks.	❏ Use a brush or small broom to loosen the debris. ❏ Use a vacuum cleaner attachment to vacuum out the dirt. ❏ Wipe the inside track with a damp cloth.

Clean Elevators (continued)

STEPS	HOW-TO'S
7. Clean the insides of elevator doors.	❑ Shut the doors by pulling them shut or by putting the elevator back in service. ❑ Wipe and polish the inside surfaces of the elevator doors with a dry cloth.
8. Put all cleaning supplies back in your cart.	
9. Place the elevator back in service.	❑ The steps to place an elevator back in service vary among properties.
10. Close the door and wipe the outside of the door with a dry cloth.	❑ Proceed to each floor and repeat the cleaning process.

Clean the Front Office and Lobby Areas

Materials needed: Stocked public-space cleaning cart, a vacuum cleaner with attachments, a disinfectant spray, cleaning cloths, a broom, mild detergent, glass cleaner, a squeegee, and a step stool.

STEPS	HOW-TO'S
1. Clean and empty ashtrays and ash urns.	❑ Make sure cigarettes are not burning. Empty ashtrays and ash urns into the trash. ❑ Wash ashtrays and liners. ❑ Return clean ashtrays to the correct spots.
2. Pick up trash and empty the trash cans.	❑ Pick up any trash on the floor. ❑ Empty trash cans and clean them as needed. ❑ Keep recyclables separate from other trash.
3. Clean the telephones.	❑ Spray an approved disinfectant on a damp cloth and clean each telephone receiver and base. Do not get in the way of front desk employees or night auditors. ❑ Pay special attention to telephone receivers. Don't forget to clean telephone receivers on fax machines.
4. Vacuum carpets and upholstered furniture.	❑ Vacuum under desks and other areas. Move furniture as necessary. ❑ Use the correct vacuum cleaner attachments to vacuum upholstered furniture. ❑ Be sure to vacuum the arms, seat, back of the seat, back of the furniture, and the areas between the seat, back, and sides. ❑ Remove and store the vacuum cleaner attachments.

Clean the Front Office and Lobby Areas (continued)

STEPS	HOW-TO'S
5. Clean handrails.	❏ Remove any cobwebs or dirt with a broom before washing the handrails.
	❏ Wipe them with a damp cloth and mild detergent followed by a wet cloth to rinse away the detergent.
	❏ Wipe them dry with a dry cloth.
6. Dust the area.	❏ When working around computers, be careful not to disturb ongoing work. Only dust keyboards when the computer is off.
7. Mop and wax hard floors.	
8. Clean windows.	❏ Spray windows with water or an approved glass cleaner.
	❏ Start at the top of each window and pull a squeegee down the window.
	❏ Overlap each stroke slightly to remove all water or glass cleaner.
	❏ Use a step stool or long-handled squeegee to reach high places.
	❏ Polish the glass with a dry, clean cloth.
9. Steam-extract carpets when scheduled to do so.	
10. If guests approach the area you are cleaning, step out of the way until they leave.	

Clean Food and Beverage Outlets

Materials needed: Stocked public-space cleaning cart, a bucket, sanitizing solution, detergent, water or an approved glass cleaner, a buffer machine, floor wax, and carpet-cleaning equipment.

STEPS	HOW-TO'S
1. Prepare the room for cleaning.	❑ Turn on as many lights as possible so you can see what you are doing. ❑ Open drapes or blinds to allow light to enter. ❑ Look at the entire area to plan your cleaning.
2. Pick up trash and empty the trash cans.	❑ Pick up any trash on the floor and put it in the bag on your cart. ❑ Keep recyclables separate from other trash.
3. Clean seats and table legs.	❑ Use a small broom to brush chairs, booths, banquettes, and stools, including seats and backs. ❑ If your vacuum has an upholstery brush, you may vacuum these areas. ❑ Wipe tables, chairs, legs, and rungs with a clean cloth dampened with a sanitizing solution. ❑ Wipe leather or vinyl with a damp cloth.
4. Sweep the edges of carpets and hard floors.	❑ Use a stiff broom to sweep food residue and other debris from the corners. Sweep hard-to-reach areas carefully to eliminate food residue that might attract pests. ❑ Note any signs of pests and report these to the executive housekeeper.
5. Clean floors.	❑ Sweep and mop hard floors. ❑ Wax floors as needed.

Clean Food and Beverage Outlets (continued)	
STEPS	**HOW-TO'S**
6. Remove food residue and spills from carpets.	❑ Look for any ground-in food or beverage spills on the carpet. The vacuum will not remove the greasy residue of food that has been ground into the carpet. ❑ Remove food and spills with a damp, clean cloth. Blot the area dry before vacuuming it. Red wine spills and other stains will require special treatment with a stain remover.
7. Vacuum carpets.	❑ Use the industrial vacuum for large areas and the smaller carpet sweeper for small areas. ❑ Move chairs away from tables. ❑ Vacuum carefully under tables and around sidework stands. ❑ Return chairs to tables.
8. Steam-extract carpets.	❑ As scheduled or as needed, shampoo or steam-extract the carpets. ❑ The type of carpet-cleaning equipment will dictate the cleaning method (shampooing or steam extracting).
9. Dust furniture and fixtures.	❑ Do not use furniture polish. Its odor may annoy diners.
10. Clean and polish glass.	❑ Follow the property's procedures for cleaning glass.

Chapter 11 Outline

Competencies

1. Identify flammability and acoustical considerations important to the initial selection of ceiling surfaces, wall coverings, and hotel furnishings. (pp. 459–460)

2. Describe critical characteristics of common types of ceiling surfaces and wall coverings. (pp. 460–466)

3. Describe general care considerations for the types of furniture and fixtures commonly found in public areas, guestrooms, and staff areas in a hotel. (pp. 466–470)

4. Describe general care conditions for such items as seating, case goods, and lighting. (pp. 471–474)

Ceilings, Walls, Furniture, and Fixtures

T HE BEST RULE OF THUMB for the care of ceilings, walls, furniture, and fixtures is easy to remember: Always follow the manufacturer's suggested cleaning procedures. Failing to follow care recommendations from the manufacturer can mean wasting valuable time researching effective cleaning methods that could be just a phone call away. It may also lead to costly damage or even the total loss of expensive items. In addition, the wrong cleaning methods could negate warranties that protect the property against faulty products.

Executive housekeepers can make cleaning and maintaining ceilings, walls, and furnishings most efficient—and contribute to property safety—by staying informed about new products on the market and making sensible purchasing recommendations.

This chapter discusses some selection criteria for ceilings, walls, furniture, and fixtures; outlines some types of ceiling surfaces, wall coverings, and appointments; and offers some general cleaning and care guidelines.

Selection Considerations

"If they had only asked me, I would have told them it was going to be impossible to keep up" is an all-too-common refrain heard in many hotels. Certainly, it makes good business sense for hotels to choose items that will make a good impression on guests. But it makes equally good sense for those choices to be practical from a housekeeper's point of view. Surfaces and items that will not wear well or cannot be cleaned efficiently will not attract many guests, no matter how much they cost initially. Flammability and acoustical factors are also important considerations when selecting ceiling surfaces, wall coverings, and furnishings.

Flammability Considerations

A number of well-publicized hotel fires in recent decades have made fire safety a primary concern for lodging property managers. As a result, many state and local governments require that ceiling and wall materials, upholstered furniture, and bedding used in commercial buildings meet certain flammability standards. Having flame-resistant furniture, wall, and ceiling materials that meet safety standards is an important part of any fire safety program. Purchasers should know what materials furnishings are made of and how flammable they are before they buy.

459

Many state and local building codes require that hotels use only Class A materials. Class A materials rate 0 to 25 on the **flame spread index,** a scale (from zero to 100) that measures how quickly flames will spread across a material's exposed, finished surface.

Some manufacturers have developed wall coverings that will trigger smoke detectors when heated to a certain temperature. Many commercial-rated vinyl coverings, for example, emit an odorless, colorless vapor when heated to 300°F [150°C]. The vapor triggers the alarm on ionization smoke detectors. (Ionization detectors are the most common type in commercial operations.)

Furnishings may be made of inherently fire-resistant materials. Or they may be treated by the manufacturer with chemicals to make them fire-resistant. Many hotels, especially those operating in states that require properties to use fire-resistant furnishings, ask manufacturers to supply documentation stating that pieces have been treated with fire-retardant chemicals. Dry-cleaning companies or other firms specializing in treating furnishings can retreat items if necessary.

Furnishings made of inherently fire-resistant materials are somewhat expensive, but they remain fire-resistant when laundered or cleaned by other processes and never have to be retreated. These materials are especially practical in buildings that cannot be evacuated quickly—for example, high-rise hotels.

Some furnishings are made of materials that produce toxic gases when burned. The National Fire Protection Association (NFPA) sets standards on fire retardancy and toxicity. Information on standards can be obtained at their website at www.nfpa.org or by calling (617) 770-3000. Interior designers usually quote NFPA specifications when they submit their finished drawings.

Acoustical Considerations

Because privacy is an integral part of hotel accommodations, **acoustical considerations** are important when choosing wall and ceiling materials. Acoustical materials are measured by a **Noise Reduction Coefficient (NRC)**. For example, an NRC of .75 indicates that the panel absorbs 75 percent of the sound waves that hit it. Most materials available for commercial use have an NRC of .60 to .95. Recommending a specific NRC for use in hotels or other settings is difficult because many factors affect sound absorption. For example, floors covered with carpet offer additional sound absorption, which may reduce the NRC needed in wall or ceiling surfaces.

Acoustical ceiling materials and wall coverings usually come in panels. The panels have a fiberglass or mineral fiber filling, which absorb the sound, and are covered with vinyl or fabric. The standard wall panel size ranges from 2 to 2.5 feet wide by 9 to 10 feet high. The panels are designed for easy installation, usually attached to **splines** (thin wooden strips), which are glued or bolted to the wall. Ceiling tiles are usually fitted together on a metal grid suspended from the ceiling.

Types of Ceiling Surfaces and Wall Coverings ——————

Ceiling, wall, and window coverings date back to the Middle Ages, when the residents of castles hung intricately woven tapestries and bed curtains to brighten up rooms and to keep out drafts. Today, ceiling, wall, and window coverings are chosen more for their acoustical properties, safety, and appearance than as insulation against the cold.

There are a wide variety of ceiling surfaces and wall coverings on the market today. Paint is by far the most common. However, vinyl manufacturers have introduced a wide variety of practical and attractive products in recent years, making vinyl a popular alternative to paint in properties of all types.

Ceiling surfaces and wall coverings include various kinds of wood surfaces such as laminated plywood, veneer, and paneling; synthetics such as carpet, paneling, and spray-on textured coatings; wallpaper; and stone such as ceramic tiles or marble. The following sections discuss more common surface coverings—paint, vinyl, and fabric.

Painted Surfaces

Much of paint's appeal derives from the fact that it is relatively inexpensive to purchase and apply to both walls and ceilings. Painted services that are stained or scratched can be easily "touched up" or quickly recoated. They can also be cleaned easily with mild soap and water. In recent years, manufacturers have greatly improved the durability and cleanability of paint by decreasing its porosity. In general, the less porous the paint, the more durable and stain-resistant it is.

Vinyl Surfaces

Vinyl is now widely used as a wall covering and also as a surface for ceiling panels. Vinyl wall coverings are made by laminating vinyl to a cotton or polycotton backing. Polycotton-backed vinyl is recommended more often than cotton-backed vinyl because it is more durable and less flammable than cotton-backed vinyl.

Like wallpaper, vinyl comes in rolls and is applied with a special adhesive. Vinyl wall coverings should be applied with adhesives that contain mildewcides—especially in areas with hot, humid climates. Mildew causes the wall covering to loosen from the adhesive, creating ripples in the surface of the vinyl. Installing wall coverings is the job of engineering personnel or an outside contractor. However, housekeeping staff may be faced with cleaning adhesive seepages off the wall, especially around seams. A solvent recommended by the manufacturer can be used to remove the adhesive.

Vinyl was once chosen strictly for practicality; it can be scrubbed with a brush and soap and water or harsher cleaning agents if necessary. Today, however, vinyl wall coverings come in a wide assortment of colors and textures, which adds aesthetic appeal to practicality.

The federal government classifies vinyl wall coverings into three types. **Type II vinyl** is the most practical for public areas because of its durability and appearance. It usually lasts about three times as long as paint. However, it is vulnerable to tears and rips from accidental bumping. Highly textured vinyls may not be scrubbable. Exhibit 1 shows the type of information available from manufacturers to help properties care for vinyl surfaces.

Fabric Surfaces

Fabric wall coverings are considered among the most luxurious. They are also expensive, tricky to install, easily damaged, and hard to clean.

Exhibit 1   Sample Manufacturer Care Recommendations for Vinyl Wall Coverings

---

WALLS/CEILINGS: Wall Coverings

Description/Characteristics:

Wallpapers usually fall into three categories. Nonwashable wallpaper is exactly that; you can't get it very wet without potentially ruining it.

Washable papers are usually plastic coated and can be wiped with a damp sponge. Scrubbable papers are vinyl or vinyl-impregnated and can withstand moderate scrubbing with nonabrasive cleansers or all-purpose household detergent.

Care & Maintenance:

- Nonwashable papers can be cleaned with commercial wallpaper cleaner, a puttylike substance that is rubbed on and removed.

- Clean washable paper with a damp sponge soaked in cool sudsy water and wipe immediately after with a clean damp sponge. Pat the walls dry with a towel. Scrubbable wallpapers can be cleaned with commercial spray foams that are wiped off with a clean sponge, then wiped with a second damp sponge and patted dry.

- Some fabric wallpapers are coated with vinyl and are scrubbable; for those that aren't, gently washing the spot with a cool sudsy solution may work. (Always test a hidden area first, even on scrubbable wallpapers, to make sure there will be no discoloration.)

- To absorb grease stains on uncoated fabric and nonwashable papers, press white paper towels onto the stain with a warm iron. Crayon marks can be removed the same way. Commercial spot removers may also be effective (make sure they're labeled as safe to use with wallpaper).

The Care and Maintenance instruction sheet is a guide. Always refer to the specific manufacturer's instructions you receive with the product.

Courtesy of Neil Kelly Design/Build Remodeling

Linen, once the material of choice for fabric wall coverings, is giving way to a wider variety of materials—cotton, wool, and silks. Sometimes two or more materials may be combined to make the texture of the covering more appealing.

Fabric wall coverings may be paper- or **acrylic**-backed. Paper-backed wall coverings ravel less at the seams and are easier to install than acrylic-backed coverings. But acrylic-backed coverings are less vulnerable to wrinkling and can be adjusted more easily on the wall during installation. All fabric wall coverings should be vacuumed regularly. Stains and spots should be removed with a cleaner recommended by the manufacturer. Water should *never* be used on fabric wall coverings because shrinking can occur.

Ceiling and Wall Cleaning

Cleaning walls and ceilings can be a major money-saving operation for the hotel compared to the alternatives—painting or replacement. Painting, for example, costs more than cleaning. It also takes longer, which may mean lost guestroom sales. Painting does not kill bacteria or get rid of dirt; it simply covers them. And paint leaves odors that guests may object to. Replacement may cost ten times as much as cleaning and still requires cleaning air vents, grids, fans, and the like. Moreover, without cleaning, replacement becomes more frequent.

The best rule of thumb for caring for ceilings and walls is to follow the manufacturer's instructions. In general, ceilings and walls fall into three categories—**porous, nonporous,** and **semiporous**—which dictate how to clean the surface.

Porous surfaces are those that more readily absorb moisture. These include flat latex paint, acoustical ceiling tiles, unsealed wood, and textured ceilings. Nonporous surfaces do not absorb moisture. They include enamel paint, sealed wood, metal, vinyl wallpaper, and plastic ceiling tiles. Excess moisture must be wiped off these surfaces. Semiporous materials include brick and stone.

Tips for selecting cleaning chemicals and equipment follow:

- The more kinds of surfaces (porous, nonporous, semiporous) a product can clean, the more economical it is.

- Choose nontoxic, biodegradable, odorless chemicals that are safe for humans and pets. Solutions should not contain chlorine or heavy oxidizers (oxygen bleaches) and should not damage carpets or furnishings that they may come in contact with.

- Make sure cleaners have spray tips that can be held comfortably by the operator, usually at waist level. Cleaners should be sprayed in a fan-like motion to ensure even coverage without wetting.

- Choose equipment that allows housekeeping personnel to clean without having to use ladders or scaffolding. This not only saves time, but can cut down on accidents.

- Tools should have extenders so that operators can hold them comfortably. This will allow cleaning to be done more efficiently.

Areas around ceiling air vents, light fixtures, and fans should be vacuumed before the ceiling is cleaned. Cobwebs and soot should also be vacuumed. The most efficient way to vacuum a ceiling is to use an extension attachment that can be held by operators while standing on the floor. It is important to let the suction do the work; don't try to "scrub" at soot or dust with a brush attachment because this could grind dirt more deeply into the surface.

Furniture and fixtures should be covered before cleaning ceilings and walls to prevent moisture damage. Housekeeping personnel should be warned to wipe floors frequently if dripping occurs in order to prevent slippery spots that could cause falls and injuries.

Window Coverings

Window coverings include everything from vinyl blinds to roller shades to fabric curtains and drapes. All window coverings—but especially drapes—attract dust, cigarette smoke, and other pollutants. Vacuuming window coverings (if not proscribed by the manufacturer) can reduce the number of major cleanings

Cthe Rooms CHRONICLE®

Oil vs. Latex—A Difference?

Nearly all paints fall into one of two categories—either oil-based paints or latex paints. Choosing the right type of paint for the job at hand is the first step to ensuring an attractive and durable finish and minimizing rework and repeated maintenance.

Oil paints

Sometimes referred to as solvent-based or alkyd paint, oil paints afford a high degree of protection, durability, and generally offer excellent adhesion characteristics, especially to chalky surfaces or surfaces coated previously with multiple layers of oil-based paint. To determine if the surface is chalking, one can merely rub a hand across the surface. If a fine powder or dust is visible on the hand, an oil-based paint would be the best option.

Though referred to as "oil-based," most paints in this category are comprised of a combination of petroleum distallates and vegetable oils. Oil paints actually contain a binder, referred to as a resin, which is derived from a vegetable oil such as linseed or soya bean. This resin is usually dissolved in a petroleum-based solvent such as mineral spirits. Alkyd paints are manufactured similarly but use a synthetic resin, usually containing a vegetable oil, as the binder.

After curing, most oil-based paints are scrub resistant and offer a higher degree of stain and moisture resistance. Some interior and exterior finishes (referred to as sheen) of oil-based paints also provide vapor barrier protection from moisture penetration.

There are various drawbacks associated with using oil-based paints. Most significantly, oil paints take considerably longer to dry and cure than latex paints and often emit an undesirable odor. Depending on the amount of moisture in the air, the coating thickness applied to the surface, and the paint's sheen, interior oil paints can often take 12 to 24 hours to dry before they can be painted with a second coat of paint and three to five days before they may be scrubbed. Cleanup requires paint thinner, which is combustible and must be disposed of according to EPA or state and municipal hazardous waste guidelines. Because of the vegetable oils and lack of rubberized binding content, oil paints may yellow and crack or chip over time. Finally, oil paints tend to cost about 20 to 25 percent more than latex paints.

Latex paints

Latex paints contain a rubberized emulsifier set in a water-based solution that binds the titanium and other paint ingredients. As such, latex paints dry and cure much quicker than oil paints (often in as little as one to six hours) and can be cleaned up with warm water and soap. Hence, no need to buy paint thinner for cleanup.

The best type of latex paints contains 100 percent acrylic binders, which add to their durability, flexibility and color retention. They are less likely to blister, chip or peel and application is often much smoother and quicker. Latex paints usually emit minimal odor, are less likely to chalk and may be applied at lower temperatures than oil paints.

Because of the decreased drying time and water-based cleanup, latex paints are an excellent choice for hotels and those high-traffic areas that cannot be

the Rooms CHRONICLE®

(continued)

cordoned off for prolonged periods. Also, unused latex paint is easy to dispose of by allowing the remaining paint content to dry thoroughly and depositing the can in the trash.

Latex paint is ideal for aluminum, masonry and primed wood surfaces as well as drywall and primed plaster. It is not recommended for surfaces that will be subject to extreme moisture (i.e., ceilings above showers or bathtubs) or those areas where guests may come into frequent direct contact with surfaces (i.e. metal hand railings).

Source: *The Rooms Chronicle®*, Volume 11, Number 2, p. 7.
For subscription information, call 866-READ-TRC.

(laundering or dry cleaning for drapes; soap-and-water washing for blinds) that need to be performed.

Drapes and blinds with cords are vulnerable to breaking and damage. Often, guests don't immediately see a cord, so they pull or tug on the drape or blind itself to see out the window. Choosing curtains and blinds with batons instead of cords and opting for headings with automatic releases can help prevent damage. It is also wise to choose hardware that can be repaired without having to remove the rod or drapes.

Drapes that are easy to remove and hang increase the efficiency of room attendants. Choosing the proper hardware for drapes can make drape removal and hanging easier. The housekeeping department should keep extra drape panels on hand so that they can replace those soiled by guests if necessary.

Hotels have been paying increasing amounts of attention to their window coverings because of the benefits they offer. Good window covers can help protect furniture and carpeting from fading. They can also help the hotel's heating and cooling systems work more efficiently. Window coverings such as shutters, shades, and draperies provide insulation and can reduce the amount of sunlight and heat entering rooms.

Single-pane windows are often considered energy inefficient and are being replaced with double- and triple-pane glazing, tinted glazing, reflective glazing, spectrally selective glazing and insulated glazing with inert gas between the layers. Wood and vinyl frames offer more energy efficiency than aluminum ones.

Cleaning Window Coverings. The executive housekeeper must understand the fabric content of window coverings before deciding how they will be cleaned. The material may require vacuuming, hand washing, spot cleaning, laundering, or dry cleaning. The manufacturer can offer the best information on how to clean specific types of window coverings , but if such information is not available, cleaning methods should be tested on an inconspicuous area of the fabric. Incorrect cleaning methods can result in dye bleeding, fading, or shrinking of the fabric.

A portable canister vacuum is easiest for vacuuming drapes, curtains, and sheers. Be sure to vacuum in the same direction that the fabric is sewn.

Cleaning draperies should be simple and inexpensive. Choosing draperies that can be laundered can save the hotel time and money. If the hotel is planning to buy drapes that can be laundered, consider drapes made of washable fabric without a crinoline backing or sewn-in lining. Drapes with backing or linings sewn in need to be dry-cleaned because the drapery fabric or lining could shrink or stretch, giving the drapes a permanently rumpled appearance. Choosing drapes that can be used with a low-cost liner that hangs independently from the drapes offers some advantages. For example, it cuts down the bulk of the drapes themselves. Moreover, liners deteriorate when exposed to light, especially in west- and south-facing windows. Separate liners can be replaced much more inexpensively than liners attached to drapes.

Many hotels recommend sending draperies that must be dry-cleaned to off-premises laundries that offer warranties in case damage occurs. Generally, drapes are cleaned on an as-needed basis or every two years, whichever comes first.

Types of Furniture and Fixtures

A quick look at a detailed job list for a room or lobby attendant in any hotel will give one an idea of the mind-boggling number of furnishings that the housekeeping staff must clean and check at least once a day. Furniture and fixtures include everything from wastebaskets to bedside lamps to poolside chairs to telephones in the lobby.

The number of furnishings in the hotel and the materials from which they are made depend on the size and service level of the hotel. In general, different types of furniture and fixtures are found in three main areas of a hotel—public areas, guestrooms, and employee areas.

Following the bed wars of the 1990s, hotels began increasing their spending on all areas of guest furnishings. PricewaterhouseCoopers predicted in Spring of 2007 that the U.S. lodging industry would invest $5.5 billion in 2007 on capital upgrades, primarily amenities and guest services and systems. This spending is up by ten percent over 2006.

The most common capital investment expenditures include:

- New technology for guestrooms, including MP3-compatible sound systems and flat-screen televisions.

- High-speed wireless Internet connections, self-check-in and check-out kiosks and computers and printers in business centers.

- Upgrades of complimentary breakfasts and evening receptions, especially with more hot food and diverse menu options.

- Lodging-branded bedding.

- Special gathering spots featuring entertainment and wireless Internet connections.

- Food and specialty beverage offered in extended hours.

- Triple-draping window treatment.

- Easy-to-use clocks and clock radios, in-room exercise equipment, cordless telephones, and enhanced bathroom finishes.[1]

Public Areas

Hotels vary widely in the sizes and types of public areas they contain. In many economy properties, for example, a small lobby is the only public area. Its furnishings may consist of simple lighting, seating, and perhaps **occasional tables.** Lobbies in world-class properties, of course, will have more luxurious appointments such as chandeliers, fountains, and sculpture or other artwork.

Public restrooms contain basic fixtures such as toilets, sinks, towel dispensers, and hand dryers, but may also contain changing tables for infants, powder rooms with special makeup lights, or lounges furnished with comfortable seating and tables.

Lobby attendants are responsible for cleaning all furnishings in these areas. In addition, they must check some items to make sure they are in working order. For example, are soap dispensers and toilets in the restrooms working properly? Do any bulbs in lamps need to be replaced? Are there any fluorescent lights burned out that should be reported to engineering? Are fire extinguishers dusted and dated for inspection? (Normally, the engineering department is responsible for filling and replacing extinguishers. However, housekeeping is responsible for dusting and cleaning and notifying engineering if they notice that inspection dates are missing from extinguishers or if inspection dates have expired.)

Besides the lobby and public restrooms, many mid-market and luxury properties have meeting and reception rooms, convention space, recreation areas, restaurants, and bars. Furnishings in these areas may include seating, tables, portable platforms, and portable screens or room dividers. Party and reception items might include portable bars, dance floors, and pianos. Meeting rooms might be furnished with chalkboards, easels, projector screens, projectors, laptop computers, high-speed Internet connectors, and lecterns.

The housekeeping department, however, is not responsible for special equipment or for setting up rooms for special events. Meeting and reception rooms, for example, are generally set up by the banquet or conference services department setup staff, who also clear away tables, chairs, and other items used for the occasion. Housekeeping is responsible for daily and scheduled cleaning projects such as cleaning chandeliers, walls, and windows and shampooing and vacuuming carpets. Likewise, convention center space may be handled through the conference services department while housekeeping cleans and maintains facilities on a daily cleaning schedule. Technology needed for conventions or meetings is cared for and provided by Information Technology (IT) staff, usually attached to the conference services department. Recreation areas inside a property normally fall under the rooms division and are therefore handled by housekeeping. Exterior recreation areas, however, are usually maintained by engineering or landscaping personnel. Restaurants and bars in large properties are maintained during serving hours by food & beverage staff, and by housekeeping during off hours.

Exhibit 2   Sample Suite Furnishings

Luggage Bench
0054-2670
48W x 21D x 18H
70 lbs.

Desk
0054-2620
42W x 22D x 29H
75 lbs.

Double
4/8 Headboard
Wall Hung
0054-2637
56W x 2D x 16H
30 lbs.

Queen
5/0 Headboard
Wall Hung
0054-2638
60W x 2D x 16H
32 lbs.

King
6/8 Headboard
Wall Hung
0054-2635
80W x 2D x 16H
40 lbs.

Coffee Table
0054-2650
22W x 13D x 17H
51 lbs.

Mirror
0054-2640
27W x 45H
33 lbs.

Nightstand
0054-2645
22W x 18D x 23H
75 lbs.

4-Drawer Credenza
0054-2615
78W x 21D x 24H
178 lbs.

Corner Table
0054-2610
28W x 28D x 24H
60 lbs.

Hutch
0054-2617
37.5W x 21D x 40H
140 lbs.

6-Drawer Dresser
0054-2612
68W x 21D x 30H
185 lbs.

Activity Table
0054-2655
34Dia x 29H
43 lbs.

2-Drawer Chest
0054-2616
40.5W x 21D x 24H
95 lbs.

NOTE: *Dimensions are shown in inches.*
*D=Depth. **W**=Width, **H**=Height, **Dia**=Diameter.*
Cs. pk.: 1 ea. unless otherwise indicated.

Courtesy of Holiday Inn Worldwide

Guestrooms

Many chain companies help member properties make wise furnishing choices by offering a catalog of items from which to choose. The items in the catalog will fit the quality standards mandated by the company as well as ensure that the property will have the same "look" as other properties in the chain. In addition, these furnishings are usually chosen because of their durability, safety qualities, and ease of maintenance. In some cases, manufacturers may build furnishings according to the company's specifications.

Virtually all chain properties and many independents purchase furniture in **"suites"**, or groupings to ensure a certain level of quality among pieces and to ensure that all pieces match. Some suites come with warranties, which further guarantee the workmanship of pieces. Exhibit 2 shows various pieces of suite furniture.

Essential furnishings in sleeping areas of guestrooms include beds, bureaus, nightstands, and some sort of lighting—typically overhead and bedside. Room attendants must clean these furnishings and make sure they are properly arranged. Making sure the hotel's literature and amenities are properly arranged on desks, bureaus, and tables is also part of the job.

The types of materials from which furnishings are made dictate care and cleaning procedures and affect durability and ease of maintenance. Items may be made of wood, metal, plastic, fabric (synthetic or natural), or a wide assortment of synthetic materials.

Exhibit 3   Sample Bathroom Furnishings

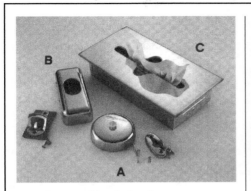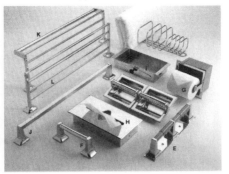

A—Retractable clothesline
B—Enclosed bottle opener
C—Recessed facial-tissue dispenser

D—Recessed twin-paper holder
E—Surface twin-paper holder
F—Surface single-paper holder
G—Recessed extra-roll paper holder
H—Shallow recessed tissue cabinet
I—Recessed vanity tissue box
J—Towel bar
K—Towel shelf with bar
L—Towel shelf

The basic design of any piece of furniture can help or hinder maintenance efforts. For example, furniture equipped with glides or carpet protectors will prevent carpet damage. Casters can make heavy pieces easier to move. **Case goods** with recessed fronts and sides will collect less dust. Bureaus and cube-shaped tables should have sealed bottoms so that moisture from spills or carpet cleaning does not seep into the material and damage them. Table, desk, and bureau tops finished with a water-repellent material will not become water damaged and are usually more resistant to stains.

Nearly all properties in the United States now offer flat-panel or high-definition television sets. Remote control televisions are standard and many televisions have wireless keyboards. Clock radios are also provided. Most properties also offer some type of Internet connection—though typically the hotel's IT department is responsible for its care. Room attendants are responsible for cleaning these items and making sure they are in proper working order. Items that are not in working order must be reported to engineering.

Bathroom areas may be as basic as a sink, toilet, towel rack, over-the-sink mirror, lighting, wastebasket, and shower stall, though most properties offer combination tubs and showers. Exhibit 3 shows some of the smaller bathroom furnishings. Often, vanities and special shower massagers are provided. Most properties, recognizing the ever-increasing number of business women who travel, now offer such amenities as wall-unit hair dryers and full-length mirrors.

Exhibit 4   Sample Living Area Suite

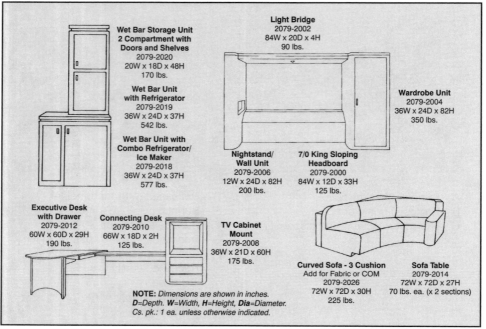

Courtesy of Holiday Inn Worldwide

Bathrooms in some mid-market hotels and many luxury properties are extremely luxurious. Bidets, whirlpools, saunas, and powder rooms may be provided. All these items must be cleaned and checked by the room attendant. Bathroom amenities must also be arranged properly around the vanity.

Increases in business travel have led all types of properties to offer living or work space, either in the same room as the sleeping area or in a separate room, as in a suite. Living areas include seating, tables, and often desks and coffee makers. Sometimes, food and beverage storage space is provided, including small refrigerators and/or wet bars. Exhibit 4 shows a suite of furniture that might be used in a guestroom with a living area.

Staff Areas

Staff areas consist of office space, lounges, and work areas. In many cases, the staff who work in various areas are responsible for cleaning their work stations and keeping them neat. Engineering and maintenance staff, for example, will clean their own shops. As noted previously, dining room servers bus and clean tables and other furnishings used in the dining areas. Office staff are usually responsible for keeping their own desks neat and clean. Housekeeping staff are only responsible for vacuuming, cleaning walls and ceilings, and emptying wastebaskets in these areas. Very large properties may even have a special office cleaning staff to clean offices daily.

Care Considerations

In general, major cleaning procedures include shampooing upholstered furnishings—usually about every six months or as needed—and cleaning washable furnishings with water and/or an appropriate cleaning solution.

Most major cleaning can be performed with very simple tools—buckets, rags, and a cleaning agent. Upholstery shampoos, however, usually require special shampooers. These machines are typically designed to be hand-held. A variety of attachments can be purchased to make cleaning easier. They can often be used to spot-clean carpets and carpeting on stairs and other hard-to-reach areas. The units usually work by feeding dry foam into a rotary brush with which soiled areas can be scrubbed. Some upholstery shampoos dry very quickly and can even be used to clean furniture in occupied rooms. Steam cleaning machines can also be used for effectively cleaning upholstered furniture.

Minor cleaning is performed more frequently than major cleaning. Minor cleaning includes such tasks as dusting and vacuuming lampshades and seat cushions and polishing metal fixtures. Paper dust cloths treated with furniture polish or microfiber cloths are generally used for dusting. Portable canister vacuums are easiest to use on upholstered furniture and other furnishings that should be vacuumed regularly.

Seating

Seating comes in many sizes and shapes, from side chairs, armchairs, and lounge chairs to love seats, sofas, sofa beds, and ottomans. Well-made seating is relatively expensive, but it will pay off for any lodging property in the long run.

In general, kiln-dried hardwood frames will resist warping and loosening. Any wooden arms, legs, or backs that are not upholstered should be finished to resist stains, mars, and perspiration. Polyurethane finishes, for example, are impervious to water and other liquids.

Upholstered seating should also be chosen for durability. Foam pad cushions will wear longer and retain their shape better than shredded foam or cotton cushions. Many times, manufacturers offer a wide range of fabrics that can be used with a particular seat frame.

Upholstered fabric needs to be vacuumed regularly and spot-cleaned. Always check with the manufacturer before cleaning pieces. Some manufacturers tag upholstered furniture with labels marked "S," "W," or "S-W." These codes mean that the piece can be cleaned with solvent only, with water only, or with either solvents or water. If a piece is marked "X," it cannot be wet-cleaned, only vacuumed. Many care experts recommend that all upholstery be pretested according to the following steps:

1. Pretest water-based cleaning solutions by mixing a small amount of the solution with the shampoo or detergent you plan to use. Follow the instructions printed on the label and use the same temperature of water that you plan to clean with.

2. Thoroughly wet an inconspicuous section of the fabric with the solution. (An ideal place to test is on one-half of the zippered panel of a cushion. Whatever

area is tested, make sure that all colors on the upholstery are included.) Blot the area with a white towel or rag. If color comes off the upholstered fabric, it is not wet-cleanable. Allow the test section to air-dry; do not hasten drying.

3. Inspect the area after drying. If one color in the fabric has bled into another, the fabric is not wet-cleanable. If the test area has puckered, shrinking will occur with wet cleaning.

4. Use wet cleaning as a last resort if the fabric shows signs of brown rings in the wetted areas after drying. If pretesting with water is successful and if the fabric has a nap (such as velvet does), wet cleaning should only be attempted as a last resort.

5. To pretest solvents, apply a small amount on a white rag, blot an inconspicuous portion of the piece, and allow it to dry. Look for color loss or other damage before proceeding.

Once upholstery has been pretested, record the results on the piece for future reference. Remember that solvents are flammable; you should therefore purchase equipment suited for solvents. Although solvents dry quickly, they may leave odors. Solvents should be thoroughly evaluated before purchase.

In general, woven nylon and good-quality vinyl are the most stain-resistant and easily cleaned upholstery materials. Seating in heavy-use areas should be upholstered in vinyl, which needs only a daily wiping, or some other fabric that is especially designed for heavy use. Satiny or lightweight fabrics should be avoided because covers made from these materials tend to shift over the cushions and do not hold up well over time.

Case Goods

Bureau drawers can pose a variety of safety threats and irritations to guests and housekeeping staff alike. Recessed handles will not snag clothes or protrude so that people bump into them. Nylon ball bearings and slide glides in drawers make opening and closing drawers quieter, reduce wear on the drawers, and eliminate jamming. Some drawers will even close all the way with a gentle push, which helps prevent people from bumping into open drawers. Better-quality bureaus have a dust panel under the bottom drawer to keep floor dust and lint out of drawers. Items that have recessed backs can be placed flush to the wall, even though electrical plugs may be behind them. Exhibit 5 outlines some factors to consider when choosing case goods.

As with seating, case goods should be finished with some durable material. Polyurethane helps protect the furniture from stains and water damage. Some finer furniture, however, is finished with less-durable materials. Waxes can protect these finishes and, to some extent, the wood below. Some hotels place glass tops with polished edges on top of of tables, bureaus, and other pieces of fine furniture for additional protection.

Lighting and Lamps

Overhead lighting is the lighting of choice in public areas. There is a wide variety of overhead lighting to choose from, including elaborate chandeliers, recessed

Exhibit 5   Case Goods Specifications

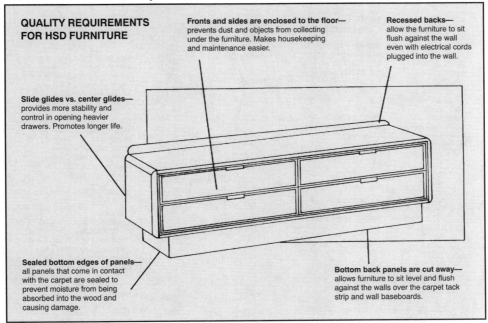

QUALITY REQUIREMENTS FOR HSD FURNITURE

Fronts and sides are enclosed to the floor— prevents dust and objects from collecting under the furniture. Makes housekeeping and maintenance easier.

Recessed backs— allow the furniture to sit flush against the wall even with electrical cords plugged into the wall.

Slide glides vs. center glides— provides more stability and control in opening heavier drawers. Promotes longer life.

Sealed bottom edges of panels— all panels that come in contact with the carpet are sealed to prevent moisture from being absorbed into the wood and causing damage.

Bottom back panels are cut away— allows furniture to sit level and flush against the walls over the carpet tack strip and wall baseboards.

Courtesy of Holiday Inn Worldwide

lighting, track lighting, and fluorescent lighting with diffuser panels. Wall lights on brackets may also be used.

The type of lighting chosen will affect how a room looks. Fabrics used for carpeting, upholstery and linens will look different under natural, incandescent, or fluorescent lights.

A variety of lighting is used in guestrooms. Overhead lights are usually installed in the bathroom and, often, just inside the door of the room. In a room with a large work area or in a suite, there may be an overhead light fixture over the worktable. The bathroom or powder room may also have a makeup mirror with wall lights.

The living room and bedroom are usually equipped with lamps on bureaus, nightstands and near seating. Metal lamp bases are more break-resistant than ceramic. Superior-quality metal bases do not have side seams. Colors in ceramic lamps will last longer if they are glazed into the surface instead of painted on. Some properties opt for lamps that can be bolted to tables or walls to eliminate breakage and theft.

Lampshades must be replaced more often than the lamp's base. Good-quality plastic-lined shades will wear longer than fabric-lined shades. Switches on the lamp base will prevent guests and staff from having to grope around under the shade to find the switch, thus damaging the shade inadvertently. **Permanent assembly** prevents loosening around the socket. Exhibit 6 shows some factors to consider when choosing lamps.

Exhibit 6   Lamp Specifications

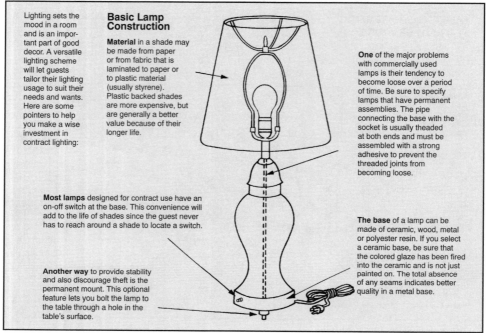

Lighting sets the mood in a room and is an important part of good decor. A versatile lighting scheme will let guests tailor their lighting usage to suit their needs and wants. Here are some pointers to help you make a wise investment in contract lighting:

Basic Lamp Construction

Material in a shade may be made from paper or from fabric that is laminated to paper or to plastic material (usually styrene). Plastic backed shades are more expensive, but are generally a better value because of their longer life.

One of the major problems with commercially used lamps is their tendency to become loose over a period of time. Be sure to specify lamps that have permanent assemblies. The pipe connecting the base with the socket is usually theaded at both ends and must be assembled with a strong adhesive to prevent the threaded joints from becoming loose.

Most lamps designed for contract use have an on-off switch at the base. This convenience will add to the life of shades since the guest never has to reach around a shade to locate a switch.

The base of a lamp can be made of ceramic, wood, metal or polyester resin. If you select a ceramic base, be sure that the colored glaze has been fired into the ceramic and is not just painted on. The total absence of any seams indicates better quality in a metal base.

Another way to provide stability and also discourage theft is the permanent mount. This optional feature lets you bolt the lamp to the table through a hole in the table's surface.

Courtesy of Holiday Inn Worldwide

Energy-Efficient Lighting. Lighting is a key component of energy savings and environmentally conscious programs at many properties. Hotels are increasingly using fluorescent fixtures where appropriate with incandescent lights used as accents. Properties are also trying to make the most of natural lighting through windows with solar glazing or reflective film. The latter two options can result in high energy savings for properties, paying themselves off quickly.

Many properties are starting to install sensors on lights so that lights are on when a person is present but turn off automatically when no one is in the room or area. This is most popular in back-of-the-house areas and restrooms, but some properties are also using them in guestrooms.

Endnote

1. Ed Watkins, "Lodging Hospitality's Guest Services Handbook," *Lodging Hospitality*, May 1, 2007, pp. 39–40.

 # Key Terms

acoustical considerations—Sound absorption quality of certain materials, usually in ceilings, walls, or floors.

acrylic—Synthetic material used in making fabric or molded transparent fixtures or surfaces.

case goods—Items with tops and sides, such as bureaus and desks.

flame spread index—A scale that measures how quickly flames will spread across a material's exposed, finished surface with zero representing a noncombustible surface such as cement-asbestos board and 100 representing untreated lumber.

nonporous—Non-moisture-absorbing.

Noise Reduction Coefficient (NRC)—A number that designates the amount of sound a material absorbs.

occasional table—Small end table.

permanent assembly—In lamps, when the base and light socket are fused together to prevent loosening.

porous—Moisture-absorbing.

semiporous—Somewhat moisture-absorbing.

spline—Thin wood slat used to attach panels to a wall or ceiling.

suite—Several pieces of furniture of similar design, usually sold together to outfit a complete room.

Type II vinyl—Commercial-grade vinyl.

Review Questions

1. List the major types of wall coverings and discuss their relative merits in terms of cost, care, and aesthetic appeal.

2. Why are acoustics important when considering ceiling materials and wall coverings?

3. What is the NRC scale? What does it mean if a wall covering has an NRC rating of .60?

4. Discuss how technology has decreased flammability in wall coverings and ceiling materials.

5. Explain why cleaning ceilings and walls can be thought of as a cost-saving operation.

6. Why is the porosity of a ceiling or wall important to cleaning?

7. Discuss some of the types of window coverings and their cleaning considerations.

8. Explain how the hotel's size and service level affect its number and kind of furnishings and how these, in turn, affect the housekeeping department.

9. Discuss some of the various types of tables, seating, and case goods found in a hotel. Discuss where various types of these items might be found.

10. Discuss some of the materials from which various furnishings are constructed.

Internet Sites

For more information, visit the following Internet web pages. Remember that Internet addresses can change without notice. If a site is no longer there, you can use a search engine to look for additional sites.

American Hotel Register Company
www.americanhotel.com

County Draperies, Inc.
www.drape.com

Fabtex, Inc.
www.fabtex.com

Hospitality Designs
www.hospitalitydesigns.com

Lutron Electronics Co Inc.
www.lutron.com

National Fire Prevention Association
www.nfpa.org

Task Breakdowns: Ceilings, Walls, Furniture, and Fixtures

The procedures presented in this section are for illustrative purposes only and should not be construed as recommendations or standards. While these procedures are typical, readers should keep in mind that each property has its own procedures, equipment specifications, and policies regarding protective gear which are designed to fit individual needs.

Vacuum Fabric and Upholstered Furniture

Materials needed: Portable vacuum or a vacuum with a hose and upholstery attachment, a damp cloth, a stiff brush, and a mild detergent solution.

STEPS	HOW-TO'S
1. Remove loose cushions and put them on furniture, not the floor.	
2 Wipe spills from vinyl or leather furniture with a damp cloth.	
3. Remove spills from fabric upholstery.	❑ Follow the property's procedures for removing spills from various pieces of furniture.
4. Use a small, stiff brush to brush debris from furniture seams, folds, and buttons.	
5. Use vacuum cleaner attachments or a portable vacuum to vacuum the fabric surface of the furniture.	❑ Vacuum vinyl or leather furniture very carefully to avoid tearing or damaging the material. Some properties use a damp cloth—not a vacuum cleaner—to clean vinyl and leather furniture. ❑ Vacuum visible surfaces. ❑ Vacuum under cushions and in cracks and crevices ❑ Pay special attention to folds, buttons, and other features that collect crumbs and dust.

Steam-Extract Fabric Upholstery

Materials needed: steam extractor, approved detergent, defoamer, a pre-spotting solution, a "wet furniture" sign, a vacuum cleaner, and a clean, damp cloth.

STEPS	HOW-TO'S
1. Vacuum fabric upholstery.	
2. Set up the steam extractor.	❑ Follow the property's procedures for steam extracting various pieces of furniture.
3. Plug in the extractor and allow the wash tank (if it has heater coils) to heat the water.	
4. Spray a pre-spotting solution to treat heavily soiled areas or spills.	
5. Inject steam into fabric.	❑ Use the extractor according to the instructions with the machine.
	❑ Inject steam into the fabric with the upholstery wand. Vacuum up the water.
	❑ Repeat the process in each area of the upholstery.
	❑ Give special attention to prespotted areas.
	❑ Do not soak the furniture. Too much water can damage the padding and takes a long time to dry. This could cause mildew.
6. Empty dirty water into a mop sink. Do not flush dirty water down guestroom toilets.	

(continued)

Steam-Extract Fabric Upholstery (continued)

STEPS	HOW-TO'S
7. Allow furniture to dry.	❑ Stand removable cushions on their ends to dry before replacing them on the furniture.
	❑ Place a "wet furniture" sign warning guests not to use furniture until it has completely dried.
	❑ Remove the sign when the furniture is dry.
8. Vacuum furniture again with a dry vacuum to remove dry detergent residue and dirt.	
9. Return all equipment and supplies to the correct locations.	

Clean Walls and Baseboards

Materials needed: Cleaning cloths, a long-handled feather duster or a broom and dust cloth, tarps or other protective material, a portable vacuum cleaner, an upholstery brush attachment, a mild detergent, and a ladder.

STEPS	HOW-TO'S
1. Dust the walls and wall coverings.	❑ Use a cloth on a broom or a long-handled feather duster to remove dust and cobwebs from hard-to-reach areas. ❑ Wipe other areas with a damp cloth. ❑ Work your way from the top of the room down.
2. Cover furniture and fixtures with tarps or other protective material before cleaning walls and baseboards.	
3. Ask your supervisor for the correct procedures for cleaning the walls and baseboards.	
4. Gather cleaning materials.	
5. Use a ladder to reach high spots.	❑ Make sure someone holds the ladder for you.
6. Clean painted walls and smooth wall coverings.	❑ Wipe with a clean, damp cloth without detergent. ❑ Spray an approved detergent on spots and stains. Rub gently with a clean cloth. Do not scrub. It can damage the wall surface. ❑ Work your way from the top the wall covering down the wall.

(continued)

Clean Walls and Baseboards (continued)	
STEPS	**HOW-TO'S**

7. Report damaged walls to your supervisor.	❑ Report to your supervisor:
	    • When cleaning does not remove stains and dirt
	    • Tears or punctures in the wall covering
	    • Areas where the wallpaper paste is not holding
	    • Other damage

8. Vacuum grass cloth and fabric wall coverings using an upholstery brush attachment.	
9. Wipe baseboards with a damp cloth.	

Clean Mirrors and Dust Furnishings

Materials needed: Stocked public-space cleaning cart and glass cleaner or water.

STEPS	HOW-TO'S
1. Dust furnishings, pictures, and signs.	❑ The steps to dust oil paintings or prints that are not covered with glass vary among properties. ❑ Dust with a clean, slightly damp cloth, followed by a dry cloth. Dust natural finished wood surfaces with only a dry cloth unless otherwise instructed. ❑ Do not use a chemical cleaner, glass cleaner, brass polish or cleaner, or furniture polish unless told to do so. ❑ If you use a chemical or polish for dusting, wipe the surface with a soft, clean cloth after dusting.
2. Clean mirrors.	❑ Follow the property's procedures for cleaning mirrors.

Clean Blinds

Materials needed: Stocked public-space cleaning cart, a small broom or brush, and heavy latex utility gloves

STEPS	HOW-TO'S
1. Wear heavy latex utility gloves.	❑ Gloves will prevent cuts from the sharp edges of blinds.
2. Use a clean cloth, a small broom, or a brush to wipe the dust from the blinds.	
3. Use a damp cloth followed by a dry cloth to clean stubborn dirt from each slat.	❑ Make sure you do not miss any slats.
4. Wipe the rods, poles, and cords of the blinds.	
5. Wipe the area behind the blinds	
6. Test blinds to make sure they work correctly.	❑ Pull the cord to raise and lower the blinds.
	❑ Twist the rod to open and close the slats.
	❑ Report any problems to your supervisor.

Clean, Straighten, Remove, and Rehang Drapes

Materials needed: *Portable vacuum cleaner or a vacuum cleaner with a hose and upholstery brush attachment, a stepladder, a hook container, and hooks.*

STEPS	HOW-TO'S
1. Vacuum drapes.	❑ Use a portable vacuum or a vacuum with a hose and upholstery brush attachment.
	❑ Stand on a stepladder to reach high areas. Never use a chair or a bar stool as a ladder.
	❑ Start vacuuming at the top of the drapes and slowly work down.
	❑ Give special attention to vacuuming valances, pinched pleats, and folds.
	❑ Move down the drapes without pulling on the fabric enough to bend or strain the drape rods.
2. Report stains to your supervisor.	
3. Gently pull the strings on the drape rods to make sure the drapes open and close correctly.	
4. Straighten the drapes.	❑ When you complete the vacuuming, straighten tie-backs and other decorative treatments.
	❑ Make sure the drapes hang evenly.

(continued)

STEPS	**HOW-TO'S**
Clean, Straighten, Remove, and Rehang Drapes (continued)	
5. Make any small repairs to the drape mechanism. Report other problems to your supervisor.	❑ The steps to fix drape mechanisms vary among properties.
6. Remove drapes when needed for repair, vacuuming, or other cleaning.	❑ Ask for help if needed. Drapes are often heavy and require two people to handle safely. Do not take safety risks.
	❑ Get a stepladder if needed. Always use caution when standing on a ladder.
	❑ Carefully lift the drapes so that the hooks detach from the rods. Lay the drapes over one arm as you release the hooks with the other hand.
	❑ Come down the ladder and remove the hooks from the top of the drapes. Place the hooks in a container so you will not lose them.
	❑ Continue this process until all assigned drapes have been removed.
7. Rehang drapes.	❑ Reinsert the hooks into the fabric on the back side of the pinched pleat headers, with one hook on each pleat. If hooks are difficult to place in the drapes, rub soap on them first.
	❑ Put the hooks evenly on each pleat. Climb on a stepladder to reach the rod. Two people may be needed to hang drapes. If so, one person will put in the hooks and hand up the sections. The other person will put the drapes on the rod.
	❑ Begin to rehang drapes on the outside end of the drape rod. Insert the first hook into the hole in the end of the rod to secure the panel.

Clean, Straighten, Remove, and Rehang Drapes *(continued)*	
STEPS	**HOW-TO'S**
	❑ Place one hook in each of the small plastic or metal cord pulls, without skipping any. Place the final hook in the hole in the metal cord pull at the end of the cord (called the carrier).
	❑ Repeat the process for the next panel. Check the operation of the pull cord and rods. Adjust the drapes so they are smooth and even.
	❑ If the rods do not have plastic or metal cord pulls, place the hooks over the rod, and keep the pleats even.

Chapter 12 Outline

Beds
    Mattresses
    Springs and Supports
    Maintenance of Beds
    The Bed Wars
    Flammability Standards
    Bedbugs
Linens
    Types of Linens
    Sizes of Linens
    Linen Care, Reuse, and Replacement
    Linen Selection Considerations
Uniforms
    Identifying Uniform Needs
    Selecting Uniforms

Competencies

1. Identify major types of bed spring and mattress construction and describe selection and general care considerations. (pp. 489–497)

2. Identify the types and sizes of linen used in hotel operations and describe general care considerations and linen recycling techniques. (pp. 497–507)

3. Outline factors to consider when selecting uniforms for hotel staff. (pp. 507–511)

12

Beds, Linens, and Uniforms

OVER THE YEARS, innovative innkeepers and hoteliers have tried to attract guests with the latest amenities—color television, air conditioning, drinking and dining facilities, pools, entertainment, and so on. But one item remains the hotel's biggest draw: the bed.

This chapter discusses the selection and maintenance of beds as well as various types of linens. Uniforms are included in this chapter because many of the selection and care criteria for linens apply to uniforms as well.

Beds

Beds, as a class, include conventional guestroom beds, cribs, and rollaways. All these beds will be discussed in this section of the chapter. Exhibit 1 lists standard bed sizes.

Most beds consist of springs, which provide resiliency and support; the mattress, which lies on top of the springs and provides extra padding; and the frame on which the springs and mattress rest. When carefully chosen, these items work together to provide a durable, comfortable bed that can be maintained and changed easily. When beds are poorly chosen, they must be replaced often, and they can be a source of guest complaints.

In most hotels, headboards are not affixed to the beds. They are typically mounted on the walls behind the beds and are designed to match the other pieces of furniture.

Mattresses

There are four main types of mattresses: **innerspring**, **memory foam**, **latex**, and **air**.

As the name implies, an innerspring mattress has an inner layer of coiled springs to provide support for the body and layers of insulation and padding to provide comfort. The quality of an innerspring mattress depends upon several factors:

- Wire gauge of the springs (the lower the number, the more durable the wire)
- The number of springs (minimum 300 for a double bed, 375 for a queen and 450 for a king)
- The shape of the springs and how they are joined together
- The number of active turns in each spring

the Rooms
CHRONICLE®

Cribs and Safety

As a courtesy for families traveling with babies, hotels generally make a child's crib available to be placed in the guestroom. By providing a crib, hotels can take responsibility for the safety and cleanliness of the bed. With these obligations, housekeeping departments must be careful to establish procedures that will ensure guests' babies are not at risk in the hotel's crib.

Safety

Not just any crib will suffice. A hotel's crib must be chosen carefully to ensure the safety of the guest. For instance, a safe crib has:

- No more than 2 3/8 inches between crib slats so a baby's body cannot fit through the slats.

- No corner posts over 1/16 of an inch above the end panels so a baby cannot catch clothing and be strangled.

- No cutout areas on the headboard or footboard so a baby's head cannot get trapped.

- A mattress support that is secured so that it does not pull apart easily from the corner posts so a baby cannot get trapped between the mattress and crib.

- A mattress that fits firmly to the edges of the crib so a baby cannot get trapped between the mattress and the side of the crib.

- No missing, loose, broken, or improperly installed screws, brackets, or other crib hardware.

- No cracked or peeling paint to prevent lead poisoning.

- No splinters or rough edges.

- Received a certification seal for meeting national standards.

The only linen that should be provided is a crib sheet which tightly fits the mattress. Loose sheets, blankets, and pillows are a hazard to the baby's safety.

Cleanliness

Prior to delivery to a guestroom a crib should be thoroughly washed with a non-toxic detergent and the mattress covered with a clean sheet. Some hotels use a full-sized sheet stitched like an envelope to fully enclose the mattress. It's a good idea to wash crib sheets with gentle detergents separate from commercial chemicals.

Exceeding expectations

To exceed expectations of guest, some hotels provide a crib gift basket containing such things as diapers, cotton swabs, baby oil, and diaper wipes. (Local businesses may provide items in exchange for a mention.) And it's a great idea to give a hotel logo item, such as a teddy bear wearing a miniature hotel T-shirt.

(continued)

The latest in crib mattresses

Three thousand babies die each year from Sudden Infant Death Syndrome in the United States. Though the "back to sleep" program has reduced the number significantly, babies who turn themselves or become entwined in blankets may still be at risk. Some experts think that the accumulation of carbon dioxide near the baby's face may be a cause of SIDS. The Halo Sleep System has developed a mattress that removes the carbon dioxide by pumping fresh air from the side of the mattress up through the mattress top surface.

Source: Gail Edwards, CHHE, *The Rooms Chronicle*®, Volume 8, Number 1, p. 5.
For subscription information, please call 866-READ-TRC.

- Type of padding (foam, latex, memory foam, down, or wool, etc.)
- Quality of "pillow top" plush top layer for featherbed-like comfort
- Cover fabric or ticking (usually quilted polyester and can be stain resistant). Mattress ticking should be sturdy fabric—at least six ounces per square inch.
- Rolled or reinforced seams around the edges of the mattress
- Handles on the sides of the mattress make moving and turning it easier

Memory foam mattresses, also known as viscoelastic, are based on technology from the National Aeronautics and Space Administration (NASA). Made from polyurethane, memory foam is less elastic than other foams and is slower to recover its form after compression. It is sensitive to temperature and weight and manufacturers claim it provides relief from pressure points of the entire body.

Latex mattresses can be made of natural rubber from the sap of rubber trees, or more commonly from a blend of natural and synthetic rubber. Respected for their durability, latex mattresses are usually five to six inches thick. Generally a layer of softer latex or memory foam is added to the top for increased comfort. Latex mattresses are less likely than innerspring mattresses to harbor mold or dust mites.

Air mattresses are being used in some hotels as a luxury upgrade. With air chambers in place of springs, the mattress is equipped with a pump to add or release air to the guest's own comfort level. The air chambers are enclosed and protected within layers of foam. In recent years, the manufacturers have made available plush pillow tops as an add-on feature.

Springs and Supports

Box springs are the sturdy frames generally sold as a unit with a mattress to provide a flat and firm structure for the mattress to lie upon. They can help absorb shock and extend the life of the mattress. In general, springs are made by joining wire springs or coils together and covering them with padding.

Exhibit 1   Standard Bed Sizes

Crib	28 × 52 inches
Rollaway	39 × 75 inches
Twin	38 × 75 inches
Double	53 or 54 × 75 inches
Queen	60 × 80 inches
King	76 × 80 inches

Exhibit 2   Folding Rollaway Bed

Flat bed springs are simply strips of metal attached lengthwise to a frame with helical hooks (small coils with hooks at both ends). Flat bed springs are most frequently found on rollaway beds, such as the one shown in Exhibit 2.

A bed frame supports the box springs and mattress. The frame consists of four metal bars joined at the corners to make a rectangular frame with an extra bar placed in the center of queen- and king-size mattresses for added support. These metal bed frames are often on wheels to make it easy to move the bed for cleaning purposes.

However, some properties prefer a box frame that sits tight to the floor, meaning the area under the bed does not have to be vacuumed or cleared of trash. These frames can receive scuffs and dents which must be cleaned and repaired.

Sometimes hotels choose to place the mattress directly on a raised platform without box springs or bed frame. This platform provides a streamlined

Exhibit 3   Bed Inspection Checklist

Mattress
    Ticking
        ☐ Check for tears
        ☐ Check for soil
    General Condition
        ☐ Check center
        ☐ Check edges
        ☐ Check for lumps
        ☐ Check to see if handles are in good repair
Springs
    Ticking
        ☐ Check for tears
    General Condition
        ☐ Check edges for firmness
        ☐ Check corners for frayed fabric
        ☐ Check for broken springs
Bed Frame (metal frame)
        ☐ Check casters or furniture glides (if any)
        ☐ Check joints
        ☐ Check for crossbar support on queen- and king-size frames
Bed Frame (box)
        ☐ Check for scuffs and dents in the box frame

appearance while supporting the mattress and raising it to a comfortable height for guest access.

Maintenance of Beds

Turning a mattress is a simple maintenance task that can add years to the useful life of a bed. Many properties routinely flip an innerspring mattress four times per year. (Flipping a mattress means to turn it over by putting the bottom to the top as well as rotating the head to the foot of the bed.) Latex or memory foam mattresses are not improved by flipping, though rotating the head to the foot of the bed can prolong its useful life. Mattresses can also be cleaned with a hand-held vacuum attachment or spot cleaned as necessary. Exhibit 3 offers a bed inspection checklist.

The Bed Wars

Up until the late 1990s, beds were fairly simple affairs in hotels. Hotels supplied mattresses, sheets, bedspreads, and pillows. Then in 1999, Westin Hotels and Resorts changed that. It introduced the Heavenly Bed® as a way of differentiating itself from the competition.

Managers at Westin spent about a year developing the Heavenly Bed® once the concept was hit upon. They filled a hotel ballroom with 50 beds from 35 different hotel chains. For months they tested hundreds of mattresses, pillows, and bed linens, determined to come up with the best bed in the industry.

Most metal frames are easy to assemble and sturdy enough to support larger-size box springs and mattresses. (Courtesy of The Hotel Source, Boston, Massachusetts)

Some box frames are all-steel construction with sturdy, center-supported bars. (Courtesy of The Hotel Source, Boston, Massachusetts)

The Heavenly Bed® was an all-white ten-layer bedroom set that included:

- A Simmons custom-designed no-flip pillowtop mattress set with 900 coils in the box springs.
- Three crisp sheets on the bed ranging in thread count from 200 to 250.
- One of three different types of down blankets depending on the climate at the hotel.
- A comforter and a white duvet.
- Five goose down/goose feather pillows.

Guests were thrilled. Westin's marks of overall guest loyalty and satisfaction underwent dramatic increases for the next five years. The bed has become the highest-rated guest satisfaction score on Westin's internal survey. In 2004, J.D. Power and Associates conducted a North America Hotel Guest Satisfaction Study. It found that Westin ranked the highest in guest satisfaction among upscale hotel chains.[1]

Guests liked the beds so much that they wanted the beds for their homes. Westin began selling its bedding accessories to customers, making more than $10 million in sales in 2005. They were sold both online and in retail stores through a partnership with Nordstrom.

In 2001, Hilton created its own brand of beds with specially designed mattress pads, down pillows, linens, decorative bed pillows and bolsters. In 2006, it announced a $1 billion renovation effort to add those beds to many of its properties. Hilton worked with Serta and created a plush-top mattress that is posturized — it provides more coil support in the center of the bed where the most weight is concentrated. They advertise that the patented quilt design of the Hilton Serenity Bed by Serta reduces tossing and turning and helps to improve circulation while sleeping. It also has a broader internal rod to provide extra edge support. Their added coils and taller mattress also raise the bed four inches higher than their previous model. Hilton also opened an online store at hiltontohome.com.

Other hotel companies soon followed suit in part because the changes were so well-received by their guests. Doubletree upgraded its beds in 2004, creating the "Sweet Dreams" bed with a plush-top mattress with extra coils, baffle-box down blankets, 300-thread count linens with triple sheeting, contemporary bed covers with matching bed skirts, four jumbo down pillows for queen-size beds and five for king-size beds, and a "Sweet Dreams" embroidered bed pillow.

Also in 2004, Embassy Suites and Hampton Inn rolled out new bedding collections with the latter raising the bed between 28 and 31 inches.

Radisson Hotels pioneered the use of air mattresses when they introduced the Select Comfort beds on their club level floors system wide. Other properties, such as Hilton Garden Inns, also offer air mattresses with their Garden Sleep System™.

In 2006, Marriott International upgraded its beds, adding 300-thread-count sheets, a feathered mattress topper, stylish pillow shams, a decorative bed scarf, and extra pillows.

Even economy and limited-service brands have gotten in on the bedding wars. Microtel Inns and Suites have introduced a new bedding system that they've dubbed "Dream Well." They outfitted all their beds with a triple sheet set of 200-thread count sheets in 2007. Holiday Inn Express Hotels & Suites upgraded their bedding with the "Simply Smart Bedding" concept that also uses triple sheets of 200 thread count. Hampton Inn has a "Cloud Nine" bed with 200-thread count sheets and a duvet cover.[2]

Flammability Standards

Many years ago the federal government instituted mandatory standards on cigarette ignition of mattresses (16 CFR Part 1632) but further regulations have been enacted more recently. New regulation (16 CFR Part 1633) will ensure mattresses are manufactured with materials to limit the spread and intensity of a fire started by an open flame such as a candle, match, or lighter. Every mattress manufactured after July 1, 2007 is labeled with a statement that it meets the federal flammability requirement.

Bedbugs

In recent years, hotel managers have been cringing at headlines announcing that hotel beds are often infested with bedbugs, whose scientific name is *Cimex lectularius*. Bedbugs are pests that were fairly common up until the early 1950s. They were nearly unheard of until around 1999 when Orkin, an exterminating company, said they began to make a resurgence and have been thriving since.

In 2006, the American Hotel & Lodging Association and the National Pest Management Association partnered to hold an International Bed Bug Symposium. It discussed what could be done to prevent and treat the problems, the legal ramifications, and public relations issues. The symposium also issued a few tips for travelers. It suggested they place luggage on a hard surface instead of the floor or bed and that if they detect bedbugs to inform the front desk and request another room.

Bedbugs will travel in guest luggage, spreading an infestation quickly. Phil Koehler of the University of Florida specializes in bedbugs. He told the *Orlando Sentinel* that a contributing factor to the spread is that pest control firms stopped using baseboard sprays in the mid-1990s and switched to bait traps. Bait traps are highly effective against roaches and ants but do nothing to prevent bedbugs.[3]

The most common variety of bedbug is a quarter-inch long, flat brown insect. It usually comes out at night—often right before dawn and is drawn to human heat. Once it bites, it will suck blood for anywhere from four to 12 minutes, taking in as much as three times its body weight. It can then go for up to six months without feeding again.

One of the best defenses a hotel has against bedbug infestations is a well-trained housekeeping staff that knows how to identify the signs that bedbugs have invaded. These signs include small reddish-brown stains on sheets and mattresses and stains near locations that could be hiding places for these shy bugs. The stains are the defecated remains of a bedbug meal. They should also look for the molted skins of the bug. Also, guests may complain of small bites or red lumps on their skin similar to mosquito or flea bites. A common pattern is for there to be a line of three bites right in a row.

At the AH&LA symposium, an attorney, Timothy Wenk, said that hotels need to be able to prove that their housekeepers were trained to look for bugs, that they used a checklist, and that the hotel had contracted with a professional pest control firm.

Bedbugs are able to hide in extremely small places and will often hide in floorboards, bed frames, and mattress seams. When inspecting, room attendants should examine the mattress seams, especially at the corners, bedboards, nightstands, and carpeted edges where the floor meets the wall close to the bed. If there is a large infestation, there may be a sickly sweet odor that could be similar to coconut, sweaty socks, or raspberries.

Sniffing Out Bedbug Infestations

Excelsis Detections uses dogs to help find bedbugs in hotels, resorts, and cruise ships. In 2005, the owner, Joe Cascone, asked his canine trainer to begin training dogs to sniff out bedbugs.

"Detection is key because the female bedbug needs only to be fertilized once in her lifetime, and she can lay up to five eggs a day," said Cascone. "That means one female can cause an infestation of over 4,000 in just six months! Finding newly introduced bugs in an environment while numbers are low help eradication efforts tremendously."

A dog can inspect a hotel room in four to five minutes once it has been properly trained. Once the dog finds the infestation, Excelsis gets rid of them by using heat to kill the adult bedbugs, their nymphs, eggs, and other insects. They clear the room of things that can melt and then deliver 140 degrees of heat throughout the room, keeping it at that temperature for more than four hours. With this process, a room is typically out of inventory for only two days to set up and administer the treatment.

Source: *The Rooms Chronicle*®, Volume 14, Number 6, p. 6.
For subscription information, please call 866-READ-TRC.

It is important that hotels promptly respond to guest complaints and any evidence of a bedbug infestation. One Chicago hotel that ignored the problems and even rented out rooms that had been identified as having heavy infestations was ordered by a court to pay $372,000 in punitive and compensatory damages. A New York hotel settled with complainants for $150,000.[4]

Once an infestation is identified, it can take up to two weeks to eradicate the bedbugs. A professional exterminator is typically called and the room must be cleaned, sprayed, aired for a week and then the entire process is repeated.

Linens

Effective communication between housekeeping and other departments within the hotel is important for purchasing and controlling the supply of linens. For example, the dining room manager is probably the best person to determine how many **par** of tablecloths and napkins are needed for effective operation, to monitor the performance of table linens, and to measure guest satisfaction with the products.

Because having the right amount and type of linens and bedding is so important, many larger hotels form a linen committee to help choose and review the current types, sizes, and uses of linens.

The linen committee helps all departments make their linen needs heard. This committee might include the executive housekeeper, linen room supervisor, laundry supervisor, chief engineer, dining room managers, and the hotel's general manager. Other staff whose tasks are affected by the supply of linens should also be included. At smaller hotels, the linen committee may consist simply of the executive housekeeper and general manager or owners.

Effective communication helps to pinpoint where linen loss is occurring since everyone then knows the procedures of other departments. Similarly, the source of linen damage can be found more easily if all staff who handle linens are in close contact with the housekeeping department. Good communication with the front desk and the reservations department will alert the housekeeping department when extra linens may be required for banquets, parties, meetings, and other special functions.

Types of Linens

Linens can be classified by where they are used: on beds, in bathrooms, or in dining rooms.

Imagine the effect on a hotel's business if a guest pulled back the blankets and bedspread to find worn, stained, and wrinkled sheets. Hotel sheets and pillowcases must not only be clean; they must *look* clean, crisp, and new. In addition, sheets and pillowcases must be comfortable.

Many properties use plain white sheets and pillowcases. Some properties color-coordinate sheets and pillowcases with the bedspread and other room decor to add a touch of elegance. World-class properties may keep a special supply of monogrammed sheets and pillowcases in various luxurious fabrics such as Egyptian cotton or satin.

Like sheets and pillowcases, blankets and comforters need to look clean and new and feel good. Climate is an important consideration in choosing blankets and comforters, and hotels in very cold or unpredictable climates may stock guestrooms with extra blankets.

Mattress pads protect mattresses. They may be made of a woven, quilted fabric or of felt. Because guests rarely see mattress pads, properties typically choose those that provide the best protection for the mattress at the best price. Felt pads are generally the least expensive, but do not hold up well under repeated washings. Other types of pads include cotton-and-synthetic blends or 100 percent polyester.

Bedcovers and pillows are usually purchased in new hotels as specified by the interior designers. It is best to follow manufacturers' specifications for cleaning and care.

Pillow content can be down, feather, acrylic fibers, or hypoallergenic foam. Down or feather pillows are more luxurious and costly. Acrylic and foam are less expensive, more durable, and are sought out by individuals with allergies to feathers.

Terry cloth is the most common fabric used for bath linens. Velvet towels may have a smoother hand (meaning feel), but they are less absorbent. Better quality towels have **selvaged edges**—that is, edges that are woven, not hemmed. Some properties recommend buying towels with hemmed selvages for extra strength. Selvaged towels last longer; they do not unravel as quickly as nonselvaged towels after repeated washing and drying. Loops should be one-eighth of an inch high.

Bath towels used to often come with the hotel's logo or initials woven into the fabric, though this is rarely the practice any more as too many hotel guests have permanently "borrowed" monogrammed towels as a souvenir of their hotel stay. In 2004, a book about Holiday Inn's iconic green-striped towels was released that traced a 52-year history of Holiday Inn through stories from guests who "borrowed" its towels. The book is appropriately titled, "About the Towels, We Forgive You: Absorbing Tales of Borrowed Towels."[5]

Extra-large towels (called bath blankets or bath sheets) may also be stocked. Many properties see bath blankets as a luxurious amenity. And they are—for large or tall people. Some guests, however, find bath blankets difficult to handle and too heavy to manage easily. Many properties now provide bathrobes to guests as a bath amenity.

Shower curtains should be washable and able to be sent through the ironer. Bath mats generally have the same characteristics as other terry items, but they are usually heavier.

Table linens have both practical and aesthetic uses. Practically speaking, tablecloths, place mats, or runners provide a sanitary eating surface, and napkins help guests stay neat while they eat. Aesthetically, a table set with crisp, fresh linens and fancy, folded napkins lend an air of elegance to the dining room.

A hotel that offers a dining room and banquet service needs a large assortment of tablecloths. Table skirts, which fit under the cloths, are often used for banquets. Silence cloths may be used under tablecloths to protect the table surface and to absorb noise. Silence cloths are generally cotton felt or oil cloth backed with polyurethane foam.

Runners and place mats can make inexpensive and attractive alternatives to tablecloths. These items come in a variety of styles and weaves, from elegant to homespun.

Sizes of Linens

Sheets, blankets, tablecloths, etc., have to be sized according to the sizes of the mattresses and tables. Other items can be chosen on the basis of appearance and price. Exhibit 4 shows standard linen sizes for various bed and table sizes.

Tablecloths come in a wide variety of sizes. To make an attractive presentation, the edges of a tablecloth should have a sufficient corner drop off the end of the table.

If many different sizes of sheets are purchased, the labor cost to sort them will be high. The careful selection of standard sizes makes purchasing, counting, storing, and maintaining inventories much easier. Sizes can be color-coded for easier sorting. Sheets are usually available with color-coded hem threads.

Linen Care, Reuse, and Replacement

Because linen is a major investment, it is particularly important to minimize its disappearance or **shrinkage** as it is sometimes called. Shrinkage may occur from wear, improper use, and theft. The cost of linen can be reduced by minimizing wear. One important way to reduce wear is by properly laundering items. Fabrics laundered the wrong way wear much faster because of the damage done to them.

Exhibit 4   Standard Linen Sizes

Bed Items	Size in Inches
Sheets	
Twin	66 × 104
Double	81 × 104
Queen	90 × 110
King	108 × 110
Pillowcases	
Standard	20 × 30
King	20 × 40
Pillows	
Standard	20 × 26
King	20 × 36

Bath Items	Size in Inches
Towels	
Bath Sheets	36 × 70
Bath	20 × 40
	22 × 44
	24 × 50
	27 × 50
Hand	16 × 26
	16 × 30
Washcloth	12 × 12
	13 × 13
Bath mat	18 × 24
	20 × 30

Napery Items	Size in Inches
Napkins	17 × 17
	22 × 22
Tablecloths	45 × 45
	54 × 54
	64 × 64
	54 × 110
Place mats	12 × 18
	14 × 20
Runners	17 × variable lengths

Improper use of linen—using a guest towel to mop up spills, for example—can cause permanent damage and increase linen costs. Many properties color-code linen to reduce improper use. For example, sheets, spreads, and blankets might be white; table linens, yellow; and cleaning rags, blue. When items are color-coded, supervisors can easily spot an item being used improperly as a rag.

Housekeeping staff may repair linens that are not beyond repair. Blankets and bath mats, for example, can often be patched. Sheets may be saved by rehemming. And, depending on their construction, bedspreads can sometimes be pieced together. However, at some point it becomes more economical to buy new linen than to repair the old.

Selecting Shower Curtains: Make the Change Easy

The key to housekeeping is installing systems that make it easy for employees to do their jobs with efficiency and excellence. One often overlooked part of the guest-room is the shower curtain. This item most likely receives daily use, but sometimes is changed infrequently. To a customer, there are not many worse things than a shower curtain gone stiff and smelly from weeks of frequent use.

Several years ago, when the heavy, vinyl curtains were popular, room atten-dants were trained to soak the bottom of the curtain in a bucket of sudsy, hot water while they cleaned the rest of the room. They were instructed to then pull the cur-tain up against the bathroom door while firmly wiping it down.

Today, with the advent of the light, washable, nylon curtains, it is more sani-tary to simply replace the curtain. In addition, guests prefer a clean, dry curtain over used, damp ones that hold moisture and promote the growth of mildew on the curtain and walls.

Replacing curtains may be more sanitary than cleaning them, perhaps, but is it easier? To make changing shower curtains easy and time effective, the hotel must make a supply of clean curtains and shower curtain hooks that make chang-ing simple readily available to each room attendant.

Shower Curtain Pars. Computing par levels always assumes that for each item in the guestroom there should be one in the laundry and one moving from the laundry to the room. Since hotel policy probably provides for changing the shower curtains in each check-out room (or as needed), the par level can be based on the average length of stay rather than the number of rooms. For instance, a hotel with 120 rooms that runs 60 percent occupancy has 72 rooms occupied per night on average. If their average length of stay is 1.8 nights, only 40 of those rooms are check-outs on any given day. That hotel, therefore, would need to have a minimum of 40 clean shower curtains readily available (on the room attendants' carts) each day and 40 more being laundered for the next day. This formula would have to be adjusted if the occupancy were irregular—that is, a full house during the week and low occupancy on weekends—or if the hotel tended to have full house turns.

Shower Curtain Hooks. If room attendants have to struggle to open and/or close the shower curtain hooks, it would be easier for them to simply not change the curtains. Or, if the room attendant has to fight a heavy decor curtain while trying to remove the nylon curtain, it might not seem worth the effort. Make it easy for employees by purchasing hooks that make curtain exchanges efficient.

Distribution of Shower Curtains. Although curtains can be folded and placed on the room attendant's cart with other linen, because of the nylon content, the curtain is slippery and hard to keep folded. A simple solution is to use a wire coat hanger with a sticky cardboard roll such as those used by dry cleaners to hang slacks. Folded in half over the cardboard, the shower curtains stay straight and can be hung at any position on the cart. Each room attendant should have a supply each day, just as he or she has towels and sheets.

(continued)

C the Rooms HRONICLE®

(continued)

Making it easy for the room attendant to provide clean shower curtains for the new check-ins will mean higher employee morale and higher guest satisfaction.

Source: Gail Edwards, CHHE, *The Rooms Chronicle*®, Volume 4, Number 1, p. 5.
For subscription information, call 866-READ-TRC.

Linen reuse or recycling can save properties a great deal of money. Turning discarded items into rags is probably the simplest and most common type of recycling. Discarded sheets can also be used to replace torn or worn dustcovers on the bottoms of box springs. Large sheets can be cut down for use as crib sheets, aprons, and other items. Tablecloths can be cut into ironing board covers. Some properties, in a final attempt to recoup linen costs, sell discarded linens to staff at a reasonable price. Besides generating revenue that can help replace linens, this policy may significantly reduce employee theft. Many properties donate used linens to charities and often realize a tax benefit.

Linen Selection Considerations

Getting linens to the hotel is a long process. It begins in cotton fields, on sheep farms, and in chemical factories where the raw materials used to make linens are produced. From there, the raw materials are shipped to textile mills where they are spun and woven according to a variety of methods. The process continues in finishing plants where various techniques are used to dye, cut, and sew the final products. And the final products themselves are tested at hundreds of sites in mills, factories, and laboratories by manufacturers, professional groups, consumer organizations, and government agencies.

Anyone responsible for purchasing linens and other textiles should be aware that the American National Standards Institute (previously known as the American Standards Association) has developed and issued Minimum Performance Requirements for Institutional Textiles since 1956. The standards cover breaking strength, shrinkage, colorfastness, permanency of finish, seam strength, chlorine retention, components (that is, zippers, grommets, snaps, and other fasteners), thickness and resiliency of blankets, weathering resistance, shape retention after laundering, resistance to mildew and rot, resistance to wetting, and yarn distortion. Standards are available by writing to the American National Standards Institute, 25 West 43rd Street, New York, NY 10036, or calling (212) 642-4900.

While this chapter cannot cover every aspect of linen manufacturing, it can offer some practical information that will help hotels select the best materials for their guests. This section will cover fabric materials, fabric construction, and finishing.

Fabric Materials. All fabrics begin with raw materials that are spun into long strands of fibers called yarns that are woven or knitted into cloth.

A large number of synthetic fibers were developed during World War II. These fibers were frequently stronger than natural fibers and could often be spun to resemble luxurious materials like silk. To make fabrics easier to identify, the U.S. government passed a law in 1960 requiring that all textile products carry labels stating their fiber content.

Today, yarns can be made from dozens of different materials that fall into three basic groups—natural, synthetics, or blends.

Natural fibers. Linens generally come in one of three natural fibers: cotton, wool, or linen. Cotton is by far the most common of these fibers.

Before synthetics and blends became widely used, most of the linens in hotels were made of cotton. Cotton is strong, absorbent, and available in a wide range of grades. Blends and synthetics have replaced the bulk of cotton linens in most hotels. But this trend may be reversing. Natural fibers have enjoyed a renaissance in the clothing industry, and consumers are expressing a preference for other natural-fiber items.

Despite the extensive use of synthetics for some items, cotton has continued to be the fabric of choice for napery (table linens) and towels. Cotton's superior absorbency makes it a good choice for napkins and bath towels. It can also be starched (synthetics cannot), which helps it retain a crisp appearance and makes napkins easier to fold into fancy shapes. Mercerized cotton, while more expensive, reduces cotton's tendency to produce lint. Cotton blends combine many of the advantages of cotton with the durability of synthetics (mostly polyester). Egyptian cotton is considered by many to be the longest fiber and the best quality of cotton.

Wool, once the fabric of choice for blankets, is not as soft as, and does not wear as well or wash as easily, as synthetic fabrics. It also has a tendency to **felt**, which means that its surface fibers mat together. As a result, most blankets are now made from a variety of synthetic materials.

Cotton and wool can be either carded or combed and then spun. Combed fibers generally make stronger, more lustrous yarns and better quality fabrics. Carded fibers are coarser and shorter, rougher to the touch, and yield duller fabrics (for example, cotton muslins) that produce more lint and pills.

Linen, made from the fibers of the flax plant, is another natural material. It is generally used only for napery today. Linen is smooth, durable, lintless, fast-drying, and absorbent. It is also expensive. A less costly natural fiber can be made by combining linen and cotton, which resembles 100 percent linen.

Synthetics. Blankets, bedspreads, and shower curtains are most frequently made from all-synthetic fabrics. Synthetics may be less absorbent than cotton or actually moisture repellent. This makes them particularly attractive fabrics for shower curtains and bedspreads. Synthetics also have good thermal qualities that make them a good choice for blankets. And many synthetic fabrics are stronger than natural fabrics. As a result, some uniform items are made from woven or knit synthetics. There are dozens of synthetic fibers on the market today. A list of some of them is offered in Exhibit 5.

Blends. In the last two decades, many hotels have purchased "no-iron" sheets and pillowcases made of cotton/synthetic (usually polyester) blends. Whether these products can truly be called no-iron, however, is debatable. Usually, laundering erodes the wrinkle resistance of these linens about halfway through their useful

Exhibit 5   Generic Names and Some Common Trade Names of Synthetic Fibers

Generic	Trade Names
Acetate	Celanese, Celaperm
Acrylic	Acrilan, Creslan, Orlon
Polyester	Dacron, Fortrel, Kodel
Spandex	Lycra
Nylon	
Rayon	
Vinyl	Vinylon

lives. Moreover, if no-iron sheets and pillowcases are not removed from dryers and folded immediately, wrinkles generally set in.

Nevertheless, no-iron linens are often stronger than those made of 100 percent cotton—and they get stronger after more washings. A blended fabric can last for more than 500 washings; a 100 percent cotton fabric can last for only 150 to 200 washings. This fact alone represents a considerable savings to the hotel. Also, if ironing can be eliminated when the linens are new, then the hotel need not purchase as many ironers as it might if it were using all-cotton linens. No-iron linens can represent considerable labor savings for the property as well.

Some hotels have also found that using a small percentage of polyester fibers in the base of bath linens and all-cotton nap on the **face** offers a product with all the absorbency of cotton and some of the added strength of synthetics. Doing so also yields a fabric that tends not to shrink as much as 100 percent cotton.

Napery made of polycotton blends is widely available. These napkins and tablecloths initially have some of the absorbency of cotton and the easy-care characteristics of polyester. With repeated washings, however, the cotton wears out, reducing the absorbency of the item.

Fabric Construction. Some linen items may not be made of woven fabric. Blankets, for example, may be bonded or made by a process known as fiberlock. Nylon fibers are flocked to a foam backing to make a bonded blanket. These blankets wash well and have a velvety look and hand.

Woven fabrics. Woven fabrics have two kinds of yarns. The yarns that run the length of the fabric are called **warp yarns**, and the yarns that run sideways are called **fill** (or **weft**) **yarns**. The strength and durability of the fabric depend not only on the material from which the yarn is made, but on how thick the yarns are and how close together the yarns are placed on the loom. When yarns are placed close together, the fabric is strong, heavy, and stiff; when yarns are placed further apart, the fabric is weaker, looser, and more limp.

Balance of warp and fill yarns is an important indicator of fabric quality. Better-quality fabrics are well-balanced; that is, they have approximately the same number of warp yarns (no more than 10) as fill yarns per square inch. Balance determines how well the fabric will stand up under repeated stretching with a flat-work ironer.

The number of yarns per square inch of fabric is the fabric's **thread count**. Thread count may be written to reveal the number of both warp and fill yarns, for example: 80 × 76. Or the number of warp and fill yarns per square inch can be added together to yield the fabric's total thread count per square inch, for example: T120. (The latter way of expressing thread count, of course, does not tell you whether the fabric is well-balanced. You may have to go directly to the manufacturer or sales representative for more information.)

Thread counts can range from 80 to 700, but most sheets are between 180 and 320. Economy class hotels used to use linens with a thread count of 150 or lower. However, guests are far more demanding today and most properties have upgraded to linens with a thread count of 180 to 200. Limited service and select-service hotels typically have sheets with a minimum of 200-thread count. Full-service hotels typically buy sheets that have thread counts between 250 and 280. These sheets are typically more comfortable and more durable. World class and luxury hotels have even higher quality linens. The minimum is at least a 280-thread count linen with others as high as 400-thread count. The Ritz Carlton uses 400-thread count sheets while many Hyatt's use 300-thread count sheets.

Thread counts over 500 usually use plied yarn that is made by twisting together multiple finer threads. These may mean that the fibers are thinner so that while the linen is softer, it is more delicate and won't hold up to wear and tear as long as others.[6]

Thread count is a good indicator of fabric durability only if one is comparing linens made from the same kind of fabric. Fabrics can have the same thread count but different weights. If you are comparing two fabrics, weight per square inch is a better way to determine which fabric is more durable. Towels are sometimes measured by the number of pounds per dozen.

Yarns can be woven into three basic fabric types called weaves: **plain weave**, **twill weave**, and **satin weave**.

Fill yarns in plain weave are simply woven under and over the warp yarns in a crisscross pattern. Twill weaves, somewhat more durable than plain weaves, are woven so that a diagonal pattern of yarns emerges. Most sheets, pillowcases, towels, tablecloths, and napkins are made in plain-weave fabrics. However, some properties opt to purchase some of these items in more luxurious—and more expensive—satin weaves. In satin weaves, the warp and filling threads interlace to produce a smooth-faced fabric.

Terry cloth is made with a plain- or twill-weave base with extra warp yarns pulled up on either side of the base to form the loops on the face of the towel. The face loops may be sheared to make a **velvet**. **Jacquard** towels are those in which a raised terry or velvet pattern is woven into the fabric for a sculpted effect.

Napery (table linens) may be made of plain weave fabric (also called crash cloth). Dobby cloth is another kind of plain weave fabric into which repeating geometric patterns are woven at regular intervals. Momie cloth is a type of dobby. Damask is a patterned cloth in which the pattern emerges in a twill weave; the background or field is made by passing warp yarns over several fill yarns for a satin effect. While the effect is elegant, the more fill yarns the warp thread passes over, the weaker the fabric. In single-damask construction (as opposed to

Purchasing Facts and Tips for Terry Cloth

- The terry cloth industry is unusual in that only a handful of mills exists.

- Mills generally shut down for two weeks in July to allow maintenance on equipment and vacations for employees.

- Price adjustments usually occur twice a year, in January and July. Cotton prices have been on the rise recently. This has meant significant increases in the price of terry.

- Terry cloth towels have two types of borders: cam (a plain, cloth border) and a more expensive type, dobby (a twill, designed edge).

- A chain-stitched towel is of lesser quality because it allows stitching to unravel. A lock stitch is becoming the industry standard because it hinders loose ends and is more efficient to produce than other types.

- The most popular towel sizes have become known as the "institutional standard" and have increased in size over the years from a 20-inch by 40-inch bath towel weighing 4 pounds per dozen to a 24-inch by 50-inch bath towel weighing 10.5 pounds per dozen.

- Purchasing through a consortium can produce savings. Also, the purchasing arms of some large hotel companies are eager to sell to independent hotels and can pass along these savings.

- Use due diligence when purchasing imported linen to ensure the stitching, construction, durability, and colorfastness meet the hotel's standards.

- Weigh towels by the dozen upon delivery to ensure that the order is correct.

- The institutional standard calls for ROM (run-of-the-mill) linen that is case-packed with 10 percent seconds. First-quality linen (without flaws) is generally reserved for retail standards.

- Order early to avoid costly express shipping charges.

Make price adjustments as follows:

Dobby border:	add 20%
Beige:	add 8%
Other colors:	upgrade to retail or order 100 dz min; add 25%
Name woven:	order 100 dz min and add 25%
Ship from mill:	case pack only, allow 4 to 6 wks lead time
Ship from warehouse:	no minimum, ship within 72 hours; add 3% to 4%

Source: *The Rooms Chronicle*®, Volume 3, Number 6, p. 16.
For subscription information, please call 866-READ-TRC.

double-damask construction) fewer fill yarns are passed over. This is why most properties prefer to use single damask linens.

Woven blankets come in plain weaves for summer and winter. Thermal weave, a type of plain weave, is designed for cold weather. The blanket surface has small depressions, giving the blanket a waffled texture, that trap warm air next to the body.

Fabric Finishing. Other factors will affect a fabric's quality besides weave. A sheet with a high thread count and good balance, for example, is not worth buying if its colors fade quickly or run during washings or if its hems will not hold. Finishing, dyeing, and sewing are therefore important considerations.

Dyeing. Color-coordinating linens with a guestroom or dining room's decor often seems like a good way to enhance the appearance of the property. However, colored linens complicate purchasing, laundering, and inventory procedures.

Purchasers should find out how a particular item has been dyed before buying it. Linens that have been vat-dyed in the yarn stage (before being woven) are the most colorfast fabrics available. In addition, the purchaser should make sure to purchase linens in the same dye lot. Items should be from the same dye lot to avoid minor color differences between pieces. Long-term replacement of these items may become a problem when the dye lot becomes obsolete.

While vat-dyed linens retain colors better, all dyed, natural fibers will fade after several washings. This fading will be more immediately noticeable in bright colors than in pastels. Moreover, chlorine bleach, used frequently to remove stains, can erode the color further. Laundering procedures must be established and carefully followed to help linens retain their original color.

Because linens will fade with washing, housekeeping staff in charge of storage and inventory should rotate colored linens carefully so that all pieces fade at the same rate. When linens become too faded to use, they will have to be discarded and new linens will have to be purchased.

Sewing. Most linens are woven in standard widths on the loom so that the piece need only be hemmed at the ends to prevent unraveling. However, for appearance' sake, it is a good idea to purchase napery that has been hemmed on all sides.

In general, hem threads should be made from some type of fabric that will shrink at the same rate as the piece itself. Otherwise, the piece will pucker after laundering. Hem stitches should be close together so that the hem lasts for the life of the item. Hems that pull out must be repaired by housekeeping staff, and if this happens frequently, the cost of rehemming items can become excessive.

Uniforms

Hotel staff may use many different types of uniforms. Door attendants, parking attendants, guest hosts and hostesses, male and female front desk personnel, bell attendants, chefs and kitchen personnel, wait staff, banquet servers, engineering personnel, room attendants, laundry workers, and others may have their own special uniforms, perhaps even with seasonal variations. Each uniform may have a number of components. A door attendant may need an overcoat, a summer jacket,

Workers and Employers Appreciate New Uniform Fabrics

Hotel employees want uniforms that will look good and feel comfortable through long hours on the job. Physically active employees need apparel in which they can move easily. Those assigned to warm locations such as kitchens, boiler rooms, spas, or outdoors in warm weather need fabrics that breathe easily and help them stay cool.

Managers and owners are seeking to ensure that employees comply with uniform requirements and that morale is not affected by problems associated with uniforms. They also want to ensure a consistent appearance among all employees that reflects the brand image of the facility, whether it is professional, upscale, fun, sport, etc.

Uniform service companies

Developing a uniform program that meets all of these requirements is a time-consuming and complex job. Uniform service companies (those who rent, lease, and sell uniforms) can help. They provide assistance to customers that goes beyond simply providing them garments, picking up dirty uniforms, washing them, and delivering clean ones.

Uniform service companies also consult with hotel managers to make sure that they are choosing the uniform fabrics that best meet their objectives, offering performance-related information about the latest textile technologies, or new fabrics for workwear that are available from textile manufacturers. If a revamped uniform program is still in the early planning phases, they can also provide information about fabrics that will soon be available for uniform applications.

In addition, uniform service companies also help customers explore options for uniform design that will help make the desired visual statement. The Uniform and Textile Service Association (UTSA) is an international trade organization that represents these companies and works to convey information about new uniform textile options.

New choice for wearability and durability

In recent years, 65 percent cotton/35 percent polyester blends have been popular uniform fabrics for hotel and resort employees. These blends have many advantages, including durability. It is not uncommon for a uniform that is 65/35 blend to last two to three times longer than one that is 100 percent cotton. They also have another advantage that appeals to managers: wrinkle resistance. The reduced wrinkling helps keep the uniforms looking crisp and sharp resulting in employees who look neat and project a more professional image.

Blends produced for the uniform market also have excellent soil release properties built into them, making it possible to eliminate even the worst stains.

Blends may be less breathable than 100 percent cotton however, so employees in warm environments may feel their apparel does not stay fresh on the job. In addition, the reduced softness of blends may frustrate workers whose tasks require a great deal of movement.

More new-tech fabrics

New textiles being introduced now into the uniform marketplace combine the advantages of both all-cotton fabrics and cotton/polyester blends. Known as

(continued)

hydrophilic fabrics, they have become familiar to consumers under brand names such as Nike's Dri-FIT.

Hydrophilic fabrics used in work apparel are 100 percent polyester knits. These are not 1970s-style polyesters. These fabrics use spun yarns that give a truly cotton-like feel, creating soft garments that allow for plenty of freedom of movement. They also help athletes and outdoor enthusiasts, and hot, busy hotel employees, stay cool and dry. This is because these fabrics allow perspiration to be moved away from the skin and evaporate. Thus, they enhance comfort and provide odor resistance, because without moisture, odor-causing bacteria cannot survive in large numbers.

Wicking properties also enhance safety for employees who work indoors in hot environments and outdoors in hot or cold weather, or who work in conditions in which temperatures can fluctuate between hot and cold. Color-retention, durability, and wrinkle resistance of hydrophilic uniform fabrics ensure that these new uniforms can be kept very clean.

Stretch features also constitute an emerging option for uniform construction. Lycra, which is commonly incorporated into fabric blends in consumer clothing to add stretch capability, is less suited to workwear, because it can be hot to wear during extended activity. Also, its limited durability may make it unattractive to employers. However, wicking Lycra is now available and may increase the wearer's comfort during active work. Instead of using Lycra, a mechanical stretch can be woven into uniform textile fabrics. The result is a garment that stretches comfortably and also has soil release and other features found in 65/35 blends.

Getting the best value from a uniform program

To ensure that they are getting the most from their uniform program, hotel managers should consider the following:

- Use the most durable fabrics possible given employee tasks and the desired appearance of the uniforms. Frequent laundering will quickly take its toll on less durable fabrics.

- Keep all uniforms in good repair, seeing that rips and tears are repaired quickly. By contracting with a uniform service provider, repairs typically will be included, along with basic laundering, steam-pressing and stain removal. Uniform companies also will see that worn uniforms are replaced with new ones and that larger or smaller-sized uniforms are delivered promptly if needed.

- Encourage employees to provide feedback about their experiences with their uniforms. Do they have to strain seams and fabrics to perform their normal job duties? If so, stronger fabrics or reinforced seams may be needed. If employees frequently become too warm, more breathable fabrics are in order.

- Hotel logos or other unique, identifiable business elements such as slogans or departmental names, should be incorporated into all possible employee wear items, including uniforms, coveralls, gloves, headgear, and other ancillary products. This step will help discourage theft of uniform items, and will also aid in security within the property while reinforcing the hotel's brand image among guests.

(continued)

C the Rooms
HRONICLE®

(continued)

- Store uniforms collected for laundering in a secure location so non-employees may not obtain them and use them as cover for committing illegal acts on property.

- Make certain that all department managers collect uniforms distributed to employees who have resigned or who were terminated.

A textile service company can help hotel managers identify the impact of each job activity on clothing and select uniform textiles that will meet the specific needs of the hotel and its workers, so that all of the property's employees can look professional and be comfortable while doing their jobs.

Source: Jennifer Kellar, *The Rooms Chronicle®*, Volume 12, Number 3, pp. 1, 14–15.
For subscription information, call 866-READ-TRC.

pants, a hat, and a vest. A hostess may require a skirt, blouse, vest and/or jacket, and scarf.

In many hotels, nametags are also considered part of all uniforms. Nametags are the one common element that unites all of a property's employees. Nametags convey a sense of hospitality to those who wear them and to those who see them. It is standard practice in most lodging properties that all employees, from room attendant to the general manager, wear their issued nametag. No staff member is exempt from this responsibility. A nametag coupled with a warm welcoming smile is the most important element of any employee's uniform.[7]

Identifying Uniform Needs

Identifying uniform needs is much like determining linen needs. Staff members may be canvassed by managers to find out whether they wish to wear uniforms and what styles they would prefer. In most cases, especially in chain properties, corporate management decides which staff members will wear uniforms and what styles they may choose from. Staff who wear uniforms need to help track the quality of the items. The hotel must also decide who will pay for uniforms—the employee or the property—and how they will be maintained.

Par levels must also be determined and, again like linen, a number of factors will affect par: Will the hotel's laundry service or on-premises laundry take care of cleaning uniforms? Or will employees be responsible for laundering their own? Is turnover high among employees who wear uniforms? How effective are the property's measures to control uniform loss and damage? What kinds of work do staff members wearing uniforms perform that could damage or ruin uniforms?

Selecting Uniforms

Hotel managers like employees to wear uniforms because it gives managers more control over how employees dress. Staff uniforms also allow managers to create an image for the property through the kind of uniforms they choose. Guests like uniforms because they identify staff members who can offer assistance and information. And many staff members like wearing uniforms because

Exhibit 6   Designing a Uniform

Most hotel employees wouldn't think their uniforms were the stuff of high-fashion catwalks, yet more and more designers are competing for hospitality business.

Blame it on reality television shows such as The Apprentice, Donald Trump's show in which teams compete to gain business success, and Project Runway, where fashion designers compete to see whose designs are the best.

In 2006, the runner-up for one of the Project Runway seasons landed a contract with NYLO, a new North American hotel chain. They contracted with Daniel Vosovic to design clothing for staff members at the proposed hotels. The uniforms are planned to be an extension of the décor that employees will enjoy wearing. The hotel will also sell the uniforms to guests online and at hotel gift shops.

Likewise, one of the Project Runway judges, Michael Kors, has signed with Starwood to design uniforms for their W hotels. His uniform design is similar to that of his clothing line found in his stores.

Also in 2006, the task for the final four Apprentice candidates was to design a uniform for the Embassy Suites hotel brand. The winning uniform was then rolled out to the entire hotel chain.

"As a hotel brand, we continually strive for innovation, comfort and high quality for our guests," notes John Lee, Vice President, Brand Marketing & Communications, Embassy Suites Hotels, "but our team members are at the heart of everything we do," said Lee. "So, we decided to arrange the task to focus on them."

Focus groups of Embassy Suites employees were brought in to explain what they needed in terms of fit, functionality, and a professional look. Embassy Suites employees were the ones who voted on which design would win.

Other fashion designers getting in on the uniform game are Cynthia Rowley, who has designed concierge and housekeeping uniforms for the Hotel Monaco in Denver, and Narcisco Rodreguez for Gramercy Park Hotel.

it eliminates the need for employees to choose, buy, and, sometimes, care for their own work clothes.

Uniforms must be chosen with caution, however. Food & beverage servers may refuse to wear revealing uniforms that could attract unwanted attention from guests. Staff members may balk at wearing uniforms that are unfashionable, uncomfortable, or ill-fitting. Managers must remember that uniforms should make staff feel well-groomed, neat, and confident about meeting the public. When employees are unhappy with what they are wearing, their dissatisfaction will be transmitted to guests. Some hotels are getting creative about the design of their uniforms and contracting with well-known fashion designers. See Exhibit 6.

Fortunately, the marketplace offers a wide variety of uniforms in a range of styles, colors, and fabrics. Most of today's uniforms are made of polycotton that is durable, is easy to care for, holds its color well, and offers much of the comfort of all-cotton fabrics. Polyester or other synthetic fabric is often used for jackets, coats, scarves, vests, ties, and other accessories. In some areas of the hotel, however, all-cotton uniform items are still preferred. All-cotton kitchen aprons, for example, are more absorbent and more easily cleaned than those made of synthetics or blends.

Endnotes

1. "Westin Heavenly Beds Celebrates Fifth Anniversary; 19 Million Guests Agree—Westin is Still the Best in Bed," *Business Wire*, August 30, 2004.

2. Lindsay Otto, "Threadcount Basics that Every Housekeeping Manager Should Know," *The Rooms Chronicle®*, Volume 15, Number 2, pp. 1, 14. For subscription information, call 866-READ-TRC.

3. Tim Barker, "Bedbugs Finding Their Way into Hotel Beds Throughout Orlando," *The Orlando Sentinel* via www.hotel-online.com, July 1, 2001.

4. "Unique Technology Introduced for "Sniffing Out" Hotel Bedbug Infestations," *The Rooms Chronicle®*, Volume 14, Number 6, p. 6. For subscription information, call 866-READ-TRC.

5. "The Holiday Inn Green-striped Towel Earns a Permanent Place in Americana; Tracing the 52-year History of Holiday Inn," via www.hotel-online.com, October 19, 2004.

6. Otto, pp. 1, 14.

7. "Why Employee Nametags Are So Important," *The Rooms Chronicle®*, Volume 13, Number 4, p. 11. For subscription information, call 866-READ-TRC.

Key Terms

box springs—Type of bed springs fastened to a wood frame.

fill (or weft) yarns—Yarns running the width of the fabric.

flat bed springs—Bed springs made of metal slats linked with helical hooks.

helical hooks—Small coils with hooks on both ends.

innerspring mattress—Mattress in which springs are sandwiched between layers of padding.

latex mattress—Mattress made of natural rubber from the sap of rubber trees, or more commonly from a blend of natural and synthetic rubber.

napery—Table linens.

par—The standard quantity of a particular inventory item that must be on hand to support daily, routine housekeeping operations.

plain weave—Type of weave in which fill yarns are alternately woven under and over warp yarns.

satin weave—Type of weave in which warp threads interlace with filling threads to produce a smooth-faced fabric.

selvaged edges—Towel edges that are woven, not hemmed.

shrinkage—Linen disappearance caused by wear, improper use, or theft.

terry cloth—Fabric made with a plain or twill base with extra warp yarns pulled up on either side of the base to form the loops on the face of a towel.

thread count—Number of warp and fill yarns per square inch.

ticking—Sturdy fabric used to cover mattresses and springs.

twill weave—Type of weave in which a diagonal yarn pattern emerges.

warp yarns—Yarns that run the length of the fabric.

 Review Questions

1. Name the main parts of a bed.

2. Name the principal kinds of mattresses and discuss the advantages and disadvantages of each. Which kind would be most suitable for your property and why?

3. Review some of the factors that affect the quantity of linens that must be kept on hand. What specific factors affect the supply of linens at your property?

4. How does good communication between housekeeping and other departments affect the purchase and control of linens?

5. Discuss some of the main types of fabrics for linens, advantages, and appropriate and inappropriate uses for each type.

6. What is linen reuse and why is it important? How are linens reused at your property?

7. What are some of the advantages of uniforms?

8. Discuss how uniforms are related to employee morale.

 Internet Sites

For more information, visit the following Internet sites. Remember that Internet addresses can change without notice. If the site is no longer there, you can use a search engine to look for additional sites.

American National Standards Institute
www.ansi.org

Harbor Linens
www.harborlinen.com

Hilton to Home
www.hiltontohome.com

Hospitality Index Database
www.hospitality-index.com/
 category.html

Marriott Store
www.shopmarriott.com/index.aspx

Mission Linen and Uniform Service
www.mission-linen.com

Sealy, Inc.
www.sealycontract.com

Sleep Products Safety Council
www.safesleep.org

Sobel Westex
www.sobelwestex.com

Uniform & Textile Service Association
www.usta.com

The W Store
www.whotelsthestore.com

Westin at Home
www.westin-hotelsathome.com

Chapter 13 Outline

Carpets
    Carpet Construction
    Carpet Problems
    Carpet Maintenance
    Carpet and Floor Care Equipment
    Carpet Cleaning Methods
    Special Carpet Treatments
Floors
    Resilient Floors
    Wood Floors
    Hard Floors
    General Floor Maintenance
    Floor Cleaning Methods
    Green Floor Care

Competencies

1. Identify factors of carpet construction that affect the durability, texture retention, and serviceability of a carpet. (pp. 515–519)

2. Identify carpet care and maintenance issues. (pp. 519–525)

3. Identify the carpet and floor care functions of vacuums, wet vacuums, wet extractors, and rotary floor machines. (pp. 525–534)

4. Describe common carpet cleaning methods and special treatments. (pp. 534–542)

5. Distinguish resilient floors from hard floors and describe appropriate cleaning and maintenance methods for each. (pp. 542–553)

13

Carpets and Floors

UNTIL HUMAN BEINGS LEARN to defy the laws of gravity, carpets and floors will be walked on, spilled on, tracked in on, crushed, and eventually worn down. In a lodging operation, carpets and floors are walked on by thousands of feet every day. As a result, they can become worn and dirty very quickly. A soiled, stained, or faded carpet or floor creates one impression in the minds of guests: poor care and maintenance. No wonder, then, that most lodging properties rate durability, appearance, and ease of maintenance as the major concerns when choosing carpets and floors.

New kinds of floor coverings, cleaning solutions, and maintenance equipment appear on the market every year. Executive housekeepers must keep up with these advances to develop effective cleaning procedures and make wise recommendations about purchasing equipment or contracting carpet or floor cleaning services. For example, many properties can save money by purchasing equipment that can be used on both carpets and floors.

In this chapter, the term "floors" is used to refer to all floor surfaces other than carpeting. After a brief discussion of general carpet and floor care considerations, this chapter focuses on the types of carpets and floors found in lodging properties; common preventive and routine carpet and floor maintenance procedures and equipment; and typical carpet and floor cleaning methods. This chapter also includes a brief discussion of special carpet treatments such as antimicrobial treatment and electrostatic dissipation, and examines "green" floor care.

Carpets

Carpeting offers a number of benefits over other types of floor coverings. Carpeting reduces noise in halls and guestrooms, prevents slipping, and keeps floors and rooms warmer. Carpeting is also easier to maintain than many other floor coverings. Most lodging properties use commercial-grade carpet specially designed to withstand more wear and tear than the retail- (or consumer-) grade carpets people install in their homes.

Carpet Construction

In general, carpets have three components: the **face**, the **primary backing,** and the **secondary backing**. Exhibit 1 shows a cross section of these components.

The face or **pile** of the carpet is the part people see and walk on. The face may be made of synthetic fibers or yarns such as polyester, acrylic, polypropylene (olefin), or nylon. The face may also be made of such natural fibers as wool or cotton, though cotton is seldom used as a face fiber today. Some carpets are made of blends of synthetics and natural fibers, or blends of different kinds of synthetics.

Exhibit 1   Cross Section of Carpet Components

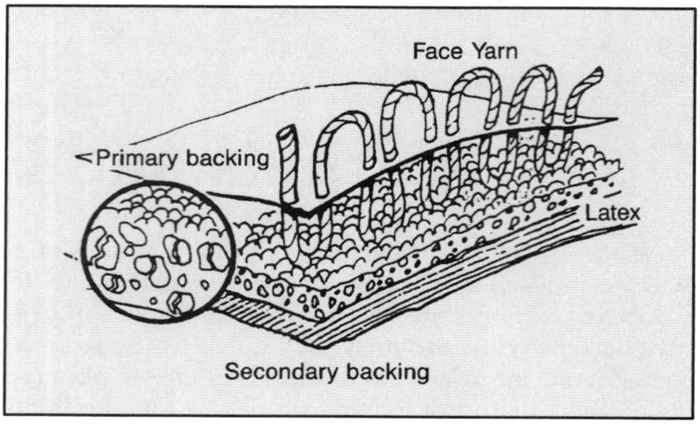

The carpet's face fibers, as well as its density, height, twist, and weave, will affect the carpet's durability, texture retention, and serviceability.

The density of the carpet's face fibers is the best indicator of durability. In general, the greater the density, the better grade of carpet. Dense carpets retain their shape longer and resist matting and crushing. They also keep stains and dirt at the top of the fibers, preventing deeply embedded soiling. To determine how dense a carpet is, bend a corner of the carpet and see how much backing shows underneath the pile. The less backing that shows, the denser the carpet.

In carpets of equal density, the one with the higher pile and tighter twist will generally be the better product. Carpet that is more tightly twisted is more resilient and will retain its appearance better. When examining a carpet, one should be able to see the twist. The tips of the fibers should not be flared or open. Good quality cut pile carpets have a heat-set twist.

Pile weight, while not as important as density, can affect the carpet's durability. Pile weight is measured in **face weight**—the weight of the face fibers in one square yard of carpet. The greater the weight, the more durable the carpet.

Face fibers are attached to a primary backing which holds the fibers in place. This backing may be made of natural material (typically jute) or synthetic material such as polypropylene. Jute backings are durable and resilient but may mildew under damp conditions. Polypropylene has most of the advantages of jute and is mildew-resistant. Both jute and polypropylene are suitable for tufted or woven carpets.

Usually, the primary backing of the carpet has a backsize. A backsize is a bonding material made of plastic, rubber, latex, or other adhesive that holds the fibers in place. This material is spread in a thin layer over the back of the primary backing and prevents the carpet tufts or loops from shifting or loosening after installation. Some carpets have a secondary backing that is laminated to the primary backing to provide additional stability and more secure installation.

In the past, all carpeting was installed over a separate pad. Today, carpeting may be glued directly to the floor or installed over one of a variety of pads. Sometimes, particularly with carpet tiles, a pad may be bonded directly to the backing in the manufacturing process.

In general, pads should be chosen with as careful an eye toward quality as toward the carpet itself. A cheap pad will reduce the life of the carpet as well as its insulating, sound-absorbing, and cushioning abilities. A thick pad will prevent the carpet from shifting unless the carpet is installed in an area where heavy equipment will be rolled over it frequently; in this case, a thinner pad, or no pad, is preferred.

Tufted Carpet. Nonwoven or **tufted carpet** is constructed with either **staple** or **bulk continuous filament (BCF)** fibers. Staple fibers are short (approximately seven to ten inches long) and are twisted together to form long strands. BCF fibers form one continuous strand. Of course, wool and other natural fibers are only available as staple fibers. The reason some carpets shed or pill (pills are small, round fibers appearing at the tips of the tufts or loops) is that not all the fibers in a staple construction are attached to the primary backing as well as the fibers in a BCF construction. Carpets that do not shed are almost always made of BCF fibers.

In tufted construction, needles on a large machine pull the face fibers through the carpet's backing to form tufts or loops. These tufts or loops form a thick pile or plush. Cut pile may be long, short, or cut in various lengths to provide a sculpted effect. Or, the tufts may be pulled to different lengths and left uncut to give a pattern to the finished carpet. Sometimes, both methods are used to create a cut-and-loop effect.

Berber carpets have short, nubby tufts and are available in a variety of textures. Level loops are the most common commercial carpets, usually tufted in short continuous rows. Lodging properties typically use a level-cut pile carpet in guestrooms to approximate the appearance of residential carpet. Other types of carpeting may be used in public areas, depending on the individual design requirements of the property.

Woven Carpet. In a woven carpet, a machine or loom weaves the face fibers and backing together as the carpet is being made. Generally, woven carpets are available only in narrow widths or strips that are attached or seamed together. Woven carpets do not have secondary backings, but they can perform as well as or better than tufted carpets if properly installed and maintained.

The weaving consists of warp (lengthwise) and weft (widthwise) yarns interwoven to form the face pile and backing at the same time. Different weaves include Velvet, Wilton, and Axminster. Many variations are available with the Velvet weaving method, including plushes, loop pile, multilevel loop, and cut-and-loop styles. Wilton refers to the special loom used to produce intricate patterns (sometimes multicolored) using perforated pattern cards. Axminster weaves are made from prearranged spools of different colored yarns that are fed into a mechanical patterning device. This method places most of the pile yarn on the surface and leaves a ribbed back.

Different types of carpets and various characteristics are shown in Exhibit 2.

Face Fibers. In general, synthetic fibers are more durable, more sanitary, and less expensive than natural fibers. These advantages help explain why synthetic fibers make up 90 percent of the carpets used in commercial operations. Face fibers are judged on their appearance, springiness and texture retention (ability to hold their shape), resistance to wear, resistance to soil, and cleanability. Typical face fibers include wool and other natural fibers and nylon and other synthetics.

Exhibit 2   Typical Carpet Types and Characteristics

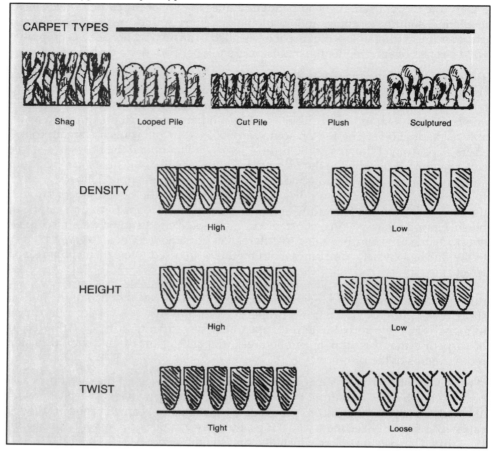

Wool and other natural fibers. People who buy and sell carpets agree that wool is good-looking, resilient, durable, and easily cleaned. It is also expensive.

Despite the cost, wool is especially well-suited for lodging properties because of its natural resistance to flame and its ability to shed soil. Indentations caused by furniture legs, sometimes permanent on synthetic carpet, can be removed easily from wool by applications of moisture and low heat.

Wool fibers are also water-loving, which means they are responsive to wet cleaning. Unfortunately, this also means that they provide a better breeding ground for microorganisms than do synthetic fibers. Molds, mildew, bacteria, and other growths can mar the carpet and/or cause odors. Cleaning solutions for wool should be chosen carefully; ammonia, salts, alkaline soaps, chlorine bleach, or strong detergents can damage the fabric.

Other natural fibers available but rarely used today are cotton, sisal (hemp), and silk.

Nylon. More than 80 percent of all carpets manufactured in the United States are nylon. Nylon holds its shape and color well, cleans easily, and costs much less than wool. When properly maintained, nylon carpet fibers are less likely to promote bacterial growth than wool ones; they are easily treated for resistance to mold, mildew, and other organic growth. Nylon is particularly attractive because of its durability and its flexibility in construction and design. It is also comfortable underfoot and is more resistant to stains and soil than wool.

Nylon fibers normally have a shiny appearance. However, a "baking" process is now available that gives the carpet a duller or **delustered** finish that looks more like wool. Delustered carpets have the added advantage of soiling less quickly.

Other synthetics. Acrylic fibers were developed in the 1950s to approximate the appearance and durability of wool. Generally, acrylic carpet is not as easily cleaned or as resilient as other synthetics. It can also turn brown during cleaning. It has poor resilience and a tendency to pill and fuzz. Oil may leave permanent stains if not treated quickly. Acrylic does, however, resist most acids and solvents. **Mod acrylic** is similar to acrylic, but has less resistance to stains and abrasions than acrylic.

Olefin (or polypropylene) fibers wear very well. They can be cleaned very aggressively without damage and are not as susceptible to sun fading as nylons and wools. Olefin carpets are solution-dyed, which means that color is added to the olefin in its liquid state. Olefin resists acids, solvents, and static electricity buildup. Olefin is, however, susceptible to heat or friction damage and is not as comfortable to walk on as other fibers.

Polyesters offer an appearance similar to wool. They are also very durable and clean easily. They do, however, have a tendency to mat under heavy traffic and are not very resilient.

Acetate is a low-cost silky fiber. It is colorfast and resistant to mildew, but it is relatively easy to soil and is vulnerable to abrasion. Spot-cleaning should be handled with care, because acetate may dissolve when dry-cleaning fluid or solvents are applied.

Rayon has many of the same characteristics as acetate—poor resistance to soil and abrasion but good color retention and resistance to mildew. Dense, high-grade rayons have adequate resilience for hotel use. Rayon is vulnerable to oil stains.

Carpet Problems

To keep carpets as attractive and clean as possible, housekeeping staff in charge of carpet cleaning should learn to recognize and remedy the following common carpet problems:

- Pile distortion

- Shading

- Fading

- Wicking

- Mildew

- Shedding/pilling

Pile Distortion. Pile distortion is a general term for a number of problems with the carpet's face fibers. Fibers can become twisted, pilled, crushed, or flared and matted. Pile distortion occurs when the carpet receives heavy foot or equipment traffic. Improper cleaning methods can also cause pile distortion. For example, the pile can lose its twist when it is subjected to cleaning solutions that are too hot or methods that are too aggressive.

Pile distortion is hard to remedy. It may be impossible to remedy in high-traffic areas. Mats, runners, and furniture glides can help prevent crushing. Regularly vacuuming or using a pile lifter or pile brush on high-traffic areas will help to remove dry soil, which can wear on fibers and cause pile distortion. A pile lifter will help pick up crushed pile while removing gritty soils, which can damage the carpet. Pile distortion can also be prevented by grooming high-traffic areas with a carpet rake. Using a pile lifter or carpet rake before corrective cleaning will improve the effect of the cleaning.

Shading. Shading occurs when the pile in a carpet is brushed in two different directions so that dark and light areas appear. Shading is a normal feature of almost all carpets. Vacuuming or pile-lifting the carpet in one direction can help to reduce a shading problem, but probably will not eliminate it. Some properties instruct room attendants to leave shading marks purposely in the carpet while vacuuming. The notion behind this practice is that guests will see the vacuuming pattern and feel that the room has been properly cleaned.

Fading. Every carpet will fade with time. Sunlight, wear, cleaning, and natural aging can combine to accelerate color loss. Some professional carpet service companies can dye carpets that have faded prematurely. Premature fading may occur if the carpet is improperly cleaned. Improper cleaning or spot removal can actually do more damage than some permanent stains. Always pretest carpets before using aggressive spot-removal techniques.

Wicking. Wicking (sometimes called browning) occurs when the backing of the carpet becomes wet and the face yarns draw or wick the moisture and color of the backing to the surface of the carpet. Wicking can often be prevented by promptly attending to spills and by following proper cleaning procedures that avoid overwetting the carpet.

Wicking occurs most frequently in jute-backed carpet that has a light-color face fiber. Vinegar or synthetic citric acid solutions used in postcleaning treatments or added to certain cleaning chemicals can help prevent or cure browning problems. As always, check with the manufacturer and/or pretest the application before proceeding with an antibrowning treatment.

Mildew. Mildew forms when moisture allows molds in the carpet to grow. Mildew can cause staining, odor, and rotting. Natural fibers are especially prone to mildew, but all carpets should be kept dry and/or treated with an antibacterial to prevent the problem. Proper cleaning procedures that avoid overwetting the carpet can help prevent mildew from forming.

Shedding/Pilling. Short pieces of face fibers are often trapped in the carpet when it is manufactured. As the new carpet is walked upon, these pieces work themselves to the surface of the carpet and can make a new carpet look littered and unkempt. Shedding will eventually stop. In the meantime, frequent vacuuming will prevent the carpet from looking littered. Pilling, often the result of cleaning, can be removed by heavy vacuuming or by gently cutting loose fibers from the carpet with scissors.

Carpet Maintenance

The aim of any carpet maintenance program is to keep the carpet clean and like new for as long as possible. To some extent, the carpet's fiber, backing, and construction will dictate the maintenance program required to keep it looking good. Most floor care experts encourage executive housekeepers to develop a cleaning schedule for all carpet and floor areas. The most efficient cleaning schedules are based on studies of the amount of traffic in the various areas of the property.

Heavy soiling typically occurs in high-traffic public areas, track-off areas, and funnel areas. Track-off areas are those directly in front of doors leading to the outside. Funnel areas, identified by their distinctive funnel-shaped soil spots, are those in which traffic converges into a narrow space. Funnel areas typically occur around elevators and stairways and in front of vending machines.

High-traffic and heavy-soil areas can be indicated in colors or shades on a property floor plan. For example, one color or shade could indicate high-traffic areas—those that need to be cleaned at least once a day. Areas with less traffic that soil more slowly can be depicted with other colors or shades to indicate weekly, monthly, or quarterly cleaning. Exhibit 3 shows such a floor plan for a hospitality operation.

Once the floor plan is completed, a calendar plan can be devised. The calendar plan should list the cleaning tasks—vacuuming, spot-cleaning, deep cleaning—to be performed on specific days and the time required for each task. Implementing a regular cleaning schedule has a number of advantages:

* Housekeepers can accurately forecast monthly and yearly cleaning costs.

* Regular maintenance will prevent major problems from occurring and will extend the life of the carpet.

* Regularly scheduled carpet and floor cleaning allows the executive housekeeper to budget time for other major department projects.

Before implementing any maintenance programs or purchasing equipment or cleaning chemicals, the executive housekeeper should consult with the carpet supplier or manufacturer and follow the suggested cleaning procedures.

Routine Inspection. Inspection is an important part of all carpet and floor care programs. Housekeeping staff generally inspect carpets and floors in all areas of the property each day. All hotel employees should be instructed to help preserve carpets and floors by promptly reporting spots and spills to the housekeeping department. Good maintenance depends on immediate removal of spots and spills.

Exhibit 3   Sample Floor Plan of Carpet Traffic Areas

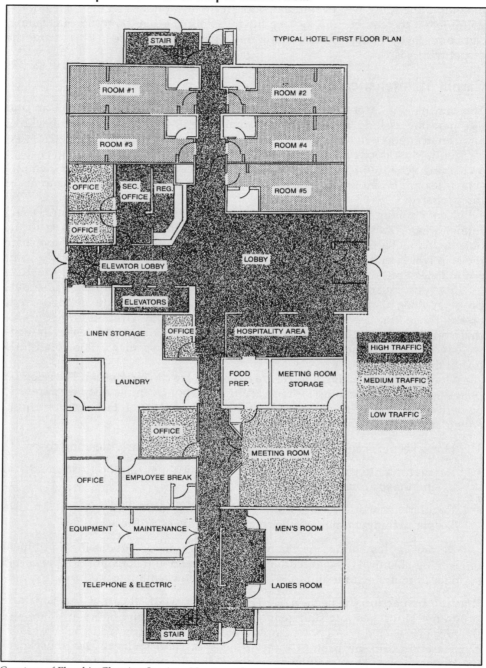

Courtesy of Flagship Cleaning Services, Newtown Square, Pennsylvania

Housekeeping supervisors should routinely review the property's carpet cleaning procedures and ensure that employees follow these procedures properly. At many properties, supervisors routinely inspect cleaning equipment to make sure that all items function safely and efficiently.

Preventive Maintenance. Lodging properties can prevent carpet soiling and damage with frequently changed mats and runners in high-traffic, track-off, and funnel areas. Furniture glides on the bottoms of chairs and tables can help reduce pile distortion or tearing. Damage from food and beverage spills around self-serve bars in dining rooms or near vending machines can be reduced by using waterproof plastic carpet protectors or, if preferred, regularly cleaned customized mats. Carpet tiles, which can be easily replaced or rotated in high-use areas, can be used to reduce pile distortion.

Routine Maintenance. Most housekeeping departments vacuum all carpets once a day—or even more often—as part of routine maintenance. Routine maintenance also includes periodic deep-cleaning (shampoos and hot or cold water extraction), spot-cleaning, and stain removal as necessary. Spots should be removed quickly before they set into the fabric as more-stubborn stains.

The executive housekeeper should develop a manual for spot and stain removal, stating the proper procedures and cleaning fluids to use on the carpets throughout the property. This task can be simplified by contacting the carpet supplier for care and maintenance instructions and spot removal techniques especially suited for carpets on-site.

A sample spot and stain removal chart is provided in Exhibit 4. Some general guidelines for spot-cleaning are included in the following list. Because not all cleaning techniques are suitable for all carpets, the following instructions are presented for illustrative purposes only:

1. Identify the source of the spot or stain. This makes removal easier.

2. If you can't identify the source of the stain, carefully remove solid particles from the spot or stain with a hand-held scraper or soup spoon and vacuum thoroughly. Use a wet vacuum whenever possible to pick up large wet spills. After removing as much of the wet spill as possible, blot up remaining moisture by pressing a clean, dry towel against the spot or stain.

3. If vacuuming the spill is impossible, blot carefully from the edges to the center of the spot or stain to remove as much as possible of the staining material before adding a cleaning solution. *Never rub to remove a spot or stain;* you may cause irreversible fiber distortion, such as fuzzing, loss of twist, or loss of fiber.

4. Always try to remove the spot or stain with plain water alone, which will remove many spills. Gently blot excess water as noted above.

5. If unsuccessful with water, spot-test an inconspicuous portion of the spot or stain with another cleaning agent. Blot some of the agent on the affected area with a clean rag. Be sure to apply the solution *to the rag only,* then blot.

Exhibit 4   Sample Spot and Stain Removal Chart (Carpets)

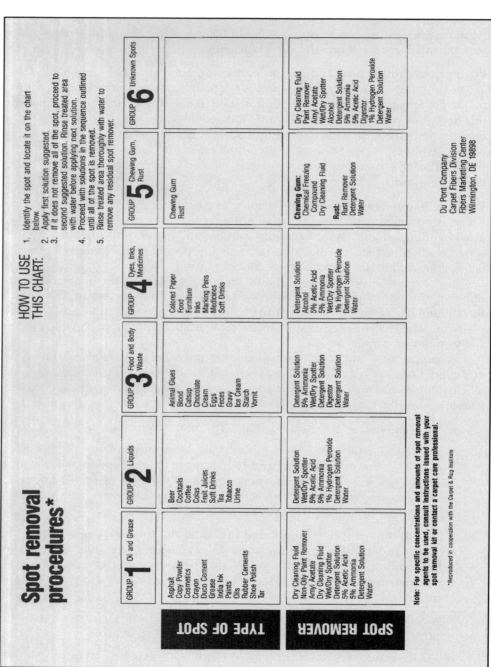

Spot removal procedures*

HOW TO USE THIS CHART:

1. Identify the spot and locate it on the chart below.
2. Apply first solution suggested.
3. If it does not remove all of the spot, proceed to second suggested solution. Rinse treated area with water before applying next solution.
4. Proceed with solutions in the sequence outlined until all of the spot is removed.
5. Rinse treated area thoroughly with water to remove any residual spot remover.

TYPE OF SPOT	GROUP **1** Oil and Grease	GROUP **2** Liquids	GROUP **3** Food and Body Waste	GROUP **4** Dyes, Inks, Medicines	GROUP **5** Chewing Gum, Rust	GROUP **6** Unknown Spots
	Asphalt Copy Powder Cosmetics Crayon Duco Cement Grease India Ink Paints Oils Rubber Cements Shoe Polish Tar	Beer Cocktails Coffee Colas Fruit Juices Soft Drinks Tea Tobacco Urine	Animal Glues Blood Catsup Chocolate Cream Eggs Feces Gravy Ice Cream Starch Vomit	Colored Paper Food Furniture Inks Marking Pens Medicines Soft Drinks	Chewing Gum Rust	
SPOT REMOVER	Dry Cleaning Fluid Non-Oily Paint Remover Amyl Acetate Dry Cleaning Fluid Wet/Dry Spotter Detergent Solution 5% Acetic Acid 5% Ammonia Detergent Solution Water	Detergent Solution Wet/Dry Spotter 5% Acetic Acid 5% Ammonia 1% Hydrogen Peroxide Detergent Solution Water	Detergent Solution 5% Ammonia Wet/Dry Spotter Detergent Solution Digestor Detergent Solution Water	Detergent Solution Alcohol 5% Acetic Acid 5% Ammonia Wet/Dry Spotter 1% Hydrogen Peroxide Detergent Solution Water	**Chewing Gum:** Chemical Freezing Compound Dry Cleaning Fluid **Rust:** Rust Remover Detergent Solution Water	Dry Cleaning Fluid Paint Remover Amyl Acetate Wet/Dry Spotter Alcohol Detergent Solution 5% Ammonia 5% Acetic Acid Digestor 1% Hydrogen Peroxide Detergent Solution Water

Note: For specific concentrations and amounts of spot removal agents to be used, consult instructions issued with your spot removal kit or contact a carpet care professional.

*Reproduced in cooperation with the Carpet & Rug Institute

Du Pont Company
Carpet Fibers Division
Fibers Marketing Center
Wilmington, DE 19898

Courtesy of Du Pont Company, Wilmington, Delaware

6. If a small amount of cleaning solution works, do not add more; it will only increase the amount of rinsing required to remove the residual cleaning agent. If you are using a water-soluble detergent, you will need to rinse the spill to remove the cleaning agent. If you are using a solvent, rinsing is not necessary. Be sure to rinse out detergent residues with water before trying solvent cleaning agents.

7. If the spot or stain lifts with a water-soluble solution, rinse the area frequently with water to hasten the cleaning without adding more chemical. After the spot or stain is gone, a minimum of three rinses is suggested to prevent any residual detergent from attracting new soil to the clean area. Use the blotting procedure previously described.

8. If the spot or stain lifts with a solvent, continue to work with solvent on a rag. Do not pour solvent directly on the area. Do not introduce water to a spot or stain that is lifted with a solvent. Solvents are volatile and will dry without a residue.

9. In all cases, do not overwork the spot or stain. Work only for short periods and allow the area to dry before returning later to continue spot or stain removal.

Carpet and Floor Care Equipment

Deciding when and how carpets and floors should be cleaned is an important task. This task is complicated by the great number of cleaning machines, supplies, and solutions now available. Commonly used small equipment is described in Exhibit 5. Major equipment is discussed in the sections that follow.

Because carpet and floor cleaning equipment is a major expense, equipment should be cared for properly. A sample equipment inspection checklist is provided in Exhibit 6.

Outlining all of the kinds of carpet and floor care equipment individual properties should have is beyond the scope of this chapter. However, a property's arsenal of dirt-fighting equipment typically includes wet vacuums or wet extractors and rotary floor machines as well as vacuums. Each of these items can be used on carpets and floors and will be discussed in the following sections. To maintain the warranty on a carpet when using this equipment, be sure to follow the manufacturer's suggested cleaning guide.

Vacuum Cleaners. Many types of vacuums have been developed for different types of carpets. Beater-bar vacuums, for example, use a rotating bar to agitate the carpet to loosen dirt. These vacuums are best for carpets installed over pads. Brush vacuums agitate the carpet with a brush and are best for carpets glued to the floor. Pile-lifter machines have a strong suction capacity and a separate brush motor which helps restore crushed carpet pile.

Commercial vacuums can be upright, canister, or carried/mounted. An upright sweeper has a large agitator/suction head that pulls dirt up into a bag attached along the handle of the machine. In hospitality properties, uprights with a dual-motor are most often used. This combined motor system provides greater suction and agitation while not overtaxing the

Exhibit 5 Commonly Used Small Equipment for Carpet and Floor Cleaning

Small waterproof tarp—used for mixing cleaning solutions

Nylon nap brush—used to restore carpet pile after cleaning

Carpet rake—used after cleaning or used to restore very long carpet pile that has become crushed

Hand shampoo brush—used on stairs and edges

Mixing buckets—used to mix and carry cleaning solutions

Stirring paddle—used to mix cleaning solutions

Traffic lane paper—used to protect just-cleaned carpets from guest traffic; can be used to protect floor-length drapes from wet carpet

Clip-on floodlights—used to light dark hallways and stairwells that must be cleaned

Sprayers—may be manually pumped or electric-powered; used to spray solutions and water onto carpet

Measuring cups—used with cleaning solutions

Mop—used for daily cleaning of floors or for rinsing and applying polishes and strippers

Mop bucket—may be a simple stainless steel bucket or a bucket on casters with a wringer attached

Hand wringer—used to squeeze excess moisture out of mop heads and bonnets

Squeegee—a tool with a rubber blade, like a windshield wiper, used for picking up excess moisture from floors

Pickup pan—works like a dustpan; used with a squeegee

Mats, runners—used to protect carpets and floors from traffic or to protect guests and employees from slippery surfaces

Furniture glides—typically small disks or squares that fit under furniture legs to protect carpet pile

Pill shearer—small shaver-like machine that shaves pills from carpets

vacuum's motor. The single-motor vacuum should be reserved for guest-rooms or areas that require light to medium cleaning.

Canister models collect dirt in a tank which moves on casters for easy maneuvering. Canister models provide little agitation to loosen dirt, but they are handy for cleaning hard-to-reach corners and spaces that upright models cannot reach. They are more versatile than upright vacuums and are ideal for hard floors. Filter bags in canister vacuums can be filled to capacity without causing the vacuum to loose performance.

Backpack and hip vacuums were designed for cleaning professionals. They are great for fast and light cleaning jobs. They can be worn either like a backpack or a fanny pack. They are a lightweight tool that is ergonomically designed and affords great efficiency and mobility. They are not as strong as upright or canister vacuums nor do they agitate as well. They are good for lightly soiled areas, stairway and upholstery cleaning, and constricted areas.[1]

Exhibit 6   Sample Equipment Inspection Checklist

Casters and wheels:
- ☐ Clean wheels of litter and dirt, string, hair, etc.
- ☐ Replace broken wheels that could snag or tear carpet.

Hoses:
- ☐ Check for leaks.
- ☐ Check for loose dirt or cleaning solutions caught inside the hose.

Electrical cords:
- ☐ Check cords and plugs. Do not use machines with frayed cords or cords without insulation.

Brushes and mops:
- ☐ Replace brushes that are worn down to less than $1/8$ of an inch.
- ☐ Be sure all machine and hand-held brushes are clean.
- ☐ Make sure the mop handle is in good condition and the mop head is clean and dry.
- ☐ Use a new mop only after soaking it for 30 minutes in clear water to remove sizing.
- ☐ Use only clean, dry bonnets.

Tanks, buckets, and bags:
- ☐ Make sure extractor and wet vacuum tanks are clean and empty before using.
- ☐ Make sure extractor tanks are rinsed of solutions before using.
- ☐ Replace torn vacuum sweeper bags or those that are more than half full.

Choosing the right vacuum cleaner. The prudent housekeeping or engineering manager performs an internal needs assessment survey to decide on the best vacuum cleaner for the hotel. The following issues should be addressed before purchasing a vacuum cleaning system for the property:

- The type of debris to be picked up by the vacuum cleaner

- The type of floors being vacuumed

- The type and availability of attachments

- The importance of the maneuverability of the equipment

- The weight of the equipment

- The primary operators of the equipment

- The ease of operation and maintenance

- The useful life of the vacuum in relation to its acquisition costs

For a vacuum to clean most effectively, it should be matched to the intended cleaning tasks and the person(s) who will be doing the cleaning.

Housekeeping managers should keep in mind the challenges that house-keeping staff members have experienced with present and past vacuuming systems when making the decision.

Types of commercial vacuums. The different types of vacuums that are used in commercial cleaning operations are:

- Hip-vac and back-pack vacuum cleaners with tool attachments, which include upholstery, round brush, and a crevice tool.

- Upright single- and dual-motor vacuum cleaners. These vacuums should have a detachable hose and tools.

- Canister-tank wet and dry vacuums. In order to increase the cleaning efficiency of these types of vacuums, there should also be attachment tools and a power nozzle available.

- Wide-area walk-behind vacuums or sweepers that can be powered by battery, power cord, gasoline, or propane motor.

Types of surfaces to be cleaned. Additional factors to keep in mind before purchasing a vacuum cleaner are:

- What type of surfaces will be cleaned?

- Are these surfaces carpeted or hard floor?

- Are they interior or exterior surfaces?

- What is the size of the area(s) to be cleaned?

Interior floors: There are many different types of carpets. The critical issue to consider is the nap thickness. Long and short fiber carpeting need different height settings in order for the vacuum's brush head to clean most effectively. Therefore, the ideal vacuuming tool for indoor applications will come with an adjustable height-setting mechanism. Hard floors are vacuumed at the lowest height setting.

Outside surfaces: Typically, these would include concrete sidewalks as well as asphalt parking lots. These are usually large, very high-profile areas and should be maintained at all times. They are often the first and last areas of a hotel that any guest sees, thus leaving lasting impressions about the hotel's image and its commitment to providing a clean and sanitary living environment.

Types of areas to be cleaned. When choosing a vacuum cleaner the most important decision-making criteria should be the area and application where it will be used.

Front entrances, hallways, and corridors: These are usually large areas and need large vacuum cleaners. There are vacuum cleaners designed to maintain large floor areas but they are not always effective in picking up small pebbles or rock salt (in regions where snow is an issue), which tend to accumulate in doorways. Small debris is best picked up with a powerful two-motor upright or a canister vacuum with a power nozzle. Hallways and corridors are cleaned most effectively with a large-area walk-behind

Selecting Vacuum Cleaners—Effectiveness and Ease of Use

Without question, the workhorse of the housekeeping department is the vacuum cleaner. Efforts to move the vacuum, unwrap or wrap the cord, change the bag, or contend with a broken belt can be time-consuming and frustrating. Here are some issues to consider when selecting the appropriate machine.

Cleaning Effectiveness

A vacuum should have a power head with a brush that whisks the carpet surface to help loosen and remove the dirt.

Consumer Reports testing reveals no correlation between cleaning performance and claims of amperage, peak horsepower, or cleaning effectiveness per amp. However, suction varies depending on the condition of the bag. Cleaning effectiveness can be limited not only by full bags, but also bags in which the air vents have become plugged.

Canister and upright vacuums are nearly the same in cleaning effectiveness, except that uprights are most effective on carpet, and canisters are most effective on hard floors or upholstery.

For air cleanliness, some companies are selling disposable, microfiltration bags. Again, *Consumer Reports* found that the specially designed bags did not significantly cut emissions.

Ease of Use

The weights of upright vacuums range from approximately 10 to 24 pounds and do not correlate to cleaning efficiency.

The heavier vacuums are often equipped with self-propelling drive wheels that make pushing ease equivalent to that of the lighter machines.

Vacuums are normally sold with cords that range in length from 20 to 30 feet. The required cord length should be determined by the configuration of the guestrooms or public space to be cleaned. A cord that is too long will get in the way, but one that is too short will cause difficulty in completing work efficiently.

Review the cord storage efficiency of the vacuum. Wrapping and unwrapping the cord can be facilitated by the design of the cord storage hooks or mechanism.

The location of the on/off switch should be considered as well. Many room attendants prefer a foot switch (which is also easier to replace) to something on the handle that might require stooping to operate.

Is the dirt sucked into a cloth bag, a dirt cup, or a disposable paper bag? Cloth bags are difficult to empty. Dirt cups can crack. Disposable paper bags are an additional expense. Choose the vacuum that uses the easiest, yet most affordable, method.

The ease of replacing beater-bar belts varies across vacuum types. Some vacuum heads require screwdrivers to remove the casing, while others have simple knobs.

Room attendants usually move the vacuums from room to room by dragging them on their back wheels, regardless of whether they should. Since this habit is hard to break, buy a vacuum with sturdy wheels.

(continued)

Cthe Rooms
CHRONICLE®

(continued)

Headlights may seem funny, but room attendants who vacuum the corners between beds and walls appreciate the extra light on the subject.

Few uprights are designed to slide under beds or chairs, although most canister models do so easily.

Other Considerations

- **Price.** Upright models may vary greatly in price. Many hotel companies have national purchasing contracts that offer significant savings over retail prices, but even independent hotels can save if they buy in volume. For instance, buying 12 vacuums at once can save 10 to 15 percent of the purchase price.

- **Model.** Most manufacturers make commercial versions of their vacuum cleaner lines. Such models include denser plastic casings, more amperage, and more easily accessible maintenance areas.

- **Noise.** "Quiet vacuum cleaner" is an oxymoron. Such things just don't exist, regardless of advertising claims, but there are differences in noise levels to consider.

- **Attachments.** Upright vacuums are now manufactured with built-in hoses to make cleaning edges and upholstery easier. Consideration should be given both to the length of the hose and the stability of the vacuum while the hose is in use.

(Thanks to Randy Ticer, The Harloff Company; and Hoover Vacuum Company)

Source: Gail Edwards, CHHE, *The Rooms Chronicle®*, Volume 3, Number 5, p. 5. For subscription information, call 866-READ-TRC.

vacuum. During the winter or wet season, wet and dry vacuums are both needed to keep the front entrance clean and dry.

Banquet rooms: Banquet rooms are usually large rooms that include hard-to-reach areas. As such, banquet room surfaces might call for both large and small vacuums. Hard-to-reach areas are best vacuumed with a commercial-grade upright, canister, or backpack vacuum. Large-area vacuum cleaners should be used to clean large open areas. These vacuums should be equipped with a brush height adjustment in order to ideally operate on hard floors and different types of carpets.

Guestrooms: Guestrooms are areas that typically have many obstacles such as beds, credenzas, tables, and closets. Guestroom floors are cleaned most effectively with a commercial-grade dual-motor upright vacuum. These upright vacuums should have a height-adjustable brush to agitate the carpet and to allow the vacuum to effectively clean on both the carpet and hard floors. Attachments allow room attendants to use upright vacuums for curtain and furniture vacuuming (canister vacuums, which are operated with a vacuum hose and wand might also be used). For guestrooms that only need light and quick vacuuming, a commercial-grade single-motor upright vacuum is appropriate.

Stairways: Stairways are best vacuumed with a back-pack or hip vacuum cleaner. These vacuums were designed to be carried on the operator's back with attachments carried on the belt. This set-up allows the operator to work with both hands free and get into hard-to-reach places without the need to pull or carry a vacuum up and down the stairs or around obstacles. The flexible hose and attachments allow for better cleaning in restrictive areas.

Sidewalks and parking lots: These typically large areas can be effectively maintained with a walk-behind sweeper or a large industrial vacuum designed for picking up large debris. These outside sweepers and vacuum cleaners are available with gasoline or propane engines or are battery powered. Outside vacuums should have large openings to pick up large debris, while outside sweepers are designed with large, stiff brushes. Both types typically have large debris bags or recovery hoppers.

The cost of mismatched equipment. Labor cost is a major factor to consider before purchasing vacuum equipment. If debris cannot be picked up quickly with a few passes of the vacuum, much time will be wasted going over the same area with the same poor results. For this reason, it is very important that the correct vacuum cleaner be used in the right application.

Another factor is the human one. Who is the person responsible for the cleaning? If, for one reason or another, the room attendant or houseperson does not like to use the available vacuum cleaner (perhaps the vacuum is too heavy or cumbersome, it is always breaking down, the electrical cord is too short, the vacuum emits odors or dust, or otherwise performs poorly), the likely outcome will be poor cleaning results and discouraged cleaning personnel. If, however, a well-performing and appropriate vacuum cleaner is available for the job, the user will likely be more satisfied using the equipment, and better cleaning results will be achieved in less time.[2]

Wet Vacuums. Wet spills will damage many carpets and floors. They also pose safety hazards for guests and employees. **Wet vacuums** are used to pick up spills or to pick up rinse water used during carpet or floor cleaning. Many wet vacuums can also be used on floors to pick up dry soils. Conventional vacuuming equipment must *never* be used to pick up wet spots because electrical shock can occur and the machines can be destroyed.

Wet vacuums may have only suction or they may also have a water sprayer that can rinse soiled areas immediately. Squeegee attachments on wet vacuums can make floor cleanup, stripping, and scrubbing more efficient.

Wet vacuums come in a variety of shapes and sizes. Some canister models are small enough to be strapped onto the cleaner's back. Canister vacuums have a collection tank which stores the water, the hose, and cleaning head. Typically, the tank rests on casters for easy mobility. Many canister models can be adapted to pick up dry soil on floors. Some manufacturers and most cleaning experts recommend canister models with bypass motors. These units prevent moisture from condensing on the machine's motor, thus reducing mechanical problems over time.

Walk-behind wet vacuums pick up water quickly in very large areas. These models are a little larger than a grocery cart and are often self-propelled for easy handling. Some models come with cords; others are battery-powered.

Wet Extractors. While some wet vacuums have only suction capability, wet extractors have a capacity for both suction and water injection. These units can simultaneously rinse and vacuum the soil from carpets or floors.

Wet extractors spray water and detergent onto the carpet. The extractor then uses suction to remove the water, detergent, and dirt from the carpet. Some machines have a special tool that agitates the carpet before spraying, to loosen dirt. Such attachments as specialty drapery and upholstery cleaning tools are also available.

Wet extractors come in a variety of shapes and sizes. Tank and walk-behind models are available. These machines can often be used on floors for dry pickup. Self-contained extractors, which resemble upright vacuums, cannot be adapted to floor use (that is, they can be used only on carpets). There are no hoses on a self-contained extractor; this makes the machine more compact to use in small areas such as guestrooms.

Rotary Floor Machines. Rotary floor machines can be used for a wide variety of surface cleaning jobs. Those that accommodate both brushes and pads are the most versatile. On carpets, rotary floor machines can be fitted with pads or brushes to perform dry-foam cleaning, mist pad cleaning, rotary spin pad cleaning, bonnet shampoos, or brush shampoos. On hard surface floors, rotary floor machines can be used to buff, burnish, scrub, strip, and refinish. Most manufacturers and floor care businesses offer specially made pads for particular tasks, which makes the floor cleaner's job easier.

Housekeepers should note that manufacturers use a color code for floor pads according to the job they perform. Stripping pads are black and brown, scrubbing pads are blue and green, polishing pads are white, and spray cleaning pads are red. Burnishing pads are not universally color-coded.

Some rotary machines come with a cleaner-dispensing tank and disk holders or "blocks" that are used to hold bonnet pads. By changing from a bonnet block to a brush block, the same machine can be used to shampoo carpets. One machine can even be fitted with a small vacuum and used to vacuum the foam while shampooing. Bonnet pads are made for both hard-floor and carpet maintenance and may be used on the same machine and bonnet block after changing chemicals.

High-speed machines (300 rpm to 1,000 rpm) reduce buffing time and create a more durable buff coat. Burnishers run at extremely high speeds (700 rpm to 1,500 rpm), further reducing buffing time. Rotary floor machines that exceed 175 rpm should *never* be used on carpets; high-speed machines will cause enormous damage.

Rotary floor machines can be tricky to use. Inexperienced employees, for example, may overwet the carpet when shampooing. This can lead to a host of problems, such as seam separation, delamination of the backing, buckling, shrinkage, premature face fiber wear, mildew formation, and other conditions.

What to Look for When Choosing Extraction Equipment

Before buying equipment, a manager should ask for a demonstration of the product. Also, ask for business references and for locations where the results can be seen. The following checklist will help any purchaser compare available systems and find which best meets the needs of the hotel:

☐ **Productivity**
How many square feet of open-area carpet can be cleaned in one hour?

☐ **Quality**
What percentage of soil is removed? What is the appearance of the carpet immediately after extraction, after 24 hours, after one month, and after one year?

☐ **Washing Efficiency**
With what amount of pressure is the fluid forced through the carpet fibers? Equipment with fluid pressures as little as 100 PSI or as much as 1,000 PSI is available.

☐ **Solution Recovery**
How much of the fluid injected into the carpet is recovered? To compare suction or vacuum capabilities, ask for the product's cubic air displacement and its water lift.

☐ **Drying**
How long does it take the area to thoroughly dry after treatment? This is the best indicator of the power of the vacuum function.

☐ **Refill Procedure**
How difficult or easy is it to load fluid or chemicals? How many square feet can be cleaned before the tank has to be changed or refilled?

☐ **Cost**
What is the actual purchase price of the equipment, including attachments and chemicals?

☐ **Appearance**
What impression might guests have if they see the equipment in use?

☐ **Handling**
How easy is the equipment to turn and operate? How much does it weigh? Can it be used in tight areas, such as guestrooms, as well as in open areas, like ballrooms? When in use, does it "drag" or does it move easily across the surface?

☐ **Accessories**
What accessories are necessary or available? Can the system be adjusted for different types of carpet? Can it handle upholstery, small areas, stairs, office panels, fabric wall coverings, or hard surfaces such as tile grouting or floors?

(continued)

the Rooms
CHRONICLE®

(continued)

☐ **Chemicals**
What chemicals are required? What is the effectiveness of these chemicals as cleaners? Are the chemicals affordable, biodegradable, pleasant-smelling, and solvent-free whenever possible? Remember that quality chemicals will rinse out of the fibers easily.

☐ **Service**
What training programs are in place for staff? What service warranties are included? What service can be expected?

Source: *The Rooms Chronicle®*, Volume 3, Number 2, p. 5.
For subscription information, call 866-READ-TRC.

Improper use of rotary machines on floors can cause abrasions or inadvertent removal of sealant and/or finishes. Many properties allow only experienced housekeeping personnel to operate rotary machines and other large pieces of equipment.

Carpet Cleaning Methods

There are a number of kinds of carpet cleaning methods, from simple vacuuming to hot- or cold-water extraction. Carpet experts frequently disagree over which cleaning methods are most effective and which methods produce less wear on the carpet itself. For example, some say that shampooing can wear down the carpet and leave soap residues that will actually attract dirt.

Complicating the situation is the fact that the many types of carpets and floors sold today have very different care and maintenance requirements. For example, simple ammonia solutions which work on most synthetic carpets will cause immediate and irreversible damage to natural fibers. Similarly, olefin carpets can be cleaned with bleaching solutions that would damage nylon carpets.

Executive housekeepers should carefully follow the carpet manufacturer's recommendations regarding cleaning methods. Improper carpet cleaning procedures will not only void the manufacturer's warranty in many instances, but might also cause accelerated soiling and deterioration of the carpet. Carpet suppliers are able to provide specific data on carpet care requirements that will help executive housekeepers select the correct cleaning methods, products, and services offered by carpet care suppliers and/or carpet cleaning contractors.

The following sections describe basic carpet cleaning methods. The method(s) appropriate for a property will depend on the specific requirements set by the manufacturer.

Vacuuming. Carpet experts do agree on one thing: you can't vacuum too much. Daily vacuuming prevents abrasives (gritty materials such as sand and gravel) from working into the carpet and causing stains and wear over a long period. It also helps restore the carpet's pile. The most effective vacuuming equipment agitates the carpet to loosen the dirt and removes it with suction.

the Rooms
CHRONICLE®

Carpet Cleaning: When, How, and Why

Yards and yards of carpet throughout the hotel. Thousands and thousands of people walking across the carpet. Hundreds and hundreds of opportunities for drips, spills, and stains. Expectation of management for the life of the carpet? Seven years. What's a housekeeper to do?

In addition to being a visual detraction from the hotel's appearance, a dirty carpet is a contributor to poor air quality as well. Carpet fibers capture a great number of impurities, including microorganisms such as germs, bacteria, dust mites, molds, and spores; organic substances such as food, cellulose, hair, skin, and decaying plant cells; and inorganic substances such as solvents, detergents, and pollutants.

When humidity is introduced into these impurities, the moisture sustains the growth of microorganisms. The result is the introduction of gases, excretions, and decomposed matter into the air.

Sound scary? Don't give up! Many methods for cleaning carpets are outlined below:

Begin Outside. Installing good walk-off mats for a measured distance into the hotel will ensure that minimal amounts of dirt are tracked onto the hallway or lobby carpet.

Vacuum Regularly. An upright vacuum cleaner with a rotating brush or beater bar will remove dry soil from the carpet very quickly and efficiently. The action of the brush agitates the carpet pile and brushes soil from the fibers. Suction from the vacuum motor removes the loosened soil from the carpet. A carpet's life is extended by regular (daily) vacuuming and the removal of soil that otherwise might be ground into the fibers.

Limited Fluid Methods of Cleaning: *Absorbent Compound Method.* A powder cleaning compound is spread on the surface of the carpet, agitated, allowed to dry, then removed by vacuuming. This compound is a surface cleaner. The advantage of this method is that spills and spots can be quickly treated. The disadvantage is that absorbent powders fail to emulsify and remove dirt below the surface of the carpet.

Bonnet Method. The bonnet method requires that a liquid cleaning agent be applied to the carpet, allowed to soak into the carpet for a short time, and then buffed with an absorbent bonnet pad. This system resembles the absorbent compound method and is also a surface cleaner. The advantage of the bonnet method is speed and fast drying time. The disadvantage is that this method fails to reach and remove the soils that fall into the fibers and backing.

"Dry" Foam or Shampoo Cleaning Methods. These methods use a limited amount of liquid (a high-foaming detergent or shampoo), which is applied to the carpet nap with a reel- or rotary-type brush to suspend soils and emulsify oils. The carpet can then be vacuumed with a wet vacuum.

(continued)

C the Rooms HRONICLE®

(continued)

The advantage of these limited-fluid methods is speed and a short drying time. Also, the top surface looks clean. But the disadvantage is the insufficient amount of fluids introduced into the fibers to penetrate, emulsify, and remove dirt below the surface of the carpet. Surface soils are driven deeper into the carpet's pile. And if the shampoo is not thoroughly vacuumed out of the carpet, it could leave a residue that attracts dirt.

Continual use of these limited fluid methods can result in a dull, matted, flat carpet appearance caused by the buildup of dirt and chemicals.

Free Fluid Method: Extraction Method. This is the deepest cleaning method available—it forces water and chemicals into the carpet fibers under pressure. Considered a wet or restoration method, it involves the application of a soil-releasing detergent (preconditioner) to the carpet followed by soaking time and subsequent removal with a hot- or cold-water or chemical treatment.

The advantage is that a good extractor can deliver adequate pressure to loosen the soil in the carpet's pile and enough extraction power to remove as much as 90 percent of the water or solution. The disadvantage is that drying time can range from one hour to one day, depending on the equipment selected. Some extractors recover only a portion of the dirty solution that soaks through fiber and backing, thus extending drying time, providing a breeding ground for bacteria, and promoting resoiling.

So What's a Housekeeper to Do?

In situations that require an immediate turnaround of the space (for instance, a spill in a busy restaurant), one of the methods listed earlier for quick application and drying might be used. But the area should be noted for later follow-up cleaning by extraction to remove the dirt below the surface. When extraction is done with quality equipment, which will loosen and remove all dirt, the carpets will look good throughout their life.

The bottom line is to evaluate the investment in cleaning systems carefully in terms of budget, results, and protection of the hotel's valuable fabric and carpet assets.

(Thanks to Andy Holt of CFR Corporation in New Brighton, Minnesota, and Tom Messmer of Clean Sweep Carpet Care in St. Louis, Missouri, for contributing information for this article.)

Source: Gail Edwards, CHHE, *The Rooms Chronicle®*, Volume 3, Number 2, p. 4. For subscription information, call 866-READ-TRC.

Frequent vacuuming contributes to the carpet's appearance, the property's hygiene, and prolongs the life of the carpet. Carpets that are walked on every day should be vacuumed every day. Some carpets in high traffic areas may need even more frequent vacuuming. Whenever carpets display signs of soil, they should be vacuumed before the foot traffic pushes dirt between the carpet's fibers.[3]

Dry Powder Cleaning. With the dry powder carpet cleaning method, dry powder or crystals are sprinkled onto the carpet and worked into the pile with a hand brush or a special machine that dispenses and brushes in the powder. The powder absorbs oily soils, which are then removed by vacuuming. Since no drying time is required, carpets in high-traffic areas need not be closed off. Properties may schedule dry powder cleaning between deeper cleaning activities.

Dry powder cleaning may be a good way to clean carpets that should not be cleaned with water. Dry powder cleaning also does not leave a soap residue on the carpet or excess water that could give rise to mold or mildew. The brushes in the dry powder machine, however, may cause cut pile fibers to flare. Periodic extraction or wet cleaning is suggested to remove dry powder residue from carpets. Some experts also caution that dry powder cleaning will not remove some types of dirt very well.

Dry Foam Cleaning. With this dry cleaning method, dry foam is sprayed on the carpet and a rotary floor machine brushes the foam into the carpet. The foam is then removed with a wet vacuum. Machines are available that will apply the foam and vacuum away the moisture. Dry foam can also be sprayed and brushed into carpets by hand. Since this method requires little drying time, housekeepers often use dry foam cleaning in high-traffic areas as frequently as once a day.

Dry foam cleaning can cause flaring in some cut-pile carpets. If proper cleaning procedures are not followed, overwetting can occur, which could lead to shrinking, mildew, fading, and other conditions. A sample dry foam carpet maintenance program from a carpet-care product manufacturer is shown in Exhibit 7. Some manufacturers provide similar materials in languages other than English.

Bonnet Spin Pad Cleaning. Bonnet spin pad cleaning is similar to the dry foam method in that it can be used daily for surface cleaning. With this method, a rotary floor machine with a special holder and pad agitates the tips of the carpet fibers as it moves across the carpet. The bonnet pad lifts and absorbs soil as it rotates. Pads are made of synthetic or natural fibers and can be laundered and reused as often as necessary. Bonnet spin pad cleaning should be followed by vacuuming after the carpet has dried.

Rotary Shampoos. Rotary or brush shampooing offers more effective cleaning than dry powder or dry foam cleaning. With this method, a rotary bristle brush is used instead of a pad or bonnet. (Before using new bristle shampoo brushes on fine carpets, the brushes should be broken in by running them on concrete floors.) The brush design allows the shampoo to drain down through the bristles directly onto the carpet. The shampoo is agitated by the machine into a foam which can then be left to dry or be vacuumed by a wet vacuum or extractor. When the carpet is vacuumed, it is necessary to use a defoamer in the wet vacuum or extractor tank. As with all carpet cleaning machinery, caution should be exercised so as not to damage the carpeting by using too little solution, too much solution, or too much agitation.

A sample rotary-brush carpet maintenance program from a carpet care product manufacturer is shown in Exhibit 8. Some manufacturers provide similar materials in languages other than English.

Exhibit 7 Sample Dry Foam Carpet Maintenance Program

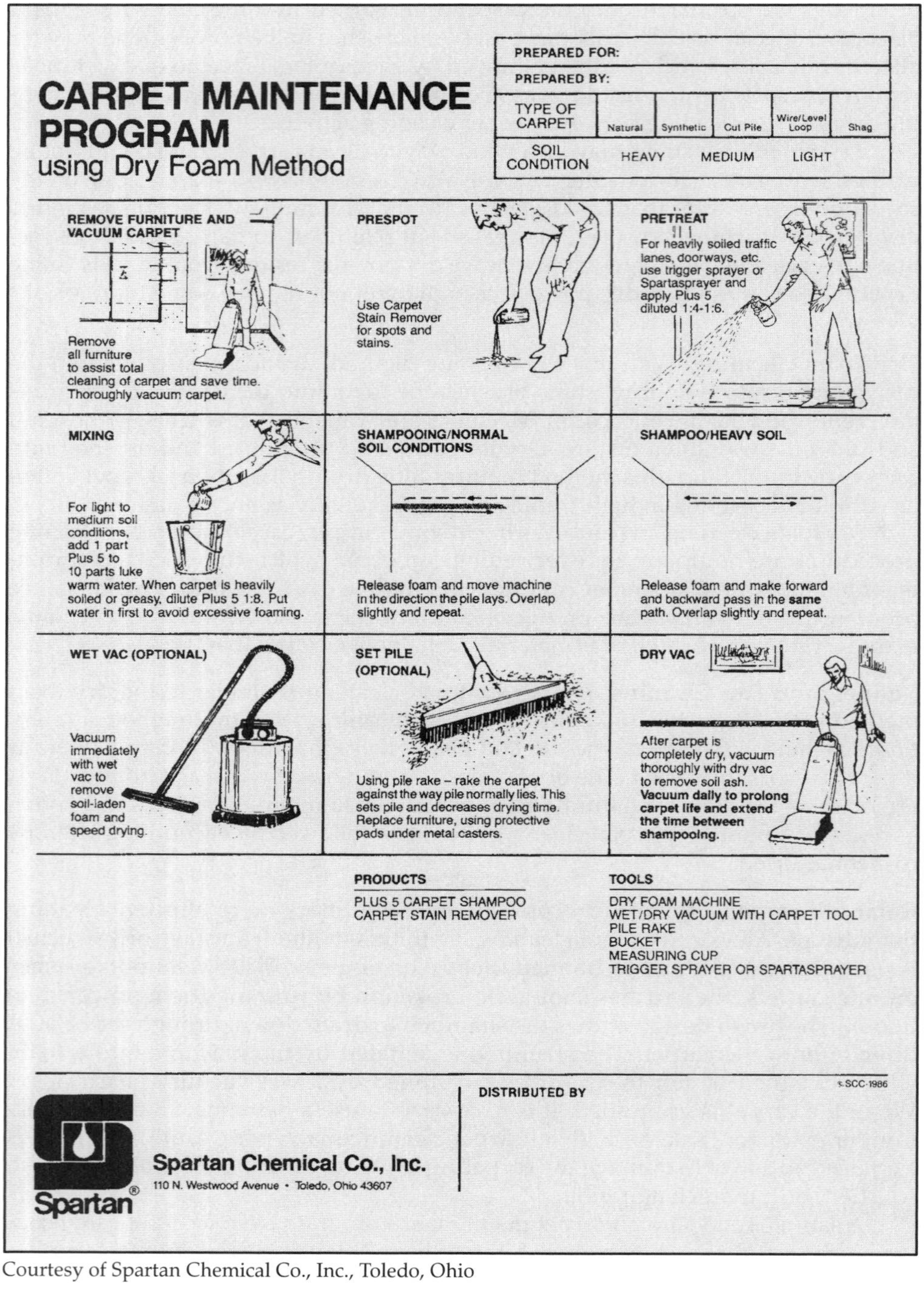

CARPET MAINTENANCE PROGRAM
using Dry Foam Method

PREPARED FOR:					
PREPARED BY:					
TYPE OF CARPET	Natural	Synthetic	Cut Pile	Wire/Level Loop	Shag
SOIL CONDITION	HEAVY		MEDIUM		LIGHT

REMOVE FURNITURE AND VACUUM CARPET
Remove all furniture to assist total cleaning of carpet and save time. Thoroughly vacuum carpet.

PRESPOT
Use Carpet Stain Remover for spots and stains.

PRETREAT
For heavily soiled traffic lanes, doorways, etc. use trigger sprayer or Spartasprayer and apply Plus 5 diluted 1:4-1:6.

MIXING
For light to medium soil conditions, add 1 part Plus 5 to 10 parts luke warm water. When carpet is heavily soiled or greasy, dilute Plus 5 1:8. Put water in first to avoid excessive foaming.

SHAMPOOING/NORMAL SOIL CONDITIONS
Release foam and move machine in the direction the pile lays. Overlap slightly and repeat.

SHAMPOO/HEAVY SOIL
Release foam and make forward and backward pass in the **same** path. Overlap slightly and repeat.

WET VAC (OPTIONAL)
Vacuum immediately with wet vac to remove soil-laden foam and speed drying.

SET PILE (OPTIONAL)
Using pile rake – rake the carpet against the way pile normally lies. This sets pile and decreases drying time. Replace furniture, using protective pads under metal casters.

DRY VAC
After carpet is completely dry, vacuum thoroughly with dry vac to remove soil ash. **Vacuum daily to prolong carpet life and extend the time between shampooing.**

PRODUCTS
PLUS 5 CARPET SHAMPOO
CARPET STAIN REMOVER

TOOLS
DRY FOAM MACHINE
WET/DRY VACUUM WITH CARPET TOOL
PILE RAKE
BUCKET
MEASURING CUP
TRIGGER SPRAYER OR SPARTASPRAYER

DISTRIBUTED BY

Spartan®
Spartan Chemical Co., Inc.
110 N. Westwood Avenue • Toledo, Ohio 43607

Courtesy of Spartan Chemical Co., Inc., Toledo, Ohio

Exhibit 8   Sample Rotary-Brush Carpet Maintenance Program

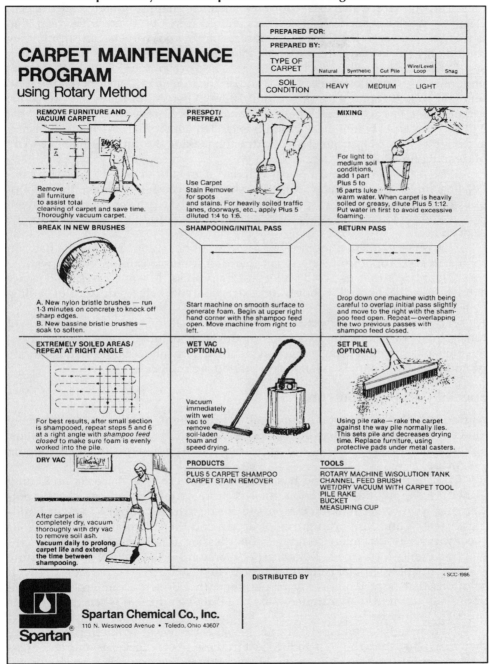

Courtesy of Spartan Chemical Co., Inc., Toledo, Ohio

Water Extraction. Water extraction is the deepest cleaning method available for most carpets. **Hot water extraction** is sometimes inappropriately called steam cleaning. Actually, hot water extractors should never be filled with water that is higher than 150°F [66°C] in temperature. Since wool carpets can shrink, they should only be cleaned with warm or cool water.

Hot water extractors spray a detergent and water solution onto the carpet under low pressure (less than 200 psi) and, in the same pass, vacuum out the solution and soil. A good extractor can pull 70 to 90 percent of the water out of the carpet. Some extraction machines have a special tool called a power head that agitates the carpet before the solution is extracted. Other tools, such as upholstery and stair tools, can be attached to the extractor, making the unit useful for a variety of cleaning functions.

With proper extraction, a carpet will dry in an hour or two. However, housekeeping staff using hot water extraction should be careful to control the amount of water that goes into the carpet. Overwetting can be a problem if the equipment is underpowered or if the operator does not take care to thoroughly vacuum the cleaned area.

Hot water extraction requires a great deal of hot water. This can be hard on some carpets. Properties trying to cut their hot water consumption may want to consider models that use cold water in this process. In some cases, cold water extraction works as well as hot-water extraction and helps reduce color fading, running, and shrinking.

Excessively soiled carpets are most effectively cleaned with a combination of rotary shampoo and water extraction methods. A manufacturer's sample carpet maintenance program using extraction is shown in Exhibit 9. Some manufacturers provide similar materials in languages other than English.

Special Carpet Treatments

Antimicrobial Treatment. Antimicrobial treatment in carpets kills many kinds of bacteria, fungi, and the odors they cause. First introduced in hospitals, antimicrobial-treated carpets are appearing more and more often in lodging properties.

Tight building syndrome has increased concern over bacteria and fungi growth. A "tight" building is one that is more or less sealed against the outside and requires ventilation systems to freshen the air supply. In tight buildings, bacteria and fungi can grow in carpets and then circulate through the air supply. As a result, many lodging properties are now considering antimicrobial treatments for carpets. Many carpets come from the factory treated with a permanent antimicrobial solution. Carpets can also be treated periodically with solutions that offer temporarily or permanently bonded antimicrobial protection. Keep in mind that antimicrobials will only be effective when the carpet is properly maintained.

Even though bacteria and fungi are less likely to live in synthetic carpet fibers, they may flourish in the soils that collect in these fibers. Locker rooms and areas around hot tubs and pools are especially good breeding grounds for bacteria and fungi that can cause carpet damage and odors.

Exhibit 9 Sample Carpet Extraction Maintenance Program

CARPET MAINTENANCE PROGRAM
using Xtraction Method

PREPARED FOR:					
PREPARED BY:					
TYPE OF CARPET	Natural	Synthetic	Cut Pile	Wire/Level Loop	Shag
SOIL CONDITION	HEAVY	MEDIUM	LIGHT		

REMOVE FURNITURE AND VACUUM CARPET

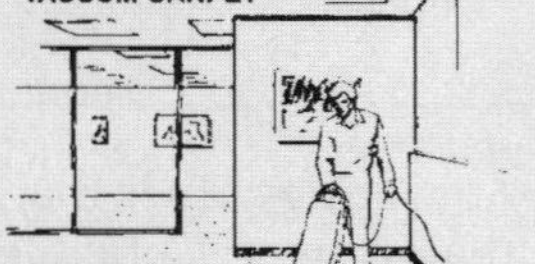

Remove all furniture to assist total cleaning of carpet and save time. Thoroughly vacuum carpet.

PRESPOT

Use Carpet Stain Remover for spots and stains.

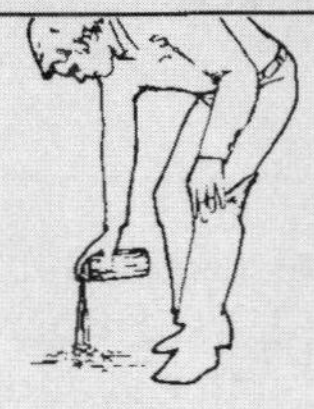

PRETREAT

For heavily soiled areas, doorways, etc., use trigger sprayer or Sparta-sprayer and apply Xtraction II diluted 1:16 or 1:32.

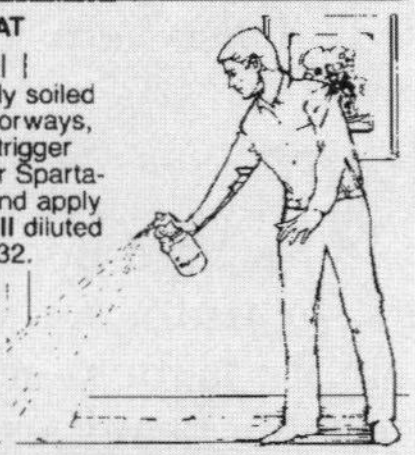

MIXING

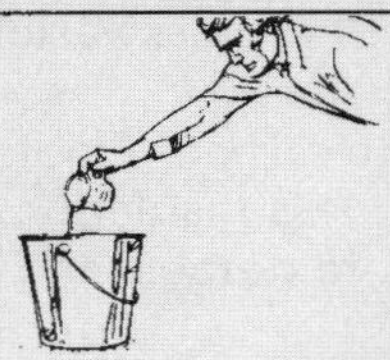

Add 2 oz. of Xtraction II for every gallon of water in solution tank.

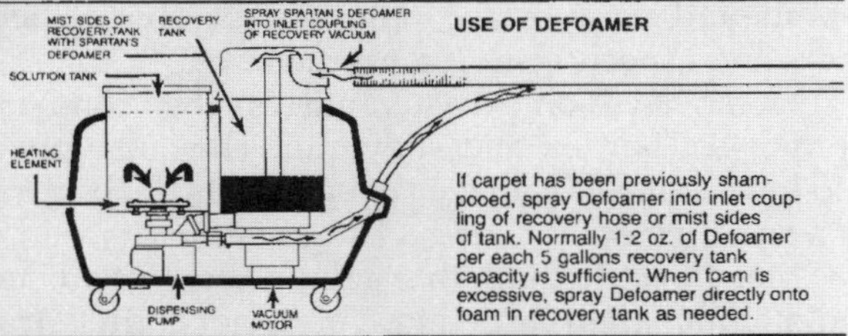

USE OF DEFOAMER

If carpet has been previously shampooed, spray Defoamer into inlet coupling of recovery hose or mist sides of tank. Normally 1-2 oz. of Defoamer per each 5 gallons recovery tank capacity is sufficient. When foam is excessive, spray Defoamer directly onto foam in recovery tank as needed.

CARPET CLEANING PROCEDURE

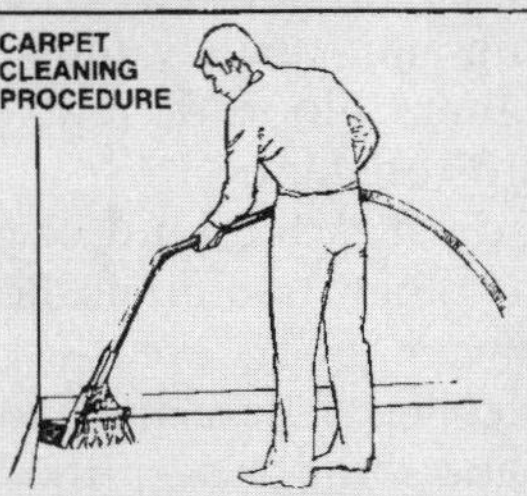

1. Begin carpet cleaning at corner of room farthest from the door.
2. Reach out with wand at moderate distance, making certain floor tool is always perpendicular to the carpeting.
3. Open cleaner dispensing valve and slowly pull cleaning wand toward you. Close cleaner dispenser valve just prior to completion of first "pass" to eliminate "puddling" of cleaning solution.
4. Lift wand and return to original position. With cleaner dispensing valve closed – vacuum up excess solution. (Repeat for wool carpet.)
5. Always slightly overlap "passes".
6. Always avoid overwetting carpet.

SET PILE

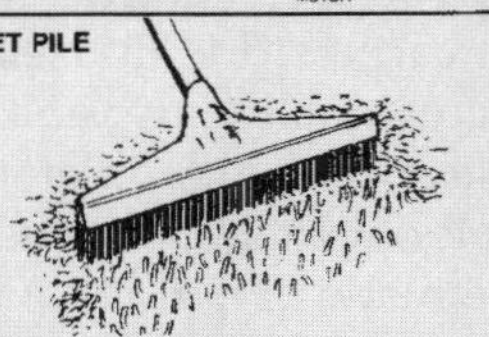

Using pile rake – rake the carpet against the way pile normally lies. This sets pile and decreases drying time. Replace furniture, using protective pads under metal casters.

DRY VAC

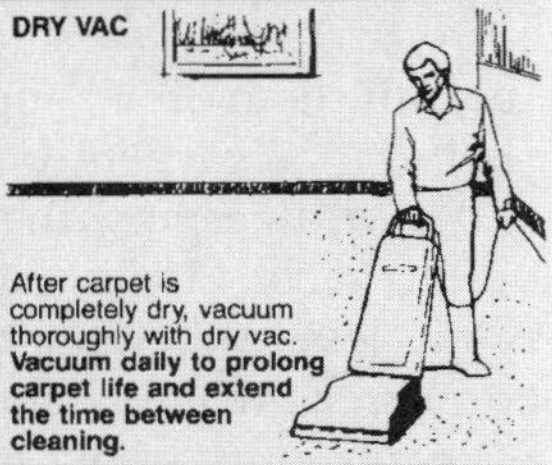

After carpet is completely dry, vacuum thoroughly with dry vac. **Vacuum daily to prolong carpet life and extend the time between cleaning.**

PRODUCTS

CARPET STAIN REMOVER
XTRACTION II
SPARTAN DEFOAMER

TOOLS

HOT AND/OR COLD WATER EXTRACTOR
MEASURING CUP
PILE RAKE
TRIGGER SPRAYER OR SPARTASPRAYER

DISTRIBUTED BY

Spartan®

Spartan Chemical Co., Inc.
110 N. Westwood Avenue • Toledo, Ohio 43607

Courtesy of Spartan Chemical Co., Inc., Toledo, Ohio

Electrostatic Dissipation. Static electricity in carpets irritates guests and employees and can cause real harm to computers. Microchips used in electronic equipment are more sensitive to static electricity than people are, especially when computers are opened for repair or other operations. Static electricity can wipe out information stored by the microchips or reduce a computer's memory capacity.

Many carpets receive an **electrostatic dissipation** treatment from the manufacturer. Antistatic solutions can be applied by housekeeping staff. Humidity control will also help reduce static.

Floors

The term **hard floor** is sometimes used to describe floor coverings other than carpets. In truth, some so-called hard floors are harder than others. Concrete, for example, is the hardest floor material and is reserved chiefly for areas that receive extremely heavy use. Cork, by contrast, is a springy natural material that is easy to walk and stand on for long periods. This section will discuss various types of floors and aspects of caring for them.

Floors have some disadvantages when compared to carpets. Floors are generally noisier, harder, and slipperier. They also provide less insulation. But floors also have some advantages over carpets. Floors are more durable and more sanitary, and they do not conduct static electricity.

Many people think that a floor's biggest advantage is that it is easier to clean and maintain than carpeting. This is not entirely true. Floors in lodging properties require frequent care just as carpets do. Housekeeping staff usually mop floors daily, buff them often, and, occasionally, strip and wax them. Floors do repel stains far better than carpets, but they are not completely stain-resistant.

As with carpets, the material a floor is made of dictates the kind of care it should receive. Floors may be made of natural and/or synthetic materials. Because they are less vulnerable to moisture and stains than carpet, floors are most often used in areas where water, soils, and stains frequently collect. These areas include guest bathrooms, public areas (lobbies and restrooms), and some back-of-the-house work spaces (kitchens, garages, repair shops, etc.).

There are three basic types of floors: **resilient** (or springy), **wood**, and **hard floors**. Floors are judged on resilience (how easy the floors are to stand and walk on), cleanability, resistance to stains and abrasions, and safety.

Resilient Floors

Resilient floors are easier to stand and walk on and may reduce noise better than hard floors. Resilient floors are often, however, less durable. Types of resilient floors include:

- Vinyl.
- Asphalt.
- Rubber.
- Linoleum.

Vinyl. Vinyl floors may be made of pure vinyl or a blend of vinyl and some other material. Pure vinyl floors cost about twice as much as vinyl blend floors.

Vinyl may be a conventional or no-wax type. Conventional vinyl is used most often in commercial operations like hotels because the wax and finish on the floor protects heavy-use areas from undue abrading and soiling.

The vinyls best suited for commercial use are thick and have **homogeneous color**—that is, color that permeates the entire layer of vinyl so that the color does not wear off with use. White vinyl may yellow if it gets too much direct, strong sunlight or if it is covered by a rug or appliance for a long period. Not much can be done about this condition. Yellowing may also occur with soiling; this can sometimes be corrected with a good cleaning.

Vinyl is impervious to most stains and substances. Vinyls with cushioned backing add to the material's natural resilience and noise absorption. Vinyl is also easy to care for and provides good traction.

Asphalt. Asphalt flooring is decay- and mildew-proof, resists ink stains, and is very fire-resistant. It also resists damage from alkaline moisture, which means that it can be installed directly over concrete. Asphalt is relatively inexpensive and durable. It also cracks and chips easily, which calls for careful installation. Harsh cleaners should be avoided.

Some asphalt floors contain asbestos. Asbestos has been outlawed in many states due to health risks. When asphalt floors with asbestos (or vinyl asbestos tiles) are torn up, the remains are considered hazardous waste and must be treated as such. Disposal of this hazardous waste can be expensive.

Rubber. Rubber, whether natural or synthetic (synthetic rubber is far more common today), is the most resilient, sound-absorbent flooring available. It is also relatively expensive. Rubber is durable and provides good traction, even when wet. Oil, grease, high heat, and detergent may injure rubber flooring.

Linoleum. Linoleum may be made from a variety of materials. It has been around so long that it has become an almost generic term for any kind of resilient floor. It is made from linseed oil, ground cork or wood, mineral fillers, and resins. It may be bonded to a burlap or felt backing for extra resilience and strength. Linoleum is inexpensive, easily installed, and easy to maintain, but it can be damaged by strong detergents.

Wood Floors

Oak is the wood of choice for most **wood floors** because it is hard and attractively grained. Maple, walnut, and teak, which tend to be more expensive than oak, may also be used. Softer woods such as pine are sometimes used. Depending upon the finish, soft woods may be more susceptible to dents and scratches. Cork, another soft wood, may be shaved, pressed, and baked into tiles that make a very resilient, but somewhat vulnerable, floor surface.

Because all types of wood are porous and absorbent, they are especially susceptible to water damage. Such alkaline substances as sudsy cleaners or ammonia can cause dark spots that must be removed with vinegar applications. Proper installation, sealing, and finishing are essential to the durability of a wood floor.

Wood may be laid on the floor in a number of ways. Parquet floors are made of wood "tiles," usually oak or maple. Wood block floors resemble butcher block surfaces and also come in tiles. Strips of end grain, which can weather heavy blows and use, are laid together to make up the floor's surface. Plank floors are long strips of wood fitted together to make a smooth surface. The planks may be of similar or varying widths to make an attractive pattern on the floor.

Wood costs considerably more than most other kinds of floors. Much of its use in commercial operations is probably due to its luxurious appearance.

Hard Floors

Hard floors are made from natural stone or clay. They are sometimes called stone floors and masonry floors. Hard floors are among the most durable of all floor surfaces, but also are among the least resilient. Types of hard floors include the following:

- Concrete
- Marble and terrazzo
- Ceramic tile
- Other natural stone

Concrete. Concrete floors are most often found in utility areas or areas that will receive a great deal of traffic from heavy equipment. Lodging properties often have concrete floors in parking areas, garages, and trade show areas. Concrete floors may be covered, painted, or sealed.

Marble and Terrazzo. Marble is a type of crystallized limestone and comes in many colors and patterns—white, black (onyx), gray, pink, green (verd antique), brown, orange, red-orange, banded (serpentine), or mottled. Marble is relatively durable, but lighter colors often yellow with age. Oil stains are extremely difficult to remove.

Marble can be finished in a variety of ways. Polished interior marble has a high-gloss finish and is usually used on tabletops, vanities, or other furniture. Since polished marble usually requires a great deal of maintenance, it is generally considered impractical for commercial floor use. Honed marble (satin-finished with little or no gloss) is recommended most often for commercial floors. Sand-blasted or abrasive-finished marble has a matte or nonreflective surface and is best suited for exterior use.

Sheet marble is very expensive because it is difficult to mine. Even with careful mining techniques, about half the marble that is quarried crumbles to rubble.

Marble rubble is often salvaged and used in terrazzo floors. The rubble is made into small tiles or pieces that are embedded into mortar like a mosaic. Terrazzo can also be made from granite, a less expensive natural stone. Granite may be pink, gray, or black. The mortar, not the stone, gives terrazzo its durability. Like most porous surfaces, terrazzo floors must be sealed.

Ceramic Tile. Ceramic tile is made from combinations of clay, marble, slate, glass, and/or flint. It is very durable and easy to maintain. It does not require sealant or wax.

Marble Care for Large Floor Areas

Start-Up and Twice a Year (Quarterly in High-Traffic Areas)

- Begin with a clean, undamaged surface. If the floor is old and has grooves, lippage, scratches, and/or pitting, it must be honed prior to beginning.
- Sweep, dry-mop, and wet-mop the floor with a clean mop head and neutral cleaner.
- Using a 175-rpm machine, polish the floor with polishing powder until the desired level of shine is achieved. Work on small areas, 72 square feet at a time.
- Immediately rinse off the remaining polishing powder with a wet mop and bucket or automatic scrubber.
- Rinse the floor at least three times with clear, cold water.
- Inspect the floor to ensure there is no residue left on it.
- Let the surface dry completely.
- Mop it with a clean mop head and polish preserver.
- Polish the floor with a white pad to increase its shine (if desired).

Daily Maintenance

- Dry-mop the floor at least twice per day.
- Wet-mop it with the recommended conditioner added to water. Each third day, use polish preserver instead of conditioner, and buff the floor with a white pad.

Source: Vera Juestel, *The Rooms Chronicle®*, Volume 1, Number 2, p. 9.
For subscription information, call 866-READ-TRC.

Other Natural Stone. Slate, a gray or blue-gray stone, is another popular natural stone floor. Slate forms when layers of mud and silt build up and solidify over millions of years. These layers allow slate to be "sliced" rather easily into floor pieces. But these floor pieces may split with excessive use or if heavy objects fall on them.

Quarry tile is less durable than slate and has a rougher texture. It is related to slate, however, being made of clay or shale.

There are two types of russet or brown clay floors. Terra cotta is a hard-baked tile, while brick is clay that is molded into rectangular blocks and hard-baked. Terra cotta tiles and bricks are typically left their natural color.

General Floor Maintenance

Floors require regular cleaning and finishing to retain their appearance and durability. Some housekeeping departments caution that soap should not be used on

the Rooms
CHRONICLE®

Marble Floors

Marble floors are one of the most beautiful assets of the hotel—but they are the most difficult part of the cleaning regimen. Any housekeeper who has struggled to keep a high gloss surface on the marble knows that there are many things to consider before deciding how to maintain the floor.

In fact, stone expert Evan Conklin affirms that not all marble floors are created equal and that consequently there is not one recommended cleaning procedure to fit every situation. Conklin, known in the industry as the "stone doctor," says, "Marble is composed primarily of calcium carbonate. It is relatively soft and can be scratched by common silica-containing soils carried by wind and tracked onto floors from outside. It is absorbent to liquids and sensitive to chemical attack, especially from food acids and harsh caustic cleaning agents."

Executive housekeepers face the following challenges:

- Designers choose a highly polished marble tile for high traffic areas of the hotel.
- Owners insist on keeping a high gloss on the floor.
- General managers want to keep maintenance costs low.
- The marble floor industry is divided on what cleaning procedures to recommend.
- Local floor care experts may not be very expert at all.

Understanding the marble

In the United States, designers tend to choose marble with a high gloss. After installation in high-traffic areas, the gloss immediately begins to dull. "When the only maintenance process used on a polished marble floor under commercial traffic conditions is washing, the mirror finish soon becomes dull, lifeless, and loses definition," says Conklin. "The floor becomes abraded (scratched), the polish disappears, and the stone surface becomes opaque."

Meeting the owners' expectations

Of course, the hotel owners want the floor to be beautifully shiny.

"So your marble is dull, scratched, and in major need of help! Out come the Yellow Pages; you call several marble refinishers and set up a few appointments. How hard can it be? You'll get a few estimates, check some references, and select a professional to do the job. And then the fun begins. The first professional tells you that your floor needs to be ground flat. The second professional tells you he can hone and polish it—no grinding required. The third professional tells you he only needs to recrystallize the marble to make it look like new. Now that you're totally confused, how do you determine who's right?"

To further complicate the situation, the refinishers start quoting very high prices for their services.

Keeping costs low

The general manager balks at the high quotes and the housekeeper is starting to feel trapped. Unfortunately, these people are caught in a common situation—the operating budget was not written to include the substantial costs of maintaining a highly reflective marble floor.

One reason the costs are high is that most maintenance procedures are very labor-intensive. Second, the care given must be provided by experts. And third, usually the condition of the floor has deteriorated due to lack of proper care.

The operator must make a decision based on up-front costs, long-term maintenance costs, and preservation of the life of the floor.

Deciding on a remedy

To keep it simple, there are three methods of marble care: mechanical restoration, chemical restoration, and surface coatings.

Mechanical restoration is the process of polishing the stone with a series of abrasive grits the way the stone was originally polished at the factory. If the scratches are quite deep or the tiles are uneven, the abrading process begins with grinding the stone down until it is quite flat. This is a very time-consuming, expensive, and messy process involving water and potential splashes of slurry on adjacent carpet, wallpaper, and furniture. But the result is a completely flat floor that will be easier to maintain.

After grinding, the abrading process uses increasingly less abrasive grits to sand the entire floor. This part of the process is known as "honing" and leaves the stone smooth and beautiful, but not reflective.

For those who wish to achieve a high polish, the floor must be polished after honing with a fine abrasive powder mixed with water.

If the operator wishes to avoid doing anything further to the floor, daily upkeep of the mechanically restored floor would involve dust mopping and wet mopping with clear water.

Chemical restoration is better known as crystallization. Used in the United States since the 1970s, crystallization has generated controversy among experts. The process consists of spraying silico-fluorides onto the marble floor and buffing with a high-speed buffer using special pads. The spray, heated by the action of the buffer, reacts chemically with the stone to produce an extra hard surface which is highly reflective.

Conklin advises that although this method of bringing a polish to a natural marble surface has potential as a problem-solving tool in the hands of an expert familiar with the particular stone and the chemicals involved, silico-fluorides chemically change the composition of the marble surface and can seriously damage some marble.

Although crystallization requires professional floor care specialists, the routine maintenance involves only dust mopping to remove loose debris and damp mopping with special chemicals.

(continued)

C the Rooms
CHRONICLE®

(continued)

Surface coatings are the third way of maintaining a marble floor. This process involves coating the surface with acrylic floor chemicals. Conklin refers to this as "sacrificial coatings" installed on top of the stone surface to act as a physical barrier to the environment. "All abrasive wear and staining liquids are physically separated from the polished marble surface by a thin membrane or film coating," Conklin writes. "When the coated surface is abraded by foot traffic or when liquids are spilled onto the floor, the abrasion or stain never touches the marble surface and the film is damaged instead of the stone surface. The advantage of the film coating is that it is more easily repaired or replaced than the ground polish of the marble surface." The negative to a sacrificial coating is the look. An acrylic-coated floor has a plastic look that is shiny, but quite different from the natural gloss of polished stone.

Routine maintenance involves applying more acrylic and spray buffing or burnishing the floor as needed. When the coating is badly damaged, the water-based acrylic can be stripped with ammonia-based products and the process restarted.

Source: Mary Friedman, *The Rooms Chronicle*®, Volume 7, Number 2, pp. 4–5. For subscription information, call 866-READ-TRC.

---

floors. Hard water often fails to rinse soap residue adequately; this residue can soften finishes or make the finishes unnecessarily slippery.

While floors generally resist stains far better than carpets, housekeeping staff should note floor spills and correct them quickly. Some general rules follow:

- Identify the stain and determine how to treat it. (See your property's cleaning manual.)

- Remove solid particles with a hand-held scraper. Be careful not to scratch or gouge the floor.

- Use a wet vacuum on large wet stains.

- Spot-test the stain remover and apply it according to the manufacturer's directions.

In today's world of no-wax floors, floor polish may seem like a thing of the past. However, floor care experts advise that proper waxing not only makes the floor more attractive, but is vital to its survival in commercial operations. Waxing protects all floor surfaces—even no-wax surfaces—from abrasions. It also strengthens porous floor materials such as wood.

Despite their stain resistance, floors still need protection against scuff marks and abrasives. Mats can help reduce scuffing and scratching—especially in entryways where the greatest number of abrasives is found. As with carpets, routine floor maintenance involves a regular cleaning schedule and prompt attention to problem spots. Exhibit 10 provides a sample form that distributors and/or manufacturers may supply to their customers. These kinds of forms can be used not only to set up a regular maintenance schedule, but also to train employees in the

Exhibit 10 Sample Floor Maintenance Schedule

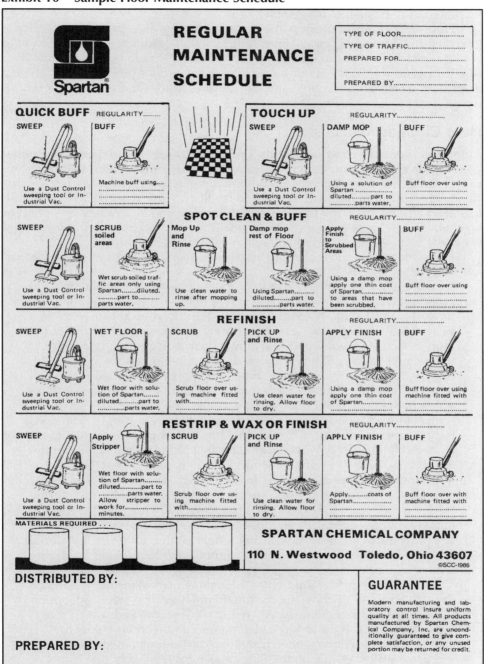

Courtesy of Spartan Chemical Co., Inc., Toledo, Ohio

importance and techniques of basic floor care. Some manufacturers provide similar materials in languages other than English.

Floor safety is also a major part of floor maintenance—especially in the face of an increasing number of lawsuits resulting from falls. Housekeepers may want to consider purchasing commercial floor-slip testers which can help determine floor safety. In addition, asking about liability coverage of floor care products can help determine which products are safer—and even reduce the insurance premiums for users of those products.

Floor Cleaning Methods

Mopping. Floors in most hospitality operations must be mopped daily, either with a damp mop or, on floors that cannot tolerate much water, with a chemically treated dust mop. Staff should be careful not to overtreat mops, because the chemical on the mop head will transfer to the floor. This can create a haze or dulling effect and may destroy the finish. Mop heads come in a variety of natural or synthetic fibers. Some properties recommend rayon. Soaking new mop heads in water for 30 minutes before use will remove the sizing chemicals.

Floor cleaners should make sure mop heads are rotated so they can be cleaned and dried after each use.

One of the recent advances in mopping was the development of flat mopping systems in Sweden in the early 1990s, with additional advances in Korea and China. It caught on quickly in Europe because it was a system that allowed for cleaning without chemical use. Microfiber flat mops are created with fibers that attract dust, dirt, and bacteria, holding them on the map until it is laundered. Microfiber mops are lightweight, easy to use, and can reduce the time and energy spent maintaining all types of flooring surfaces. Each microfiber cloth is comprised of thousands of synthetic split fiber yarns that are smaller in diameter than a typical human hair and can hold 10 times their own weight. The need for presweeping is virtually eliminated as hair, dust, and loose dirt are gathered by the finely woven cloth attached to the end of an aluminum telescoping pole. If needed, chemical cleaners may be sprayed on the floor or the mop head prior to using. The microfiber cloths, which may be rewashed for several uses, are typically held into place by spring loaded hinges, pins, or even Velcro fasteners, allowing housekeepers to quickly change out soiled microfiber cloths for clean ones. Special laundry procedures are necessary, as microfiber cloths cannot be laundered with bleach or fabric softener and cannot have high water or drying temperatures.

The UC Davis Medical Center in Sacramento, California, researched the effectiveness of these mops and found that they reduced opportunities for cross-contamination, reduced chemical and water usage, increased productivity, reduced staff injuries and workers compensation claims, and cleaned more effectively than conventional mops.[4] They also leave less water residue on the floor, making it less likely that someone will slip and fall on it.

Some hospitality housekeeping managers have resisted converting to micro-fiber mops, because the costs seem high. Both wet and dry microfiber cloths start at about $6 apiece. However, they can be washed and reused and typically outlast the traditional string mop by years.[5]

Buffing and Burnishing. Buffing involves spraying the floor with a polishing solution and buffing the floor with a rotary floor machine. Some rotary machines can spread the polishing solution as well as buff the floor. Spray buffing effectively removes scuff marks, heel marks, and restores the gloss to the floor. High-speed rotary machines are available that will make buffing quicker and the buff coat more durable.

Burnishing (polishing) is a floor care technique similar to buffing except that it is a dry method. Another difference between buffing and burnishing is the speed of the rotary floor machine. Burnishing requires faster rotation of the machine head. Some properties recommend burnishing only in low-traffic areas. Burnishing can only be used on hard floors.

Whether to buff or burnish a floor depends on the wax, sealer, or finish on the floor itself. Also, before a floor is buffed or burnished, it must be clean.

Scrubbing. Scrubbing usually requires a stiff scrubbing brush or pad, a suitable cleaning mixture, and a rotary floor machine. Scrubbing is often followed with buffing or burnishing, depending upon how much of the old wax comes off the floor during scrubbing.

Stripping and Refinishing. Housekeepers agree that stripping and refinishing are expensive and time-consuming tasks. However, to ensure proper floor care, they should be done on a regular basis. Stripping solutions may be water- or ammonia-based. Ammonia is a very powerful chemical and should be used carefully on floors. A rotary floor machine can be used to strip the old finish and spread the new finish on the floor. Exhibit 11 provides a sample form that distributors and/or manufacturers may supply to their customers. These kinds of forms can be used to train employees in floor stripping and refinishing techniques. Some manufacturers provide similar materials in languages other than English.

Finishes come in two types—wax-based or polymer finish. Wax-based polishes require at least two coats of wax to attain maximum protection for the floor. Many manufacturers and housekeeping departments recommend three or more coats. Almost all finishes can be spray-buffed. Wax-based finishes are buffable.

Metal-interlocking (or **cross-linking**) **polymer finishes** contain a dissolved metal, usually zinc, which strengthens the floor finish. Some properties use only solutions with at least 18 percent to 20 percent solids. This kind of finish is virtually impervious to heel marks, detergents, and abrasions. A polymer finish is also easily touched up with fresh coats to keep the floor glossy and restore the protection of the original finish. Metal interlocking finishes also make stripping easier because ammonia (the active ingredient in many strippers) attracts the metal. This unseals the finish, making removal easier.

Green Floor Care

Increasingly, hospitality managers understand that being environmentally conscious isn't a matter of simply buying a few "green" products, but of implementing

Exhibit 11   Sample Stripping and Refinishing Techniques

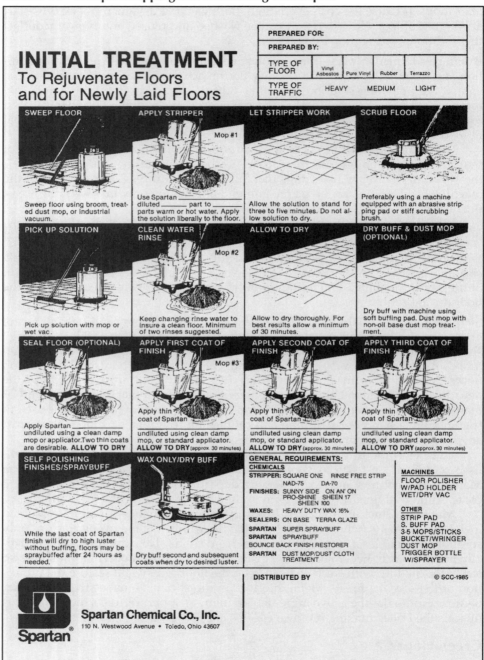

Courtesy of Spartan Chemical Co., Inc., Toledo, Ohio

an overall program that works throughout the property. The same is true with floor care. Environmentally responsible floor care requires that the executive housekeeper implement a system that achieves high quality, functional floors that don't harm the environment or the health of those who walk on them and clean them.

Several traditional floor care finishes contain chemicals that we now know cause health and environmental problems. These can include finishes that contain zinc, phthalates, solvents, and flourosurfacants. Likewise, many traditional strippers contain such environmentally and health hazardous ingredients as 2-butoxyethanol, ammonia, sodium hydroxide, and akylphenol ethoxylate surfacants.

Green Seal, Inc., created an environmental standard for floor-care products in 2004. It focused on finishes and strippers used for industrial and institutional purposes. Green Seal established performance requirements for these products that included slip resistance, removability, soil resistance, and detergent resistance. Green Seal insisted that undiluted product:

- Cannot be toxic to humans
- Cannot contain any ingredients that are carcinogens, mutagens, or reproductive toxins
- Cannot be corrosive to the skin or eyes
- Cannot be a skin sensitizer
- Must have a flash point above 150 degrees Fahrenheit

Green Seal also says that the product as used cannot contribute significantly to producing photochemical smog, tropospheric ozone, or poor indoor-air quality. It also should not be toxic to aquatic life, and should be biodegradable. Other requirements are that a product's primary package be recyclable and not contain any of the following ingredients:

- Alkylphenol ethoxylates
- Phthalates
- Zinc or other heavy metals, including arsenic, lead, cadmium, cobalt, chromium, mercury, nickel, selenium, optical brighteners, and ozone-depleting compounds (ODCs)

Any floor care product that meets Green Seal's standards is able to put the Green Seal certification mark on its packaging. The seal usually includes wording such as: "This product meets Green Seal's standard for industrial and institutional floor-care products based on its reduced human and aquatic toxicity and reduced smog production potential."

Floor care experts also point out that part of being environmentally sound is not just in the careful use of products but in the overall floor care plan. The U.S. Green Building Council's Existing Buildings Rating System mandates what it calls a sustainable floor care system that reduces the frequency of stripping and refinishing. It calls for floors to be designed so that stripping and sealing can take place less frequently. Sustainable floor care systems can include entrance mats, burnishers with vacuum attachments, microfiber floor mops, mop buckets, etc.

Endnotes

1. Source: Doug Scouten, *The Rooms Chronicle®*, Volume 12, Number 2, pp. 6, 11. For subscription information, call 866-READ-TRC.

2. Source: Doug Scouten, *The Rooms Chronicle®*, Volume 12, Number 3, pp. 6–7. For subscription information, call 866-READ-TRC.

3. Scouten, pp. 6–7.

4. "How to Evaluate and Select Microfiber Mops" www.vpico.com/articlemanager/printerfriendly.aspx?article=60321, August 1, 2005

5. "Cleaning bathroom floors in guestrooms…Are microfiber mops the answer?", *The Rooms Chronicle®*, Volume 12, Number 1, p. 6. For subscription information, call 866-READ-TRC.

 **Key Terms**

acetate—A low-cost silky fiber. It is colorfast and resistant to mildew, but it is relatively easy to soil and is vulnerable to abrasion.

acrylic—Synthetic material used in making fabric or molded transparent fixtures or surfaces.

antimicrobial treatment—Carpet treatment in which a solution is applied to the carpet to kill many kinds of bacteria and fungi and the odors they cause.

bulk continuous filament (BCF) fibers—Continuous strands of fiber that are used to construct nonwoven or tufted carpet.

delustered—A process used on nylon carpet to lessen the shine and to give the surface a duller finish that looks more like wool.

electrostatic dissipation—Carpet treatment in which a solution is applied to make the carpet resistant to static electricity.

face—The pile of the carpet.

face fibers—Yarns that form the pile of the carpet.

face weight—The measure of a carpet's pile. Equal to the weight of the face fibers in one square yard of carpet.

hard floor—Noncarpeted floor. These floors are among the most durable of all floor surfaces, but also the least resilient. Types of hard floors include concrete, marble and terrazzo, ceramic tile, and other natural stone.

homogeneous color—Color that permeates the entire layer of vinyl flooring so that the color does not wear off with use.

hot- or cold-water extraction—A deep-cleaning method in which a machine sprays a detergent-and-water solution onto the carpet under low pressure and, in the same pass, vacuums out the solution and soil.

metal interlocking polymer finish—A type of polymer floor finish that contains dissolved metal, usually zinc.

modacrylic—Acrylic fiber that is less resistant to stains and abrasions.

pile—The surface of a carpet; consists of fibers or yarns that form raised loops that can be cut or sheared.

pile distortion—Face fiber conditions such as twisting, pilling, flaring, or matting caused by heavy traffic or improper cleaning methods.

primary backing—The part of the carpet to which face fibers are attached and which holds these fibers in place.

resilient floor—A type of floor that reduces noise and is considered easier to stand and walk on than hard floors. Types of resilient floors include vinyl, asphalt, rubber, and linoleum.

rotary floor machine—Floor care equipment that accommodates both brushes and pads to perform such carpet-cleaning tasks as dry-foam cleaning, mist pad cleaning, rotary spin pad cleaning, or bonnet and brush shampoos. On hard floors, these machines can be used to buff, burnish, scrub, strip, and refinish.

secondary backing—The part of a carpet that is laminated to the primary backing to provide additional stability and more secure installation.

shading—A carpet condition that occurs when the pile is brushed in two different directions so that dark and light areas appear.

staple fibers—Fibers approximately seven to ten inches long that are twisted together into long strands and used to construct non-woven or tufted carpet.

tufted or looped carpets—Carpet constructed by pulling face fibers through the carpet's backing to form a thick pile of tufts or loops.

wet vacuum—Floor care equipment used to pick up spills or to pick up rinse water that is used during carpet or floor cleaning.

wicking—A carpet condition that occurs when the backing of the carpet becomes wet and the face yarns draw the moisture and color of the backing to the carpet's surface.

wood floor—A type of floor in which hard or soft woods are cut and laid in planks, blocks, or tiles (parquet) to make attractive patterns.

Review Questions

1. What are the differences between a carpet and a floor?

2. What are the basic components of a carpet?

3. What kinds of carpets would be most practical in a guestroom? A lobby? A dining room? Why?

4. How can such carpet problems as pile distortion, wicking, and fading be prevented?

5. What are some of the main considerations in planning floor and carpet maintenance schedules and procedures?

6. What are some of the basic pieces of equipment used to clean carpets and floors and how are they used?

7. What are various kinds of carpet cleaning methods?

8. What should be considered when choosing floor surfaces for a lodging operation?

9. What are three basic types of floor coverings?

10. What are various kinds of floor cleaning methods and their applications?

11. What elements can contribute to environmentally sound floor care?

Internet Sites

For more information, visit the following Internet sites. Remember that Internet addresses can change without notice. If the site is no longer there, you can use a search engine to look for additional sites.

First Finish
www.firstfinish.net/portg_loews1.html

Green Seal Certified Floor Care
  Products
www.greenseal.org/findaproduct/
fcp.cfm

Kinsley Carpet Mills
www.kinsleycarpets.com

Leggett & Platt Hospitality
www.lphospitality.com

Milliken Hospitality Floor Covering
www.millikencarpet.com/
americas/hospitality/pages/default.aspx

Stainmaster Carpet Care
www.stainmaster.com

Templeton Hospitality Carpet
www.templetoncarpet.com

Task Breakdowns: Carpets and Floors

The procedures presented in this section are for illustrative purposes only and should not be construed as recommendations or standards. While these procedures are typical, readers should keep in mind that each property has its own procedures, equipment specifications, and policies regarding protective gear which are designed to fit individual needs.

Sweep Hard Floors

Materials needed: A broom, a dustpan, a trash bag, and a stocked public-space cleaning cart.

STEPS	HOW-TO'S
1. Move equipment and furniture as necessary to expose all areas of the floor.	
2. Start in the back corner of the room, away from the door.	
3. Use a broom to sweep dirt into a small pile.	❏ Keep the broom's bristles on the floor as much as possible to avoid stirring up dirt.
4. Pick up the dirt using a dustpan before sweeping further.	
5. Empty the dirt from the dustpan into the trash bag on your cart.	
6. Continue to sweep and pick up dirt until the entire floor is clean.	

Mop Hard Floors

Materials needed: *Caution signs, floor cleaner, a mop bucket, a spray bottle, and a mop.*

STEPS	HOW-TO'S
1. Set up Caution signs.	
2. Select the appropriate cleaner.	❑ The cleaners used in the following areas vary among properties: • Bathroom • Corridors • Closets • Food and beverage areas
3. Mop the floor with a damp mop.	❑ Begin in the back of the room, away from the door. ❑ Mop from left to right in three-foot sections, working toward the door. Each three-foot section should overlap the previous one. This method of overlapping, often called "the figure 8," will prevent you from walking on the cleaned area and will make sure that the entire floor area is clean. ❑ Use Method 1 or Method 2 to mop the floor: **Method 1:** • Mix the appropriate cleaner with water in the mop bucket and apply it to the floor. • Dump dirty water and refill the mop bucket with clean rinse water. • Mop the floor with rinse water, changing the water as needed. • Wring the mop and soak up excess water so the floor is just damp. **Method 2:** • Mix the appropriate cleaner and water in a spray bottle. • Fill the mop bucket with clean rinse water. • Spray the floor with the cleaner. • Dip the mop in the rinse bucket, wring the mop, and mop up the cleaning solution.

(continued)

Mop Hard Floors (continued)

STEPS	HOW-TO'S
4. Let the floor air dry.	
5. Empty and clean the mop bucket.	
6. Rinse the mop in clean water and hang it to dry.	
7. Put away Caution signs and other equipment and supplies.	
8. Dust-mop floors that cannot tolerate much water.	❑ Never wet-mop wood or marble floors unless they have been treated with a waterproof sealer. ❑ Always check with your supervisor if you are in doubt about whether to mop a floor.

Use a Rotary Floor Machine

Materials needed: *Caution signs and a rotary floor machine with brushes or pads.*

STEPS	HOW-TO'S
1. Place Caution signs in the work area.	
2. Check electrical cords on the rotary floor machine.	❏ Check cords to be sure they are untangled and free of damage. ❏ Try not to run cords through traffic areas.
3. Attach a scrub brush or pad to the rotary floor machine.	❏ Make sure the machine is unplugged. ❏ Tilt the rotary floor machine backward until the operating handle rests on the floor. ❏ Make sure the brush or pad is clean, or you could damage the floor. ❏ Twist the brush or pad on the studs counterclockwise.
4. Run the rotary floor machine over the floor.	❏ Plug in the rotary floor machine. ❏ Buff the floor with the rotary floor machine, working from the far side of the room to the entrance. ❏ Work backward slowly in a fanning motion from left to right. ❏ Operate the rotary floor machine with one hand, and use your other hand to move the electrical cord out of your path.
5. Check the pad or brush at set intervals, and change dirty pads or brushes.	
6. If a film is left on the floor, mop the floor. Then buff it again using a clean brush or pad on the machine.	

(continued)

Use a Rotary Floor Machine (continued)	
STEPS	**HOW-TO'S**
7. Remove the buffer pad or brush from the machine, clean all buffer pads or brushes, and hang them to dry. 8. Put away the rotary floor machine and Caution signs.	❑ The steps to clean buffer pads vary among properties. ❑ The steps to clean brushes vary among properties.

Clean and Wax Tile Floors

Materials needed: *Caution signs, a rotary floor machine with brushes or pads, detergent, a stripping chemical, white vinegar, floor sealer, floor wax, a putty knife, cleaning cloths, a broom, a mop for wet-mopping, a mop for waxing, a wrung-out mop or wet vacuum, a mop bucket, a dust mop, a dustpan, heavy latex utility gloves, protective goggles, a bucket, a spray bottle, and a small brush.*

STEPS	HOW-TO'S
1. Place Caution signs in the work area.	
2. Sweep or dust-mop the area.	❑ Clear the floor of movable equipment.
	❑ Remove all loose dust and dirt using a broom or a clean, dry dust mop and dustpan.
	❑ Follow all safety rules to protect guests, employees, and yourself.
	❑ Twist the brush or pad on the studs counterclockwise.
3. Remove any stains from the floor.	
4. Wet-mop tile floors when instructed by the supervisor.	❑ Keep floors dry in busy public spaces. Wet mop floors when traffic is light.
	❑ Do not mix up mops for wet-mopping and waxing.
5. Strip built-up wax from tile floors.	❑ Wear heavy latex utility gloves and protective goggles.
	❑ Mix water and an approved floor stripper.
	❑ Apply a heavy coat of the solution with a mop. Let this stand for 10 minutes or until a haze appears.
	❑ Hand-scrub edges with a brush.
	❑ Scrape the wax loose from corners with a small putty knife.

(continued)

Clean and Wax Tile Floors (continued)	
STEPS	**HOW-TO'S**
	❑ Pick up residue in corners and along edges with a hand cloth if needed.
	❑ Scrub the wax loose using a rotary floor machine with a brush or nylon pads.
	❑ Use warm, clean rinse water and a wet vacuum or a wrung-out mop to pick up wax and dirt.
	❑ Change rinse water as needed.
	❑ Use a final rinse to get rid of any film from the wax and stripping solution. Be sure to reach corners and edges.
	❑ Air-dry the tile floor.
6. Apply sealer and liquid wax.	❑ Ask your supervisor what you should use to apply liquid wax.
	❑ Apply according to the property's procedures.
7. Touch up the wax finish.	❑ Mix one part liquid wax with one part water in a spray bottle.
	❑ Spray the solution lightly on the floor just ahead of the rotary floor machine. Buff the floor until a glossy finish appears.
	❑ Maintain the floor by sweeping, mopping, and light buffing.
8. Rinse all mops well and hang them to dry.	
9. Clean other supplies and equipment and hang them to dry as necessary.	
10. Put away Caution signs and other equipment and supplies.	

Remove Stains from Tile Floors

Materials needed: *Caution signs, heavy latex utility gloves, protective goggles, paper towels, cleaning cloths, liquid detergent or disinfectant, a sealable plastic container, a trash can, all-purpose detergent, a putty knife, and a sponge.*

STEPS	HOW-TO'S
1. Set up Caution signs in your work area if necessary.	
2. Wear heavy latex utility gloves and protective goggles to remove stains.	❑ Always wear protective items when you clean with strong chemicals or when you clean blood or other body fluid stains.
3. Test the stain removal process.	❑ Test the stain remover by applying it to a small area out of sight.
	❑ If the remover damages the floor, do not continue. Report the damage to your supervisor immediately.
	❑ If you are unable to remove a stain, report it to your supervisor. It may be necessary to contact the tile manufacturer for instructions.
4. Remove bloodstains.	❑ Follow safety procedures for removing bloodborne pathogens.
	❑ Wash your hands immediately after removing gloves.
5. Remove burns.	❑ Follow the property's procedures for removing burns from tile.
6. Remove candy or chewing gum.	❑ Scrape up gum or candy with a putty knife. Be careful not to scratch or gouge the floor. (Some properties use "gum remover." Ask your supervisor if this is available.)
	❑ Apply an all-purpose detergent solution.
	❑ Rinse the spot with a wet cloth or sponge.

(continued)

Remove Stains from Tile Floors (continued)

STEPS	HOW-TO'S
7. Remove heel marks using the property's procedures.	
8. Remove ink stains.	❑ Follow the property's procedures for removing ink stains.
9. Remove nail polish.	❑ Blot as much of the polish as possible using a dry cloth or sponge. ❑ Clean the spot using the property's procedures.
10. Remove urine stains.	❑ If the stain is fresh, use absorbent paper towels to blot it until you can't soak up any more urine. ❑ The materials used to clean up urine stains vary among properties.
11. Rub unknown stains with all-purpose detergent solution and #0 steel wool.	
12. Strip and wax the floor or touch up the wax finish if necessary.	

Clean and Wax Hardwood and Parquet Floors

Materials needed: *Caution signs, a broom or dust mop, a dustpan, floor wax, a cloth, and a rotary floor machine with pads.*

STEPS	HOW-TO'S
1. Place Caution signs in your work area.	
2. Sweep or dust-mop the area.	❑ Clear the floor of movable equipment. ❑ Remove all loose dust and dirt using a broom or a clean, dry dust mop and dustpan. ❑ Do not use water to clean the floors. ❑ Follow all safety rules to protect guests, employees, and yourself.
3. Check electrical cords on the rotary floor machine.	❑ Make sure cords are untangled and free of damage. ❑ Try not to run cords through traffic areas.
4. Attach a buffer pad to the rotary floor machine.	❑ Make sure the rotary floor machine is unplugged. ❑ Tilt the machine backward until the operating handle rests on the floor. ❑ Make sure the pad is clean, or you could damage the floor. ❑ Twist the pad on the studs counterclockwise.
5. Work small amounts of wax into the rotary floor machine pad with your fingers or a cloth.	
6. Buff the floor until it shines.	❑ Plug in the rotary floor machine. ❑ Buff the floor with the rotary floor machine, working from the far side of the room to the entrance.

(continued)

Clean and Wax Hardwood and Parquet Floors *(continued)*

STEPS	HOW-TO'S
	❏ Work backward slowly in a fanning motion from left to right.
	❏ Operate the rotary floor machine with one hand, and use your other hand to move the electrical cord out of your path.
	❏ You may need to add more wax to the pad if the floor is large.
	❏ Wait for the wax on the floor to completely dry.
	❏ Apply a second coat of wax to difficult areas to get an even finish. Wait for the wax to dry.
	❏ Attach a clean, unwaxed buffer pad to the rotary floor machine.
	❏ Buff the floor again, working from the far side of the room to the entrance.
7. Remove the buffer pad from the machine, clean all buffer pads, and hang them to dry.	❏ The steps to clean buffer pads vary among properties.
8. Put away the rotary floor machine, Caution signs, and other equipment and supplies.	

Vacuum Carpets

Materials needed: *Caution signs, a stiff broom, a vacuum cleaner, and a vacuum bag.*

STEPS	HOW-TO'S
1. Place Caution signs if necessary.	
2. Remove dirt from room corners and carpet edges.	❑ Use a small, stiff broom to brush dirt from room corners and carpet edges to a carpeted area that a vacuum can reach. ❑ Push down on the broom and pull it toward you-away from the wall.
3. Plug in the vacuum cleaner.	❑ Try to use an outlet near the door. ❑ Make sure the cord is in an out-of-the-way place so that no one trips over it.
4. Vacuum from one side of the room to the other.	❑ Begin vacuuming in a back corner of the room. Don't stand in wet areas while vacuuming. ❑ Vacuum toward the door so that you vacuum over your footprints. ❑ Carefully vacuum room corners, edges, and high-traffic areas. ❑ Report any rips in the carpet to the supervisor so staff members can repair them.
5. Check and empty the vacuum bag, and clean beater brushes periodically.	❑ The steps to empty the bag and to clean brushes vary among properties.
6. Unplug the vacuum, wind the cord correctly, and return the vacuum to your cart.	❑ Pull on the plug, not the cord, when unplugging the vacuum. ❑ The steps to wind the vacuum cord vary among properties.

Clean, Seal, and Wax Marble Surfaces

Materials needed: Caution signs, a dust cloth, a dust mop, a waxing mop, a wet mop, a mop bucket, water-resistant sealer, approved detergents, floor wax, a rotary floor machine with brushes or pads, and clean, soft cloths.

STEPS	HOW-TO'S
1. Place Caution signs in your work area.	
2. Use a dry dust cloth or dust mop to remove dust.	
3. Wash marble.	❑ Dip a clean, soft cloth or mop into a mixture of fresh, warm water and a mild detergent.
	❑ Scrub the marble to remove any ingrained residue.
	❑ The schedule to wash marble varies among properties.
	❑ Wipe the marble with a dry cloth until it is completely dry. Water will discolor the surface if it soaks into the stone.
4. Use a waxing mop to apply a clear, water-resistant sealer to the marble floor.	❑ The sealer to use on marble floors varies among proper-ties.
5 Wax the marble.	❑ Use the buffer to apply an approved non-yellowing floor wax evenly to the marble.
	❑ Make even strokes with the rotary floor machine.
6. Rinse all wet or waxing mops used and hang them to dry.	
7. Remove pads or brushes from the buffer, rinse them, and hang them to dry.	
8. Put away Caution signs, equipment, and supplies.	

Extract Carpets

Materials needed: *Caution signs, a water extractor, carpet prespotting solution, an approved detergent, defoamer, and a vacuum cleaner.*

STEPS	HOW-TO'S
1. Place Caution signs in your work area.	
2. Move equipment and furniture.	❏ Carefully lift and carry all portable equipment and furniture to an area approved by your supervisor.
3. Vacuum the carpet.	❏ Carefully move furniture to expose all areas of the carpet that need to be cleaned.
4. Spray heavily soiled areas or spills with a carpet prespotting solution.	
5. Remove candle wax.	❏ By hand, gently remove as much of the wax as possible, being careful to not pull or damage carpet fibers. ❏ Cover the remaining dried wax deposit with absorbent paper towels. ❏ Apply a hot flat iron to the top side of the paper towel. This should make the towel absorb the wax. ❏ Repeat as necessary until all wax is absorbed.
6. Set up the water extractor.	❏ The steps to fill the water tank with water and detergent vary among properties.
7. Plug in the extractor and allow the wash tank to heat the water (if the tank has heater coils).	

(continued)

Extract Carpets (continued)

STEPS	HOW-TO'S
8. Add defoamer to the extraction tank to prevent excess foaming.	
9. Use the extractor according to the manufacturer's instructions.	❑ Start at the far side of the area and work back to the entrance. ❑ Inject water into the carpet. ❑ Work quickly to prevent overwetting the carpet. Do not soak the carpet. ❑ Give special attention to prespotted areas. ❑ Don't stand in excess water while using the extractor.
10. Empty dirty water in a mop sink or dock area drain, not down guestroom toilets.	
11. Allow the carpet to dry completely.	
12. Vacuum the carpet again.	
13. Put the room back in order.	❑ Replace equipment and furniture that you moved out of the way or removed from the room.
14. Clean the water extractor.	❑ The steps to clean the water extractor vary among properties.
15. Store all equipment and supplies in the correct locations.	

Chapter 14 Outline

Types of Bathroom Furnishings and Fixtures
    Tubs and Showers
    Toilets
    Vanities
    Fixtures
    Amenities
Handicap Accessibility
Care Considerations
    Tubs
    Toilets
    Vanities
    Floors
    Shower Curtains
Safety in the Guest Bathroom

Competencies

1. Describe the types of fittings and furnishings used in guestroom bathrooms. (pp. 575—583)

2. Identify the elements necessary to make a bathroom handicap accessible. (pp. 583—587)

3. Explain the proper cleaning and care procedures for guestroom bathrooms. (pp. 587—594)

4. Identify safety concerns connected with cleaning and using guest bathrooms. (pp. 594—597)

14

Tubs, Toilets, and Vanities

In 1829, THE TREMONT HOTEL in Boston announced that its rooms featured indoor plumbing. Thanks to the 26-year-old architect, Isaiah Rogers, bathrooms had arrived in hotels. The rooms had copper or tin bathtubs and the eight rooms with "water closets" were all found on the ground floor. The bathtubs were heated with small gas furnaces and cold water was supplied to the sink. Five years later, Rogers designed the Astor House in New York City and managed to get water closets on the top floors and bathrooms in all 300 guestrooms.[1]

Today's bathrooms are far more advanced, yet they still speak to that same desire for luxury. Lodging properties are still luring guests to their rooms with ever-more up-to-date bathrooms. Some properties, such as the Fairmont Chicago, have gone so far as to hire a bath sommelier who sets up a bathroom according to the guest's choices from a bath menu.

The bathrooms are often the gauge that guests use to determine how clean the entire guestroom is. This makes it an essential concern for every executive housekeeper. Also, as designers create ever-more elaborate bathrooms, cleaning needs continue to increase and executive housekeepers must come up with new routines and procedures.

This chapter examines the type of furnishings and fittings found in bathrooms: tubs, toilets, vanities, fixtures, and amenities. It discusses some of the latest design trends in each of these and some of the new challenges that executive housekeepers and room attendants face. It also discusses the importance of handicap accessibility in bathrooms, care considerations, and guest bathroom cleaning safety.

Types of Bathroom Furnishings and Fixtures

With most of the shots already fired in the bed wars, the next battle between brands is being waged over bathrooms. Properties are seeking to create better, more appealing bathrooms. This can mean anything from redesigning the entire bathroom to providing new and unique amenities and bathroom-related services. The upgrades have been limited only by the creativity of the designers.

In upscale and luxury properties, bathrooms are getting bigger and owners are rethinking such basics as the bathtub, sometimes replacing them with walk-in spa-like showers. Other properties are creating luxury bath experiences by hiring famous designers to create unique looks for their property. Exhibit 1 describes the urban spa experience that the Park Hyatt Washington created with its bathrooms.

However, bathroom renovations aren't limited to upscale or resort properties. Midscale properties are also getting into the game. Holiday Inn Express asked

Exhibit 1   Urban Spa Experience in the Bathroom

The Park Hyatt Washington redesigned its hotel in 2006 to meet modern demands. One of the more dramatic changes in the $24 million renovation was the bathroom.

Designer Tony Chi created the spa-inspired bathrooms because there was no room to add a spa at the hotel. The bathrooms are 618 square feet with dark gray limestone on walls, floor, and ceiling. The walk-in bath is made of limestone. The hotel offers sybaritic soaks in a deep tub, a rain shower overhead, and hand-held showers.

Amenities are created by Parisian artisan perfumer Blaise Mautin. In keeping with the Washington D.C. theme, each shampoo is infused with the scent of cherry blossoms.

Harris Interactive to conduct a poll, which found that nearly three-quarters of U.S. adults are dissatisfied with hotel bathrooms. Their top complaint was that water pressure in hotel showers was either too low or too high. Others were unhappy with linen quality or the amount of room in the shower.

In response, Holiday Inn rolled out a $20 million SimplySmart^{SM} bathroom upgrade that would reach all of its 1,300 North American properties. It involved replacing shower heads and adding new towels. The new shower heads let guests choose among spray settings, while the bathroom linens have been upgraded in size, softness, and absorbency. It also installed a curved shower rod and a new line of amenities that have a proprietary scent: fresh-baked cinnamon. Holiday Inn Express now offers its shower heads for purchase online.

Some other examples of property initiatives in bathroom upgrades include:

- Starwood introduced the Heavenly Bath® at Westin Hotels to complement its Heavenly Bed®. The Heavenly Bath® includes a shower with a curved shower rod and multiple shower heads, larger and fluffier towels, velour bathrobes, and spa-quality amenities.

- Harrah's redesigned its bathrooms in the late 1990s. It created a four-fixture bathroom with a vanity/dressing area, glass-enclosed shower, whirlpool tub, and private toilets. It also featured a full-length mirror, artwork above the whirlpool tubs, and chrome- and brass-plated hardware fixtures. The tubs are six inches longer and six inches wider than a standard bathtub.

- Gansevoort South on Miami Beach built showers with multiple shower heads and six-foot-long tubs.

- Sofitel in Los Angeles designed oversized showers surrounded by glass walls that change from clear to opaque with the flip of a switch.

- The Rihga Royal Hotel in New York renovated its bathrooms to include all Waterworks bathtubs, fixtures, and linens.

- Hotel Valley Ho in Scottsdale placed Philippe Starck-designed bathtubs in 21 of its 194 rooms. The tubs are located next to the bed, behind a curtain.

- The InterContinental Playa Bonita Resort in Panama has suite bathrooms with shutters that open to the rest of the room so guests can lounge in the tub and watch television.

- The Mykanos Grace, a boutique hotel in Greece, won a prestigious European design award in November 2007, in part because of its bathrooms. The spacious bathrooms include walk-in showers and hydro-massage plunge pools that are on private terraces.

- The Calistoga Ranch in California's Napa Valley has a bathroom that opens out to an enclosed private garden with a shower.

- The Las Vegas MGM Grand has a boutique hotel on its upper floors called Skylofts. These rooms have an oversized 32-inch deep tub with bubbles and chromatherapy lights that emanate a rainbow of hues. It also has a walk-in shower/steam room with a handheld wand and simulated waterfalls and rain showers. There is a remote control to dictate temperatures, mood lighting, and customized music/video library. Guests can also watch high-definition television in a mirror facing the tub. A spa butler can be called to draw the bath, add scented infusions, light candles, and serve champagne.

- In Mexico, the Paraiso de la Bonita has a room-sized shower with multiple wall jets that lead to a separate skylit garden shower. There is also a deep marble tub that is surrounded with candles and covered in red rose petals daily.

Other properties are taking advantage of lighting and mirrors to add depth to their guest bathrooms by doing such things as using lighted glass as a vanity top.

As mentioned previously, another trend that some major hotel chains have been exploring is eliminating the bathtub altogether. Hotel baths are typically shallow for safety reasons—too shallow for an adult to comfortably use. Customer research indicated that most guests weren't using the bathtub. For this reason, many properties are switching to larger shower areas when they renovate or build. In several major chains, designers have removed the tubs and replaced them with large shower stalls and multiple shower-head sprays. These properties typically split their room blocks so that some rooms are still available with bathtubs.

Some experts have pointed out that the move toward showers instead of bathtubs is a move that will save hotels money while contributing to a more sustainable property. Showers use less water, something especially important in drought-stricken areas. They also require less space and can result in lower insurance premiums.

Other properties, particularly luxury and boutique hotels, are choosing to upgrade the bath to make it more attractive. Some options include several varieties of whirlpools and soaking tubs. Some use air injection fixtures to create effervescent, champagne-like bubbles in a whirlpool.

Tubs and Showers

Bathtubs are most frequently made of enameled cast iron or acrylic. Acrylic models are often reinforced with fiberglass and may come in combination tub/shower units that include shower-stall walls. Ceramic tile is frequently used around the enameled cast-iron tubs and in the shower stall.

Many designers and owners select enameled tubs and tile walls. But house-keepers often prefer acrylic tubs or tub/shower units because they are cheaper, easier to care for, and at least as durable as enameled cast-iron tubs. An inexpensive vinegar solution cleans acrylic tubs quickly and easily (though some hotels prefer to use a mild all-purpose cleaner to prevent the bathroom from smelling like a salad). Moreover, the tub/shower units do not require the attention that tile and grout do. Scratches or cigarette burns, too, can be sanded out without loss of color or finish. All in all, housekeepers say they can clean an acrylic unit in half the time it takes to clean a conventional, enameled, cast-iron/tile tub and shower.

As properties become more sensitive to expensive mold and mildew problems, they're taking closer looks at the tub surrounds and liners. Traditional tile and other surfaces were attractive to mold, whereas an **acrylic tub liner** is non-porous and resists mold and mildew. Most of the new ones are also durable, scratch-resistant, and available in a number of colors. There are also non-porous cast-polymer surrounds on the market now that are designed to look and feel like ceramic tile and grout.

Properties also must determine how they are going to make their tubs slip-resistant. Rubber mats used to be fairly common, but they had several drawbacks. They had to be washed frequently, incurring additional costs in water, chemicals, and energy. They also took up room on the housekeeping cart. Other properties use strips or decals that are permanently installed in the tub.

Some tubs are now designed with non-skid bottoms. The challenge with these is that they eventually become discolored. Special cleaning substances have been designed to eliminate any graying. These substances usually must be applied on a monthly basis as part of a special-project or deep-cleaning schedule.

Upgraded shower heads have also become common in all lodging segments—especially as demands for an indulgent, spa-like experience become more common. The upgraded shower heads also take environmental concerns into account and balance low-flow requirements with guest desires.

Curved shower rods are becoming more popular in many properties. They've been adopted by such chains as Westin, Hampton Inn, and Park Inn. The curved rods give the guest more elbow space in the shower—typically around nine more inches. The way it is designed keeps water from escaping onto the floor. With less water escaping, there is a reduced risk of mold, mildew, and slips and falls.

Some properties are also turning to natural fiber shower curtains, which both create a luxury feel and are more friendly to the environment and to people with allergies and chemical sensitivities. Vinyl curtains release chemical gases and odors and are made with non-renewable resources. Natural fiber shower curtains can be laundered and are appealing. Some fibers are naturally mold-resistant and are quick drying so that they don't leak through. Some properties are also installing clear glass shower doors.

Toilets

Toilets are most often made of vitreous china. Models with elongated bowls often use space more efficiently. Because the bowl protrudes out farther, a shelf can be built behind the toilet.

the Rooms CHRONICLE®

Hookless Shower Curtains and Curved Shower Rods for Guestrooms

One of the most frustrating and potentially dangerous tasks for room attendants involves changing out shower curtains and their liners. The standard sized 72-inch shower curtain is typically hung at a height of 6.6 to 7 feet, so many room attendants resort to various daring feats of balance atop bathtub edges and toilet seats while they align the curtain's holes with the pins on the shower rings.

As any room attendant can attest, working with one's arms overhead to hang shower curtains is physically demanding. Analogous to threading a needle twelve times over, it can take several minutes for a shorter room attendant to complete the overhead task. Two recent bathtub innovations change the face of the guest bathroom. One benefits the room attendant and the other provides more comfort and overall satisfaction to the hotel guest.

Easy-to-install shower curtain

Arcs & Angles has introduced a hook-free shower curtain and liner system that room attendants can change out in under a minute. In fact, it takes only about ten seconds to completely hang the Hookless® shower curtain thanks to the exclusive, patented "Flex-on® Rings" which are built into the top of the shower curtain pins. It is so simple that a housekeeper can actually install it with one hand. No more waiting for assistance to hang the shower curtain or balancing on the edge of the tub or toilet for prolonged periods of time.

Also gone are torn curtains and missing or broken rings. Since the patented "split ring" design is built directly into the curtain itself, all that remains is the Hookless® shower curtain pleating back and forth across the shower bar. There is nothing else to buy. Available in a wide range of colors, sizes, and materials, to date more than one million hotel guest bathrooms have replaced traditional shower curtain and liners with the Hookless® shower curtain, thus reducing the time needed to service the bathroom and minimizing risk and discomfort to housekeeping personnel.

Curved shower rod

Another innovation that is appearing in more guestroom baths is the curved shower curtain rod. By replacing straight shower rods with arced bars, hotels can offer guests up to 30 percent more elbow room in the shower, thus contributing to guest comfort and satisfaction. Indeed, most guests do not wish to brush up against the shower curtain nor the wall of the bathtub while showering. Arced shower curtain bars help prevent this problem.

Source: *The Rooms Chronicle*®, Volume 14, Number 1, p. 4.
For subscription information, please call 866-READ-TRC.

Because water is a precious resource that must be conserved, low-flow toilets are mandatory according to building codes. Before these water regulations, toilets consumed as much as three to four gallons of water per flush. Water standards now require that toilets consume no more than 1.6 gallons per flush. It is also possible to buy high-efficiency models that use as little as 1.28 gallons per flush.

High-efficiency toilets can save thousands of gallons of water per guestroom over a year's time, reducing expenses and preserving valuable natural resources. High-efficiency toilets, including dual-flush models, have been used for years in places like Australia, but have been slower to catch on in the United States.

What makes a toilet high-efficiency? According to Phil Schrieber, a senior sales engineer with Kohler Co., it uses at least 20 percent less water than a 1.6-gallon-per-flush model and effectively removes 350 grams of waste with that lower amount of water.

A **dual-flush toilet** offers two flush options: one for liquid waste (0.8 gallons per flush) and one for solid waste (1.6 gallons per flush). Dual-flush toilets can save up to 40 percent of the water used by 1.6-gallon-per-flush models.

Gravity-fed high-efficiency toilets can be very effective at removing large amounts of waste without clogging the toilet. Pressure-assist toilets use air pressure to help remove waste and some toilet models employ electric pumps to ensure a clean flush. Whereas pressure-assist toilets once were unreasonably loud as they flushed, they now are almost as quiet as gravity-fed models.

To ensure the effectiveness of high-efficiency toilets, bowl designs have changed and flush valves are larger than they once were. Greater amounts of water flow faster to eliminate the waste.

Larger trap configurations help to eliminate clogging. When purchasing a toilet, the executive housekeeper should always ask whether the toilets are going to be clog free and how that is ensured.[2]

At some properties, earlier low-flow toilets (not the high-efficiency models) caused problems with clogging. Low-flow toilets sometimes must be flushed more often. The instructional cards shown in Exhibit 2 shows the solution that one property devised. The message reduced the number of clogged toilet calls by 78 percent within the first 30 days of implementing the card program.

Other properties, such as the Detroit Marriott Renaissance Center, fixed their low-flow flush problems with newly engineered toilets designed with a larger flush valve and new chambers that have a more powerful siphoning action. The toilets were specifically designed for the upper floors so that gravity would assist in removing waste.

Increasingly, hospitality properties have been adopting **RFID technology**. RFID technology is a system of transponders (tags), circuits and antenna, and a transceiver (radio). It is typically used as a wireless monitoring device for a vast variety of uses. One of its newest uses is in the bathroom. Properties have been installing RFID-enabled monitoring devices to help recognize when a toilet is leaking or overflowing and to automatically shut off the water source.

The RFID device is small enough to be barely visible and operates without wires. The system consists of a tank sensor, a bowl sensor and a control unit that is an electronically operated valve that attaches to the pipe that supplies the toilet with water. The control unit typically has an RFID reader. The tank sensor can detect such problems as a silent leak, an open flapper, or a fill valve leak. The bowl sensor can detect the rise of water level. If the sensors detect a problem, the tag

Exhibit 2   Low-Flow Toilet Information Card

DON'T MAKE ME COME UP THERE!

We're kidding, of course, but this is fair warning. Per building code, our toilets are low flow—designed to save water. So please flush often when using in order to eliminate the chance of congestion.

We're more than happy to assist if you experience toilet congestion but frequent flushing will prevent the old plunger procedure.

CLAYTON
ON THE PARK
A Hotel and Residence

PLUMBER

Your Friendly Toilet Technicians

Source: Clayton on the Park, used with permission.

transmits the information to the control unit. Traditional units would then set off an audible alarm—something that disrupts hotel guests. To meet this challenge, modern RFID systems have a housekeeping unit that room attendants can carry with them. The room attendant can press a button when in the hotel bathroom to be alerted if the toilet is malfunctioning.

Vanities

Vanities (bathroom countertops) are usually made of marble or a synthetic material. Acrylics, polymers, and combinations of the two are the most popular synthetics. Marble is more expensive and more vulnerable to damage than acrylics or polymers. Synthetics are easier to care for; scratches or other damage can often be sanded out. Granite is growing in popularity as a choice for hotel bathrooms because of its durability. It's a material that looks good, wears well, and has been decreasing in cost. Vanities are typically purchased in classic colors because they last a long time and will need to work with changing décor.

As properties look to upgrade their bathrooms, many of them are turning to the vanity as a way of creating a more luxurious bathroom without making major structural changes. One popular choice is to create storage space underneath the vanity. This space can hold towels, hair dryers, and other items that have traditionally been put on the vanity top. This frees up space on the vanity, giving the guest more room for personal items.

Another trend in vanity design has been to surround the mirror with a decorative frame. This provides a more residential feel that is intended to be appealing to guests.

Fixtures

Lavatories most often come in vitreous china or enameled cast iron. However, very luxurious models may be made of marble, glass or even teak, which is water-resistant and can be treated with a water-tight seal. Sinks can also be made in a variety of synthetics designed to look like natural materials such as granite or marble.

Faucets and handles on tubs, showers, and lavatories may be made of nickel, chrome, or, on the most elegant fixtures, brass. Brass and chrome should never be exposed to acidic cleaners.

Hoteliers are also taking second looks at the faucets that they use in guestrooms. Single-handle models were often unfamiliar to guests and a source of frustration. Some hotels are choosing to go to brand-name faucets that are more familiar to their guests. They're also choosing alternative finishes such as brushed chrome or satin nickel. Some properties are also looking for plumbing fixtures and levers that are artistic touches as well as being easy to use.

Lighting in bathrooms is also receiving more attention. Throughout the 1980s, bathrooms often had light boxes above the sink vanities. If incorrectly designed, these boxes cast shadows and provided poor light. Guests frequently complained about bathroom lighting. More recently, properties are installing sconces on either side of the sink for a more residential design style. If equipped with correct lamps, sconces can provide better quality lighting.

Night lights are starting to appear in guestroom bathrooms as both an amenity and an energy-saving device. Many hotel guests will turn the bathroom light on and leave it on for their entire stay. This wastes energy, but provides guests with the security of being able to find their way around an unfamiliar room. Night lights attempt to meet the guests' needs while reducing energy usage.

Some night lights come with motion sensors. The standard wall switch in guest bathrooms is replaced with infrared technology to turn lights on and off based on whether the room is occupied. When the room is vacant, a highly efficient, super bright LED provides a night light as a convenience and comfort to guests.

Technology is also changing the face of bathrooms. Some hotels are now offering televisions that are embedded in the bathroom mirror. When the television is turned on, the picture appears in the mirror. It vanishes when the television is turned off.

Amenities

Bathroom **amenities** can include anything from shampoo to sewing kits. Most properties provide soap, shampoo, and conditioner while others will add hand lotion, shower gel, shoeshine cloths, or any of a number of other products.

Two major trends that are changing the look of amenities in lodging property bathrooms are bulk dispensers and luxury amenities.

Bulk Dispensers. Many properties are turning to bulk dispensers for such things as soap, bath gel, shampoo, and conditioner. Vendors have developed dispensers that are tamper proof and allow a wide range of options for guests.

Properties have found bulk dispensers appealing because they save a great deal of money and reduce labor costs. They are also considered to be environmentally friendly because they reduce the amount of wasteful packaging and the need to throw away partially used soap or other amenities.

As of 2006, it was estimated that more than ten billion shower amenity packaging pieces are thrown away each year by hotels around the world. According to a survey done by the U.S. Travel Data Center, 83 percent of travelers thought that the amenity bottles were wasteful. However, early designs of dispensers were unappealing and unattractive.

Individual amenities also carve a chunk out of the bottom line. Individual amenity bottles can cost anywhere from 15 cents to a dollar or more. In comparison, a single use of shampoo from a dispenser may cost just a few cents. Some properties that have switched to dispensers have realized a cost savings of 70 percent.

When dispensers were first introduced to the lodging industry, design was not a priority. Today's dispensers are more durable, tamper-proof, and can offer several varieties of products. Each dispenser comes with a lock to prevent tampering. They also come in different colors and finishes to match bathroom décor.

Maintenance is minimal. Dispensers need to be wiped regularly and filled as seldom as once a month, depending on usage. Since room attendants no longer have to clean up and reset the individual bottles, they save time cleaning the guestroom.

Tent cards and clear product identification on the dispenser itself are often used to educate guests. The cards can be used to communicate the quality of the product in the dispenser.[3]

Luxury Amenities. One of the fastest-growing segments of the hospitality industry is spas. Their influence has had a tremendous effect on hotels and that effect has begun to spread to guest bathrooms. Guests are seeking a more indulgent and restorative experience from their baths. They demand more from skincare and soap products. Hotels have responded by purchasing name-brand spa amenities and making them available in guestrooms.

Some properties have even teamed up with beauty industry experts to create private label products that have a signature scent or ingredient—whether it be geraniums in Mackinac Island's Grand Hotel amenities or the scent of Holiday Inn's trademark cinnamon rolls infused into their amenities.

Handicap Accessibility

The Americans with Disabilities Act requires that lodging properties make a certain percentage of their rooms handicap accessible. This includes very specific instructions for accessible bathrooms that have properly fitted tubs and roll-in showers. Exhibit 3 lists the required number of rooms that must be accessible.

Exhibit 3   Number of Rooms Required to Be Fully Accessible

Number of Rooms	Total Accessible Rooms
1 to 25	1
26 to 50	2
51 to 75	4 (1 with roll-in shower)
76 to 100	5 (1 with roll-in shower)
101 to 150	7 (2 with roll-in showers)
151 to 200	8 (2 with roll-in showers)
201 to 300	10 (3 with roll-in showers)
301 to 400	12 (4 with roll-in showers)
401 to 500	13 (4 with roll-in showers)
501 to 1000	2 percent of all rooms (plus 1 room with a roll-in shower for each 100 rooms)
1001 and over	20 plus 1 for each 100 over 1000 (plus 1 room with roll-in shower for each 100 rooms)

Source: Americans with Disabilities Act.

Lawsuits are increasingly being brought against properties that do not offer handicap-accessible rooms and building inspectors are often strict about exactly what makes a bathroom accessible. Some properties have had to demolish rooms and rebuild them because they did not meet the code standards—even after blueprints had been approved by regulatory authorities.

ADA requirements include:

- Clear floor space at least 48 inches wide by 66 inches long around a toilet that is approached from the front.

- Clear floor space at least 48 inches wide by 56 inches long for a toilet that is approached from the side.

- Grab bars for toilets that are at least 36 inches long with the end closer to the side wall mounted at least 12 inches from the centerline of the toilet.

- Space between the grab bar and the wall of exactly 1½ inches.

- The toilet seat must be between 17 and 19 inches from the floor.

- Flush controls must be automatic or able to be operated with one hand without tight grasping, pinching, or twisting of the wrist.

- The toilet paper dispenser must be mounted below the grab bar no more than 36 inches from the back wall and at least 19 inches from the floor. It must not obstruct the use of the grab bar and must allow for continuous paper delivery.

- Hot water pipes and drain pipes must be insulated against contact.

the Rooms
CHRONICLE®

Serenity Bath: Something from Nothing

What happens when a guest reads the words: luxury, serenity, warm, inviting, luscious, invigorating, soothing, and relaxing? Mental pictures begin to develop—pictures that interrupt the hassle of travel. Pictures that draw a guest into the idea of being pampered.

The Fairmont Chicago understands pampering and they have developed a concept to coddle their guests with a unique offer of lavishness: The Fairmont Serenity Baths. When guests enter the elevator at the Fairmont, they see a poster of a Bath Sommelier preparing a sumptuous bath in a guestroom. When they open their guestroom directory, they see the bath "menu." By the time they walk into the bathroom, they are dreaming about what luxury they might experience right in their own guestroom.

Think about it. This hotel has created something from nothing. They've taken the standard hotel bathtub and turned it into a profit center.

Serenity Bath Procedures

From the guest directory, guests may choose from a menu of invigorating, soothing, therapeutic, or relaxing baths. For instance, the "Tranquility—Bloom Chamomile Infusion Bath" description reads as follows:

> Immerse yourself in therapeutic natural mineral waters. Mineral salt is helpful in assisting the body to detoxify and condition the skin. This bath includes:

- Tranquility Sea Salt Soak
- Tranquility Bubble Bath
- Purity Relaxing Hand and Body Lotion
- Waves 100 percent Glycerin Soap
- Votive Candles
- Loofah Scrubber
- Two Cucumber Slices
- Neck Pillow
- Choices of music
- Fresh sliced tropical fruit
- Glass of Kendall Jackson Merlot
- Large Evian water or flavored Perrier water

Guests dial room service to order and schedule their baths. The service is available from 4 P.M. to 11 P.M.

The room service attendant calls the room fifteen minutes before the scheduled hour to inquire if the guest is ready for the bath. At the appointed hour, the Bath Sommelier (room service attendant) arrives with a special bath cart to set up the bathroom according to the guest's choice.

The bath water is drawn, infused with suitable balms and checked with a thermometer to be exactly 110 degrees Fahrenheit. Scented votive candles are set and lit.

(continued)

the Rooms
CHRONICLE®

(continued)

Fruits and beverages are placed beautifully on a tray beside the bathtub. The other amenities (including cucumber slices for covering the guest's eyes) are arranged.

The Bath Sommelier presents a choice of music CDs and inquires which the guest prefers. The music is played on a small CD player placed in the bathroom. The Sommelier informs the guest that all items will be retrieved in the morning (no call will be necessary), obtains the guest's signature on a charge slip similar to a room service ticket, wishes the guest a lovely bath and exits the room.

A charge of $50 plus gratuity is placed on the guest's room account.

Menu items

The bath menu lists such enticing items as:

- Archipelago Botanicals Milk Bath with soy and rice salt milk for health benefits.

- Ecologique Natural Spa Essentials European Style Bath with lemon-oil elixirs and chamomile for relaxation.

- Archipelago Botanicals Excursion Collection Bath with Fresca for skin nourishment and spirit revitalization.

- V'tae Peppermint Series Bath designed to cleanse and promote sleek skin and a healthy glow.

Not to miss an opportunity, the bath menu contains upgrades that are available for an additional charge. Noted as Bath Enhancements, these upgrades include a 60-minute in-room massage ($90), a glass of champagne ($7) or a Fairmont Signature Bath Robe ($90).

Something from Nothing

What's really involved in this program? The costs include a few amenities and the labor of a staff member already on duty for room service responsibilities. If a hotel like the Fairmont sold 20 luxury baths per week, it would gain $1,000 in revenue it would not have otherwise. Traveling businesswomen buy a bath for themselves. Husbands buy a bath for their wives as part of a getaway weekend. Families buy a gift certificate for a room and a bath for their mothers or favorite aunts. This bath package is extremely "sellable." And it is extremely simple and memorable for guests. One guest remarked about the program, "I slept like a baby. It was worth every penny." The Serenity Bath program proves once again, customers will pay for service.

The best hotel managers will examine every aspect of their operation—looking for clever ways, like the Serenity Bath, to provide new services their guests can buy.

Source: *The Rooms Chronicle®*, Volume 10, Number 4, p. 5.
For subscription information, please call 866-READ-TRC.

- The sink faucet must be operated with one hand without tight grasping, pinching, or twisting of the wrist.

- At least one mirror must have a bottom edge of the reflecting surface no higher than 40 inches from the floor.

- There must be sufficient knee and toe clearances under a sink. This includes a minimum of 8 inches measured from the front edge underneath the sink back toward the wall and a toe clearance 9 inches minimum high. A minimum of 27 inches clear space is required underneath the sink bowl.

- The door swing must not intrude into the clear floor space of any fixture.

- A mounted in-tub seat or built-in seat must be provided at the head of the tub and securely mounted.

- Faucets and other controls must be able to be operated with one hand and without tight grasping, pinching, or twisting of the wrist.

- A shower spray unit must have a hose that is at least 60 inches long and can be used both as a hand-held and a fixed shower head.

- A roll-in shower must have a folding seat and grab bars.

- Shower stall enclosures must not obstruct the controls or transfer from a wheelchair into the shower seat.

There are many additional requirements, so properties should consult ADA experts when designing or redesigning a bathroom and selecting furnishings for the bathroom. Most vendors will try to make it easy for their customers by indicating which of their products meet ADA requirements.

Care Considerations

The Opinion Research Corporation conducted a survey asking lodging guests how they determine whether a hotel room is clean. Nearly three-quarters of the survey respondents said they judged the room by the condition of the bathroom. This same survey found that the number one pick of what guests wanted to find when they arrived was a truly clean room and bathroom—ranking above all other in-room amenities.

The survey also asked guests what bothers them the most about stays at hotels. The number one answer—at 28 percent—was dirty guest-room bathrooms.[4]

Almost as important as what to clean is what not to clean. A local network channel in 2007 did an exposé that showed guestroom attendants rinsing out glasses in the bathroom sink using highly unsanitary practices. Guestroom attendants should always remove used glassware from the bathroom (or wherever else in the guestroom they are kept) and take them to the dishroom to be washed and sanitized through the dishwasher. Glasses and glass covers should never be wiped out and reused. Room attendants should also handle clean glassware as little as possible, always touching them on the outside.

Tubs

When it comes to cleaning the bathroom, the tub and tile area takes more time and energy and can be the cause of more problems than any other area of the guestroom. Many guest complaints and employee injuries begin in this area.

the Rooms CHRONICLE®

Grab Bar Rules of Game

Horizontal. Vertical. Slanted. Doubled. L-shaped. U-shaped. Stainless steel. Chrome-plated. Nylon. Bending stress. Shear stress. Shear force. Tensile force.

Welcome to the world of grab bars in hotel bathrooms. While some managers may remember a simpler day when a wall-mounted ceramic soap dish had a little handhold, those days are over. Today the rules of "accessibility" govern the why and how and where of handholds—grab bars—and there is not one hotel manager in America who can be exempted from knowing these rules.

The official guideline for grab bar regulations is number 4.26, "Handrails, Grab Bars, and Tub and Shower Seats" of the Americans with Disabilities Act Access Guidelines (ADAAG). These regulations apply to the guestrooms and public spaces designated as accessible according to law. Twelve specific types of buildings must comply with the ADA guidelines. They include schools, restaurants, hotels, retail stores, stadiums, theaters, convention facilities, museums, parks and hospitals, banks, gas stations, and laundromats.

So what about non-ADA guestrooms in hotels? Many managers are adding grab bars to every guestroom. Must they meet the specifications of ADAAG? No, but to limit the hotel's liability, all grab bar installations must meet two very important considerations:

- Grab bars must be installed according to manufacturer's instructions, local building codes, and standard architectural procedures.

- Grab bars must be maintained properly.

The ADA requires grab bar installation because people with disabilities use them to maintain balance, transfer from the tub to a wheelchair, and prevent falls. Grab bars are an important component of a barrier-free design and are specified, by the ADA, in both new and existing buildings. When hotel management wishes to appeal to guests with disabilities or even to the booming senior market, grab bars will be an essential room amenity.

Source: *The Rooms Chronicle*®, Volume 11, Number 3, p. 16.
For subscription information, please call 866-READ-TRC.

Here are some tips for cleaning the tub and surrounding tile:

1. Turn on the fan or open a window, if possible, to provide ventilation to the area.

2. Remove towels and amenities from the tub area. Properly dispose of soiled linens and used amenities. Be very careful with guests' personal amenities.

3. Spray the tub and tile surfaces, including the shower head, faucets, and soap dish, with disinfectant cleaner. Using a wet sponge, spread the cleaner evenly to cover all surfaces. Allow the surfaces to remain wet according to label instructions for activation of the disinfectant.

4. Scrub areas with a brush or white pad. Keep the brush or pad very wet with hot water while working.

5. Rinsing the areas is a very important step. Using hot water, rinse all the surfaces to remove the cleaner. Some workers attach a hose to the spigot or shower head while others use an ice bucket or wastebasket to collect water for rinsing. If rinsing is faithfully done with each cleaning, there will be no buildup of soap film.

6. Upscale properties often keep an inventory of nylon shower curtains to allow them to be changed with every check-out. If plastic shower curtains are in use, they must be scrubbed with disinfectant and rinsed as above. If decorative curtains are used, managers should have a rotation program to remove the curtains regularly for laundering. Glass doors should be sprayed with the disinfectant, scrubbed, rinsed, and dried. Be sure to clean the door tracks. Glass doors are usually deep cleaned on a regular schedule by removing them from their tracks and cleaning with a bleach solution.

7. Dry the tub and tile area completely, especially the corners. Dry bath areas are not susceptible to mildew. Also dry or polish the fixtures to remove water spots.

8. Wipe the shower curtain rod, towel racks (if present), and the front of the tub.

9. Replace towels, amenities, and guest items.

Abrasive cleaners should never be used in the tub. It cuts soap film, but it erodes the porcelain surface of the tub. This results in a dull, gray tub that has to be resurfaced or replaced.

Mildew removal requires special chemicals that must dry in place. When treating mildew, the housekeeping department may need to take the room out of service.

Abrasive dots etched into the tub bottom will require extra effort if they have not been properly cleaned continuously. The etching permits soap scum and body oils to collect in the dots, resulting in a dark gray or black appearance. This accumulation requires special cleaning chemicals and scrubbing. Some hotels will use a power sander with a custom white-pad accessory to perform this special cleaning.

Fiberglass surfaces should never be scrubbed with abrasive cleaners or tools as these cleaners could create scratches that will hold dirt. Most chemical companies offer liquid cleaners for fiberglass, but non-abrasive powders will also be effective as paste cleaners.

Tub drains should be cleaned when possible by housekeeping. If the design of the drain requires engineering assistance, a plugged drain should be reported immediately. A slow drain is a nuisance to guests and a time-waster for employees.

Grab bars are usually made of stainless steel with a polished or satin feature. They are typically easily cleaned with a damp cloth. Room attendants should not use abrasive or chemical cleaning agents on them.

There are two tests to check the cleanliness of the tub area. When cleaned properly, the tiles should visually sparkle. Second, if a person runs her hand anywhere along the surface, no white powder soap residue should be felt. The walls should squeak as a hand is pulled across the surface.

Management needs to provide adequate cleaning materials (especially cleaning cloths) and excellent training for staff. The executive housekeeper can prepare a training bulletin for tub and shower cleaning, including pictures of the correct method.[5]

Toilets

Cleaning a toilet may be one of the least coveted jobs in housekeeping. Yet it is done hundreds of thousands of times every day in hotels around the world. When cleaning is properly done, the toilet is a gleaming feature of the bathroom. When cleaning procedures are less than proper, the toilet is not only unappealing, it can be a dangerous source of germs.

Many hotels recommend flushing the toilet as the first cleaning step. Other hotels wish to preserve their water usage and leave it to the cleaner's judgment of whether the toilet needs to be flushed before cleaning begins. Many hotels also recommend lowering the water level in the toilet bowl to let the disinfectant work more effectively. To accomplish this, room attendants may push their toilet mop into the trap three or four times quickly until the water drops into the trap. A plunger may also be used.

Spray all the surfaces of the toilet including the handle, toilet seat and lid, bowl, and exterior. When using disinfectant, the surfaces must be sprayed and allowed to remain wet for ten minutes (or an amount of time recommended on the product label) for the disinfectant to activate. For this reason, spraying down the toilet becomes one of the first things to do in the proper routine for cleaning the bathroom. The tub and other areas can be cleaned while the toilet is soaking.

Using the bowl brush or mop, begin swabbing under the rim and working down into the trap. Do not flush until the ten minutes or recommended time has passed. After the appropriate time, flush the toilet. Using the cloth or sponge wet with cleaning solution, wipe down the outside surfaces including the toilet seat, handle, tank, and lid. Some hotels recommend using the bowl brush for exterior surfaces, allowing extra cleaning solution and water to reach the floor and be wiped up later when the floor is cleaned.

Using a clean cloth, dry the surfaces for a sparkling clean toilet. Report to supervisors immediately any water leaks or drips, broken seats, or bumpers, as well as tough stains.

Rust stains or scaly film can be removed with stronger acid cleaners or with a pumice stone. Though toilet bowls are made of **vitreous china**

the Rooms
CHRONICLE®

New Product for Tubs and Showers Makes Cleaning Easier and Safer

Showers and tubs have frequently been the bane of hoteliers, not just for the risk they pose for slip and fall accidents by both guests and the room attendants who must clean them, but for the inordinate time that is required to maintain them. Typical cleaning procedures may require a room attendant to spray disinfectant on the walls and tub and to wipe down all surfaces to remove dirt, hair, and soap scum. This cleaning regimen typically requires the room attendant to initially stand in the bathtub to clean the higher surfaces and then to bend, kneel, and stretch in order to reach those areas below waist level. All in all, there is a very good possibility that the room attendant may incur an on-the-job injury, especially a back strain, performing this task several times a day.

Some hotel managers have embraced a new product to make tub and shower cleaning easier for their room attendant employees. It is a scrubber that incorporates a 32-inch wand with a versatile scrub brush on one end and a ten-foot supply hose on the other that connects directly to a diverter valve. The diverter valve adapts to all standard household shower heads. The 32-inch wand with trigger handle allows the room attendant to stand outside the tub and clean without bending or stretching. A variable pressure water stream can be delivered through the scrub brush and controlled by the attendant by squeezing the trigger handle. The same trigger handle allows the user to squeeze harder, forcing an intense jet to spray from the bottom of the brush to aid in cleaning those hard-to-reach areas as well as stains.

Source: *The Rooms Chronicle*®, Volume 13, Number 3, p. 5.
For subscription information, please call 866-READ-TRC.

(a hard, acid-resistant material) use of strong acids is not recommended on a regular basis.

Tablets or solutions made for toilet tanks and designed to enter the bowl with every flush are not recommended for commercial use. The harsh chemicals in the tablets will deteriorate the rubber parts of the tank.

It is not safe to leave cleaning solution in the bowl after cleaning. There is no need for the chemical to be in contact with the china surface longer than the recommended cleaning time.

Managers must provide adequate cleaning materials, especially cleaning cloths, to room attendants. Employees must not use the toilet cleaning cloths, brushes, or sponges in any other part of the guestroom.

Executive housekeepers may wish to prepare a training bulletin for room attendants that includes photos of the hotel's bathrooms and specific instructions on the chemicals and supplies that are needed for cleaning.[6]

Vanities

Chemical labels should be examined to ensure their safe use on the surfaces present in the bathroom. Most acid-based cleaners are safe for cultured marble, tile, and porcelain, but are not recommended for natural marble.[7]

Vanities are typically cleaned with a short-handled brush. Disinfectant is sprayed on the surface and allowed to set while the rest of the guestroom is being cleaned. The countertop and basin is then cleaned with a clean cloth. The room attendant needs to remove any hair from the sink stopper and drain and wipe up any spilled toothpaste or soap. Fixtures are then polished and the mirror is cleaned with glass cleaner or water. The room attendant will also need to wipe the light fixture, towel rack, and other bathroom fixtures.

A stiff brush can be used to clean overflow holes in the sink. This is an area in which dirt often collects.

Room attendants should be trained to handle guest toiletries as little and as respectfully as possible. Many properties will train room attendants to place a clean washcloth or hand towel on the vanity top and place guest toiletries on it using a clean washcloth or towel.

Extensive research has gone into ways to polish and restore stone and marble. Recently, some properties have been using a process that involves ultraviolet energy that reacts with the stone and creates a new finish rapidly. Surfaces treated in this way are impervious to stains and can be cared for by wiping with a damp cloth.

Floors

The conventional way of cleaning a bathroom floor is to spray the floor and baseboards with an all-purpose cleaning solution. The room attendant then kneels on a towel on the floor to protect his or her knees and prevent slipping. Starting in the farthest corner, room attendants then work toward the door and scrub the floor with a sponge or cleaning cloth, wiping the baseboards as they go. They pay special attention to the areas around the toilet, behind the door, and in corners. They then dry the floor with a clean cloth.

One of the reasons that hotels continue to require room attendants to wash the floor on their hands and knees is because room attendant carts were not designed to hold mops and water pails. Reusing a mop for each room with a mop bucket is unsanitary for the guests and a potential hazard for both the employee and the guestroom.

Some executive housekeepers have room attendants use a tool that is a combination of a broom handle and a cleaning cloth. The floor is sprayed with a neutral cleaner and then the rag is placed at the end of a broom handle and changed out with each guestroom.

A more recent innovative technique is the use of microfiber mops. Microfiber mops are lightweight, easy to use, and can reduce the time and energy spent maintaining all types of flooring surfaces. Each microfiber cloth comprises thousands of synthetic split fiber yarns that are smaller in diameter than a typical human hair and can hold 10 times their own weight. The need for presweeping is virtually eliminated as hair, dust, and loose dirt are gathered by the finely woven cloth, which is attached to the end of an aluminum telescoping pole. If needed, chemical cleaners may be sprayed on the floor or the mop head prior to using. The microfiber cloths, which may be rewashed for several uses, are typically held into place by spring-loaded hinges, pins, or even Velcro fasteners, allowing room attendants to quickly change out soiled microfiber cloths for clean ones.[8]

Urine stains in bathrooms can be a sore point for many guestroom attendants. Not only are the stains unpleasant sights and breeding grounds for unsanitary conditions, but the odors associated with them are objectionable. Urine is made up of three main compounds: urochrome, urea, and uric acid salt. The urochrome and urea components of urine are water-soluble and can be cleaned up with detergent as they don't form a hard bond like uric salt does. It is the uric salt that attaches the urine to a surface and makes it difficult to remove the stains and the odors.

Detergents and solvents usually clean only the surface as they cannot break the bonds of the uric salt that hold the urine in place. Likewise, using scouring powders with bleach and deodorizers to clean urine buildup on tile and grout only has a temporary, surface cleaning effect. The freshly cleaned look and scent has a short lifespan. As soon as water comes in contact with the urine, the odor will return. Although bleach kills bacteria and visually whitens the area initially, it is only a surface improvement. Bleach, like detergents, cannot effectively remove urine buildup that has been drawn deep into the porous surface of the grout.

One way of effectively removing urine stains from tile and grout surfaces is to use a small auto-scrubber. An auto-scrubber is a device designed to put down cleaning solution, scrub the floor, and then pick up the dirty solution all in one pass. This leaves the floor very clean without leaving a filmy layer on the surface. It also allows the floor to dry in a short time. A second and more critical point is to use a cleaner that has enzymes that will eat the uric salt. These types of cleaning compounds are designed with enzymes that get into the same hiding places as the uric salts, break down the chemical bonds, and dissolve the salts so they can be washed away with the solvent in the cleaning compound.

These bio-enzyme cleaners require time for the enzymes to work. It usually takes about 20 minutes with the enzymes doubling in growth every 20 minutes thereafter. If the first application of the bio-enzyme solution does not clean out the urine buildup completely, the process may have to be repeated until the odor is gone.

The enzyme portion of these chemicals is designed to both clean the surface and kill bacteria by removing the urine medium in which they grow. These chemicals are not to be mixed or used with any other cleaning chemicals, unless instructed.[9]

Shower Curtains

Shower curtains are areas of the bathroom that are sometimes missed by otherwise thorough room attendants. The room attendant needs to stand in the bathtub in order to properly see the inside of a shower curtain liner. This is especially important as the room attendant needs to check for hair, soap and shampoo buildup, and mildew growth.

To prevent mildew, room attendants can spray the liner with a bleach disinfectant and wipe it down with a damp rag to remove unwanted debris and prevent scum buildup. The shower curtain liner then needs to be rinsed clean with water and then wiped dry with a different but clean housekeeping cloth.

Shower curtains and liners also need to be laundered on a rotating basis. During high occupancy periods, shower curtains and liners should be changed out with greater frequency than during low occupancy periods. Pulled and dirty shower curtains and liners should be sent to the laundry. The curtains have to be laundered separately from the liners using a non-chlorinated laundry detergent.

After laundering, shake the excessive water from the curtains or liners and place in the dryer for a maximum of 25 to 30 seconds, set at medium temperature. This will sufficiently dry the curtains or liners without melting or scorching them. Immediately pull from the dryer while still warm and place flat on a six-foot folding table. Smooth out any wrinkles by hand and fold into a six square for storage. Curtains and liners must be folded while still warm to prevent wrinkling.

Safety in the Guest Bathroom

An area of particular concern in guest safety is the guest bathroom. Some of the safety concerns are:

* Hot water temperatures.
* Slip resistance of bathtubs, showers, and bathroom floor coverings.
* Electrical shock.
* Proper bathroom construction.

The scalding of guests in lodging bathrooms has resulted in injury and death. This problem occurs primarily in older establishments due to system design and operation. The resulting lawsuits can bankrupt smaller operations and significantly affect the bottom line of larger ones. To prevent scalding, it is suggested that hotel managers:

* Set guest-use water temperatures no higher than 120°F (49°C) at the source and 110°F (43°C) at the tap.
* Separate hotel water systems supplying commercial facilities, guestrooms, and locker rooms from those supplying kitchens and laundries.
* Install bath and shower valves that provide pressure and temperature compensation. These "anti-scald" valves maintain a preset mix of hot and cold water and automatically adjust to system changes.

The slip resistance of bathtubs is also a concern, since slippery bathtubs can cause injuries. The American Society for Testing and Materials (ASTM) has defined indices of "slipperiness." When purchasing new bathtubs and showers, ask for a nonslip surface per ASTM F462.

Exhibit 4 The Position and Mounting of Grab Bars

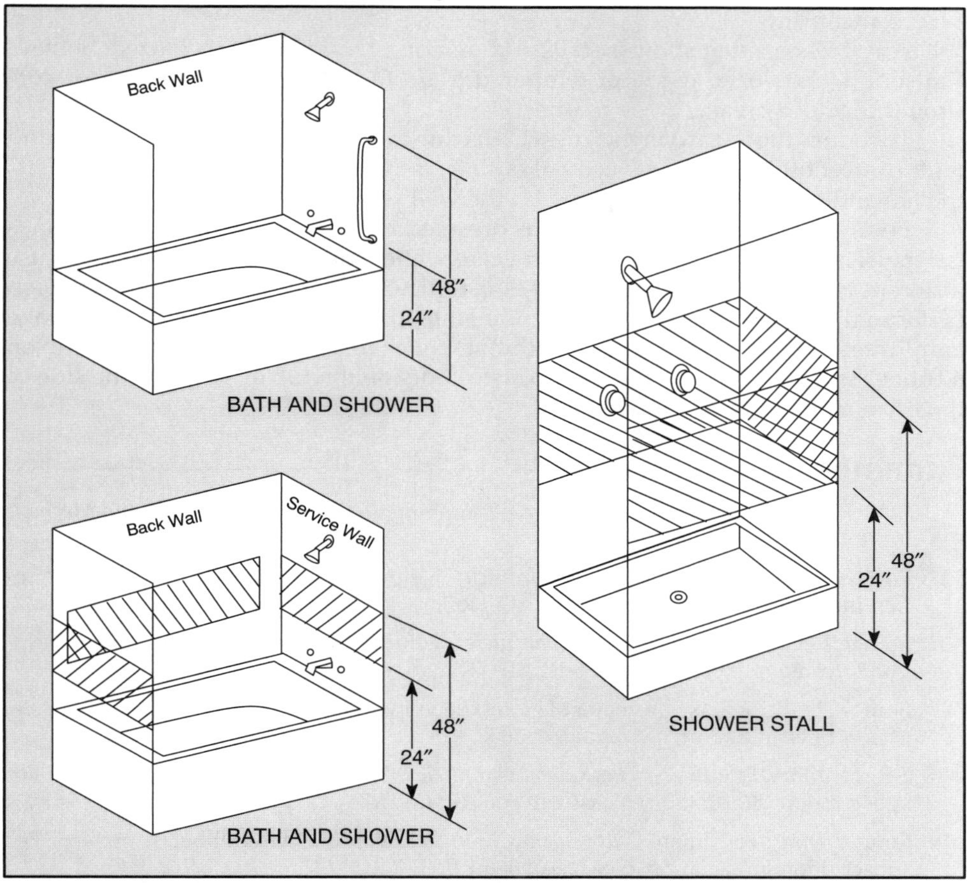

Source: Robert L. Kohr, "The Safety Factor in Bathroom Design," *Lodging,* May 1989, p. 28.

The slip resistance rating of a bathroom tub and shower can decrease over time due to wear and the effects of cleaning chemicals. Tub and shower suppliers can recommend cleaning materials and methods. When resurfacing these fixtures, be sure to specify the required slip resistance as part of the contract; require the contractor to submit test results per ASTM F462 on samples of the finished product.

Bathroom flooring should also have proper slip resistance. When specifying floor surfaces, require the manufacturer to submit certified copies of slip resistance test results from independent laboratories. The test results should represent conditions appropriate to the expected use of the flooring material. The manufacturer can also recommend cleaning materials that maintain the floor's slip resistance. These steps will help minimize slips and falls.

The location and installation of grab bars is also important in bath safety. Suggested guidelines for positioning and mounting grab bars appear in Exhibit 4.

All wall-mounted items need to be installed with adequate blocking to ensure secure anchoring.

Any glass used in shower stalls and mirrors should be safety glazed. Shower stall doors should be made of tempered glass to reduce the possibility of cuts should the door break.

To reduce the hazard in the guest baths due to electrical shocks, furnish ground fault protection on selected electrical outlets. If the property provides hair dryers, the fan and coil should be mounted on the wall with a built-in GFCI capability.

Because wet tub and shower areas present a definite opportunity for slip-and-fall injuries, employees must take extra care while working. Various managers use different techniques to help employees complete their tasks, including provision of long-handled scrub brushes or mini-stepladders. It is proper to encourage employees to kneel in the tub on a bathmat while working or to stand in the tub on a rubber suction mat. It is not safe to stand outside the tub or to sit on the side of the tub and lean into the tub to clean.[10]

Endnotes

1. "The History of Plumbing—Part Two—Plumbing in America," *Plumbing and Mechanical Engineer,* July 1996.

2. Source: Glenn Hasek, *The Rooms Chronicle®*, Volume 15, Number 3, p. 5. For subscription information, please call 866-READ-TRC.

3. Source: Glenn Hasek, *The Rooms Chronicle®*, Volume 14, Number 3, p. 10. For subscription information, please call 866-READ-TRC.

4. Source: "Bathroom is Barometer of Hotel Cleanliness According to New Survey," *Hotel Online* Special Report, November 6, 2002.

5. Source: Mary Friedman, *The Rooms Chronicle®*, Volume 10, Number 2, pp. 4–5. For subscription information, please call 866-READ-TRC.

6. Source: Mary Friedman, *The Rooms Chronicle®*, Volume 10, Number 1, pp. 4–5. For subscription information, please call 866-READ-TRC.

7. Mary Friedman, "Vanity/floor cleaning tips for sparkling rooms", *The Rooms Chronicle®*, Volume 10, Number 3, p. 5. For subscription information, please call 866-READ-TRC.

8. Source: *The Rooms Chronicle®*, Volume 12, Number 1, p. 6. For subscription information, please call 866-READ-TRC.

9. Source: Doug Scouten, *The Rooms Chronicle®*, Volume 12, Number 6, pp. 4–5. For subscription information, please call 866-READ-TRC.

10. Friedman, Volume 10, Number 2, pp. 4–5.

Key Terms

acrylic tub liner—A tub surround that is non-porous and resists mold and mildew.

amenities—Complimentary items given to guests that can include anything from shampoo to sewing kits. Most properties provide soap, shampoo, and conditioner while others will add hand lotion, shower gel, shoeshine cloths, or any of a number of other products.

bulk dispensers—A method for giving out bathroom amenities such as soap, bath gel, shampoo, and conditioner without having to use disposable bottles.

dual-flush toilet—A water-saving toilet with two flush options: one for liquid waste and one for solid waste.

high-efficiency toilets—Toilets that use at least 20 percent less water than a 1.6-gallon-per-flush model and can remove 350 grams of waste.

RFID technology—A system of transponders (tags), circuits and antenna, and a transceiver (radio). It is typically used as a wireless monitoring device.

vitreous china—A hard, acid-resistant material often used for toilets.

 Review Questions ─────────────────────────

1. In what ways have lodging properties been upgrading their guestroom bathrooms?

2. What materials are most commonly used for tub and shower surrounds?

3. How have energy-efficient research changed guestroom toilets?

4. What are two major trends in bathroom amenities?

5. What must a property do to meet Americans With Disabilities Act requirements for accessible bathrooms?

6. What are the proper ways to clean tubs, toilets, vanities, floors, and shower curtains?

7. What are some of the major safety concerns in a guestroom bathroom?

 Internet Sites ────────────────────────────

For more information, visit the following Internet sites. Remember that Internet addresses can change without notice. If the site is no longer there, you can use a search engine to look for additional sites.

Arcs & Angles
www.arcsandangles.com

Courtesy Products
www.courtesyproducts.com

Grab Bars Online
www.grabbarsonline.com

Hospi-tel MFG Co.
www.hospitel.com

Hotel Vanities International, LLC
www.hotelvanities.com

Plumbing World
www.plumbingworld.com

WingIt Innovations, LLC
www.wingits.com

Index

599